victory *in defeat*

victory *in defeat*
THE WAKE ISLAND DEFENDERS IN CAPTIVITY
1941–1945

GREGORY J. W. URWIN

NAVAL INSTITUTE PRESS
Annapolis, Maryland

Naval Institute Press
291 Wood Road
Annapolis, MD 21402

This book has been brought to publication with the generous assistance of Marguerite and Gerry Lenfest.

© 2010 by Gregory J. W. Urwin
All rights reserved. No part of this book may be reproduced or utilized in any form or by any means, electronic or mechanical, including photocopying and recording, or by any information storage and retrieval system, without permission in writing from the publisher.

First Naval Institute Press paperback edition published in 2021.
ISBN: 978-1-68247-670-3 (paperback)
ISBN: 978-1-61251-004-0 (eBook)

The Library of Congress has cataloged the hardcover edition as follows:
Urwin, Gregory J. W.
  Victory in defeat : the Wake Island defenders in captivity, 1941-1945 / Gregory J.W. Urwin.
    p. cm.
  Includes bibliographical references and indexes.
  ISBN 978-1-59114-899-9
  1. Wake Island, Battle of, Wake Island, 1941. 2. World War, 1939–1945—Prisoners and prisons, Japanese. 3. World War, 1939–1945—Concentration camps—Japan. 4. World War, 1939–1945—Concentration camps—China—Shanghai. 5. World War, 1939–1945—Wake Island. 6. Prisoners of war—United States—Biography. 7. Prisoners of war—Wake Island—Biography. 8. Wake Island—History, Military—20th century. I. Title.
  D767.99.W3U79 2010
  940.54'7252092273—dc22

                                                 2010022123

♾ Print editions meet the requirements of ANSI/NISO z39.48-1992 (Permanence of Paper).
Printed in the United States of America.

9 8 7 6 5 4 3 2 1

To the Borromeo Seminary High School Class of 1973,
the band of brothers that first taught me
the sustaining power of community

contents

Abbreviations		ix
Introduction		xi
1	"Issue in Doubt" *The Siege of Wake Island*	1
2	"The Emperor Has . . . Presented You with Your Lives" *The Shock of Capture*	22
3	"Very Odd People Indeed" *The First Twenty-four Hours in Captivity*	40
4	"The Japanese Continue to Treat Us with Respect" *A Deceptively Gentle Transition to POW Life*	58
5	"A Real Hell Ship" *From Wake Island to Yokohama on the* Nitta Maru	75
6	"Never Had I Felt so Desolate or so Weary" *From Murder at Sea to Despair on Land*	92
7	"The Most Painful Days We Spent in Prison Camp" *Hitting Bottom at Woosung*	110
8	"The Japanese Army . . . Will Improve Your Conditions" *Turning the Corner at Woosung*	130
9	"Without Red Cross Help . . . We Would Never Have Pulled Through" *The Impact of Outside Aid*	149

10	"I Thought They Handled Themselves Reasonably Well" *Japanese–POW Relations at Woosung*	169
11	"You God Damn Americans Don't Understand Anything" *Strains, Outrages, and Departures*	188
12	"This Camp Is the Best One That the Japs Have" *A New Commandant and a New Camp*	210
13	"A Hellacious Damn Deal till We Finished" *Pushed to the Edge on Mount Fuji*	232
14	"Optimism . . . Is Running High" *Hope Revives at Kiangwan*	254
15	"The Pleasure of Raising Our Flag over the Enemy's Homeland" *To Japan and Liberation*	277
16	"98 US PW, 5-10-43" *The Wake Island Diaspora, 1942–1945*	304
17	"We Had a Bond There That's Still Going" *Why so Many Came Home*	333
Notes		351
Bibliography		443
Index		463

abbreviations

AVG	American Volunteer Group
BAR	Browning automatic rifle
CINCPAC	commander-in-chief of the U.S. Pacific Fleet
CNO	chief of naval operations
CP	command post
CPNAB	Contractors Pacific Naval Air Bases
CRB	Central Reserve Bank of China
ICRC	International Committee of the Red Cross
NCO	noncommissioned officer
PBY	long-range patrol plane
POW	prisoner of war
SNLF	Special Naval Landing Force
UNT	University of North Texas
USAAF	U.S. Army Air Forces
USAMHI	U.S. Army Military History Institute
VMF-211	Marine Fighting Squadron 211

introduction

In December 1941 a small atoll called Wake Island became a beacon of hope for Americans plunged into a Christmas season darkened by defeat. A token garrison of U.S. Marines supported by some sailors, soldiers, and civilian construction workers held that isolated outpost two thousand miles west of Pearl Harbor for more than two weeks against numerically superior Japanese forces. On December 11 Wake's defenders treated their countrymen to an early Christmas present by winning America's first tactical victory of World War II. With only six 5-inch guns and four fighter planes, they repulsed a Japanese landing attempt—the first and only time a major amphibious assault failed in the Pacific theater. The Japanese returned on December 23 with even heavier numbers and firepower, and Wake fell after several hours of savage ground fighting.

With that defeat Wake Island soon faded from the nation's headlines, and the 1,621 Americans trapped there disappeared into the bowels of Japan's Asian empire. They would spend the next three and a half years in captivity, though not completely forgotten by their fellow Americans. Wake's defense inspired a successful 1942 feature film and numerous publications, and it also became a potent symbol for Marine Corps recruiting and war bond drives. When Allied forces liberated the Wake Islanders from various prison camps in September 1945, it turned out that those men had won a second notable victory—a surprisingly low death rate. For a variety of reasons, that second achievement has attracted little attention and has never been fully explained until now.

In 1995 I accompanied three Marine survivors of the Wake Island fight on a trip to Japan. Ed Borne, Tom Kennedy, and Wiley Sloman went to face a former Japanese naval officer who had held their lives in his hands soon after they became prisoners of war (POWs). My elderly companions did not make the long flight across the Pacific Ocean to hunt down a war criminal. Theirs was a mission of friendship. They came to thank former Sub-Lieutenant Shigeyoshi Ozeki for his decency and kindness, which helped them survive the start of an often harrowing captivity.

History, literature, and film depict Japanese POW camps of World War II as places of unmitigated horror run by adherents to a fierce military code that countenanced the heartless treatment of helpless foes. The shockingly high death rates suffered by Allied personnel captured in the Pacific theater and the many memoirs produced by survivors of those camps amply support this dark view of the Japanese military.

On the other hand, the three and a half years that the Americans captured on Wake Island spent in enemy custody revealed that not every Japanese soldier or sailor was an unfeeling brute. The Wake defenders emerged from confinement with one of the highest survival rates of any group of Caucasians overrun by the Japanese war machine. These American Marines, soldiers, sailors, and civilians earned their salvation through their own discipline, toughness, stamina, and caring, but most also benefited from occasionally encountering Japanese like Shigeyoshi Ozeki. Ozeki and men like him chose to deviate from established cultural norms and exhibit a quality all too rare on both sides in the racially charged Pacific War—compassion.

Victory in Defeat tells the story of the Wake Islanders' prolonged struggle to preserve their lives under circumstances that must beggar the imagination of their descendants. The servicemen among this group were taught to defend themselves with weapons, and they did that with lethal efficiency during America's first sixteen days at war. For the rest of the conflict, they had to rely only on their wits, willpower, and sheer luck to shape their destiny. They and the construction workers captured on Wake formed interlocking networks based on affection and mutual interest in order to sacrifice, steal, and bargain for another day of life. The Wake Islanders would open their networks to other POWs they encountered in the course of their confinement. They also formed relationships with some of their captors, who often contributed in surprising ways to these lifesaving communities.

Readers seeking a story of American courage, grit, and self-sacrifice will find much to like in this book. They will also encounter reminders that Americans do not inhabit this planet alone. The Wake Islanders owed their lives to assistance from a wide assortment of foreigners, both friend and foe. While the Wake Islanders would point with pride to their survival for the rest of their lives, they retained enough humility to acknowledge the assistance they received from non-Americans. That is a lesson that has escaped too many children of the so-called "Greatest Generation." It is hoped that *Victory in Defeat* will broaden their awareness.

Speaking of acknowledging debts, this book owes its existence to the kindness of many people. First and foremost, I must acknowledge the many Wake Island survivors who consented to share their memories with me in person and via correspondence. They also allowed me the use of their wartime papers and photographs. Many of these same materials were made available by Wake Islanders' widows, children, grandchildren, and other relations. This latter group includes June Faubion, Christopher Andrews, Gregory R. Cunningham, Anne Freuler Loring, James Bair, Peter Russell, Harold A. Futtrup, Inge Futtrup, Ileen B. Lent, Harold W. Smith, Pam Durrwachter, Bill Phillip, Joseph P. Commers, Herbert Highstone, F. Wayne Mills, and Al Thurmond. To save space, most of the items from my personal archive cited in the endnotes are not listed in the bibliography. In due course, I shall donate the Wake-related interviews, correspondence, and other papers in my possession to the archives of the Marine Corps University in Quantico, Virginia.

I am indebted to many friends and colleagues for their advice and support. For reading and commenting on the entire manuscript, I thank James M. McCaffrey, University of Houston—Downtown; Ronald E. Marcello, formerly of the University of North Texas (UNT); Mark E. Hubbs, environmental protection specialist and archaeologist, U.S. Army Space and Missile Defense Command; Cecilia Schneider, widow of Pfc. LeRoy E. Schneider, a Wake Marine; and Paul Astle. Joanne Grossey and historical consultant Dan King interpreted for me during interviews with Japanese veterans. William F. Kauffman of Aviator Pictures generously shared the transcripts for all the interviews conducted for his documentary *Those Who Also Served: The Civilian Construction Men of Wake Island*. In addition, my colleagues Beth Bailey and William I. Hitchcock at Temple University; Gunter Bischof and the late Stephen E. Ambrose of the University of New Orleans; Eugene J. Corcoran, University of Central Arkansas; Robert von Maier, executive editor of *Global War Studies*; independent scholars Dennis M. Giangreco, Gavan Daws, Gregory F. Michno, Bonnie Gilbert, David H. Lippman, Greg Leck, and Roger Mansell; Wake Islander descendants Christopher Andrews and Gregory R. Cunningham; and Bernard R. O'Brien, B. J. Omanson, Bob Tiernan, and Mrs. G. Trupin deserve my gratitude for either reading portions of this work or rendering other assistance. Finally, four of my professors at the University of Notre Dame—Robert L. Kerby, Vincent P. DeSantis, and the late Leon Bernard and Bernard Norling—read this account in its original dissertation form many years ago and saved me from many youthful pitfalls. At the Naval Institute Press, my editor, Adam C. Kane, and my copyeditor, Ed Lamb, expertly purged the manuscript of many lingering imperfections.

A University of Central Arkansas Summer Research stipend enabled me to work with Ron Marcello's vast collection of POW oral histories at UNT. A Marine Corps Heritage Foundation research grant funded a final visit to the Marine Corps Historical Archives on the eve of its transfer to Quantico. A Summer Research Fellowship from Temple University permitted me to examine important materials held by the Howard Gotlieb Archival Research Center at Boston University and the many POW papers at the U.S. Army Military History Institute (USAMHI) at Carlisle Barracks, Pennsylvania.

Archivists and librarians are among a historian's most valuable allies, and I have benefited from my association with this generous and ingenious breed. Among those whose efforts were essential to this project are Richard A. Long, Jennifer L. Gooding, Danny J. Crawford, Robert V. Aquilina, and the late Benis M. Frank of the old Marine Corps Historical Center; F. W. Pernell, Maida H. Loescher, and Wilbert B. Mahoney of the National Archives; Richard L. Himmel, University Libraries, UNT; David Keough and Richard J. Sommers, USAMHI; Dale Sauter, Special Collections Department, Joyner Library, East Carolina University; and Alison Beck, Archives and Manuscripts, Barker Texas History Center, University of Texas at Austin.

Quotations from primary sources appear in this book in their original form to preserve their flavor. In a few instances, minor edits have been inserted within brackets to ensure clarity.

I close, as always, with joyous recognition of the constant encouragement and inexhaustible patience of my wife, Cathy Kunzinger Urwin, and our son, Edward. Their love gives meaning and purpose to my work.

CHAPTER ONE

"issue in doubt"
the siege of wake island

"OH, SHUCKS!"

When 2nd Lt. Arthur A. Poindexter, USMCR, glanced at his watch around 11:15 AM, December 23, 1941, he must have been amazed at how good he felt. He had been awake and on his feet since before midnight. At 3:00 AM, his world erupted with the chaos and carnage of close infantry combat. Poindexter had never experienced ground fighting before, but he performed like a champion during the next eight hours. He seemed to pop up anywhere his men most needed him, ambushing the left flank of a Japanese beachhead, conducting a skillful withdrawal, and directing firefights. At one point, he even struggled through pounding surf to throw hand grenades into an enemy landing barge.

Yet it was not only Poindexter's athletic physique or adrenalin that kept him going as a blazing sun rose directly over Wake Island, it was the exaltation generated by standing on the verge of victory. With a scratch-built force of Marine machine gunners, Navy ratings, civilian volunteers, and rear-echelon personnel, Poindexter established a line by 7:00 AM that checked Japanese efforts to overrun the American garrison's camp on Wake's southern leg. Within two hours, Poindexter began sensing that the steam had gone out of the enemy drive, and he decided to push back. "To hell with that old saw about 'a gallant last stand' like George Armstrong Custer at the Little Big Horn," he thought. Being a Marine taught him "that the only way to accomplish anything is to take the offensive." Quickly organizing a strike force consisting of fifty-five riflemen, Poindexter launched a counterattack at 9:35 AM that compelled the Japanese to recoil for nine hundred yards in less than two hours.

After Poindexter reached the west end of Wake's airfield, he sent a runner to bring up four machine guns to consolidate his position. Before those reinforcements arrived, however, one of the second lieutenant's Marines reported a large party of Japanese approaching under a white flag. Poindexter assumed that the enemy wanted to capitulate. "Stay in place," he called to his men, "and be ready to fire, if I'm fired on." Poindexter stepped out into the open, holding his Model 1903 Springfield rifle at the ready, but the pleasure of the moment caused his face to crease into a grin.

As Poindexter neared the Japanese, however, he heard a familiar voice shout in perfect English, "Drop your rifle." The order came from the shocked officer's immediate commander, Maj. James P. S. Devereux, who was tramping across Wake under enemy escort to get his men to stop fighting. The white flag that had thrilled Poindexter moments earlier actually heralded an American surrender.

This unexpected turnaround left Poindexter so stunned that he forgot how to swear. "Oh, shucks!" he exclaimed. Without further protest, Poindexter dropped his rifle, automatic pistol, and hand grenades and joined more than 1,600 other Americans on Wake Island in becoming a POW.[1]

"WE HAD TO WORK HARD TO GET READY"

Human beings have fought and died for more appealing places than Wake Island. It is not an island, strictly speaking, but an atoll—a broken, low-lying **V** formed by three islets situated in the Central Pacific and situated two thousand miles west of Hawaii. The atoll's main islet, also called Wake, forms the apex of the **V**, which opens toward the northwest. The other two islets—Peale Island on the north and Wilkes Island to the south—resemble feet lopped off the main islet's legs. A coral reef encircling the atoll blocks access to the lagoon from its open end. Counting all three islets, Wake Island runs nearly nine miles from tip to tip, but its narrow landmass amounts to only about two and a half square miles. Rough seas and the reef make landfalls at Wake both difficult and dangerous.

During the 367 years that followed Wake Island's entrée into recorded history, it attracted relatively few visitors, and none tarried there for long. An inhospitable surface that offered coral boulders and rock, coarse sand, scrub brush, and no potable water caused most mariners to shun the place. The Spanish discovered the atoll in 1568, a British merchant captain bestowed his name on it in 1796, and an exploring expedition sponsored by the U.S. Navy accurately charted its position in December 1841—exactly a century before it became a battlefield. On January 17, 1899, a landing party from the gunboat USS *Bennington* officially claimed the uninhabited atoll for the republic.

For more than three decades the United States found no practical use for Wake Island. Then advances in aerial technology and deteriorating relations with

Japan turned a desolate pile of coral into a strategic asset. In 1935 and 1936, Pan American Airways converted Peale Island and a portion of the lagoon into a stop on its new aerial clipper route from San Francisco to Manila. The U.S. Navy secretly encouraged the establishment of Pan Am's Pacific Division, cognizant that marine runways and other facilities that serviced commercial flying boats could be easily adapted for military purposes. On December 1, 1938, a board of American naval officers chaired by Adm. Arthur J. Hepburn recommended a system of bases to guard their country's interests in the Pacific. "From a strategic point of view," the Hepburn Board asserted, "Wake Island is next in importance to Midway in the mid-Pacific area." Hepburn and his colleagues advocated the immediate expenditure of $11,902,000 to convert Wake into a naval air station equipped with one squadron of long-range patrol planes (PBYs) and one division of submarines.

Isolationists in Congress delayed Wake's development for military purposes until World War II broke out and Adolf Hitler's easy victories in 1939 and 1940 alerted Americans to their country's vulnerability. Finally, in January 1941, Contractors Pacific Naval Air Bases (CPNAB), the powerful combine created to translate the Navy's defensive plans into reality, landed an advance party of seventy-seven men on Wake. The Navy called those civilian construction workers "Contractors," and there were 1,146 of them swarming across the atoll within eleven months. In addition to erecting a seaplane base on Peale Island and a complex of barracks and other buildings on the main islet's northern leg nearby, the Contractors massed their heavy excavating and grading equipment to lay out a triangular airstrip for landplanes at the atoll's apex, the one area just wide enough for that purpose.

Morrison Knudsen Company, one of CPNAB's member firms, oversaw Wake Island's eleventh-hour base construction program. Some of the men it sent to the atoll were rugged veterans of earlier projects at Boulder Dam, Bonneville Dam, or Grand Coulee Dam. The rest were largely refugees from the Great Depression, men so desperate for work they would live on a distant strip of coral grit to get it. They found plenty of work on Wake. Nathan D. "Dan" Teters, the project's general superintendent, kept his men on the job ten hours a day, seven days a week, with every fourteenth day off. He also offered his Contractors as much overtime as they could stand.

To ensure workforce stability at this forlorn site, CPNAB provided its employees with high pay, time-and-a-half for overtime, opportunities for promotion, training in skilled trades closed to new workers on the American mainland, and a schedule of bonuses that kicked in once a man began the fourth month of his nine-month contract. The Contractors also enjoyed plenty of good food served by Chinese mess boys and many forms of entertainment and recreation. A ban on women, alcohol, and narcotics promoted both health and order. Although some men could not endure Wake's heat, barrenness, and isolation, most thrived on the CPNAB lifestyle.

As Dan Teters and his Contractors labored through the first half of 1941, Wake Island increasingly occupied the thoughts of Adm. Husband E. Kimmel, the energetic and aggressive commander-in-chief of the U.S. Pacific Fleet (CINCPAC) at Pearl Harbor. Along with three other American atolls—Palmyra, Johnston, and Midway—Wake belonged to the Hawaiian Naval Coastal Frontier. The PBYs and submarines that the U.S. Navy wanted to position along that thin perimeter of outpost islands would presumably give Kimmel early warning of any Japanese thrust toward Pearl from the South Pacific or Central Pacific. What made Wake so special in Kimmel's eyes was its proximity to Japanese-held territory. It sat just six hundred miles north of the Marshall Islands. That accident of geography made Wake a likely target in the event of war, but that pleased CINCPAC as much as it worried him. As Kimmel confided to Adm. Harold R. Stark, the chief of naval operations (CNO), with emphasis, "Should its capture be an early objective of Japan, such an effort might be supported by a substantial portion of their Combined Fleet, which would create for us, a golden opportunity *if we have the strength to meet it.*"

The trap Kimmel intended to set at Wake hinged on preventing the Japanese from swallowing the bait before the Pacific Fleet could steam to the atoll's relief and surprise the enemy. The admiral believed Wake should be garrisoned with 1,851 U.S. Marines, 760 sailors, two fighter squadrons, one PBY squadron, half a squadron of dive-bombers, and half a squadron of torpedo bombers. The first 176 Marines assigned to the atoll arrived there in mid-August 1941. By that time the Contractors inhabited Camp 2, the permanent barracks they had built on the main islet's north leg. The Marines settled on the main islet's south side and moved into Camp 1, the rude tent city that the civilians had occupied during their first four months on the atoll. Lodging was the least of the Leathernecks' worries. Armed mainly with hand tools, they began toiling to fortify Wake. Their primary task was to emplace, sandbag, and camouflage twelve 3-inch antiaircraft guns, six 5-inch seacoast guns, six searchlights, eighteen .50-caliber antiaircraft machine guns, and thirty .30-caliber machine guns. A 1939 Marine Corps defense survey allocated one two-gun coastal battery and one four-gun antiaircraft battery to each of Wake's three islets.

Kimmel sent Wake Island every Marine and sailor he could spare from the Pacific Fleet's many other commitments, but he was running a race he could not win. By December 7, 1941, the atoll contained only 524 military personnel. Four hundred and forty-nine officers and men belonged to two Marine units. The U.S. Navy supplied sixty-eight officers and men to help get the PBY base operational or to handle the Marines' small boats. A patrolling submarine put another sailor ashore for emergency medical care. In addition, the U.S. Army posted six radiomen on Wake to help flights of B-17 heavy bombers negotiate the long haul across the Pacific to the Philippines. This relatively puny band fell far short of the 2,611 Marines and sailors that Kimmel deemed necessary to stop a strong Japanese raiding force from easily seizing Wake.

On November 25, 1941, Secretary of the Navy Frank Knox announced, "The United States Naval Air Station, Wake Island, is hereby established, effective 22 November 1941." A 1926 law specified that only qualified naval aviators could command such installations. Accordingly, Cdr. Winfield Scott Cunningham, the navigator on the PBY tender USS *Wright*, debarked at Wake on November 28 to assume the role of island commander. Cunningham was a Wisconsin native born in 1900. He graduated from the U.S. Naval Academy in 1919, and friends from an early sea assignment nicknamed him "Spiv." His career in naval aviation began in 1924, and he acquired considerable experience with fighters and seaplanes. Second Lt. Arthur Poindexter, who became acquainted with Cunningham on Wake, called him "a nice, gutsy guy" and a "good man's man."

The largest contingent in Cunningham's garrison was the Wake Island Detachment, 1st Defense Battalion—388 U.S. Marines and attached Navy medical personnel under Major Devereux. Though an unimpressive five feet five inches tall, Devereux came from a privileged background. He was born in Cabana, Cuba, on February 20, 1903. His mother was a Philadelphia heiress, and his father was an Army doctor who eventually returned to his old job as a medical professor at Georgetown University. Young Jimmy Devereux received a cosmopolitan education in America, Germany, and Switzerland, but he compiled a poor record as a student. His unwavering devotion to his parents' Catholic faith, however, revealed a serious side to his nature. Devereux enlisted in the Marine Corps on a whim in July 1923, and he entered Officer Candidates School after about eighteen months in the ranks. Commissioned as a second lieutenant on February 19, 1925, Devereux received a succession of assignments that included service at sea, stateside naval bases, and foreign postings in Nicaragua and China. Devereux's largely ordinary career took an important turn in the autumn of 1933 when he joined the first class of Marine officers to study base defense methods at the U.S. Army's Coast Artillery School at Fort Monroe, Virginia. His mastery of this important specialty led to promotion to captain in 1935 and major in 1940, as well as a billet in the 1st Defense Battalion. The defense battalion was a new type of Marine unit designed to hold the island bases that CPNAB was building in the Pacific.

As the 1st Defense Battalion's executive officer, Major Devereux inherited the unenviable job of maintaining discipline, which included meting out summary punishments to errant enlisted men. Devereux performed his duties with a zeal that made many in the lower ranks loathe the very sight of him. "I would say that Devereux was very G.I.," recalled Sgt. Donald R. Malleck, "very strict in every sense of the word & probably one of the least liked officers in any Bn. [battalion] prior to the war." Soft-spoken, aristocratic, and aloof, Devereux struck many of his men as an uncaring martinet. One barracks wit joked that the major's first three initials—J.P.S.—stood for "Just Plain Shit." That nickname would follow Devereux to Wake Island.

Devereux earned a reputation as a slave driver on Wake. After he landed on the atoll on October 12, 1941, he opened standing orders from Pearl Harbor to "fire on all unidentified and suspicious aircraft" and to stop unauthorized vessels "from entering the Naval Defense Sea Areas." Devereux instantly recognized the need to fortify Wake as quickly as possible, and he worked his grumbling subordinates twelve to sixteen hours a day, seven days a week. Even the Contractors noted the merciless pace that Devereux imposed on his Leathernecks. "Those poor fellows just worked their hearts out," remarked Earl R. Row. With a Catholic as devout as Devereux violating the sanctity of the Sabbath, a few Marines began to appreciate the precariousness of their situation. "Well, we had to work hard to get ready," explained Pfc. Mackie L. Wheeler, "because we knew something was going to happen."[2]

Devereux's Marines may have groused about their accelerated work schedule, but they stood it well enough. Pfc. Robert Shores went so far as to claim that the major's regimen left him and his comrades "all stout and in the best of physical shape." As Marines, these men considered themselves America's warrior elite, and that meant they had to be tough. That attitude had been drummed into their heads during the intensive and deliberately traumatic recruit training that initiated them into the Corps at either Parris Island or San Diego. Howling drill instructors also bombarded their charges with this injunction: "Marines don't surrender." That was practical advice in an organization that frequently dispatched its members to international trouble spots where the enemy did not always observe the conventional rules of war. It also fostered an ethos that made every Leatherneck his brother's keeper in a combat zone.[3]

The Wake Island Detachment contained a scattering of seasoned noncommissioned officers (NCOs), but most of the rank and file had joined the Corps between early 1939 and mid-1941, when its authorized strength rose from 19,354 officers and men to 53,886. The Great Depression was still acting as a potent recruiter for all of America's armed forces. That permitted the Marines to more than double their numbers in two years without sacrificing selectivity. Out of 205,338 new applicants who presented themselves at recruiting stations during fiscal years 1939 through 1941, only 38,080 were enlisted. These high standards permitted Capt. Bryghte D. Godbold, the commander of one of Devereux's antiaircraft batteries, to describe the Wake Island Detachment in these terms: "Obviously, there were some who had not been in the Marine Corps a long time, but . . . the troops were exceedingly well trained and prepared for combat."[4]

No matter how highly Devereux's men rated as fighters, there were not enough of them to properly defend Wake if war broke out. Admiral Kimmel had equipped the atoll with all the artillery and 80 percent of the machine guns allotted to a defense battalion, but he sent less than half of the 859 Leathernecks normally required to crew those weapons. Godbold's Battery D on Peale Island could only operate three of its four 3-inch guns. Battery E, the 3-inch antiaircraft battery on Wake proper, was in roughly the same shape, and Devereux left Battery F, his 3-inch battery on Wilkes Island, completely unmanned. The rest of the Wake Island Detachment's batteries had only skeleton crews.

Kimmel realized that the Japanese might strike Wake before he could station a full Marine defense battalion there. Casting about for a quick fix to forestall the atoll's easy capture, CINCPAC informed Admiral Stark as early as August 1941, "It is contemplated that in a sudden emergency civilian personnel, which includes a considerable number of ex-service men, will augment the efforts of the Marines." Soon after the first Leathernecks arrived that same month, they invited the Contractors to train on the Wake Island Detachment's artillery and machine guns. In addition to tapping the American male's fascination with technology and firepower, the Marines offered their pupils something that was illegal in Camp 2—3.2 beer. There are no firm figures on how many Contractors enrolled in this impromptu base weapons school, but anywhere from 150 to 225 attended training sessions during the last month of peace.

Regardless of the shape of Devereux's detachment, Wake Island could not be considered a functioning naval air station until it became home to some mili-

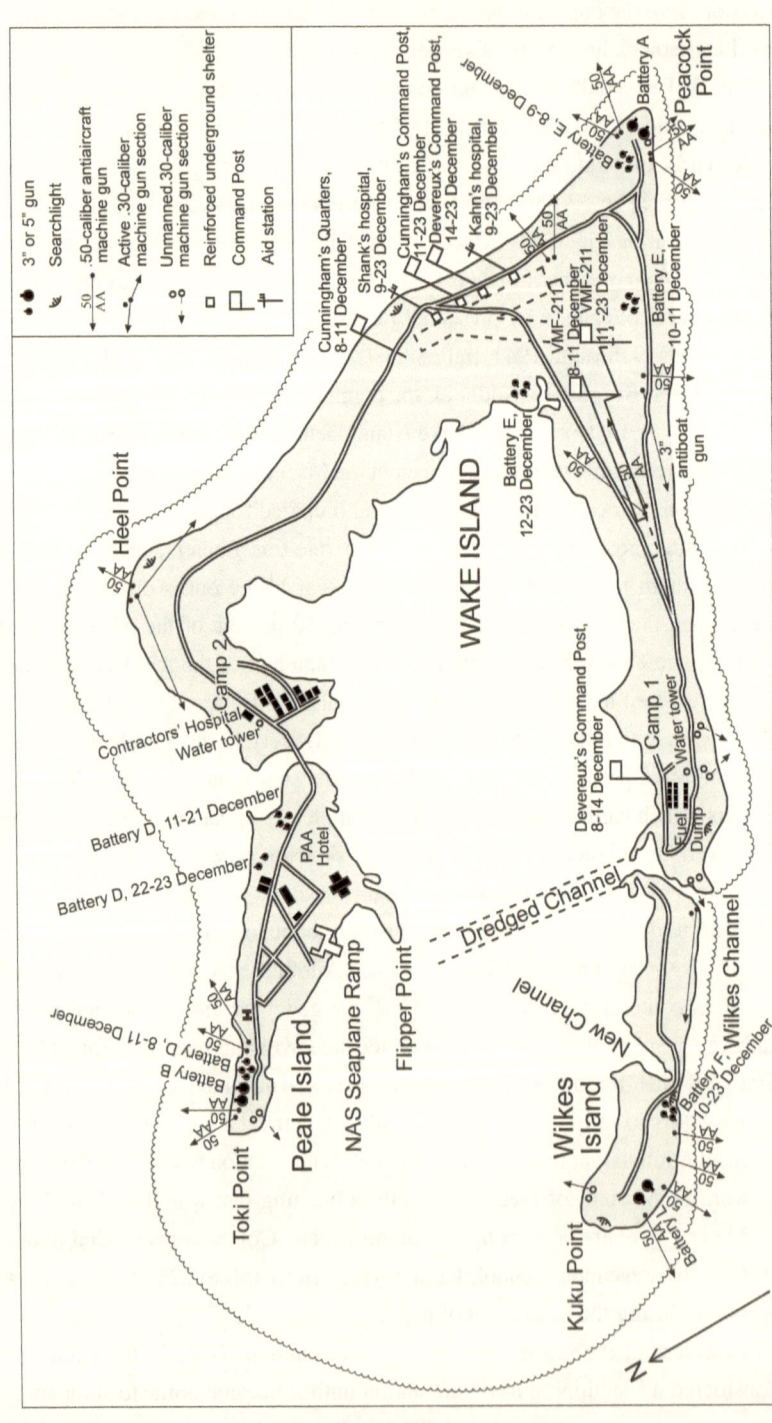

Defense Installations on Wake Island, December 1941

Map by Charles Grear. Modified from Robert D. Heinl Jr., The Defense of Wake Island (Washington, DC: Historical Section, Division of Public Information, Headquarters, U.S. Marine Corps, 1947) and Gregory J. W. Urwin, Facing Fearful Odds: The Siege of Wake Island (Lincoln: University of Nebraska Press, 1997), 207.

tary aircraft. This finally occurred when the last contingent of Marine reinforcements reached the atoll scant days before the outbreak of war. On November 27 Admiral Stark wired Admiral Kimmel that Japanese–American negotiations had broken down and warned that "an aggressive move by Japan is expected within the next few days." CINCPAC responded to Stark's injunction to "execute an appropriate defensive deployment" by tasking the aircraft carrier USS *Enterprise* to ferry Marine fighters to Wake. One week after Stark issued his alert, twelve stubby Grumman F4F-3 Wildcats from Marine Fighting Squadron 211 (VMF-211) put down on Wake's sole finished runway. Two officers and forty-eight enlisted men from Marine Air Group 21 (MAG-21) had preceded VMF-211 to Wake by six days to service whatever kind of Marine aircraft Kimmel decided to station there.

Maj. Paul A. Putnam, VMF-211's no-nonsense commander, spent much of what remained of December 4, his first day on Wake, inspecting the airstrip. He did not like what he saw. The installation was primitive and far from complete. It lacked revetments to shield parked aircraft from attack, and the crushed-coral runway was too fragile to accommodate more than one plane at a time. All of Putnam's aviation fuel and oil sat in the open in two 2,500-gallon tanks and hundreds of 55-gallon drums rather than in protected underground storage facilities. None of VMF-211's ground personnel were experienced mechanics, and most of them had little previous experience with fighters. Two-thirds of the limited Marine aviation stores on Wake belonged to dive-bombers, which left VMF-211 short of tools and spare parts. Finally, Putnam and the twelve other pilots present had switched only a month earlier from obsolete biplanes to F4F-3 monoplanes. They had yet to fully familiarize themselves with their new machines. None had ever fired a Wildcat's machine guns or dropped a bomb from one.

"THIS HAS TO BE A BIG FOUL UP"

Monday, December 8, 1941, opened like any other workday in Camp 1. Reveille rang out at 6:00 AM, and Major Devereux's Marines shaved, dressed, and headed to the mess hall for breakfast. Roughly forty minutes later, the Army K-19 radio trailer at the airfield received this jarring message from Pearl Harbor to the east of the International Date Line, where it was Sunday morning, December 7: "SOS ISLAND OF OAHU ATTACKED BY JAPANESE DIVE BOMBERS. THIS IS THE REAL THING." As soon as Devereux heard the news, he bade Field Music First Class Alvin C. Waronker to sound "Call to Arms."

It may have been the allure of the mess hall's hotcakes, sausages, and eggs or the rattled Waronker playing some incorrect calls, but most of the Wake

Island Detachment reacted lethargically to his bugle's urgent bleating. Devereux spurred his subordinates into action by shouting, "We're now under attack. Pearl Harbor is being bombed.... Break open the ammunition, arm yourselves, and get to your gun positions as fast as you can." Excited Marine sergeants took up the cry, "This is no drill." Devereux's Leathernecks raced to their tents and emerged wearing helmets and field packs and with their hands grasping Springfield rifles or Browning automatic rifles (BARs) and their cartridge belts, bandoliers, and pockets stuffed with ammunition. The Marines quickly boarded trucks and roared off toward their battle stations. They reached their posts on Peale Island and the main islet within forty-five minutes of the first alarm from Hawaii, but it took another forty-five minutes to man the artillery, machine guns, and searchlights on Wilkes Island, which was accessible only by a cranky ferry.

Even with every Marine in his appointed place, the Wake Island Detachment was far from war-ready. Only the 5-inch seacoast battery and the 3-inch antiaircraft battery on Peale were fully sandbagged. Not only were many gun positions poorly protected, but they had little or no camouflage. In addition, the Marines had yet to dig any foxholes or slit trenches to protect themselves from enemy fire. Finally, no one thought to alleviate the Wake Island Detachment's shorthanded condition by promptly mobilizing the Contractors.

Still preoccupied with peacetime construction deadlines, Commander Cunningham decided to avoid unnecessary panic by keeping most Contractors in the dark about the war. Those who had trained with the Marines would be quietly informed of the situation and given permission to report to Devereux for military service. The delayed availability of this additional assistance forced Devereux to lower his guard at 10:00 AM. He telephoned his battery commanders to release most of their Leathernecks to fill sandbags, dig foxholes, or disperse artillery ammunition in small dumps in the brush to ensure that large quantities could not be destroyed by a single hostile bomb or shell. Even though these trained fighting men had been sweating day in and day out to prepare Wake for hostilities and had gotten word of the Pearl Harbor attack, they still found it hard to believe that little Japan, a supposedly backward Asian nation, would dare strike at the United States. As 1st Lt. Clarence A. Barninger, the commander of Battery A, the 5-inch seacoast battery on the main islet, scanned the ocean that morning from Peacock Point, he muttered audibly to himself, "This has to be a big foul up. Those little Yellow Bastards haven't got the guts to attack us."

The Wake Island Detachment possessed no radar, which left VMF-211 as the atoll's only early warning system. Major Putnam opted to keep four Wildcats in the air at all times during daylight. The other eight planes would be refueled and undergo maintenance until their turn came to go on patrol. Commander Cunningham devised an inspired expedient to augment Putnam's efforts. Pan American's *Philippine Clipper* had lifted off Wake's lagoon at dawn bound for Guam, but Cunningham recalled it by radio. The island commander wanted the big M-130 flying boat to conduct a long-range scouting circuit around the atoll escorted by two F4F-3s.

As noon approached on that hectic Monday, massive columns of cumulus clouds began rolling over Wake's south shore. VMF-211's four-plane patrol climbed to 12,000–13,000 feet above the overcast, which blocked the Marine pilots' view of their base. Malfunctioning radios ensured the fliers' total insulation from the catastrophe that would soon engulf their unsuspecting comrades below.

Taking advantage of the clouds, twenty-seven Japanese medium bombers approached Wake from the south, passing unseen beneath VMF-211's airborne Wildcats. The Mitsubishi G3M2 Type 96 Attack Bombers, later code-named Nells by the Allies, belonged to the Chitose Air Group, which was part of the Imperial Japanese Navy's 24th Air Flotilla. They had taken off from their airfield in the Marshalls at dawn and steered a steady course toward their objective. As if guided by an omniscient hand, the Nells burst out of the cloud bank at 11:58 AM less than two thousand feet above the main islet's south beach. The elated pilots could see the American airfield, their main target, dead ahead.

Wake's defenders had only fifteen seconds to react before hell erupted around them, but they hesitated, mistaking the Mitsubishis for an anticipated flight of B-17s. By the time the Americans realized those were enemy planes dropping bombs and firing machine guns, the airfield had turned into a massacre site. The Japanese destroyed seven Wildcats as they sat helpless on the ground and left the eighth badly damaged. Thirty-two of VMF-211's officers and men—more than half its personnel—became casualties, including three pilots and sixteen others killed or mortally wounded. The Japanese torched the Marine squadron's main fuel dump and obliterated half of its other materiel. Nine Nells saved their bombs for the Pan Am complex, where they killed ten Chamorros from Guam who were employed in the airline's hotel as domestics. The G3M2s also strafed Camp 2 and Marine positions on Wilkes Island and Peale Island before departing virtually unscathed by fire belatedly directed at them by Marine antiaircraft batteries and machine guns.

In a single stroke the Chitose Air Group had all but annihilated Wake Island's primary means of aerial defense. The Japanese had also dealt a stinging blow to the American garrison's assumption of racial superiority. "We were amazed," exclaimed Pvt. Ewing E. LaPorte, a machine gunner on Peale. "We had always been told they [the Japanese] were inferior people. We was amazed at how well they were bombing."

Wake's defenders rebounded with remarkable speed from the pain, terror, and humiliation caused by the first enemy air raid. Major Putnam refused hospitalization for a back wound and reorganized VMF-211's remnants to meet the Japanese the next time they appeared over the atoll. With the squadron's engineering officer killed, Putnam entrusted the daunting task of keeping his few intact Wildcats flyable to 2nd Lt. John F. Kinney, an electrical engineering major from Washington State College and a former mechanic with Pan Am. Commander Cunningham assigned three sailors with aviation experience to assist VMF-211 and eighteen other sailors to augment Devereux's Wake Island Detachment.

The garrison received even more reinforcements from the Contractors, the atoll's largest manpower source. Dan Teters permitted 186 of his underlings to serve alongside the Marines while retaining them on CPNAB's payroll. Many of the Contractors were alumni of the Marines' prewar training program, but close to half were simply Americans who wanted to hit back if the Japanese returned. These patriots made indispensable contributions to the Wake Island Detachment's combat effectiveness. Over on Peale's Toki Point, Sgt. Walter A. Bowsher formed sixteen civilians into a crew for Battery D's fourth 3-inch gun. Other Contractors took on equally vital duties at the rest of the atoll's batteries. As First Lieutenant Barninger of Battery A testified, "Without the aid of the civilians who acted as ammunition handlers, I seriously doubt that we could have maintained fire for any length of time." Sixteen Contractors headed straight to the airfield—the most dangerous post on the atoll—and attached themselves to VMF-211. As the majority knew something about engines, they proved a welcome addition to Second Lieutenant Kinney's maintenance and repair effort. Enough Contractors reported to Second Lieutenant Poindexter, the commander of Devereux's .30-caliber machine guns, for him to assign two or more to each of those weapons.

In gun pits across the atoll, Marines and civilians would forge the kind of bonds that can only result from sharing the dangers and hardships of combat. "It was a satisfying feeling being with the Marines," explained John R. Hoskins, who served with Battery E on Wake proper. "They gave a feeling of competence, of bravery, everything. So, you really felt safe with them."

Most Contractors, however, sought safety by hiding in the brush. Some thought it best to stay out of the way and leave the fighting to the experts. Many lacked the mental conditioning necessary to enter combat. Others feared the consequences if they violated their noncombatant status and the Japanese took the atoll. These men must have wished they worked for Pan Am. Less than two hours after the raid, the *Philippine Clipper*'s crew, passengers, and all but one of the atoll's twenty-seven white airline staff crowded into the big seaplane and took off for Midway. The airline's thirty-five surviving Chamorro employees and one tardy passenger were left behind to fend for themselves.

In contrast to these displays of human weakness, at least 250 Contractors who did not take up arms found ways to assist Wake's defenders. Many did what they knew best, utilizing their heavy equipment to build sturdy bomb shelters at Marine battle stations, as well as airplane revetments and personnel dugouts at the airfield for VMF-211. The military found a multitude of other tasks for civilian hands: belting machine-gun ammunition; filling sandbags; fabricating camouflage and portable barbed wire barriers; building latrines; dispersing food, water, and ammunition to caches all over the atoll; and replenishing ammunition stores at various Marine positions. When enemy bombers later spotted Marine antiaircraft batteries, large Contractor work gangs turned out at dusk to move the heavy 3-inch guns and their massive sandbag parapets to new locations by dawn. Finally, Dan Teters organized an all-civilian catering service that strove to serve the entire garrison two hot meals a day.

"A PERFECTLY MAGNIFICENT JOB"

When twenty-seven Nell bombers bore down on Wake at 11:45 AM, Tuesday, December 9, the atoll's defenders were ready for them. Two Wildcats managed to flame one Mitsubishi, and 3-inch fire forced a second Japanese bomber to drop out of formation trailing smoke. Nevertheless, the enemy executed their bombing runs across Peacock Point and Camp 2. At the former, they killed one Marine and knocked out the range finder belonging to Battery A. At the latter, they hit the hospital, finishing off three NCOs from VMF-211 who had been wounded the day before. Japanese bombs and strafing also cut down an unspecified number of Contractors who disregarded Commander Cunningham's advice to steer clear of Camp 2 as a likely target. A Marine officer not stationed on that part of the atoll reported that fifty-five civilians died during this raid—a spurious claim that would be repeated in subsequent histories.

The Chitose Air Group adhered to its pattern of midday raids by pouncing at 10:45 AM on December 10, but the Nells exhibited a newfound respect for the Marine 3-inchers and attacked from the higher altitude of 18,000 feet. That change in tactics could not shield the Japanese from the deadly fury of VMF-211's best pilot. Capt. Henry T. Elrod met the approaching V formations out at sea and shot down two G3M2s in rapid succession. That feat earned Elrod the nickname "Hammering Hank" from thrilled Marines watching below. Undeterred by these losses, the Japanese pressed on. They scored near misses on Battery A and Battery E at Peacock Point, set fire to the Marines' tents at Camp 1, and bombed Wilkes Island—where they detonated a CPNAB shed containing 120 tons of dynamite, destroyed Battery L's range finder, and damaged both of that battery's 5-inch guns—but killed only one Leatherneck.

According to Japanese timetables, the Wake Island campaign should have lasted less than a week. On the war's first day Rear Admiral Sadamichi Kajioka sailed from Ruotta anchorage near Kwajalein in the Marshalls at the head of the Wake Invasion Force, consisting of three older light cruisers, six destroyers, two transports, two patrol boats, two submarines, and 450 troops from the Special Naval Landing Force (SNLF). It was hardly a formidable armada, but the Japanese did not deem Wake a formidable target. The Chitose Air Group boasted that its raids had destroyed the atoll's coastal defenses and virtually wiped out VMF-211. Those overly optimistic claims were just what the Imperial Japanese Navy's high command wanted to hear. With its ships and planes spread thin across the broad Pacific to deliver simultaneous blows against more important objectives, the Japanese navy could afford no close air support for Kajioka's invasion attempt.

Major Devereux became aware of this new threat a little before 3:00 AM, December 11, when Capt. Wesley McCoy Platt, the strong point commander on Wilkes Island, phoned in a report of movement at sea far to the south. As the enemy ships drew closer, Devereux realized that he was not only outgunned but probably outranged by Kajioka's light cruisers. With the two Marine 5-inch batteries on Wake's south shore recently deprived of their range finders, Devereux knew that a duel at maximum or even moderate range would be a losing proposition. He decided to play possum in hopes of drawing the enemy near enough for his gunners to have a chance of hitting something. Luckily for the stern little major, faulty intelligence and sheer hubris made the Japanese play right into his hands.

Since Admiral Kajioka believed he had nothing to fear, his flagship, the light cruiser *Yubari*, steamed impudently to within 8,000 yards of Peacock Point before it began its first firing run at 5:30 AM along the main islet's southern leg. Kajioka's other light cruisers and six destroyers followed suit, steadily closing the range as they banged away at the silent atoll. The shriek and explosions of incoming shells made Devereux's Marines fighting mad, and they grew impatient to start shooting. One frustrated 5-inch battery commander shouted into his field phone at the corporal manning the switchboard in Devereux's command post (CP), "What is the little son-of-a-bitch doing? Goddam it! We've been hitting targets at Pearl Harbor at 12,000 yards and the bastards are in to 7,000! What the hell is he waiting for?" Devereux stood calmly on top of his CP watching the Japanese and had the corporal pass these instructions to his fuming subordinates: "Repeat the order. You will not uncover camouflage until I give the word. You will not fire until I give the word."

As the *Yubari* swung into its third firing run just 4,500 yards off Peacock Point at 6:15 AM, Devereux uttered the order every Marine on Wake ached to hear, "O.K. Open fire." Barninger's Battery A let loose at the Japanese flagship, and Kajioka immediately knew that he had charged into an ambush. The *Yubari* made a run for the open sea, but two 5-inch shells caught it amidships at 5,500–6,000 yards, causing it to limp off spewing smoke and steam. Second Lt. John A. McAlister's Battery L engaged three Japanese destroyers off Wilkes' Kuku Point. McAlister's third salvo connected with a magazine on the leading destroyer, the *Hayate*. A terrible explosion raised the ship out of the water, and it cracked in half, sinking with all hands. Devereux's coastal batteries hit more ships before Kajioka's flotilla could scurry out of range. It had taken the Marines' six 5-inch guns less than two hours to rout the would-be invaders. Now the Japanese had to run an aerial gauntlet before they could feel completely safe.

Shortly before the Japanese started shelling Wake, Major Putnam decided to get VMF-211's four Grumman fighters into the sky. The Wildcats took off with one 100-pound bomb attached to each wing. As the battered Japanese flotilla fled south, Putnam and his comrades screamed down on it, releasing bombs and emptying their .50-caliber machine guns. Then they returned to Wake to rearm and refuel, while VMF-211's other pilots awaited their turn for a crack at the enemy. During the next hour or so, the squadron flew nine more sorties against the Wake Invasion Force. A bomb dropped by the indefatigable Captain Elrod detonated some depth charges on the destroyer *Kisaragi*, which exploded and sank. Unfortunately for VMF-211, Japanese antiaircraft fire caused one Wildcat to crash land on the main islet's south beach, and a second barely reached the airfield before its shot-up engine died.

Although VMF-211's flying strength had been halved, the repulse of Kajioka's flotilla was a sweet victory for the Wake garrison. At a cost of only five Marines slightly wounded, the Americans had sunk two destroyers; damaged three light cruisers, two destroyers, one patrol boat, and one transport; and slain more than three hundred enemy sailors. Before the day ended, Major Putnam reported that one of his pilots had sunk a Japanese submarine that surfaced twenty-five miles off the atoll. That news only boosted the euphoria filling the American garrison. "You'd have thought we'd won the war," recalled Cpl. Bernard E. Richardson of Battery L. The American public reacted in much the same way after the Navy Department informed the press of the glorious events at Wake. Still reeling from the Pearl Harbor disaster and other Allied setbacks in the Pacific, Americans took renewed pride and hope from their country's first clear-cut victory over Japan. President Franklin D. Roosevelt spoke for millions of his fellow citizens on December 12 when he credited the Wake garrison with "doing a perfectly magnificent job."

"A FEELING THAT WE WERE DOOMED"

Set against the broad context of the Pacific War, Admiral Kajioka's botched landing attempt registered as only a minor setback. For an organization as unaccustomed to failure as the Imperial Japanese Navy, however, any reverse had to smart. Kajioka's superiors were determined to save face, and they gave him enough additional resources to ensure his next try at taking the atoll succeeded. The Japanese Fourth Fleet replaced the Wake Invasion Force's two lost destroyers and added four powerful heavy cruisers to its order of battle. Kajioka's landing force received nearly 1,600 additional SNLF troops, raising its size to 2,000. Finally, the high command radioed the six aircraft carriers that had devastated Pearl Harbor and diverted two of them and their escorts to support the Wake operation.

While the Wake Invasion Force licked its wounds and reorganized, the Chitose Air Group continued bombing the atoll, delivering attacks almost every day. The 24th Air Flotilla augmented the aerial war of attrition with the gigantic Kawanishi H6K4 Navy Type 97 flying boats of the Yokohama Air Group at Majuro. The Mavises, as the Allies came to know them, would strike before dawn, depriving the Americans of much-needed sleep. This bombardment campaign inflicted relatively few casualties on Wake's garrison, but each raid took a toll on the defenders' nerves, physical endurance, and materiel.

Bad weather deterred Japanese fliers from pounding Wake on Saturday, December 20, but the clouds and rain did not stop a lone PBY out of Pearl Harbor from landing in the atoll's lagoon at 3:20 PM. The three ensigns aboard brought Commander Cunningham the welcome news that help was on the way. Despite the severe drubbing the U.S. Pacific Fleet took on December 7, Admiral Kimmel had not lost his fighting spirit or his resolve to keep Wake Island out of Japanese hands. On December 15 and 16, a relief force built around the carrier USS *Saratoga* sortied from Pearl and headed toward Wake. Kimmel intended to reinforce the atoll with a second Marine fighter squadron, 209 more Leathernecks from the 4th Defense Battalion, early-warning and fire-control radar, and additional weapons, ammunition, and equipment. The relief force also carried orders to evacuate all but 350 Contractors. If all went well, the relief force could be expected by December 23 or 24.

The PBY slipped away from Wake at 7:00 AM the next day. It carried one passenger, a Marine communications officer who had been working with VMF-211. Two hours later the Americans the PBY had left behind learned that the aid promised them might not arrive in time. Eighteen fighters and thirty-one bombers from the Japanese carriers *Soryu* and *Hiryu* swooped down on the atoll and subjected Marine positions to harrowing, low-level attacks. The proximity of enemy carriers also informed Wake's defenders that a second amphibious assault attempt had to be imminent. The *Soryu* and *Hiryu* hurled thirty-nine aircraft against the atoll on December 22, and VMF-211 sacrificed its last two Wildcats in an uneven duel with six Japanese fighters. That double loss depressed the surviving Marines more than anything that had happened since the war's first day. "When that last Wildcat was gone it was like loosing all the best friends one has," reflected TSgt. Charles A. Holmes of Battery E. "It began to give me a feeling that we were doomed."

Sergeant Holmes did not know it, but his enemies also faced the future with trepidation. The Japanese officers who had witnessed the disconcerting marksmanship of Major Devereux's coastal batteries on December 11 could not believe that so much damage had been wrought by only a few medium guns. They came away from that encounter convinced that Wake had been armed with ordnance much heavier than 5-inch guns—most probably 12-inchers taken off older American battleships.

As Admiral Kajioka developed his plans for a second amphibious assault, he took pains to spare his flotilla from exposure to another close-range ship-to-shore duel. The 900 SNLF troops composing the admiral's first assault wave would storm the atoll's south shore hours before dawn on December 23. To guarantee that a substantial number of invaders reached dry land, *Patrol Boat 32* and *Patrol Boat 33*—a pair of converted destroyers containing more than half of the first wave—were to run aground on the main islet opposite the airfield. Kajioka also directed the light cruisers *Tenryu* and *Tatsuta* to circle around to the north and unleash a brief bombardment against Peale Island at 1:00 AM. He hoped that would distract the Americans and draw their reserves to the wrong side of the atoll. Aside from that token gesture, the assault troops assigned to breach Wake Isand's defenses could expect no more protection as they approached hostile beaches than the cover of darkness and roar of the surf. Kajioka intended the 1,100 SNLF troops he held in reserve to enter the fight once daylight disclosed the location of the first wave's beachheads and close air support became available from the

Soyru and *Hiryu*. If the SNLF lacked the power to subdue Wake's garrison, Kajioka was prepared to run his six regular destroyers aground, arm their crews with rifles, and hurl them against the Americans.

Kajioka's tactics smacked more of desperation than sound amphibious doctrine. Like most military plans, his began to go awry the moment they went into operation. The *Tenryu* and *Tatsuta* apparently lost their bearings and ended up shelling an empty stretch of ocean. The light cruisers' distant muzzle flashes spooked the Americans enough to prompt a mistaken report of small boats off Peale's Toki Point. Second Lieutenant Poindexter, the commander of Devereux's mobile reserve at Camp 1, loaded two trucks with twenty Marines, fourteen civilians, and four .30-caliber machine guns and set out for the supposedly threatened sector. The little convoy rumbled east along the main islet's southern leg and then turned north to follow the road past the eastern edge of the airfield. As Poindexter's lead truck approached the partially buried magazine that had housed Devereux's CP since December 14, a Marine flagged it down. Since Poindexter's departure from Camp 1, the major had received a flurry of reports telephoned from Wilkes Island and various stations on the main islet that persuaded him the Japanese meant to land on Wake's lee shore—just as they had tried on December 11. Devereux instructed Poindexter to deploy the Mobile Reserve between Camp 1 and the airfield's west end.

Even though the Japanese had bungled their deception stratagem, a moonless night cloaked their invasion troops until they were so close inshore that Batteries A and L could not bring their 5-inchers to bear on them. At 2:45 AM, Marine Gunner Clarence B. McKinstry heard the thrum of a motor over the noise of waves crashing against Wilkes. A few seconds of illumination from a Marine searchlight revealed two Daihatsu landing craft packed with approximately one hundred SNLF men. The hulking McKinstry and civilian crews converted two 3-inch antiaircraft guns belonging to Battery F into antiboat weapons, cutting the fuses on their shells to explode at pointblank range. At the same time, bursts from Marine machine guns began ringing off the Daihatsus' steel sides. The whirr of shrapnel and streaming tracers could not stop the landing craft, however, and they rammed into the boulder-strewn beach, lowered their ramps, and disgorged their occupants. Rallied by screaming officers and warrant officers, the SNLF troops charged Battery F, forcing McKinstry and his Contractors, who had no small arms, to abandon their position.

Over on the main islet, 2nd Lt. Robert M. Hanna spotted *Patrol Boat 32* as it came looming out of the darkness west of Peacock Point. Hanna led a Marine corporal and two Contractors in a frantic race to a damaged 3-inch gun that had been moved to Wake's south beach for just such an exigency. The four Americans slammed at least twenty shells into the grounded vessel, setting off the ammunition in its small arms magazine. The resulting pyrotechnics provided illumination for Marine machine gunners, and they opened fire on the SNLF men tumbling over the patrol boat's gunwales or struggling through the surf below. As Sub-Lieutenant Shigeyoshi Ozeki slid down a rope hanging off *Patrol Boat 32*, streams of tracers told him that the Americans "were well entrenched and waiting for us." Ozeki felt like he and his comrades were being flung "into the jaws of a hungry beast that made its lair on Wake Island."

The exploding ammunition bursting over *Patrol Boat 32* also revealed its sister ship, *Patrol Boat 33*, sitting grounded some seven hundred yards to the west, which made that boat a fine target as well. Dozens of battle-maddened Japanese crawled across the rocky beach and groped their way through the brush toward Hanna's barking gun, eager to silence it. They met with a blistering check from Major Putnam and a dozen Leathernecks from VMF-211, fighting now as infantry. Faithful to the end, fourteen of VMF-211's civilian helpers trailed their Marine comrades, toting extra ammunition for the latter's Thompson submachine guns and BARs. Captain Elrod, the squadron's chief hero, did fearful execution with his Tommy gun in fierce, close-quarters action. A Japanese bullet finally killed him when he paused to throw a hand grenade.[5]

Poindexter's mobile reserve succeeded in reaching the west end of Wake's airfield ahead of the Japanese. The lieutenant's four machine-gun crews and supporting riflemen announced their presence by ambushing some SNLF troops from *Patrol Boat 33* as they tried to launch an advance toward Camp 1. The mobile reserve held its ground until an hour before daylight, finally retiring after the Japanese began working their way around the Americans' left flank. Poindexter pulled back to Camp 1, where he formed a line with ten .30-caliber machine guns straddling the main islet's southern leg and stopped the enemy cold. Then he mounted a counterattack that regained all the ground he had recently abandoned, forcing the Japanese to retire nine hundred yards.[6]

Poindexter was not the only officer of the Wake Island Detachment to exhibit such aggressive instincts or tactical acumen. As the sun rose over Wilkes Island, Captain Platt rounded up eight Marine riflemen and a pair of .30-caliber machine guns manned by two more Leathernecks and six Contractors. Platt placed his squad in a thin skirmish line behind the perimeter the Japanese had established around Battery F. The SNLF men already had their hands full and their backs to Platt. Second Lieutenant McAlister and Gunner McKinstry had mobilized Battery L and some Marine searchlight operators to meet the enemy as infantry.

Accompanied by five Contractors carrying grenades, they started pressing the other side of the Japanese beachhead as soon as it grew light enough to tell friend from foe. Platt commenced his attack around the same time. Struck from two directions at once, the bewildered Japanese soon succumbed to panic and bunched up. The Americans exterminated them with ruthless efficiency, taking only two prisoners for intelligence purposes.[7]

From a reinforced concrete CP on the lower shank of Wake's northern leg, Major Devereux endeavored vainly to monitor the morning's fighting. The atoll's garrison depended on a field telephone network for its communications, but Japanese troops cut the lines wherever they found them. Hence, Devereux lost contact with his subordinates from Peacock Point west, and he had no inkling of what Poindexter or Platt had accomplished. All he knew was that enemy troops had crossed the airfield and were filtering into the brush along its eastern fringes to snipe at Battery E. Concluding that the Japanese had overrun Wilkes and the main islet's southern leg, Devereux deployed a skirmish line south of his CP, bolstering it with sixty Marines and Contractors trucked down from Peale Island.

Commander Cunningham relied on Devereux for his knowledge of how the garrison was faring, which resulted in the blind leading the blind. In addition to a string of increasingly pessimistic briefings from the Marine major, Cunningham received bad news that desperate morning from another quarter. At 2:50 AM, the island commander radioed his superiors at Pearl Harbor, "ISLAND UNDER GUNFIRE X APPARENTLY LANDING." That message elicited a terse but shattering response: "NO FRIENDLY VESSELS SHOULD BE IN YOUR IMMEDIATE VICINITY TODAY X KEEP ME INFORMED X."

Admiral Kimmel, Wake's best friend at Pearl, had been relieved of his command on December 17 by Vice Adm. William S. Pye, a temporary replacement. Rattled by the Pearl Harbor disaster, Pye did not want to risk any of the Pacific Fleet's remaining ships for a lightly manned, faraway stronghold on the verge of capture. Pye's wavering support for saving Wake evaporated completely after Cunningham flashed this ominous message at 5:00 AM: "ENEMY ON ISLAND ISSUE IN DOUBT." The *Saratoga* received Pye's recall order when it was just 425 miles from Wake. The task force's sailors and their Marine passengers reacted with curses and tears, but they obeyed orders and abandoned their embattled comrades on the barren coral pile that had embodied America's pride for nearly two weeks.[8]

Five hours after the Japanese landed on Wake, Cunningham and Devereux arrived at an agonizing decision. By that time, the island commander and his senior Marine subordinate believed that the Japanese held half of the atoll and had killed or captured that sector's defenders. The two American officers expected an all-out attack on the skirmish line guarding Devereux's CP at any moment. Cunningham was convinced that he confronted overwhelming enemy power on land, at sea, and in the air. Informed that no help could be expected for twenty-four hours, he judged that further resistance would produce only needless casualties. Sometime around 8:00 AM, he ordered Wake's surviving defenders to surrender. What remained to be seen was whether an enemy that had suffered tremendous losses in winning the atoll would deign to take prisoners.[9]

CHAPTER TWO

"the emperor has . . . presented you with your lives"

the shock of capture

"WE HAD NO IDEA OF SURRENDERING"
After Commander Cunningham ordered Wake Island's surrender, he exited his CP alone. The island commander tossed his .45 automatic pistol into a nearby latrine, slid into the cab of a pickup truck, and drove to his prewar quarters—a wooden cottage on the main islet's northern leg. Cunningham wearily removed the soiled khaki uniform he had worn day and night since December 8. He shaved, washed his face, and donned a set of dress blues. He was gambling that a dignified appearance might make a positive impression on the Japanese. He then attached a white flag to his truck and headed south with "no particular hopes" the enemy would spare him or any of Wake's other defenders. Nevertheless, Cunningham felt obligated to try to arrange a capitulation for the sake of the hundreds of unarmed Contractors entrusted to his care.[1]

In the meantime, Major Devereux struggled to inform his hard-fighting Marines that Wake Island now belonged to their foes. Implementing the surrender order turned out to be one of the darkest moments in Devereux's life. He referred to it ever after as "the death of pride." Surrender ran counter to everything Devereux believed in as a Marine. Until Cunningham's final phone call that hectic morning, Cpl. Robert McCulloch Brown, a member of Devereux's headquarters staff, remained certain that the major would fight to the death. But Devereux was either too good or conventional an officer to defy a direct order.

Devereux turned sadly to his munitions officer, Marine Gunner John A. Hamas, and said, "Commander Cunningham has ordered us to surrender. Fix up a white flag and pass the word to cease firing." A sullen Hamas strode toward the skirmish line of Marines and armed Contractors deployed outside Devereux's

CP. "Major's orders!" he shouted. "We're surrendering. . . . Major's orders." Devereux's temper snapped when he heard himself credited with the decision to surrender. Lapsing into unaccustomed profanity, he protested from the CP door, "It's not my order, God damn it."[2]

Once Devereux regained his composure, he instructed every American position still linked by field phone to his CP, "Cease firing. Destroy all weapons. The island is being surrendered." Among the few battle stations to receive that call were Battery B on Toki Point, Battery E on the north side of the airfield, and Battery A and some .50-caliber machine-gun pits on Peacock Point that repaired a break in the line just in time to catch the bad news. Devereux also got through to the half-buried concrete magazine south of his CP that Lt. (j.g.) G. Mason Kahn, the Wake Island Detachment's Navy surgeon, had converted into a hospital for the garrison's sick and wounded. Even though the hospital now lay behind enemy lines, the SNLF men had not yet discovered it nor cut its communications wire. With no friendly troops on hand to protect the hospital's patients, Dr. Kahn raised a white bed sheet over his installation and closed its heavy steel door.[3]

If ordering the Wake Marines to stop fighting came hard for Devereux, his subordinates found it just as difficult to obey. Like all Leathernecks, they subscribed to the same inflexible warrior creed as their major. As Cpl. Guy J. Kelnhofer explained, "We had been indoctrinated, I don't mean trained, I mean indoctrinated, there was no such thing as surrender. Marines didn't surrender." Pfc. James O. King, a communicator assigned to Devereux's CP, shared Kelnhofer's incredulity. "I had heard it from the commander [Devereux] himself," King recalled, "and I still found it hard to believe." Pfc. John R. Himelrick, a machine gunner posted on the main islet's south beach, scribbled similar sentiments in his diary: "We had no idea of surrendering. We all figured this was our last day & we were going out fighting." TSgt. Charles A. Holmes gauged the impact of the surrender order on his comrades in Battery E: "The reaction of the men . . . was complete astonishment. . . . Some broke down and wept like children and others were just mum and stunned, including myself."[4]

It was not just Marine Corps pride that made Wake's defenders reluctant to lay down their arms—it was fear. "Surrender is not always a way to escape the hazards of the battlefield," Corporal Kelnhofer later observed. "Many who surrender in combat are killed as soon as they put down their weapons." Winston S. Churchill, who suffered capture himself during the Second Anglo-Boer War four decades earlier, would have known exactly what Kelnhofer meant. "The position of a prisoner of war is painful and humiliating," Churchill wrote. "A man tries his best to kill another, and finding that he cannot succeed asks his enemy for mercy." The Wake Marines and their Army, Navy, and civilian comrades had not only tried to kill their assailants—they had succeeded all too well. According to Sub-Lieutenant Shigeyoshi Ozeki, the only doctor in the Japanese landing force, the Americans slew three hundred invaders and wounded many more on December 23. "Many of our wounded men were soon to die from the horrendous wounds they received from the enemy's large caliber machine guns," Ozeki testified. "As a doctor it was a nightmare trying to treat all the brave men who had thrown themselves on enemy machine gun nests."[5]

When the Japanese finally finished securing the atoll, they were shocked to discover that they had suffered much heavier casualties than the Americans. Counting the 300 to 350 SNLF troops slaughtered that last desperate morning, the Wake Island campaign cost the Imperial Japanese Navy as many as 900 to 1,000 dead, along with two destroyers and one submarine sunk, two converted destroyers deliberately sacrificed, and twenty-one aircraft shot down. American deaths totaled only ninety-six, and forty-seven of those were of civilians. Among the heaps of Japanese who fell on December 23 lay only fourteen Marines and fourteen Contractors. "We were told several times that it was unfair that they [the Japanese] lost so many more men than we," gloated 1st Lt. Woodrow M. Kessler, Battery B's commander. The growing awareness among Wake's conquerors that they had suffered such disproportionate losses must have plunged them into an ugly frame of mind.[6]

Even if the Japanese had purchased Wake at a comparatively low price, the atoll's defenders still would have had good reason to expect little mercy. Next to "Marines don't surrender," the battle cry most commonly sounded by Wake's defenders for the previous sixteen days had been, "The Japs don't take prisoners." Since the start of the Second Sino–Japanese War in 1937, the Western news media had carried lurid accounts of the numerous atrocities that the Japanese military committed against captured Chinese soldiers and the general populace. Every American on Wake had read stories or seen film or photographic evidence of terror bombings, mass machine gunnings and beheadings, bound prisoners used for bayonet practice, and the rape and murder of unarmed civilians. U.S. Marines stationed in North China or Shanghai before the Pearl Harbor attack purchased snapshots of bestial war crimes from Japanese soldiers, and those disgusting images were soon circulating through the Corps' stateside barracks. This perception of the Japanese fighting man as an inhumane beast became so prevalent that many Leathernecks assumed it enjoyed official sanction. "Marine

Corps propaganda drummed into our heads that the Japs never bothered to take prisoners," claimed Cpl. Bernard E. Richardson of Battery L.[7]

That strong preconception explains why the surrender order filled most in the Wake garrison with dread rather than relief. "We didn't know what we were surrendering to," related 2nd Lt. Robert Hanna. "We didn't know what treatment we might get. We hadn't the vaguest idea. We'd heard a lot of rumors." Cpl. Franklin A. Gross, a .50-caliber machine gunner on Peacock Point, expressed his anxieties in these words: "So here you're surrendering to people who don't take prisoners. Do you know what a conflict that was that morning?" News of the surrender made Pvt. Edward V. Sturgeon of Battery B and many of his comrades feel sick. Pfc. James C. Venable of Battery E called that moment "probably the lowest point of my life."[8]

Deep down, the majority of Wake's defenders considered surrender a big mistake. "We anticipated that we were all going to die where we were," remembered Corporal Kelnhofer. "It was just a matter of how many people we were going to kill before they killed us." Cpl. Eschol E. Davis, a communications specialist on Peacock Point, harbored the same fatalistic resolve, recalling, "My idea was to take as many as you could with you." Cpl. Thomas W. Johnson of Battery D later confided these glum thoughts to an interviewer, "I feel that we give up too easy. . . . I'd rather died in combat, I think."[9]

On top of everything else, it galled the Wake Islanders to submit to an enemy they saw as racially inferior. Every man in the atoll's garrison and the vast majority of the Contractors were Caucasian, and all but a few of them had been born in the United States. They grew up in a Jim Crow country where whites took their dominance for granted and people of color challenging the social order risked persecution, arrest, or even lynching. The U.S. Marine Corps was still an all-white organization, the U.S. Army confined African Americans to a few segregated units, and the Navy enlisted them mainly as domestic help and menial laborers. The Americans trapped on Wake had thought they inhabited a white man's world, but the Japanese turned that world on its head. Contractor Edwin Darby "Ned" Nye captured his comrades' chagrin and bewilderment when he exclaimed, "It's a shame these great big Americans being captured by these midgets."[10]

Some Wake Islanders rose above their cultural biases and concluded that surrender represented their only chance for survival. "We all hated to do it," admitted Cpl. Henry L. Durrwachter, a Battery D Marine who fought on the skirmish line near Devereux's CP, "but it was either that or annihilation." Many others, however, never got over the humiliation of becoming prisoners. "I did not surrender and neither did my fellow marines," insisted Corporal Kelnhhofer. "We were . . . surrendered by our commanding officers." Technical Sergeant Holmes, another member of Battery E, felt that he had been "just plain sacrificed . . . thrown to the enemy. After so gallant a fight, how could my country do this to me and my fellow marines?"[11]

"THAT HUMILIATING AND ONEROUS JOB"

Shortly after Major Devereux phoned Dr. Kahn about the surrender, the line to the hospital went dead. Concerned about the safety of the American wounded, Devereux called to some Marines standing beside his CP, "Rig a white flag you can carry. We'll have to go down there." Sgt. Donald R. Malleck, a radioman from the CP staff, volunteered to accompany the major. Maj. George H. Potter Jr., the Wake Island Detachment's executive officer and commander of the CP skirmish line, also wanted to go along, but Devereux waved him away. "Under the circumstances," an awed Potter remarked, "I considered that an act of great courage and under any circumstances who in hell would have ever wanted that humiliating and onerous job?" Sergeant Malleck tore up a white sheet and attached a piece to a mop handle. "I remembered thinking it wasn't very neat," Malleck quipped, "but its purpose wasn't altogether that honorable." Then he and Devereux started down the road to make contact with the Japanese.[12]

Devereux's mission almost came to a tragic halt before it barely began. Spotting two Americans approaching under a flag of truce, a lone SNLF man stepped out of the brush and onto the road. The Japanese wore a steel helmet with camouflage netting, greenish khaki tropical combat dress, and split-toed canvas shoes with rubber soles. What most impressed Devereux and Malleck, however, was the enemy seaman's Arisaka rifle and fixed bayonet, which he leveled at them as he drew closer. Motioning with his bayonet, the Japanese made Devereux remove his helmet and pistol belt. He forced Malleck to do the same and had the sergeant peel off his shirt for good measure. Satisfied that the two Marines had been rendered harmless, the Japanese signaled them to resume their trek south.

A few seconds later a second SNLF man appeared on the road and a Springfield rifle barked from Potter's skirmish line. That shot was fired by Cpl. Leon A. Graves of Battery D. Exhausted by a night of hunting Japanese through the brush, Graves had dozed off just before Devereux passed the word to cease fire. Awakening with a start, he saw an SNLF man in the open and reacted instinctively. "Watch this," Graves hissed to another Marine as he squeezed the trigger. The .30-caliber round hit the second Japanese between the eyes, throwing him on his back as his brains spilled from his shattered skull.

A furious Devereux hollered at his subordinates, "I gave an order to cease fire and God damn it I mean just that!" Incredibly, the first SNLF man kept his cool and stifled any impulse to exact retribution from Devereux or Malleck. He simply ascertained that his comrade was dead and then gestured at the two Americans to keep moving.[13]

Devereux reached Dr. Kahn's hospital several minutes after the Japanese had occupied it. A squad of nervous SNLF troops stumbled across the magazine and banged on its steel door with their rifle butts. Capt. Herbert C. Freuler, a Marine pilot wounded in VMF-211's last dogfight the day before, was the senior American officer present. He took it upon himself to admit the enemy to the hospital. As he cracked open the door, those patients who could stand or sit up on their cots raised their hands to signify submission. Seeing sudden movement inside the dimly lit chamber behind Freuler, a Japanese seaman thrust his rifle through the opening before the captain had moved the door more than six inches and fired. A bullet whizzed past Freuler's head and ricocheted off the hospital's curved concrete ceiling. That single round hit three patients. It wounded one Contractor in the buttocks, winged another American in the shoulder, and killed a civilian cook when it smashed into his forehead.[14]

Devereux encountered a young SNLF officer who spoke a little English standing outside the hospital and informed him, "We are surrendering." Moments later, Commander Cunningham pulled up in his pickup truck. While the island commander attempted to arrange formal surrender terms, Devereux offered to take Malleck and coax the other Americans still at large on the main islet and Wilkes Island to stop fighting. Devereux set out escorted by the English-speaking SNLF officer, another who held a samurai sword against the Marine major's back, and twenty Japanese riflemen. It would take Devereux five hours or so to make his way along the atoll's south shore to most of the points where Americans were still battling Wake's invaders. As expected, the trip was fraught with tension, peril, and heartache—and not a few surprises.[15]

Due to the communications breakdown that bedeviled the atoll's garrison in the final hours of fighting, Devereux expected to find a few scattered remnants of his command alive and resisting the Japanese. He soon discovered that he had seriously underestimated the Wake Marines and the sailors and Contractors who stood with them in the field. The badly decimated SNLF companies had failed to overrun any important American positions. Not only were the Leathernecks and their auxiliaries holding their own, but they had even gone on the offensive in places and attained spectacular results. Captain Platt's victory on Wilkes Island,

and Second Lieutenant Poindexter's advance to the west edge of the airfield, inclined many of their men to conclude that the Japanese were losing the battle. That hunch made those Americans all the more reluctant to accept the necessity of surrender. When Devereux hailed some Marine positions, their occupants initially suspected that he was acting under duress and the Japanese were trying to trick them.[16]

Whatever Wake's defenders may have thought at the time, many later thanked their maker that they served under Maj. James P. S. Devereux on December 23, 1941. If the Marine Corps possessed one officer capable of compelling men animated by combat frenzy to abruptly throw themselves on the mercy of a supposedly merciless enemy, it was Devereux. His Leathernecks feared him almost as much as they did the enemy. As Private First Class Himelrick declared, "When the Major gave the word we automatically surrendered without thinking." Cpl. John S. Johnson Jr., a .30-caliber machine gunner who played a leading role in Platt's counterattack on Wilkes Island, offered a similar assessment: "You just didn't think about disobeying the major."[17]

In reality, Devereux did not have as easy a time ending the fighting as Himelrick and Johnson implied. The surrender process was jeopardized from beginning to end by battle-crazed men who either did not realize what was happening or refused to accept it. Both sides exchanged pot shots after the white flags went up. Devereux himself attracted several bullets from Japanese seamen who did not seem to care about endangering his SNLF escorts. All of those shots missed, and Devereux carried on with unflinching coolness. He maintained the same impassive mien whenever he and his party neared a source of American gunfire. "This is Major Devereux," he would shout. "Drop your arms. Surrender. The island has been surrendered."[18]

Devereux faced some of his most suspenseful moments at Camp 1. As the major neared the camp, a floatplane from a Japanese cruiser swooped low overhead. A Marine machine gunner still unaware of the surrender raked the enemy aircraft, and it flew away trailing smoke and losing altitude. The stricken machine burst into flames and crashed on or just beyond the eastern end of the main islet. It was just as well for Devereux and the other Americans with him that the plane's demise could not be seen from Camp 1.[19]

When the SNLF troops finally swarmed into the Marine camp, they spotted the Wake Island Detachment's American flag waving from a fifty-foot water tower. Emitting exultant cries, some Japanese seamen rushed over to the tower and cheered one of their number as he climbed up and cut down the Stars and Stripes. Pfc. George G. Hubley never forgot that moment of symbolic emasculation: "That was the hardest part of the whole war for me—watch[ing] that flag go down."

S2C Cassius E. Smith shared Hubley's distress and outrage: "When they took that flag down, the flag was dropped . . . dropped on the ground. I think if somebody had said, 'Let's get them sons of bitches,' they all would have done it right there. No arms, no nothing." Devereux could read those thoughts in the furrowing brows and clenched fists of the Marines, sailors, and Contractors clustered around him. He called them back to their senses by growling, "Hold it! Keep your heads all of you."[20]

Devereux almost had a mutiny on his hands after he reached Wilkes Island, his last stop. By then, it was past 1:00 PM, and the afternoon sun raised beads of sweat on the major's bald head. Spying some Marines as they came out of the brush ahead, Devereux launched into what had become a well-rehearsed routine: "It's me, Major Devereux! Lay down your arms! Lay down your arms! The island has been surrendered! Lay down your arms! The island has been surrendered!"

Too far back in the brush to see Devereux or hear him identify himself, an angry Captain Platt roared, "Who in the hell gave that order?"

"It's me, Major Devereux."

Platt pushed forward until he stood face to face with the major, who repeated the surrender order. Platt snapped back that Marines never surrendered.

Devereux rose to the challenge. "I'm not asking you," he emphasized. "I'm telling you. That is an order, Captain. You will surrender."

Devereux's firm tone abruptly reminded Platt that he was addressing a superior officer. The captain's insubordinate glare melted away and tears filled his eyes. Devereux knew the argument had swung his way, and he switched to a more soothing approach. He assured Platt that the Japanese would treat their prisoners humanely, conveniently concealing the fact that the enemy had yet to commit to such a pledge. "It's an honorable surrender," he promised Platt.

"Major," the captain asked bitterly, "do you know what you are asking us to do?"

"Yes, Cutie," Devereux answered with rare fatherly warmth. "Tell your men to lay down their arms. It's an honorable surrender."[21]

It required about another hour for the Japanese to root all of Platt's men out of their foxholes and dugouts and concentrate them by the Wilkes ferry for transfer to the main islet. By 2:00 PM all firing on the atoll had died out. The battle for Wake Island was over. Its defenders now commenced a much different and much longer struggle, but one that would prove just as desperate as their sixteen days in combat.[22]

"THEY STRIPPED US DOWN BALLS AND ASS NAKED AND HOGTIED US"

In many cases, the Wake Island defenders enjoyed at least a few moments of grace between the time they learned of the surrender and when the Japanese actually took them into custody. The Marines and their auxiliaries put those precious minutes to good use. The Americans' first priority was to disable their own weapons, spitefully depriving the enemy of the most valuable victory trophies on the atoll. Riflemen made their Springfields inoperable by disengaging the bolts and firing pins. They either flung these small parts into the brush or buried them in the sand. Some Leathernecks smashed their rifles against coral rocks, bending steel barrels and shattering wooden stocks. Marine artillerymen worked together to deny the Japanese the future use of their big guns and range equipment. At Battery A and Battery B, gunners removed the firing locks from their 5-inch guns. They threw those mechanisms into the ocean at the former location, and into the lagoon at the latter.[23]

The personnel manning Battery E at first tried to blow up their 3-inch antiaircraft guns by loading them with live rounds, stuffing the barrels with blankets, sand, and coral chunks, and then yanking the lanyards. The resulting explosions only succeeded in polishing the inside of the 3-inchers' barrels. The Marines next tried dropping hand grenades down the muzzles, but that made no noticeable impression either. In the end, the sky gunners emulated their comrades in Batteries A and B. They removed the firing locks from the ordnance and heaved those mechanisms into the lagoon. The men also drained hydraulic fluid from the guns' recoil cylinders and smashed their telescopes, prisms, and data receivers. First Lt. William W. Lewis, Battery E's commander, drew his .45 automatic and emptied a clip into his outfit's height finder. He fired seven more rounds into the director, another range instrument. Lewis' subordinates delivered the coup de grâce by chopping up the electrical cables that transmitted data from the range section to the guns. Surveying the wreckage, Sergeant Holmes noted with grim satisfaction, "I doubt if our equipment was worth anything to the Japs . . . other than scrap metal."[24]

After Battery E completed its destructive work, First Lieutenant Lewis had a Marine tie a white undershirt to a long pole. Holding this improvised flag of truce high in the air, Lewis and his men marched toward Devereux's CP to turn themselves over to the Japanese. On that walk, Cpl. Guy Kelnhofer hungrily drank in what he feared were the last sights of his life. "I can remember the devastation," he recounted forty-five years later. "It was just very impressive. There were trucks all shot up, . . . windshields smashed, and lying on their sides on the side of the road. There were shell craters all over, ammunition boxes, debris, weapons lying here and there along the road."[25]

The commanders of two of the Wake Island Detachment's coastal batteries decided to let the enemy come to them. First Lt. Clarence Barninger permitted the men of Battery A to gorge themselves on the canned food cached near Peacock Point. At Battery B on Toki Point, First Lieutenant Kessler broke out his unit's remaining stores of canned food and candy bars and urged his Marines to eat as much as they could hold. He also instructed them to keep their rifles in firing condition until the last possible moment just in case the Japanese came with murder on their minds. An equally pessimistic Sgt. Jack B. Cook of Battery A pulled the few dollars he had in his pockets and scattered them to the four winds. In contrast to Cook, Sgt. Ernest G. Rogers, an Army radioman stationed at Commander Cunningham's CP, hid $100 in a crack in a big boulder, hoping to retrieve the money later. Other soldiers in Rogers' detail lit their cigarettes with $20 bills as they sat and waited for the Japanese.[26]

The first sizable groups of Wake Islanders to meet their captors face to face were those located closest to Major Devereux's CP. These consisted initially of the servicemen and Contractors from Major Potter's skirmish line and the occupants of Dr. Kahn's military hospital. The Marines from Battery E and a few civilian helpers joined this POW concentration after several SNLF troops intercepted them roughly fifty yards to seventy-five yards from Devereux's CP.[27]

Since the Americans had disarmed themselves and lacked the capacity for effective resistance, they were willing to do almost anything their captors demanded. As the SNLF men took their opponents into custody, however, a serious obstacle presented itself. None of the Americans spoke Japanese. A handful of SNLF troops knew a little broken English, but they could not be present everywhere a translator might be needed. In addition, Wake's conquerors could hardly be expected to exercise much patience. Six hours of continuous fighting had strained their nerves and sapped their vitality. These Japanese had seen hundreds of their comrades cut down by the men they now held in their power, and they were mortified to count so few dead Americans on the ground they had taken. Gunfire still crackled angrily to the west, and the SNLF men could not be sure if the Americans still fighting would respect Devereux's authority and surrender.

Contractor Earl R. Row thought the Japanese who took him prisoner looked frightened. They were certainly apprehensive, even after they ascertained that the Americans no longer possessed weapons. "We had been instructed that in hand-to-hand combat to never allow an American 'gorilla' to come within an arm's length," revealed Sub-Lieutenant Ozeki, "as they were all trained boxers. We were told that one solid punch was enough to break a man's neck."[28]

When unintelligible shouts failed to produce the reactions the Japanese desired, they resorted to the universal language of the rifle butt and naked bayonet. One SNLF man jabbed his bayonet into the leg of a Marine for being too slow to drop a BAR. Two other Japanese beat a second Leatherneck unconscious for some unintentional offense.[29]

No sooner had the Japanese secured the military hospital than they herded Dr. Kahn and his ambulatory patients outside. The SNLF men lined up the Americans on the road and directed them to strip. Some prisoners were compelled to remove every stitch except their socks and shoes, while others retained their underpants. The defenders of Potter's line and Battery E's personnel underwent the same treatment, but survivors from those two outfits cannot agree on whether they were stripped at Devereux's CP and then marched to the hospital, or if they lost their clothes after they reached the latter position. Before, during, and after the stripping process, the Wake Islanders suffered another indignity much more common to battlefield capture. Individual Japanese would confront a prisoner and demand he give up his wristwatch or other valuables. If a POW protested that a ring fit too tightly to remove from his finger, an SNLF man only had to whip out his bayonet, which invariably enabled the threatened party to instantly divest himself of his property.[30]

After the Americans disrobed, their captors made them cross their wrists behind their backs. The Japanese lashed together each prisoner's wrists with a piece of communications wire appropriated from the Marines' field phone network. They next took a second strand of wire, looped it around the American's neck, and tied the ends to his wrists, tugging them high up his back. This arrangement subjected its victims to acute discomfort. The wire bit into their wrists, which made their hands grow numb. If an American tried to struggle out of his bonds or just lower his wrists to relieve an ache in his shoulders he would choke himself.[31]

Corporal Brown of Devereux's staff distilled the Japanese method for confining freshly caught prisoners into a concise formula: "They stripped us down balls and ass naked and hogtied us." Many Wake Islanders viewed such conduct as proof of Japanese barbarity, but it was actually an effective way for a limited quantity of captors to neutralize growing numbers of captives. "When you are stripped naked," remarked Contractor Don W. Ludington, "you don't put up much of a fight." As an added precaution, the Japanese cut up more communications wire and tied some Americans together by their ankles. One SNLF man celebrated the Wake Islanders' helplessness by pulling a fist full of bills from a confiscated wallet and throwing them away. "American money no good," he crowed. "Japanese money number one."[32]

After the Japanese finished restraining their prisoners, they formed the Americans in tight rows on the road and directed them to sit down. Coral chat bit into the POWs' buttocks and lower legs, compounding their misery. "We were defeated, very unhappy, you know," remembered Private First Class Venable. "We were tied up in this wire and everyone was feeling bad."[33]

Demoralization took second place to cold, gnawing fear when the Japanese placed three to six machine guns in front of the immobilized column of naked Americans, loaded the weapons, and cocked them as if preparing to fire. Second Lt. John F. Kinney of VMF-211, a dysentery patient dragged from the hospital, decided that "the guards were making preparations to dispose of us with the least expenditure of ammunition." The other Americans massed around Kinney leaped to the same conclusion. "I had read of how the Japs executed the Chinese in the China war," noted Sergeant Holmes, "so I figured we were to suffer the same fate."[34]

Curiously, the prospect of imminent death elicited little outward reaction from the Americans. "There we were, . . . naked with our hands wired behind us," Corporal Kelnhofer later exclaimed, "in front of people who were preparing the execute us, and I can't think of anybody being excited, visibly nervous, visibly panicky." Kelnhofer himself felt "fatalistic numbness, acceptance" over his impending fate. Nature seemed to conspire with the Japanese at that moment to deepen the POWs' despair. The skies opened, dousing the Americans with one of those short squalls that frequently drenched the atoll. Corporal Durrwachter called that rain "the coldest I have ever felt." Cpl. Terrence T. McAmis of Battery E, a former carnival boxer and wrestler, tried making light of the situation. "God," he blurted, "I hate cold showers." A shivering Marine seated next to the wisecracking corporal snarled, "If my hands were loose, I'd hit you." Major Potter sat a row or two ahead of McAmis, and he immediately made it clear that this was not the time or place for levity. "If looks could have killed," testified Private First Class Venable, McAmis would "have never gone through prison camp because Major Potter took care of him on the spot."[35]

Just when all seemed lost for Potter and his subordinates, a Japanese landing craft beached itself a little east of the supposedly doomed prisoners. The bow ramp slammed down, and out stepped a senior enemy naval officer resplendent in a spotless white uniform and trailed by an attentive staff. The Americans later learned this was Admiral Kajioka, the commander of the Wake Invasion Force.

Fortunately for these prisoners and their comrades elsewhere on the atoll, the admiral had left his flagship and hastened ashore to prevent a massacre. He uttered some sharp commands to the SNLF machine gunners, and the latter removed the ammunition magazines or stripper clips from their weapons. The POWs on that corner of Wake Island had been granted a timely reprieve.[36]

While the SNLF troops may have received strict orders to spare their prisoners, nobody said anything about making the Americans comfortable. After Kajioka departed for other parts of the atoll, the guards prodded the POWs to their feet. The Japanese herded the mystified Marines and Contractors into Dr. Kahn's hospital and shut the steel door behind them. Jammed into a limited space with no windows and inadequate ventilation, the POWs began experiencing new torments. Gunner Hamas accurately conveyed their predicament in a postwar report: "The hospital become crowded to the point of suffocation." Routine griping gave way to a rising chorus of emphatic curses, and then bedlam exploded inside the hospital as the men at the rear of the structure started shouting they could not get enough air and shoving the men wedged against them. A few cool-headed Marines managed to wriggle out of their bonds and untied their buddies, which provided at least a small measure of relief.[37]

After what seemed like hours, the Japanese finally released the POWs from the hospital. They also freed those Americans still wearing wire restraints and permitted them to redress from the piles of clothing heaped haphazardly beside the road. Hardly anyone succeeded in reclaiming his own garments, and several grabbed items that did not fit very well. Cpl. Robert F. Haidinger of Battery E weighed only 145 pounds, and he ended up with size 44 trousers, which required considerable engineering to keep from sliding off his waist. With the SNLF men yelling, "Speedo, speedo," the Americans had no time to swap shirts and pants to obtain better fits. Once most of the POWs had covered themselves, the guards had them fall in on the road. The Japanese then marched Devereux's staff, Potter's skirmishers, and the men of Battery E toward the airfield, their superiors having deemed that big open space the ideal site to concentrate their prisoners.[38]

"I WAS SORRY AS HELL I EVER PUT MY RIFLE DOWN"

As the Japanese extended their control over the rest of Wake Island, the surrender scenes first enacted around Major Devereux's CP and Dr. Kahn's hospital repeated themselves, but with considerable variation. The meeting of captors and captives still pulsated with nerve-racking tension, but the greater number of men on either side exhibited remarkable restraint, which minimized the possibility of misunderstandings and accidents triggering unnecessary bloodshed.

The SNLF troops subjected each batch of freshly surrendered defenders to rough searches. They also kept helping themselves to whatever valuables caught their eye. Rank protected no Americans from robbery. A Japanese officer demanded Commander Cunningham's wallet, promising to return it after examining the island commander's papers for intelligence purposes. Cunningham never saw his wallet, or the $200 it contained, again. The SNLF men who took Battery B into custody knew only one word of English, and they barked it incessantly as they frisked their new charges: "Money! Money! Money!" The badgered Marines turned out their pants pockets, but enemy seamen scooped up only the silver coins that fell to the ground and threw away the paper currency. The Japanese especially coveted American watches. Sergeant Rogers, the Army radioman, saw one invader with eight to ten stolen timepieces strapped to one arm. Two Japanese who spoke a little English slyly asked five Contractors they encountered to tell them the time. When two of the Americans naively pulled out their pocket watches, the SNLF men took them.[39]

The Japanese continued to strip and bind prisoners, but they seemed to weary of both precautions as the day wore on. Marines, sailors, and Contractors rounded up in the vicinity of Camp 1 lost everything save their shoes and undershorts and had their hands tied together. The Leathernecks captured in a group on Wilkes with Captain Platt had to pull off their shirts and undershirts to confirm they carried no hand grenades or other concealed weapons. The Japanese then forced them to stand with their hands held high for a lengthy period, but these Americans escaped getting tied up. By contrast, the Marines and Contractors that the Japanese had to roust out of dugouts and gun pits elsewhere on Wilkes were stripped of every stitch. On Peale Island at the other end of the atoll, the Marines belonging to Battery B experienced a far less unpleasant introduction to captivity. The Japanese did not strip the Leathernecks, and they did not even have to march to the airfield. Their captors drove them there by truck.[40]

First Lieutenant Barninger and Battery A waited several hours at Peacock Point on the main islet for Japanese troops to come and fetch them, but no SNLF men ventured into that foliage-shrouded corner of the atoll. Barninger noticed the lengthening afternoon shadows and judged his most prudent course would be to seek out the enemy. "I did not want the men to be at the position in the night," he reasoned, "and have the Japs come for us." Barninger marched his Marines to the outskirts of the airfield, where the Japanese spotted them and placed them under guard. The Battery A Marines had to give up their web cartridge belts with attached canteens and first aid pouches, but kept their clothing.[41]

The majority of Wake Marines capitulated as military units. That was the way they trained and how they fought. A Leatherneck could also find some comfort by undergoing such a trial with his shipmates or buddies. In addition, the Marines believed they were less likely to be murdered if they stuck together.[42]

To a large extent, however, the Contractors became prisoners in a far less organized or orderly fashion. Those who had fought alongside the Marines usually surrendered with them. Others converged on Camp 2—some in compliance with their foremen's instructions, and others from the herding instinct that takes over during severe crises. A substantial number of civilians opted to lie low in the brush, a dugout, or some other hiding place until the Japanese found them. Alexander Pay adopted a decidedly unhurried approach to surrender. After Pay learned of the battle's outcome, he took a bath in the lagoon, shaved, and then retired to his dugout to whip up a meal of rice and tea. He did not come out into the open until 6:00 PM. "Was eventually picked up & taken to the airport," Pay noted laconically in his diary. A pair of Contractors with less savoir faire than Pay helped themselves to some moonshine from an illegal still and went to greet the Japanese singing and as merry as lords. Fourteen or more civilian holdouts delayed presenting themselves to the enemy until the following day. A pair of particularly stubborn Contractors would remain at large until March 10, 1942—more than two months after Wake capitulated.[43]

The Americans caught on Wilkes Island probably constituted the last large organized group of POWs to file onto the airfield before night fell on December 23. It took two ferry trips across Wilkes Channel to transport the eighty-odd Marines and civilians to the main islet. The Japanese formed these men into a column of fours and started them toward Camp 1 and the airfield beyond.[44]

As the Americans from Wilkes Island moved out, their downcast faces and slumped shoulders reflected how they felt about becoming prisoners. The first of them to snap out of this despondent spell was TSgt. Edwin F. Hassig, a former North Dakota sodbuster whose skill with a rifle earned him the honored nickname "Peepsight" during his twelve years in the Marine Corps. Hassig never explained what prompted him to do it, but he began to call cadence while en route to the airfield, just as he had done numerous times in the past during routine drill sessions. At the sound of Hassig's voice, the Leathernecks in the column automatically fell into step, and the familiar rhythmic ritual rekindled a pride they thought forever extinguished. "Four abreast, we marched up the road," recounted Corporal Richardson, "trying to make this the best marching we had ever done.... We must have been impressive.... We were marching along on parade—quick snappy steps, squared shoulders, arms swinging, heads erect, eyes to the front."

The SNLF men guarding the column were shorter than most of their prisoners, and they had to trot to keep up. The sight of the Japanese puffing and sweating filled Richardson and his comrades with an additional sense of satisfaction. The Wilkes defenders could also not help noticing the many funeral pyres they passed along Wake's south beach, where the enemy were burning their dead in stacks. As the POWs neared the 3-inch gun that had demolished *Patrol Boat 32*, Hassig saw Commander Cunningham and other senior American officers being interrogated about the atoll's defenses. "Eyes left," Hassig thundered, and every head in his column snapped toward the island commander in a smart marching salute.[45]

If there could ever be a way to enter captivity like a U.S. Marine, Peepsight Hassig had just invented it. Sgt. Walter Bowsher, the commander of Battery D's all-civilian gun crew, put his finger on what the Wilkes defenders were feeling. As Bowsher gazed at the SNLF men scowling ominously at the prisoners already on the airfield, he muttered under his breath, "We've already whipped you. Now you can do your damnedest—you can't hurt us." Even if the Japanese butchered their prisoners, Bowsher assured himself that would not change one salient fact: "We've had our victory. Now what are you going to do about it?"[46]

The Wake Islanders needed every particle of inner strength they could muster because the threat of execution continued to hang over them. After the Japanese finished securing Wilkes Island, some captors confided to Platt's Marines that no prisoners would be spared unless Tokyo approved. An SNLF man waited until the fighting had ceased and then told Sergeant Malleck, Devereux's flag bearer, "You have one hour to live." During the Wilkes defenders' defiant march to the airfield, Cpl. John Johnson sighted the corpses of two decapitated Americans, the victims of a deliberate execution, lying beside the road.[47]

By 4:00 or 5:00 PM, the Japanese had assembled close to 1,600 Americans in a corner of the airfield against a small embankment created when the Contractors leveled that area before the war. As each group of defenders or noncombatants arrived, the Japanese seated them on the ground in rows. To Corporal Johnson, the mass of largely naked or half naked prisoners resembled "a square field of human flesh." SNLF troops placed six to eight machine guns to the south of the Americans, and they set up a second line of machine guns along the POWs' eastern flank. Caught in a potential crossfire, hardly any Wake Islander present believed that the preparations represented mere crowd control.[48]

"It was a very uncomfortable situation there," commented Sgt. Jack Cook. SSgt. Clifford E. Hotchkiss, an Army radioman, expressed identical qualms: "It didn't look good, I'll say that. It looked like the possibility existed that we might not get off of there." Sergeant Rogers, a member of Hotchkiss' communications detail, harbored no doubts regarding the enemy's intentions: "This is it. They're going to wait until they get us all down here in these big rows and then they're going to . . . go down the row and wipe us all out."[49]

As this sickening realization sank in, some POWs grew angry. "Why the hell did we give up in the first place?" wondered Pfc. Henry H. W. Chapman, a participant in the defense of Wilkes Island. Pfc. Luther Williams of Battery B faced death with just one regret: "I was sorry as hell I ever put my rifle down. I said, 'Well, I might as well have killed a few more of them before they got around to killing us.'"[50]

A greater number of Americans lapsed into the fatalism evinced earlier by those apprehended near Devereux's CP and Dr. Kahn's hospital. For one of those prisoners, Corporal McAmis of Battery E, this was his second time that day to stare into the muzzle of an enemy machine gun, and he no longer felt like joking. "Well, this looks like it's it," McAmis whispered to the Marines surrounding him. "So let me tell you. When they start pulling the trigger let's just jump up and get a gut full. Let's not get caught here in a pile and have them come through shooting us." McAmis' plan to seek a quick and clean death made perfect sense to Private First Class Venable, and he nerved himself to follow the corporal's lead. "And I think," Venable admitted, "that I felt that I was closer to death at that point than at any time in my life." The same instinctive urge gripped Pvt. Joe M. Reeves and a few other .50-caliber machine gunners captured on Wilkes Island. "We sort of crowded up a little to get up to the front so we'd be the first ones to get the bullets," Reeves related. "If they were going to shoot us, we didn't want to get wounded and have them come by and shoot us again."[51]

As the latest arrivals among the prisoners seated themselves on the airfield, Admiral Kajioka drove up in an American vehicle. The admiral walked over to a khaki-clad Japanese officer who seemed to be commanding the landing force and engaged him in conversation. In no time at all, the two officers started shouting at each other at the top of their voices. This argument raged for fifteen to twenty minutes. When it ended the SNLF commander, visibly upset, stomped to the top of an airplane revetment and issued a verbal order. The Japanese troops manning the machine guns immediately uncocked their weapons and assumed a more casual stance.[52]

A little bit later a Japanese interpreter wearing white shorts and socks held up by garters approached the POWs. The Americans later learned his surname was Katsumi, but they would insist on calling him "Garters."[53] He held a piece of paper dated December 23, 1941, which he proceeded to read aloud to his captive audience:

Here it is proclaimed that the entire islands of "WAKE" are now the property of the Great Empire of Japan.

PUBLIC NOTICE

The Great Empire of Japan who loves peace and respects justice has been oblidged to take arms against the challenge of President Roosevelt. Therefore, in accordance with the peace loving spirit of the Great Empire of Japan, Japanese Imperial Navy will not inflict harms to those peoples though they may have been our enemy—who do not hold hostility against us in any respect. So they may be in peace!

But whoever violates our spirit or whoever are not obedient shall be severely punished by our Martial law.

Issued by
The Headquarters of the
Japanese Im[p]erial Navy[54]

To ensure that the Wake Islanders grasped the full import of that clumsily worded manifesto, Katsumi ad-libbed, "The Emperor has gracefully presented you with your lives." A Marine near Private First Class Chapman muttered in response, "Well, thank the son-of-a-bitch."[55]

In the next few seconds, however, five pilots from VMF-211 realized that a Japanese emperor's magnanimity had its limits as Katsumi announced, "Certain individuals will be shot for military reasons—Major Putnam, Captain Tharin, Captain Freuler, Lieutenant Kinney, Lieutenant Kliewer." The Wake Islanders would learn that being prisoners of the Japanese did not guarantee they would sit out the war in either safety or reasonable comfort.[56]

CHAPTER THREE

"very odd people indeed"
the first twenty-four hours in captivity

"WHY WE THOUGHT SO LITTLE OF THE POWS"

Shigeyoshi Ozeki had just graduated from medical school when the Imperial Japanese Navy sent him a draft notice on March 20, 1940. Though feeling honored to take the naval medical exam, he knew that 98 percent of those who attempted did not pass. Failed applicants had to join the Japanese army in China, where medical officers did not survive long. To Ozeki's relief, he scored sufficiently high marks on the naval exam and received the title "honorable naval doctor."

Ozeki took pride in his sub-lieutenant's commission and his assignment to an SNLF company in Admiral Kajioka's Wake Invasion Force. The withering losses Japanese landing troops sustained during the ground fighting on December 23, 1941, rattled the impressionable, twenty-three year old. As the lone Japanese medical officer on Wake, Ozeki also had to grapple with the overwhelming task of treating hundreds of maimed men. "I was so busy tending the wounded," he admitted, "that my head spun constantly." At the same time, however, Ozeki exulted in his countrymen's bloody victory. He took possession of the U.S. flag that had flown over Camp 1 and delighted in showing that trophy to relatives and friends when he returned to Japan on leave in February 1942.

Faced with trying to repair the damage inflicted by American marksmanship, Ozeki had as much right to hate Wake Island's defenders as anyone who served with Admiral Kajioka. Nevertheless, Ozeki regarded what he called "our American 'guests'" with curiosity rather than hostility. Like most other Japanese, he was fascinated with American popular culture—movies, music, baseball, and other things. Ozeki's status as a medical officer gave him considerable freedom of movement on Wake, and he mixed freely with the POWs. He came away from these interactions both amused and perplexed. Among the traits that puzzled him the most was the speed with which the Wake Islanders recovered from the shame of capture.[1] As Ozeki explained in his old age:

> The Americans and Japanese had very different concepts about the idea of becoming a prisoner. To us, it was the most humiliating thing that could happen. We were educated to never allow ourselves to fall into the hands of the enemy....
>
> This is why we thought so little of the POWs we had taken on Wake. These men had allowed themselves to become captives and were not worthy of honor. They surely must feel ashamed to ever return to their families. The Americans were under the impression that they had done their best and had been ordered to surrender. This is why [their] compound was so lively. Men were joking, laughing, talking in loud voices, and generally not acting like POWs at all.[2]

"THE OFFICERS SLAP THE NONCOMS, THE NONCOMS SLAP THE PRIVATES"

To better understand the ordeal Americans captured on Wake Island would endure from December 23, 1941, to mid-August 1945, it is necessary to probe the collective mind of their captors. The values of the Japanese fighting man and his society heavily influenced the treatment the Wake POWs received. Any attempt to summarize Japanese values, however, must rest on generalizations, and no generalization is safe from legitimate challenge. Nevertheless, many, if not most, of the Japanese that the Wake Islanders encountered during their three and a half years in enemy custody would justify these generalizations. For want of better criteria, the following observations must serve in assessing what happened to this group of POWs.

In 1941 Japanese popular culture consisted of a volatile mixture of religious fervor, national chauvinism, imperialistic aspirations, and seething resentment against the West. A remarkable degree of racial and cultural homogeneity prompted the Japanese to view themselves as a chosen people—the "pure Yamato race," which was doubly privileged to be ruled by a divine emperor. Since the emperor ranked as a god, his people felt duty-bound to extend his rule to wherever their leaders decreed. These convictions endowed the Japanese with an impressive sense of national unity and purpose. Their educational system and mass media extolled *kodo*, the "imperial way," and denounced the "chaotic individualism" of the democratic United States and the "godless materialism" of communism. Many Japanese accepted the emperor's will as their guide in all matters—the arbiter of both their individual lives and national destiny.

In theory, at least, the emperor ruled as an absolute monarch. His word was law, even though the strong men who ran Japan from behind the imperial throne usually fed him his lines. All Japanese officials—high or low—were seen as the emperor's personal representatives. Whenever a government minister, a commissioned or noncommissioned officer in the armed forces, a factory foreman, or anyone else in authority issued a command to a subordinate, it was as if the emperor had spoken. Any self-respecting Japanese was expected to comply immediately, regardless of the consequences to his or her person. Loyalty, obedience, and conformity stood foremost among Japanese virtues. This held true especially in the military. As Sub-Lieutenant Ozeki discovered, "One did not doubt the wisdom of one's superiors in the Imperial Japanese Navy, where independent thought and reasoning were not cultivated."[3]

The cult of the emperor and the hierarchical social system it supported emerged largely in reaction to living conditions in the Japanese homeland. Japan's lack of living space and its limited natural resources had long conditioned its people to approach life as a struggle. In order to survive, the Japanese had to develop sharp competitive instincts. Weakness, sickness, or failure had no place in Japanese life. Consequently, the Japanese evolved into a tough and aggressive people. Cdr. Edwin T. Layton, an American naval officer who studied the Japanese language in Japan from 1929 to 1932, noted how hard the emperor's sailors trained ashore when their ships put into port. "It left me," Layton recalled, "with the indelible impression that the Japanese never rest."[4]

To keep those competitive urges from tearing the nation apart, discipline and order had to be imposed on the Japanese populace. The cult of the emperor served this purpose with admirable effectiveness, reinforcing the collectivism that made Japanese society so cohesive, industrious, and productive. The vast majority of Japanese felt a keen need to belong, and their desire to prove their value to the group inclined some Western observers to conclude they were addicted to work.[5]

From these cultural roots sprang Bushido, the Japanese code of martial conduct. "Bushido" is a term that resists precise definition in Western terms. The word itself is most commonly translated as the "way of the warrior." In its earliest incarnation, Bushido belonged exclusively to the samurai, the warrior class of feudal Japan. Bushido evolved as a code to govern the conduct of those Japanese knights. It demanded the samurai's absolute loyalty to their respective feudal lords, along with such high-minded qualities as righteousness, courage, propriety, sincerity, honor, and compassion toward the weak and defeated. At its best, this code fostered self-discipline, tolerance, and humanity.[6]

Japan's feudal period ended in 1867, and the country's subsequent rush to modernize led to a broader application of Bushido. With the introduction of conscription and European-style military training in 1872, Japanese leaders envisioned a people's army equipped with modern weapons but permeated with the ancient warrior spirit. Bushido thus became the privilege of all Japanese. Its tenets formed an integral part of the nation's educational system, and everyone was schooled in this creed. The mass dissemination of Bushido required considerable simplification, and that quickly resulted in the venerable code's corruption. By the eve of World War II, Bushido's essential elements had been reduced to blind loyalty to one's superiors, absolute disregard for death in pursuing one's duty, the spirit of continuous attack, unsleeping revenge, and the conviction that the ends justified the means. A Japanese military writer captured these radical changes in emphasis by redefining Bushido as the "art of seeking death."[7]

By Western standards, the revised version of Bushido imposed impossible demands on its adherents. A good soldier chose death at the enemy's hands or his own rather than submit to defeat or capture. "Glorious self-annihilation," or *gyokusai*, for the emperor or the nation assured a Japanese soldier or sailor immortality. His spirit would become part of the emperor's spirit, or the national body (*kokutai*). The dead warrior would also be forever honored by his descendants. This exalted fatalism made the Japanese feel morally superior to their enemies. Since Japanese soldiers supposedly harbored no fear of death, they possessed an edge in élan; they were willing to run more risks and expend more lives than their opponents. Such aggressiveness often meant the difference between victory or defeat on the battlefield.[8]

To prepare for self-immolation, Japanese troops led Spartan lives devoid of comforts that many Westerners regarded as bare necessities. Japanese basic training has been aptly described as "socialization for death." Recruits entered a realm governed by a harsh disciplinary code that remained in force for the length of their service. Corporal punishment was the most common penalty for all infractions whatever their gravity, even innocent mistakes. Enlisted men had to submit to savage beatings without a whimper or complaint. After more than three years in Japanese army custody, Cpl. Bernard Richardson quipped, "If a no-star private offended a one-star private, the one-star private stood the poor bugger at attention and beat him up one side and down the other. And if a corporal was offended by a one-star private, he did the same." Major Devereux confirmed Richardson's observation: "That is the custom in the Japanese service. The officers slap the noncoms, the noncoms slap the privates." The Japanese military depicted *bentatsu*, the routine striking and beating of soldiers, as "character building" or an "act of love." A Japanese warrior was simply supposed to be oblivious to pain — his own, a comrade's, and the enemy's.[9]

Japanese soldiers and sailors were taught that sickness was shameful and a form of dereliction of duty to the emperor, that it was better to perish quickly on the battlefield than surrender to human frailty and waste away in a hospital. The average Japanese did not seek medical aid unless absolutely necessary. Consequently, the medical profession did not enjoy much prestige in prewar Japan, and many of its members were not particularly well-trained. Instead of viewing the sick as objects of compassion, many Japanese despised them for their weakness. Indeed, ailing Japanese soldiers received reduced rations because feeding the disabled and unproductive was seen as wasting scarce resources. Some Japanese guards expressed that harsh outlook after a few Wake Contractors later complained about having to endure winter cold in an unheated ship's hold. "If you are sick," they taunted the Americans, "you should die."[10]

The typical Japanese serviceman cherished his sense of personal honor, or face, and his family's esteem more than anything else. These two notions were intertwined. Family ties were all important to the Japanese, and the state exploited those sentiments to advance the national war effort. If a soldier or sailor shirked his duty in any way — such as consenting to be taken prisoner — he brought dishonor on himself and his loved ones. To blot out the disgrace, one or more family members might feel obliged to commit suicide. Sub-Lieutenant Ozeki insisted that he and his comrades eschewed the merest thought of surrender not "out of fear or what they [the enemy] would do to us," but because of "the shame that our families would bear if it were learned that we were POWs." Ozeki reinforced that point by adding, "I know this is very difficult for westerners to understand, but shame plays a significant role in this society." The relatively few Japanese servicemen captured by the Allies believed that all their bonds to their families and country had been permanently severed. Desperate to establish a new sense of belonging, large numbers of Japanese POWs would collaborate with their captors.[11]

When a Japanese serviceman left home for the front, he went with the determination to conquer or die. To prevent backsliding, his farewell to his family frequently resembled a funeral ceremony. From the moment that warrior departed, he was considered dead. He could only return to life if he and his country achieved victory. Relatives made no effort to seek news of their serviceman, and his superiors discouraged him from writing home. This custom brought heartache to countless Japanese, but they observed it with stringent fidelity. Later in the Wake Islanders' captivity, they met a Japanese guard in China who told them that he had not seen his family in six years and harbored little hope of returning home. Though such mores appeared heartless in Western eyes, they constituted the ultimate expression of a Japanese fighting man's love for his emperor, country, and family.[12]

Like other peoples, the Japanese judged their enemies by their own standards. It did not take Corporal Richardson long to discern this: "According to Japanese ways of thinking we were already worse than dead, having disgraced ourselves irretrievably by bein[g] taken prisoner." Sub-Lieutenant Ozeki was more broad-minded than many of his countrymen, but closer acquaintance with Wake's defenders scandalized him. As the shock of surrender wore off, most American Marines and their comrades absolved themselves of any blame for their situation. The POWs began exhibiting a cheerfulness and optimism that baffled the young naval doctor. "How could they laugh and joke," Ozeki wondered. "Why not take their own lives in shame at becoming prisoners? These *Amerika-jin* were very odd people indeed."[13]

"YOU GAVE UP EVERYTHING WHEN YOU SURRENDERED"

The preceding description of Bushido and the forces that shaped it make it easier to see why the Japanese military acquired an infamous reputation for its mistreatment of Allied prisoners during World War II. It also helps explain the fast-and-loose attitude the Japanese adopted toward the Geneva Convention of 1929.

Formally titled the Convention of July 27, 1929, Relative to the Treatment of Prisoners of War, this agreement resulted from a praiseworthy effort to devise enlightened standards to regulate the confinement and care of military personnel captured in wartime. Forty-seven countries, including the United States and Japan, signed the undertaking. In the Western world, the Geneva Convention gained rapid acceptance as part of international law. The Geneva Convention placed its signatories under numerous obligations. POWs were to be "humanely treated and protected, particularly against acts of violence, insults and public curiosity." The convention expected a "detaining power" to provide the POWs in its custody with the same rations, clothing, and shelter furnished to its own troops. Prisoners were also entitled to full medical care. Captured officers were to receive the same salary paid to officers of equivalent rank in the detaining power's forces. All prisoners had the right to retain their personal effects. Belligerents were bound to promptly inform each other of the identity, location, and physical condition of their prisoners. In addition, POWs were supposed to be able to correspond with their families on a regular basis.[14]

In 1929 three distinguished Japanese diplomats affixed their signatures to this high-minded document, but the ratification period ran out five years later without their government giving the Geneva Convention official assent. Japanese scholar Yuki Tanaka ascribed the refusal to ratify to Japan's military leaders. Since Japanese forces theoretically lacked the capacity to surrender, ratifying the Geneva Convention would saddle Japan with commitments that promised no reciprocal benefits to its own soldiers and sailors.

Shortly after the Pearl Harbor attack, the Japanese government released a curious announcement. Although not legally compelled to do so, Japan pledged to observe the Geneva Convention and apply its guidelines to the treatment of Allied POWs. The Japanese slyly added, however, that they would interpret these provisions mutatis mutandis—a legal nicety meaning "necessary changes having been made." That seemingly innocent disclaimer gave the Japanese a loophole to ignore any part of the agreement they found inconvenient. In actual practice, the Japanese ran their POW camps as if the Geneva Convention had never been written—something the Wake Islanders would soon discover. After the bulk of the atoll's garrison ended up in a camp in China, Commander Cunningham reminded the Japanese commandant that Tokyo had promised to abide by the Geneva Convention. The enemy officer shrugged off that proclamation as only so much "journalese."[15]

This ambivalence toward the Geneva Convention is why so many of the POW camps Japan opened during World War II degenerated into death camps. In Japanese eyes, the sole justification for maintaining such facilities was to provide slave labor to support the island empire's war effort and the Greater East Asia Co-Prosperity Sphere. For example, the Wake Islanders who ended up in China had the following sentence pronounced on them by one of their camp commandants: "From now on, you have no property. You gave up everything when you surrendered. You do not even own the air that is in your bodies. From now on you will work for the building of Greater East Asia. You are slaves of the Japanese." A glimpse at a few statistics registers the consequences of this harsh policy. The Japanese captured 27,465 personnel from the U.S. Army and U.S. Army Air Forces (USAAF), and 11,107 of them—or 40 percent—died as POWs. In German POW camps, on the other hand, American and British inmates normally enjoyed the protection of the Geneva Convention and suffered a death rate of only 4 percent.[16]

Many Western writers have roundly condemned the Japanese for their brutality toward Allied POWs. It warrants mentioning, however, that kind treatment for POWs was a relatively novel notion in the West. World War II stood merely eighty years removed from the American Civil War, which produced such notorious hellholes as Andersonville, Danville, Fort Delaware, Camp Douglas, and Elmira. More than 56,000 of the 409,608 Federals and Confederates who fell into enemy hands perished in these or other camps. Many of these victims succumbed to deliberate neglect and abuse, as both sides exploited POWs as pawns—frequently sacrificing them over petty disputes in the name of national pride. The Civil War's POW death rate of nearly 14 percent would have been far worse without an erratically applied parole and exchange system that facilitated the release of thousands of captives before their health broke. Tragically, Allied servicemen taken in the Pacific theater between 1941 and 1945 could not count on that form of relief from their torments.[17]

While harsh treatment of Allied POWs may have been consistent with the Japanese military's rigid code, it also represented a sharp break with recent practice. As a modernized Japan began flexing its imperial muscle in the late nineteenth century, it also attempted to impress Western powers with its humanity. Red Cross representatives and lawyers versed in international law accompanied the units the Japanese army committed to the First Sino–Japanese War of 1894–1895 to ensure they fought in "Christian style." The Japanese troops that helped relieve the Beijing legations during the Boxer Rebellion of 1900 won praise for not emulating the bloody reprisals that their Western allies visited on the defeated Chinese. The Russo–Japanese War of 1904–1905 established the image of the chivalrous Japanese soldier who respectfully buried the enemy's dead, ministered to the enemy's wounded, and handled prisoners with decency. The Japanese military lavished similar care on the German soldiers it captured during World War I.

In the two decades that followed the Great War, this humane standard fell out of favor as Japan embraced a bitter brand of xenophobia. Repeated snubs generated by European and American racism extinguished the old desire to win the West's approval. When Japan went to war with the Allies in December 1941, it aimed to expel all Westerners from East Asia and simultaneously demolish the myth of white supremacy. Once that struggle commenced, Emperor Hirohito's subjects proved to be a passionate and demonstrative people. They hated their enemies, and they despised their prisoners. To the Japanese, any soldier who allowed himself to be taken prisoner was a loathsome weakling lacking any shred of honor. They could not bear to furnish such cowards with the same food, clothing, quarters, or medical care as their own brave troops. Under the best conditions, the Japanese usually felt obligated to provide no more than the barest minimum necessary to keep their prisoners alive. In return, they felt free to work POWs to the bone. The Japanese could also not believe that anyone as contemptible as a POW would want his friends and family to know about his disgrace. Consequently, they adopted a lax approach to releasing POW information and processing POW mail.[18]

Even if the Japanese had followed the Geneva Convention to the letter, Allied POWs still would have suffered a multitude of hardships. The Japanese standard of living was much lower than that to which most Westerners were accustomed. As an American civilian, repatriated from an internment camp near Shanghai in 1943, informed the U.S. State Department, "Japanese standards are so far below ours that what are legitimate complaints to us, appear ridiculous to the Japanese." Second Lieutenant Kinney of VMF-211 brought back a similar tale: "The poorest most poverty stricken people in the United States are fortunate when compared to the POW of an Asian country with a low standard of living. A scrap of paper, a piece of tin, a bottle or a piece of wire are treasures. . . . There was no litter left on the paths since it was all picked up and used, if it had even been discarded in the first place."[19]

Paradoxically, the Japanese strove throughout World War II to maintain the illusion that they scrupulously observed every article of the Geneva Convention. When they finally permitted the Wake defenders to write home, they demanded that the Americans paint a rosy picture of prison life. POWs ignoring those instructions risked having their letters torn up by enemy censors. Japanese camp officials cynically assured the International Committee of the Red Cross (ICRC) that they fed the Wake Islanders the same rations as Japanese officers. The prisoners themselves were told that they ate as well as the emperor's soldiers, but some guards let it slip that the Americans were actually subsisting on convicts' rations.[20]

The Japanese not only deprived their prisoners of the basic rudiments of life, but they also strove to purge the ostensibly soft Americans of their self-indulgent, individualistic, and dishonorable ways by schooling them in Bushido. Guards routinely subjected their charges to the savage discipline reserved for Japanese recruits. That boiled down to conditioning by terror—a man had his undesirable traits beaten out and Japanese virtues beaten in. "It is not surprising what we were put through," remarked Contractor John R. Hoskins, "mainly because of what the Japanese were used to. . . . They seemed to feel that discipline was by violence."

Pfc. Robert Shores soon realized that a POW had no right to question his captors' orders. "You either did it or they'd beat you pretty bad," Shores recalled.[21]

Many Japanese took extra pains to rub their prisoners' faces in the humiliation of surrender. They would try to break the Westerners' pride, sour their spirits, and deprive them of comforting news. A guard could choose at almost any moment to plunge a POW into pain or to strip him of his dignity. "I can still remember . . . how I hated the Nips," testified FN2C Dare Kibble, "when they would hit us with a club or gun butt and then smirk as if daring us to give them provocation to stick a bayonet in our gut." Pfc. Floyd H. Comfort of the 1st Defense Battalion claimed that the Wake POWs took frequent beatings from their guards. "There did not have to be a reason," Comfort explained. "Usually for some minor infraction of some rule, but if there was no infraction, they could always dream one up." The Japanese even banned harmless possessions that could bring POWs some degree of solace and diversion, such as diaries or playing cards, confiscating such items as contraband.[22]

This analysis seems headed toward the conclusion that Emperor Hirohito's soldiers and sailors were prisoners of their own culture and acted accordingly. The danger in such thinking is that it can be manipulated to excuse war crimes. During the three and a half years the Wake Islanders spent in Japanese custody, the more perceptive among them figured out that it is wrong to write off an entire people with sweeping generalizations. Nations consist of individuals, and human nature can express itself in varied and unpredictable ways. Many, if not most, of the Japanese the Wake POWs met largely conformed to what the Japanese considered their nation's traditions, as well as other social pressures. Others, however, rose above established cultural norms and deviated from them in either major or minor ways. When Marine Corps historians queried Maj. Paul Putnam, VMF-211's commander, about his POW experiences twenty years after the war, he responded with this surprising appeal: "I would feel better if greater and broader recognition were given to the really surprising number of Japanese who went far out of their way, and even risked their own safety, to make things a little better for the prisoners."[23]

A select few among Wake Island's defenders benefited from Japanese sympathy shortly after they laid down their arms on December 23, 1941. Cpl. Ralph J. Holewinski sustained severe leg and back wounds from grenade fragments and a strafing Japanese dive-bomber while defending 2nd Lt. Robert Hanna's 3-inch gun on the main islet's south beach. After the surrender some SNLF men dragged him from under the gun platform to the nearby coastal road. An unendurable thirst due to blood loss eventually prompted Holewinski to point at the canteens on some passing enemy seamen. An SNLF officer took pity on the mangled Marine and directed a subordinate to give him a drink.[24]

As the fighting subsided, Sub-Lieutenant Ozeki appropriated an American truck to search the main islet for Japanese wounded. Because Ozeki could not immediately locate an enlisted SNLF man who knew how to operate a manual transmission, he pressed a naked Marine truck driver, Pfc. Joseph E. Borne, into service. "Moments before," the doctor mused, "we were enemies locked in a life or death struggle, but when the fight was over, he worked hard to help his former enemy save the lives of the wounded. That impressed me." Over the course of the next seven hours, Ozeki shared some of his rations with Borne. He also came to Borne's rescue when four SNLF men dragged the frightened Louisianan from the truck cab and began beating him. After Ozeki found a Japanese driver, he personally returned Borne to the latter's buddies on Wake's airfield. Before this improbable duo parted, Ozeki allowed Borne to smuggle two cartons of Lucky Strike cigarettes into the POW area by wrapping them inside a shirt picked up during their travels.[25]

Following the surrender on Wilkes Island, an SNLF man guarding Captain Platt's Marines opened a shiny tin can containing his personal stash of cigarettes. He extracted a handful and held them toward Corporal Richardson, saying, "*Tobako ka?*" Not quite sure what the guard meant, Richardson took a chance and helped himself to a cigarette. Delighted at having made himself understood to an American, the SNLF man offered cigarettes to the other POWs around him. He then produced a box of matches and helped Richardson light up. The Marine corporal would always remember that moment as "my first lesson from the Japanese. . . . It taught me that the individual Jap could be friendly and kind."[26]

"DURING THE DAY YOU'D ROAST . . . AND AT NIGHT, YOU'D FREEZE"

During the anxious hours that initially followed Wake Island's surrender, few of the atoll's inhabitants dared to expect the slightest mercies from their captors. Their outlook brightened somewhat when they heard the proclamation that Admiral Kajioka did not intend to execute them. But the hope those words inspired proved fleeting. The nearly 1,600 Americans herded onto the airfield were soon wondering if the Japanese had decided to subject them to a slower, more excruciating end than death by machine gun.

Once Kajioka received authorization to spare the Wake Islanders, his subordinates cut the bonds of those who were still hogtied. Aside from that, however, the Japanese did nothing else to make their prisoners more comfortable. Katsumi, the interpreter also known as Garters, told the Americans they could not speak to each other, smoke, or even move about without permission. In addition, Cpl. Guy Kelnhofer complained, "There was no food, no drink, no shelter, and most of us were naked."[27]

Wake Island's white coral surface reflected the sun's heat, and that gave the airfield an oven-like quality from mid-morning until dusk. "It was hotter than all get out during the day," remembered Pfc. George G. Hubley. Hundreds of naked or half-naked Americans suffered horrible burns. "The boys who weren't tanned had blisters all over their backs and arms," noted Contractor John Burton. "Some of those blisters were as big as my fist." Private First Class Shores, a fair-skinned blond from Oklahoma, admitted, "I blistered like a son of a gun, there, when . . . they kept us on the airfield." As painful reddish-purple splotches sprouted on the POWs' exposed torsos and limbs, the rough coral chat on the airstrip bit into their buttocks and any other body parts they rested on the ground. "Coral was sorta sharp," noted Contractor Don W. Ludington, "and when you're sitting on your bare hind-end out there . . . , it's not very comfortable."[28]

To make matters infinitely worse, most prisoners had not received anything to eat or drink since the evening of December 22, close to twenty hours earlier. The Americans' bodies, drained by the rigors of combat and the emotional trauma of capture, desperately needed nourishment. The Japanese, however, evinced no interest in bringing the POWs either food or water. Fireman Second Class Kibble believed the Japanese were deliberately starving their prisoners to reduce the Americans' capacity for escape or resistance. It is probably more likely that the decimated SNLF companies needed time to regroup and assess the atoll's resources before they could begin to succor their enemies. Whatever the reason for Japanese neglect, the misery of the Americans broiling on the airfield grew more acute with each passing minute. The POWs suffered most especially from thirst. Sgt. Ernest Rogers, an Army radioman, felt his lips crack and his tongue swell, and he feared he would soon die. Cpl. John Johnson, a Marine machine gunner, became so badly dehydrated that he did not have to urinate or defecate.[29]

In one respect, Johnson was lucky. A fourth affliction joined heat, thirst, and hunger to bedevil the POWs. Dysentery had made its appearance among the Wake defenders toward the end of the siege—an inevitability given that so many Americans were subsisting on canned food and drinking water from any container they could find. Now, with all those exhausted and dejected men crowded together on the airfield, the infection spread among them with epidemic speed. The Japanese provided the POWs some relief by digging a slit trench on the airfield's lagoon side. This primitive facility made a barely adequate latrine. Concerned as the Japanese were about keeping the POWs under control, the guards restricted traffic to and from the slit trench, especially after dark. An untold number of sick Americans lost control of their aching bowels before their turn came to make a latrine run. They ended up soiling themselves and their neighbors, and lay in their own filth.[30]

The POWs yearned for nightfall, but darkness brought new tortures. As the sun sank beneath the western horizon, Wake cooled down. Having baked as much as half the day, the famished and semiclad prisoners were in no shape to withstand the chilling breezes that swept in from the ocean. Contractor Alec Pay sketched the defeated garrison's predicament in his diary, writing, "Slept on ground, some without any covering & all without sufficient clothing." Pfc. Erwin D. Pistole, a Marine captured on Wilkes Island, explained, "Now Wake is warm, but at night, nude, . . . it got pretty chilly." Contractor Joe Goiceochea could not decide what was worse. "During the day you'd roast to death," he spat, "and at night, you'd freeze." Sergeant Rogers developed such a bad case of the chills that his teeth chattered incessantly and his body shook and bounced on the hard coral.[31]

In such straits, instinct takes over, and the Wake Islanders did whatever they could to ward off the cold. "At night everybody would have to huddle together trying to keep warm," confessed SSgt. Clifford E. Hotchkiss, another Army radioman. Pfc. Leonard G. Mettscher, a Marine antiaircraft gunner, gave a more explicit description of this survival technique: "We lay on top of each other and around each other as close as possible to get warmth from each other." Many POWs scooped shallow depressions out of the ground to gain a little protection from the wind. TSgt. Charles Holmes occupied one of these sleeping holes. "I was tired out and slept fairly well that night . . . although I woke up several times cold," he related. "Since I had nothing to cover my body with there wasn't anything to do but suffer through it." Some Contractors tried to shield themselves by piling pieces of coral to form rude windbreaks, but those low walls afforded only partial relief. Other POWs got their hands on some rolls of tar paper, which they tore into pieces to cover themselves or draw over their sleeping holes. Cpl. Thomas W. Johnson spotted a bedsheet caked with blood from some casualty and wrapped the repulsive thing around himself. "I'll always remember that blood, how stiff it was," exclaimed the Marine from Missouri, "but how that sheet kept the air off me."[32]

As if to mock these pathetic efforts, a squall blew across Wake sometime between midnight and 1:00 AM, dumping cold rain on the shivering POWs. For many Americans, that was the last straw. They began complaining to the guards about being left out in the open. The Japanese eventually permitted the prisoners to take shelter in an unfinished maintenance hangar built by the Contractors for VMF-211. That humane gesture promptly backfired, however, as the SNLF men endeavored to force almost all their prisoners into a space forty by forty feet. As more and more POWs squeezed into the hangar, those in the back started screaming that they could not get enough air. Some passed out in the stifling crush and had to be passed to the front to be revived. Most of the others decided they preferred freezing to being trampled or smothered, and they began chanting, "Let us out!" It took the Japanese even longer to decide to let the clamoring Americans exit the hanger than enter it. At last, the SNLF men released enough POWs to allow those remaining in the structure enough room to sit down. The rest returned to their hard, open-air beds and a few more hours of fitful sleep.[33]

The highest-ranking officers in the Wake garrison and several of their subordinates avoided having to spend their first night in captivity on the airstrip. Late on the evening of December 23, the Japanese confined Commander Cunningham to the whitewashed guest cottage adjacent to his old quarters. He shared this one-room dwelling with two officers and a civilian official from Washington, DC. Capt. Wesley Platt had conducted the defense of Wilkes Island, and Capt. Henry S. Wilson headed the atoll's small U.S. Army radio detachment. Herman P. Hevenor from the U.S. Bureau of the Budget had landed at Wake in the *Philippine Clipper* on December 7 for a one-week inspection of CPNAB construction and costs. The hapless bureaucrat missed his plane when Pan Am hastily evacuated its passengers and white employees right after the first Japanese air raid on December 8.

Although some sources indicate otherwise, Dan Teters did not end up residing in the guest cottage with Cunningham. The Japanese permitted the CPNAB general superintendent to reoccupy his own bungalow, which stood nearby, but they also forced seven roommates on him. Those included Major Devereux and three junior officers from his Wake Island Detachment—1st Lt. Woodrow Kessler, 2nd Lt. John McAlister, and 2nd Lt. Arthur Poindexter. Sgt. Donald Malleck also remained with Devereux. In addition, two naval officers joined Teters and the six Marines. Cdr. Campbell Keene was Cunningham's second-in-command, and Lt. Cdr. Elmer B. Greey of the Civil Engineers Corps had been posted to Wake to oversee the Contractors' progress. Devereux and his companions would dub their crowded quarters the "White House."[34]

The Japanese never explained why they segregated so many officers from the other Americans, but these arrangements made the garrison's senior leadership more easily available for questioning. As Sergeant Malleck recalled, "We were treated well, interrogated much, and were not aware of the poor treatment given the men on the airstrip for several days."[35]

"WE HAD TO ESTABLISH DISCIPLINE"

The sun that shone on Wake Island on Wednesday, December 24, awoke a bleary-eyed rabble of some 1,600 Americans sprawled on the airfield. Stinging from sunburn and achy from lying on what one Contractor called "the rock pile," they feared that the enemy would do no more to alleviate their suffering than the day before. "We were hungry," remarked 1st Lt. Clarence Barninger, "and a bit depressed at the prospect of the future."[36]

The POWs lacked either the internal organization or the will to do much to help themselves during their first twenty-four hours in captivity. Several elements of the Wake garrison had entered confinement as units, but the Japanese made no effort to separate servicemen from civilians as they delivered groups of prisoners to the airfield. First Lieutenant Barninger managed to keep his Battery A together. With Maj. Paul Putnam nursing a painful face wound, Capt. Frank A. Tharin did his best to look after VMF-211's surviving personnel. As that dejected throng of prisoners mushroomed in size from a steady flow of new arrivals, however, Marines, sailors, and soldiers became intermixed with the Contractors. Many servicemen lost all sense of military discipline and identity.

The Japanese contributed to the deteriorating cohesion by secluding Cunningham, Devereux, several other officers, and Dan Teters in the two cottages on the main islet's northern leg. The POW officers confined on the airfield were either too groggy from combat or too intimidated by their captors to assert any authority over the other Americans. Sharp-eyed SNLF guards with loaded rifles and fixed bayonets watched their charges closely, and no officer wanted to be mistaken for a ringleader fomenting revolt. "We were forbidden to talk to each other," commented Second Lieutenant Hanna. "We weren't supposed to say a word, unless we were talking to a Japanese to ask permission to . . . go to bathroom or whatever."[37]

The POWs' need for a semblance of internal order manifested itself with disturbing force on the twenty-fourth. Sometime between noon and 3:00 PM, the Japanese backed a truck to the edge of the airfield. The vehicle's bed contained 55-gallon fuel drums, formerly the property of VMF-211. The Japanese had filled them with water at a desalinization plant. The prospect of getting a drink at long last jerked the Americans out of their depressed languor and filled them with an almost frantic energy. With no officers or foremen exercising control, the least disciplined prisoners refused to wait their turn and rushed the truck. "Men hard to control while . . . water being passed out," a shocked CPNAB supervisor named Leal Henderson Russell scratched in his diary. "Act like wolves." The Japanese panicked at the sight of this unruly crowd, rolled the drums off the back of the truck, and zoomed away. Much of the precious water spilled as the drums bounced onto the coral, and the POWs wasted more by pushing and fighting for what was left. Many Wake Islanders did not get to taste a drop from that first water shipment. They were luckier than they realized.[38]

The Japanese had neglected to clean those fuel drums before converting them into water containers. Consequently, all the water the POWs received carried a strong taste of gasoline. "If you tried to drink the water," reminisced Kibble, "which I did, it burned your throat and mouth." The Wake Islanders realized that such a concoction could make them sick, but they were too parched to resist. After Pvt. Earl M. Broyles Jr. took a swig, his stomach started to swell. All he could do to obtain relief "was just belch, belch, belch, belch." FN1C James H. Cox experienced a similar reaction: "Every time you took a swallow of water you belched gasoline for a couple of hours." POWs cursed with more sensitive digestive systems retched and vomited, which expelled more fluid than their bodies took in. Others came down with diarrhea mixed with blood.[39]

Few things can frighten a professional soldier more than the sight of his men degenerating into a mob. The lawless scene triggered by the water truck's arrival finally galvanized the Marine officers on the airfield into taking command of the situation. They could see that their survival and that of every other American depended on reinstating discipline and order. Unless the current state of anarchy was curbed, each prisoner could not count on getting his fair share of water or anything else the Japanese might bring to the airfield. The next delivery would set off yet another mad-animal scramble, with the strong and selfish trampling the weak. And if the men continued to run amuck, the Japanese might mistake such behavior for an uprising and start shooting. Second Lieutenant Kinney recognized that he and the other POW officers could not afford to lie low any longer. "We had to establish discipline," he recalled thinking.[40]

Maj. George Potter, the ranking American officer on the airfield, risked Japanese ire by moving to resolve this crisis. He held a hushed conference with his commissioned subordinates. They decided that the first step in restoring order was to separate the American servicemen from the Contractors. Henceforth, civilian superintendents and foremen would keep their men under control, and Marine officers would answer for the military POWs. To implement this scheme, Potter enlisted the assistance of Raymond R. "Cap" Rutledge, a CPNAB office clerk and World War I veteran who earned the Marines' respect by fighting heroically beside Second Lieutenant Poindexter a day earlier. Once the POWs were segregated, the officers and foremen positioned themselves between the two groups. This permitted both forms of American leadership to readily confer should other problems crop up. If the guards noticed Potter's efforts to subject the POWs to some basic control, they must have sensed that this also buttressed their authority and did not interfere.[41]

The truck eventually returned to the airfield with more gasoline-tainted water and a load of either hardtack or stale bread that the Japanese discovered in Camp 2. This time, the POWs waited to be served. Everyone who thought he could stomach some water received a little drink. The Japanese also handed each prisoner a small piece of bread. Potter's system had worked. Meager as it was, the Wake Islanders had received their first meal as POWs.[42]

Conditions improved in other ways on December 24. After the Japanese finished rifling through the piles of clothing scattered across the atoll, they dumped them beside the airfield and allowed the prisoners to help themselves. No one recovered his own garments, but a man could feel lucky if he succeeded in grabbing a shirt or a pair of pants near his size. Many Wake Islanders had to continue living without underwear or socks. Marines ended up garbed like civilians, and civilians like Marines, with dozens from both groups attired in a random variety of clashing styles. Pfc. Carl E. Stegmaier Jr. got stuck with a blood-stained shirt to go with his Marine trousers and low-top sneakers. Cpl. John R. Dale, a short and skinny Oklahoman, picked up a pair of size 42 overalls, a white shirt, and a pair of Florsheim shoes. Sergeant Rogers made do with khaki trousers, a khaki shirt, and some bedroom slippers. Second Lieutenant Kinney found a pair of trousers and two oversized, hip-length rubber work boots designed to be pulled over shoes. An unknown POW near Kinney happened to snatch the latter's summer flight jacket with his name and wings embroidered on the front. Not wanting to be mistaken for a Marine pilot targeted for execution, the other fellow had the jacket slipped quietly to the surprised lieutenant. Despite the eclectic nature of Kinney's wardrobe, he fared better than many of his comrades. Even after all the newly delivered clothing had been distributed, many POWs were still left with no more than T-shirts, shorts, and tennis shoes.[43]

The Japanese also exhibited unexpected compassion toward the captured garrison's wounded, who lay clustered along the north side of the airfield near the latrine. The guards handed POW medics some canvas and wood to furnish shade for their patients. The Japanese also outfitted this primitive hospital with two cots and a few mattresses. That concession permitted a handful of stricken prisoners to rest more comfortably. Corporal Holewinski, one of the most critical cases, received several cans of evaporated milk to drink—which was much more conducive to recovery than downing gasoline-tainted water and yet more evidence that individual Japanese could treat defeated enemies kindly.[44]

Finally, the Japanese consented to pleas from the Marine officers that the POWs be permitted to bury their dead. One burial detail headed to Camp 2, where fatalities incurred before December 23 had been stored in the Contractors' big reefers. Captain Tharin and Gunner Hamas led an additional thirty Marines armed with shovels in the opposite direction to the ground south of the airfield, where most of the Americans slain on December 23 fell. SSgt. Robert O. Arthur, a noncommissioned pilot with VMF-211, accompanied that second burial detail, and he stumbled across a sight that drove home how capricious his captors could be. Slightly wounded by a sniper on the final morning of resistance, Arthur had been left behind by his squadron mates to care for three civilians who were too badly wounded to walk. When the Japanese secured that part of the atoll, they forced Arthur to abandon the three Contractors and join the POWs they were concentrating on the far side of the airfield. Arthur found his former companions dead. As he helped inter them, he noted their corpses were punctured with numerous bayonet thrusts.[45]

Later on December 24, Katsumi, the interpreter, must have rekindled Sergeant Arthur's sense of dread by calling out the names of four of VMF-211's commissioned pilots—Major Putnam, Captain Tharin, Second Lieutenant Kinney, and 2nd Lt. David D. Kliewer. Garters had announced the day before that the Japanese intended to execute these officers. Nonetheless, the four bravely responded to his summons and boarded a truck that whisked them to Camp 2. Instead of facing a firing squad, however, the flying Leathernecks merely had to submit to a cordial interrogation conducted by an enemy naval officer and a pilot who spoke English.[46]

As darkness gathered over the airfield, some POWs remembered it was Christmas Eve and started singing carols. That feeble chorus of raspy voices did not go over well with many fellow prisoners. "We were so disgusted and so mad at them," remarked Pfc. Henry Chapman. "Not enough sense to be scared." When the carolers persisted, the Japanese stepped in and insisted the Americans observe a silent vigil. Facing a second night exposed to cold and rain understandably sapped most Wake Islanders of their holiday spirit. Despite that grim prospect, the POWs now had more grounds for hope than twenty-four hours previously. They could see that their captors were now expending an effort to keep them alive, and that was as good a Christmas present as Wake Island's defenders had any right to expect.[47]

CHAPTER FOUR

"the japanese continue to treat us with respect"

a deceptively gentle transition to POW life

"WHAT A GODSEND . . . TO BE ON A SMOOTH FLOOR"

The Wake Islanders may have been surly when they turned in on Christmas Eve, but their self pity evaporated in the sun's warming glow the following morning. Leal Henderson Russell, the CPNAB superintendent in charge of base buildings, informed his diary that cries of Merry Christmas "could be heard thru out the whole gang." With revived American pride, he declared, "Pretty hard to dampen the spirits of free men." As the highest ranking Contractor on the airfield, Russell conducted a quick count of the POWs clustered around him and arrived at a total of "1110 of us and 450+ of the military."[1]

The Japanese made Christmas Day all the more memorable by bestowing two tangible blessings on Wake Island's defenders. First, they gave the prisoners a second meal. The beverage remained water contaminated by aviation fuel and the entrée was still bread, but each hand-sized chunk of the latter came with a dab of jam. A few POWs, luckier than the rest, received a sip of canned tomato juice and a small piece of cheese. The Japanese followed this pale imitation of Christmas dinner with the gift of shelter. Around 6:00 PM, they got the Americans on their feet and marched them some two miles to Camp 2. The Japanese loaded Cpl. Ralph Holewinski and eight other seriously wounded POWs on a truck for the trip, but they forced many sick men to walk. Dysentery had so depleted SC2 Cassius E. Smith that he collapsed onto his hands and knees before he could reach Camp 2. Two Marines marching behind Smith came up on either side of the ailing sailor, grabbed him by the upper arms, and dragged him the rest of the way without breaking stride.[2]

On arrival at Camp 2 the POWs noticed the enemy's Rising Sun flag flapping from the water tower in place of the Stars and Stripes. That sight depressed

Contractor Theodore A. Abraham Jr. because it drove home the reality that he was no longer a free man. John O. Young, a CPNAB carpenter from Idaho, reacted similarly after he learned that a Japanese officer had stuffed the camp's American flag into a net to prop open his office door in an appropriated administration building. "One cannot imagine what a horrible and helpless feeling that was to see our flag so desecrated," Young reflected.[3]

Unlike Abraham and Young, most POWs focused on where they were going to live. The Japanese had converted the residential section of Camp 2 into a large holding facility by surrounding several barracks with a post-and-barbed-wire fence ten feet tall. A road ran through the center of this area, and the Japanese erected fences on either side to create separate compounds for the military and civilian prisoners. They also segregated Major Potter and the other American officers who had originally been confined on the airfield from the rest of the POW population. Commander Cunningham, Major Devereux, and their ten companions remained in the two cottages over a mile and a half away. In a surprise show of chivalry, the Japanese deposited Corporal Holewinski and his wounded comrades in a hospital they had established elsewhere in Camp 2 for their own officers.[4]

Each of the H-shaped barracks set aside for the POWs consisted of two parallel wings connected by a center section containing flush toilets and saltwater showers. Up until December 8 those buildings housed eighty men apiece, with the Contractors occupying two-man cubicles equipped with bunks and plenty of storage space. The barracks had boasted other amenities as well, such as screened porches, watercoolers, electric lights, writing desks, chairs, radios, and bed lamps. Sub-Lieutenant Ozeki marveled at the presence of so many modern conveniences—"something that only the richest families in Japan had"—on a distant tropical outpost.[5]

After a sixteen-day siege and two days of enemy occupation, however, the Contractors' camp bore little resemblance to the posh island resort of prewar days. Those barracks still standing had sustained varying damage from Japanese bombing and strafing. Allan A. O'Guinn, a civilian plumber, discovered that one wing in his old barracks had been reduced to splintered wreckage. While O'Guinn's cubicle was largely intact, his bunk had been blown off the wall. "Pictures of my family hung askew on the wall," he recalled, "riddled in weird patterns by the machine gun bullets." The barracks had also been plundered of much of what made them so inviting. At the outbreak of the siege, the Contractors had dragged mattresses and other bedding to their hiding places in the brush. Next, the Japanese swept through after the Wake defenders' surrender, snatching any item that caught their eye. SNLF officers even ordered the destruction of the pictures of scantily clad females decorating the Contractors' quarters. Sub-Lieutenant Ozeki wryly observed that not all the rank and file complied with this attempt to insulate them from American decadence: "We tried to keep our men from liberating the posters, but the pin-ups of these American women were most invigorating."[6]

Since the Japanese reserved much of Camp 2 for their own use, the barracks space available inside the POW compound proved insufficient for nearly 1,600 inmates. Three hundred men were jammed into structures designed to hold little more than a quarter of that number. Dozens of Americans had to sleep outside, where they fashioned shabby shelters from plywood and debris left by enemy air raids. Those prisoners who found room in the barracks counted themselves extremely lucky even if they had to sleep on the floor in a hallway or on a porch. After two nights on the airfield, Cpl. John Johnson consoled himself with this thought: "What a godsend to be off the . . . coral chat and to be on a smooth floor." He promptly stretched out and slept for sixteen hours straight.[7]

While Corporal Johnson slumbered, one of the POWs' fondest dreams came true. Their rations suddenly increased in quantity and quality. The wizard chiefly responsible for that transformation was Chester A. "Chet" Riebel, the CPNAB steward who had run the Camp 2 mess hall before the war. After the Japanese moved the Americans from the airfield, they allowed Riebel and his cooking crew to return to their galley. Much if not all of the Contractors' perishable foodstuffs had spoiled since Wake's fall, but the civilian chefs had plenty of dried cereals and canned food at their disposal. After taking a day or two to get organized, the chefs proceeded to turn out two hot meals a day for the entire POW population. Breakfast usually consisted of mush made from oatmeal or cream of wheat. At noon, the Wake Islanders sat down to a rich stew, a creamed tuna dish that proved extremely popular, or beans. In the evening the POWs received a snack of freshly baked bread with a little jam washed down by tea or cocoa. Riebel also arranged to have these meals delivered to the Americans confined with Commander Cunningham and Major Devereux in the cottages outside Camp 2.[8]

Leal Russell derived considerable gratification from how well his subordinates met the challenge of feeding some 1,600 POWs. "Chet Riebel and his crew are sure doing swell work under big handicaps," Russell bragged to his diary on January 5, 1942. Not every POW proffered such effusive praise for the dining situation, however. Pvt. Ewing E. LaPorte grew tired of living on oatmeal and stew. "It wasn't the best," he said of Riebel's bill of fare, "but it was American made and American food." Contractor Theodore Abraham opined that "the food tasted good enough." His only complaint was he did not get as much to eat as he wanted.[9]

The Japanese issued no mess gear, but the POWs converted empty food cans into bowls or improvised other solutions. Sergeant Rogers had his first hot meal plopped into a cone that he fashioned from pages torn out of a discarded magazine. Rogers possessed no eating utensils at that time, so he lapped the food out of his paper container like a dog. After two days the Army radioman secured a piece of tin and folded up its edges to form a primitive pan. Most prisoners managed to obtain spoons, but Rogers made do initially with his fingers and, later, a piece of cardboard. The Americans realized the importance of keeping their ersatz dining equipment clean. They rinsed their tin cans with any available water and applied coral sand as an abrasive. Such methods were less than ideal, however, and some Wake Islanders developed diarrhea or ptomaine poisoning.[10]

Thanks to Japanese intervention, one fortunate Marine ended up with a personal chef. During Captain Platt's counterattack against the doomed SNLF foothold on Wilkes Island on December 23, a Japanese bullet struck Pfc. Wiley W. Sloman on the right side of the head as he stood to throw a hand grenade. The wound did not kill Sloman, but it temporarily paralyzed his left side and caused him to drift in and out of consciousness. When the Japanese transferred Platt's Leathernecks to the main islet after the surrender, they thought the stricken Texan was a goner. Despite the protests of 2nd Lt. John McAlister and Gunner Clarence McKinstry, the SNLF men left Sloman behind to die.

Sloman lay alone in a small clump of brush for three days until his comrades prevailed on the Japanese for permission to visit Wilkes and check his condition. Captain Platt and an English-speaking SNLF officer headed the rescue party, which was amazed to find Sloman still alive. The enemy officer personally brought the filthy, unshaven, and blood-covered Texan to the Japanese hospital in Camp 2, where Sloman instantly became the center of attention. Enemy medics tried feeding him Japanese rations, but he could not stomach the fish, rice, pickled daikon (a kind of radish), and pickled fruit that they offered him. Sub-Lieutenant Ozeki learned of the weak and woozy Marine's refusal to eat Japanese food during his rounds on the morning of December 27. "I will take care of this," the doctor announced and then exited the hospital.

Ozeki reappeared at Sloman's bedside with a nervous-looking cook from Chet Riebel's galley in tow. The cook asked Sloman what he wanted for breakfast.

"Are you kidding?" Sloman rasped. "What I'd really like to have is soft-boiled eggs and toast and coffee."

"Well, you'll get it," the cook replied. "This doctor has been to the mess hall and . . . I've been given instructions . . . to feed you while you are here in the hospital."

The civilian returned shortly with Sloman's order, along with two unexpected extras—some cereal and a glass of milk.

From that moment on Sloman received three specially prepared meals a day. His cook also provided the same service for the other American patients in the Japanese hospital. These POWs enjoyed additional perks while under Ozeki's protection. The Japanese stored all the canned pineapple and pineapple juice they found around the atoll in the hospital for their own consumption, and they shared this nutritious bounty with the wounded POWs. An enemy officer wounded while piloting a flying boat over Wake got his hands on a large supply of cigars. He gave one to each of his American ward mates every day they convalesced together.[11]

"JAPANESE TREATING US WITH REASONABLE CONSIDERATION"

Besides full bellies and shelter, the thing the Wake Islanders most liked about life in Camp 2 was the lack of constant tension that had characterized their wretched existence on the airfield. Once the Japanese thought they had their prisoners securely penned up, they grew more relaxed. "Japanese treating us with reasonable consideration," a relieved Leal Russell told his diary on December 27. Armed guards still patrolled the perimeter of the POW compound, but they only entered when they had official business to perform—and then they usually behaved with surprising courtesy. "The Japanese continue to treat us with respect," Russell observed on January 8. A handful of SNLF men tried taunting their charges by falsely claiming the Imperial Japanese Navy was about to snap up Midway or had already occupied Honolulu, but such juvenile behavior was the exception rather than the rule. Most Japanese adopted a live-and-let-live attitude where the POWs were concerned. "Some of the guards are pretty friendly," reported Pfc. John Himelrick, "and give us cigarettes now & then."[12]

One Japanese who delighted in fraternizing with the Wake Islanders was Sub-Lieutenant Ozeki. As the atoll's chief medical officer, Ozeki could enter the POW compound at will, and he fully exploited that privilege. "I came to enjoy my daily visits," Ozeki recalled. "The Americans were very cheerful and confident that their Navy would steam up any day and take back Wake." Smiling POWs would warn the friendly doctor, "I wouldn't stick around here if I were you. Our friends will be here any minute to offer you some more hospitality." One American prophesied, "We're losing now, but you just wait and see, we'll beat you in the end."

Occasionally, Ozeki's visits assumed a more professional nature. He enjoyed talking shop with two medical colleagues from America—Lt. (j.g.) G. Mason Kahn, the Navy surgeon assigned to the Wake Marines, and Lawton E. Shank, the Contractors' physician. "They were both gentlemen in the highest sense of the word," Ozeki commented. He listened admiringly to the American doctors' descriptions of the complicated operations they had performed "on this tiny backwater island." As Ozeki confessed afterward, his conversations with Kahn and Shank taught him some important lessons. "It made me realize how much importance the Americans placed on the well being of their people," he recalled. "It made me stop and seriously consider how little the Japanese valued the lives of their own soldiers."[13]

Ozeki was not the only perceptive man on Wake Island. Charles L. Myers, a CPNAB steam shovel operator, quickly deduced that the Japanese had an ulterior motive for keeping the POWs well-fed, healthy, and reasonably content. "We weren't mistreated that much on the island," Myers explained. "They needed us."[14]

No sooner had the Wake Islanders taken up residence in Camp 2 than the Japanese began sending them on work details to every corner of the atoll. At first, the POWs tackled cleanup jobs. They restored the airfield and Wake's road network to usable shape by filling in bomb craters and clearing away debris. Other crews searched for stray corpses to bury or carried discarded clothing and cached canned goods to warehouses in the Japanese sector of Camp 2. The enemy also relied on POW labor to gather up the many small arms littering the atoll. For the most part, the guards who went with these details did not pressure the Americans to work very hard. One road repair crew got to rest five minutes for every thirty on the job. The POWs also came to appreciate the Japanese custom of refreshing workers on break with hot tea.[15]

John D. Rogge, a CPNAB office clerk, drew light duty when the Japanese assigned him to Commander Cunningham as an orderly. The gangly young Contractor from Idaho occupied a dugout near Cunningham's CP during the siege, and the island commander had taken a liking to him. Rogge moved into Cunningham's cottage and puttered around the place as a combination janitor and handyman.[16]

Once the Japanese became fully aware they had a highly trained work force at their command, their agenda grew more ambitious. In addition to tapping American ingenuity, supplies, and equipment to complete or repair base facilities, Wake's new owners decided to use the CPNAB organization to fortify the atoll. On the evening of January 3, 1942, Katsumi summoned Russell and other

Contractor superintendents to a meeting. "The Japanese wanted us to go on with the job," Russell learned. "Asked us to figure how many men it would take in our various departments." To determine which Americans would be of most use, the Japanese had them fill out questionnaires concerning their job skills. Even captured servicemen were required to disclose what they had done in civilian life.[17]

The Japanese launched their fortification campaign by having the Contractors erect barbed wire fences on the atoll's beaches. Then civilians with construction experience went to work on dugouts, pillboxes, CPs, and magazines made of reinforced concrete. One detail toiled on a coral emplacement to shield a cannon the enemy had landed on the atoll. James Allen, a quick-thinking carpenter from California, convinced a guard that the emplacement would look prettier if the POWs lined the inside with white coral. The SNLF man did not suspect that Allen wanted to make the gun position easier for American planes to spot when they returned to bomb Wake.[18]

The Japanese evinced intense interest in repairing the Wake Island Detachment's artillery for incorporation into their own defense system. They took Marines from the 5-inch and 3-inch batteries to their former battle stations and demanded that the Americans produce the firing locks and other parts they had removed from their ordnance before surrendering. The Japanese also urged these prisoners to reassemble the heavy weapons and demonstrate how to load and fire them. Invariably, the Marines played dumb and disclaimed any knowledge of such matters. One SNLF officer tried penetrating this veil of silence by interrogating a POW in isolation from his comrades. He escorted Pfc. Otis T. Jones, an antiaircraft gunner, back to Battery E. Feigning friendship, the officer plied Jones with extra food and a cigarette while questioning him, but the stubborn Marine insisted, "I did not know anything about these guns." The stymied officer ultimately lost his patience. He denounced Jones as a liar, drew his pistol, and punched the barrel into the frightened American's stomach, knocking the wind out of him. The enraged Japanese viciously pistol-whipped Jones for several minutes, drawing blood from his mouth, nose, and ear. A second Japanese officer subjected Jones to the same treatment on another day at a different battery. Bruised and bleeding, the steadfast Leatherneck never deviated from his story and pled ignorance until the enemy despaired of breaking him.[19]

Perhaps another sky gunner cracked under such abuse, or the enemy just got lucky, but they eventually found one or two of the firing locks that Battery E's personnel had tossed into the lagoon. The Japanese promptly conveyed some Marines down from Camp 2 and ordered them to put the 3-inch guns back together. Two hard-boiled corporals—Robert F. Haidinger and Michael N. Economou—were selected for that detail. Haidinger and Economou waited until the guards looked away and then drained the recoil fluid from the cannon they were supposedly fixing. Haidinger also tinkered with the traversing gear on one artillery piece. Once the Japanese judged the 3-inchers restored to working order, they had one loaded and pulled the lanyard. With a sharp boom, the barrel tore loose and shot backwards through the gun platform, ramming itself into the ground like a giant javelin. Other POWs dabbled in sabotage whenever they thought the enemy was distracted, but no one else achieved such spectacular results.[20]

As much as it went against the grain to assist the Japanese, most POWs liked being chosen for work details. A man felt less like a prisoner beyond the crowded confines of the POW compound, and any kind of activity broke up the day and made time seem to go faster. Ranging across the atoll also gave the Wake Islanders a chance to supplement their diet by foraging among numerous caches of canned food. Many guards did not relish American edibles, and they allowed the POWs to keep as much of the salvaged food as they could carry. Work details usually returned to Camp 2 laden with a wide assortment of goodies. Private First Class Himelrick cataloged the cornucopia he collected on January 9 alone as two 1-gallon cans of tomatoes, one can of tomato juice, two cans of fruit cocktail, one can of sliced dried beef, ten smaller tins of sardines, and one of shrimp.[21]

"As a result," recounted Cpl. Henry Durrwachter, another Marine diarist, "it wasn't long until we were . . . cooking over an open fire in the compound. The place looked for all the world like a hobo jungle with everyone over his fire cooking in a tin can." Occasionally, the POWs turned the cookouts into social affairs. "We had a couple of community stews cooked up here," related Himelrick. "Everybody chipped in a couple of cans of something & we cooked it up & rationed it out to everybody."[22]

Wake's frequent rains had washed the paper labels off many food cans while they sat outdoors. Hence, the POWs often had no idea what kind of groceries they recovered until they pried open the lids. That produced some disappointing potluck dinners. Sergeant Rogers once ended up with a two-gallon can of sauerkraut. Two Marine buddies got stuck with three gallons of tomato puree and three gallons of canned asparagus, which they refused to eat. They would soon reproach themselves for being so picky.

A large number of Wake Islanders were young men in their twenties and late teens, and they always seemed to be hungry. Such fellows refused to restrict their foraging to daytime or to pilfer only American food. The barbed wire fence enclosing the POWs' barracks was not as formidable a barrier as the Japanese assumed. Several daring Wake Islanders regularly slipped under it at night to raid a nearby dugout used to store canned food. Private LaPorte got a kick out of these midnight adventures, although it later dawned on him that he could have been shot had the guards been more vigilant. Pvt. Edward V. Sturgeon belonged to another band of Marines whose stomachs overruled their common sense. Detailed to stack Japanese hardtack in a warehouse, they stuffed their pockets with the thick crackers whenever they could get away with it. "And they were three times better than the ones we had," Sturgeon asserted, "'cause they had this sweet taste."[23]

Foraging yielded treasures other than additional food. Some Americans rendered their quarters a little more comfortable by bringing back mattresses and blankets. Others expanded their meager wardrobes with pieces of clothing they found here or there. Six or seven Contractors struck it rich after they came across the mail shipment that Pan Am's *Philippine Clipper* left behind when it flew out of Wake for the last time on December 8. The civilians discovered lots of cash in the letters and packages they tore open, and they decided to retain it as insurance against whatever uncertainties awaited them. They sewed the money inside their shirt collars and trouser waistbands to hide it from the enemy and spare their comrades the temptation of stealing it.[24]

"RUMORS, RUMORS, RUMORS THAT IS ALL WE HEAR"

POWs not chosen for work details led a monotonous existence. "We just lay around waiting for something to eat and for night time to arrive," remembered TSgt. Charles Holmes. Even prisoners who got out to work still spent a lot of time caged at Camp 2. Every American with time on his hands worried about the future. "You didn't know from one day until the next what the hell was going to go on," groused TSgt. Edwin "Peepsight" Hassig. Leal Russell, the head Contractor in Camp 2, had to deal with a torrent of questions from anxious underlings. "Men all asking for news," he jotted in his diary on December 26. "None to give them. None of us know anything."[25]

In the absence of trustworthy information, the POWs automatically resorted to speculation and rumor. Robert C. Maple, a civilian electrician, related that the main source of amusement in Camp 2 "was just treating each other to all the scuttlebutt and rumors we would hear." Some stories attained wild proportions as they circulated. One predicted that the United States would trade Japan two or three full oil tankers in exchange for the Wake Islanders' release. Unaware of the crippled state of the U.S. Pacific Fleet at Pearl Harbor, many Marines and civilians awoke each day expecting to see an American task force steaming over the eastern horizon to recapture Wake and liberate them. "Rumors, rumors, rumors that is all we hear," a disgusted Russell carped on January 3. "I believe none of them."[26]

A large number of Contractors clung to the naive belief that the Japanese would recognize their civilian status and repatriate them. They were disappointed when their captors inexplicably classified them as convict labor, as that bit of legerdemain freed the Japanese to treat the Contractors as POWs. Jack Snipes, a level-headed civil engineer from California, suspected his captors must have had a more legitimate reason for their decision: "The Japs figured that the islands were so small that anyone there would be helping the Marines or Navy and classified them all as POWs."[27]

Russell preferred spending his evenings in conversation with the two POW doctors. Mason Kahn and Lawton Shank were both mature, educated men with a diversity of interests. They also possessed a bottle of sake given to them by the Japanese, which the doctors gladly shared with the CPNAB superintendent. Russell may have despised rumormongering, but he recognized how difficult it was for the Wake Islanders to go without news from the outside world. "It is no fun," he conceded.[28]

Not all of Russell's fellow prisoners were as news-deprived as he thought. After the Wake Islanders settled in at Camp 2, Cpl. Eschol E. Davis, a communications technician with Battery A, discovered a radio hidden in a barracks attic. He would steal up there at night to monitor news broadcasts from the United States. Several other POWs found another hidden radio in their barracks, and they succeeded in raising station KGEI out of San Francisco. Second Lieutenant Kinney, VMF-211's ingenious engineering officer, picked up a portable radio with a cracked case and punctured speaker diaphragm. Thinking the apparatus beyond salvaging, the SNLF guards left it lying in the POW compound, but Kinney had a knack for fixing all kinds of gadgets. A little fiddling produced a loud hum. Under the right atmospheric conditions, Kinney was soon able to tune in American stations. To avoid detection by the Japanese, he would listen with the set pressed to his ear at low volume and a mattress folded over his head. On one occasion, Kinney heard Secretary of Labor Frances Perkins repeat President Roosevelt's pledge that American industry would turn out 50,000 warplanes in 1942. The jubilant American shared that snippet of braggadocio with his brother officers, and it significantly bolstered their morale. Unfortunately, Kinney's radio caused interference on a set that the Japanese used on the same frequency. The guards searched the POWs' quarters, discovered an improvised antenna Kinney had rigged, and followed it to his radio, which they promptly confiscated. Kinney missed his radio, but he was thankful that the Japanese did not punish him for this transgression.[29]

Even as the Japanese strove to deny the POWs contact with the outside world, they probed them for information of military value. Wake's conquerors concentrated primarily on Dan Teters and the American officers. The Japanese especially sought intelligence on American aviation and artillery, devoting much of their attention to VMF-211's pilots and the commanders of Major Devereux's 5-inch and 3-inch batteries. Second Lt. Robert Hanna of the Wake Island Detachment was astonished by how much data the enemy had obtained on the garrison's officers prior to the atoll's capture. "They knew what each of us, his job was," Hanna exclaimed. "They knew that before they got there. . . . I don't know where they got it from, but they . . . knew what our assignments were."[30]

These interrogations tended to be cordial, with Japanese officers even congratulating their American counterparts on certain aspects of Wake's defense. At times, the Japanese seemed more concerned with justifying their country's decision to go to war than tricking their guests into revealing anything. Commander Cunningham received several reminders that Bushido dictated that the commander of a defeated garrison should commit suicide. He interpreted these comments as taunts, but his captors were actually complimenting an enemy they respected by hinting he seek an honorable death.[31]

The Japanese quizzed Major Devereux on how American radar worked. When Devereux stated that he knew only about radar's "general functions," his interrogators politely took him at his word. During another session, however, an enemy officer tried to bluff First Lieutenant Kessler into yielding more information by threatening to lop off his head. Kessler persuaded the Japanese that he had nothing else to tell and was sent back to the White House with a case of canned sardines to share with his roommates.[32]

The most persistent question the enemy directed at the Wake Islanders had to do with the whereabouts of the garrison's "big guns." The Japanese just could not accept that the Wake Island Detachment had dealt so much damage to Admiral Kajioka's ships with only six 5-inch guns. What really rubbed salt in the Imperial Japanese Navy's wounded pride was that those antiquated 5-inchers originally belonged to the auxiliary batteries on American battleships and cruisers that had been handed down to Marine defense battalions after the U.S. Navy replaced them with heavier and more modern armament. The Japanese believed that Devereux's seacoast batteries had actually fought with 12-inch or 16-inch guns that could be retracted into the ground to protect them from enemy counterfire or detection from the air.[33]

By January 7, 1942, the Wake Islanders had spent nearly two weeks lodged at Camp 2. Leal Russell paused toward the end of that day to take stock of the POWs' overall state. The Americans had established an agreeable relationship with their captors, who apparently bore them no ill will for the lethal tenacity of the atoll's defense. Although the enemy required many prisoners to work, the hours were not overly long and the pace was anything but grueling. The Japanese also ensured that their charges ate regularly, gave them access to medical care, and met most of their other basic physical needs. Russell and his companions could not know it at the time, but they had undergone a far gentler transition to captivity than the vast majority of American and British Commonwealth troops snapped up by the Japanese in the Pacific War's opening rounds. Nonetheless, a bitterness gnaws at every imprisoned soul, and Russell perceived it as he stared into the darkness gathering outside his barracks that January evening. He echoed the thoughts of the hundreds of Americans gathered around him when he scratched in his diary, "Many men already asking when it will end."[34]

The end had come earlier that day for Pfc. Alexander Branch Venable Jr., the first Wake defender to die while a POW. Venable belonged to the 1st Defense Battalion's Battery E, and he weathered the siege without a scratch. A friendly and considerate young man from Pennsylvania, he dreamed of a career as a forest ranger after completing his stint in the Marine Corps. Yet like the wild things he loved, he could not thrive in a cage. The atoll's surrender sank him into deep depression, and he could not become reconciled to an existence without freedom. While the move to Camp 2 raised other Americans' spirits, it had the opposite effect on Venable. Afflicted by both dysentery and stomach pains, he simply laid down in the barracks occupied by his battery mates and waited to die. Solicitous comrades repeatedly encouraged him to take some nourishment or medication, but he paid no heed. "He decided that he'd rather die than be a prisoner," testified Cpl. Guy Kelnhofer, a chum from before the war. On January 5, two days before Venable expired, Dr. Shank charitably diagnosed his malady as diarrhea and "other complications." The forlorn Leatherneck's unnecessary demise constituted a vital lesson for every other American on Wake Island. Not even halfway decent treatment from the Japanese could save a POW if he lost the all-important will to live.[35]

Life behind barbed wire weighed heavily on Second Lieutenant Kinney's spirits, too, but he sought release in a manner consistent with his code as a Marine Corps officer. Kinney felt duty bound to get back into the war, and he focused an electrical engineer's calculating mind on making that happen. The primary reason he risked operating a radio in Camp 2 was to gather intelligence for an escape attempt. Kinney also figured that he needed help. Accordingly, he enlisted Capt. Frank Tharin as a coconspirator. The two fliers had known each other for eighteen months, and they forged a close friendship during VMF-211's valiant fight to deny the Japanese control of Wake's airspace.

Tharin and Kinney decided early on to keep their aspirations secret. They did not want their plans becoming the object of idle gossip, which might be overheard by English-speaking Japanese nosing around the prisoners' quarters. It also appeared that most POW officers thought escape from Wake was impossible. Some, still expecting rescue by the U.S. Navy, saw no need to hazard anything so foolhardy. Tharin and Kinney feared that one of these cautious souls might turn informer in a misguided effort to save them from the enemy's wrath.

Initially, Tharin and Kinney plotted to steal a small boat and either rig a sail or row more than two thousand miles to Hawaii. That was a fantastic idea that easily crossed the line from daring to reckless. Fortunately, the would-be escape artists aborted that plan for want of information. Neither Tharin nor Kinney knew if any American small craft had survived the siege. Since POW officers did not accompany work details, the two Marine aviators could not conduct their own search of the atoll. At the same time, their commitment to secrecy prevented them from asking enlisted or civilian prisoners about the locations of any boats.

No sooner had Tharin and Kinney discarded their original escape plan than the Japanese provided them with another option. Once Wake passed into enemy hands, the Yokohama Air Group began operating its massive Kawanishi H6K4 Navy Type 97 flying boats from the marine airport that the Americans had dredged and blasted in the lagoon. Tharin had shot down one of these four-engine Mavis seaplanes when the Japanese attacked the atoll before dawn on December 12. Of greater pertinence to escape planning, however, both Tharin and Kinney had qualified to pilot twin-engine seaplanes during their flight training at Naval Air Station Pensacola in Florida. In addition, Kinney had worked as a mechanic for Pan Am before entering the Marine Corps. That experience familiarized him with the electrical, mechanical, fuel, and oil system on the airline's four-engine flying clippers, and he assumed that knowledge would apply to the inner workings of an H6K4.

Tharin and Kinney enjoyed a good view of Mavis operations from Camp 2. Resolving to commandeer a seaplane and fly it to Pearl Harbor, they studied the routines followed by enemy aircrews. They spotted two surfboards lying on the lagoon beach 150 yards from their barracks, which would enable them to paddle out to the Mavises. Their maturing plans involved slipping out of the POW compound after dark, boarding an empty flying boat, familiarizing themselves with its controls and operating systems, and taking off just as the sky grew light enough to allow them to see. Tharin and Kinney estimated the odds against their success as 10,000 to 1, but nothing could dissuade them from pressing ahead. Before the Leathernecks could complete their preparations, however, the Japanese inadvertently foiled their scheme by removing them from Wake Island.[36]

"THE GREAT JAPANESE EMPIRE WILL NOT TRY TO PUNISH YOU ALL WITH DEATH"

Russell did not hear a rumor he thought worthy of preserving in his diary until January 9, 1942, which was exactly one year after he had landed on Wake with the first contingent of Contractors. "Little did we think then what the anniversary date would be like," he quipped. Turning to the day's news, he wrote, "Rumored that part of us to be shipped off. I think they intend to keep some here to help in reconstructing several of the buildings."[37]

Less than forty-eight hours later, a young Marine from Missouri, Cpl. John Johnson, received verification from an unlikely source that a move was indeed imminent. Johnson's buddies in the 1st Defense Battalion called him "Junior" because he made corporal while still in his teens, which was a rare occurrence in the prewar Marine Corps. A practicing Catholic with an earnest nature and a deep respect for authority, Johnson turned twenty on December 23, 1941, his last day as a free man. At that time, he commanded another Marine and six Contractors manning two .30-caliber machine guns on the western tip of Wilkes Island. As Johnson went off watch at midnight on the twenty-third, he promised the civilian who relieved him that they would celebrate his birthday after sunup. The Japanese navy had other plans, and the Americans on Wilkes Island found themselves locked in combat with the one hundred SNLF troops who intruded on their small domain shortly before 3:00 AM.

Corporal Johnson helped turn the tide in that contest by leading his .30-caliber section against the rear of the enemy beachhead. Japanese resistance soon collapsed, and roughly thirty SNLF men crawled under a bomb-damaged searchlight truck in a frantic scramble for cover from a closing circle of lethal Marine rifle and BAR fire. Despite the hopelessness of their position, the Japanese gave no sign of surrendering. Shots continued to come from the writhing mass of panic-struck men until Johnson hosed it with a stream of slugs from his machine gun. Marine riflemen then bounded forward to finish off any survivors. Captain Platt, the quick-thinking commander of Wilkes' defenders, intervened in the mopping-up process by insisting his men spare two wounded Japanese for interrogation. Platt entrusted his terrified prisoners to Corporal Johnson, and they were still alive when Wilkes surrendered later in the day.

From the moment Junior Johnson became a prisoner himself, he saw neither of his former charges until the day before he departed Wake Island. An agonizing case of athlete's foot accompanied by chronic fatigue kept the corporal from getting out of Camp 2 on work details. Johnson adopted a simple treatment to battle his physical complaints. He would hobble outside after breakfast, select a spot likely to stay in the sun most of the day, cover his feet with warm sand, and nap.

Johnson began January 11 in this sedate manner, but an unexpected visitor interrupted his routine. A tapping sensation on his arm roused the corporal from a short sleep, and he opened his eyes to see an unarmed SNLF man poking him softly with a walking stick. The Japanese motioned at Johnson to stand. After closely examining the puzzled American's face, he pointed his stick twice in the direction of Wilkes Island to the southwest. The SNLF man then held his stick like a firearm and said, "Tat-tat-tat." Frustrated by Johnson's blank expression, the Japanese yanked up his shirt, exposing a bandage on his lower back. Johnson gave an involuntary start as it finally dawned on him that he was face to face with one of the prisoners the Marines had taken on Wilkes.

Once the SNLF man established his identity, he gripped Johnson by the wrist and led him out of the POW compound. Johnson feared that his escort desired revenge for the bloodbath on Wilkes. The wounded seaman said something while passing the guard at the gate that elicited laughter from both Japanese. That exchange only deepened the American's apprehension. Johnson's visitor conducted him to a building in the Japanese section of Camp 2 and beckoned him inside. The nervous corporal expected to be greeted by a hostile court of enemy officers eager to have him executed, but the structure contained nothing but piles of American clothing. The SNLF man sorted through the garments until he extracted a double-breasted suit and two long-sleeved shirts that fit Johnson. He handed those items to the mystified Marine and then held his own shoulders and pretended to shiver as if he were cold. Johnson could not decipher the meaning of that brief charade, other than that his companion meant him no harm. The Japanese seaman returned the relieved Missourian to the POW compound, where he gave the latter's arm an affectionate pat and said in farewell, "*Tomodachi*," which means "friend."

Johnson received no time to ponder what had just happened, as he had just stepped out of one bewildering situation and into another. He found his fellow prisoners in a state of high excitement. The Americans held printed sheets of paper and were engaged in agitated conversation.[38] Someone handed Johnson a copy, and he began reading a set of mimeographed instructions:

COMMANDER OF THE PRISONER ESCORT
NAVY OF THE GREAT JAPANESE EMPIRE

REGULATIONS FOR PRISONERS

1. The prisoners disobeying the following orders will be punished with immediate death.
    a. Those disobeying orders and instructions.
    b. Those showing a motion of antagonism and raising a sign of opposition.
    c. Those disordering the regulations by individualism, egoism, thinking only about yourself, rushing for your own goods.
    d. Those talking without permission and raising loud voices.
    e. Those walking and moving without order.
    f. Those carrying unnecessary baggage in embarking.
    g. Those resisting mutually.
    h. Those touching the boat's materials, wires, electric lights, tools, switches, etc.
    i. Those climbing ladder without order.
    j. Those showing action of running away from room or boat.
    k. Those trying to take more meal than given to them.
    l. Those using more than two blankets.

2. Since the boat is not well equiped and inside being narrow, food being scarce and poor you'll feel uncomfortable during the short time on the boat. Those losing patience and disordering the regulation will be punished for the reason of not being able to escort.

The ominous tone of these passages worried Johnson. Most of the rest of the document described sanitary provisions and how food would be distributed aboard ship. The final paragraph tried to strike a reassuring note, but the wording must have made the POWs shudder, and then chuckle.

6. Navy of the Great Japanese Empire will not try to punish you all with death. Those obeying all the rules and regulations, and believing the

action and purpose of the Japanese Navy, cooperating with Japan in constructing the "New Order of the Great Asia" which lead to the world's peace will be well treated.[39]

By the time Johnson finished reading, the scales had fallen from his eyes and he understood what the wounded SNLF man had been trying to tell him. The Wake Islanders were about to board a ship that would transport them to a colder climate. Johnson's visitor credited the corporal with saving his life on Wilkes. He went out of his way to ensure his American *tomodachi* would be appropriately garbed when the POWs reached their new home. What Johnson and his comrades could not know was that the comparatively kind treatment that had graced most of their confinement on Wake Island was coming to an abrupt end.[40]

CHAPTER FIVE

"a real hell ship"
from wake island to yokohama
on the nitta maru

"YOU BLINKED YOUR EYELID YOU'RE DEAD"
The release of the Regulations for Prisoners plunged the Wake Islanders into a frenzy of rumor and speculation. Japanese guards confirmed the arrival of a troopship to transport the POWs to an undisclosed location. That bit of information prompted the Americans to give free rein to their imaginations. Many Contractors leaped to the conclusion that they would soon be back in the United States. "Oh, we're gonna be repatriated," they congratulated each other.[1]

Other POWs guessed they were headed for Japan or someplace else deep in the enemy's empire. That disappointed the servicemen and civilians who still believed the U.S. Pacific Fleet would soon recapture Wake Island. "We thought the American forces would be back at any time to rescue us," explained 2nd Lt. John McAlister, "but we lost hope when we were told to prepare to leave the island."[2]

The draconian nature of the enemy's boarding instructions left most Wake Islanders wondering if they would survive the coming voyage. "We didn't know whether we was going to make it to China or wherever they was going to take us," exclaimed Pfc. Mackie Wheeler. As Cpl. Robert Brown surveyed all the trivial offenses that could result in capital punishment, he thought, "You blinked your eyelid you're dead."[3]

The Japanese waited for the POWs to gather in the Camp 2 mess hall for their noon meal before ordering them to return to their barracks to pack for the trip. The enemy limited the Americans to one piece of hand luggage per man, but that elicited few complaints. A Wake Islander was lucky if he could claim a change of clothes and a couple of cans of food as his own. Aside from the shirt and trousers that TSgt. Charles Holmes wore day in and day out, his other possessions consisted of two blankets and one Marine sun helmet. Leal Henderson

Russell easily fit his few belongings into a pair of trousers that he converted into a bundle by tying off the legs.

Once the POWs had collected their things, the Japanese marched them back to the mess hall. Instead of finally getting some food, the Wake Islanders learned that they would be divided into two groups. The guards herded the Contractors into a nearby field, where an interpreter stood on a raised platform. The interpreter produced a long list and called out the names of 367 civilians, most of whom were heavy equipment operators or specialists in various forms of construction. The Japanese intended for these men to remain on Wake to build base facilities and defense installations. The POWs now realized the purpose behind the questionnaires the enemy had given them. The Japanese selected Leal Russell, the CPNAB buildings superintendent, to head their new American labor battalion. They also retained Dr. Lawton Shank to attend to this group's medical needs.

The POWs received nothing to eat until after their captors completed this reorganization. The Japanese fed Russell and his 367 "key men" first and escorted them to their quarters. The remaining POWs ate in shifts. The last of them to pass through the mess hall finally crawled under their blankets around midnight.[4]

After sunup on Monday, January 12, the prisoners selected to remain on Wake congregated in the mess hall. Except for some two dozen sick or wounded men in the POW hospital, the rest of Camp 2's American population turned out for evacuation. The Japanese thoughtfully provided trucks to haul the Wake Islanders to Wilkes Channel, where they would embark on the waiting ship. Clutching nondescript bundles, the POWs boarded the vehicles and took their last ride around Wake Island.[5]

The patients at the hospital expected to follow their comrades to the atoll's south side, but they were in for a disappointment. "Each of you are staying here," Dr. Shank told his charges. "In my opinion, you would have a horrible trip. . . . The ship is not equipped to take care of sick or wounded people." Shank was being more diplomatic than truthful. The decision to leave behind the American wounded had actually emanated from a Japanese officer, Lieutenant Toshio Saito, the commander of the detail that would guard the POWs aboard ship. Saito had landed on Wake the day before to finalize embarkation plans. Before he went ashore, he pledged to the ship's doctor, "I will not bring any sick prisoners." Saito communicated this determination to Shank on the morning of January 12, and the American doctor apparently thought it would cause his patients less alarm if he claimed the idea as his own. Shank also realized that he needed help to care for so many bedridden men. He had the Japanese recall three civilian nurses from among the departing POWs to give him a suitable staff.[6]

Not everyone left in the hospital abided by Shanks' ruling. Capt. Herbert Freuler of VMF-211 had taken a machine-gun bullet in the upper back during his last dogfight on December 22, and the wound had still not healed. Nevertheless, the Marine pilot insisted on leaving Wake with the bulk of his comrades. Another Marine with a nasty back wound, Pfc. Joseph E. Terfansky from the 1st Defense Battalion, also went along. At least two injured Contractors were permitted to embark. One of them, Mick D. Johnson, a truck driver from Olympia, Washington, had a broken arm set in a cast. Despite Lieutenant Saito's vow to accept no sick prisoners, some dysentery cases slipped into the ranks of the evacuees, as well.

Altogether, Dr. Shank kept twenty American service personnel in his hospital. They included Cpl. Ralph Holewinski, Pfc. Wiley Sloman, and six other Leathernecks from the Wake Island Detachment; a pilot and six enlisted men from VMF-211; and four Navy Bluejackets. The twentieth patient to stick with Shank was Capt. Henry Wilson of the Army radio detail. Wilson had weathered the siege without a scratch, only to be immobilized by acute dysentery.[7]

As the 1,235 prisoners chosen for departure detrucked on the main islet's south shore, their eyes swept the sea for the ship they were supposed to board. A mile or so away sat the stately *Nitta Maru*, a relatively new luxury liner and the pride of the Nippon Yusen Kaisha Line. Launched on May 20, 1939, the 17,100-ton ship was rated at an impressive 22.2 knots. The *Nitta Maru* soon set a speed record for crossing the Pacific Ocean, and the 100 stewards in its 225-man crew acquired a reputation for gracious service to Western passengers. On the outbreak of war with the United States, the Imperial Japanese Navy commandeered the *Nitta Maru* as a troopship and pressed its crew into service. On December 23, Kiyoshi Ogawa, the liner's captain, received orders to sail from Yokohama to Japan's Kure Naval Base to pick up Lieutenant Saito's guard detachment. The *Nitta Maru* called next at Shanghai to embark five hundred SNLF troops to reinforce Wake Island's Japanese garrison.[8]

Saito's detachment contained one additional officer, eight petty officers, and forty enlisted men drawn largely from the 3rd Replacement Company. The men under Saito's command were trained as SNLF troops, and they carried rifles and bayonets. Both Japanese and American eyewitnesses would later describe these guards as a tough bunch, and that was no accident. With the Imperial Japanese Navy unwilling to allocate more than fifty men to control some 1,200 prisoners, Saito needed personnel who could project an intimidating presence and dominate any situation. He personally chose tall, muscular men for this assignment, exhibiting a preference for sailors skilled in one of Japan's traditional martial arts, such as sumo, judo, or kendo (fencing). Chief Petty Officer Asaichi Yoshimura, a middle-aged warrant officer with a handlebar mustache, was a veteran of the Second Sino–Japanese War. He had taught kendo at a Japanese high school and was rated as an expert with a sword. Petty Officer Third Class Tokuichi Takamura placed third among Japan's judo experts. Petty Officer First Class Tamotsu Takezoe taught judo to recruits at the Kure Naval Base.[9]

A tall, thin officer who had graduated from the Imperial Japanese Naval Academy at Eta Jima, Saito ran a tight outfit. After he selected his detachment, he called together its members and reminded them "that all would obey him, that their lives were in his hands and that he would be responsible for them." Saito's handpicked band would not disappoint him. Having seen no action thus far in this new war, these men yearned to demonstrate their prowess against the emperor's enemies. As the *Nitta Maru* steamed toward Wake, Tsumori Misaka, the ship's second purser, overheard some ominous mutterings among Saito's personnel. "Because many Japanese soldiers had lost their lives in the original attack on Wake Island," Misaka later related, "the Guards would attempt to seek revenge from the captured Prisoners of War in the event the Prisoners of War were not obedient to every command." Saito and his scrawny, inexperienced second-in-command, Ensign Toshio Jinno, reflected this antagonistic attitude when they drafted the boarding instructions that so chilled the Wake Islanders. The lieutenant also remarked ominously to Jinno that some of their subordinates "would like to be permitted to cut the enemy."[10]

"AS SOON AS WE GOT INSIDE . . . THEN HELL BROKE LOOSE"

The POWs scheduled to leave Wake Island arrived at Wilkes Channel sometime after 8:00 AM, January 12. Their embarkation was delayed as the Japanese used the available lighters to send ashore the five hundred SNLF troops and assorted supplies the *Nitta Maru* had brought to the atoll. The day turned hot, and the Americans roasted as they sat waiting on an open beach. The Wake Islanders who had dressed in layers at Camp 2 stripped down to T-shirts, shorts, and tennis shoes and stuffed the garments they removed into their bundles. Some inner voice prevented FN1C William O. Plate from following suit, and he continued to swelter in a leather jacket, wool Navy jumper, Navy blue wool trousers, and Marine combat boots. As a Leatherneck, Pvt. Ewing LaPorte felt "stupid" to be wearing a woolen sailor's uniform, but he would come to cherish his incongruous wardrobe in a matter of days.

The Japanese finally finished unloading the *Nitta Maru* around midday, which freed their landing craft and motorboats to start ferrying the POWs to the ship. The limited number of small craft dictated that the Americans would have to embark in contingents. Lieutenant Saito returned to the *Nitta Maru* with the first group of three hundred prisoners.[11]

The Americans knew that boarding any ship off Wake Island could be difficult and even dangerous. The sea surrounding the atoll tended to be rough, and that was the case on January 12. Heavy swells tossed barges and boats full of POWs up and down like bathtub toys. Many men grew violently seasick and vomited into the water or on each other. Underestimating the power of the ocean, the *Nitta Maru*'s crew lowered a heavy gangplank to take on their American passengers. Pfc. James Venable stood in the first landing craft to approach that apparatus, and he described the jarring results this way: "Our coxswain wasn't a very good driver, and he managed to bring the boat up under the gangplank . . . which . . . slammed into this little conning tower in the back, and everyone damned near went over to one side, and we almost capsized the boat." The collision not only disabled the landing craft's steering mechanism, but the heaving Pacific turned the gangplank into a club that knocked down several POWs. Fortunately, the landing craft drifted clear, and the Japanese eventually transferred the shaken Americans to a motorboat.[12]

In the meantime the Japanese adopted a different boarding procedure. They raised the gangplank and opened a watertight cargo hatch on the side of the *Nitta Maru*. From this opening, crewmen hung a cargo net. As a lighter pulled alongside the hatch, the POWs threw their bundles to Japanese sailors standing inside. Then the Americans had to leap from their small craft one at a time and grab hold of the net.

This business required the split-second timing and nerveless agility of an acrobat. If a Wake Islander missed, he would be crushed between the ship's steel hull and the pitching lighter. The waves that day could lift small craft as high as twenty feet in nothing flat. "The lighter'd go up, and then down," recalled Contractor Leo L. Nonn, "and the ship was up and the lighter was down, and so forth." The trick was to jump just as the lighter reached the top of a wave. Real safety, however, could only be attained by scrambling up the cargo net before a stronger wave dashed the lighter against the *Nitta Maru* at the very spot where the POW clung. The sea was so choppy that a Wake Islander would often spring from a lighter, clear the cargo hatch, and land inside the ship.[13]

It was a miracle that no POW suffered death or serious injury during that hair-raising operation. One of the ship's officers sensibly stationed some good men at the cargo hatch to help the Americans aboard. Edwin Darby Nye, a CPNAB canteen clerk, was a bookish sort, not an athlete. The mere idea of jumping from a tossing lighter terrified him. When he finally made his leap, however, a Japanese sailor leaned out, caught him, and pulled him into the ship. Pfc. Carl Stegmaier got confused just before he pushed off and hit the *Nitta Maru* lower than he intended, but his hands managed to grip the bottom of the open hatch. Two enemy crewmen instantly seized hold and yanked the young Marine out of harm's way a second or two before a rebounding lighter would have squashed Stegmaier flat.[14]

Just before Cpl. John Johnson left his lighter, he took one last look at Wake Island. "What a worthless piece of ground to have cost so much in blood, suffering and materiel," he mused as he clambered up the loading net. As Johnson ended his climb, a Japanese sailor knocked all thoughts of Wake out of his mind by whacking his left shoulder with a long bamboo club. The impact nearly sent Johnson tumbling backward onto the barge below, but he made a convulsive lunge forward through the cargo hatch and fell on one knee on the deck. The bewildered corporal wondered if he had done the right thing as more blows rained down on his back, shoulders, and head while a chorus of angry voices shouted unintelligible curses and commands in Japanese.[15]

Private First Class Sturgeon preceded Johnson through the cargo hatch, and he later related, "As soon as we got inside there, then hell broke loose." POWs who kept hold of their luggage while boarding had their bundles clubbed from their hands. Both they and the Wake Islanders who threw their belongings through the cargo hatch never saw them again. Before the Americans could gain their bearings, the Japanese promptly deloused them using hand-pumped canisters of disinfectant, taking special care to aim the nozzles at their victims' faces.[16]

Beyond the foul-smelling mist that engulfed the POWs stood a double line of snarling Japanese drawn both from Saito's guard detachment and the ship's crew. These men flanked the passageways that led into the *Nitta Maru*'s bowels, and most of them brandished pick handles, mop handles, and bamboo clubs. The sight reminded Pfc. Edwin Borne of the initiation rituals he had endured growing up in New Orleans. "It was like . . . one of these high school belt lines," Borne recalled. The Japanese forced the Wake Islanders to run a gauntlet from the cargo hatch to the different holds set aside as their quarters. "They had the crew lined up there," remembered Pfc. George G. Hubley, "and just beat the hell out of us as they rushed [us] down in the hold." In addition to clubbing the POWs, the Japanese kicked and cuffed them. Lieutenant Saito had also stationed guards armed with rifles and bayonets at intervals along the passageways. These men freely used their weapons to harass the prisoners. "As we passed these [Japanese]

Marines," attested SSgt. Eugene W. Shugart, "they struck at us with rifle butts and some of them made passes at the prisoners with fixed bayonets."[17]

Most Wake Islanders would remember that welcoming gauntlet simply as an example of gratuitous cruelty. "We run into a bunch of mean Japs there, I'll tell you," commented Sturgeon. The Japanese, however, had practical reasons for their conduct. The longer the *Nitta Maru* sat off Wake, the more it chanced being spotted and sunk by an American submarine or long-range patrol plane. "As the Prisoners of War were distributed to their various holds aboard ship," testified Second Purser Misaka, "they were told to hurry because there was fear of enemy attack. . . . It is a Japanese custom to encourage haste, for officers to beat the soldiers to get them to respond more readily to duty."

Pfc. Grover Thaire noted that the POWs received more whacks "if we dident move fast enough." The gauntlet also permitted Saito's undermanned detachment to establish its dominance by literally beating the POWs into submission. In view of the grudge Saito's subordinates bore against Wake's defenders, it is possible that some guards tried to provoke the prisoners into doing something that would justify more drastic treatment. As Sergeant Holmes reported, "A Jap sailor hit me above the right temple and I bounded off the bulkhead . . . of the ship. My reaction was to come back fighting . . . but I recovered my senses to realize that they were looking for an excuse to kill us."[18]

For reasons the Japanese never divulged, they separated the American officers from the other prisoners and had them board the *Nitta Maru* last. Around 3:00 PM, a station wagon pulled up beside Commander Cunningham's cottage and drove him, his civilian orderly John Rogge, Captain Platt, and federal bureaucrat Herman Hevenor to the boat landing at Wilkes Channel. Major Devereux, Sergeant Malleck, Dan Teters, and their roommates from the White House followed in a truck. The Japanese spared the POW officers the ordeal of jumping through a cargo hatch, but the means employed to get them aboard was no less undignified. The ship's crew swung out booms and lowered cargo nets into the motor boat that brought the officers alongside. Cunningham, Devereux, and their companions climbed into the nets, and the Japanese hoisted them into the air, ultimately dumping the Americans onto the ship's deck like a load of fish.

Once aboard the *Nitta Maru*, the officers encountered a reception similar to that extended to the other prisoners. For starters, the Japanese deprived the officers of their baggage. Major Devereux tried to retain a big envelope containing genealogical papers tracing his lineage to Robert Devereux, Earl of Essex—the dashing but ill-fated paramour of England's Queen Elizabeth I. The major released his grip when an impatient guard gave him a resounding slap across the face. Cunningham, Devereux, Platt, Hevenor, and Rogge did not have to run a gauntlet, but the other officers sustained considerable battering en route to their quarters. "The Japs took great delight, laughing and chattering in glee every time they had an opportunity to kick or hit a prisoner with a club," related 1st Lt. Woodrow Kessler.[19]

Saito's guards lodged the thirty POW officers in the *Nitta Maru*'s steel-walled mailroom, a windowless space no more than twenty-four feet deep and fifteen feet wide. This unventilated chamber near the ship's engine room contained a few shelves, which the senior officers appropriated as bunks. The other officers slept on the hard steel deck. The enemy issued the mailroom's residents two blankets apiece, and most of the officers also received thin, cot-style mattresses. The Japanese opted to confine the civilians Teters and Hevenor separately in a small compartment nearby, but they sent Sergeant Malleck and John Rogge to the holds to join their lower-ranking comrades.[20]

"SO, THIS IS WHERE WE GOT THE EXPRESSION 'HELL HOLE'"

Compared to the accommodations occupied by the majority of Wake Islanders, the *Nitta Maru*'s mailroom represented the lap of luxury. The Japanese placed the Contractors and enlisted American servicemen in dimly lit holds. As CPNAB plumber Al O'Guinn peeked into one, he muttered, "So, this is where we got the expression 'hell hole.'" Each of these cavernous chambers contained three levels—the lowest just above the ship's keel, and the highest directly below the main deck.[21]

The Japanese did not believe in wasting much space on prisoners. "We's crowded up just like sardines in a can," complained Private First Class Hubley. TSgt. William J. Hamilton of VMF-211 claimed that the number of POWs jammed into his section "permitted only room enough for the prisoners to lie down shoulder to shoulder." Surrounded by 290 men in a space that could house only 100 comfortably, Cpl. Robert Brown discovered, "It was therefore impossible for us to lie down without lying on top of one another." Benjamin F. Comstock Jr., a CPNAB carpenter from Iowa, ended up in an area so crowded that the POWs had to sleep in shifts. Conditions were most cramped in the lowest levels, where the sharp slope of the hull left little flat space to lie or sit down. Some POWs found lengths of straw rope and lashed themselves to the two-by-eight timbers bolted to the side of the ship so they could sleep or relax without sliding down on their neighbors. "That's where I hung for [twelve] days," remembered Don W. Ludington, a sheet metal foreman.[22]

As the POWs got settled in the holds, the guards issued them their bedding. "We were given 2 blankets and a thin piece of straw hallway runner as a bed," Cpl. Henry Durrwachter scratched in his diary. "The straw and blankets weren't much help on those steel deck plates tho." Especially unfortunate was the Wake Islander forced to lie on a row of protruding rivets. Some prisoners received only one blanket, and Sergeant Holmes disclosed that he and the men in his section received none.[23]

The number of blankets issued and their thickness did not initially concern the POWs. Keeping warm was the least of their worries. Wake's tropical climate endowed the overcrowded holds with a furnace-like quality, and the Americans soon became drenched in sweat. Conditions were worst in the lower levels, where the air was particularly stale. Once the *Nitta Maru* got under way, the Japanese would open the hatches over the holds, but that afforded minuscule relief only to the prisoners in the top levels.[24]

The Japanese fed their charges twice daily, normally at 7:00 AM and 5:00 PM. Each meal consisted of a small bowl containing a teacup of watery rice or barley gruel. "There was not over one tablespoon of rice in this gruel and the rest was starchy water," groused Sergeant Hamilton. On one occasion, Fireman First Class Plate counted only eleven whole rice grains in his bowl before he started eating. Pfc. Mackie Wheeler dismissed the gruel as "so tasteless," with no hint of salt or other seasoning. The Japanese sometimes tried flavoring the gruel with a piece of rotten fish or a slice of daikon, but that hardly improved the taste and provided little additional nutrition. Every POW also received a teacup of water to drink with his meal. The guards occasionally ladled out a third cup between meals, but the Americans still felt deprived. Sergeant Shugart estimated that each prisoner downed less than a pint of water per day.[25]

This niggardly ration, which was personally set by Lieutenant Saito, had a debilitating effect on the POWs' bodies and morale. Contractor Fred R. Rumpel believed the Japanese fed their prisoners "barely enough to keep us alive." Herbert Papock, a CPNAB foreman from Los Angeles, jotted in his diary, "Everyone terribly hungry." For many Wake Islanders, thirst proved much more agonizing than hunger. "The hold was stifling and hot," explained Pfc. S. L. Baker, "and all of us were thirsty constantly."[26]

In addition to dehydration and malnutrition, the insipid fare visited one more torment on the Wake Islanders—widespread constipation. Contractor Nye managed to defecate only once during his twelve days on the *Nitta Maru*. Many POWs went up to seventeen days without experiencing a bowel movement. One Contractor remained constipated for twenty-two days, but another American set the group's record by not moving his bowels for another week or more. In view of the rudimentary sanitary facilities that the enemy provided, however, the constipation epidemic was a blessing is disguise.[27]

Lieutenant Saito's Regulations for Prisoners had promised the Wake Islanders that "toilet will be fixed at the four corners of the room." The document also conveyed this solemn injunction: "Everyone must cooperate to make the room sanitary. Those being careless will be punished." Once the POWs beheld what the enemy considered a proper waste disposal system, however, Saito's admonition about cleanliness seemed like a cruel joke. For toilets, or *benjos*, the Japanese provided four-sided, five-gallon cans with open tops and wire handles. They allotted a maximum of four of these primitive contraptions per hold level, and a few sections appear to have been equipped with no more than two or even one. Despite the prevalence of constipation, it did not take the two hundred or more men packed into most POW compartments long to fill their benjo cans, especially since several left Wake in the throes of dysentery or diarrhea.

The Americans were supposed to signal their keepers when the benjos were full so the cans could be emptied, but the guards liked to wait until the cans overflowed. They thought it funny to keep the POWs waiting as long as four hours. Consequently, a ghastly stench filled the holds as each roll of the ship sent urine and excrement splashing on or under the prisoners. Seasickness added vomit to this unholy recipe. "We were lying in this filth," grumbled FN2C Dare Kibble, "with . . . the attitude of 'what-the-hell-difference-does-it-make-anyway' to men who believed they were at the tailend of their lives."[28]

Eventually, the Japanese permitted the POWs to drag the brimming containers to the center of their respective compartments beneath a hatch. A couple of Americans would go up on deck, lower a line, haul the cans topside, and then dump their contents overboard. The men chosen to empty the benjos relished the chance to enjoy some fresh air, but theirs was a thankless job. Because the nauseous receptacles were full, the slightest motion of the ship produced spillage as they lurched upward. If a can caught on the edge of a hatch, it would tip sideways and douse the prisoners directly below. Petty Officer Third Class Takamura tried to make this happen more frequently by deliberately bumping into POWs raising benjo cans.

Since the Wake Islanders received no soap or water to wash their persons or living spaces, the atmosphere in their compartments grew increasingly fetid. "There really was a terrific smell down there," shuddered Fireman First Class Plate. Cpl. Thomas Johnson identified another common complaint: "The deck was just a slimy, filthy mess." All of Cpl. Franklin Gross' exposed skin except for his fingertips turned black from accumulating layers of grime. The Americans lived without eating utensils on the *Nitta Maru*, and Gross inadvertently licked his fingers as he scooped gruel, fish, and daikon into his mouth at meal times.²⁹

During the *Nitta Maru*'s first few days out from Wake, the weather remained hot and humid. The POWs marinated in their own sweat and refuse while hunger, thirst, and stink ate away at their spirits and vitality. "I could tell I was getting weaker by the minute," admitted Fireman Second Class Kibble, "and my zest for living was diminishing rapidly. All the laying around with about 300 calories a day . . . for body nourishment and breathing the foul air . . . kept your gut wrenching twenty-four hours a day." Soon, however, the Wake Islanders noticed that the ship's decks and bulkheads had started cooling. This came as a relief, but any relief was short-lived. In another day or two, the holds felt like refrigerators. "Then we liked to froze," exclaimed Private First Class Thaire. After months of life in a tropical climate, the prisoners were unaccustomed to cold. Except for a fortunate handful, they had left Wake garbed in lightweight summer clothing. Some were so scantily clad that they lacked underwear and socks.³⁰

The Japanese left the lights burning in the POW compartments all the time and rarely opened the hatches over the holds. These arrangements robbed many Americans of the ability to tell night from day. Some learned to determine the approximate time from when meals were served. As Cpl. Bernard Richardson related, however, most prisoners had ceased to care about that or anything else: "The cramped positions, the gnawing hunger, the stench, the stifling heat of the tropics, followed by the penetrating cold as we steamed north, together with the uncertainty of our destination, of our very lives—all combined with the cruelty of the Japs to plague us. The result was that we fell into gentle stupors. It was practically impossible to distinguish between dreaming done while awake and dreaming done in sleep."³¹

With the *Nitta Maru*'s mailroom situated directly over the ship's engines, the POW officers did not suffer too badly from the cold. The Japanese also showed Commander Cunningham, Major Devereux, and their brother officers the courtesy of placing their benjo cans in the passageway outside their quarters. The officers even received access to water to wash themselves on three occasions. Despite these amenities the atmosphere inside the mailroom could hardly be described as pleasant. The Japanese provided minimal treatment for Captain Freuler's wounded back, which became infected. They would let Freuler go without fresh dressings for two or three days, compelling him and his companions to live with the smell of puss and rotting flesh.³²

At some point in the trip, the guards returned the officers' luggage. Cunningham and the others noticed that the enemy had pilfered any valuables from their bags and bundles. The Japanese had also confiscated Dr. Kahn's small stash of medical supplies, negating his ability to help Captain Freuler. Nevertheless, the officers were glad to recover a little extra clothing and anything else Saito's men did not covet. One officer had packed some books, which enabled his comrades to kill time reading the Bible, a volume of Dorothy Parker's short stories, and Marjorie Rawlings' novel *The Yearling*.[33]

"THE BLOWS OF THE CLUB COULD BE HEARD IN THE PASSAGEWAY"

Neither rank nor any other consideration shielded the POWs from the reign of terror orchestrated by Lieutenant Saito and his subordinates. From the day the Wake Islanders boarded the *Nitta Maru* to the day they disembarked, they could be brutalized at any moment. Saito's men were preoccupied with crowd control, and their methods reflected the harshness typical of the Japanese military.

Security was tight on the *Nitta Maru*. The guards enforced every article in the Regulations for Prisoners and added several new rules to the list. After the enlisted POWs and Contractors entered the holds, the Japanese directed them to lie down and abstain from talking. The Americans had to obtain permission to sit up or use the benjo. When the weather turned frigid, POWs began huddling together in twos, threes, or larger clusters, but the guards put a stop to that as soon as they noticed it. The Japanese made the Americans kneel in ranks twice a day to receive their rations. The Wake Islanders had to get on their knees again after each meal and remain in that position while their captors conducted interminable head counts to ensure no one had achieved the impossible and escaped. The Japanese also required their prisoners to kneel once every day and bow to the west in a galling show of respect for Emperor Hirohito.[34]

The guards subjected the Wake Islanders to constant surveillance from passageway openings overlooking the holds. Scowling Japanese armed with clubs or rifles regularly descended into the POW compartments to search for rule breakers. If they spotted the slightest infraction, they meted out swift and savage punishment. Twenty prisoners who had silently squeezed together to share body heat were accused of talking. The guards lined the men up and worked them over with pick handles. Fourteen other Americans each received three licks against the spine for the crime of sitting up slightly by resting their backs against the ship's curved bulkhead. Convinced that Pfc. Herman A. Todd had broken the no-talking rule, the Japanese ordered him to stand, jump up, and grab an overhead beam.

That left the Marine dangling in midair with his toes just inches off the deck. An enemy petty officer then gripped a pick handle with both hands and beat Todd on the back. The pain must have been excruciating, but Todd did not dare release his hold on the beam. Another Japanese stood in front of him with a rifle and bayonet leveled at the Leatherneck's belly.[35]

Private First Class Terfansky received the same punishment with even less justification. A piece of shrapnel had struck this Marine machine gunner just below his left shoulder blade during the fighting on Wake, opening a jagged hole about six inches across and eight inches down his back. The wound had not yet closed completely, and the vile conditions in the space where Terfansky lay bred a septic infection. Growing tired of the intense pain from lying on his back, the stricken Marine raised himself a little on his elbows. A guard detected the movement, and the Japanese forced Terfansky to hang from a beam or pipe while they deliberately struck him on his wound as many as forty times, according to other prisoners' reports. Incredibly, Terfansky stood this inhuman abuse without a whimper. Cpl. John Johnson prided himself on being a tough Leatherneck, but watching the enemy torture Terfansky reduced him to tears for the first time in the war. Other Marines found inspiration in Terfansky's courage. Corporal Richardson credited him with restoring "our confidence in ourselves."[36]

Not every prisoner exhibited Terfansky's grit. After a guard administered a few whacks to another Marine with a club, the American fell to his knees screaming, "Oh, Mary, Mother of God, take care of me! Mercy! Don't hit me. Oh, God! Please don't hit me!" The unforgiving guard made the POW resume his hold on an overhead beam as a second Japanese pressed a bayonet against their victim's gut. At that, the blubbering Marine braced himself and accepted the rest of his chastisement without plea or protest. SSgt. John F. Blandy of VMF-211 saw an American sailor collapse and beg for mercy after sustaining a much worse beating.[37]

Saito's seamen often brought erring POWs into the passageways outside the holds, where four or five guards might drub a Wake Islander. The Japanese habitually aimed their blows at a prisoner's lower spine, which could paralyze his legs for days thereafter. Though sequestered inside the mailroom, the American officers knew how their men were being treated. "The blows of the club could be heard in the passageway," reported Captain Platt.[38]

Platt was a rarity in the prewar Marine Corps—an officer who openly empathized with the rank and file—and he ultimately got a taste of what his men were experiencing. Whenever Japanese inspection parties entered the mailroom, American officers were expected to kneel and bow. During one of these visits,

Platt failed to execute this salute quickly enough to satisfy his captors. An enemy petty officer returned minutes later and summoned Platt into the adjoining passageway. Two guards seized the captain's arms as the petty officer aimed a dozen blows across the small of his back.[39]

Much of the violence inflicted on the Wake Islanders had no rhyme or reason. Saito's seamen picked on numerous prisoners simply because they despised their country's foes and had the power to abuse them. Pfc. Robert Shores received two beatings on the *Nitta Maru* because his reddish blond hair made him conspicuous. Pvt. Earl Broyles was beaten unconscious six different times after one Japanese took a dislike to him. Many guards made a point of demonstrating their prowess at judo by choosing prisoners at random and throwing them around. After the weather turned cold, a few sentries dumped a pile of extra blankets beside a group of twenty Contractors. The Japanese waited outside the hold until the shivering prisoners helped themselves. Then the guards came back and beat the civilians for taking more than their share. Some Japanese prowled the POW quarters at any hour of the day or night, conducting shakedowns for the last few rings, watches, pens, and other valuables the Americans had concealed since their surrender.

The POWs never learned the names of most of their persecutors, but they remembered their appearances and tagged nicknames on the most sadistic. The "Sword Waver" repeatedly frightened the Americans by acting as if he was about to cleave them with a sword. Tiring of that sport, he would subject a helpless Yank to judo holds and flips. The "Snake" entered the holds at frequent intervals to catch prisoners talking, whispering, or standing without permission. He won his sobriquet by hissing as he stalked his prey. The guard called "Babe Ruth" swung his club against a POW's back as if he were trying to knock a home run out of the park.[40]

The guards committed their depredations with the encouragement of Lieutenant Saito, who collected the loot they gathered. Saito later presented his petty officers with American wristwatches and rings as souvenirs, but he reserved a healthy share of the stolen property for himself. He personally had Commander Cunningham and Major Potter relieved of their Annapolis class rings, explaining disingenuously that "the Emperor needed the gold to help finance the war effort." The lower-ranking prisoners also came in for plenty of Saito's attention. He inspected their holds at least once a day, sometimes staging additional surprise inspections at night to annoy his charges and deprive them of sleep. He would linger for an hour or more in a single POW compartment, as if to test how long the Americans could stand the pain of kneeling on bare steel plating.[41]

Saito also delighted in toying with his prisoners' minds. Two or three days out from Wake, the lieutenant, who spoke English, entered the compartment where Private First Class Hubley was being held with a big smile on his face. "He asked us how we liked it aboard one of the great Imperial Japanese Navy's ships," Hubley attested, "and said he had some good news for us. He then showed us some photographs of the bombing of Pearl Harbor. They were real photographs for we could identify several of the buildings. Then he said our Navy had been wiped out." On this or another visit, Saito commanded Second Purser Misaka to announce the receipt of a radio report that the Japanese had just torpedoed the aircraft carrier USS *Lexington*.[42]

Assailed incessantly both body and soul, the Wake Islanders slid steadily into despair. Reynold Carr, a Contractor with a poetic bent, dubbed the *Nitta Maru* "a real hell ship." Pfc. Henry Chapman would always remember the voyage from Wake as "the most depressing incident" in his three and a half years as a POW. To avoid going insane, Cpl. John Johnson imagined himself attending dances and other pleasant events back when he was enrolled at a Catholic military school in St. Louis.[43]

Besides demoralizing the Americans with propaganda, Lieutenant Saito employed Second Purser Misaka, another English speaker, to collect information from the Americans. A couple of days into the voyage, Misaka and ten to twelve assistants distributed printed questionnaires prepared by Saito to the POWs. Misaka thought he was obtaining the prisoners' "personal and military histories" to compile a more comprehensive roster. He would learn that Saito had a sinister use in mind for the information collected.[44]

"I AM IN PERFECT HEALTH AND EXPECT TO STAY THAT WAY"

On January 17, 1942, the Wake Islanders who had not lapsed totally into listless trances felt the *Nitta Maru* ease into a dock. The ship had just arrived at Yokohama, one of Japan's major ports, to refuel and take on supplies. It was snowing, and the guards opened the hatches and pelted the prisoners with snowballs.[45]

Soon after the *Nitta Maru* stopped moving, the guards rousted Dan Teters, Commander Cunningham, and several other POW officers from their quarters. The Japanese bade these men to wash their hands and faces and comb their hair. At the same time, Lieutenant Saito had several enlisted prisoners removed from the holds. The guards waited for the Americans to make themselves semipresentable and then herded them to the main deck. With dramatic effect, Saito's seamen marched the Wake Islanders into an unheated salon filled with Japanese reporters, photographers, and newsreel cameramen. Guessing that Japanese authorities wanted to show their people images of dejected enemy prisoners, Cunningham met the press with the widest smile he could muster. The other POWs followed his lead. Undaunted by this unexpected display of American moxie, Japanese journalists co-opted it to depict Wake's defenders as shameless buffoons. An English-language propaganda magazine with the improbable name of *Freedom* claimed that the Wake Islanders celebrated their first sight of Yokohama "with no trace of war consternation" and shouts of "Here we come Japan!" The same article told this incredible lie: "This group was . . . rowdy and boisterous . . . for they sang and danced, happy to find a new haven."[46]

For Private Broyles the press conference seemed to last forever, especially when the assemblage went out on deck for pictures. A short-sleeved shirt and khaki trousers afforded Broyles little protection from sleet driven by twenty-mile-per-hour winds. "Our hands were turning blue and our noses," he grumbled. To create the impression of Japanese magnanimity for the cameras, the POWs received cigarettes to smoke, but the sudden ingestion of nicotine by their starved bodies produced more dizziness than pleasure.[47]

Freedom admitted that the POWs had lived on short rations since leaving Wake, but it depicted the *Nitta Maru*'s passage to Yokohama as an epic of Japanese courage. "The vessel had a hazardous voyage," the magazine assured its readers, "zig-zagging through numerous enemy submarine infested lanes." The *Nitta Maru* did sail an evasive course, and it experienced more than one submarine scare—no doubt the result of nervous lookouts mistaking waves or shadows for the periscope of an underwater predator. What *Freedom* omitted to mention, however, was that Saito's guards dogged down the hatch covers to the holds and secured the door to the mailroom whenever the alarm bell and siren sounded. If the *Nitta Maru* took an American torpedo in its vitals, 1,235 Americans would go down with the ship.[48]

After the press conference broke up, the Japanese required several prisoners to record messages for radio broadcast. The selected POWs were eager to notify their loved ones that they were still alive. Commander Cunningham once again set an example by putting up a brave front before the microphone, saying, "Since the capture of Wake the prisoners, including myself, have been fairly treated and all in good health, looking forward to getting back to our homes. To my wife in Annapolis, I wish to send my best greetings and hopes for her welfare and that of our child, and I also wish to assure her that I am in perfect health and expect to stay that way a long time."

Once the Japanese finished exploiting the Wake Islanders for propaganda purposes, their thoughts turned to intelligence. They removed twenty Americans from the *Nitta Maru* for extended interrogation and confinement in Japan. The prisoners singled out for this special treatment were all servicemen—Major Potter, a Marine warrant officer, and a platoon sergeant from the 1st Defense Battalion; Major Putnam, three other pilots, and a corporal belonging to VMF-211; Cdr. Campbell Keene, Cunningham's second-in-command at Naval Air Station Wake Island; three Navy ensigns; one aerographer; six radiomen; and Sgt. Ernest Rogers from the Army radio detail. All of these prisoners possessed technological specialties, the majority in aviation and coded communications. These skills and knowledge made them prize catches for the Imperial Japanese Navy.[49]

By January 20 the *Nitta Maru* had wrapped up its business at Yokohama and it put out to sea again. As on the first leg of the trip, the POWs had no inkling where they were headed. "Destination unknown," Cpl. John Johnson noted glumly in his diary. The Wake Islanders were just four days away from setting foot once more on dry land. Before that happened, however, five would die in a bizarre revenge ritual staged by their unflagging nemesis, Lieutenant Toshio Saito.[50]

CHAPTER SIX

"never had i felt so desolate or so weary"
from murder at sea to despair on land

"YOU ARE NOW GOING TO BE KILLED FOR REVENGE"

After the *Nitta Maru* slipped its moorings and exited Yokohama harbor, it steered a southerly course toward Shanghai. In the POWs' holds, life followed the same dismal routine it had since the liner bid farewell to Wake Island. Elsewhere on the ship, Lieutenant Saito moved to consummate a design he had been contemplating since January 11, the day he landed on Wake to oversee preparations for his prisoners' embarkation. During that busy layover, Saito encountered an officer from the 24th Air Flotilla, the naval bomber force that suffered substantial losses while pounding the atoll December 8–21, 1941. That officer had asked permission from his superiors to avenge the death of a favorite subordinate by executing Major Putnam, the commander of VMF-211. Admiral Kajioka or some other senior Japanese officer rejected the request, but the vindictive airman would not take no for an answer. He sought out Saito and privately implored him to kill Putnam and two or three more Americans once the *Nitta Maru* put out to sea.[1]

Saito wished to oblige his comrade, but his hands were tied to a certain extent. With Japanese naval intelligence eager to interrogate Putnam and VMF-211's other pilots, Saito did not dare kill any of them. Yet sometime on the *Nitta Maru*'s outward voyage from Wake, he concocted a way to extract symbolic vengeance for the Chitose Air Group. On January 21 the lieutenant asked Ensign Jinno, his second in command, for the roster derived from the questionnaires distributed earlier to the POWs. Saito scanned the list and selected two Marines and three sailors with some connection to aviation. TSgt. Earl R. Hannum and SSgt. Vincent W. Bailey belonged to VMF-211, but they were not pilots and had spent the siege repairing and servicing the squadron's Wildcat fighters. S1C John W. Lambert, S2C Theodore Franklin, and S2C Roy J. Gonzales had been sent to Wake by Patrol Wing 2 to perform maintenance for a PBY squadron that never arrived. Later that evening, Saito confided his intent to execute these five Americans to Jinno.[2]

At 1:00 PM, January 22, Saito summoned Warrant Officer Asaichi Yoshimura to his cabin. "There are five POWs to be killed," the lieutenant announced. Saito told Yoshimura that the executions would be carried out at 4:00 PM that very day. He detailed the middle-aged warrant officer as an executioner and named four petty officers to share that duty. Saito opted to slay the Americans in time-honored Japanese style—with the sword—and he designated B deck, a former recreation area on the ship's stern, as the execution site.[3]

Around 3:00 PM, members of Saito's guard detachment entered the POW compartments and called out the names of the five doomed men. When the latter answered, the guards instructed them, "Bring blanket and shoes." The Japanese escorted Hannum, Bailey, Franklin, Lambert, and Gonzales to a steward's pantry off B deck without a word of explanation. Warrant Officer Yoshimura gave the baffled Americans some cigarettes and left them to speculate as to what was going on.[4]

Nearly an hour later the *Nitta Maru*'s loudspeaker system crackled with this invitation: "The execution is taking place now. Everyone come. Everyone who are free come." Approximately 150 Japanese assembled under an overcast sky to witness the spectacle, including more than two dozen of Saito's off-duty guards. Some congregated on B deck, while others overlooked the proceedings from A deck. Among them stood the *Nitta Maru*'s skipper, Kiyoshi Ogawa, ship's doctor Fukashi Sakurai, Chief Engineer Nishiki Juta, and Second Purser Misaka. The spectators could see that five straw mats had been laid on B deck in front of a deckhouse near the stern. A wooden box three feet wide sat between the mats and the waiting crowd. The four petty officers chosen as executioners bedecked themselves with the ceremonial *hachimaki*, a white cotton cloth pulled tight across the forehead and knotted behind at the base of the skull. Shortly before 4:00 PM, five guards carrying rifles and fixed bayonets brought out the prisoners, who were now blindfolded with their hands bound behind their backs.[5]

Lieutenant Saito appeared at the appointed time in full naval uniform. He mounted the box, drew his sword, rested the back of the blade against his right shoulder, and pulled a large piece of paper covered with Japanese characters from his pocket. In a solemn voice, the lieutenant uttered the names of the condemned. The five Americans were shivering—probably as much from fear as the cold—but each answered his name by saying "Here" or "Yes." Saito then read his victims their death warrant, speaking in Japanese without the benefit of an interpreter. "You have killed many Japanese soldiers on Wake Island," he said. "Since you have done it, it is a custom in the Japanese way to revenge ourselves. For what you have done you are now going to be killed in payment for the blood you caused from the Japanese soldiers and you are now going to be killed for revenge. . . . You can now pray to be happy in the next world—in heaven."[6]

Having pronounced sentence, Saito tersely beckoned Warrant Officer Yoshimura to perform the first execution, ordering, "Squad Leader, Proceed." A guard guided an American in a khaki uniform to the leftmost mat and made him kneel with his torso bent forward. Yoshimura came up behind the prisoner, raised his gleaming sword, and swung it down on his victim's right shoulder. Second Purser Misaka heard the blade give "a swishing noise as it cut the air," ending with a snap like "a wet towel . . . being flipped" as it sliced into the Wake Islander's flesh. Despite Yoshimura's reputation as a kendo expert, he failed to cut his man deeply enough to kill him. The stricken American emitted a deep groan and sagged sideways. A visibly irritated Saito directed Yoshimura to position himself on the prisoner's left side and deliver a second blow. This time, the warrant officer clove through the base of his victim's neck and split open the American's chest, causing him to fall forward as his blood gushed onto the deck. The POW straightened his legs, gave a slight quiver, and then lay still.[7]

Without wasting a moment, Saito cued his second executioner: "Petty Officer Takamura, go to it." Tokuichi Takamura strode toward an American who stood on a mat beside his slain comrade. Recalling that Takamura was a judo instructor, Saito bade him to demonstrate his skill by barking, "*Atemi*." Takamura obediently took one hand, landed an atemi blow with extended fingers just below the prisoner's breastbone, and then sat the stunned man on the mat. Takamura wanted to decapitate his victim, but he was no swordsman. He struck the American's neck without removing the latter's head or killing him outright. To Takamura's added embarrassment, his sword was defective, and the blade bent on impact. Quickly extricating the weapon, the petty officer slashed the American again in the same place, finishing him off.[8]

Undeterred by the botched nature of the first two executions, Saito called to Petty Officer First Class Yasuo Kohara, "Senior Guard." After witnessing the clumsiness of Yoshimura and Takamura, Kohara nervously approached the red-haired American kneeling before him. Twice Kohara raised his blade, only to lower it without striking. "Then," as he later confessed, "realizing I was acting on orders from the Emperor . . . , I closed my eyes, raised my sword, and swung it downwards. When I opened my eyes, the body of the American . . . was laying at my feet. His head was severed from his body." A ripple of applause emanated from the watching Japanese—most of them relieved to finally see a man killed properly. Captain Ogawa, Chief Engineer Juta, and Dr. Sakurai had been so sickened by the butchery, however, that they slipped away to other parts of the ship.[9]

Lieutenant Saito did not seem to mind that his audience was shrinking. Kohara's lucky stroke broke the spell that had been marring the lieutenant's bloody homage to Bushido. Petty Officer First Class Yoshio Asakawa followed Kohara's lead perfectly by removing the fourth American's head from his body with a single chop. Petty Officer First Class Yamotsu Takezoe did not succeed in completely beheading the fifth prisoner, but he sunk his sword far enough in the man's neck to kill him.[10]

After the POWs were dead, Saito found one additional use for them. Under the supervision of Petty Officer First Class Usaji Hida, the guards dragged the corpses over to B deck's port side, where a wooden grate had been placed on top of some empty sake barrels. One after another, four of the lifeless Americans were thrown on the grate. A petty officer who had not bloodied his sword during the executions now used that weapon to mutilate the first body. He let his subordinates thrust their bayonets into the other three. Once the guards had satiated their bloodlust, they dumped the remains of Hannum, Bailey, Franklin, Lambert, and Gonzales into the sea below.[11]

Although Toshio Saito staged the executions on the *Nitta Maru* as public entertainment, he took immediate steps to cover up his crime. He kept the other Wake Islanders in the dark concerning the fate of their five slaughtered comrades. Prisoners quartered near the two Marines and three sailors knew only that those men had been taken from the holds and never returned. The POW officers mistakenly assumed that Saito's victims left the ship with the twenty other Yanks removed for intelligence purposes at Yokohama. Saito misled his own superiors by falsifying his records. He had Ensign Jinno prepare a new POW roster with the dead Americans' names left off and cautioned him, "There will be no reports of the execution . . . made to anyone. Deleting the names from the roster will be sufficient."[12]

When the five dead men failed to turn up after the war, Capt. John Hamas, formerly a Marine gunner on Major Devereux's staff, pressured American occupation authorities in Japan to investigate. American agents interrogated thirty-five members of the *Nitta Maru*'s crew and the POW guard detail. The truth emerged with startling quickness. Unfortunately, the Americans made the mistake of questioning Saito early in the investigation before they uncovered sufficient evidence to arrest him. When they revisited his home to take him into custody, they found he had gone into hiding. Saito successfully evaded capture, but investigators caught his wife trying to hide the booty he acquired on the *Nitta Maru*, including the class rings he stole from Commander Cunningham and Major Potter.

A military commission acting on behalf of the U.S. 8th Army convened at Yokohama on December 19, 1947, to try Usaji Hida, Yasuo Kohara, Tokuichi Takamura, Tamotsu Takezoe, and Asaichi Yoshimura for war crimes. The trial lasted until February 2, 1948, when the commission found all of the defendants but Hida guilty of murder. The four executioners received sentences of life at hard labor. As wartime passions cooled and Japanese–American relations improved, however, Saito's swordsmen eventually became the beneficiaries of clemency. Between September 19, 1956, and July 25, 1957, Kohara, Takezoe, Takamura, and Yoshimura were released on parole.[13]

"I WAS SO GLAD TO GET OFF OF THAT HELL SHIP"

The 1,210 Wake Islanders still aboard the *Nitta Maru* completed their horrific Pacific crossing on January 23, 1942, when the liner docked at Shanghai—the Paris of the Orient, China's largest city, and the world's fifth largest seaport. Situated at the mouth of the Yangtze River and with an estimated population of 5 million, Shanghai ranked second in size only to Tokyo among Asia's great metropolises. The city's fabled International Settlement was home to thousands of Britons, Americans, and other Westerners. The Japanese thought this longtime center of Euro-American economic domination would make the perfect backdrop to highlight the new order they hoped to impose on East Asia. They wanted to humiliate the newly arrived POWs by parading them through the city before the Chinese populace. When word of this leaked to the International Settlement, the local Swiss consulate general filed a stiff protest. Switzerland had shouldered the thankless task of representing British and American interests in East Asia after Japan declared war on those two powers, and no self-respecting Swiss diplomat could tolerate such a blatant violation of the Geneva Convention. The Japanese placated the consul by canceling their victory celebration, but they may have been more influenced by the threat of inclement weather, which would have adversely affected spectator turnout.[14]

The *Nitta Maru* remained tied up at Shanghai through the morning of January 24. Around noon, the liner embarked more than forty British and American naval personnel who had been captured at Shanghai on the war's first day. Most of these men belonged to the crews of two Yangtze River gunboats, the HMS *Peterel* and the USS *Wake*. Worsening relations with Japan had inclined Great Britain and the United States to drastically reduce their military presence

East China and Korea, 1942–1945

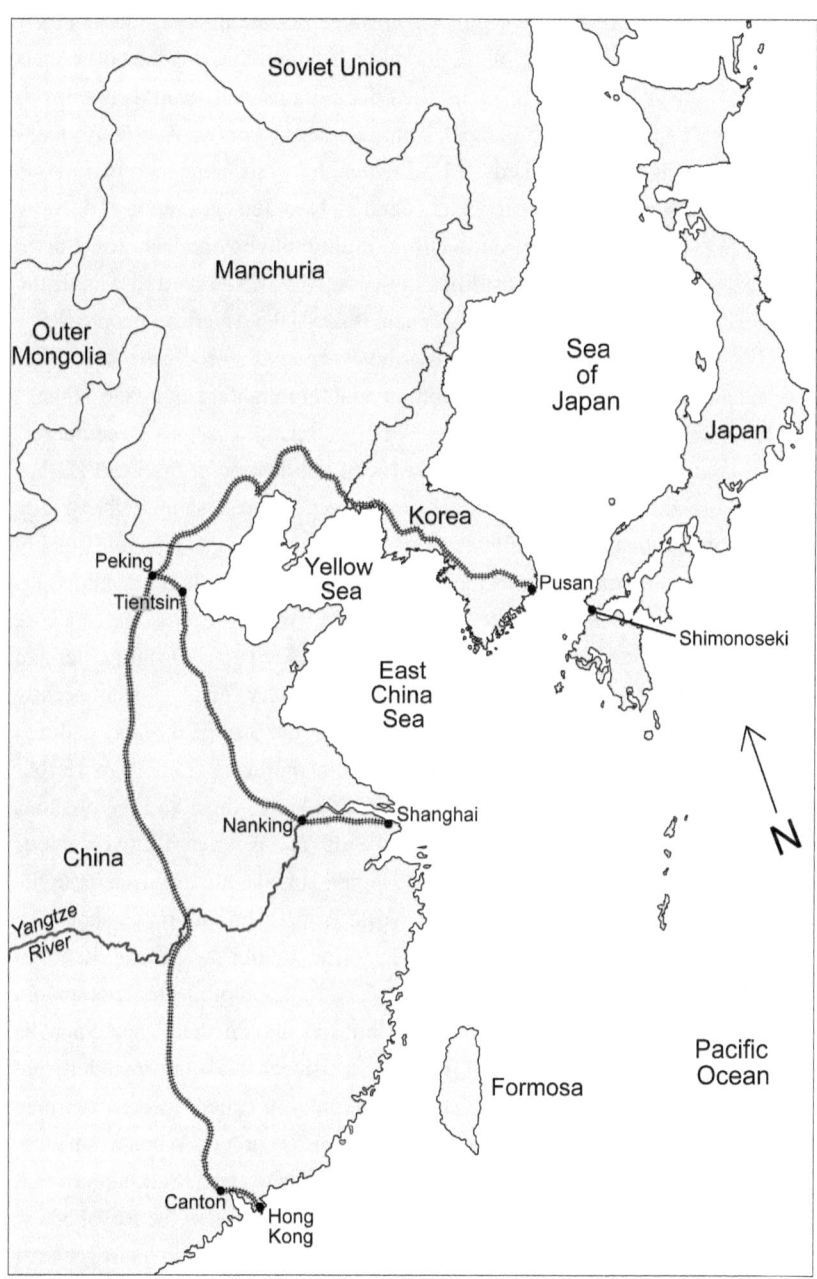

Map by Charles Grear.

in Japanese-occupied China, but they left the *Peterel* and *Wake* at Shanghai with skeleton complements. The two gunboats operated as station ships, utilizing their radios to transmit intelligence on the looming Japanese threat gathered by their respective consulates. Both crews installed demolitions charges in their ships to prevent their capture if war broke out. Throughout most of the *Wake*'s fourteen-year existence, it had been called the USS *Guam*. It lost its name in January 1941 to a battle cruiser under construction at Camden, New Jersey, and the U.S. Navy rechristened the gunboat after an even more diminutive American possession. When Japan finally initiated hostilities, however, the *Wake* failed to exhibit the fierce fighting spirit that so endeared its namesake to the American people.[15]

By the eve of war, the *Peterel* and the *Wake* sat moored near each other beside the Shanghai Bund, the city's commercial thoroughfare along the Whangpoo River, a tributary of the Yangtze. Shortly after 4:00 AM, on December 8, 1941, a radioman on the *Wake* received official notification of the Pearl Harbor attack. He rushed on deck to discover that armed Japanese sailors had already swarmed aboard and overpowered the lone Yank on watch. The Japanese quickly secured the other American crewmen before they could scuttle the gunboat. Lt. Cdr. Columbus Darwin Smith, the *Wake*'s skipper, was ashore when the Japanese seized his ship. A veteran of thirteen years on Chinese rivers as a shipmaster and a pilot, Smith held a commission in the U.S. Navy Reserve and had been recently recalled to active service. He preferred sleeping at his Shanghai home, and that was where a frantic phone call awoke him with the news from Pearl Harbor at 4:20 AM. Smith took a taxi to the Bund to find his gunboat and the precious radio ciphers it contained already in enemy hands. The *Wake* earned two dubious distinctions that day, as it became the only American warship to surrender to the Japanese and the only one seized during World War II without firing a shot.[16]

The Japanese did not have such an easy time taking the *Peterel*. Its commander, fifty-five-year-old Lieutenant Stephen Polkinghorn, was another old China hand and reactivated reservist. He bunked aboard the *Peterel*, and he responded with alacrity when a call from the British consulate informed him that Japan was at war with the United States. Polkinghorn called his eighteen-man crew to battle stations and issued cutlasses to repel boarders. When a Japanese naval officer came on board to demand the *Peterel*'s surrender, Polkinghorn sent him packing with a reply that echoed the proudest traditions of the Royal Navy: "Get off my bloody ship!" No sooner did Polkinghorn's unwanted guest get clear of the *Peterel* than a Japanese cruiser, destroyer, and gunboat opened fire. Japanese army field batteries on both sides of the Whangpoo also boomed into action, while the *Peterel* resisted briefly with its only workable armament—two Lewis machine guns. In twenty minutes the Japanese turned the British gunboat into a flaming wreck, and Polkinghorn ordered his crew to abandon ship. As the British sailors swam through water glowing from burning oil slicks, Japanese troops fired on them with rifles. Six of the *Peterel*'s crew died that day, but courageous Chinese sampan operators ignored the danger to fish a wounded Polkinghorn and twelve more survivors out of the Whangpoo.[17]

The Japanese confined the crews from the *Peterel* and *Wake*, along with other Allied naval personnel rounded up in Shanghai, at the Kiangwan Road Naval War Prisoners Camp. The latter included Commander John B. Woolley, the senior Royal Navy officer in the city. The Britons and Americans lived in sturdy brick buildings, with each officer being allocated his own room and charcoal stove. The POWs received a daily ration of two meals, plus ten cigarettes per man. The Japanese also provided the wounded with proper medical care, even amputating the smashed third finger on Polkinghorn's right hand. This comparatively privileged existence came to an end on January 24, when these prisoners joined the Wake Islanders on the *Nitta Maru* for transfer to a larger prison camp outside Shanghai.[18]

No sooner did the *Nitta Maru* board its newest passengers than it cast off and turned up the Whangpoo River. Roughly two hours and thirteen twisting miles later, the liner reached its ultimate destination, a village named Woosung. The Japanese began disembarking their prisoners at 2:30 or 3:00 PM, and they conducted that operation much like the embarkation at Wake twelve days earlier. As Cpl. Guy Kelnhofer put it, "We got beat off the ship, too." Contractor Herb Papock jotted some additional details in his diary later that day: "Big Jap. Guards throw men about (Judo)—Run gauntlet again—(hitting and kicking)." As the POWs headed down a gangplank, the Japanese assailed them with delousing spray, invariably aiming at the Americans' faces. Other guards grabbed each prisoner as he cleared the gangplank on the dock below and shoved him into what grew into a formation five ranks deep.[19]

Once the Wake Islanders stopped moving, they took stock of their new surroundings. Many found them as grim as the foul holds they had just vacated. "The China sky was overcast, grey and gloomy," wrote Cpl. Bernard Richardson, "with just a single break in the drabness of the clouds permitting a pale sliver of sky to accentuate the general murkiness by contrast." Having dwelt below decks for the entire voyage from Wake, a number of Richardson's comrades fixated on that solitary sun ray to the exclusion of the sky's general appearance. "Light of day dazzling after 12 days in the hold," acknowledged Herb Papock. The late afternoon temperature hovered around 35° Fahrenheit, and brisk winds made Cpl.

Thomas Johnson and the other thinly clad Wake Islanders feel "colder than hell." Snow lay on the ground, which induced the POWs to feel even sorrier for themselves. In addition, nearly two weeks of enforced immobility and insipid rations rendered the mere act of walking or standing an exercise in misery. "I was shivering," recalled TSgt. Charles Holmes, "and I noticed the weakness in my legs after 11 days in the hold . . . sitting down except when I had to go to the benjo." For some Wake Islanders, however, being anywhere but inside the *Nitta Maru* was a godsend. "I was so glad to get off of that hell ship I hardly felt the cold," rejoiced Pfc. Grover Thaire.[20]

Despite optimists like Thaire, apprehension prevailed in the prisoners' ranks, especially after they determined where they had landed. Sergeant Holmes had a hunch, and he sought confirmation from MGySgt. John W. Krawie, Battery E's senior NCO and a veteran of China service in the 1930s. When Holmes asked if Krawie knew where they were, the latter whispered, "Shanghai." The two noncoms furtively communicated that news to the men around them. The revelation that the prisoners had ended up so far from home and friendly forces—along with the harsh, alien nature of their new environment—caused the Wake Islanders' spirits to plummet to new lows. "I can remember what a shock it was to see China," remarked Corporal Kelnhofer. The wharves and buildings that lined the Woosung waterfront impressed Corporal Richardson as depressingly battered and shabby. The area also still bore scars from the fighting between Japanese and Chinese troops four years earlier. Pfc. Jack Skaggs never forgot his first sight of China—an old Chinese man sitting out in the open defecating into an earthen pot, which the Oklahoma Marine interpreted as a bad omen.[21]

Another worrisome portent turned out to be the enemy's continuing lack of concern for their charges' comfort and welfare. They kept the Wake Islanders standing exposed to the elements for the duration of a ninety-minute formal ceremony marking the prisoners' turnover to the Imperial Japanese Army. The Americans had to endure repeated head counts before Lieutenant Saito satisfied himself that the number of POWs present jibed with his amended roster. Then came two long speeches, each transformed into semi-intelligible English by an interpreter. The first, a farewell delivered by an enemy naval officer, was not particularly memorable. After that, a bandy-legged officer from the Japanese army addressed the Wake Contractors and their military comrades. He began with the announcement that they were now prisoners of "the Great Imperial Japanese Army." They would be expected to cooperate in building "the Greater East Asia Co-Prosperity Sphere," the self-serving label the Japanese had slapped on their newly enlarged empire. Finally, the officer warned that any prisoners disobeying their new masters "would be promptly shot." Then amid seemingly endless bowing by various enemy officers, Saito's naval guards stepped away from the men they had tormented since January 12, and Japanese soldiers replaced them.[22]

The Wake Islanders' new keepers formed them into a column of fours for the march to camp, which the interpreter indicated was only two miles away. As the POWs moved out, a cold drizzle started falling. That was the last straw for Corporal Richardson, who wrote, "I looked about me at the disheveled prisoners and . . . at the Japanese guards in their ill fitting uniforms and at the rain. For a minute I thought of home. Never had I felt so desolate or so weary."[23]

"GIVE UP ALL HOPE"

The Wake Islanders' suffering was far from over. The next two hours would plague them with a succession of tests, pushing some prisoners beyond the limits of their endurance. The camp lay much further from the POWs' point of debarkation than the Japanese said, which made the march seem to drag on forever. "Those 2 miles turned out to be closer to 5," revealed Cpl. Henry Durrwachter, "and just about killed the men." The sun set and the temperature dropped as the Americans and Britons tramped along. The drizzle that heralded the prisoners' departure from Woosung village alternated with bursts of heavier rain, and the precipitation eventually turned into sleet. Attired in only a skivvy T-shirt and shorts, Pfc. Marshall E. Fields felt his naked arms and legs smart as a stiff wind lashed them with tiny ice particles. The precipitation changed the dirt road on which the prisoners trudged from a hard, dusty surface into what Richardson characterized as "a queasy sludge of mud, ankle deep and adhesive."[24]

The Japanese placed the crews of the *Wake* and *Peterel* at the head of the column. Eager to get out of the cold and wet, the gunboat sailors walked as fast as their legs could carry them. That set an agonizing pace for the Wake Islanders, who had not yet begun to recover from their mistreatment on the *Nitta Maru*. Pfc. George Hubley remembered that march as "real torture." "You know," he elaborated, "you sit [twelve] days all cramped up, your knee up under your chin and you don't move—your body just don't react as it should." Sergeant Holmes felt as if his legs had turned against him. "As time went on," Holmes explained, "the bitter cold caused 'charlie horses' in my legs. . . . It was very painful trying to get where we were going." With cranky guards urging the Wake POWs to keep up with their fitter comrades from Shanghai, the bedraggled Yanks tried to double time, which fatigued them even more. It took most Wake Islanders all their willpower just to put one mud-encrusted foot in front of the other, and the column stretched out more than two miles in length.[25]

Some of the prisoners struggling through the muck were older men, and others still nursed unhealed wounds and injuries from Wake. Many marchers were sick. Earlier in the day, each Wake Islander received a small can of salmon as an aloha dinner before exiting the *Nitta Maru*. Pfc. S. L. Baker's can was contaminated, and the full effects hit him after he had walked for a while. "Some of my fellow prisoners had to carry me at intervals," he related, "as I would become blind and become unconscious at times." Not every ailing POW could count on having comrades as strong or solicitous as Baker's. Men began collapsing on the road. Fortunately, the Japanese had thought to send a couple of trucks to follow the column, and those Yanks too lame, ill, or exhausted to walk were hauled the rest of the way.[26]

The POWs' route led through a few small Chinese hamlets, and the locals turned out to watch the humbled Westerners. Some Chinese laughed at the passing prisoners, but not many. These fleeting contacts provided most Wake Islanders with their introduction to China's endemic poverty. Corporal Richardson noticed the peasants' ragged and dirty appearance. Pvt. Edward Sturgeon saw one man pulling lice off his body, snapping them in half, and throwing away the pieces. Corporal Kelnhofer gasped at the human skulls and other bones sitting in the ditches on either side of the road.[27]

At length, the head of the column reached an area seemingly devoid of human habitations. As the POWs plodded into their fifth mile, they spotted something manmade sticking out of the flat landscape ahead. Corporal Richardson initially thought it was "indistinguishable from a trash-garbage dump." FN2C Dare Kibble's first glimpse of the place reminded him of "the old hog hutches" on the farm where he had worked in Ola, Idaho, two years earlier. The Wake Islanders forced themselves to keep walking toward those dilapidated structures, sensing without being told they now had their destination in view. At approximately 6:00 PM, they passed through an unimpressive gateway consisting of two granite pillars and a patched wooden door hanging open at an awkward angle. The POWs sloshed into what Capt. Bryghte Godbold termed "a rather depressing type of compound" covered with dirty brown weeds, horse manure, and icy puddles and enclosed by a barbed wire fence. The guards halted the column in front of a row of seven sagging, unpainted barracks. The Imperial Japanese Army tried to dignify this sorry installation with an ostentatious name—Shanghai War Prisoners Camp. The men caged there would refer to it simply as Woosung.[28]

With shelter close at hand, the prisoners could hardly wait to place a roof and four walls between themselves and the inclement weather. The Japanese, however, kept the POWs in formation while they handed each one a typed, single-spaced, four-page document titled "Directions for the Daily Life of the War-Prisoners." To ensure that the Americans and Britons understood all thirty-four regulations, the camp's temporary commandant, a first lieutenant named Takamoto, mounted a wooden platform, called the prisoners to attention, and subjected them to a lengthy harangue. As Corporal Durrwachter grumbled, "We were made to stand ankle deep in horse manure while some Jap jabbered at us for an hour or so." Takamoto spoke through an interpreter. The latter sported a big pair of horn-rimmed eyeglasses and a tweed sports coat, which inspired the Wake Islanders to instantly dub him "Joe College."[29]

Joe College was not much of a linguist, but the POWs caught the gist of what he said. For the most part, Takamoto repeated the same threats the Americans and Britons had heard quayside at Woosung village. He warned that the camp's inmates could not expect to "eat the bread of idleness," but would work for the Greater East Asia Co-Prosperity Sphere "so the world could have peace and prosperity." Takamoto admonished his audience to rise immediately each morning at "the voice of the cornet," and he had Joe College stress more than once, "You must obey." The lieutenant promised death to anyone attempting escape, but the interpreter's poor English pronunciation diluted the impact of that threat. It was all the Wake Islanders could do to refrain from laughing as Joe College stammered, "You must not try to escape. You will be shit, shit . . . you know, shot?" The interpreter struck a more sobering note when he alerted his listeners to the fact that the fence surrounding them was electrified. "You know," he emphasized, "you touch the fence, you die." Takamoto also hastened the POWs' returning glumness by announcing that Japan did not feel obliged to abide by the Geneva Convention. The lieutenant closed his tirade by advising the POWs that their survival depended on each man's ability to preserve his own health. "Finally," related Ramon Menique, a Contractor from Boise, "way after dark, wet, weak and hungry, we were allowed to enter our barracks."[30]

Under other circumstances the Wake Islanders would have greeted the end of Takamoto's speech with relief, but they were too downtrodden to feel good about anything. "I know I wasn't happy about being there," confessed Pfc. James King, "nor was anyone." Corporal Richardson's first close look at Woosung filled him with "a really depths of despair feeling." S2C Cassius Smith decided the camp constituted the end of the line for him and his comrades. "Give up all hope," he muttered to himself.[31]

Before the Japanese permitted the POWs to enter their barracks, they separated the British naval contingent from the rest and divided the Americans into five groups containing slightly more than two hundred men apiece. They then counted off the Contractors and enlisted Allied service personnel into thirty-six-man sections. In a nod to the Geneva Convention's prohibition against mixing different nationalities, the Japanese housed the *Peterel*'s crew and the other Royal Navy prisoners in Barracks 1. The USS *Wake*'s crew and the U.S. Marines, sailors, and soldiers from Wake Island occupied Barracks 2 and Barracks 3. The Japanese assigned Barracks 4, 5, and 6 to the Wake civilians. Without explaining why, First Lieutenant Takamoto left Barracks 7 vacant for the time being. To readily ascertain where the prisoners belonged, camp authorities issued them all individual numbers, which everyone had to wear at all times. The POWs originally displayed their numbers on armbands, but their keepers later switched to stenciled tags. SSgt. Clifford Hotchkiss, an Army radioman, received an armband bearing "2621," which meant he was Prisoner 21 in Barracks 2, Section 6. CPNAB carpenter Jim Allen became "4428"—Prisoner 28, Barracks 4, Section 4.[32]

With these bureaucratic preliminaries out of the way, the Wake Islanders and their comrades were finally free to straggle into their barracks. What they encountered did little to revive their sunken spirits. Pfc. Leonard Mettscher from rural Reno County, Kansas, thought the POWs' quarters resembled the inside of a barn. Sergeant Holmes immediately decided that his barracks "was without a doubt the dreariest looking place I have ever seen."[33]

The Wake Island defenders would make more unpleasant discoveries in the minutes, hours, and days that followed. During that period, they would have to choose whether they would adapt to their current surroundings and start devising survival strategies or surrender to the despair that accompanied their introduction to Woosung.

"ALL OF SOUTHERN CHINA SMELLS LIKE A CESSPOOL"

The Japanese army constructed the Woosung camp after it drove Chiang Kai-Shek's Chinese forces from the Shanghai area in a series of bloody battles in August, September, and October 1937. The Japanese located the installation at a strategic spot fifteen miles north of Shanghai and five miles northeast of the Woosung forts on the Whangpoo River. The barracks had originally housed an infantry battalion, as evinced by the rifle racks that still lined their walls in January 1942. The prevalence of animal droppings around the barracks fooled some POWs into assuming that Woosung had been either a Japanese or Chinese cavalry post. Japanese troops abandoned the camp long before the Wake Islanders saw it, and it had since fallen into a state of advanced decay. To convert the place into the Shanghai War Prisoners Camp, the Japanese erected four 15-foot guard towers and an electrified barbed wire fence. It would take more than these simple modifications, however, to make Woosung habitable or escapeproof.[34]

The seven drab barracks standing inside the compound were single-story frame structures. They were run down and dirty and had leaky metal roofs. Cracks in the walls and too many windows with shattered panes exposed occupants to the slightest draft. "They were damn cold," confirmed Corporal Kelnhofer. The barracks had no understructure and sat directly on flat delta ground possessing a high water table. This geological condition frequently turned the compound into a muddy mess and ensured a perennially damp atmosphere indoors. The POWs were relieved to find the barracks had wooden plank flooring, but Fireman Second Class Kibble noted, "You could see through the knot holes to the ground. The mice and rats loved these escape hatches." The barracks contained heating stoves when the POWs first arrived, but the Japanese provided no fuel for the appliances and removed them entirely from at least one barracks on February 13.[35]

Each barracks could accommodate up to 230 men. Six of these dwellings measured approximately 210 feet in length and 50 feet in width. The seventh was a little shorter. A hallway six feet to eight feet wide ran down the center of each barracks. This feature split six large rooms, better known as sections, which the Japanese reserved for Allied enlisted men and common Contractors. The sections reminded Pfc. Leonard Mettscher of stalls, prompting him to wisecrack, "It looked more like a stable in there than . . . our type of barracks." Two wooden platforms raised eighteen inches to twenty-four inches off the floor were built into a corner of every half section. These sleeping platforms projected eight feet from the wall, and each was long enough to permit nine men an average space of twenty-two inches to twenty-eight inches apiece. Hence, a single section could sleep a maximum of thirty-six men, which is why the Japanese organized the POWs into subunits of that size.

In addition to the platforms, a half-section's furnishings included a rude wooden table and two benches. Shelves ten inches wide ran above the Wake Islanders' hard plank beds, providing the men with more than enough space to store their meager possessions. POW officers and higher-ranking Contractors occupied smaller rooms at one end of their barracks. Seniority determined the amount of space and privacy the prisoners' leadership received. Lieutenants slept eight to a room, captains bunked in groups of four, and field grade officers were quartered in pairs.[36]

Two smaller structures sat behind every barracks—a wash rack and a benjo, or latrine. The wash rack consisted of a long galvanized tin trough set under twelve leaky faucets with rags or ropes wrapped around their joints. A tin roof

The Layout of the Woosung Site of the Shanghai War Prisoners Camp as Sketched Right After the War by Contractor Gurdon H. Wattles

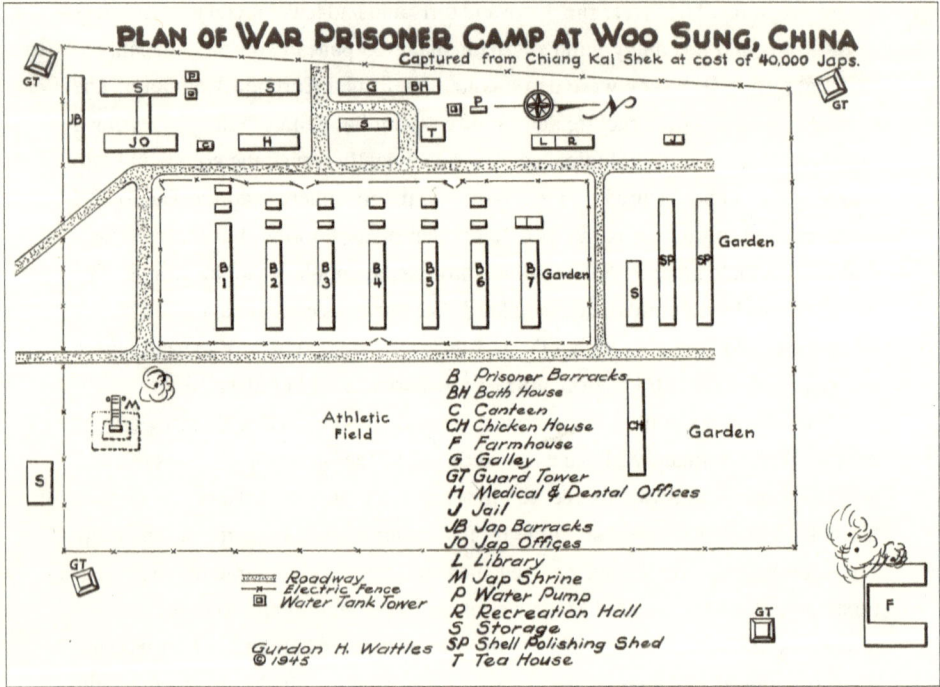

Author's collection

held up by rickety timbers offered minimal protection from snow or rain. This feature mattered little to the POWs, as the faucets released cold water only. Although most Wake Islanders arrived at Woosung caked with grime from the *Nitta Maru* and their muddy march to camp, they hesitated to make much use of the wash rack while winter remained in full swing. "In freezing weather," commented Sergeant Holmes, "it took a lot of guts to just go out there and wash one's hands." Besides, the Japanese issued no soap for the next several weeks, which rendered it difficult for even the hardiest prisoners to get really clean.[37]

A row of seven benjos—rectangular wooden shacks—stood just beyond the wash racks. Inside these large outhouses, urinals lined one wall, and ten stalls lined the opposite one. A stall contained nothing recognizable to the Wake Islanders as a toilet—just a hole cut through the floor. This was typical Japanese lavatory design, but the Americans viewed it as backward and demeaning. To defecate, a POW had to squat over the hole and let his feces fall through into a large earthenware or ceramic pot positioned below. Woosung's inmates called these receptacles "honey pots," a nickname steeped in irony. "The odor," remarked Corporal Richardson "was comparable only to that of a long dead body that had been allowed to rot in the sun." Until the POWs got the hang of defecating Japanese style, however, they often missed their aim. That infused the benjos with an even more disgusting aura. During the hot summer months, especially, the camp smelled like a stockyard.[38]

The Japanese located the benjos within twenty feet of the barracks, which made them both an affront to the POWs' nostrils and a hygienic threat. The outhouses became breeding places for flies and malaria-carrying mosquitoes. The open honey pots also attracted the many rats that infested the camp. "While one squatted over the 8" × 14" opening," recounted 1st Lt. Woodrow Kessler, "flies buzzed around one's head and rats scampered here and there in search of rare tidbits." These pests could easily follow the POWs into the barracks through the latter's glassless, unscreened windows and cracked walls.[39]

The Japanese relegated the task of waste disposal to the local Chinese. Several times a week, ten thin, muscular peasants carrying wooden buckets slung from "yo-yo" or "yo-ho" poles entered Woosung to empty the honey pots. As this "honey bucket brigade" exited the compound, its members emitted the singsong chant "Hye-huh, hye-huh, hye-huh," which meant "Get out of the way." Sergeant Holmes considered the warning gratuitous. "As the honey bucket brigade cleaned out the benjos we gave them plenty of space," he chuckled. Chinese farmers fertilized their fields with night soil, which made them regard the refuse produced by more than 1,200 POWs a precious resource. The Wake Islanders were appalled by this practice. "The smell of human excreation being spread is awful," Pfc. John E. Pearsall told his diary later that year. "All of Southern China smells like a cesspool filled with human excrement," blurted Fireman Second Class Kibble. In addition to the stench created by Chinese agricultural techniques, the POWs also had to worry about the possible health hazards. "Well," whistled Contractor H. Jay Tice, "we'll all be dead in three weeks from cholera." Other POWs with a less-fatalistic bent realized that everything they ate had to be boiled first.[40]

The fence enclosing the barracks, wash racks, and latrines carried an electric current that the POWs estimated as anywhere from 2,300 volts to 35,000 volts. Whatever the actual voltage, it was strong enough to kill anyone who touched it. The Japanese erected this lethal obstruction ominously close to the prisoners' barracks and benjos. Camp officials posted no warning signs around the fence or barriers to prevent accidental contact. The Japanese announced they would charge the fence only at night, presumably when the POWs were safe in their quarters, but they usually turned on the juice before sunset and often forgot to turn it off after sunrise. Despite the danger, most of Woosung's inmates came to view the fence as a source of occasional entertainment. As Sergeant Holmes explained, "If anything touched [it] an alarm was set off in the Jap guard house and sentries would come pouring out the door on the double with rifles and fixed bayonets. Sometimes a big rat would try to go under the bottom of the wire, . . . and set off the alarm. It was amusing to see the guards scramble for nothing."[41]

The camp's other structures stood outside the electrified fence. Most were clustered along the compound's west side. These included an administration building, the guards' barracks, a galley with an attached bathhouse, a teahouse, a brig or guardhouse, a water tower with an electric pump to draw water from the camp's only well, and several storehouses. An additional storehouse and two long shacks bordered the compound to the north. A Japanese shrine sat outside the fence to the southeast of Barracks 1. These nondescript and weather-beaten edifices completed the installation that the majority of Wake's defenders would call home for the next ten months.[42]

"WHAT A TERRIBLE FEELING OF UTTER DESPAIR"

After the shivering Wake Islanders filed into their barracks, they congregated instinctively beneath the light bulbs in their sections to enjoy at least the illusion of warmth. By a fortuitous coincidence, the Japanese chose that moment to start issuing blankets to their prisoners. Each American and Briton drew four. The blankets were made of light cotton fabric, and they had gotten damp and mildewed while sitting in storage. Contractor Fred R. Rumpel took one whiff and joked that his blankets felt and smelled "like they had just come from a sweaty horse." The dampness made the blankets seem heavier at first than they actually were. Sergeant Holmes, for one, was not fooled. "One USMC wool blanket would have been warmer than all four of the Jap blankets," he scoffed. The POWs also discovered that the blanket fabric was shot through with wood fibers, which left the coverings anything but soft to the touch. Cpl. Thomas Johnson remembered that his blankets "felt like cardboard." Since those objects had been manufactured for Japanese soldiers, they proved too short for most POWs. Whenever the average Wake Islander pulled his blankets up to his chin, he uncovered his ankles and feet.[43]

The Japanese neglected to provide the POWs with mattresses for several weeks. Eventually, they gave their charges small cotton bed ticks to fill with rice straw. Any improvement was hardly noticeable as winter rains, ceiling leaks, and the region's prevailing dampness prevented the POWs from completely drying their clothing, blankets, and sleeping mats.[44]

Whatever misgivings the POWs harbored about their bedding dissolved temporarily at 11:00 PM. The barracks doors slammed open and Japanese soldiers tramped in with something the Americans and Britons craved as much as warmth—food. "Our eyes bulged and our mouths watered as the buckets were carried in . . . and the Jap guards began issuing the rations," related Corporal Richardson. Many Wake Islanders would remember that occasion as their first decent meal since leaving the atoll and the only decent one they would get at Woosung. The Japanese handed their charges bowls filled with rice and vegetables mixed with a strong-smelling sauce foreign to all but a handful of Wake Islanders. The guards also provided the prisoners with chopsticks. Most of the men from Wake did not know how to use them and ate with their hands.[45]

In the next few seconds, the Wake Islanders experienced their first taste of curry. "It burned like the devil going in," testified Pfc. Henry Chapman. The curry sauce "just wanted to make the top of your head fly off," Corporal Richardson claimed. "It was hot," agreed Contractor Joe Goiceochea, "but god, it was good." Curried stew was what the Japanese army fed sentries in the wintertime, and its warming effects delighted the POWs. As Cpl. Thomas Johnson downed a heaping bowl of the stuff, he mused, "Boy, if this is the way they feed us, we're going to be in good shape." Even the normally pessimistic Fireman Second Class Kibble dared to hope "maybe life in China wasn't going to be too bad."[46]

Not every Wake Islander derived as big a lift from that meal as Johnson and Kibble. For some, the curry was just too hot to swallow. The very smell of the sauce nauseated Corporal Kelnhofer, and he gave his bowl to a buddy who was still hungry after emptying his own. Other Wake survivors, their stomachs shrunken by the starvation diet on the *Nitta Maru*, could not down a full serving. They placed the bowls containing their leftovers on shelves projecting over their sleeping platforms. In some barracks, the Japanese gave too much food to the men in the front sections, which left less for those in the rear.[47]

By 1:30 or 2:00 AM, January 25, the POWs had finished eating. They crawled under their blankets on the sleeping platforms, and the guards turned out the lights. There, in the darkness, the pervasive cold and dampness leeched any remaining warmth generated by the curry out of the prisoners, and many men must have felt abandoned, helpless, and alone. "And then for the first and only time in my life," confessed Corporal Kelnhofer, "that night, . . . I knew I was going to die and I just gave up. I knew that I would never be alive in the morning. I never had that happen before or since. What a terrible feeling of utter despair."[48]

CHAPTER SEVEN

"the most painful days we spent in prison camp"
hitting bottom at woosung

"I THOUGHT I WAS GOING THROUGH HELL"
Cpl. Bernard Richardson later characterized the Wake Islanders' first few weeks at Woosung as "the most painful days we spent in prison camp." Contractor Alec Pay said essentially the same thing shortly after his arrival, complaining that "conditions were very unpleasant due to cold, lack of organization & inadequate & poor facilities & insufficient food." Second Lt. John Kinney recreated the prevailing mood during this period in his memoirs, writing, "We spent many days feeling sorry for ourselves and complaining to each other. This only contributed to our depression."[1]

During the Wake Islanders' initial two months at Woosung, the temperature frequently dipped to 15–20° Fahrenheit. To make matters worse, the Americans reached the Shanghai area at the height of the winter rainy season. "This made the temperature . . . seem colder than it really was," averred TSgt. Charles Holmes. It rained for long stretches almost daily, and snow fell on several occasions. The POWs did not experience any breaks in the cold until late March, and spring weather did not really take hold until the second half of April. Even then, rain remained a regular occurrence, leaving the camp compound a muddy mess glistening with numerous puddles.[2]

Getting a good night's sleep in Woosung's damp, drafty, and unheated barracks would have challenged a man possessing a full winter wardrobe and a pile of thick wool blankets, but the prisoners from Wake were not equipped for roughing it in the cold. As on the *Nitta Maru*, the lightly clad Americans reverted to instinct, huddling together on their sleeping platforms to share body heat and pool their blankets. "Most of us 'shacked up' with others to keep warm," remarked Sgt. Donald Malleck. A dozen or more officers crowded into a single room at the end of one barracks, hoping their body heat would raise the temperature by a couple of degrees. The enlisted ranks bedded down in twos, threes, or fours. Sometimes all nine men on a sleeping platform would spoon together, everyone facing in the same direction for maximum warmth. POWs on the outer ends of these clusters felt the cold more than those sandwiched between them. Bunkies learned to rotate every night to ensure each man spent equal time in the group's most exposed positions. Lying on a hard wood shelf without a decent mattress led to soreness, but a spooning prisoner could not roll over whenever he felt like it. "After so long on one side," explained FN2C Dare Kibble, "someone would say 'SHIFT' and everyone would switch sides. You either cooperated or got fists in the ribs."[3]

Some Wake Islanders decided that spooning did not generate enough warmth to make it worth their while. These men wrapped themselves in their flimsy Japanese blankets and withdrew to a corner of the platform to shiver through the night. Others draped their blankets over their heads and shoulders and tramped up and down the center aisle dividing each barracks. More Americans participated in this seemingly endless procession during daylight hours. Sergeant Holmes quipped that he and his comrades "looked like a bunch of early American Indians." In light of the Wake Islanders' actual condition, that was a flattering description. Holmes had not taken a decent bath since the war's start, and he had gone more than a month without a shave and haircut. When Contractor Al O'Guinn shuffled into Woosung, soap and water had not touched his body for thirty-one days.[4]

A growing number of Wake Islanders joined the nocturnal barracks traffic not by choice but necessity. The ingestion of solid food began easing the constipation that had gripped so many of them aboard the *Nitta Maru*. Deliverance did not visit everyone at once. Some POWs managed to defecate their first night at Woosung. Others had to wait another two to four days. In quite a few cases, the blockage persisted with alarming stubbornness. Contractor Bill Charters went twenty-six days without a bowel movement, and Herbert K. Jaffe, another CPNAB man, went twenty-eight. Cpl. Guy Kelnhofer may have set the record for the Wake Marines by remaining constipated for thirty-three days.

When relief finally came, it was difficult and painful. "I thought I was going through hell when my bowels first started to move," recalled Cpl. Thomas Johnson. Nearly every Wake Islander discovered that the stool that had accumulated in his colon was rock hard and too big to pass easily. The POWs flocked to Dr. G. Mason Kahn for assistance, but the Japanese had confiscated his medical kit while he was on the *Nitta Maru*. He possessed no laxatives or instruments that might have spared his comrades considerable suffering. With the prisoners left to their own devices, each had to face a private moment of truth in the weeks that followed. Herb Jaffe, an ex-Marine turned rigger, chose an aggressive method for ending his discomfort. "I had to put my fingers up my rectum," he disclosed, "to literally tear it [the stool] out. It was like concrete. I bled like a stuck pig." Pfc. Carl Stegmaier Jr. and other Wake Islanders likewise dug pellets of hard fecal matter out of their rectums until their bowels could expel what was left.[5]

The camp's benjos reminded Corporal Richardson of torture chambers. "The floors in the toilets were spotted with blood," he recounted. "More than one time, while in the toilet, I heard cries . . . of pain from those Marines who had but recently faced death without flinching." No one howled louder than 1st Sgt. Paul R. Agar, who remained impacted for thirty-one days. "When he finally got his bowels to move," Corporal Johnson related, "you could hear him screaming out there in the head. Later he came in and water was running off of his forehead, and it was wintertime." Agar noticed the sympathetic looks from his barracks mates, which caused him to gasp, "I thought I was passing great big cinders. It felt so sharp. It really tore up my butt." Several Wake Islanders discovered during their travails that they had developed hemorrhoids. That condition made defecation a daily agony for some time afterward.[6]

"NO RESPITE FROM THE DEMANDING VOICE OF THE CORNET"

On January 25, just as Joe College, the enemy interpreter, had announced the night before, the "voice of the cornet" summoned the Wake Islanders to face their first full day at Woosung. Reveille sounded sometime after dawn. Joe College had warned the POWs to rise immediately at that bugle call, and squads of grim-faced guards swept through the barracks to roust any shirkers from their bunks.

As the prisoners rubbed the sleep out of their eyes, those unable to finish dinner the previous evening experienced a nasty surprise. These men had placed their leftovers on the shelves overhanging their sleeping platforms, with some covering the bowls with their hats. Rats had eaten all the curried rice, even gnawing through the POWs' headgear to get at the food underneath. Those big rodents scavenged through the camp every night, and they became bolder on closer acquaintance with the inmates. Rats often dropped on top of sleeping prisoners, creating repeated commotions in every barracks. No matter what camp authorities or the POWs did to address the rat problem, it only grew worse. As Contractor Emmett L. Newell noted on October 10, 1942, "Rats getting terrible—3 in bed with me last night." Another civilian awoke one morning to discover that rats had chewed the calluses off his feet without disturbing his slumber. Cpl. Frank Gross called these unwelcome visitors "the most clever rats in the world." Some POWs later tried to outsmart their four-legged antagonists by stringing wires over their bunks to hang any extra food they accumulated in bags. That precaution did not deprive the rats of a meal. "They'd even walk the wire to get to it," marveled Pfc. George W. McDaniel.[7]

Woosung's residents momentarily forgot about the rats as the guards hectored them to prepare for morning inspection. The Japanese regarded this ritual as much more than a mechanism for keeping tabs on their prisoners. The printed regulations handed to the Wake Islanders on their arrival contained this injunction: "Roll call or inspection is one of the most important and solemn times in the military forces." As instructed by the guards, the POWs folded their blankets, stored their personal effects as neatly as possible, and wet-mopped the barracks floors. They then stood quietly beside their bunks, awaiting the appearance of the enemy officer of the day, an interpreter, and an escort of four soldiers armed with rifles and bayonets.[8]

Inspection normally began at 7:00 AM that winter. The officer of the day conducted roll call by section, and he expected the prisoners to take their orders and utter all responses in Japanese. As the inspecting party drew near, a POW designated as section leader would call his roommates to attention by barking, "*Keoki!*" At the command, "*Banco,*" the POWs were supposed to sound off by number—*Ichi, Ni, San, Shi, Go, Roku, Shichi, Hachi,* and so forth—until every man in the section accounted for himself.

Once the Japanese judged the Americans had sufficient time to learn this routine, they tolerated no slipups. Memorizing just one number did not suffice, as the count changed with the absence of a section mate. If a POW forgot his number, shouted it out of order, or mispronounced it, he could expect to be cuffed or slapped. Then the section had to sound off again until everyone completed the procedure without a mistake. The Wake Islanders received plenty of practice, as their captors subjected them to a second banco, or *tenko,* each evening at either 7:00 or 8:30 PM. Between the two inspections, the Japanese used bugle calls to alert the prisoners to meal times and guide them through the rest of their daily schedule. "Everything in prison . . . was done by the voice of the cornet," reminisced Corporal Richardson. "There was no respite from the demanding voice of the cornet."[9]

At first contact, the Japanese soldiers who welcomed the Wake Islanders to Woosung seemed almost friendly—a refreshing change from Lieutenant Saito's brutes aboard the *Nitta Maru*. These new guards mixed amiably with the weary Americans as the latter settled into their barracks late on January 24. Curious young Japanese tried communicating with their charges in pidgin English—a cultural legacy of generations of Western trade and imperialism in East Asia. Corporal Richardson labeled the resulting conversations as the "*wifo* routine." The Japanese got things started by asking the prisoners several one-word questions, such as "*Wifo* (wife)?"; "*Bebe* (baby)?"; "*Caru* (car)?"; and "*Beisbol* (baseball)?" In common with young men the world over, the main thing the guards had on their minds was *skivvy*, or sex. Pfc. Henry Chapman smiled as they babbled on about "*skivvy-skivvy chi-si cunya ichi-ban*," or "sex with number one girl." A POW could elicit gales of laughter from his keepers by simply affirming or denying he ever had sexual relations.[10]

When the guards burst into the POWs' barracks on January 25, their mood had changed from the night before, and they were all business. The Wake Islanders and Allied naval personnel from Shanghai had lost their novelty, and the Japanese soldiers now treated them as irritants. First Lieutenant Takamoto and his men were combat troops. They regarded guarding creatures as craven as POWs as far below their dignity. The Imperial Japanese Army usually assigned that job to second-class troops and such misfits as drunkards, troublemakers, and the mentally imbalanced. A Japanese interpreter confirmed this when he testified at a war crimes trial in 1946: "If the officer has a good ability the Japanese army never sends them to the prison camp—they go to the front."[11]

Takamoto's detachment had been temporarily posted to Woosung until a permanent guard detail could be assembled, but that did not prevent the first lieutenant and his subordinates from resenting the assignment. They frequently took out their unhappiness on the prisoners. Guards eager to demonstrate their prowess as martial artists liked placing an American in a judo hold or throwing him to the ground. The fact that they preferred victimizing older Contractors rendered these feats unimpressive. Nevertheless, when Cpl. John Johnson updated his secret diary on January 25, he inserted this observation: "Precautions exercised by all hands in order to please our guards."[12]

Despite these foul-tempered episodes, Takamoto's soldiers did not persecute the Wake Islanders with the same zeal as their counterparts on the *Nitta Maru*. The Woosung guards stayed outside of the prisoners' compound much of the time. They also refrained from taking the POWs out on any work details. Consequently, the Americans and Britons could expect to live free of harassment for most of each day.[13]

With nothing else to do, the Wake Islanders devoted their waking hours to getting warm. Those few with more than one change of clothes put on every stitch they owned. During long spells of inclement weather, the POWs trudged back and forth inside their barracks with numbing repetition. The less-energetic sat wrapped in their blankets for hours on end. Whenever the sun poked through the clouds, the Americans would flock outside to bask in its feeble rays. Sockless and shoeless men wrapped rags and scraps of paper around their feet. Those with shoes rarely removed them—even when they slept. FN1C William Plate wore his shoes continuously until the weather turned warm. When he finally tugged them off, he was able to peel chunks of dead, black flesh from his feet.[14]

Nothing the POWs tried to ward off the cold worked especially well. A desperate Cpl. Eschol Davis adopted a mind-over-matter strategy. "I just thought . . . if I could just deny reality, just escape from that," he explained. When that method failed, Davis resorted to exercise. Incessant shivering caused SSgt. Clifford Hotchkiss to walk around camp with his shoulders perpetually hunched. Most, if not all, of the Wake Islanders suffered from chilblain or minor frostbite, especially in their feet. Such cases experienced acute pain at night after their lower extremities warmed up beneath their blankets. Pfc. Leonard Mettscher would awake from a sound sleep to find his feet hurting "like the devil."[15]

The cold also discouraged the Wake Islanders from paying proper attention to personal hygiene. The Japanese issued each POW a paper bag containing a rudimentary toiletry kit. Corporal Richardson inventoried its contents as "a toothbrush comparable to a wet feather, a large bag of toothpowder of the same consistency as Dutch Cleanser, a tiny piece of soap, and a piece of cheese cloth a foot long and a yard wide to be used as a towel." The Japanese also gave the prisoners a month's allotment of toilet paper—four sheets per man. Second Lt. Kinney dismissed those brittle, eight-inch squares as "about as soft as 00 sandpaper." When the Americans exhausted this meager supply, they wiped themselves with their fingers, which they rinsed off at the wash rack.[16]

A single bar of soap was supposed to last a POW one month. That seemed no problem as long as frigid temperatures prevailed because most Wake Islanders could not bear to wash much more than their hands and faces. By February 1, however, Alec Pay tired of smelling like a pig, and he ventured out to the camp bathhouse. Connected to the galley, that dilapidated wooden edifice contained one section for officers and another section for enlisted men and Contractors. Each section housed two large tubs—one filled with hot water and the other with cold. Pay drew a bucket of hot water to lather up his soap and scrub his body.

Then he rinsed off with dippers of cold water. "Took bath," he recorded tersely. "Weather very cold."[17]

Many Wake Islanders waited three weeks before daring to follow Pay's lead. More postponed visiting the bathhouse for two or three months. Once bathing became popular, the POWs learned that sections failing to reach the bathhouse early in the day ended up washing with lukewarm water. The Wake Islanders also delayed washing their clothes because most lacked a second set to wear while the first dried. In addition, most feared those ragged garments would fall apart if exposed to soap and water.[18]

"WE WERE BEING FED BARELY ENOUGH TO SUSTAIN LIFE"

With morning inspection out of the way on January 25, Woosung's occupants wondered what they would get to eat. The enemy had promised them three meals a day based on the standard Imperial Japanese Army ration. Camp authorities heightened the prisoners' anticipation by distributing mess kits that morning. They handed each man a canvas drawstring bag containing two bowls and a Japanese teacup made of enamelware or aluminum, plus a pair of wooden chopsticks. The Wake Islanders found chopsticks difficult to master. After several days, the Japanese heeded the Americans' complaints by replacing those utensils with forks and spoons. The prisoners never received any table knives, which made good sense from a security viewpoint, but some of them sharpened the edges on their spoons or forks to cut any solid food they might receive.[19]

The mess kits went unused through the morning of the twenty-fifth and into the afternoon. Finally, at 2:00 PM, the Japanese served the famished prisoners a late lunch of rice and onion stew. A second meal featuring the same entrees was not ready until 8:00 PM. On January 26 the Japanese once again managed to provide only two meals rather than three.[20]

The POWs felt cheated, and they looked for someone to blame. Suspicion immediately fell on the Chinese civilians that the Japanese hired to operate the camp's galley. Rumormongers charged the Chinese with pilfering large amounts of food, especially meat and vegetables. The Japanese warrant officer overseeing the galley spoke English, and he divulged a different explanation. He claimed he had been told to expect only three hundred prisoners. The arrival of nearly 1,300 enemy mouths caught him short-staffed and with insufficient stores on hand. Some POWs bought this story, but many others suspected the Japanese of pilfering, too.

The kitchen crew finally got its act together on January 27 and put out breakfast, lunch, and dinner on schedule. Each meal consisted of a teacup's worth of rice, a bowl of something the Japanese called stew, and a couple of cups of Chinese tea. By February 11 the Japanese began substituting bread baked in Shanghai—when available—for rice at one daily meal. This new addition to the menu came in the form of two small buns or a slightly larger single loaf per man.[21]

Rice made up the staple element in the Woosung diet. The POWs believed that the brown, unpolished rice they consumed was the poorest grade to be had. It actually possessed more roughage and vitamins than the white, polished variety, which made it more nutritious than most Wake Islanders initially realized. The rice also contained a great deal of debris, however. That inspired the rumor that the camp was being fed floor sweepings from Shanghai warehouses. First Lt. Woodrow Kessler observed, "The quality of the rice varied considerably; often it contained large quantities of hulls which we found almost impossible to pick out and, at times, small bits of gravel and even chips of glass." Some Americans claimed they turned up rocks, tacks, nails, and rat droppings in their rice bowls. POWs who chewed their rice quickly risked cracking their teeth on pebbles. The presence of so much extraneous matter also precipitated appendicitis attacks. In addition, the rice was often crawling with small rice worms, which were discernible only by their tiny black heads.[22]

The usually high liquid content of the POWs' "stew" made it resemble a weak vegetable soup more than anything else. The Wake Islanders immediately dubbed the concoction "Tojo Water." The recipe varied according to which vegetables were in season, but Chinese cabbage appeared most often in the brew, along with slices of daikon. Corporal Richardson likened eating that Chinese radish to "chewing on a slice of boiled two-by-four lumber." On rare occasions, a prisoner might find one, two, or three minuscule cubes of meat in his soup. On other days, he might spoon up small pieces of dried or rotten fish. After the galley got better organized, the Tojo Water that accompanied the evening meal was sometimes thick enough to approximate stew.[23]

In a country where human waste served as fertilizer, tea was the only thing that Woosung's populace could drink safely. Camp facilities included a freestanding teahouse, and the POWs were pretty much free to imbibe as much as they wanted. Some Wake Islanders remembered the beverage had a bitter taste. Cpl. Thomas Johnson felt otherwise. "You couldn't tell it was tea," he insisted, "but it was the color of tea."[24]

The bread the Japanese obtained for the POWs had a sweet quality. "To us it tasted like cake," mused Herb Jaffe. The buns and loaves delivered to Woosung arrived in barely palatable shape. They were stale and covered with mold, indicating they could no longer be sold to civilian consumers. The Americans soon discovered that Shanghai bakers stooped to underhanded means to stretch their flour stocks. Herb Jaffe characterized the bread as "about half sawdust.... Must have been made with wood pulp as well as flour. Funny looking strings of wood in there." When First Lieutenant Kessler later tried to diminish the sweet taste of his bread by toasting it, the pervasive wood fiber caused it to catch fire "very very easily."[25]

The Japanese chose not to equip Woosung with a mess hall, which compelled prisoners to dine in their barracks. Whenever meal call sounded, one POW from each section headed to the teahouse to fetch a two-gallon porcelain teapot. At the same time, two-man chow details lined up in front of the galley to bring their respective sections a wooden bucket full of rice and another containing soup or stew.

The job of ladling out the food rotated among the inmates, and with good reason. No other role in camp attracted closer scrutiny. "Each man took his turn serving the other 35 men the rice and soup," Sergeant Holmes recalled. "It was a matter of great accomplishment to make the rice 'come out even' among the 36 men." A server had to carefully avoid packing down the rice in one comrade's bowl more tightly than any other lest he be accused of playing favorites and giving some more to eat than others. Likewise, a server had to thoroughly stir the soup bucket or plunge the ladle to the very bottom to make sure he plopped the same amount of solids in everyone's soup bowl. Every now and then, a conscientious chow man would dip a dead rat out of the soup. The rodents fell off rafters in the galley and landed in the large cauldrons in which the prisoners' food cooked. Either the kitchen crew did not notice or did not care enough to remove the thrashing creatures as they boiled to death.[26]

No matter how honest a server tried to be, many POWs insisted they were being shortchanged. "If you watched the rationing process you were sure that every bowl contained more than yours," Corporal Richardson explained. "If you did not watch you were equally positive you would be slighted." Pfc. George Hubley conceded that perceived inequities triggered violent reactions. "God help you if you got a little too much in one [bowl] and short the other one," he noted. "I've seen some knock down drag out fights over there." The same thing happened in the civilian barracks. "I've seen some good fights over a grain of rice," remarked Contractor Shirley "Tex" Akin. Under the circumstances, Contractor Ned Nye had every right to boast that his comrades trusted him to dole out equal portions when he wielded his section's ladle. John O. Young, a CPNAB carpenter from Boise, gloried in his section mates calling him the "King of the Ladle" for the same reason.[27]

Disposing of leftovers constituted possibly the most delicate part of the food distribution process. If a server ended up with any extra rice or soup after going all around the section, he would return to where he started and hand out smaller portions until he had emptied the bucket. The next man owed leftovers would receive some sort of "buck," or token, to guarantee he got the first crack at an extra portion during the next meal.[28]

Even if every prisoner received his fair share of the available food, no one felt full. "All the meals did, it seemed, was to make us hungrier," maintained Contractor John H. Burton. Despite enemy claims to the contrary, a POW did not subsist on the same quantity of food as a Japanese soldier. The latter also enjoyed tastier and more varied fare. The guards eventually let it slip that the POWs were actually receiving convicts' rations. The Wake Islanders came up with different estimates regarding the nutritional value of their ration, but it appears most likely that three servings of rice and soup provided an intake of no more than 1,000 calories per day. That represented only about 25 percent of what the U.S. Army thought an active soldier required to keep healthy. "We were being fed barely enough to sustain life," declared Tex Akin.[29]

On such paltry rations, malnutrition and its attendant complications quickly manifested themselves. Most Wake Islanders were already slim and trim at the time of capture. They began losing weight on the *Nitta Maru*, and that continued after they reached Woosung. Fireman Second Class Kibble dwindled to between 115 pounds and 105 pounds during his early days in camp, and there he stayed for the rest of his captivity. As the prisoners' bodies adjusted to a starvation living standard, they suffered a wide range of nutritional disorders, including beriberi, neuritis, pellagra, impaired vision, blistered mouths, and boils. In the Americans' weakened state, they fell prey to other afflictions, as well, such as dysentery and tuberculosis. Dr. Kahn predicted that the Woosung diet would kill every man in camp within six months.[30]

As if to prove Kahn a prophet, Woosung suffered its first death less than a month after opening its gates. Mark E. Staten, a young CPNAB canteen clerk from California, expired on February 17, 1942. Kahn identified malnutrition as the cause of death, but there was more to the story than that. Staten's stomach rebelled against the wormy, pebbly rice. He claimed he could not eat the standard POW ration. Skeptical camp authorities refused to give him any other food. They also rejected a request to send him to a Shanghai hospital as his condition deteriorated. After Staten died, the Japanese trucked his remains to the city for cremation.[31]

"YOU CANNOT HAVE PEOPLE JUST SITTING AROUND"

Most POWs blamed Mark Staten's death on the Japanese, but some suspected he had lost the will to live and starved himself to death. And it appeared that other Americans were on the verge of following suit. Deprived of life's barest necessities, beaten down by cold and hunger, and subject to the whims of an unpredictable enemy, the Wake Islanders increasingly succumbed to self-pity. The moxie and adaptability that so many of them exhibited during combat drained away in Woosung's joyless confines. Even the most gung-ho Marines lost their spirit and sense of collective identity. "We were not in Batteries or any form of military organization," commented Sergeant Holmes. "It made a man feel that he was sorta on his own. Some men thought their NCOs and officers had no power over them now they were POWs." No one seemed to know how to improve matters. Worse than that, no one seemed to care. Second Lieutenant Kinney of VMF-211 admitted that he and his brother officers had lost the capacity to think clearly. The Japanese contributed inadvertently to the prisoners' plight by giving them nothing constructive to do with their time.[32]

The Wake Islanders quickly tired of their sole source of physical exercise—keeping warm. One by one, they plopped onto their sleeping platforms, gazed vacantly into space, and sank inexorably into despair. Throughout the month following surrender, Wake's occupants had often been too terrified or too busy to dwell on much more than present problems. But now, stranded in China beyond the easy reach of potential rescuers, the prisoners had ample time to brood, gripe, and wallow in misery. As Major Devereux inspected the servicemen's barracks, he recognized the lifeless expression creeping into his men's faces. Leathernecks stationed on island outposts called it the "thousand-yard stare," "going Asiatic," or the "Wake Island Wacky Woo." American gangster films referred to it as "going stir-crazy." By any name, this surrender to hopelessness threatened to destroy the Wake Island defenders and their civilian companions. Devereux had found a new enemy to fight, and he promptly took up the challenge.[33]

Devereux reacted in a manner consistent with his character. The U.S. Marine Corps and much of the Navy knew him as an incorrigible martinet. Devereux believed that discipline—his patent cure-all for military problems—could arrest deteriorating morale at Woosung. "I think anybody would recognize that you must maintain discipline within a group even if you are prisoners," the little major asserted. "You cannot have people just sitting around."[34]

Almost as soon as the Wake Islanders got settled at Woosung, Devereux put out the word that he expected his subordinates to conduct themselves as military men. "You're still Marines," he reminded them. "Act like it." That included keeping clean and observing all forms of military courtesy, such as greeting their officers with snappy salutes. At the same time, Devereux urged his officers to smarten up their appearance and conduct themselves as gentlemen. Second Lt. Arthur Poindexter expressed amazement at Devereux's insistence on such niceties as superiors presenting junior officers with their compliments and the latter replying with their respects. "Here we're sleeping on a pile of rags," Poindexter exclaimed, but the major "maintained that all through the war."[35]

Devereux's crusade to revive discipline exemplified more than the habits of a lifetime or adherence to tradition. He believed that he and his Leathernecks were still at war with the Japanese. Surrender on Wake Island had altered the nature of the struggle, but not its intensity. Devereux interpreted Woosung's shoddy conditions and the enemy's indifference to POW suffering as cold-blooded and nefarious. The major would convey these thoughts in his memoirs, writing, "Hidden behind the routine, under the surface of life in prison camp, was fought a war of wills for moral supremacy—an endless struggle, as bitter as it was unspoken, between the captors and the captives. The stake seemed to me simply this: the main objective of the whole Japanese prison program was to break our spirit, and on our side was a stubborn determination to keep our self-respect whatever else they took from us."[36]

Back on Wake, surviving combat had depended on teamwork; the same principle applied to surviving prison camp. Devereux considered discipline the prisoners' last remaining weapon "to use against the breaking of pride." It would save his men from degenerating into a mob and make them think and act once again as members of a military organization. The major strove ceaselessly to rekindle a team spirit among his Leathernecks. "This is a unit," he would say. "This is the 1st Marine Defense Battalion, Wake Island Detachment." Devereux did not want his men feeling abandoned and free to fend for themselves. His soldierly instincts told him that such attitudes were dangerous. They would transform Woosung into a dog-eat-dog world where POWs preyed on each other instead of working together for the common good. Devereux wanted the Wake defenders to remember that they had buddies who cared about them and officers who were solicitous of their best interests. The POWs could not afford to worry solely about themselves, Devereux believed. The group could support the individual only if he gave his allegiance to the group.[37]

Devereux would never admit it, but the Japanese did him a favor by organizing the Wake Islanders into thirty-six-man sections. In the servicemen's barracks, Devereux appointed his senior NCOs as section leaders. These men served a dual function and answered to two sets of masters. The Japanese expected them to keep tabs on the prisoners under them, have their subordinates make their bunks and clean the barracks, and account for them at roll call. At the same time, Devereux relied on section leaders and other noncoms to enforce order and discipline among the rank and file on a day-to-day basis. "Discipline was maintained essentially as you would maintain it if you have not been in a prison," expounded Capt. Bryghte Godbold. "We worked through the noncommissioned officers." Sergeant Holmes confirmed Godbold's comments, noting, "Marine officers of that day . . . depended almost entirely on the senior NCOs to run things. . . . Up the line of Command the officers usually got the credit . . . but it was the 'old salty' NCOs that really got the job done." The efficacy of this approach highlighted the fact that noncommissioned rank conferred much higher prestige in the smaller prewar Marine Corps than afterward. Frank Gross described the status he and his brother corporals enjoyed in the "Old Corps." "You was just a little Jesus, that's what you was," he said. As for the next level in the Marine pecking order, Gross quipped, "The sergeant was God."[38]

For most of Devereux's men, reinstituting the old command system diluted the uncertainty of POW life with comforting doses of the normal via familiar rituals. Working through the noncoms also enabled the major to reimpose control without making himself too conspicuous. If he had gone around Woosung constantly barking orders, the Japanese might have seen him as a threat to their authority. The enemy did provide POW officers with a sanctioned role in camp management, though, by requiring that each barracks have its own adjutant. Barracks adjutants acted as the chief liaisons between the prisoners and their keepers, relaying orders from the commandant's office to their respective section leaders. Devereux named two of his officers as the adjutants of Barracks 2 and Barracks 3. Whenever they received instructions from the Japanese, those officers would confer with the major on how best to phrase them to the enlisted men.[39]

By and large, the Marines, sailors, and soldiers from Wake fell into line and complied with Devereux's dictates. For many of them, obeying one's superiors was an automatic reflex. When the major began to snap the whip again, Pfc. James King simply shrugged and told himself, "I'm a Marine and he's the boss." Pfc. George McDaniel responded in a like fashion, and with emphasis. "We were given orders to maintain discipline," he recalled, "and our commanding officer *was* Major Devereux." Others fell into step because of the major's personal example. "I was quite proud of the man," volunteered Pfc. Jesse E. Nowlin, "because he would be out there marching around the compound in the dead of winter getting his exercise. He . . . conducted himself as a gentleman."[40]

A number of POWs recognized the wisdom in Devereux's regimen and willingly embraced it. "There's no doubt that discipline was needed," conceded Pfc. Joseph Borne. "That's what brought us through prison camp," asserted Pvt. Edward Sturgeon, "respect." Sgt. Donald Malleck addressed this point with greater clarity. "I would say there was very little difficulty—or no difficulty in maintaining discipline among the Wake Island Marines," Malleck reminisced. "I think The Major & our other officers were respected enough to ensure this. . . . It was quite evident that they had our well being in mind—it was also evident that discipline was . . . beneficial to our cause." FN1C William Plate, a Navy man, offered even stronger praise for the milieu Devereux fostered. "We had our own officers, our own noncoms, and we had our own military discipline regardless of the fact that we were POWs," Plate testified. "We knew that anything that we did . . . if we did anything that was unmilitary like, that we would . . . get disciplinary action after we got back to the States. And I think this is one of the things that held our men together, held our camp together—tighter, and gave us a sense of respectability even though we were prisoners."[41]

Military men—no matter how well-trained—are not unthinking automatons, and not every Marine welcomed Devereux's efforts to reassert his authority. First Lieutenant Kessler later spoke of "a very short lived feeling of rebellion against all authority in Woosung, which was quickly squelched by Major Devereux's actions." Devereux dealt harshly with the insubordinate, disobedient, quarrelsome, and dishonest. He put offenders on report and swore to court-martial them after they returned home. When a Marine section leader complained he was losing control over his men, Devereux snapped, "You pick up a pick handle and use it, and don't forget I said that, because you have to maintain discipline." The iron-willed major justified such drastic methods with their results. "Our morale was good because I insisted on military courtesy," Devereux contended. "If I went in to one of the barracks where the men were, they all got up."[42]

The Marines' resumption of military protocol reaped unexpected dividends. "We soon learned that the Japs respected a military man," surmised Sergeant Holmes. He grew convinced that weaklings and undisciplined gripers attracted more harassment from the guards. Devereux's agency in his subordinates' transformation did not go unnoticed by the Japanese. Instead of arousing his keepers' ire or suspicions, however, the major's conduct received their tacit blessing. "All our guards . . . showed much respect for Devereux & always went into their goose step and salute when they met him," bragged Sergeant Malleck. On a more practical level, camp authorities decided that Devereux's activities reinforced their own control over Woosung's inmates. In return, the American officers gained sufficient credibility in enemy eyes to act as advocates for their subordinates. As Devereux put it, "It was only by maintaining the officers' status that we could properly represent our men in dealing with the Japs and get things for them from our captors."[43]

Devereux took this reciprocal relationship a step further by involving the Japanese in punishing his worst miscreants. One day, a Marine corporal lost his composure and started a fistfight with a sergeant. The major reacted by having the Japanese place the corporal in solitary confinement. Devereux then assembled his Marines and warned them, "I will sacrifice a few of you to get the rest back."

"And he meant it," recalled Pvt. Ewing LaPorte. "There's going to be discipline here." Private First Class Borne remembered Devereux pledging that "he only wanted the good Marines, the people that behaved like Marines, and he was going to bring them back—even if he sacrificed the other half."[44]

The Japanese would have been far less cooperative had they realized Devereux's agenda extended beyond making more tractable prisoners. The little major never ceased hoping that the Allies would someday capture Shanghai and liberate him and his men. When that day came, he wanted to reenter combat as swiftly as possible. Devereux had his clerk, Cpl. Robert Brown, draw up a table of organization for the Wake Island Detachment, assigning each man to a specific battery and battle-related task. He had Brown keep those secret rosters throughout the war. Devereux also searched out SSgt. Clifford Hotchkiss, an Army communicator, and directed him to rig a signal light. The major desired to speak in Morse code to any Allied planes flying over Shanghai.[45]

Devereux assumed that the example set by his Marines had a salutary effect on the Contractors. "With the predominance of Marines we set the pattern even among the civilians," he opined. "They were under their own people in their own barracks, but their senior civilian constructor, Dan Teters, had been in the Army during World War I, . . . and he was able to handle those people all right." To be sure, many Contractors admired the Leathernecks for their reborn esprit de corps. Al O'Guinn, a plumber from California, spoke warmly of "the spirit of the Marines, their brotherly comradeship." After watching Devereux's men execute a little close-order drill, Theodore Abraham, a CPNAB secretary, remarked, "Their performance made us shiver and also made us extremely proud of our Marines."[46]

In actual fact, keeping order among the Contractors proved a tricky business. The Japanese initially acknowledged that Dan Teters, the CPNAB general superintendent, was the Contractors' headman, but he left Woosung in less than two months. Raymond Rutledge, an office clerk who had fought heroically beside the Marines on Wake, then tried to fill Teters' shoes. Rutledge either failed to exercise sufficient control over his fellow Contractors or otherwise displeased the Japanese. They removed him as "civilian commander" by May 2, 1942.

The Contractors' barracks adjutants and section leaders tended to be CPNAB superintendents and foremen. The retention of such positions, however, depended more on respect, popularity, and a man's willingness to accept responsibility than his place in the corporate hierarchy. Although civilian barracks adjutants and section leaders performed the same duties as their military equivalents, they could not draw on military conditioning and tradition to bolster their authority. In some instances, the Contractors elected their section leaders. Appointed or elected, the civilian *honchos*, as the Japanese called them, needed to cultivate their comrades' good will. If one made himself obnoxious, his subordinates only had to do something to anger the Japanese and that would get him into trouble. Civilian leaders also needed group backing to restrain "camp bulls." These malcontents, bullies, and other predators respected no authority aside from Japanese bayonets and only behaved themselves under compulsion.[47]

Curiously, Commander Cunningham took little if any part in the campaign to construct an inner POW organization. Posted to Wake Island just ten days before the outbreak of hostilities, Cunningham was not well acquainted with most of the American garrison's personnel, and he did not appear eager to alter the situation once he landed in China. "I saw no indication of Cunningham wanting to assume command over the men as POWs," reported Sergeant Holmes. "It seemed to me he shied away from us and spent most of his time with the Shanghai Navy officers in our camp." Unfolding events would soon make Major Devereux the Wake defenders' main leader by default.[48]

"I HATED MOST OF THE SON OF BITCHES"

On the morning of February 1, 1942, a large contingent of new prisoners entered Woosung. The 202 men looked like nothing the camp had ever seen before, and their arrival brought the original inmates streaming from their barracks. Herb Jaffe could not get over the group's unbowed manner and smart appearance. "They were marching in close order, very military in bearing," Jaffe exclaimed. "I couldn't believe it. I thought what are you going to do—liberate us?" The newcomers sported dark green woolen overcoats and luxurious fur caps. Most of them had seabags crammed with extra clothing, canned food, and other treasures perched on their shoulders. Sergeant Malleck drank in this inexplicable sight with his mouth agape. "Those beautiful winter uniforms, fur caps, shoes," he thought, "a guy could nearly warm up just looking at them." Standing a few feet away, Contractor Herman G. "Dutch" Raspe shouted with evident glee, "Hey, the Rooskies are in the war! They all wear fur caps."[49]

Raspe got it wrong. The newcomers' headgear bore the bronze eagle, globe, and anchor device of the U.S. Marine Corps, not the red star of the Soviet Union's Red Army. The magnificently dressed specimens turned out to be the North China Marines, the guard details from the American embassy at Peking (now Beijing), American legation at Tientsin, and firing range outside the seaport of Chinwangtao. The North China Marines represented the cream of the Old Corps, each man being chosen for his looks, stance, and intelligence. As a reward for such qualities, those Leathernecks received a coveted assignment. The dollar went a long way in prewar China. Even enlisted men could afford to hire houseboys to make their bunks, clean their quarters, and keep their shoes, belts, and brass gleaming, and still have enough left over to enjoy their pick of local women. Japan's 1937 invasion of North China pronounced a death sentence on that idyllic existence by placing the American legation guards in an untenable position. After four years of festering tension, the American government finally faced reality and ordered the North China Marines to close their posts and assemble at Chinwangtao. There they would board a passenger ship, the SS *President Harrison*, on December 10, 1941, for transfer to the Philippines. Unfortunately, the Japanese initiated hostilities against the United States two days before the Leathernecks could effect their escape.[50]

Despite the North China Marines' elite status, they came to Woosung stained with a double shame. Not only were they the first American troops to lower their flag in the Pacific War, but they did so without firing a shot. That was not to say they were cowards. They awoke on December 8 to find themselves surrounded by thousands of Japanese soldiers demanding their immediate capitulation. Lacking prepared defenses, weapons heavier than machine guns, and any hope of relief, the North China Marines declined to mount a pointless battle against impossible odds.[51]

In any event, those Americans expected they would soon get a chance to fight their captors. They believed that the Boxer Protocol of 1901 classified them as diplomatic personnel, and they anticipated speedy repatriation. In fact, the North China Marines' superiors had advised against offering resistance if war erupted to avoid jeopardizing their supposedly privileged position. As it turned out, the Boxer Protocol did not elevate the legation guards above the level of ordinary combatants, and they were destined to spend the entire conflict behind barbed wire.[52]

Initial uncertainty regarding the North China Marines' diplomatic standing led the Japanese army to treat them with kid gloves. The Japanese permitted those Leathernecks to retain their cash, jewelry, and other personal possessions. They housed the North China Marines in their own quarters and let them dine on American food. The Japanese eventually concentrated all the legation guards in the American barracks at Tientsin, but they did not stay there long. On January 27, the North China Marines climbed into boxcars for a four-day ride to Shanghai. An enemy interpreter assured the departing Americans that a repatriation ship would be awaiting them at that port. The Marines' still-indulgent captors gave them leave to haul along considerable baggage—two trunks per officer, one trunk or footlocker per enlisted man, and all the hand luggage that the latter could carry. The items the legation guards packed for the trip would shortly make the Wake Islanders' eyes bulge—several changes of clothing per man, underwear, soap, towels, toothpaste, shaving equipment, thousands of dollars in Chinese and American currency, and a phonograph with a selection of musical recordings. The Japanese were so lax that the North China Marines succeeded in smuggling twenty bottles of Black Label scotch and Gordon's gin out of Tientsin for their officers, along with the parts for a contraband shortwave radio. The satisfaction the legation guards enjoyed from these small victories dissipated as soon as they detrained outside Shanghai. Instead of reporting to the city's Bund for embarkation, the Marines marched eight miles to the isolated and barren location of the Shanghai War Prisoners Camp.[53]

First Lieutenant Takamoto assigned the North China Marines to Barracks 7, which had remained vacant since Woosung opened. The other Americans followed the legation guards to their quarters and watched them move in. The Wake Islanders could not help envying their new neighbors. "They had lots of clothes, and scarves, and earmuffs, several pair of shoes, and plenty of money and cigarettes," vouched Pvt. Joe Reeves. A noticeable stir swept the onlookers when they spied the innerspring mattresses that accompanied the North China Marines' three most-senior officers. The more the Wake Islanders stared at those well-fed, well-clothed, and well-provisioned Leathernecks, the more it reminded them how far their own standard of living had dropped. "Here we were," reflected Dr. Kahn, "we looked like a bunch of tramps. . . . It was just horrible."[54]

The cruel contrast did not completely dampen the Wake Marines' elation at seeing their comrades from North China. The event contained all the ingredients for a family reunion. Up until 1939 the Marine Corps had been a small and remarkably close-knit organization. Many of Major Devereux's officers and men had trained or served with various legation guards sometime in their military careers. They looked forward to rekindling old friendships and expected that their affluent fellow Leathernecks would share the wealth with the less fortunate. Private First Class Borne felt a thrill of recognition when he bumped into his old drill instructor, PlSgt. Holland Cash, who had been taken prisoner at Peking. Cash invited Borne into Barracks 7 for a chat. A few minutes later, Cecil M. Dietz, Cash's sergeant major, spotted Borne and other Wake Marines inside the North China Marines' quarters. Instead of extending a hearty welcome, Dietz flew at them in a fury, bellowing, "Get them goddam scroungers out of here! We don't want them around! Get them out of here!"[55]

Signs went up immediately declaring Barracks 7 off-limits to any Wake Islander. The North China Marines also posted guards at each entrance to enforce this inhospitable decree. Their officers tried to justify the quarantine by claiming they did not want the other POWs to contaminate Barracks 7 with lice and other vermin. This charade failed to fool the Wake Islanders. They knew this was a case of the haves protecting their property from the have-nots. "They thought they was in Hollywood," sneered Pvt. Edward Sturgeon. "There was rumors they wanted nothing to do with us pigs." The legation guards confirmed those stories by openly mocking their scruffy Wake counterparts as "Raggedy-Ass Marines."[56]

Such behavior stunned the survivors of the Wake Island Detachment and VMF-211. "It kind of tears at your heart," elaborated Cpl. Thomas Johnson, "to think that the [North China] Marines would treat their fellow Marines like this." Like the rest of Devereux's men, Johnson had been schooled in the creed that all Leathernecks were brothers and should share and share alike. On top of the apparent selfishness, nothing galled the Wake Marines more than the legation guards' superior attitude. After all, the latter had laid down their arms without putting up a fight, while the men they scorned had bloodied the enemy considerably. It did not seem right that the Japanese should grant privileges to the North China Marines and deny them to genuine combat heroes. The Contractors viewed the situation with the same sense of injustice, and they registered their disapproval by lauding Devereux's men as "fighting Marines" and dismissing the legation guards as "Ten-Cent Marines"—a play on Tientsin, the latter's former station. What most riled the Wake Islanders was hearing the North China Marines speak with such assurance about getting repatriated in the near future.[57]

Pfc. James Venable later conceded that the North China Marines had acted wisely by excluding the Wake POWs from their barracks. "We probably would have stolen from the North China Marines," Venable acknowledged, "for their food initially, . . . and seriously, we wouldn't have really considered it theft." Few Wake Marines were as philosophical or forgiving. Their early encounters with the North China Marines engendered a bitterness in some that lasted a lifetime. Cpl. Thomas Johnson judged the legation guards' conduct "a real black spot in the history of the Marine Corps." It was as if an economic class system had sprung up within Woosung. Private Reeves expressed his resentment in scathing terms: "I hated most of the son of bitches."[58]

The only comfort the Wake Islanders derived from this inequitable situation was the thought that time would level the distinctions that placed the North China Marines higher in Woosung's social order. "Our day will come," Private First Class Hubley told himself. And Private Reeves uttered this grim vow: "I would like to get out of this prison camp, but I hope we stay here long enough where these damned guys are as bad off as we are." Unless the POWs reconciled, they would battle for survival divided rather than united, and that stacked the odds against any of them living long enough to be liberated.[59]

CHAPTER EIGHT

"the japanese army . . . will improve your conditions"

turning the corner at woosung

"HE NEVER QUIT TRYING TO MAKE LIFE BETTER FOR US"

The presence of the North China Marines, despite the tensions it bred, also conferred tangible benefits on Woosung's other prisoners. The legation guards' arrival turned out to be the first in a series of events that ushered in a noticeable betterment in the quality of life at the Shanghai War Prisoners Camp.

The first blessing attributable to the North China Marines was short-term and hardly endeared the newcomers to their fellow prisoners. As long as the legation guards' canned goods and other provisions held out, they often refrained from eating all the food that the Japanese gave them. They would send much of their rice ration to the barracks occupied by Devereux's servicemen and the Contractors. The Wake Islanders chafed at this finickiness, but they were not too proud to accept the additional nourishment. "That was alright with us," affirmed SSgt. Clifford Hotchkiss. "They were eating sausages and cheeses, and everything they brought with them."[1]

Old friendships and a sense of solidarity with all Leathernecks inspired several North China Marines to rediscover their compassion for the poor. In proper military style, the officers led the way. Capt. John A. White from Tientsin handed his best pair of sky blue dress trousers to a threadbare Navy ensign captured on Wake. Second Lt. James D. McBrayer from Peking had attended Basic School in Philadelphia in 1939 with VMF-211's 2nd Lt. John Kinney. McBrayer presented his pilot friend with an overcoat, a heavy shirt, and other clothing. Capt. Herbert Freuler, Kinney's squadron mate, also witnessed North China officers sharing clothes with their peers from Wake. In addition, a dozen or more enlisted legation guards gave some garments and a little American food to buddies among the Wake Marines. Such acts of largesse might have been more commonplace had not the Japanese—resistant to letting any captives live too comfortably–locked up most of the North China Marines' surplus garments and other possessions in a warehouse. During the new arrivals' first few days in camp, they slept without their own wool blankets, which partially explains why so many balked at parting with the slightest stitch of clothing. The Japanese eventually granted the North China Marines access to their belongings, but on a restricted basis.[2]

On the other hand, several legation guards took advantage of their relative wealth to extract compensation from the Wake Islanders. Major Devereux received a full uniform from one North China Marine officer, but he had to write a check before a second would part with a spare overcoat. A sergeant quartered in Barracks 7 wanted extra cups of hot tea but did not want to expose himself fully to the winter cold. He paid Cpl. Thomas Johnson in stateside cigarettes to make trips to the camp teahouse for him. Other Wake Marines hired themselves out to run errands for their North China comrades.[3]

After the legation guards exhausted their private food stores, hunger altered their business dealings with the Wake Islanders. They not only kept every morsel that they got from the Japanese, but they began offering clothes to the other prisoners for some of their sustenance. "When their food supply ran out they dealt in bowls of rice, too," chortled Sergeant Hotchkiss. The narrowing economic gap deflated the North China Marines' superior attitude. So did the dawning realization that the Japanese were not about to grant them an early release. The erasure of class distinctions led to warmer relations between the Wake Islanders and the legation guards, although some of the former never forgave the latter's initial haughtiness. By early June 1942, the two groups of Leathernecks had bonded sufficiently for a civilian comrade to remark, "Well, I could think of far worse company, and might have to do a lot of hunting before I could find better."[4]

The North China Marines made their weight felt most keenly in matters of POW leadership. The cadre of experienced NCOs that accompanied them into captivity usually kept demoralization and disorder at bay on the grassroots level. Foremost among the legation guards' noncoms loomed the most formidable warrant officer in the Old Corps, Marine Gunner William A. Lee. A tall and athletic bruiser who joined the Marines in 1919, Lee received the Navy Cross and the nickname "Iron Man" in the early 1930s while battling Sandinista guerrillas in Nicaragua alongside another living legend, then-1st Lt. Lewis B. "Chesty" Puller. A disgruntled private had to think twice before disregarding orders from someone with Lee's fearsome reputation.[5]

The North China Marines also appropriated the top slots in Woosung's interior hierarchy. Col. William W. Ashurst, the legation guards' commanding officer, outranked Commander Cunningham and supplanted him as senior POW. Ashurst obtained a second lieutenant's commission in the Marines on May 21, 1917, a month after America entered World War I. Wounded while charging a German machine-gun nest at Belleau Wood on June 10, 1918, he received the Silver Star and France's Croix de Guerre. The colonel was only forty-eight in February 1942, but arthritis and a heart condition made him appear older than his years. Although Ashurst retained his command prerogatives, he realized that he lacked the energy and stamina to actively oversee approximately 1,400 prisoners or effectively defend their interests before the Japanese.[6]

Ashurst wisely delegated considerable authority to his executive officer, Maj. Luther A. Brown. A 1921 Annapolis graduate, Brown was still fit and trim at the age of forty-one. The major also possessed a dynamic personality and impeccable military bearing. No matter how rugged conditions grew in prison camp, Brown looked as if he had just stepped out of a recruiting poster. "He always had on [a] polished Sam Brown belt, in full 'Greens' [the winter dress uniform] and shined shoes, neatly shaven and a well trimmed 'Ronald Coleman' . . . mustach[e]," enthused Pfc. Jack R. Williamson of Devereux's 1st Defense Battalion. When it came to proper POW conduct, Brown preached the same message as Devereux. "We are a military organization," Brown lectured his Marines, "and I intend to see that we remain one. To do that, there must be discipline." None of Brown's hearers doubted his qualifications for judging how Leathernecks should behave. The prewar Corps knew him as "Handbook Brown" for his authorship of *The Marine's Handbook*, the enlisted man's primary guide to service life. The major demonstrated at Woosung that being a man of letters did not rob him of the toughness required in a man of action. When one of his enlisted subordinates responded to a reprimand by snarling, "Goddam the Marine Corps!" Brown flattened him with a roundhouse punch to the face.[7]

Brown encountered less success when he tried imposing Marine disciplinary methods on the Wake Island civilians. The Contractors rebelled at the major's proposal that they start practicing close order drill. They also resisted Brown's efforts to regulate barracks life. One civilian sneered at the meddlesome officer as "God's personal representative here in camp." Civil–military relations at Woosung grew so strained that word leaked out of camp. According to A. B. Henningsen, a prominent member of Shanghai's American community, "It was apparent there was a great deal of friction between the civilians and the Marines the first few months. . . . The fault was on the part of the civilians who were unwilling to listen or cooperate with the Marine officers' administration of the Camp."[8]

Brown ultimately established a rough sort of authority by sending his brawniest Marines to strong-arm defiant Contractors. He also threatened to turn recalcitrants in to the Japanese. Though the civilians grudgingly conformed to the new social order, they let Brown know that his control was not total. Whenever the major ventured into the compound to take his constitutional, a Contractor would shout, "What color is horseshit?" At that, another would answer, "Brown!" and all civilians within earshot would guffaw.[9]

Despite Brown's headstrong approach to POW management, he earned the respect of several critics with his performance as camp representative to the Japanese. He served his fellow prisoners superbly as an advocate. The first time the Japanese permitted the North China Marines to open their baggage, Brown retrieved his copy of the U.S. Army training manual *Rules for Land Warfare*. That book contained excerpts from the Geneva Convention on the proper treatment of prisoners of war. Whenever the major's keepers violated the convention, he would stomp into the commandant's office to file a protest. "He never quit trying to make life better for us," remembered Cpl. Terence S. Kirk from Chinwangtao. "Every time I saw him heading for a conference with the Japs, he clutched his international law book like a preacher going to church with a bible. . . . Th[r]ough his persistence we received a few favors from the Japs we would not have gotten otherwise." Brown quoted from *Rules for Land Warfare* so incessantly that Pfc. Chester H. Biggs Jr. from Peking ruminated, "It is a wonder the Japanese did not confiscate the manual."[10]

Brown's efforts did not go unnoticed by the Wake Islanders, and many praised him as effusively as his own Marines did. Y3C Glenn E. Tripp, Commander Cunningham's secretary on Wake, later confided to his old boss, "It was Major Brown who . . . did all he could for the men of our camp." TSgt. Charles Holmes referenced the major's denigrators when he proclaimed, "Major Brown did a good job as our Camp representative and if he hurt somebody's feelings along the way . . . so be it." Pvt. Ewing LaPorte chimed in: "He helped us. He did. Major Brown did help us." Pfc. Jesse Nowlin divulged that Brown's admirers among the Wake Marines called him "the Diplomat" because he always cited international law.[11]

Whenever Brown interacted with the Japanese, he behaved with utter fearlessness. He got away with saying and doing things that would have garnered any other POW severe beatings, if not worse. Some prisoners assumed that Brown had friends in the enemy high command and that this immunized him from retaliation. The year Brown spent in North China before the war allowed him to mix with Japanese army officers and gain some insights into their collective mind-set, but there is no evidence these acquaintances did him any personal favors after he landed in Woosung. He probably derived more protection from his fuzzy diplomatic status and the forbearance of the Japanese officers at the Shanghai War Prisoners Camp.[12]

Next to Handbook Brown, no other officers attached to the North China Marines mattered more to Woosung's POWs than the three Navy doctors captured at Peking and Tientsin. The new health care team consisted of two physicians—Cdr. Leo C. Thyson and Lt. (j.g.) William T. Foley—and dentist Lt. (s.g.) Eric G. F. Pollard. Second Lt. Robert Hanna, a leading hero of Wake's defense, thought highly of this trio. "The medical personnel that come in with the North China Marines were outstanding," he declared. Hanna tactfully omitted mentioning Commander Thyson's reputation as an alcoholic who had been banished to China. Regardless of the gossip, Thyson turned over a new leaf in prison camp. He may not have been a great surgeon, but he could assist with an operation, and his training as a pharmacist made him an undoubted asset. Lieutenant (junior grade) Foley impressed many POWs as a caring and competent physician. Lieutenant (senior grade) Pollard proved good at his job, too, and also exhibited skills with anesthesiology.[13]

Until the arrival of Thyson, Foley, and Pollard, the burden of keeping Woosung's inmates well had fallen entirely on Dr. G. Mason Kahn, and he had little to work with. The Japanese forced him to leave his instruments on Wake and confiscated the small amount of drugs he brought aboard the *Nitta Maru*. At Woosung, camp authorities gave Kahn a few Japanese instruments and medications, but this did not gladden his outlook. The low state of enemy medical technology appalled the Wake Island Detachment's surgeon. He dismissed Japanese instruments as not "worth a damn." The clamps he received did not close arteries but snapped through them. The drugs the enemy first shared with him possessed little more potency than snake oil. Kahn was reduced to prescribing grains of burnt rice scraped from the bottom of cooking cauldrons as a charcoal substitute for treating dysentery.[14]

Having the North China Marines in camp struck Kahn as a veritable godsend. No longer a lone healer, he now belonged to a qualified medical staff large enough to attend to the POWs' needs. Best of all, Thyson, Foley, and Pollard entered Woosung with their own instruments and American medications. Major Brown wasted no time in persuading the Japanese to clear a few small rooms at one end of Barracks 4 for use as a hospital.

Japanese arbitrariness still left Kahn and his new colleagues waging an uphill battle against sickness and injury. Their hospital was small and sparsely furnished. It contained no separate bunks for contagious cases—just the same old sleeping platforms installed elsewhere in the barracks. Sick men had to lie on their own blankets rather than uncontaminated bed linen. The hospital also lacked a proper operating room. The American doctors commandeered a table for performing emergency surgeries, but they had to get along without sheets, towels, aprons, and rubber gloves. In a fit of unreasonable peevishness, the Japanese locked up much of the North China Marines' medical stores with the rest of the detachment's luggage for several weeks.[15]

Illness did not wait for the cessation of this foolishness before striking the POW population. A diet dominated by debris-laden rice set off a wave of appendicitis attacks. Fully equipped or not, the Navy doctors had to start removing inflamed appendixes or watch their fellow prisoners perish in agony. Out of sheer desperation, Kahn went to work with the only implements he could find. On February 28, 1942, Contractor Alec Pay noted in his diary that Kahn operated on Pfc. Irving R. Silverlieb for "acute appendicitis" with "a dbl. edged razor blade." The only anesthetics available were the local variety—supplemented at times by Dr. Pollard's ether—and the doctors tried to make their limited supplies stretch as far as possible. Contractor John Young, another appendicitis case, described how it felt to undergo surgery with only a shot of Novocain to kill the pain this way: "I was awake during the process. It was somewhat painful. When they got to cutting on the appendix it kinda hurt and felt like someone cutting gristle."[16]

Removing a ruptured appendix was just half the battle. Conventional practice dictated that a surgeon insert a drain in the patient's abdomen to facilitate an infection-free recovery. Kahn recalled reading an article in the *Journal of the American Medical Association* about a year before the war that advised a different treatment—simply sprinkling the antibiotic sulfanilamide inside the incision and sewing it up tight. Dr. Thyson agreed to assist the first time Kahn experimented with this technique. To the relief of both doctors, it worked like a charm and became standard practice for the rest of their confinement. Kahn and his colleagues also attained positive results when they improvised sutures out of common thread, string, and fishing line.[17]

Not every prisoner at Woosung admired the American medical staff. A few civilians accused the Navy doctors of lavishing preferential treatment on servicemen and slighting everyone else. The vast majority of the inmates, however, realized that Thyson, Foley, Kahn, and Pollard pulled off a miracle in keeping the camp's death rate as low as they did. As Cpl. Bernard Richardson aptly put it, "I think that the . . . medical capabilities were minimal, but the service was maximum."[18]

"HE WAS TRYING TO MAKE OUR CAMP A MODEL CAMP"

Two days following the arrival of the North China Marines, Woosung opened its gates to a permanent Japanese guard detachment. Colonel Goichi Yuse relieved First Lieutenant Takamoto as commandant on February 3. The 150 soldiers accompanying Yuse included a Captain Endo, who assumed the role of executive officer, and a Lieutenant Akiyama, who supervised the daily guard postings. The detachment's NCOs were Japanese, but many enlisted men were Korean and Taiwanese conscripts, which was a sure indicator of the low status that the Japanese army attached to shepherding prisoners.[19]

Every inmate at Woosung intently studied the man who now held their lives in his hands. The POWs were not bowled over by what they beheld. A reservist in his sixties who made his living as a lawyer, Colonel Yuse was a small man even by Japanese standards. He reached less than five feet in height and barely tipped the scales at one hundred pounds. He had a wooden platform placed in the compound so he could look down on his charges when he addressed them, but that only accentuated his diminutive stature. Yuse wore his cap with the visor pulled down to shade his eyes and his coat with the collar buttoned around his short, thin neck. The rest of his wardrobe looked like something drawn for a madcap cartoon. "His old boots would come up above his knees," chuckled Pfc. George Hubley. "And his crotch would hang down almost to his knees. It was comic as all get out. His ears held his hat up. His sword would drag behind him when he walked. You couldn't help but laugh at him."[20]

Yuse did not enjoy robust health, but he tackled his responsibilities at Woosung with a diligence fueled by nervous energy. A micromanager, he personally handled a multitude of tasks he should have entrusted to his subordinates. His obsession with security and making sure everything ran smoothly kept him prowling the compound morning, noon, and night.[21] Yuse's devotion to duty elicited only laughter from most POWs, especially whenever anyone recited this verse by an anonymous American or British poet:

> There was a camp commander named USELESS
> He was old, bald and toothless

> When he was young he suffered a very bad fall
> For the rest of his life he was juiceless.[22]

Perhaps to compensate for deficient command presence, Yuse inaugurated his tenure at Woosung in a snarling manner. He bluntly informed Major Brown that Japan's treatment of war prisoners was not governed by international law. He disregarded the Geneva Convention by directing the POWs to salute all Japanese camp personnel—even their inferiors in rank—or take a beating. He also talked about putting the entire camp population to work, including Allied officers.

Upon closer acquaintance, however, the POWs learned that Yuse's bark was worse than his bite. This became manifest during an early interview between Major Brown and Captain Endo in the latter's office. Neither officer spoke the other's language. The camp's head Japanese interpreter, an inept fellow named Mikani, tried vainly to bridge the communications gap. Growing exasperated, Brown ultimately told Mikani that he did not understand English well enough to warrant his appointment. Stung by such impertinence from a prisoner, Mikani struck the major in the face. The Diplomat did not respond diplomatically. Brown automatically delivered an uppercut to Mikani's chin that sent the interpreter crashing into a corner. Then the incensed Marine stuck his finger in Endo's face and told him to get a decent interpreter. In any other Japanese-run camp, such a defiant deed would have signed Brown's death warrant. Yuse not only let the pugnacious major go unpunished, but he arranged for Mikani's transfer.[23]

The POWs found Yuse agreeably flexible on a matter dearer to their hearts than Major Brown's personal safety. The colonel quickly acceded to the American officers' request that he discharge the camp's Chinese galley crew and permit the prisoners to cook their own food. Colonel Ashurst named one of his own, Capt. James F. Climie from Peking, as Woosung's first Allied mess officer. Another North China Marine, SSgt. Raymond E. Smith, actually ran the kitchen for Climie.

The POWs did not get any more rice in their bowls by eliminating alleged Chinese pilfering, but they noticed a change in quality. Eager to spare their comrades more broken teeth, the POW cooks tried picking pebbles and small stones out of the rice by hand, but they never had enough time to perform that monotonous task thoroughly. Eventually, Captain Freuler of VMF-211 designed a sluice box to clean the rice before it went into the cooking pots. Water separated the rice from the debris, washing away the lighter grains while pebbles and stones lodged against cleats nailed to the bottom of the box. The same Contractor carpenters who built this apparatus from Freuler's plans also equipped the galley with other cooking tools, such as large paddles to stir the boiling rice.[24]

Without any prodding from Ashurst and Brown, Yuse noted the discrepancy between the warmly clad North China Marines and the destitute Yanks from Wake Island. On February 9 the tiny colonel issued Japanese army uniforms and hobnailed shoes to the Contractors and Major Devereux's servicemen. This unexpected windfall included brown wool uniform tunics and pants, long cotton underdrawers, cotton shirts, and white cotton socks. All this clothing was worn out and condemned, full of patches and holes, however, which sparked murmurs among the POWs that it had been stripped from soldiers killed in battle. Devereux's Leathernecks hesitated at donning the enemy's uniform, but the cold winds whistling across the Woosung flats banished those scruples almost instantly.

Excited Wake Islanders rummaged through the clothing and footwear dumped in their barracks by the guards, searching for objects at least close to their size. The results fell short of everyone's expectations. "You never saw such a rag-tag, motley bunch in your life," exclaimed Pfc. Jesse Nowlin. "Sleeves ending at the elbows and pant legs terminating at the knees. No trouble fitting elsewhere. We were all so skinny we could have worn a stovepipe if need be." The stiff, heavy shoes were far less forgiving than wool and cotton, and sore, blistered feet became a common affliction across camp. Sergeant Holmes shuddered at the idea of wearing dead men's raiment, but he and his comrades were glad to have anything "warm enough to keep from freezing to death."[25]

Characteristically, the Japanese spoiled this magnanimous gesture by issuing a churlish new regulation. They now expected all Wake Islanders, excepting officers, to turn out for roll call garbed in the emperor's uniforms and looking as military as possible. If a POW forgot to close all the buttons on his tunic, he could expect slaps or cuffing.[26]

Those Wake Islanders able to surmount their detestation for everything Japanese discerned that Colonel Yuse's gruff exterior masked a predominantly benign disposition. Pfc. Marshall E. Fields considered the commandant "a pretty good fellow." Cpl. Bernard Richardson testified that "on one occasion, he beat a subordinate officer for maltreating a prisoner." The one legitimate complaint that could be laid at Yuse's door was an inability to be everywhere at once, which often freed underlings with frayed tempers or sadistic impulses to get away with abusing POWs.[27]

While Yuse attracted more critics than admirers, his medical officer, Captain Yoshiro Shindo, became the object of universal praise. Winford J. McAnally, one of Devereux's hard-bitten corporals, called Shindo "the only 'white man' I met among the Japanese." Dr. Kahn remembered his Japanese colleague as "a nice young man." The Contractors felt the same. John Young described Shindo as "a fine fellow" who did "all the good that he could do." And John Burton credited this "one good Japanese" with going "out of his way to be good to the prisoners, especially the sick ones."[28]

Slender, handsome, and six feet tall, Shindo towered over most of his countrymen. He came from a wealthy family, which sent him to study medicine in Germany. He had even visited the United States to attend a medical conference. Shindo's professional education and his exposure to the West help explain why he treated sick POWs compassionately, which put him at odds with the standard Japanese view of such people as useless drains on scarce resources. Called to military service, Shindo pulled strings to obtain a billet behind the lines. Since the Japanese army considered its doctors primarily infantry officers, Shindo's appointment to Woosung vastly improved his chances of surviving the war. He still had to take his turn as officer of the day once or twice a week like Yuse's other officers. On those occasions when Captain Endo had to be absent, Shindo filled in as Woosung's second in command.

A quiet, gentle man, Shindo exhibited such deep reserve that some POWs thought he feared looking them in the face. Shyness, however, did not deter him from aiding the sick. Unlike Japanese medical officers in other camps, Shindo did not pester the POWs' doctors. He left them free to perform their duties as they saw fit and attempted to furnish them with the instruments, drugs, and other supplies that they needed. "Now, he took his doctoring seriously," pointed out Second Lieutenant Hanna. "From within his limits, he did help a lot." Success did not always crown Shindo's efforts, but the POWs never doubted his good intentions. No one ever saw Shindo strike or abuse a prisoner. He even lent the North China Marines his prized set of Stephen Foster records to play on their phonograph for the entire camp's entertainment.[29]

The POWs met regularly with Dr. Shindo through his initiatives to preserve their health. Under Shindo's auspices, the Japanese administered several mass inoculations to prevent the outbreak of epidemic diseases at Woosung. Between March 29, 1942, and August 19, 1942, the entire inmate population received five different shots to ward off typhoid, cholera, and dysentery. The serum used for typhoid inoculations on March 29 and April 5 produced severe side effects. Contractor Alec Pay complained of an extremely sore throat and arm after getting stuck on the twenty-ninth. Another civilian said that the inoculation "had the bucking power of a mule. My arm from the elbow to the shoulder is still as tender as though it had been hit with a baseball bat." First Lt. Woodrow Kessler claimed that the typhoid serum brought camp life to a standstill. "Most of us suffered temperatures near 105°," Kessler wrote, "and an enormous swelling at the needle site." Other Japanese medications also packed an unpleasant wallop. After Second Lieutenant Hanna gashed his hand, for instance, he received a tetanus shot that caused the worst case of hives he ever had.[30]

Shindo also monitored the POWs' condition by weighing them all in April, May, July, and September. If their weight dipped too low, the Japanese temporarily increased the camp's rations. A physical examination also accompanied the first weigh-in. When Shindo finished checking out Cpl. Henry Durrwachter on April 18, the latter told his diary, "I've lost about 35 lbs since I left Wake, and my eye's are not so good otherwise I'm O.K." As Shindo weighed the prisoners in September, he also questioned them regarding past or present ailments.[31]

The inoculations, weigh-ins, and Shindo's numerous acts of mercy convinced 2nd Lt. Richard M. Huizenga of the North China Marines that the tall Japanese physician "did everything in his power to cooperate with our doctors in maintaining a good health record in our camp. He was a favorite of the prisoners in that respect." Huizenga concluded his observations on Shindo's conduct with this supreme compliment: "He was trying to make our camp a model camp from the health standpoint."[32]

"THE JAPANESE ARMY WISHES TO MAKE THIS A GOOD CAMP"

Additional evidence that the Japanese contemplated transforming Woosung into a model camp accrued through the month of February. They confined six more U.S. Marines there before the month ended. The handling received by these newest inmates lent credence to the notion that the enemy regarded the Shanghai War Prisoners Camp as someplace special.

When the Japanese announced the transfer of the North China Marines from Tientsin to Shanghai in late January 1942, two Leathernecks decided they did not want to go. Sgt. George B. Stone and Cpl. Donald R. Marshall grabbed some water containers and canned food and secreted themselves in the cavernous attic atop their barracks. The Japanese failed to locate the holdouts' hiding place, but Stone and Marshall had not reckoned on braving a North China winter in an unheated space. Their provisions froze rock hard, and frostbite attacked Stone's feet. The two miserable fugitives finally gave themselves away by descending from their unlit refuge to search for more food. The Japanese seemingly forgot their threat to shoot escapees. They roughed up Stone and Marshall a little but sent them to Woosung, where they arrived two or three weeks after the other legation guards. This episode breathed some extra life into the North China Marines' hope that the Boxer Protocol assured them privileged treatment.[33]

The Wake Island and North China Marines were not the first Leathernecks to reside at Shanghai. The spread of the Chinese Revolution in early 1927 induced Washington to dispatch an entire Marine regiment to Shanghai to protect American lives and business interests. Known as the 4th Marines, this outfit became a fixture in the International Settlement for nearly fifteen years. Mirroring events in North China, four years of tension with the Japanese troops that overran the Shanghai area in 1937 ultimately forced the termination of this prolonged deployment. On November 27–28, 1941, the eight hundred-man regiment boarded the SS *President Madison* and SS *President Harrison* to reinforce the garrison of the Philippines. The 4th Marines left behind its assistant quartermaster, WO Paul D. Chandler, and three other men to close out the regiment's leases, pay late bills, and dispose of other unsettled business. The Japanese took Chandler and his subordinates into custody on the first day of the war and moved them to Woosung two months later. For some inscrutable reason, Chandler's captors regarded him and his detail as diplomatic personnel attached to the American consulate. The Japanese resolved to repatriate the four Leathernecks by the earliest possible means—a courtesy not extended to their surviving comrades after the 4th Marines surrendered on Corregidor in May 1942.[34]

Five more American soldiers who had also hoped to reach the Philippines ended up at Woosung instead. After the outbreak of war turned the Philippines into a Japanese military objective, the U.S. Army placed SSgt. John C. Minnick, four other radar technicians, and some advanced aircraft detection equipment on the unarmed freighter SS *Malama*, which then tried to slip undetected to the archipelago. This desperate mission came to an end on January 1 when a bomb-laden Japanese seaplane intercepted the *Malama* in the South Pacific. The *Malama*'s crewmen scuttled the ship to deny the radar aboard to the enemy and took to their lifeboats. A Japanese raider picked up the Americans, and they were eventually transported to Shanghai. They arrived at Woosung on February 17, 1942, the same day as the crew of the SS *Vincent*. That freighter had been stopped and sunk by another Japanese commerce raider on December 12, 1941. Altogether, the *Malama* and *Vincent* contributed seventy-six additional Americans to Woosung's POW community.[35]

The Japanese produced a much bigger sensation when they lodged a genuine Allied VIP at the Shanghai War Prisoners Camp. February 21, 1942, became a noteworthy date in Woosung's short history with the arrival of Sir Mark Aitchison Young, knight commander of the Most Distinguished Order of St. Michael and St. George and governor-general of the British Crown Colony of Hong Kong. The third son of Sir William Mackworth Young, he was born in India on June 30, 1886, while his father held the post of chief secretary of the Punjab. Mark Young received an upper-class education at Eton and Cambridge University. He followed in his father's footsteps by entering the colonial service in 1909 but interrupted his career to put on a uniform during World War I. During the interwar period, he received a succession of increasingly responsible imperial postings at such stations as Sierra Leone, Palestine, Barbados, Trinidad and Tabago, and Tanganyika. He assumed control at Hong Kong scarcely two months before 20,000 Japanese troops descended on his 10,000-man garrison. Following seventeen days of resistance and the deaths of 4,500 British, Canadian, and Indian soldiers, Sir Mark surrendered to Lieutenant General Taikaishi Sakai.[36]

The British statesman who subsequently entered Woosung gave no sign of being beaten. Tall, slender, and ramrod straight, Sir Mark bore himself with a dignified self-assurance befitting his privileged background and exalted position. At the same time, he behaved with a gracious courtesy that charmed even the most egalitarian of his new American neighbors. "He was a fine gentleman," remarked Sergeant Holmes. "Was friendly to all regardless of who we were."[37]

The Japanese treated Sir Mark with a deference shown to no other prisoner at Woosung. They brought him into camp with his own orderly, Private J. Waller of the British army. Camp authorities cleared two large rooms in one barracks for Young's use. They furnished his quarters with an overstuffed easy chair, a radio, and a real bed with a spring mattress. They even hung drapes on his windows so he could bathe in privacy with water drawn by his batman.[38]

Sir Mark accepted these perquisites as his due, but he balked when the Japanese offered him better quality food and much larger portions than the rest of the camp. Young's show of integrity won him the other POWs' respect. Herb Papock jotted in his diary that the former governor "refuses special officers portions." To the twenty-four-year-old Contractor, the proud Briton was "a real man," an opinion voiced by other Wake Islanders. The news-starved Americans also appreciated the fact that Young deliberately played his radio loud enough for POWs standing outside his quarters to hear.[39]

Sir Mark attained heroic status in his fellow prisoners' eyes by chiding the Japanese any time they violated the Geneva Convention. The Americans came to regard him as the living embodiment of the British lion—unbowed by defeat and unafraid of his captors. "That was when I started to appreciate the 'Sir' on the British," commented CPNAB carpenter Jim Allen. "He was quite an Englishman," concurred Sergeant Hotchkiss.[40]

Woosung experienced its final thrill that crowded February 1942, when it hosted a visit from a Japanese dignitary. On the twenty-sixth the POWs stood inspection in their respective sections by General Shunroku Hata, the newly appointed commander-in-chief of Japan's largest ground command, the China Expeditionary Army. The general swept through the barracks too quickly to take in much. As Corporal Durrwachter aptly summed up the event in his diary, "Well the inspection yesterday was very short."[41]

After General Hata completed his whirlwind tour, Second Lieutenant M. Matsuda, an enemy officer in his mid-twenties, delivered a speech to Woosung's occupants. Matsuda proudly identified himself as a graduate of the University of Missouri School of Journalism, and he spoke a brand of English that did honor to his alma mater. Adopting a cordial tone, he began by sharing some bad news with his audience. He announced that the British had surrendered their supposedly impregnable stronghold at Singapore on February 15, and he predicted the imminent defeat of Gen. Douglas MacArthur's Filipino and American forces on Bataan and Corregidor. Having dropped these bombshells, Matsuda closed on a more comforting note, saying, "We wish that you know the news of the world. Therefore, the General presents each barracks with a radio. The Japanese Army wishes to make this a good camp and will improve your conditions. We shall issue more rice and today, we have brought an extra sweet roll which you will like. Also here are Shanghai and Tokyo newspapers and we shall send in more."[42]

In addition to these prepared remarks, Matsuda invited the POWs' senior military leaders and a few American civilians to join him for an informal conference at some tables and chairs set outside the barracks. The ostensible purpose of this gathering was to provide these prisoners with a forum to air "their opinions on Nipponese treatment and things in general." All the while, however, a photographer from General Hata's entourage snapped pictures to preserve the moment and Matsuda's earlier speech as a propaganda coup. The article that appeared with these shots in *Freedom*, the Japanese English-language magazine, purported that the POW officers urged Matsuda to "tell the public that we are all well and are receiving good treatment from the Japanese."[43]

The camera kept clicking as selected prisoners lined up to record short messages for subsequent broadcast by the enemy. "There was much preliminary discussion among us as to the pros and cons of making such recordings," conceded First Lieutenant Kessler. "We realized that the Japs were not being nice guys, but they intended to use our message for propaganda purposes." Despite such misgivings, the Wake Islanders and their comrades could not forego telling the world they were alive and well. The Japanese allowed the men to state their names and addresses, which enabled ham radio operators in the United States to pass their messages to the appropriate parties.[44] Consequently, a little more than a month later, Louise Cunningham received a letter conveying the following tidings from her husband:

> This is Commander Winfield Scott Cunningham, United States Navy, age 43 years. At Wake Island I was in command of all Navy and Marine forces. My home is Annapolis, Maryland. Since capture at Wake, the prisoners, including myself, have been fairly treated and all are in good health and are looking forward to getting back to their homes. To my wife at Annapolis, Maryland, I wish to send my best greetings and I hope for her welfare; also I wish to tell her I am in perfect health and expect to stay that way for a long time.[45]

Woosung had ceased to be a mere POW camp. Tokyo was presenting it to the world as a symbol of Japanese humanity.

"WE HAVE SETTLED DOWN TO A RATHER PLEASANT EXISTENCE HERE"

The radios mentioned by Lieutenant Matsuda arrived at Woosung by March 18, but there were only three of them instead of seven as promised. Colonel Yuse handed over the compact shortwave sets to Colonel Ashurst, Major Devereux, and Contractor Raymond Rutledge—whom the Japanese recognized as the leader of the civilians—in a little ceremony staged as another photo opportunity. The radios had been adjusted to pick up only stations in occupied Shanghai, but they still became an immediate hit. The POWs welcomed getting daily doses of American jazz and older swing tunes, classical music, and Chinese and Japanese songs. They also discovered that a Vichy French station and a Russian station broadcast news in English. The Russian announcer covered the fighting in Europe with a Soviet slant, but both stations adhered to the Japanese line in reporting the Pacific War, which left the prisoners feeling frustrated, isolated, and frequently depressed. "I do wish I could get hold of some good news that wasn't Jap inspired," Corporal Durrwachter complained on March 22.[46]

During cold weather the POWs could tune in Allied stations from Chunking. Desiring reliable news on a steady basis, Second Lieutenant Kinney of VMF-211, Second Lieutenant McBrayer of the North China Marines, Sergeant Holmes of the Wake Marines, and several Contractors improvised an adaptor and wire antennas that widened the radios' range. The improved sets picked up the BBC out of New Delhi and American news straight from San Francisco. The North China Marines also reassembled the shortwave radio they had smuggled into camp, which provided additional access to Allied news outlets. Stealth and Yankee ingenuity ensured that these POWs learned about the Doolittle Raid, the U.S. Navy's slim victory in the Coral Sea, and the U.S. 1st Marine Division's landing at Guadalcanal. To avoid detection by the guards, loose-lipped comrades, and possible collaborators, the shortwave broadcasts had to be monitored late at night with the volume turned low or otherwise muffled. Other than a small circle of trusted friends who received direct reports, information gleaned from Allied sources circulated through camp as anonymous rumors.[47]

Camp authorities also distributed three different English-language newspapers to the POWs. The *Shanghai Times* and another sheet came off local presses, and the *Japan Times and Advertiser* originated in Tokyo. The propaganda all three papers contained was so over the top that the prisoners considered the publications more amusing than illuminating. "The Japanese had a lot of trouble with the truth," sneered Pfc. Henry Chapman, who recalled reading "some of the craziest stories" during his confinement. Headlines like "500 American Planes Shot Down" and "200 U.S. Ships Sunk" failed to fool the POWs. "We knew this was a line," related Sergeant Holmes, "and laughed at the silly propaganda." Yet even these ludicrous fantasies betrayed glimpses of the truth. The Americans and Britons became practiced at reading between the lines, noting that the glorious enemy victories trumpeted by the disingenuous rags were occurring closer and closer to the Japanese homeland.[48]

The Japanese also kept their pledge to upgrade their charges' rations. The POWs began getting larger servings of rice, and they noticed a thicker mix of vegetables in their Tojo Water. In addition, bread became a regular part of the menu except for a brief interruption in late March after a flour shortage hit Shanghai. The increments were not dramatic enough to banish all hunger pangs, but they had a cumulative effect. By May 27, 1942, Corporal Durrwachter could boast, "I have gained 7 lbs since I [was] weighed last" on April 18.[49]

Camp authorities occasionally surprised the POWs with extra treats. For Easter Sunday, April 5, 1942, the Wake Islanders and their fellow prisoners received small turnovers filled with jam made from carrots. Three additional spoonfuls of carrot jam accompanied each man's dinner that evening, which gave an appetizing flavor to the ordinarily unseasoned rice. On April 15 the Japanese issued two tablespoons of sugar to every inmate. Colonel Yuse waited until Emperor Hirohito's birthday on April 29 to spoil the POWs with what Contractor Herb Papock termed the "First 1/2 very decent meal since Dec. 8th." Each American and Briton got two apples, half a pound of butter, twenty cigarettes, and even some coffee. "A very enjoyable day," exulted Alec Pay. "The best yet." "Some feed I'll say," agreed Contractor Emmett Newell. The next day, Newell admitted in his diary to suffering a "belly ache all last night" from overeating—a complaint few POWs thought would ever plague them at Woosung. Corporal Durrwachter assessed the value of these seemingly minor improvements by reminding his diary, "If you have never been in a fix like this you can't appreciate those things as we did."[50]

Along with improved nutrition, decreasing rain, and rising temperatures, Woosung's occupants began benefiting from the physical and psychological effects of organized activity. The hardier Marine NCOs were already emulating Major Devereux and Major Brown by taking brisk daily walks around the compound. On March 18 the entire camp turned out at 10:00 AM for exercise, and this soon became a daily event. One week later Colonel Yuse set his charges to clearing litter from camp with the promise of extra food for a job well done. The POWs buried all the trash they found. They also pulled the weeds sprouting around their barracks and the other camp buildings.[51]

The Japanese supplied the prisoners with tools and materials to improve Woosung's appearance and comfort. Contractor carpenters replaced missing panes in empty window frames and repaired existing sidewalks. On March 21 some CPNAB men built a handsome brick walk linking their barracks and latrine. Camp authorities took advantage of this burgeoning energy by having the POWs fill all the puddles in the compound. The Japanese next tasked their charges to clear and level a large field east of the barracks for softball and baseball diamonds, a soccer field, and a volleyball court. "It reminds me of a W.P.A. job the way it is done," Corporal Durrwachter mentioned on April 12. "In other words the leveling is done a shovel full at a time. It is all done with shovels and hoes. No one is overworking himself but it passes time faster."[52]

As spring turned into a season of near contentment, the Japanese introduced new batches of prisoners to Woosung. Twenty-five officers and seamen from the British merchant marine entered the camp on March 17. Five of those officers and fifteen sailors belonged to the SS *Ben Nevis*, which the Japanese captured on December 8 before it could deliver a load of munitions to Singapore. The other five Britons were skippers off ships crewed by Russians or Chinese. The Japanese released those seamen in Shanghai and bundled off their captains to Woosung.

These latest additions motivated Contractors Alec Pay and Herb Papock to conduct an unofficial census of the camp's population. Pay recorded the following count of 1,529 prisoners in his diary on May 10:

746   Contractors
34   Pan American Airways employees
208   North China Marines
367   Wake Marines
47   American naval officers and enlisted men
71   American merchant sailors
25   British merchant sailors
7   British consulate employees
13   Royal Navy officers and men
Governor-General Sir Mark Young and his orderly
9   U.S. Army personnel.[53]

These figures had to be readjusted on June 3 when fifty-four more prisoners joined the Woosung community. Twenty-four of the new men were Chinese boat boys from the HMS *Peterel* and USS *Wake*. Unable to shake their loyalty to the Allied cause, the Japanese finally classified them as POWs and clapped them into prison camp. Eleven other fresh faces belonged to members of Shanghai's British consulate staff. This group included six naval officers, two enlisted Royal Marines, and two noncoms from the British army's Royal Corps of Signals. The nineteen remaining new arrivals came from the SS *President Harrison*, and they had a thrilling tale to tell.[54]

The *President Harrison* had helped spirit the 4th Marines from Shanghai to the Philippines between November 28, 1941, and December 1, 1941. After debarking its passengers at Subic Bay, the *President Harrison* turned westward to pick up the North China Marines at Chinwangtao. On December 8, however, the liner steamed into a jarring rendezvous with a Japanese bomber about sixty miles northwest of Shanghai. The plane strafed the ship's bow and dropped marker bombs on the boat deck to emphasize an order to halt. A few hours later the *President Harrison*'s radio operator picked up a transmission announcing that Japan had declared war on the United States. Capt. Orel A. Pierson declared he would run his ship aground rather than wait idly for a Japanese prize crew. Pierson steered a course for the Shaweishan Island lighthouse at the mouth of the Yangtze River and tore open the *President Harrison*'s side on a rock at 2:25 PM.[55]

Japanese salvage teams succeeded in saving the *President Harrison*. The repaired liner entered enemy service as the *Kakko Maru*. The Japanese had forced Captain Pierson and his 150-odd crewmen to assist with the recovery work. On March 5 most of these Americans transferred to a detention center located in a former Chinese hospital near Shanghai's Hongkew Park. The Japanese sent Pierson to Japan in April. Two months later they removed the *President Harrison*'s mates, engineers, surgeon, purser, linen keeper, and saloonman to Woosung. The majority of the ship's crew, however, was set loose in Shanghai until they were finally interned in January 1943 and February 1943.[56]

The *President Harrison*'s purser, William Kay Kantzer Sr., welcomed this change in accommodations. Three days into his residence at Woosung, he confided to his diary, "We have settled down to a rather pleasant existence here—pleasant . . . because of the relatively better food and greater space to move around in down here." Kantzer did not fully appreciate it at the time, but the life he led at Woosung depended as much on outside assistance as on Japanese benevolence.[57]

CHAPTER NINE

"without red cross help . . . we would never have pulled through"
the impact of outside aid

"THE RED CROSS HAS BEEN VERY GENEROUS TO US"
When the Japanese army decided to create a showcase to convey the impression it treated POWs humanely, Woosung stood out as an ideal choice. The camp's proximity to Shanghai made it easier to supply than many other such facilities in Japan's newly expanded empire. Furthermore, that cosmopolitan port contained a plentitude of Westerners glad to underwrite much of the cost of burnishing the Imperial Japanese Army's image. The outbreak of war on December 8, 1941, caught some 10,000 British, American, Dutch, French, and Russian civilians in Shanghai. A large number of these people were diplomats, businessmen, and journalists. Many enemy nationals qualified for repatriation, and the emperor's generals did not want these influential people returning home to spread tales of Japanese barbarism.[1]

The presence of a fully staffed Swiss consulate general in Shanghai presented an extra incentive to afford Woosung's inmates better than average treatment. As noted earlier, Switzerland stepped forward to watch over American and British interests in Japanese-occupied East Asia. The Geneva Convention mandated that the Swiss pay special attention to the welfare of Allied POWs. "Representatives of the protecting Power . . . shall be permitted to go any place, without exception, where prisoners of war are interned," the convention reads. "They shall have access to all places occupied by prisoners and may interview them, as a general rule without witnesses, personally or through interpreters." Swiss diplomats took these provisions seriously and exhibited an abiding interest in the men confined at the Shanghai War Prisoners Camp. Consul General Emile Fontanel or a representative from his office inspected the installation three times between 1942 and 1945. Fontanel utilized firsthand observation and other sources to insert detailed descriptions of POW conditions in his regular cables and diplomatic correspondence. Swiss officials turned over this information to the American legation at Bern, which relayed it to the U.S. State Department in Washington, D.C.[2]

Intent on avoiding negative reports, Japanese officers cooperated with Fontanel and his colleagues, but they rarely did so with good grace. Three camp visits in three years fell pathetically short of the kind of access the Geneva Convention expected. The Japanese denied any Swiss diplomat admission to Woosung until camp staff could issue the prisoners extra food and spruce up their quarters and the rest of the compound. Even after the gates swung open, the Japanese did not relax their control. They reclaimed the food put on display in the barracks as soon as the outside inspectors departed. Camp authorities restricted where Swiss representatives could go inside the compound, what they saw, which prisoners they met, and what they heard. The day before each visit, Colonel Ashurst had to prepare a list of topics he wanted to discuss. Colonel Yuse or another enemy officer would censor this list, and a Japanese interpreter would attend Ashurst's interview to ensure he did not deviate from the approved script. The POWs could file no complaints or protests with Swiss inspectors, and the Japanese denied Ashurst's repeated requests to send messages to Fontanel in Shanghai.[3]

Despite the desire to impress the Swiss, the Japanese army signaled that it would run its prison camps as it saw fit regardless of what meddling Westerners thought. One such instance occurred fairly early in Woosung's existence. In June 1942 the State Department notified the Swiss that it was prepared to provide each American at Woosung with a "comfort loan" of $6.50 per month. The modest sum would allow these men to purchase much additional food and other necessities. To prevent misappropriation of these funds, the State Department required that each POW sign a personal receipt. The Japanese rejected these conditions, and the Swiss could not disburse the aid.[4]

A sharper spur for ameliorating the POWs' lot came from a nongovernment organization headquartered in Switzerland—the ICRC. The Red Cross not only acted with greater insistence than American or Swiss diplomatic apparatuses, but it also achieved more success at improving daily life inside Woosung. When Cpl. Henry Durrwachter looked back on his first seven months in that camp, he gratefully noted, "The Red Cross has been very generous to us." Second Lt. Richard Huizenga of the North China Marines summed up the importance of ICRC efforts in these words: "Without Red Cross help in the matter of food, we would have never pulled through."[5]

Immediately after Pearl Harbor, the ICRC presented itself to the Japanese government as the protector of all POWs and civilian internees held in East Asia.

The ICRC's initiative fit with the Geneva Convention, which envisioned just such a mission for the humanitarian relief agency. The Red Cross requested the right to inspect Japanese POW camps to check on compliance with the convention. The ICRC also attempted to organize the delivery of extra food, clothing, and medical supplies sent or financed by Allied Red Cross chapters to succor Japan's captives.

The story of ICRC activities in East Asia from 1941 to 1945 evolved into a saga of remarkable persistence, and even heroic martyrdom. The Japanese mistrusted all foreigners, even neutrals. They tended to suspect Red Cross agents of spying for the Allies. Aid workers and their helpers suffered frequent harassment by the Kempeitai, the Japanese secret police. The Imperial Japanese Navy executed Borneo's unofficial ICRC delegate in December 1943. Even at the best of times, Japanese officials imposed severe limitations on the transportation of Red Cross relief supplies through their lines. Only four shipments of mail, food parcels, clothing, and medical supplies from Allied countries reached East Asia between 1942 and 1944. To further curb ICRC operations, Tokyo acceded to the appointment of just three Red Cross delegates in Japanese-controlled territory. One lived in Japan's capital, the second toiled at Hong Kong, and the third was Edouard Egle, a Swiss resident of Shanghai.[6]

Tokyo approved Egle's appointment in March 1942, and he set right to work. He soon became the most successful Red Cross operative to deal with the capricious Japanese. A well-built man who stood five feet eleven and weighed 190 pounds, Egle possessed a friendly face and winning smile. His years of doing business in Shanghai equipped him with invaluable contacts and insights. He also acted with the instincts of a born diplomat. He knew when to plead, when to prod, and when to bide his time. He demonstrated a knack for identifying the needs of Woosung's inmates without implying the Japanese were neglecting their obligations. He mollified local authorities by praising them in his dispatches. Whenever he reported deficiencies at the Shanghai War Prisoners Camp, he would deflect any possible criticism of the Japanese by closing with emphatic disclaimers like this: "THIS DOES NOT REFLECT ANY LACK OF GOODWILL OF CAMP AUTHORITIES." Although the Japanese hampered Egle and his assistant Hans Jost in many small ways, they never deterred these ICRC men from their mission of mercy.[7]

Colonel Yuse at first refused Egle admittance to the Shanghai War Prisoners Camp, as well as the right to communicate with its occupants. This obstructionism arose from something more than Japanese xenophobia. Yuse seemed to have trouble accepting that anyone would have a legitimate reason to assist beings as contemptible as POWs. Egle went over the commandant's head to the liaison bureau of the Japanese army. After repeated applications Egle obtained authorization in June 1942 to institute fortnightly relief deliveries to the POWs. The Japanese also granted Egle permission to correspond with Colonel Ashurst and to visit Woosung on August 18 and November 10 of that year.

In light of Second Lieutenant Matsuda's promise of improved treatment on February 26, it appears curious that the Japanese should have thrown any obstacles in Egle's path. The obstructionism was probably a face-saving gesture rooted in reluctance to admit that the Imperial Japanese Army would or could not give the POWs everything they needed. Once Egle won access to the Shanghai War Prisoners Camp, however, the Japanese grew dependent on his help.[8]

Egle realized that outflanking Colonel Yuse signified no more than a partial victory. He now had to come up with vast quantities of relief supplies on a regular basis if he was going to make a difference to the more than 1,500 POWs. Channeling Allied funds into Shanghai proved extremely difficult, which forced Egle to rely largely on his delegation's limited resources, preexisting stocks of American Red Cross supplies, and contributions from the International Settlement. Runaway wartime inflation and a stiffening American submarine blockade made clothing, shoes, medicines, and most foodstuffs increasingly scarce and costly. Fortunately, Egle turned out to be a brilliant organizer with a fertile imagination and a nose for smelling out hidden resources. He quickly discovered that the American Red Cross had sent a large quantity of cracked wheat to Shanghai several years earlier to feed civilian refugees. For some unaccountable reason, the precious cereal never reached its intended recipients but sat locked away in local warehouses. Egle promptly appropriated the cracked wheat to augment POW rations at Woosung. Thus, the Wake Island defenders profited from initially misdirected American charity.[9]

Egle found ready allies for his POW relief campaign among the enemy nationals left at large in Shanghai. Though at war with the United States and Great Britain, the Japanese refrained from interning many of the International Settlement's American and British residents, especially businessmen. The latter's enterprises kept the city's faltering economy afloat. Occupation authorities could not afford to shut them down—at least not until they trained their own people to fill the gap. In the meantime, the well-heeled Westerners and their families demonstrated both their humanity and patriotism by aiding Allied POWs and civilian internees. Shanghai's American Association and British Residents Association each formed committees dedicated to upgrading living conditions at Woosung.[10]

The American Association published the following appeal in a local English-language newspaper on April 4, 1942: "Permission has been obtained from Japanese Military Authorities for delivery of necessities to American prisoners-of-war. Warm clothing of all types for these men such as sweaters, underwear, socks as well as candies & canned goods are desired for American prisoners & refugees from Wake Island. Donations are earnestly requested & should be delivered to The Shanghai Evening Post & Mercury . . . between the hours of 8:30 AM & 6:00 PM. Collection can be arranged for if necessary."[11]

This and similar calls fell on receptive ears. American and British civilians donated much money and personal property to POW relief. Many Shanghai residents responded to motives stronger than national allegiance. Allied consular officials and naval personnel captured in Shanghai had left close friends and even some family dwelling in the International Settlement. The sailors from the USS *Wake* and the HMS *Peterel* included several old China hands who had married local Chinese girls and female White Russian exiles. These women gave as much as their means allowed to send their husbands a few amenities. The junior leadership of the SS *President Harrison* and other imprisoned merchant mariners knew people in Shanghai who gladly helped them, too.[12]

"ALL THE CHAMPIONS EAT THIS STUFF"

By June 1942 Egle's relief network was in place and ready to go into operation. On the tenth and twenty-fifth of every month he sent a one-ton truck loaded with food and other supplies to Woosung. The contents of each shipment varied according to the season of the year and availability of goods on the Shanghai market. A typical load contained approximately 1,000 pounds of meat, 1,500 pounds of cracked wheat, 1,000 pounds of beans, 50 pounds of sugar, and 50 pounds of salt. The delivery for August 25 included 1,800 pounds of tomatoes. "They have made new culinary masterpieces out of our daily soup," commented William Kantzer, the purser of the *President Harrison*. While visiting Woosung on November 10, Egle saw the Red Cross truck pull into camp with five hundred pounds of smoked sausage, five hundred loaves of dark whole wheat bread, and a live pig weighing sixty pounds for the POWs to fatten and slaughter. "Needless to say," Egle related, "that our fortnightly delivery trucks are the high-spot in the life of the prisoners and the truck is every time eagerly awaited."[13]

Numerous POWs acknowledged the indispensable effect of Egle's activities. "I would like to express my deep gratefulness to the work which was carried out by the Red Cross in behalf of . . . all war prisoners in our camp in Shanghai," Major Devereux professed. "Through the International Red Cross we were furnished from one-fourth to one-third of all the food we consumed." Cpl. Bernard Richardson offered a no less laudatory assessment of Egle's contribution: "It is my opinion that these beans sent in by the Red Cross contributed more to bringing most of us through prison alive than any single factor." Pfc. Floyd H. Comfort was even more adamant: "If it had not been for the International Red Cross, I guess we all would have starved to death."[14]

Other voices, however, argued that Japanese pilfering diluted the benefits of Egle's deliveries. The Japanese army's desire to run Woosung as a model camp clashed with a deep-seated national belief that POWs did not deserve a soft life. The idea that defeated enemies should enjoy delicacies denied to their captors rubbed the Japanese the wrong way. Greed played a role, too, as foodstuffs commanded increasingly high prices on the black market. Colonel Yuse and some of his officers also seemed to think they had a right to share in anything the Red Cross brought into camp. "Evidence of misappropriation were apparent in the vicinity of the Japanese officers quartered at Woosung," Colonel Ashurst complained. "Boxes of Red Cross supplies were seen in Japanese officers quarters."[15]

Camp authorities went to great lengths to convince Egle that everything he trucked into Woosung went to the POWs. During Egle's visit of November 10, 1942, his hosts fed him soup they claimed came from the prisoners' midday meal. The Red Cross man found his bowl full of beef and vegetables. The Japanese assured him that each POW received two hundred grams of beef or chicken per day. They also said they served eggs to hospital patients or other inmates needing an extra jolt of protein. On another occasion, the Japanese issued oranges to the prisoners just before Egle came calling, and then repossessed the fruit after he left.[16]

Colonel Ashurst and Major Brown refrained from informing Egle about this peculation for fear of retaliation. Left alone with their captors, however, the two senior Marines kept up a running argument with Yuse and his officers to give the POWs all the aid the Red Cross sent them. Japanese pilfering tapered off with time, and Egle's relief shipments eventually reached the camp's inmates virtually intact.[17]

Yet even when the Japanese were on their best behavior, the POWs rarely felt like they were being pampered. One thousand pounds of meat divided among 1,500-odd men over two weeks did not make for large portions. Contractor Emmett Newell's diary spells out how lightly the five hundred pounds of smoked sausage delivered on November 10, 1942, registered in the Woosung diet: "Nov. 11—.... Got small piece of baloney, half loaf of black bread, 2 1/2 oz. of gum drops from R.C. Nov. 12—Got another small piece of baloney." At the same time, the introduction of Red Cross food inclined camp authorities to reduce their own contribution to their charges' rations.[18]

Regardless of the spurts of Japanese perversity and mendacity, Red Cross food shipments did cause the POWs' standard of living to inch upwards. Colonel Ashurst reckoned that Egle's contributions resulted in each inmate ingesting an average of three thousand calories per day. While the colonel appreciated any improvements, he pointed out that his subordinates still had to exist on an "unbalanced diet" that never equaled Japanese rations. Purser Kantzer corroborated Ashurst's claims. "We are hungry now, 24 hours a day," he wrote on August 7. "We got enough to live on, but that is all." The Red Cross remained sensitive to this situation, and it occasionally managed to boost the POWs' caloric intake with special treats. In late November 1942 the prisoners snacked for several days on Red Cross apples. Egle also donated 640 yen a month—$192 in U.S. currency—to the POW officers' mess, allowing Woosung's interior leadership to eat slightly better than the rank and file.[19]

One of the most noteworthy changes that the Red Cross introduced to the POWs' daily fare occurred shortly after the inauguration of Egle's relief campaign. William Kantzer noted this event in his diary on July 11, 1942, "The Red Cross has started to send in cracked wheat, the first of which we got this morning. A hundred bags or so of the cereal arrived yesterday. Cooked up with sugar into a sweet mush, it is very tasty, and so filling that we don't need the stew that accompanies it."[20]

For the next two years or so, breakfast at the Shanghai War Prisoners Camp usually consisted of a cup of cracked wheat. The cereal made an awfully bland dish whenever sugar ran out, but that was not its least-appealing quality. "It looked like grain that was for cattle or horse food," snorted 2nd Lt. Robert Hanna. No amount of boiling could conceal the fact that mold and mildew had spoiled much of the cracked wheat during its years in storage, and all of the stuff teemed with vermin. "It was half worms," shuddered Corporal Richardson, "little white worms." Other Wake Islanders remembered the cereal as a habitat for weevils and maggots.[21]

Initially, some POWs refused to eat their cracked wheat. Chronic hunger, however, almost invariably functioned as a cure for squeamishness. First Lt. Woodrow Kessler placed the acclimation process in a humorous light: "One of the jokes [in camp] was that it was very easily possible to determine how long a man had been a POW by his attitude toward the cracked wheat and weavil combination. A short timer would turn away from the disgusting sight of dead weavils sprinkled like bits of cocoanut over the cereal; a man with more time as a POW would pick out the weavils and eat the cereal; but the longtime POW would eat it all and then reach for the weavils discarded by others—weavils were protein."[22]

Major Devereux's NCOs, a practical breed, adopted the last approach Kessler mentioned. "They're born in the bran, they live in the bran, they die in the bran," Cpl. Robert E. McQuilling would coo to section mates repelled by worms and weevils. "They're bran." Corporal Richardson agreed with McQuilling but still likened a meal of cracked wheat to dining on "pieces of chopped up rubber bands."[23]

Sgt. Raymon Gragg, an ebullient soul, made light of the cracked wheat's unpalatable characteristics by constantly urging his comrades to gobble up the "Breakfast of Champions."

Another prisoner finally got fed up with Gragg's cheery spiel and challenged him. "What champions?"

"They all eat it," Gragg roared back. Then, without missing a beat, the sergeant rattled off the names of famous racehorses: "Man-of-War, Whirlaway, all the champions eat this stuff."[24]

Beneath this clowning lay a profound truth. A POW had to take nourishment wherever he found it. Sadly, Pfc. Joseph F. Commers, one of Corporal Richardson's friends, could not adjust to that reality. Imprisonment left him homesick and depressed, and that eroded his will to live. "Joe came from a . . . very congenial, close-knit family," Richardson explained, "and when Japanese food came, Joe didn't see it as . . . something that had to be eaten no matter what to keep us alive. He apparently saw his mother's dining table, with steaks or hamburger or pies or cakes. . . . He could never eat Japanese food." As Commers starved himself into frailty, he contracted tuberculosis. Colonel Yuse had Commers hospitalized in Shanghai, but the doctors there could not save him. Death finally ended the unhappy Marine's pining for home on August 20.[25]

Egle and Shanghai's Anglo-American community did not attempt to enrich the Woosung diet solely with donated food. They also encouraged the POWs to feed themselves. Around the same time that Egle assumed his duties as Red Cross delegate, Colonel Yuse permitted the prisoners to convert portions of their compound into a vegetable garden. The ground allocated for this purpose lay at the north end of camp and in strips along the south side of each barracks. FN2C Dare Kibble estimated that he and his comrades ended up placing a total of forty acres under cultivation.

What Kibble called "the great 'Farm' experiment" kicked off in late March 1942. As many as three hundred POWs armed with shovels turned out to level plots that the Japanese placed at their disposal. They also turned over the soil to a depth of twenty-four inches. Local Chinese had used Woosung and its environs as a cemetery, covering the area with burial mounds. Displaying utter disregard for native sensibilities, the Japanese had the POWs demolish the mounds and smash the half-rotten wooden caskets they contained. The Americans and Britons unearthed a lot of bones, which the guards directed them to pitch unceremoniously into garbage piles. The prisoners also discovered modest treasures that the Chinese interred with their dead, such as coins, jade, jewelry, and pottery. The Japanese demanded that all valuables be turned over to them, but inmates with agile fingers pocketed much of this loot for trading purposes. Some mounds harbored poisonous vipers, which the POWs killed on sight.

The Red Cross relief network supported the prisoners' agricultural pursuits to the best of its ability. Farm tools were scarce in Shanghai, but Egle sent Woosung whatever he could find. The POWs took up the slack by fabricating some of their own implements. These handmade tools included harrows fashioned from timber and railroad spikes that teams of sixteen to twenty men pulled with lengths of rope to prepare the ground for planting. The Red Cross shipped in the seeds that the POWs needed to start growing the additional food they craved so keenly.

Marine Gunner John Hamas, who had been Major Devereux's munitions officer on Wake, supervised the gardening detail at Woosung. A Czech national captured while fighting for Austria-Hungary during World War I, Hamas seemingly revered the seeds obtained from Egle. "You've got to love the little fellers," the grandfatherly gunner lectured his underlings, "love them to grow." Planting commenced on May 1, when the POWs put in potatoes and onions. Other crops included cucumbers, spinach, cabbage, eggplant, tomatoes, and watermelons. In July the prisoners turned to cultivating beans.[26]

Hamas' methods, combined with Woosung's rich delta soil and ample moisture, brought the POW farmers the payoff they desired. Every piece of ground they tended bloomed with something edible. "It was the most beautiful garden you'd ever seen," bragged Pvt. Edward Sturgeon, the son of an Illinois farmer. Although the Japanese withheld some of their own food stores whenever the prisoners harvested a crop, the latter still ate more than would have otherwise been the case. On November 7, for instance, Pfc. John E. Pearsall wrote something in his diary that inmates at other Japanese camps could only dream about: "Made a hot bread-tomato sandwitch for a midafternoon snack."[27]

Egle made the Americans and Britons at Woosung feel like they were running a real farm by providing them with livestock. By early June the POWs possessed their own chicken coop with incubators for hatching eggs. In addition to the chickens, the Red Cross brought in ducks, pigs, and goats. The latter supplied milk to strengthen sick inmates. After the goats arrived, the POWs formed a hay detail. Men wielded hand scythes to cut grass in the fields surrounding camp. Then they dried the grass, tied it into bales, and carried it back to feed the goats.[28]

Camp authorities encouraged POW participation in those bucolic pursuits by promising workers extra food. In reality, many of the fruits yielded by the prisoners' labor ended up in enemy stomachs. The Japanese took ten of the sixteen hogs furnished by the Red Cross for their own consumption. The same thing happened to all of the POWs' watermelons. Much of Woosung's bean crop likewise disappeared into the guards' cooking pots or the shadowy regions of the black market.[29]

"SO WE ARE VERY WELL OFF INDEED"

Deuteronomy and the Gospels of Matthew and Luke declare that man does not live by bread alone. Edouard Egle and his Anglo-American angels of mercy took that injunction to heart. Word of the Wake Islanders' destitution and Woosung's primitive facilities led the Red Cross to send the prison camp much more than food.[30]

Egle succeeded in gathering copious amounts of clothing for the POWs. Thinking perhaps of the many summer days the Americans and Britons would toil in their vegetable patches, the Red Cross man made procuring headgear an early priority. "Today we got another gift of the Red Cross—straw hats," Purser Kantzer reported on July 11, "and the whole camp is going around greeting each other in Spanish like a bunch of rancheros." Egle filled out the inmates' summer wardrobes by sending them all khaki shirts, khaki shorts, and blue cotton shirts before mid-August. As winter approached Egle scrambled to find warmer garb for the Wake Islanders and their comrades. By November 10, 1942, he had shipped 3,100 sweatshirts into camp. Egle also scrounged up corduroy and wool trousers, heavy shirts, and different types of leggings to protect the POWs from the coming cold. In every season of the year, the Red Cross truck also dropped off batches of socks, shoes, and tennis shoes.[31]

The Japanese played many of the same petty games in distributing Red Cross clothing as they did with the food Egle turned over to them. Instead of immediately releasing everything that came from Shanghai, camp authorities dribbled out certain items in small installments, as if to fool the prisoners into thinking that there was not enough to go around. On August 4, 1942, for example, each thirty-six-man section received only nine pairs of socks and eleven pairs of shorts. Every POW drew one sweatshirt on October 28, but the guards handed out just three pairs of socks to each section. On November 27 Contractor Emmett Newell noted the issuance of "10 shirts, 10 pr. legins, 8 pr. wool legens per section." The temperature dropped below freezing that night, and Newell saw the Japanese dole out "six pairs of new wool breeches and 4 pairs of shoes per section" the following day. To add to the POWs' inconvenience, the Japanese insisted that they surrender their Red Cross summer wear before they took possession of new winter garments. The opposite happened when spring 1943 rolled around, and a seasonal clothing exchange became a regular ritual at the Shanghai War Prisoners Camp.[32]

On top of the additional clothing, Egle helped Woosung's occupants improve their personal hygiene. Through the Red Cross, the POWs received toothbrushes, toothpaste, toothpowder, hand towels, bath towels, bars of hand and laundry soap, safety razors, razor blades, shaving cream, mirrors, and handkerchiefs at irregular intervals. A gift of six hair clippers facilitated the establishment of a camp barbershop. The Wake Islanders welcomed the removal of the beards and shaggy manes that caused them to resemble tramps during their first months at Woosung. A decent GI haircut made many of Devereux's men feel like Marines again. Closely cropped hair, together with clean clothes, impeded the spread of lice. Numerous Contractors went so far as to have their heads shaved.[33]

Egle devoted considerable attention to bettering the quality of health care at Woosung. He presented the POW doctors with a genuine operating table, additional instruments, and an x-ray machine. On September 30 a special truck from Shanghai rolled into camp bearing the contents of a complete dental parlor, down to a pedal-powered drill. This setup was donated by an American dentist who had been practicing in Shanghai but was scheduled for imminent repatriation. Having relatively modern equipment on hand contributed enormously to Dr. Pollard's reputation as an effective dentist. Even enemy guards went to him for treatment. In fact, camp authorities grew so proud of the prisoners' hospital that they made a point of showing it to all visitors.

Dr. Kahn soon felt well enough equipped to schedule optional surgery. On June 12, 1942, he began operating on Wake Islanders who still carried small bits of shrapnel in their bodies. He developed another specialty after some POWs, concerned about comfort and cleanliness, requested circumcisions. Kahn carried out so many of these procedures that his fellow prisoners took to calling him the "China Clipper"—a play on the name of one of Pan Am's massive seaplanes.[34]

One gift from the Red Cross actually impaired the prisoners' health. Ignorant of the risks later generations associated with smoking, Egle took every opportunity to supply the Wake Islanders and their imprisoned neighbors with additional cigarettes. His first truck to Woosung carried enough cigarettes for camp authorities to issue seventy-five packs per section on June 17. Each POW received thirty more Red Cross cigarettes on October 9. Nonsmokers welcomed these deliveries because they furnished extra currency for purchasing food and other property from comrades addicted to nicotine.[35]

Not everything the Red Cross hauled into Woosung was meant for mass distribution. Each payload also contained items for specific individuals or smaller groups within the camp's population. The privileged minorities owed their preferential treatment to having friends or family in Shanghai.

From the start of the Red Cross relief effort, the British Residents Association reserved much of its charity for Woosung's British occupants. In June 1942 these civilians started sending their fellow subjects comfort parcels every two weeks. The British prisoners got to eat 750 more calories a day thanks to these deliveries, which caused them to stop losing weight. The British Residents Association also graced those privileged POWs with razors and razor blades, board games, dozens of books, some sports gear, and a phonograph with a selection of records.

The crewmen from the HMS *Peterel* and the USS *Wake* benefited on a more modest level from care packages put together by their wives. The White Russian wife of the *Wake's* Chief Radioman William B. Ganci would send him food and thermos bottles filled with beverages unavailable in camp. The spouses of the other gunboat sailors did likewise. "Oh, them guys used to get parcels every week," blurted SSgt. Clifford Hotchkiss with pardonable exaggeration. "We envied that naturally."[36]

The mates and other POWs from the *President Harrison* also enjoyed a steady stream of private aid courtesy of their Shanghai friends and loyal shipmates not yet confined in a civilian internment camp. Purser Kantzer detailed the contents of the shipment that reached Woosung on November 10, 1942: "I am now luxuriating in tobacco, having two more cartons of cig[arette]s, 25 cigars and a half pound of pipe tobacco. Besides that there was jam, chewing gum, honey, cocoa and glycine. So we are very well off indeed." Other trucks brought Kantzer and his shipmates canned jam, soup, candy, towels, and matches to light their tobacco.[37]

Sometime in June 1942 Mrs. Beatrice Coyle Widdup, an American socialite in Shanghai, learned that the Wake Islanders—the neediest prisoners in camp—were not sharing in this bounty. She secured the names of Major Devereux and thirteen other American officers. Then she rounded up a corresponding number of well-off American women to join in brightening those prisoners' existence.

Acting in concert with the Red Cross, Widdup requested permission to write her countrymen and send them aid. Japanese authorities must have been in a contrary mood when they heard from her, because they shot back that only relatives could have such contact with the POWs. Widdup met this lie with one of her own. She claimed that the fourteen officers were her nephews, and, as she later told the story, "the silly Japs let me write them all without question!" With this inspired bit of legerdemain, the determined matron assumed the identity of "Auntie Bee."

Auntie Bee and her associates made the most of the opening. They stuffed their comfort parcels with jam, sugar, tea, coffee, cocoa mix, canned milk, canned meats, canned sardines, vitamin tablets, and chocolate bars. Widdup adopted Major Devereux as her personal favorite and outfitted him with woolen underwear, brown corduroy trousers, a brown sweater, and flannel pajamas. When the Wake officers asked for something to warm their heads and hands in chilly weather, Widdup's group obliged with fourteen wool berets and fourteen pairs of knitted gloves. Some officers responded with thank-you notes that said they proudly wore those gifts to identify themselves as "Auntie Bee's Boys." While the officers' expressions of gratitude did them credit, flouting their good fortune did not go down well with the vast majority of Wake Islanders—men who lacked personal benefactors of their own.[38]

"THE WHOLE CAMP CAME OUT TO WATCH THE GAMES"

Food, clothing, and medical care are all essential to a person's welfare, but prisoners also require recreation and entertainment to sustain their physical and mental health. Edouard Egle and his Anglo-American allies recognized this need. The Red Cross relief system came up with multiple ways for the POWs to use their spare time constructively and prevent boredom from crushing their spirits. The Wake Islanders and Woosung's other inmates eagerly exploited the facilities and supplies given them. Some prisoners also exhibited a flair for devising their own diversions—both licit and illicit.

Aware of the inclinations of an all-male community, the POWs' benefactors flooded Woosung with large quantities of sports equipment. The first gift of this type consisted of some volleyballs donated by the International Settlement's small Dutch population. Many prisoners were so excited that they ventured out into the lingering cold, wet, and mud of late March 1942 to play with their new toys. Volleyball persisted as a common time killer through April and May, but it soon took second place to America's favorite pastime.[39]

The American Association scoured Shanghai to outfit the POWs with everything necessary to establish fully functioning softball and baseball leagues. By

September 18, 1943, the Shanghai War Prisoners Camp possessed 198 softballs, 80 baseballs, 35 softball bats, 35 baseball bats, 32 fielder's gloves, 9 first baseman's mitts, 7 catcher's masks, 4 chest protectors, 4 pairs of shin guards, 10 base bags, 2 rubber home plates, 1 pitcher's rubber, and enough baseball jerseys, shirts, pants, stockings, and cleated shoes to completely garb more than three teams. So much gear for softball, baseball, and other sports flowed into Woosung that Colonel Yuse permitted CPNAB carpenters to convert the north end of a big building on the west side of camp into a recreation hall. No mere storage space, that facility also housed two ping-pong tables supplied by the Red Cross, which afforded the POWs an outlet for their pent-up energy during inclement weather. "It will be pretty nice when our carpenters finish building it," Purser Kantzer said of the recreation hall on August 16, 1942. Two days later, Egle noted, "ARRANGEMENTS FOR INDOOR . . . SPORTS [were] EXCEPTIONALLY WELL ARRANGED."[40]

Whenever the sun shone, however, Woosung's denizens flocked to the ball diamonds. The POWs preferred softball to hardball, but not because they considered the former less challenging. They played a fierce brand of fast-pitch softball at Woosung. One captured merchant sailor happened to be one of the world's premier softball pitchers, and he set a high standard of play. Each barracks formed two teams, and Colonel Ashurst appointed a Marine recreation officer to organize leagues and schedule games. Intense rivalries arose between various teams and different groups of prisoners. "We w[ould] bet on that," reminisced Contractor Tex Akin. "I once laid 10:1 that we w[oul]d beat another team. I had 13 [cigarettes] bet, it cost me 130 to pay off." Still nursing old grudges, the Wake Island Marines vied to beat their North China brothers in every contest. The servicemen presented a united front, however, whenever one of their teams faced off against a civilian club. For years afterward surviving Contractors bragged that they won more of these games, while the Marines maintained exactly the opposite.[41]

The Japanese loved baseball, and Woosung contained no bigger fan than Colonel Yuse. He encouraged POW play, and he and his guards took in every game they could. In this way, softball became a bonding experience not only for the prisoners, but for the entire Woosung community. "The whole camp came out to watch the games in the evening along with all the Japanese," recalled Capt. Bryghte Godbold, one of Ashurst's earlier recreation officers, "and there was a great deal of enthusiasm for it and betting and a lot of animation about it, and it took the minds of the prisoners off their own plight. . . . And this went on every night during the spring, the summer, and the fall."[42]

Woosung received some basketballs, but most POWs found that sport too strenuous even on a Red Cross-supplemented diet. Curiously, a shipment of boxing gloves ignited a mania for that brutal martial art. According to Emmett Newell's diary, the camp witnessed boxing matches every night in mid-August. Some barracks fielded soccer teams, but that European craze never matched softball's popularity. In the autumn American prisoners turned to their country's version of football, although they wisely opted for touch rather than tackle. Football season opened at Woosung on October 10, 1942, but it did not last long. Two civilian barracks, 3 and 5, battled for the camp championship on November 15, and Barracks 3 prevailed. An entry one week later in Pfc. John E. Pearsall's diary chronicled football's last hurrah for 1942 but also revealed that baseball stayed in season as long as the weather permitted outdoor activities. "Watched football game between allstars," Pearsall wrote. "Played some baseball awhile."[43]

For those moments when the prisoners did not feel like team sports or individual exercise, the Red Cross enabled them to enjoy a range of sedentary activities. Egle's most conspicuous achievement in this respect was to bestow the Shanghai War Prisoners Camp with the finest library owned by any such installation run by the Japanese. The library got its start with the three hundred volumes that the British Residents Association had donated by July 10, 1942. That total soon soared to three thousand, as additional enemy nationals responded to relief drives by thinning their bookshelves and magazine racks. The collection ultimately encompassed close to six thousand titles. The POWs housed their library in the same building as the recreation hall, and Contractor Howard Cook took charge as librarian. The son of a wealthy businessman, Cook had received an impressive education before the family fortune ran out in the 1930s and he had to go to work for a living. He made an ideal librarian, conscientiously cataloging each book and guiding his fellow prisoners to titles he knew would interest them.

The camp library offered a wide enough selection to suit almost any taste. Prisoners with an intellectual bent reveled in the works of H. G. Wells, the *Treatises* of David Hume, and Sir Edward Creasy's *Fifteen Decisive Battles of the World*. They could also sample textbooks like *Modern Business and Government*. Fiction outnumbered nonfiction on Cook's shelves many times over. That larger section of the library ran the gamut from established classics by Charles Dickens to works by more contemporary masters, such as John Galsworthy, Thomas Wolfe, Sinclair Lewis, Pearl S. Buck, and James T. Farrell. POWs unconcerned with literary pretension could read Erle Stanley Gardner's Perry Mason series or curl up with an action-packed Western by Zane Grey. The library also held two complete years of *Fortune* magazine from the previous decade and many issues of *Reader's Digest*.[44]

Preoccupied as ever with saving face, camp authorities ordered all incoming books and magazines censored to prevent the prisoners from reading anything critical about Japan and its war effort. The sheer volume of the reading materials dropped off by the Red Cross overwhelmed Woosung's few interpreters, however, and their uneven performance caused the POWs more mirth than irritation. Purser Kantzer thumbed through "Readers' Digests that had articles torn out, but others just as anti-jap and anti-axis left in." The interpreters committed one of their biggest blunders by releasing John Strachey's prophetic 1933 tome *The Menace of Fascism* for circulation. A wry Emmett Newell took note of other titles the Japanese should have withheld: "There is two pamphlets in the library on treatment prisoners should recieve. Sure don't sound like us."[45]

Reading became a major source of comfort to Woosung's residents. "The library made the most valuable recreation feature of the camp," declared Capt. John White of the North China Marines. There was nothing like a good book to make a POW forget his current surroundings and transport him to worlds far more pleasing. "There was hardly a day went by that I didn't read, read, read," quipped Corporal Richardson, an aspiring novelist. Richardson was not the library's only frequent patron. "The library was so popular," Second Lieutenant Kinney related, "that the men literally read the covers off many of the books, and prison officials had to send them into Shanghai for rebinding."[46]

The library's creation supported a form of mental nourishment that the POWs had already instituted themselves. Shortly after the Wake Islanders entered Woosung, Major Devereux established a school to give his men something constructive to do with their time. First Lieutenant Kessler instantly discerned the major's motive: "It was a good effort to give the group a sense of belonging." Devereux directed his officers and other better-educated prisoners to prepare courses in any subject they felt qualified to teach. A Contractor from Peru offered a course in Spanish, and another who had attended the American University in Damascus taught French. Other foreign languages on the curriculum included German, Russian, and Japanese. A merchant marine captain lectured on general navigation, and Second Lieutenant Kinney of VMF-211 taught celestial navigation. The agriculturally minded Gunner Hamas presided over a course on beekeeping. POWs could also enroll to study history, mathematics, and astronomy.[47]

Aided by the camp library and school materials provided by the Red Cross, Devereux's barbed wire academy grew increasingly rigorous. "I started taking German lessons several days ago," Corporal Durrwachter revealed on May 27,

1942, "But they are going into it pretty deep and I guess I'll end up dropping it all together." Attendance in French class dwindled for the same reason until only two students remained—Major Devereux and Corporal Richardson. On November 17 Private First Class Pearsall complained, "The math is getting stif." He cut Spanish class over the next few days, but he stuck with math and history, even though the latter required students to submit term papers for grades.[48]

Camp authorities unintentionally placed a damper on POW education by ordering all inmates to study Japanese. That directive made good sense for all concerned, as it would improve communications between the prisoners and their keepers. The plan backfired, however, because the Wake Islanders and their comrades bridled at the enemy telling them what to do with their free time. Those POWs who had opted to study Japanese earlier now turned their attention elsewhere. Most of the others refused to participate in the program for fear of being branded "Jap lovers." A few practical Leathernecks continued to study the enemy's language surreptitiously because of the obvious advantages. Cpl. Franklin Gross plugged away solitarily with an English–Japanese dictionary. Second Lieutenant Kinney and his North China pal, Second Lieutenant McBrayer, realized that knowledge of Japanese could assist them in gathering intelligence for an escape attempt. They privately quizzed each other with flash cards made from the cardboard cut from Japanese cigarette packs.[49]

In addition to education, Woosung's occupants channeled considerable energy into staging musical entertainments. Colonel Yuse opened the door to that possibility by bringing a thirty-piece Japanese army band into camp on February 21, 1942, to mark George Washington's birthday. The evening's program featured both Japanese tunes and American semiclassics. When the enemy musicians ceased playing, the grateful POWs gave them a standing ovation. Yuse arranged for a second concert on April 21, which elicited an identical response. "Band concert," Contractor Pay rejoiced in his diary. "Several popular American numbers played to great enjoyment of all men."[50]

As the POWs' strength and spirits rose, they took to making their own music. The Chamorros that Pan American had employed on Wake already possessed a reputation as a cheerful and musical bunch. They got their hands on a few guitars and regularly treated their comrades to Pacific island music. "One of the Guamanians from Wake Island visited us last night with his guitar," Purser Kantzer recorded on June 15, "and gave us a concert of spanish songs that were pretty good." Dr. Pollard, the camp dentist, organized a British–American glee club that started presenting a cappella recitals as early as April 29, 1942. A series of amateur shows allowed more prisoners to put their talents on display. The quality of these productions picked up markedly after Woosung received a Red Cross shipment of musical instruments on August 10. At first, POW performers toured from barracks to barracks, but they found a suitable home in the recreation hall by mid-November.[51]

American POWs cherished tunes that reminded them of home, but they also developed a particular fondness for ditties taught them by their British allies. The charm of these numbers lay in their novelty and eccentric humor.[52] After hearing a parody of the British wartime standard "Bless 'Em All," Pfc. John Himelrick recorded its ribald chorus in his diary:

> Cheer up my lads Bless 'em all,
> The long & the short & the tall.
> Bless all the Sgts. & W.O.'s one.
> Bless all the Cpls. & their Bloomin Sons
> So we'll say goodbye to them all
> As up the C.O.'s as[s]hole they crawl
> They'll get no promotions
> This side of the Ocean
> So cheer up my lads Fuckemall.[53]

Prisoners desiring quieter amusements could avail themselves of board games that had once graced the parlors in Shanghai's finest British and American homes. Chess attracted a wide circle of devotees at Woosung. Many POWs relaxed over checkers, dominoes, or an American variation on backgammon known as acey-deucey. At the same time, bridge emerged as an indoor pastime with enduring popularity. Once the strongest chess and bridge players became known, they entertained their fellow prisoners by competing in organized tournaments.[54]

The existence of donated or homemade playing cards fanned the spread of gambling. Pfc. Robert Shores testified that there "was tremendous gambling in camp on everything." Both servicemen and civilians ran poker and blackjack games, and some acquired the adeptness of professional croupiers. "I ran a poker game for a year or two," reminisced Don Ludington, a CPNAB sheet metal foreman, "and I learned how to play poker. I learned how to win."[55]

In most games of chance, cigarettes served as the coin of the realm. "You could buy anything with cigarettes," Ludington emphasized. Contractor Tex Akin, one of the camp's top cardsharps, defined the dollar value of this form of currency this way: "Chinese cigarettes $1.00 each. American cigarettes $3.00 each or a pack of 20 were $60.00." Some POWs grew so dependent on the thrill of gambling that they played for food. Big losers had to accept deductions from their rations for weeks at a time. Fearful that gambling addicts might damage their health, POW officers forbade food wagers, but they could not completely stamp out the practice.[56]

The Japanese tolerated bridge, but they banned gambling as a decadent Western vice. The POWs devised several subterfuges to defy this order. In addition to rigging blankets to screen playing spaces, they would post lookouts to watch for roving guards. Whenever a Japanese soldier approached, the lookout would shout a prearranged signal such as "Shake your blankets" or "Air bedding." The gamblers would then hide their cards, betting chips, and cigarettes and assume an air of feigned innocence.[57]

While practitioners might object to categorizing religion as entertainment, it served a similar purpose at Woosung by taking many POWs' thoughts off their troubles. No official U.S. Navy chaplain accompanied either the Wake Island defenders or North China Marines into captivity, but several individuals took it upon themselves to bring spiritual solace to their comrades. Forrest L. Packard, a CPNAB carpenter from Idaho, would gather his fellow Mormons in the evening to study holy scripture. There was no copy of the Book of Mormon available at Woosung, so Packard's group relied on the Bible. "Our communion with the Lord helped very much," commented Contractor John Burton, a member of Packard's flock. "What would a person do at times like these, if he couldn't turn to the Lord?"[58]

Other self-appointed lay chaplains ministered to members of mainstream Christian sects. "We got together and prayed and talked about Jesus and sang hymes in POW camps," recalled Pfc. Sylvester Gregouire, a staunch Baptist from Louisiana. Gregouire's Marine buddies had called him "Preacher" since boot camp because of his penchant for witnessing "for God, Christ Jesus and the Holy Ghost." As a prisoner, he frequently quoted memorized Bible verses to comfort his comrades. Major Devereux, a devout Catholic, had concealed his rosary when he surrendered on Wake, and he used it to lead his coreligionists in prayer on a regular basis. When Devereux's attention to his men's spiritual needs became known after the war, readers of the *Queen's Work*, a national Catholic magazine, named him Catholic of the Month for December 1945.[59]

On July 12, 1942, Colonel Yuse permitted a Protestant clergyman from Shanghai to hold services for the prisoners inside Woosung. Although the minister was Japanese and he obsequiously thanked camp authorities for the privilege of being there, some three hundred POWs turned out to hear him preach. Purser William Kantzer dismissed the sermon as "non-partisan, non-sectarian, non-controversial, non-interesting and non-inspirational." The Japanese minister subsequently returned to Woosung every month. Camp authorities also brought in some Buddhist priests to perform a religious ceremony in the recreation hall on November 16.[60]

In between sporting events, school, shows, games, and religious observances, the POWs filled their idle hours with conversation. In peacetime the leading topic had been real or imagined encounters with the opposite sex, but the scanty Woosung diet inclined the Wake Islanders and their comrades toward a new obsession. Corporal Durrwachter documented that shift on March 30, 1942, when he wrote in his diary, "Food is about the only topic of conversation we have left." This confirmed what Durrwachter had told his diary a month earlier: "From now on practically all the space will be taken up on the subject of food." In response to a question regarding what food meant to the POWs, Pfc. Marshall Fields confessed, "It was on your mind, and it was in your dreams." Fields spent more than three years behind barbed wire dreaming about donuts. One Contractor continually fantasized about pitching into a tall stack of pancakes drenched with maple syrup and ringed by spicy sausages. As Fred Rumpel, an Idaho carpenter, explained, the POWs yearned most for what they got least: "Our diet was practically free of fat and I got to craving fat."[61]

Nothing pleased most Wake Islanders more than gathering in small groups to talk about food. Pfc. Henry Chapman referred to these bull sessions as "mental masturbation." The POWs would talk about their favorite restaurants, the tastiest meals or desserts they ever ate, and what they planned to devour once they got home. More than anything else, they enjoyed swapping all sorts of recipes—anything from mom's apple pie to something a man made up on the spot. "I had recipes for cakes and pies and everything [else] that I never intended to cook," affirmed Contractor John Hoskins, "but it was the #1 conversation piece." Prisoners who kept secret diaries devoted page after page to preserving these recipes, while others compiled separate recipe notebooks.[62]

Extra food and other outside assistance could not take all the pain out of being a POW. Even after the Red Cross relief effort kicked into high gear, the very fact of confinement gnawed at each POW's soul. "Life in prison camp is certainly *miserable*," Private First Class Pearsall declared on November 16. Next to food, nothing figured more prominently in the Wake Islanders' conversation than speculation about when the war would end and they could go free. Nevertheless, Edouard Egle's ceaseless industry and ingenuity made life behind barbed wire a little more bearable, and that sufficed to keep the majority of Woosung's occupants willing participants in the fight for survival.[63]

CHAPTER TEN

"i thought they handled themselves reasonably well"
japanese–POW relations at woosung

"A BUNCH OF GUYS DOING THEIR DUTY"
Regardless of Edouard Egle's persistence, his control over Red Cross relief efforts ceased as soon as Woosung's gates closed behind his fortnightly delivery truck. From that moment, how much aid the POWs received—or whether they received any at all—was up to their Japanese overlords. The battle for survival that the Wake Islanders and their comrades waged at the Shanghai War Prisoners Camp depended on more than individual hope, group discipline, and outside aid. No factor weighed more heavily on the outcome than the relationship the prisoners maintained with Colonel Yuse, his officers, and the camp's guards. Subject to a jarring mix of personalities, clashes in cultural values, and unexpected events, Japanese–POW relations did not always go smoothly. They experienced repeated ups and downs that brought the prisoners unnecessary stress, pain, and even death. Nevertheless, most of Woosung's Japanese personnel exercised sufficient self-restraint to prevent their camp from deteriorating into one of the numerous hellholes where the Imperial Japanese Army confined other Allied prisoners.

The Wake Islanders never arrived at a complete consensus regarding their keepers, but they agreed on certain points. The guards the Japanese army posted at the Shanghai War Prisoners Camp were second-class troops, their ranks riddled with many conscripts from Formosa (now Taiwan) and a lesser number of Koreans. A large percentage of these unwilling keepers adopted a laid-back approach to soldiering, while others strove to be as tough and strict as the most Bushido-driven Japanese. Yet with rare exceptions, the guards at Woosung behaved less viciously than those on the *Nitta Maru*.[1]

In the eyes of many Wake Islanders, however, the difference between Colonel Yuse's soldiers and Lieutenant Saito's club-wielding sailors was merely a matter of degrees. "As a whole," claimed Pvt. Earl Broyles, "most of the Japanese guards were mean." Pfc. Floyd Comfort concurred. "At Woo Sung . . . prisoners were frequently beaten by guards or other Jap personnel," he testified. "There did not have to be a reason." Some enlisted Japanese made a game out of humiliating their charges. They liked to flick half-smoked cigarettes at the feet of passing POWs to see who would debase themselves by picking up the butts for a few puffs of tobacco.[2]

A significant segment of Woosung's population, however, remembered the guards in a more positive light. Cpl. Bernard Richardson described his jailers as "friendly and kind." As proof he stated, "They offered us lots of cigarettes and conversation." Contractor John Young felt much like Richardson. "Most of the guard[s] were quite civil toward us," he insisted. Sgt. Jack Cook judged Japanese camp personnel as extraordinarily enlightened. Compared to the guards Pfc. Mackie Wheeler later met in Japan, he decided the ones he knew at Shanghai were relatively lenient.[3]

As far as the majority of Wake Islanders were concerned, however, their keepers swung between extremes of decency and cruelty with unsettling frequency. "The Japanese were so unpredictable you'd have no idea what the hell they were going to do next," complained Pfc. Dennis Conner. Japanese inscrutability so baffled Contractor William Gooding that he exclaimed, "They're funny people them Japs. They're not human as far as I'm concerned." Even Corporal Richardson had to concede, "Some of them were unpredictable. They might be reasonable on one encounter and seem like maniacs in the next encounter."[4]

Over time the more perceptive and mature Wake Islanders figured out that their guards were not irrational fiends. "Their main interest in life was getting out of that war and getting back home and having a family and a garden," reminisced Pvt. Joe Reeves. "So they had the same interests and hopes . . . that we had." More often than not, enemy soldiers had a rational reason when they lashed out at the POWs. "If you got out of line and you didn't do what you were told," Pfc. James Venable explained, "why, they would put you back in, and they were pretty quick to hit you. But just as a matter of course, . . . the guards were pretty much a bunch of guys doing their duty." Capt. Bryghte Godbold shared Venable's perspective on guard–prisoner relations, and he came up with this objective assessment of Japanese conduct: "I think they were sometimes brutal, sometimes stupid, sometimes kindly, sometimes thoughtful. Mostly they were indifferent in that they did their job, and I thought they handled themselves reasonably well."[5]

Smart POWs could avoid punishment by adopting a low profile and steering clear of trouble. Many of the Wake Island Marines who experienced the most friction with the Japanese had been disciplinary problems before the war, creating numerous headaches for their American superiors. Private Broyles prided himself on being one of the top thieves at the Shanghai War Prisoners Camp. He chronically stole bread, brown sugar, and rice from the enemy's food stores, and he paid a price for his daring. "I was caught six or seven times," Broyles admitted, "and beaten severely." According to Jack Hoskins, a CPNAB chainman from Okanogan, Washington, the civilian barracks housed rule breakers as reckless as Broyles: "We had several—what you might call knot heads—people who couldn't take orders, couldn't keep their noses clean, . . . and were inclined to steal whenever they could."[6]

Wisdom dictates that unarmed prisoners refrain from antagonizing their guards. At Woosung, however, wisdom did not always guide POW conduct. There was a war on, after all, and the Japanese were the enemy. Furthermore, the POWs regarded every minute spent behind barbed wire as time torn from their lives, and that kindled bitter resentment against their keepers. "I fought through . . . World War One," Contractor Robert J. Hardy later informed Major Devereux, "but feel that . . . nothing could be as tough as those long years we spent in those prison camps." It became a point of honor among the Wake Islanders to keep from looking too chummy with the Japanese. Even the best-behaved POWs could not always withstand the temptation to get away with petty gestures of defiance. "They were not disorderly," attested Corporal Tushihiko Yazawa, a member of Colonel Yuse's guard detail, "but they violated to a large extent the rules of the prisoners of war camp."[7]

Those Wake Islanders inclined to make their keepers look foolish tried exploiting the latter's unfamiliarity with English and aspects of American culture. One Wake defender numbered thirty-one (*san-jyuu-ichi*) in his section would deliberately mispronounce his number at morning and evening roll call. "Sons of bitchie," the man would shout at the uncomprehending Japanese, and sometimes, "Suck a peachy." Whenever the POWs determined a guard knew no English, they played similar games with him. A smiling prisoner would approach that soldier and proceed in a calm, conversational tone to call him every foul term in the dictionary. That stunt could backfire if the object of abuse turned out to be better educated than the prisoners realized. "We had a sentry, . . . we was always calling 'Crash Dive,'" related Pfc. Marshall Fields. "He was one of these tough guys. . . . We started making fun of him, and he said, 'You don't think I know what you mean!' And he started working a few of us over."[8]

The most celebrated escapade of this type involved Kazunori Morisako, an interpreter who reported to Woosung in April 1942. Morisako was an unusually short and thin Japanese. Corporal Richardson characterized him as a "kindly, innocuous little fellow." Although Morisako understood English well enough, he often confused his grammar and word order when speaking, which amused the POWs. The Wake Islanders and other Americans derived additional laughs from Morisako's looks. The interpreter's status as a civilian did not prevent him from wearing an officer's uniform, but it fit poorly. The jacket hung loose from his slight frame and the sleeves nearly covered his hands. Morisako's boots reached above his knees, forcing him to walk with an ungainly shuffle. His head was too large for his body, and he had a protruding jaw set off by an enormous set of buckteeth.

The Americans took one look at Morisakso and decided that he bore an uncanny resemblance to Mortimer Snerd, the moronic dummy made famous by ventriloquist Edgar Bergen. The POWs soon began calling the interpreter Mortimer to his face, which he accepted without complaint. As no one let him in on the joke, however, the practice left him increasingly puzzled.

At length, Morisako's curiosity grew too acute to contain. He cornered a prisoner he had befriended and asked, "My name is Mr. Morisako. For why do you call me Mortimer?"

The man thought for a moment and then said, "Well, Mortimer's a famous American movie star."

At those words, Morisako's face lit up with pride. "You mean," he chirped delightedly, "like Clarks Gables?"

"Yeah," the relieved Yank nodded, "sort of."

From that moment Morisako became the friendliest Japanese at Woosung. Any POW who greeted him with "Hello, Mortimer," could expect a gift of extra cigarettes and a warm salutation in fractured English: "Today I say it is a fine day hello—I presento tobacco."

This farcical scenario lasted for two or more weeks. Then one day, Morisako entered the prisoners' compound, his countenance darkened by a frown instead of the customary smile. When a POW exclaimed, "Hi, Mortimer," the interpreter slashed him across the face with a leather riding crop. Morisako stalked through camp until he found the fellow who had lied about Mortimer Snerd. As he whipped the surprised American about the head and shoulders, the humiliated interpreter screeched, "Many days I go downtown Shanghai! I look in many movie books! Mortimer is the fencepost man! Never forever do I present tobacco again!"

Word soon flashed around Woosung: "Beware of Mortimer. He knows who Mortimer Snerd is." While Allied inmates took care to address the interpreter properly from that point forward, they would retell the story of Mortimer Snerd amongst themselves to give their spirits a lift. "We sure got a bang out of that," chortled Contractor Fred Rumpel.[9]

Morisako's injured feelings healed fairly quickly, however, and he reverted to his basically amiable nature. Other Japanese personnel at Woosung also grew comfortable enough with the POWs to show a softer side. Certain guards liked to joke and banter with the prisoners when no Japanese officers or stricter NCOs were present. Those who knew English enjoyed demonstrating their varying levels of proficiency. One guard surprised a group of Contractors by saying, "Let me show you how I can sing 'My Blue Heaven.'" He smiled broadly after he got through the song without one mistake. The same soldier serenaded the prisoners with the 1933 country ballad "When It's Lamp Lighting Time in the Valley." A shorter-than-normal guard once handed his rifle to some Wake Islanders so he could use both hands to pull himself onto the back of a truck waiting to carry him and the POWs to a work detail. On another occasion, an exceptionally tall Japanese got drunk just before going on nighttime guard duty. Realizing he was in no condition to stand guard, the soldier staggered into a darkened barracks and awoke a prisoner approximately his size. He asked the surprised Yank to take his rifle, bayonet, and gear and walk his beat. The POW declined, and his befuddled visitor left.[10]

Pfc. Carl Stegmaier volunteered to assist at the camp hospital, where he worked in the pharmacy alongside two of Dr. Shindo's enlisted medics. This pair, named Tanaka and Osaka, shared Shindo's compassionate streak, and they took a liking to the studious, hard-working Stegmaier. Whenever one of the medics received a furlough, he would ask the young Marine, "Hey, I'm going into Shanghai tonight, what would you like to have?" They regularly brought him sugar-coated roasted soybeans. They also gave Stegmaier another welcome treat—handfuls of sun-dried squid, which came from care packages sent by their parents in Japan.[11]

Such gestures defused much of the tension inherent in life behind barbed wire, but the POWs learned to never take Japanese cordiality for granted. One evening a senior enemy NCO entered Pfc. Henry Chapman's barracks and regaled some Wake Marines and sailors with tales of his prewar visit to San Francisco. The following day this same sergeant headed the detail that conducted morning roll call. Somewhere in Chapman's barracks, a prisoner committed an error in counting off. The sergeant exploded and hit the American in the face with a wooden clipboard so hard that it broke in half.[12]

One Japanese–American buddy story culminated in unintended tragedy. On the evening of June 18, 1942, a CPNAB tractor operator named Lonnie B. Riddle spotted a guard he had befriended on patrol beyond the electrified fence near the POWs' benjos. The twenty-seven-year-old Californian raised his arms as if gripping a rifle and barked, "Bang, bang, bang." The guard grinned, pointed his own weapon at the playful prisoner, and repeated Riddle's words. At the last "bang," the rifle went off. The bullet tore through Riddle's throat, and he died in seconds. Because Riddle had helped install Woosung's electrical system, many Wake Islanders concluded that he had been deliberately killed to prevent him from sharing his knowledge with other prisoners. Camp authorities ruled the shooting an accident. A board of POW officers investigated the incident and arrived at the harsher finding of "criminal negligence in the handling of a firearm." Major Brown filed a protest and demanded the guard be punished, but Colonel Yuse offered no more satisfaction than an apology.[13]

"WE'VE GOT TO HAVE MORE RESPECT FROM THESE AMERICANS"

Friendly or not, the troops and interpreters that the Japanese army stationed at Woosung approached their jobs with certain expectations—and woe to any inmate who flouted them. First and foremost, the Japanese required POWs to be submissive and obedient. Colonel Yuse insisted that all prisoners bow to every Japanese they encountered, and that even applied to the American and British officers. Failure to comply, Yuse warned, meant a beating. The colonel's mandate clearly exceeded the Geneva Convention, which required that enlisted POWs salute enemy officers and that captive officers extend the courtesy solely to foes of superior rank. The Wake Marines tried to avoid bowing to camp personnel by pretending they did not see them, and they sometimes got away with it. The guards would grow lax at enforcing the bowing rule, but that could change at any time. "This was a cyclical sort of thing," explained Captain Godbold. "There would be . . . an upsurge in 'Well, we've got to have more respect from these Americans,' and so they would come around and harangue us about the need for respecting the Emperor's soldiers."[14]

When it came to obedience, the Japanese exhibited an attitude that could swiftly escalate from impatient to petulant. Programmed to respond instantly to any command, Woosung's guards assumed that their prisoners should behave in the same fashion. They did not care that many Americans and Britons knew little or no Japanese. POWs who resisted studying Japanese paid for their stubbornness throughout their stay at the Shanghai War Prisoners Camp.

Pvt. Richard P. Adams received a graphic lesson in the perils of the language gap one day in October 1942. While Adams watched, eight or ten Americans entered camp pushing a cart loaded with firewood for the galley. A short-tempered Japanese sergeant named Araki—or "Rocky," as the POWs called him—accompanied this detail. As the cart rumbled across the compound, a knotty piece of wood about two feet long and two and a half inches in diameter fell off and hit the ground unnoticed by the straining Yanks. Sergeant Rocky shouted for someone to pick up the dropped fuel, but the POWs did not catch his meaning and continued to push the cart. He rapped out the order again and received the same lack of response. At that, Rocky picked up the wood with one hand like a cudgel, overtook the cart, and walloped a Contractor called "Tex" on the side of the head. "The American staggered," recounted Adams, "and was obliged to hold on to the cart to keep from falling. The Jap then threw the piece of wood on the cart and walked away."[15]

Because the Japanese considered captivity shameful, they thought Woosung's occupants should be quiet and repentant. The Wake Islanders were certainly glum enough when they first hit camp, but warmer temperatures, along with the many improvements introduced by the enemy and the Red Cross, brightened their outlook. They and their comrades soon set the barracks and sometimes the entire compound ringing with laughter and singing. Like other young men with time on their hands, the POWs reveled in practical jokes and roughhousing. "We could always find humor in something," recalled Cpl. Thomas Johnson. "Regardless of how bad the situation was, somebody would always make a joke about it." Such antics flabbergasted the Japanese. More than once, incredulous camp personnel chided their boisterous charges, "But you don't act like prisoners!"[16]

Perhaps it was the obvious lack of contrition that accounts for some of the seemingly senseless beatings the Japanese inflicted on the POWs. If a prisoner appeared too happy and a guard was having a bad day, that could turn the former into the object of short-lived Japanese wrath. Some guards preferred picking on taller POWs, as if their height made them the embodiment of Western arrogance. "The ones the Japanese were most violent with were the larger ones," related Private Reeves, "because the Japanese were small." Whatever the pretext, it was usually wisest for a POW to shut down all emotion and endure abuse without protest or resistance. The slightest sign of defiance would incense the guards and goad them into striking their victims harder and longer. Cries of pain would arouse those Japanese infected with sadistic impulses into extending a prisoner's agony. All but the most bullheaded Wake Islanders learned early to exercise self-restraint in dealing with their keepers.[17]

The POWs may have called their souls their own, but the Imperial Japanese Army considered their bodies the emperor's property—assets to be devoted to building the Greater East Asia Co-Prosperity Sphere. While Colonel Yuse and his superiors implemented comparatively enlightened policies at Woosung, they intended inmates would earn their keep. Yuse went so far as to announce that POW officers must work alongside their men. Colonel Ashurst and Major Brown protested this decree as a violation of the Geneva Convention. They proposed that officers accompany prisoner work details in a supervisory capacity only. When Yuse acceded to this compromise, he actually handed Ashurst and Brown a small victory. Few POW officers volunteered for this duty, and the Japanese never compelled any to do so.[18]

Allied NCOs did not receive the same degree of protection from the Geneva Convention as their superiors did. Besides exempting commissioned prisoners and their equivalents from labor, that agreement also specified that "noncommissioned officers who are prisoners of war shall only be required to do supervisory work, unless they expressly request a remunerative occupation." The Japanese countered that Woosung housed too many NCOs to observe this stipulation, and Ashurst and Brown acquiesced. This was probably for the best considering the circumstances, but it was not the last time that the POW officers exhibited more solicitude for their own rights than those of their men.[19]

The Japanese waited until the latter part of March 1942—as temperatures warmed and the winter rains died off—before rousting their charges to work outside on a regular basis. In addition to leveling the compound and laying out a parade ground, playing fields, and garden plots, the POWs dug ditches to drain the camp area of excess water. This project lasted through April and possibly beyond. By early June, however, enemy administrators decided that the prisoners had dug at least one ditch too many, and they ordered it refilled. The POWs grumbled about that, but the Japanese did not push them hard enough to make the ditchdigging detail particularly onerous. As Cpl. Henry Durrwachter commented on April 28, "We are still working on the 'Great East Asia' project but not very hard. It passes the time tho and that helps."[20]

Putting the prisoners to work infused their lives with added structure by placing them on a tighter schedule. The Japanese usually required the POWs to toil six days a week, with Sundays off to relax and do laundry. In the spring reveille blew at 6:30 AM. This was pushed up to 6:00 AM by June 1, and back to 7:00 AM by October 1. In the hour after reveille, the POWs washed, stood inspection, and ate breakfast. Then they turned out for work. Lunch call sounded at noon, followed by a brief rest break. Work continued until 5:00 PM, when the prisoners returned to their barracks for their evening meal. Except for evening roll call, they had the remaining hours before lights-out to devote to their own amusements. The Japanese let the POWs stay up until 11:00 PM in the summertime, but they made them retire at 9:00 PM in the winter.[21]

Colonel Yuse precipitated a minor revolt when he directed Woosung's occupants to clean and shine spent brass casings from artillery shells. The Japanese hauled large quantities of these objects into camp in late March and deposited them at a long shed that had been originally erected north of the barracks as a stable. The building had no walls, just a roof mounted on upright beams. Some Marines familiar with heavy ordnance rated the shell casings as big enough to fit American 3-inch and 75-mm guns. The POWs guessed that the Japanese had expended those rounds on the Chinese front and now wanted them cleaned for reloading. This task made a mockery of the Geneva Convention, which stated, "Labor furnished by prisoners of war shall have no direct relation with war operations. It is especially prohibited to use prisoners for manufacturing or transporting arms or munitions of any kind."[22]

Bristling with indignation, Colonel Ashurst notified his captors that no prisoner would participate in the shell-polishing detail. Colonel Yuse initially tried to overcome his charges' scruples by dissembling. These shells would only be used to fire blanks for ceremonial salutes, he purred. Then he changed his story and asserted that the reconditioned rounds were meant solely for target practice. Yuse also tried to win the prisoners' compliance by resorting to bribery. He promised additional and more varied rations for those who worked, as well as the monetary compensation warranted by the Geneva Convention. When the Americans and Britons remained obdurate, Yuse turned punitive. He threatened to cut off the prisoners' food unless they heeded his orders. Ashurst and his officers directed their men to obey rather than risk damaging their health.[23]

Purser William Kantzer of the *President Harrison* described the shell-polishing detail as "the most primitive set up I have ever run across." The Japanese installed upright wooden boots, or posts, inside the stalls that remained in the former stable. Four POWs worked in each of the enclosures. Shell polishers received flimsy grass rope, buckets of water, and quantities of lime. A prisoner would slide a shell casing onto the post, wet a length of rope, and dip it into the lime. Then, gripping each end of the rope, he slung it over the shell casing and pulled it with a quick motion back and forth and also up and down along the length of the brass cylinder. Corporal Richardson likened the procedure to polishing shoes. Stopping now and then to apply more water and lime, the POW would keep on buffing until the brass gleamed.

The Japanese sent at least twenty prisoners to the shell-polishing shed every day. Whenever rain made outside work impossible, camp authorities would assign an entire barracks to that detail, filling the facility with two hundred men. The Japanese initially set a daily quota of one polished shell per man, but they offered extra cigarettes to crews that turned out more. Nicotine-starved POWs increased their productivity by using gravel or wet sand as an abrasive. That ingenuity only resulted in their keepers boosting each worker's quota from one shell a day to five between June 9 and 12, 1942.

Repeated exposure to acid-laden water made the shell-polishing detail rougher than it looked. The men suffered most in chilly weather, when the skin on their hands would dry out and crack. "That was a nasty cold job," averred Cpl. Thomas Johnson. "It was miserably cold," confirmed Corporal Richardson. The diary of Contractor Alec Pay yields this telling entry dated March 26, 1942: "Taken off shell polishing detail due to sore hands."[24]

Some POWs, resentful at being forced to do war work for the enemy, tried to get away with goldbricking during their shifts in the shell-polishing shed. "I can honestly say that I never shined a shell," boasted Private Reeves. "I just pitter-putted around all day during that shell shining." Like Reeves, a few other prisoners succeeded in killing time by just looking busy, but the Japanese beat many they caught shirking or doing substandard work. On June 12 several men handed in only four finished shells instead of five. The Japanese ordered the POWs back to their stalls until they met their quota and then had them stand at attention for four hours as penance.[25]

The Japanese eventually came up with some jobs that took the POWs several miles from camp. Although the Wake Islanders did not enjoy the additional work, they found it refreshing to venture beyond Woosung's confines and see the countryside. They took a keen interest in any Chinese they encountered, especially women. Whenever a pretty girl came along, Major Devereux's Marines would give her a "hubba-hubba." Malnutrition may have diminished the prisoners' sex drive, but they were glad such cravings had not been extinguished entirely.[26]

On a less pleasant note, work details outside the prison camp acquainted Woosung's inmates with the grinding poverty under which most rural Chinese lived. On November 27, 1942, Pfc. John Pearsall confided to his diary, "Had a chance to see Chinks living first hand. Boy am I glad I was born in the good old U.S.A." Witnessing instances of Japanese cruelty against the local populace furnished the POWs with an even better reason to be thankful they were not Chinese. Toward the close of one winter day, Contractor Theodore Abraham and a camp-bound detail trudged past four enemy soldiers pouring buckets of freezing water on a Chinese man they had stripped naked and tied to a post. On another occasion, a car driven by Japanese military policemen parked opposite a gang of toiling POWs. They dragged out a pair of well-dressed Chinese men, gave them shovels, and had them dig two deep holes. The Kempeitai men shot one Chinese, kicked him into a hole, and ordered his friend to cover the corpse with dirt. Then they shot the second Chinese and had a Japanese private fill in the second grave.[27]

The first prolonged work detail to draw the POWs outside the Shanghai War Prisoners Camp involved road repair. The asphalt roads serving Shanghai's outlying areas had fallen into a sorry state, with some stretches becoming pockmarked by potholes. Beginning in the spring of 1942, the Japanese mustered gangs of prisoners armed with picks, shovels, and baskets attached to yo-ho poles to eradicate those deformities. The Americans and Britons were supposed to clear holes of mud and other debris and then refill them with gravel, which they were supposed to pack tight and grade level with the road surface. If available, the POWs used rock and pieces of broken brick as part of their filling mixture.[28]

The guards assigned to the road detail liked goofing off more than watching their charges. That allowed the POWs to work at an unhurried pace, and it also provided opportunities for sabotage. The prisoners' favorite dodge was to fill a hole with mud and top it off with a thin layer of gravel. A good rain or a little bit of traffic would cause the pothole to reappear. Sometimes the Wake Islanders played dumb and filled the holes too high, leaving the road studded with jarring, axle-busting bumps. Pvt. Ewing LaPorte and his friends adopted a more drastic means to plague their keepers. "Our main pleasure was to take a piece of cardboard with a nail sticking up and puncture tires," LaPorte recalled. "We punctured a lot of tires."[29]

The most taxing part of the road detail involved reaching the work site. The POWs marched to the job at first, which posed little hardship as long as they labored close to camp. Over time, however, the trips grew longer and longer. The road gang ended up tramping ten miles to where its services were required. The POWs then had to put in six hours of work and hike ten miles back to camp. They often did not reenter Woosung and sit down to dinner until 7:00 PM. That constituted an excruciating ordeal for men whose weight had dropped as low as 110 pounds apiece. By late November the Japanese recognized the adverse impact the long days had on their charges and started trucking the road gang out and back.[30]

In October 1942 camp authorities started marching two hundred-man contingents the five miles to Woosung village to dig a series of ditches near the Whangpoo River. These excavations measured eight feet to ten feet in depth and twelve feet in width. The Japanese never mentioned the purpose of this task, but

Pfc. George McDaniel guessed they intended the ditches for either irrigation or tank traps. The Japanese increased the ditchdigging detail to three hundred men by early November, and it lasted through that month and into the next. The POWs got to rest fifteen minutes for every hour they worked, but the ninety-minute trek back to camp at the end of the day left them exhausted.[31]

"WE ARE SUPPOSED TO BE PAID FOR SIX MONTHS WORK"

In keeping with Japan's stringent social ethic, POWs classified as nonworkers were supposed to receive half rations. This penalty applied even to the sick. As the Japanese saw it, a man was supposed to stay healthy. If he fell ill, it was his fault. Besides, the Japanese reasoned, anyone avoiding work expended less energy; hence, he required less food. The Japanese imposed this harsh standard on themselves, and few of them would have dreamed of waiving it for unproductive prisoners. Fortunately for Woosung's inmates, they drew their rations in bulk and distributed the cooked meals themselves. POW officers ensured that the sick received the same portions as working Contractors and enlisted men. Whenever a large number of inmates were ailing, however, the entire camp received less to eat.[32]

Not every prisoner had to perform like a drudge to rate a full ration. Several specially trained Contractors got to utilize their skills for the benefit of both their keepers and fellow prisoners. By mid-June 1942 the Japanese allowed the civilians to open a carpentry shop and a cobbler's shop in some warehouses on the west side of camp. A few Contractors who could sew also established a tailor's shop in one of those godowns. POW carpenters repaired Woosung's barracks and other structures, and they occasionally tackled special projects such as fabricating a laboratory table and a wooden dental chair for the camp hospital. The tailors kept their comrades from going ragged, and they also had to accept patch-and-repair work from the guards. Identifying two Contractors with training as typists, the Japanese pressed them into service as clerks in the camp office. This arrangement inadvertently provided the POWs with a reliable intelligence source regarding the camp administration's mood and future plans.[33]

Despite Colonel Yuse's assurances to the contrary, the POWs did not notice a marked increase in their rations once they started working for the Japanese. The commandant thought of other ways to compensate his charges for their cooperation. Past experience had shown, however, that every boon from the Japanese came with a catch.

Sometime in July 1942 the barracks adjutants received orders to assemble thirty-two "deserving and good" POWs for a special detail personally supervised by Colonel Yuse. The Japanese transported the select group roughly ten miles by truck to the Dazang Loyalty Monument, which memorialized the troops they lost in the bloody 1937 campaign that drove Chiang Kai Shek's forces from Shanghai. The prisoners set about removing litter and weeds from the monument grounds. The job was not particularly difficult, and the Japanese let the POWs work at their own speed. At lunchtime the Japanese surprised the prisoners with unusually large servings of rice and soup, along with sweet cakes and cigarettes. "This little party rewards your good conduct," Yuse informed his surprised guests. "Sometimes I had to scold you but today we're friends." Within the next couple of days, however, the POWs learned that they had once again been used for propaganda purposes. The Japanese-controlled *Shanghai Times* ran a photograph of the POWs policing the Dazang Loyalty Monument. The accompanying caption claimed that they had volunteered for this detail and also included an invented quotation from a Marine officer paying tribute to the Japanese soldiers who had fought there five years earlier.[34]

The Geneva Convention held that prisoners undertaking work unconnected with the administration, management, and maintenance of their camps should receive wages from their keepers. In the absence of any fixed agreements between belligerents, the detaining power was supposed to provide POWs with the same amount of money owed to its own troops for the same work. For half a year Woosung's inmates toiled without the slightest hint of reimbursement. A change seemed to be in the offing on September 18, 1942, when Colonel Yuse summoned Alec Pay, CPNAB's chief accountant on Wake, and two Contractor helpers to the camp office to put together a POW payroll. On October 3 Corporal Durrwachter got wind of this development, but the news hardly fazed him: "We are supposed to be paid for six months work soon at the rate of 3 sen per day. It is so small in American money I won't even attempt to figure it out." Camp authorities kept Durrwachter and his comrades in suspense for nearly two more months. Payday did not roll around until November 28.[35]

In contemporaneous documents, memoirs, and interviews, Woosung's inmates quoted wildly divergent figures on the size of the payments the enemy gave them. This confusion stemmed partly from the POWs having their salaries computed in the Japanese yen, which was then worth thirty cents in American currency, but actually drawing their pay in occupation currency, which were dollars issued by the Central Reserve Bank of China (CRB). That institution operated as the main financial instrument for the puppet regime the Japanese installed at Nanking, and a CRB dollar was roughly equivalent to only ten American cents. It also appears that POW specialists and NCOs pocketed slightly more cash than ordinary workers. According to some Marine officers, the typical prisoner initially earned CRB$18 per month, or US$1.80. Colonel Ashurst reported that the enemy upped that sum to a dollar a day. Many enlisted men and Contractors remembered receiving much less than that. Whatever the actual amount, all POWs agreed they were not justly compensated. Not only did POW pay levels lag behind those enjoyed by Japanese soldiers, but even those of local laborers. Indignant at seeing white men paid less than people of color, Ashurst stormed, "Chinese coolies received CRB $30.00 to 60.00 per day for performing the same type of work."[36]

Curiously, the Japanese heeded the Geneva Convention's injunction to pay American and British officers at Woosung the same sums authorized for their counterparts in the Japanese army. Second lieutenants warranted ¥85 a month, captains ¥125, and Colonel Ashurst ¥312. The Japanese deducted ¥60 a month from these amounts for room and board—a galling gesture in view of how little the POW officers got for their money. The officers received the remainder owed them at a rate of CRB$5.50 for every yen.[37]

The Geneva Convention instructed a detaining power to place any funds a prisoner earned on account and pay him the total on his release. The Japanese officers who ran Woosung, however, decided the POWs should plow their paltry earnings back into the Greater East Asia Co-Prosperity Sphere. Late in February 1942 the enemy announced plans to outfit the camp with a canteen or post exchange. That promise became a reality on March 5, when the canteen opened for business in a small room set aside in a warehouse northwest of the barracks. A Chinese merchant fronted as the new establishment's proprietor, but he actually worked for some Japanese businessmen who garnered the lion's share of the profits.

Camp authorities wasted no time in boasting to the Red Cross that Woosung now possessed a "very fine canteen." The place sold foodstuffs and condiments. Items mentioned most often by POW diarists included bread, butter, margarine, salt, pepper, sugar, jam, coffee, cocoa, fruit, chocolate bars, hard candy, peanuts, peanut butter, cigarettes, and chewing tobacco. Unfortunately, transportation problems and recurring shortages in Shanghai turned the canteen into a start-and-stop affair. "The stock was always meager," Colonel Ashurst complained. Throughout much of 1942 the canteen would close for weeks at a time until it could restock.[38]

The Japanese also assured Edouard Egle that the canteen's prices "are cheaper than they are in Shanghai." True or not, the POWs found the charges exorbitant. A chocolate bar that retailed for a nickel in the United States fetched sixty cents in the canteen. A fifteen-cent bag of hard candy sold for one CRB dollar in Woosung. A hungry POW had to come up with eighty cents for a bag of stale, old peanuts that would be shunned by the typical American shopper. As wartime inflation worsened, canteen prices skyrocketed. Between September 17, 1942, and October 5, 1942, a twelve-ounce can of jam went from CRB$0.60 to CRB$1. One pound of peanut butter, which sold for CRB$85 in late 1942, climbed to CRB$845 by May 1945.[39]

The Japanese opened the canteen almost nine months before they began paying Woosung's occupants, which meant that only POWs with money already in their possession could take immediate advantage of the facility. The North China Marines flaunted their wealth by crowding into the place on opening day, March 5, 1942, to purchase all the merchandise available for sale. Several Allied naval personnel captured in Shanghai and many merchant sailors also had varying amounts of cash. A few Wake Islanders had succeeded in secreting money on their persons, and they spent part of it to add a little extra flavor to their daily rice ration. On April 28, 1942, Corporal Durrwachter wrote, "I acquired some salt and Worchestershire Sauce at these prices $2.10 & $1.20. They really improve the chow too." The Japanese tried to maximize their profits by announcing on June 24 that any prisoner holding American currency had to surrender it at the unfavorable conversion rate of three to three and a half yen per dollar.[40]

Even after the POWs began receiving pay, most derived little benefit from the canteen. "Prices were never in harmony with wages," fumed Colonel Ashurst. "The purchasing power of one month's wages equaled ten cigarettes." Private First Class Chapman quipped that the POWs were so disgusted by the relative worthlessness of their first issue of CRB script that "we wiped ourselves with it."[41]

"THE BARRACKS RESEMBLE NUT HOUSES IN A STATE OF RIOT"

The Japanese resorted to an economic incentive to motivate the POWs to perform an irksome task that turned out to promote their own health. The rich delta land surrounding Woosung lent itself to growing rice—China's staff of life—but blessings can conceal curses. The damp soil, plus the Chinese reliance on human waste for fertilizer, made the Woosung area an ideal breeding ground for flies and mosquitoes. As temperatures rose with the approach of spring, the camp began to teem with those insects. They swarmed thickly around the benjos and galley and entered the barracks through unscreened windows and knotholes in wall planks. By July 3, 1942, Purser William Kantzer had lost all patience with his winged visitors. "The flies were relentless and tireless pests," he fumed, "and they no sooner went to bed at night than the mosquitoes came out en masse."[42]

The insects also spread diseases such as diarrhea and dysentery. The mosquitoes were particularly feared as carriers of malaria, which became the most prevalent ailment at Woosung among both inmates and guards. Camp authorities distributed mosquito nets to the prisoners, but those items were compromised by holes and there were not enough of them to provide everyone with even imperfect protection.

Dr. William Foley of the North China Marines medical team later recalled that six prisoners came down with malaria in one week after the mosquitoes and flies became active. After that, men succumbed to that malady at a rate of up to six per day. The POW doctors requested quinine to treat the mounting sick list, but the Japanese claimed they had none to spare. At first, camp authorities pretended that malaria sufferers were not really ill and refused to let them be moved into the camp hospital. Those too indisposed to work had to languish on the sleeping platforms in their barracks.

The enemy's supposed complacency was actually a sham. The Japanese dreaded malaria and any other disease possessing epidemic potential. With the Imperial Japanese Army reluctant to supply Woosung with insecticide spray or other modern countermeasures, Colonel Yuse had to fall back on primitive methods to safeguard his charges' health. On April 3, 1942, he put the POWs to work filling a marshy area just outside the camp. While that move made sense, it hardly diminished Woosung's insect population and failed to check the malaria outbreak.

Yuse soon issued orders that each POW had to kill and turn in three mosquitoes and three flies every day. When Morisako, the interpreter, conveyed Yuse's desires to the barracks adjutants, he also handed each of them two empty one-quart bottles—one for mosquitoes and one for flies. "We shall weigh the bottles," Morisako pledged, "and the barracks which delivers the heaviest bottles will receive an extra ten cigarettes per man in addition to your regular issue."[43]

The POWs greeted Yuse's demand with derision, and few, if any, even feigned compliance. The Japanese initially restricted their wrath at this flare-up of insolence to the barracks adjutants, pushing and slapping those unhappy Americans. Yuse then punished the entire camp by cutting rations. At length, Dr. Shindo prevailed on the colonel to take a more positive tack. On May 6 Shindo offered the prisoners a bounty of one cigarette for every ten flies or one hundred mosquitoes killed. The Americans and Britons coveted cigarettes for their own enjoyment or as currency, and the Japanese doctor's new reward system wrought a marked change in their attitude.

The prisoners went to work at once, swatting flies with rolled up newspapers or their bare hands. One ingenious Yank fabricated a twelve-by-twelve–inch flyswatter and did his hunting in the latrines. A North China Marine discovered that dead mosquitoes accumulated by the hundreds in the shades and reflectors on the overhead light fixtures in his barracks. Capt. John White shared that secret with the other barracks adjutants, enabling the POWs to collect more bonus cigarettes from their keepers. By May 12 the fly season was at its peak, and Dr. Shindo raised the quota for the cigarette bounty to fifty flies apiece.[44]

Despite the intensified insect-killing campaign, malaria tightened its grip on Woosung. As spring receded before summer, roughly five hundred prisoners were exhibiting symptoms of the disease. Dr. Shindo finally wrested permission from his superiors to acknowledge the problem. On June 23 he admitted four malaria cases to the POW hospital. Shindo uttered a startling admission that found its way into William Kantzer's diary: "The jap doctor is reported to have said that by the end of the summer, he expects 95% of the camp to have had it [malaria]." Corporal Durrwachter validated Shindo's prognosis by jotting on June 27, "Malaria is getting very bad now and there is talk of moving the camp."[45]

The guards were no more immune to malaria than their prisoners. Many a sick Japanese solider stood his guard shift when he should have stayed in bed. "You'd see them standing there and just shiver and shake and sweat," commiserated Cpl. Thomas Johnson. "But as long as they could stand guard, they stood there and watched us. I guess it was part of the invincible Japanese spirit."[46]

In early August word reached Woosung of a major cholera outbreak in Shanghai. Colonel Yuse switched to a more urgent form of disease prevention. He somehow obtained disinfectants and had them poured into benjo receptacles. He produced a second miracle by giving the POWs a limited supply of bug spray. Flypaper appeared as if by magic in every barracks section, and strips of the stuff showed up in the urinals in every benjo. The Japanese also installed a smoldering, mosquito-killing punk in each section and placed a bowl of hand disinfectant between every two sections. In addition Yuse insisted that, beginning August 6, each prisoner kill a minimum of five flies and five mosquitoes per day.

When the POWs became fully aware that their health was on the line, they gave the commandant their fullest cooperation. "That means 8000 flies and 8000 mosquitoes less each day to bother us," Purser Kantzer commented approvingly. Prisoners assigned to lighter duties around camp killed extra insects for their friends toiling outside. When those other inmates returned from their work details, they stripped down to the Japanese-style G-strings that had replaced their worn-out Western underwear and transformed into dauntless bug hunters.[47] Their acrobatic daring filled Kantzer with an awe that he conveyed to his diary:

> To fill the quota on mosquitoes is a job. The barracks at night now look like a monkey zoo, with men all over the rafters, chasing the insect, or climbing on the beams and holding on to the stanchions with nothing but a skibby cloth on. Others hold sheets under the lights and spray in the vicinity. When the mosquitoes nose dive onto the sheets, they can be easily seen and killed. Sometimes you seen paper bags hung loosely around the light, in which the unlucky mosquitoes stray, and then proceed to desiccate, because they haven't got sense enough to find their way out. Then you see people standing on improvised ladders slapping at the walls and the roof at unwary mosquitoes as they fly by or come to rest. On the whole, the barracks resemble nut houses in a state of riot, but it is the only way of getting the quota. What fun![48]

While the POWs had mocked Colonel Yuse's insect extermination campaign, they grudgingly acknowledged the efficacy of his Stone Age techniques. As early as August 9, Kanzter observed, "Before, the flies in the rooms wouldn't give you a moments peace. Now the rooms are practically clear. At night, it was the same story with mosquitoes. Now both pests are getting hard to find." Captain White praised Yuse for doing what he had to do to maintain the prisoners' health. "By . . . requiring each man to kill five flies a day he accomplished his purpose," White argued. "We did have a semblance, at least, of good health and hygiene standards in our camp."[49]

By early August Yuse also succeeded in securing quinine pills for his charges. The supply never came close to meeting the need, though, and that forced the POW doctors to adopt some unorthodox practices. A prisoner had to suffer at least two malaria attacks to qualify for treatment. The doctors gave each patient just enough quinine—normally fifteen pills over five days—to put the malaria into remission. After two or three days of additional bed rest, the POW would return to the work force until a recurrence of fever, chills, shaking, and other symptoms drove him back to the hospital for more doses of quinine. "In time," revealed Dr. Foley, "almost all 1600 men got malaria." Nonetheless, the creative way Foley and his colleagues stretched their quinine stocks placed the disease under control. "Never lost a case," Foley boasted.[50]

Captivity is rarely, if ever, a comfortable experience. In addition to losing liberty, a prisoner exists at the mercy of his keepers, and he can become the butt of their anger, frustration, or other dark impulses without a moment's notice. Being held by an enemy whose military system rests on an inhumane ideology and sanctions fierce physical punishment only intensifies a prisoner's sense of vulnerability. All of these conditions applied to Woosung, yet that place never came near to being as hellish as many other Japanese prison camps. Most of the officers and men the Imperial Japanese Army assigned to the Shanghai War Prisoners Camp exhibited extraordinary restraint. Once the Wake Islanders and their comrades got to know and understand Colonel Yuse and his troops, life assumed a rhythm that all but a few of Woosung's inmates found tolerable. That rhythm did not always go undisturbed. It could be upset by Japanese irascibility or fickleness, forces beyond Japanese control, POW defiance or mischievousness, or a simple breakdown in communications. The slightest incident might throw part or all of the camp into tumult and raise tensions on both sides of the electrified fence. The vast majority of these upsets, however, turned out to be minor in nature and have short-term effects. The incidents also could not obscure the fact that Yuse and his officers were prepared to take any reasonable step to keep their prisoners alive.[51]

CHAPTER ELEVEN

"you god damn americans don't understand anything"
strains, outrages, and departures

"I NEVER DID VOLUNTEER TO GO ANYWHERE"

The Japanese military regarded the inmates at the Shanghai War Prisoners Camp not only as a labor resource, but also as a source of information. The Wake Islanders became aware of this during their initial confinement on the atoll and their passage on the *Nitta Maru*. During that ship's layover at Yokohama, Japanese naval intelligence removed twenty American military personnel with backgrounds in aviation and communications. Those detained for questioning in Japan included Maj. Paul Putnam, the commander of VMF-211, and three of his pilots. Curiously, the enemy permitted four of the Wake garrison's leading pilots to proceed to Woosung. They were Cdr. Winfield Cunningham and Capt. Herbert Freuler, Capt. Frank Tharin, and 2nd Lt. John Kinney of VMF-211. If these flyers hoped no one suspected they knew anything of military value, their keepers burst that illusion soon after the Wake Islanders reached Woosung.

On February 8, 1942, Colonel Yuse ordered Cunningham, Freuler, Tharin, and Kinney driven into Shanghai and turned over to the Imperial Japanese Navy. The four Yanks took up residence at 10 Kiangwan Road, the holding facility where the Japanese had temporarily confined the crews of the *Peterel* and the *Wake* on the outbreak of war. The American pilots were pleased to learn they would eat slightly better than their comrades at Woosung. The foursome also got a chance to warm up each day by taking a hot bath.

These minor luxuries did not come, however, without a price. On February 9 the enemy whisked Cunningham and the three Marines to the Cathay Mansions Hotel in downtown Shanghai for questioning. The Japanese assigned an admiral to probe the prisoners, but that officer knew little or nothing about aviation. He delegated his responsibilities to a lieutenant who seemed too polite and trusting for the job. The POWs deflected most of the latter's questions by professing ignorance.

Cunningham, Freuler, Tharin, and Kinney returned to the hotel on the tenth, twelfth, and thirteenth of February for additional interrogation. The atmosphere remained relaxed, and the Japanese even permitted the POWs to dine on the hotel's gourmet fare. The interrogations ceased after February 13, but the Japanese made the four fliers cool their heels at 10 Kiangwan Road for two additional weeks. The night before Cunningham and his brother pilots returned to Woosung, they paid a final visit to the hotel. The Japanese admiral, an avid hunter, treated them to a sumptuous pheasant dinner. It was an oddly civil interlude that indicated that some enemy naval officers still subscribed to the gentlemanly code that mandated respectful treatment for captured counterparts.[1]

While Cunningham and his companions enjoyed their stay in Shanghai, some of Major Devereux's Marines also faced questioning at Woosung. Administrative records seized on Wake Island revealed which of the men had served previously on Midway Island, an American outpost one thousand miles west of Hawaii that the Japanese hoped to seize. Enemy interrogators tried winning the prisoners' cooperation by plying them with tea, cakes, and cigarettes. These gentle methods elicited little that the Japanese did not already know. The interrogators bore their frustration with good grace except in the case of one Marine, who happened to be a Sioux Indian. "Because of his physiognomy," deduced 1st Lt. Woodrow Kessler, "the Japs were certain he was an unfaithful kin, and they were very upset that he would provide no information. He was hit and pushed around, but his only comment was, 'Those yellow sonsabitches.'"[2]

The Japanese subjected all of Woosung's inmates to an interrogation campaign that had more to do with the Greater East Asia Co-Prosperity Sphere than with ferreting out military secrets. Between the camp's opening in late January 1942 and August 9, 1942, the Japanese had the Wake Islanders and their comrades fill out seven questionnaires that inquired into their education and technical experience. It became immediately apparent that the enemy desired to identify skilled laborers to man vital war industries in the Japanese home islands. An interpreter told the prisoners that those lacking specialized training would remain in China to perform heavy labor as coolies. An older American merchant sailor urged other inmates to appear eligible for transfer to Japan. "If you get around those big industrial areas," he promised, "at least you'll keep warm."[3]

Cpl. John Johnson believed that Japan would grow too hot for comfort before the war ended. Confident in eventual American victory, Johnson did not want to relocate to an industrial city bound to be targeted for aerial and naval bombardment. Pfc. Robert Shores shared Johnson's qualms. "I knew I was safer in an occupied country than I would if I'd go over there," Shores declared. "I knew that. So I never did volunteer to go anywhere." Cpl. Bernard Richardson cited another reason to avoid transfer: "What we had in China was little enough but . . . we were fairly certain to come through alive if we could but maintain the status quo."[4]

The Wake Marines tried to mislead the enemy by classifying themselves as professional soldiers. When camp authorities countered by asking what the Marines did before enlisting, most answered "student," and Private First Class Shores described himself as "a farm kid." The Japanese then pressed these prisoners to disclose what they did when they were not studying. That questionnaire provoked an outpouring of creative evasion. "For the next three and a half years," testified Corporal Richardson, "we were actors, a Fuller Brush man, an umbrella rod repairman, an insurance adjustor, a postal clerk, a shopper, an observer, a detective, a census taker and a condom salesman."[5]

Many Contractors, on the other hand, freely admitted to possessing skill sets appealing to the Japanese. That candor produced no immediate reaction. Months passed, and camp authorities had the POWs complete more questionnaires, which were reviewed and filed away. The process took on all the appearances of another empty exercise that became emblematic of life behind barbed wire.[6]

"I PROMISE NOT TO ATTEMPT TO ESCAPE FROM . . . THE IMPERIAL JAPANESE ARMY"

Second Lieutenant Kinney enjoyed his fleeting taste of the good life at the Cathay Mansions Hotel, but what he really wanted was to leave Woosung permanently. "Escape planning became my occupation," he later wrote. After the North China Marines realized they were ineligible for repatriation, Kinney found willing confederates in 2nd Lt. Richard Huizenga and 2nd Lt. James McBrayer, his old friends from Basic School. Both Huizenga and McBrayer spoke Chinese, which would come in handy should the threesome effect a getaway. Other POWs also began plotting to burst their bonds and taste freedom again.[7]

The first step—breaking out of camp—did not appear inordinately difficult. The single barbed wire fence enclosing Woosung posed a meager deterrent to an agile or imaginative prisoner even when electrified. Pvt. Earl Broyles, one of Major Devereux's most incorrigible rule breakers, went over the fence regularly at night to pilfer food. Thanks to the lackadaisical attitude exhibited by many guards, exiting camp after sunrise also could be surprisingly easy. S2C Cassius

Smith discovered this one spring day after he had been assigned to a gardening detail. Fed up with POW life, Smith ceased working and told himself, "The hell with it. I'm going." He walked out the camp gate without anyone trying to stop him. The guards must have assumed he had permission to leave the compound. Smith covered a considerable distance before common sense kicked in and he wondered, "Where the hell am I going to?" The anxious sailor retraced his steps and reentered camp without any Japanese questioning his temporary absence.[8]

The senior Marine officers at Woosung considered the odds against escape so impossible that they counseled their men against attempting it. Major Devereux told the Wake Marines that they would have to traverse 1,500 miles of unfamiliar territory to reach Allied lines. The idea of a Caucasian traveling unnoticed through the Chinese countryside smacked of absurdity. Colonel Ashurst chimed in with the warning that his subordinates could expect no aid from any Chinese they met outside camp. Capt. Bryghte Godbold remembered Ashurst's remark: "If you did escape, the Chinese would kill you for your shoes." The Japanese further exploited the local populace's poverty by offering a cash reward for the recovery of Allied escapees. After the POWs heard this, few would have contradicted Pfc. Leonard Mettscher when he said, "A Chinese at that time would have sold his mother for 50 yen." Occupation authorities also threatened to execute Chinese assisting fugitive prisoners. Finally, Contractor John Burton realized that an escapee would have to pause to boil any water or vegetables he scrounged before consuming them or risk getting sick. That would only increase the likelihood of detection and recapture.[9]

Ever the champion of unit cohesion, Major Devereux urged his Leathernecks to stick together. If a reasonably good opportunity to escape ever arose, the Wake Island Detachment would go out as a group, the major decreed. Pfc. Sylvester Gregouire bought Devereux's arguments, which the young Cajun internalized in these terms: "We would have a better chance of making it that way instead of by ourselves."[10]

Unaware of the anti-escape policy espoused by the Marine brass, Colonel Yuse devised his own ploy to ensure no prisoners broke out of Woosung. On February 27, 1942, he mustered his charges in the compound and demanded that they sign the following pledge: "I promise not to attempt to escape from control by the Imperial Japanese Army." Backed by the recently arrived Sir Mark Young, Colonel Ashurst responded with an emphatic no. It was one thing for Marine officers to tell their men that escape was inadvisable at the present time but quite another to renounce a POW's primary duty. Rather than force an unpleasant confrontation, Yuse dismissed the formation. The commandant signified his displeasure by stopping the prisoners' cigarette ration for one day. He then let the matter drop. It was a decision he would soon regret.[11]

Regardless of what Ashurst, Devereux, and Yuse did to discourage escape, Commander Cunningham resolved to slip from his captors' clutches at the earliest opportunity. "It's in our code," explained the Wake garrison's former head. "That is one of the Ten Commandments of the Navy." The same day Cunningham returned from interrogation in Shanghai, he discovered that his roommate, Lt. Cdr. C. D. Smith, had developed an escape plan. As the last American commander of the gunboat *Wake*, Smith fancied himself an old China hand who knew the Shanghai area like the back of his hand. Smith assented to Cunningham joining the plot and revealed that he had recruited three other coconspirators. Cunningham already enjoyed a close working relationship with one of them—Dan Teters, the CPNAB general superintendent on Wake. The other two were Commander John Woolley, the senior Royal Navy officer in Shanghai who had been attached to the British consulate, and Liu, Smith's sixteen-year-old Chinese servant on the *Wake*. Smith chose Liu as the group's interpreter. Teters supervised the camp's teahouse detail, which positioned him to steal a shovel used to remove tea leaves from the vat. Rumor also had it that Teters carried a lot of money on his person that could be used to buy the assistance of any Chinese the escapees encountered.[12]

Smith and his associates waited until the moonless, cloud-shrouded night of March 11, 1942, before making their move. Sometime between 9:00 PM and 10:00 PM, they quietly dug a trench ten inches deep beneath the lowest wire in the electric fence and crawled under it. The five fugitives set out for the Whangpoo River, where they hoped to steal a sampan, pilot it to the Yangtze, and then follow that larger stream to friendly territory. The Japanese did not detect the escapees' absence until roll call the following morning, giving them a head start of eight or more hours.

Woosung's first jailbreak subjected Colonel Yuse to the fate most dreaded by Japanese officers—loss of face. Well aware that his superiors did not trust him with a combat assignment, he now appeared unfit even to run a prison camp. The disgraced commandant confined Woosung's inmates to their barracks while his guards walked the fence until they located the point where Smith's party made its exit. The Japanese questioned several prisoners to see if they had any prior knowledge of the escape. Certain that Woolley's roommate, Lieutenant Stephen Polkinghorn, had assisted the fugitives, Yuse locked him in a windowless, unfurnished shed for three weeks of solitary confinement. Yuse also sent Dr. William Foley and Wayne H. Ahlrich, a CPNAB carpenter foreman, to the guardhouse on the same suspicions.

The Japanese withheld food from Polkinghorn for forty-eight hours, and they dallied a week before giving him any bedding. They never installed a toilet in the shed, forcing the *Peterel*'s doughty skipper to sleep on a dirt floor surrounded by his own waste. In addition, they denied him medical attention for his wounded hand, which some guards struck after the stubborn New Zealander refused to tell them what he knew about the escape.

Later on March 12 Yuse released the other POWs from their quarters so they could witness a dramatic demonstration of Japanese ingenuity in recapturing runaway prisoners. The commandant brought five police dogs into camp and let them sniff some clothing the escapees had left behind. One dog ran straight to the camp galley, eliciting snickers from the watching prisoners. The remaining animals led their handlers out of camp, but that did little to assuage Yuse's shame. The sickly little colonel had a new personal mission—preventing any further escapes from marring his record at Woosung. "At night we heard Colonel Yuse on his rounds of the sentries," reminisced First Lieutenant Kessler, "his high pitched voice screamed warnings . . . lest they be negligent. His trek around the camp perimeter could be followed by the sounds of his near hysteria."[13]

Yuse did not know it yet, but the men who had disturbed his equilibrium were already back in custody. The escapees had not been tracked down by Yuse's dogs. They owed their undoing to a trick of nature and human treachery. As they neared the Whangpoo the night of March 11–12, they ran into a thick fog and lost their bearings. They eventually groped their way to the river but failed to lay hands on a boat. Smith and his party hid in a ruined, roofless building to await daylight, only to discover their refuge lay close to a Japanese army camp. The escapees headed in the opposite direction, following the Whangpoo for two miles before reaching a walled village. There, a farmer agreed to hide them. He beckoned them into a shed, locked the door behind them, and then notified a local detachment of Chinese puppet government troops loyal to the Japanese. By 5:00 PM the five dejected escape artists were en route to Shanghai with an escort of Japanese soldiers for turnover to the dreaded Kempeitai. Smith, Cunningham, Woolley, Teters, and Liu had been free for less than twenty-four hours.

On March 13 Contractor Alec Pay scratched in his diary, "Japanese announce escapees captured 12 o'clock noon today." The Kempeitai confirmed that news flash by bringing the runaways to Woosung for a brief visit the following day. The five reentered camp handcuffed and tethered together by a single cord with slip nooses pinching their necks. In full view of both guards and inmates, the Kempeitai bade Smith and his companions to reenact their escape. This further chastened Yuse and his troops for letting the escapees outsmart them. By dragging the captured men around like dogs, the Japanese hoped to demonstrate the futility of escape to the other POWs. Commander Woolley tried to spoil the enemy's intent by flashing an upraised thumb at his brother officers. Commander Cunningham also showed no glimmer of repentance. He did not enjoy parading through Woosung "ignominiously . . . at the end of a leash," as he put it, but he felt his bid for freedom "was worth all the strain and pain."[14]

The POWs subsequently learned that the Japanese tried the five escapees by court-martial in Shanghai on the fantastic charge of desertion from the Imperial Japanese Army. The three officers in the party drew sentences of ten years' confinement at the Shanghai Municipal Jail—also known as the Ward Road Jail—in the International Settlement. The court treated the two civilians with comparative leniency, sentencing Teters to two years imprisonment, and Liu to one year. All five were luckier than they realized at the time. Americans caught trying to escape in the Philippines were often tied to posts, crosses, or barbed wire fences and publicly tortured for two or three days before the Japanese put them out of their misery.[15]

Woosung never witnessed such barbarity, but Colonel Yuse seized on other means to render his camp escape-proof. He organized the POWs into ten-man "shooting squads," explaining their purpose with ominous succinctness: "Now, one escapes, the other nine die." During the second half of March 1942, Yuse had every inmate photographed and fingerprinted. The guards also took to staging surprise inspections, bursting into the barracks to rifle through the prisoners' possessions. Any man found storing food during a shakedown would be punished on the assumption he was hoarding rations for an escape attempt.[16]

A week after the breakout Yuse unveiled the linchpin in his improved security system. On March 17 the commandant called his charges into ranks in front of the camp office. He mounted a table so all could see him and announced that every man had to sign an expanded no-escape pledge. In addition to remaining in Japanese custody, the document bound the POWs to obey their captors' orders and refrain from damaging enemy property.

Once again Colonel Ashurst refused to sign away a prisoner's right to escape—one recognized by the Geneva Convention. This time, however, Yuse refused to take no for an answer. The commandant flew into a rage and threatened to confine the entire camp to barracks without food and water until the prisoners complied with his demand. Ashurst knew his men were getting little enough to eat as it was and that a showdown would damage their health. Before the Marine colonel directed his subordinates to affix their signatures to the pledge, however, he insisted on adding a disclaimer. Yuse did not care what the American did as long as the POWs signed, so Ashurst wrote on the pledge, "Signed in accordance with a direct Japanese order, under duress and with the threat of terminal punishment."[17]

Major Devereux saw the wisdom in Ashurst's qualified capitulation, and he loyally urged the Wake Marines to go along. "The Major thought it best we sign," reported Cpl. Henry Durrwachter. "So we did." Second Lt. Robert Hanna agreed: "We signed for the simple reason we knew it had to be done. It didn't mean a damn thing as far as we were concerned." As Hanna indicated, no American serviceman regarded an agreement forced on him by the enemy as binding, which was precisely why Ashurst appended his disclaimer.[18]

Despite the insertion of Ashurst's loophole, one man at Woosung still balked at submitting to Yuse without a fight. Striding to the front of the British inmates, Hong Kong Governor-General Sir Mark Young spoke defiantly to the commandant: "I presently have no intention of escaping. Nor do [I] anticipate to escape in the future. However, the right to attempt escape is sacred to all war prisoners. To sign this infamous document is incompatible with honor. I refuse to sign." Sir Mark forbade his fellow Britons to sign, as well. Astounded by such fearlessness, Cpl. Bernard Richardson thought, "There is a *man*."[19]

The Japanese immediately placed Sir Mark Young under arrest in his quarters. They also locked the other British POWs in their barracks, boarded up the windows, and cut their rations. After Sir Mark learned that the guards were beating his men and tormenting them in other ways, he permitted them to sign the pledge after a few days. The governor-general held out for four more days until he finally agreed to endorse a modified statement that said he was not presently planning an escape.[20]

Four enlisted North China Marines wasted little time in making a mockery out of Colonel Yuse's latest security precautions—and they did it in broad daylight. On the morning of March 30, Cpl. Charles W. Brimmer, Cpl. Jerold B. Story, Cpl. Connie G. Battles, and Pfc. Charles A. Stewart donned blue dungaree fatigue uniforms and joined a work detail policing the camp grounds. The four Leathernecks sneaked away without attracting attention and hid under the flooring of an old shack. After the Japanese recalled the detail for the noon meal, Brimmer and his companions crawled along a creek bed that cut through the camp and followed it under the fence, which was normally left uncharged during the day. The daring foursome stuck to the creek bed for another four hundred yards before getting up and casually strolling away without alarming any guards.

Brimmer and the three other Marines had the good fortune to meet some friendly Chinese, who bravely hid and fed them for six days. The Americans' benefactors contacted a local guerrilla band, which took the escapees under its protection. Brimmer, Story, Battles, and Stewart traveled with the guerrillas and a coterie of foreign correspondents. Then just a few days before a boat could arrive to transport the Marines to Chiang Kai-Shek's capital at Chunking, a captured Chinese courier revealed the group's whereabouts to the enemy while under torture. Japanese troops surrounded the area and closed in, recapturing the four Yanks when they made a run for it. Repeating the precedent set with Woosung's first escapees, the Japanese put Brimmer and his friends on trial for desertion. The court sent Story, Battles, and Stewart to the Ward Road Jail for four years, but Brimmer got nine because his judges decided that his cheerful and talkative nature warranted "more correction."[21]

Woosung's second escape stung Colonel Yuse and his subordinates more deeply than the first had. "Japs all worked up over escape," Alec Pay scrawled in his diary. Fortunately, Yuse did not make good on his threat to utilize shooting squads, but the POWs had to endure a ration cut for several days. "Every one very hungry," Contractor Herb Papock complained on March 31. "Men line up for scraps of food thrown out from galley." In addition Yuse crowded one hundred enlisted prisoners in a single room for twenty days. Those men went without their bedding for the first six days, which made sleeping difficult on frigid nights.[22]

As much as the commandant savored these retaliatory measures, he did not forget the need for heightened prevention. He moved at once to equip Woosung with a second electric fence to isolate the prisoners' barracks, wash racks, and latrines from the rest of the compound. The Japanese began erecting this additional barrier on March 31 and finished by April 2. In a deliberate effort to intimidate, Yuse placed the inner fence about one yard from the east end of each barracks—literally right outside the door. Like the outer fence, the new one was supposed to carry a current only between evening and morning roll call. Due to Japanese negligence or caprice, however, both fences posed a lethal peril even to inmates harboring no thoughts of escape.[23]

"AN EXCEPTIONALLY 'BLUE MONDAY' FOR ALL CIVILIANS & NO. CHINA MARINES"

Around 6:00 PM on Monday, August 15, 1942, S2C Ray H. Hodgkins, an American sailor captured on Wake Island, accompanied a buddy to Woosung's new recreation hall to borrow a baseball and a couple of gloves. The two POWs walked around to the rear of the building to play catch beside the outer fence. Hodgkins missed a throw, and the ball rolled just beyond the fence. The young sailor assumed that the guards had turned off the juice earlier in the day, but he was wrong. As he reached for the ball, his arm touched a wire, and a massive dose of electricity surged through his body. Purser William Kantzer of the *President Harrison* joined the crowd that gathered around the POW medics who fought to keep Hodgkins alive. "He was out like a light," Kantzer observed, "and although they gave him artificial respiration, adrenilin shots, and alternating hot and cold towel applications for three hours, he turned blue from the waist up and was finally given up."[24]

Seaman Second Class Hodgkins was not the first inmate to connect with a hot fence at Woosung. On June 19 another ball player stumbled and fell on the outer fence behind the galley. "He was lucky," Kantzer reported, "he only got flipped in a somersault, and burned on the arm." Dutch Raspe, a sixty-three-year-old Contractor, merely brushed the fence with his arm on August 24, 1942, but that sent him sprawling in a seemingly lifeless heap. Dr. Foley managed to revive him with artificial respiration. Even so, Raspe suffered a deep burn on his arm and severe burns on his feet where the current left his body. A third POW to survive contact with a hot fence, Contractor Thomas G. Essaff, was known thereafter as "Short Circuit Essaff." The main thing that saved those three men was that their accidents occurred on dry ground. The night of August 14–15 dumped a lot of rain on Woosung, however, and Hodgkins played his last game of catch on soil still spongy from moisture.[25]

The outer fence claimed the life of a North China Marine on August 28, 1942. Field Music Corporal Carroll W. Boucher was flinging onion plants from a small patch just outside the fence for a friend to transplant in the inner compound. Boucher lost his balance and crashed into the fence. The bugler hit the ground clear of the wire, and Dr. Foley worked on him for two hours, but all efforts to resuscitate the popular young Marine proved unavailing. Boucher's comrades honored him with a funeral service the following day, and the Japanese took his remains to Shanghai for cremation.[26]

Colonel Yuse apologized for his guards' carelessness, but his words did not allay the prisoners' resentment. "There is no doubt in my mind," raged Purser Kantzer, "that it is a case of criminal negligence on the part of the japs not to have a guard-wire several feet from the hot fence to prevent this sort of accident." Colonel Ashurst later complained to Allied authorities that Woosung's electric fences "were not equipped with safe guards."[27]

Not every death at Woosung could be blamed on the Japanese. Cancer killed Jesus Camacho, a Guamanian Pan Am employee from Wake, on August 18, 1942. Contractor Edward A. Nelson from Wheatland, Wyoming, died of a rectal tumor on October 5. Another Contractor, Louis Carr from Boise, succumbed to a cerebral tumor on October 31. A third CPNAB employee, Charles G. Helander of Lake Forest, Illinois, willed himself to die by November 13. "A peculiar psychological case," commented Alec Pay. "[He] refused all food & showed no desire to continue this earthly existence. He was physically well & normal & recovered from recent illness of malaria & diarrhea." Cancer was difficult to treat in the outside world, and Camacho, Nelson, and Carr could have died when they did had they been free. Colonel Yuse even sent Camacho to a modern hospital in Shanghai for the best available care. As for Helander, his fate underlined a hard truth that Contractor Tex Akin already appreciated: "Never give up or you've had it."[28]

Desperation, risk, or tragedy did not figure in every POW departure from Woosung. One hundred sixty-five inmates left that camp without upsetting the Japanese. This total included a lucky twenty-four who the enemy permitted to return to their homelands. In the months following the commencement of the Pacific War, the United States, Great Britain, and Japan negotiated agreements to exchange their diplomatic personnel and civilian nationals caught in hostile territory. The United States moved faster to exploit this opportunity than its ally. On June 29, 1942, the *Conte Verde*, an Italian passenger liner stranded at Shanghai since the previous December 8, left the city with 639 American, Canadian, and Latin American repatriates on board. Among its passengers were five recent residents of Woosung—American servicemen who the Japanese had lumped in with the civilian staff at the U.S. consulate in Shanghai.[29]

As early as Tuesday, June 9, the Japanese transferred WO Paul Chandler and his three-man quartermaster detail from the 4th Marines from Woosung to a holding center in Shanghai to facilitate their embarkation. A U.S. Navy radioman who had assisted with communications at the American consulate accompanied the four Leathernecks. Watching these fortunate five climb into a waiting truck cast their fellow Yanks into a glum mood. "How we envied those men," exclaimed TSgt. Charles Holmes. "It was a terrible feeling seeing them leave camp and not knowing when the rest of us would . . . if ever. It was especially a 'low blow' for the Wake civilians." The fact that the Japanese took only Chandler's party from Woosung to fill berths on the *Conte Verde* extinguished the last hope for repatriation cherished by many Contractors and North China Marines. When the Italian liner put out to sea twenty days later, Alec Pay mourned in his diary, "An exceptionally 'Blue Monday' for all civilians & No. China Marines." Chandler softened the blow somewhat by collecting the names and home addresses of all POWs who wanted their loved ones told they were still alive and well.[30]

The *Conte Verde* proceeded to Singapore, where it rendezvoused with the *Asama Maru*, which carried nearly nine hundred more Americans and other Allied nationals who had embarked at Yokohama. The two ships then sailed together to Lourenço Marques, the capital of Portuguese Mozambique. There, on July 23, the *Conte Verde* and *Asama Maru* swapped their passengers for 1,500 Japanese that the Swedish liner *Gripsholm* had carried to the neutral African port from Jersey City, New Jersey. After Chandler returned to the United States on the *Gripsholm*, he kept his word to his imprisoned comrades and wrote their wives or families.[31]

The British may have been slower off the mark, but they arranged for two exchange ships to pick up batches of their repatriates at Shanghai in the summer of 1942. On May 29 the Japanese pulled seven staff members from the British legation at Peking out of Woosung, but the *Tatuta Maru* did not sail from Shanghai with nearly eight hundred Britons, Indians, and Norwegians until August 4. Three days later, twelve members of Shanghai's British consulate left Woosung. That group had to wait only until August 17 to board the *Kamakura Maru* for its trip to Lourenço Marques.[32]

"I HAVE WRITTEN EACH TIME I AM ALLOWED"

Even though no Wake Islanders rode back to the United States on the *Conte Verde* or *Gripsholm*, the Italian liner's return to Shanghai brought home a little closer by bringing them their first mail since capture. The POWs had more than an inkling that the exchange ship would serve that purpose. In the month preceding the *Conte Verde*'s departure, the Japanese granted each inmate at Woosung permission to write home and issued him one sheet of stationery with the words "Shanghai War-prisoners' Camp" printed at the top.[33]

After food, nothing mattered more to the Wake Islanders and their fellow prisoners than communicating with their loved ones. A single letter could give an incalculable lift to a POW's morale. Purser Kantzer called the first letter he received from his family "a very welcome shot in the arm." Mail told a man that he was not forgotten, that the people who counted the most in his life still loved him and prayed for his homecoming. That restored an inmate's sense of worth, gave him reason to hope, and reinforced his will to live. Mail also enabled a prisoner to dispel any fears haunting family and friends as to his health and safety.[34]

Capt. Herbert Freuler, a pilot wounded in VMF-211's final dogfight over Wake, addressed those concerns in this opening paragraph he penned in all capital letters to his wife on May 30, 1942: "I HOPE YOU HAVE RECEIVED WORD ABOUT ME BY THIS TIME AND HAVE CEASED TO WORRY,

BECAUSE I HAVE BEEN WELL. . . . I SHOULD BE, SINCE ONE OF OUR NAVY DOCTORS IS MY ROOM MATE. THE WOUND WHICH YOU MAY HAVE HEARD . . . WAS ONLY THROUGH THE FLESH AND HAS HEALED COMPLETELY." Sgt. Jack Cook of the 1st Defense Battalion struck the same note in his first letter to his mother, writing, "I WAS NOT INJURED AT WAKE, AND HAVE BEEN IN PERFECT HEALTH SINCE YOU SAW ME LAST."[35]

Not only did the Japanese prevent the Wake Islanders from writing home until nearly six months into their captivity, but they made the privilege conditional. Camp authorities permitted a POW to write one single-page letter every three months and a postcard each intervening month. That quota did not seem overly generous to the men caged at Woosung. They carped at the arbitrary restrictions, especially since they often had hours on their hands for writing letters. "I have written each time I am allowed," Sergeant Cook swore to his parents, "so few that You must tell Everyone I CANNOT write to Other than My family." Moreover, the mail the prisoners generated could not be guaranteed a speedy trip to its proper destination—if it got there at all.[36]

The exchange of POW mail between the United States and Japan can best be characterized as a complicated, erratic, and frustrating business. The Japanese established no regular channels of communication with their enemies. They largely confined American mail shipments to civilian exchange ships, and only four such passages received authorization to traverse Japanese-controlled waters during the war. Letters addressed to prisoners sat for months awaiting transportation to East Asia, and they encountered additional obstacles once in enemy hands.[37]

All incoming and outgoing POW mail at the Shanghai War Prisoners Camp faced close scrutiny by Japanese interpreters. The enemy told prisoners and their correspondents to write solely about personal matters. Political and military subjects were off limits. "We were instructed that the only thing that you could say was your state of health and how happy you were or else it wouldn't go," explained Pfc. James Venable. "And our own officers and NCOs urged that we not try to play cute and send anything which would try to be a coded message or something." As Venable indicated, the POWs learned that letters exuding a cheerful tone and praising their keepers stood a better chance of winning the interpreters' approval. Cpl. Thomas Johnson made a habit of starting his letters this way: "Dear Mother, through the kindness of the Japanese, we are given permission to let you know we are well."[38]

Censors at every Japanese POW camp evidently prized thoroughness over speed. To make their job easier, the Japanese government demanded that all missives to and from prisoners be either typewritten or clearly printed in block capitals. In 1943 Tokyo abruptly decreed that letters emanating from the United States should contain no more than twenty-five words. The interpreters at the Shanghai War Prisoners Camp, obsessed with enforcing these and other rules, subjected incoming mail to heavy censorship. "When the Jap censor got through with it sometimes there wasn't much letter left," griped Sergeant Holmes. "I remember getting one letter from a girl friend that had so much chopped out of it that the letter didn't make sense."[39]

Practice turned the POWs and their correspondents into masters at packing a lot of information into a few, short sentences. In mid-October 1943, Louise "Lee" Hotchkiss typed these twenty-five words to her soldier husband, SSgt. Clifford Hotchkiss: "Everybody fine. Lee, Donna Lee and Sis send all their love. Hope you are well. Will try to send Picture. Keep faith with the Lord." Some home folks devised clever codes to apprise prisoners of the state of the war. This was how one Wake Islander learned about his country's June 1942 victory at Midway: "Uncle Joe and Uncle Sam met at the halfway house and had one hell of a fight. Uncle Sam won." This electrifying news spread from barracks to barracks, bringing joy to Allied servicemen and civilians alike.[40]

Woosung's interpreters had to squeeze their letter-censoring duties in between their regular tasks, and that prolonged the processing of POW mail. It was a boring, time-intensive task, and some interpreters lacked the language skills to do it quickly. The POWs did not begin receiving mail from the shipments the first exchange ships picked up at Lourenço Marques until mid-August 1942. Letters trickled out of the interpreters' office through September and October and well past mid-November. "Got letter from Eddie today," Contractor Emmett Newell exulted in his diary on November 17. "We sure appreciate them." Another mail shipment that reached the Shanghai War Prisoners Camp on December 23, 1943, did not receive clearance for distribution until April 12, 1944. The delays were partly deliberate. "The Japanese took great pleasure in holding up our ... mail due to any rule infraction—real, or imagined," insisted Sgt. Donald Malleck. Interpreters singled out obstreperous prisoners for punitive treatment. Their mail was withheld longer than the rest, and sometimes it was simply destroyed. Early in January 1943, for instance, Edouard Egle of the Red Cross discovered that the Japanese had not distributed forty-two letters out of a recently arrived shipment of eight hundred.[41]

At the bottom line, the amount of mail a Wake Islander accumulated depended on how frequently his family and friends wrote, his standing with camp authorities when a mail shipment arrived, and the mood of the censors. The stateside letters that reached the POWs varied in age from two and a half months to eighteen months. Some men got no mail at all. Others received one hundred to two hundred letters and cards during their imprisonment. Pfc. Henry Chapman, Pfc. Mackie Wheeler, and Seaman Second Class Smith ended up at the lower end of the scale, with each receiving a single letter over three and a half years. Second Lieutenant Kinney averaged one letter a year, while Pfc. Jesse Nowlin heard his name barked just four times at POW mail calls. Sergeant Cook fared much better. He received twenty letters from his mother by April 12, 1944. Cook's tally beat Major Devereux, who had only seven letters in his possession by the same date. Contractor Ned Nye set the camp record for the largest quantity of mail received in a single day. On March 8, 1944, an interpreter handed the delighted civilian more than seventy letters. Nye's mother had asked everyone she knew to drop her son a line, which resulted in this windfall. The interpreters must have also liked Nye. On another occasion a North China Marine saw a POW beaten for getting too much mail.[42]

Because of Japanese irascibility and foot-dragging, friends and family on the American home front heard relatively little from the Wake Island defenders until their liberation. Starting in late May and early June 1942, the occupants of the Shanghai War Prisoners Camp produced 1,000 to 1,500 letters or cards every month. Yet, as of September 1943, only 719 of those messages had reached addressees in the United States. As was the case with incoming mail, each POW logged a different success rate. Private First Class Nowlin wrote around fifteen letters to his family, but a dozen never got through. Only six of the letters and three postcards that Sergeant Cook posted to his parents ever reached their mailbox.[43]

Before the autumn of 1942 ended, 140 prisoners formerly confined at Woosung had to have their mail forwarded to Japan. The questionnaires that camp authorities issued earlier in the year enabled them to single out prisoners with specialized technical skills useful to Japanese war industries. By September 14 the Japanese had notified sixty-nine Contractors and one North China Marine to prepare for relocation to Japan. That seventy-man draft departed four days later.[44]

The Japanese disclosed the imminence of a second transfer the next month by requiring selected inmates to take a battery of IQ tests and trade examinations between October 23 and 27. On November 3, seventy more POWs left Woosung for the enemy's home islands. That contingent, in contrast to its predecessor, possessed a pronounced military character. Nearly fifty of its members were enlisted American servicemen. Twenty-nine came from the Wake garrison—twenty-two

Marines from the 1st Defense Battalion, two from VMF-211, four sailors, and one U.S. Army radioman. The USS *Wake* lost four crewmen, and the North China Marines sixteen of their number, to this second draft.[45]

Major Devereux worried about the Wake Marines chosen for relocation. He wanted them to remember that they still belonged to a unit and were bound by the code and traditions of the Corps. He directed his clerk Cpl. Robert Brown to type out a small card identifying each transferee as a member of the Wake Island Detachment, 1st Defense Battalion. "It didn't mean much, of course—probably nothing in itself," Devereux mused, "but I felt it was a straw of group identity to which a man could cling no matter what." That token mattered more to the men who got one than Devereux realized. A year after the war, an appreciative Pfc. Phillip W. Johnson informed his old commander, "I still have the slip of identification which you gave me in Shanghai Nov. 2, 1942."[46]

"THE TYPE OF MAN THAT WENT TO EXTREMES"

Despite occasional misunderstandings, clashes of culture, and three accidental deaths, Woosung clung to its reputation as one of Japan's most humanely managed POW camps. Colonel Yuse never recovered completely from having two escapes occur on his watch, but his initial fury gave way fairly quickly to a sort of hurt resignation. He and his guards reverted to their former live-and-let-live posture. Prisoners who kept their noses clean usually had nothing to fear from their keepers. Sergeant Araki remained a two-fisted menace with his hair-trigger temper, but he rarely pummeled a prisoner without reason.[47]

The generally harmonious atmosphere at the Shanghai War Prisoners Camp suffered a severe disturbance after Colonel Yuse got rid of Mikani—"Mickey Mouse" to the POWs—the installation's original head interpreter. Mikani's replacement, Isamu Ishihara, reported for duty on May 6, 1942. That date marked a precipitate change in the inmate population's quality of life. The new interpreter moved with speed to install himself as the dominant personality inside camp. Over the next three years, Ishihara wielded his malevolent influence to torment his charges both physically and mentally. "ISHIHARA was generally a trouble maker," testified S1C Clarence E. Wolfe, "and at every opportunity would punish prisoners directly, on the slightest provocation." Hate seemingly governed almost everything Ishihara did, and the prisoners reciprocated with undying enmity. "I could choke him now," Pfc. Marshall Fields blurted in 1972. The Wake Islanders and their comrades tagged Ishihara with several insulting nicknames. Some favored the "Snake," but the one that stuck was the "Beast of the East."[48]

Ishihara was in his early to mid-thirties when he joined the staff at Woosung. A thin man, he stood five feet eight inches in height, making him taller than most Japanese. He kept his black hair close-cropped and sported a neatly trimmed mustache. A large pair of round, horn-rimmed glasses magnified his piercing black eyes and gave them a wild cast. Though only a civilian attached to the Japanese army, Ishihara dressed like an officer but wore no rank devices on his uniform. A samurai sword hung from a leather waist belt on his left hip, and he shod his smallish feet in tight, spit-polished riding boots.[49]

Ishihara spoke much better English than the typical enemy interpreter, which caused endless speculation regarding his background. He kept his past a mystery, throwing the prisoners off the trail with several different stories. The most common placed him in Honolulu before the war, where he purportedly worked as a school teacher, taxi driver, or trucker. Other variations had him studying English at a West Coast university or selling cars in Tokyo. At a subsequent trial for war crimes, Ishihara made vague allusions to selling merchandise in China during the spring of 1938. When Ishihara offered his services to the Imperial Japanese Army as an interpreter, he expected to receive the status of a junior officer, but he had to settle for being treated as an honorary senior NCO. That filled him with resentment, as he regarded himself as more intelligent than most Japanese officers, but he had sense enough to hide that attitude from his superiors.[50]

One thing Ishihara did not bother hiding was his all-consuming hatred of Caucasians, Americans in particular. Nothing pleased him more than humiliating white men and making them grovel. "Ishihara delighted in telling us what cowards we were," remembered Cpl. Thomas Johnson, "that only cowards surrendered. Japanese warriors never surrendered." Corporal Richardson never forgot the spiteful tirade that poured out of Ishihara on the interpreter's first day at Woosung: "Why you surrender? . . . Why not kill yourselfs honorably."[51]

Ishihara regularly coupled his verbal taunts with physical assaults. "It did him pleasure to whip us or to hit one of our officers," claimed Pfc. Robert Shores. Ishihara converted his sheathed sword into a club, using it to whack POWs on their heads and backs. He resorted more frequently to the leather riding crop that he invariably carried. Its tapered end served as a whip, and he could lash a man's face with catlike quickness. On numerous occasions the crop's weighted handle doubled as a blackjack. When Ishihara lost his temper, which could happen any time, he was wont to beat prisoners with anything that came to hand. He also slapped a lot of Allied faces. Cpl. Charles H. Camp exaggerated only slightly when he said of Ishihara, "Hell, he beat the piss out of everybody." Not every American and Briton felt the interpreter's sting, but those men made up a fortunate minority at the Shanghai War Prisoners Camp.[52]

Ishihara's superiors discouraged gratuitous mistreatment of prisoners, but his appointment as chief interpreter left him ideally situated to persecute Woosung's inmates. "The guy worked hard at being mean," stated Private First Class Venable, "and in a position such as he had, he could do a pretty good job of it." Ishihara's ability to bridge the language gap made him the main point of contact between the prisoners and their captors. He cynically traded on his indispensability to assume a larger role in the camp's operation. He took over the conduct of morning and evening inspections and oversaw major work details. By Ishihara's own testimony, he rose to the level of virtual camp manager, and this often allowed him to deal with the prisoners as cruelly as he wished. A North China Marine officer who spoke Japanese discerned that Ishihara routinely distorted what his superiors wanted to tell the POWs, and vice versa. The interpreter also lied to Edouard Egle during Red Cross camp visits, portraying the prisoners' circumstances in rosier hues than warranted. Finally, Ishihara kept numerous inmates in suspense by taking much longer than other interpreters to review POWs' mail. He also went further as a censor than merely deleting objectionable words or passages. He once summoned Sgt. Walter Bowsher to his office for a beating because a letter from the Marine's father referred to the enemy as "Japs." Ishihara then ripped the offending missive to pieces without letting Bowsher read it.[53]

Ishihara's victims came up with an abundance of theories to account for his animus. Some thought he desired payback for exposure to racial discrimination or violence in Honolulu. Many POWs decided he was mentally imbalanced. Captain Freuler judged him "almost a psychotic case" exhibiting marked neurotic tendencies—someone who could converse normally one moment and fly into a rage the next. "Oh, he was just cruel," averred Private First Class Fields. "He was everything but a human. . . . I think he felt an inferiority complex." Fields' opinion received a formal endorsement from U.S. Army Maj. Maurice Levin, who spoke for the defense at Ishihara's war crimes trial in March 1946. Characterizing Ishihara as "a paranoiac with an inferiority complex," Levin argued, "The way this man was able to build up his own ego was by showing authority over people who were under his control. He felt each time he beat someone that he was a big shot." These psychological diagnoses struck TSgt. Edwin Hassig, one of Devereux's crustiest NCOs, as overblown. "He was kind of a nut in a way," Hassig admitted, "but Jesus Christ, we had some nuts in the Marine Corps who were worse than Ishihara."[54]

It may be that Ishihara simply embraced the xenophobia and unquestioning reverence for the emperor that the Japanese government strove to inculcate in its people. He derided his white charges as "turtles, pigs, and snakes"—all low forms of life in Japanese culture. Ishihara repeatedly lectured the POWs that his countrymen were destined to vanquish their enemies and monopolize the "good things of the world." Captain Godbold also commented that Ishihara "tried to make the prisoners feel that they were inferior to the Japanese in many smaller ways." The interpreter demeaned American POWs by pledging to "shit" on the Stars and Stripes in front of the entire camp after Japan won the war. Whenever he referred to Emperor Hirohito, in contrast, Ishihara would snap to attention and click his heels. He also insisted that all inmates salute him as if he were an officer.[55]

The POWs may have cursed Ishihara as a monster, but he saw himself as a moral reformer. "Ishihara was a stickler for justice," explained Corporal Tushihiko Yazawa of the camp guard detail. "He was the type of man that went to extremes." Being an interpreter was much more than a job to Ishihara, and he pursued his duties with crusading zeal. Contractor Herb Jaffe captured that side of Ishihara's personality when he said, "The guards would be on duty for 8 hours and be gone 16, . . . but this guy Ishihara took a delight in being available as many waking hours as he had." As a representative of the emperor, Ishihara expected prompt and total obedience. He acted as if it was his mission to purge the POWs of all traces of Western decadence, bend their wills to his, and convince them that the only justification for their existence was as dutiful workers for the Greater East Asia Co-Prosperity Sphere. "Why you surrender if you not work for Japan?" he would shriek at them. "He just thought he was a little tin god," seethed FN1C William Plate. "He just [did] everything he could to make it miserable for . . . all the prisoners." Corporal Richardson probably came closer to the truth by typing Ishihara as a fanatic. "His behavior was unpredictable," Richardson conceded, "but his logic was impeccable if you just followed his line of reasoning."[56]

If Ishihara possessed no scruples about harassing compliant POWs, heaven help the man he deemed deceitful, arrogant, or defiant. In such instances the interpreter became a beast in the literal sense of the word, snarling and foaming at the mouth, with no other thought than to punish, injure, and humiliate the offending party.[57]

During evening roll call on July 8, 1942, the sight of a game board sitting out on a table in one section brought Ishihara to an abrupt halt in a barracks housing Wake servicemen. A stickler for neatness, Ishihara reprimanded the section head,

PlSgt. Bernard O. Ketner, for failing to make his area presentable for inspection. "You God damn Americans don't understand anything," the interpreter sneered, giving Ketner's face a slap to drive home the lesson. Surprised by the blow, Ketner forgot himself and slapped Ishihara back. With murder in his heart, the infuriated Japanese drew his sword. Cpl. Robert Haidinger, a member of Ketner's section, watched in horror as Ishihara chased the small sergeant "halfway up the wall." Ishihara tried to split Ketner's skull, but the agile Marine turned the cutting edge sideways by grabbing the weapon's long handle. Ishihara succeeded in walloping Ketner's head four times with the flat of the blade. He also landed a few punches before Dr. Shindo, the officer of the day, pulled him away.[58]

Ishihara bided his time until inspection ended before returning to Ketner's barracks with the sergeant of the guard. The two Japanese beat Ketner with their firsts for five minutes and then marched him to the guardhouse. There, a sentry held a bayonet against the battered Marine's abdomen as the incensed interpreter and the sergeant administered another beating worse than the last. Ishihara did not relent until he smacked Ketner several times on the head and face with a heavy metal flashlight, loosening several teeth and knocking him to the ground. The interpreter kicked the semiconscious Leatherneck in the testicles at least twice, spat in his face, and called him "a white American son of a bitch." Ketner then had to endure four days in solitary for striking Ishihara—two without food. When the platoon sergeant staggered back to his quarters, his head was still so swollen his buddies could barely recognize him. It took four or five months for Ketner to recover from the most visible effects of the mauling, and he experienced recurring headaches for several years thereafter.[59]

POW officers enjoyed no more immunity from Ishihara's wrath than did their enlisted men. About a month after the Ketner affair, the interpreter accosted Colonel Ashurst's first mess officer, Capt. James Climie of the North China Marines, in front of the galley. Ishihara accused Climie of mismanaging food preparation or distribution. When the American denied the charge, Ishihara beat him in full view of the rest of the camp, starting with punches and then switching to his sheathed sword.

Another time that August, the interpreter learned that 2nd Lt. Richard Huizenga, Ashurst's first appointee as athletic officer, had asked the camp carpentry shop to make something for the POW sports program. Sources disagree over whether Huizenga wanted backboards for basketball goals, a backstop for a baseball diamond, or a sign. At any rate, Ishihara decided that the American officer had flouted regulations by not obtaining Japanese approval for his order and bade him report to the shop for retribution. "He lined up the carpenters as witnesses and commenced a hysterical denouncement of me as a prisoner of war," Huizenga related, "saying among other things, that I had no honor, should be dead, should have died at the front." Ishihara expected Huizenga to wilt under this verbal barrage, but the Naval Academy graduate gave no sign of remorse and looked his nemesis straight in the eye. Huizenga refused to flinch even after the interpreter started hitting him on the wrists and forearms with a club the size of a softball bat. "I was determined," the proud Marine declared, "not to break down and destroy what little prestige we had left." Losing control, Ishihara began clubbing Huizenga's head and shoulders. The lieutenant counted twenty-seven of these blows before blacking out. He later learned that Ishihara kicked him for several minutes as he lay senseless on the shop floor. In addition to numerous contusions on the head, neck, and shoulders, Huizenga suffered a brain concussion and had to be hospitalized for seven to ten days.[60]

The Wake Islanders had tasted a fair sampling of Japanese brutality earlier in their confinement, but Ishihara's savagery was a new experience for the North China Marines and some of Woosung's other occupants. Appalled by what happened to Huizenga, Colonel Ashurst and Sir Mark Young complained directly to Colonel Yuse. The interpreter's berserk depredations clearly violated camp policy, but Yuse hesitated to discipline him. The commandant had already gotten rid of Mikani after the latter's altercation with Maj. Luther Brown, and he could not keep on changing interpreters every time the prisoners raised a fuss. Furthermore, Yuse's health, which was frail at best, had taken a downward turn that left him less able or inclined to keep Ishihara on a tight leash. The Japanese colonel came down with malaria by the early summer of 1942, which was an ironic setback in light of his extraordinary efforts to eradicate that disease at Woosung. Dr. Shindo found no way to better Yuse's condition, and the POWs noticed the commandant growing thinner and wobblier on his feet as he conducted his daily inspections around camp.[61]

Sir Mark Young refused to accept Yuse's slide into debility as an excuse for not checking Ishihara's rampages. The governor-general presented the commandant with a typed protest that documented Ishihara's worst excesses and formally requested the interpreter's removal from the camp. The letter galled Ishihara, and he decided to compel its retraction. With his assistant, Kazunori Morisako, in tow, the head interpreter barged into Sir Mark's quarters on September 8, 1942, interrupting a visit from Major Brown. The British statesman's cool refusal to withdraw his complaint caused Ishihara's emotions to overheat. Unsheathing his sword, the frenzied Japanese lurched forward to decapitate the source of his displeasure. Luckily for Sir Mark, Major Brown sprang on Ishihara and disarmed him before he could spill a drop of aristocratic English blood. Brown flung the interpreter's sword into the hallway and neutralized the Beast of the East by pinning his arms to his sides. With Morisako's help, he ejected Ishihara from Sir Mark's room.

Ishihara's latest eruption made Colonel Yuse realize his manic subordinate had crossed the line. Victimizing ordinary prisoners was bad enough, but murdering a proconsul of the British Empire would bring ramifications the Imperial Japanese Army preferred to avoid. The commandant had Ishihara beaten with a two-by-four and deprived of his sword for a year. The mortified interpreter retained his riding crop, and he got away with whacking enough POWs to earn an alternate nickname—the "Whip." Nevertheless, Ishihara had been partially tamed, and his blowups ebbed in both frequency and intensity.[62]

Colonel Yuse endeavored to minimize friction at Woosung by getting rid of Sir Mark Young. On the evening of September 9, 1942, the camp administration informed the indomitable Briton that he was to be moved to a new camp. Within four days the Japanese put Sir Mark and his orderly on a flight to Formosa. Most of the Americans at Woosung esteemed the British statesman as the POW population's staunchest advocate. They admired him for his stand against the no-escape pledge and for having Ishihara defanged. His departure left them feeling a little less secure, and they would miss his genteel but stiff-necked presence.[63]

Few if any prisoners mourned Colonel Yuse's death less than three weeks later. Purser Kantzer saw the shriveled commandant for the last time on Thursday, September 30. "He was walking around and looked tired and weak, "Kantzer remarked, "but not alarmingly so." Yuse took to his bed sometime that day or the next. He suffered a fatal heart attack on the night of October 2–3. The Japanese gave the POWs a day off from work to attend the colonel's funeral. The Wake Islanders and their comrades found the Shinto ceremony an interesting novelty. As a hearse drove away with Yuse's corpse, however, their thoughts fixed on the future. "As a result of his death we are expecting a change in camp life," contemplated Corporal Durrwachter, "which remains to be seen." Not only was the Shanghai War Prisoners Camp due a new commandant, but the Imperial Japanese Army also planned to move it to a different location.[64]

CHAPTER TWELVE

"this camp is the best one that the japs have"
a new commandant and a new camp

"I THOUGHT HE WAS A PRETTY GOOD COMMANDANT"

The Japanese high command let more than two weeks pass before producing a replacement for Colonel Yuse. With the Imperial Japanese Army spread over some six thousand miles from the Gilbert Islands to the Burma–India border, it needed every able field officer it could muster to lead frontline units or fill important staff slots. Freeing up a colonel to run the Shanghai War Prisoners Camp hardly rated as a top priority.

In the meantime, control of Woosung went by default to Captain Endo, Yuse's executive officer. A stocky, solidly built man who stood five feet six or seven inches, Endo was a chain-smoker and an avid amateur photographer. The POWs rarely saw him without an upwardly curved cigarette holder clenched in his teeth or a camera dangling by his side. Although Endo evinced little animus toward his charges, his susceptibility to corruption earned their contempt.[1]

Endo's interim commandancy ended on October 20, 1942—seventeen days after Yuse's death—when a black Buick sedan braked in front of the Woosung camp office. A chauffeur quickly opened a rear door, and Colonel Satoshi Otera stepped out to survey his new post. Otera had served in the Japanese army for more than three decades, and he also claimed samurai lineage. His superiors sent him to Shanghai to shoulder a dual mission. In addition to acting as warden for some 1,400 Allied POWs, he soon assumed responsibility for the civilian internment camp that the Japanese opened in the city in early November at the old 4th Marines barracks on Haiphong Road. That facility would hold approximately three hundred enemy nationals, among them the most prominent Britons and Americans snatched from the International Settlement.

On October 21 Woosung's curious occupants got a good look at their new commandant as they formed ranks in the outer compound to hear his inaugural speech. The POWs beheld a heavyset man in his mid-fifties roughly the same height as Captain Endo. The colonel's face beamed with a surprising amiability undimmed by a lush white mustache terminating in meticulously waxed tips. In no time at all, the prisoners took to calling Otera "Handlebar Hank."[2]

Speaking through Ishihara, Otera addressed his captive audience with the words of a stern but caring father: "Now you must work hard and diligently, as your countrymen are working at the front and at home, and must not expect to take it easy just because you aren't there. As long as you obey orders and instructions here, I, the camp director, personally guarantee that you will be alive and well at the end of the war. But you must not think that you are guests of the Japanese government.... Now you are prisoners of war and nothing else."[3]

A cosmopolitan background set Otera apart from many other Japanese army officers. He had spent some time as a military attaché at the Japanese Embassy in Paris. That exposed him to Western racial prejudice, which would later prompt him to chide Woosung's inmates for "your sense of superiority which makes you think that the world was created for the white man and only for the white man." Nonetheless, much about the West and its people appealed to Otera, and he eschewed the knee-jerk xenophobia that infected so many Japanese. "I am spiritually and emotionally sympathetic with you," he assured his charges, "who before the war were doing your duty as best you could." Besides extolling the virtues of industry and obedience, Otera repeatedly urged the POWs to guard their health. He also liked reminding them that they resided in the Japanese military's "model camp." To foster greater harmony, the colonel awarded certificates of commendation to prisoners who made the camp a better place to live. "I thought he was a pretty good commandant," concluded Captain Godbold. Pvt. Edward Sturgeon testified that the enlisted POWs regarded Otera as "a pretty decent fellow."[4]

Otera knew no English, but he picked up a little French while an attaché, and he welcomed any chance to practice that skill. He discovered a suitable conversation partner in Major Devereux, who had received part of his schooling in Europe. The POWs noticed that the two officers spent much time together. "We always thought that was kind of neat that they at least talked together," remarked Cpl. Thomas Johnson. Devereux described his relationship with Otera in more sardonic terms: "He'd pretend like he was understanding me, and I'd pretend like I was understanding him." Although the quality of the French may have been dubious, those friendly encounters benefited the POWs by conveying the appearance that Devereux could bypass Ishihara and communicate directly with the commandant.[5]

Like other visitors to France, Handlebar Hank acquired a taste for the country's magnificent wines. Binge drinking led to alcoholism, and that vicious disease blighted Otera's career. Devereux, who got to know the commandant possibly better than any other POW, described him as "an old drunk." By 1942 most of the commandant's classmates were generals, while he was sidelined in an unimportant rear echelon job.[6]

Overseeing a pair of prisons turned Colonel Otera into a commuting commandant. He kept a house in Shanghai and divided his days between the two facilities. The colonel's chauffeur normally delivered him to the Shanghai War Prisoners Camp at 9:00 AM and then whisked him off to the Haiphong Road Camp in the early afternoon. Yet even when Otera was present, most prisoners had little contact with him. He often stayed in his office to finish off a bottle or would summon Devereux for a chat. At other times Otera neglected his duties by indulging a passion for hunting. Bemused inmates frequently spotted Handlebar Hank stalking through the distant countryside with a Japanese soldier tagging along to act as a weapons bearer or retrieve any game the colonel might bag. The POWs saw more of Otera during baseball season. "He liked softball," remembered Captain Godbold. "We played a great deal of softball, and he always came to the games."[7]

After the war Otera insisted that he had instructed his Japanese subordinates: "It is important that the prisoners be treated so that they will be happy." In actual practice, however, the colonel's absentee management style permitted any guards so inclined to harass or abuse their charges. Severe beatings remained fairly rare, but the POWs absorbed doses of excessive brutality at irregular intervals. A senior enemy NCO called "One Round Hogan" blew his stack on March 14, 1944, when he caught a section in a civilian barracks unprepared for evening inspection. He bashed the errant parties on the head so hard with a wooden clipboard that two dozen reported to the hospital for stitches or to have splinters extracted from their skin. That scene repeated itself on May 2. At another time, an irate guard aimed a bayonet thrust at Marine Gunner William Lee from North China and came close to killing him. Otera's failure to punish the perpetrators of such rampages drew criticism from the American officers. Second Lt. Richard Huizenga summed up the colonel's conduct this way: "In general, his attitude was that of a professional soldier. . . . However, he did disregard most of the things that were done by his officers and men." Huizenga and other POWs realized that Otera's detachment opened the door to the reestablishment of Ishihara's pernicious domination over camp life.[8]

While Otera never personally struck a prisoner, he did not countenance infractions of the rules, large or small. He preferred mass punishments for group offenses and those committed by unknown individuals. These demonstrations of Japanese power reminded inmates of their lowly place in the camp's pecking order. Otera also intended to pressure his charges into either policing themselves or informing on the few whose misdeeds made life miserable for the many. On April 23, 1943, a Contractor and a merchant sailor stole some canned jam from a warehouse, and the commandant threatened to stop all rations for the following day. The POWs received no breakfast or lunch on the twenty-fourth, but Otera mercifully granted them half servings of rice and stew for dinner. Three civilian barracks lost their breakfast for being unprepared for morning inspection on July 4, 1943. Otera responded even more fiercely that same month after four POWs reportedly burglarized the canteen for some extra food. He ordered every occupant of Barracks 4 to stand at attention in front of the camp office from 7:00 AM to 5:00 PM without food and water. Several men fainted during the hotter part of the day, but that only drove home Otera's lesson. The colonel also thought it a good idea to have guilty prisoners punish themselves. He once forced some Contractors caught stealing from a bean patch to pummel each other.[9]

Despite Otera's harsh side, he readily complied with his superiors' wishes to protect his prison camp's image as a propaganda showplace. The new commandant recognized the utility of the Red Cross in preserving a facade of Japanese magnanimity. In contrast to Colonel Yuse, who had to be pressured into working with the relief agency, Otera's relationship with Edouard Egle grew almost cordial. The commandant would end up beseeching the Red Cross for increased assistance, frankly admitting that he could not keep the POWs healthy on the resources allocated by Tokyo. To prove that Western aid was having the desired effect, Egle regularly received permission to see the prisoners. During Otera's first year as commandant, Egle visited the Shanghai War Prisoners Camp at least four times—on November 10, 1942, and January 9, March 24, and June 19, 1943. The commandant also allowed representatives from Shanghai's Swiss consulate general to tour his premises, but on a less-frequent basis.[10]

Otera took precautions to ensure that inspections by Egle and Swiss diplomats served the Imperial Japanese Army's agenda. Prior to every visit the POWs would drop their regular work details to concentrate on tidying up the camp. The Japanese also went to other lengths to favorably impress their European guests. As Purser William Kantzer of the *President Harrison* noted on November 4,

1943, "The Swiss Consul paid us a visit today. So the japs laid out the remaining bacon that we are going to get tonight, beautiful trays of apples—the first this year—which we also get tonight, and showed copious stores, relatively speaking, of rice[,] potatoes, salt and so forth."[11]

To prevent foreign do-gooders from seeing or hearing anything embarrassing, Otera restricted their movements inside camp. Up to eight guards escorted each visitor everywhere he went, and none could converse with a prisoner unless an interpreter and one or more Japanese officers were present. Otera extended Colonel Ashurst and Major Brown the privilege of meeting with Egle and Swiss diplomats to request specific forms of succor. The commandant stipulated, however, that Ashurst submit a written wish list well in advance, and Otera did not hesitate to delete items that might cast Japanese authorities in a negative light. Egle recognized the self-serving nature of these constraints, but he viewed Otera as basically decent and cooperative. Following the Red Cross delegate's final camp visit on February 10, 1945, he wired Geneva, "Camp commandant and his officers merit praise for their kindness and efforts [toward] maintaining camp on high standard."[12]

"WE'RE NEAR SHANGHAI & IN A LITTLE BETTER CAMP"

The POWs expected the appointment of a new commandant to trigger some changes, but one turned out to be more dramatic than anticipated. Within a month of Colonel Otera's arrival, his charges got wind of their jailers' plans to transplant the Shanghai War Prisoners Camp to a more convenient location. Woosung left much to be desired as a site for a prison camp. Its isolation and distance from Shanghai hampered the delivery of food, fuel, and other supplies. The sabotage committed by POW work details further exacerbated the poor state of the few primitive roads connecting the camp with the outside world, and Otera must not have enjoyed the long, bumpy rides to and from his home in the city. Escalating guerrilla activity in the Woosung area also concerned Japanese authorities, especially after a Chinese sniper shot a sentry walking post along the camp perimeter. The malaria epidemic that scourged inmates and guards during the spring and summer of 1942 furnished the final proof of Woosung's unsuitability. Otera accordingly received orders to transfer his entire operation to an abandoned Japanese army installation on higher and drier ground in the Shanghai suburbs near the fashionable racetrack village of Kiangwan.[13]

For manageability's sake, the commandant stretched the move over four days, from December 3 through 6, 1942. Otera organized the prisoners into four contingents of four hundred men or less, and each hiked the ten miles from

Woosung to the Kiangwan camp on a different day. Contractors composed the first group to make the march, and the Wake Marines took their leave of Woosung on December 5. The POWs spent the eve of their departure stripping their domiciles of any item that might be the slightest use to them later. Purser Kantzer, who left with the last contingent, admitted to "taking everything . . . that we could lay our hands on that wasn't nailed down too securely, including empty tin cans, buckets, brooms, mops and just plain odds and ends of metal and wood that would under any other circumstances be classified as plain junk but which is irreplaceable around these parts." The prisoners even remembered to grab all the light bulbs and reflectors hanging in their old barracks.[14]

Each POW had to tote his own blankets, extra winter clothes, and other personal belongings. Watching the first contingent trudge away burdened with blankets and bundles, Pfc. John Pearsall scoffed, "Civilian[s] moved—looked like a bunch of tramps." Colonel Otera obtained trucks to carry his charges' mattresses, sleeping mats, and heavier baggage, plus the contents of Woosung's hospital, recreation hall, library, workshops, and warehouses. He also allowed Colonel Ashurst and ailing inmates to ride to their new home. The recipients of that courtesy deeply appreciated it, as the weather did not smile on the move. Each contingent had to brave bitter cold, and the first was pelted by a driving rain.[15]

Before the Americans and Britons set out, Colonel Otera promised they would find Kiangwan a much nicer place to live. "It was supposed to be better than the one we left," reported TSgt. Edwin Hassig, "in fact a model camp." But a dismal sight awaited Hassig and his comrades at the end of their trek. "The Kiangwan Camp was little better than the Woosung Camp," the indignant sergeant snorted. "We had the same old Jap army barracks, the same stinking latrines and the same dirty galley." Contractor Emmett Newell tried adopting a sunnier tone. "We're near Shanghai & in a little better camp," he told his diary. But he could not help adding, "It is in a terrible run down condition."[16]

In many ways Kiangwan resembled a carbon copy of Woosung. "This new camp certainly looked delightful at first glance," a sarcastic Purser Kantzer noted on December 7. "Standing in a dilapidated run-down weed-patch of a compound stood seven barracks in a row, faded, rusty-roofed, broken-down buildings that had, so it seemed, as many windows out as in, and places where the walls of the building were entirely missing." Initially, the barracks had no lighting fixtures, and some sections lacked sleeping platforms and storage shelves. The camp's previous occupants also scored no points for neatness in their successors' eyes. After peering inside some barracks, Private First Class Pearsall griped, "The Japs who left hear certainly were a dirty lot."[17]

Once the POWs got over their disappointment, the majority decided that their new quarters were a little newer and in slightly better repair than their former haunts. At the very least, the barracks at Kiangwan admitted less water. The many loose boards in the walls and floors also offered inmates convenient hiding places for diaries, homemade knives, and other contraband.

Kiangwan contained the same number of barracks as Woosung, but the prisoners received slightly different housing assignments. All officers—U.S. Marine, U.S. Navy, Royal Navy, and merchant marine—were segregated from their men and lodged in the northernmost barracks. This structure became known officially as Barracks O, although antiauthoritarian inmates called it "Zero Barracks." Enlisted American and British military personnel filled the next two barracks, which were numbered 1 and 2. Barracks 3, 4, and 5 were reserved for the Wake Island Contractors and lower-ranking merchant seamen. Nonofficers still lived in thirty-six-man sections, but Barracks O was divided into smaller rooms, which provided the brass with greater privacy.[18]

The Japanese set aside the entire seventh, or southernmost, barracks for the POWs' hospital. That welcome change gave the camp's sick and their healers three times as much floor space as had been the case at Woosung. Thanks to ongoing Red Cross aid, the Kiangwan hospital became the finest health care facility in any prison camp run by the Japanese. It ended up acquiring 120 beds, many of them movable Western types. Small rooms contained one to three beds, and larger wards held eight to ten. The hospital also boasted a separate examination room, an operating clinic, an x-ray room, and a dental parlor. Besides film and a new tube for the x-ray machine, Edouard Egle equipped the POW medics with a heat lamp, an ultraviolet ray machine for sterilization, and an inductotherm machine for conducting shortwave, deep-heat therapy. The Red Cross man and his assistants constantly scoured Shanghai for medical supplies and sent the prisoners whatever he could purchase, including Novocain, thyroid tablets, adrenalin chloride, ammonium chloride, bismuth subcarbonate, calcium carbonate, alcohol, menthol crystals, mineral oil, absorbent cotton, thermometers, Vaseline, ammonium sulfate, iodine, thermometers, adhesive tape, and much, much more. Dr. Pollard also received enough dental equipment to perform extractions, fillings, and root canal and gum work, and Egle found a source in Shanghai to provide needy POWs with new dentures. The Red Cross man even hunted down some linoleum for the operating and x-ray rooms to keep out the dust that rose through the wooden floors of the converted barracks.[19]

Kiangwan could have been a much healthier establishment, however, had the Japanese paid more attention to elementary sanitation. As at Woosung, each bar-

The Layout of the Kiangwan Site of the Shanghai War Prisoners Camp as Sketched by Contractor Joseph J. Astarita

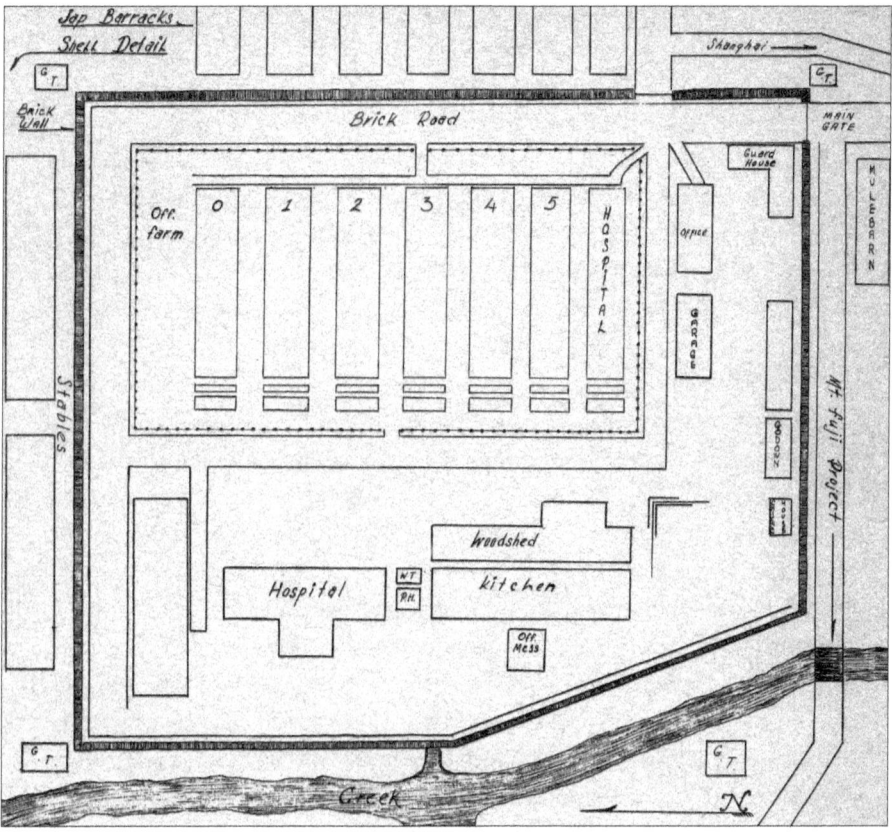

Author's collection

racks had its own latrine and wash rack standing nearby. With the benjos erected within twenty feet of the prisoners' quarters, outbreaks of dysentery and diarrhea remained a standard part of camp life.[20]

While negligent about hygiene, the Japanese took the trouble to render Kiangwan both more secure and safer for the POWs. They once again surrounded the barracks area with an electrified barbed wire fence, but this one did not sit so close to the prisoners' quarters. A stout brick wall eight feet high bounded Kiangwan's outer compound, giving the camp a total area of approximately five hundred feet by three hundred feet. A second barbed wire fence capable of carrying five thousands volts ran along the top of the wall. Both fences were supposed to be uncharged between dawn and dusk, and the wall provided inmates with additional protection against accidental electrocution. This safety precaution also constituted an effective obstacle to escape. Further, the high water table around Shanghai made tunneling under the wall impossible. "This Camp was virtually escape proof," conceded TSgt. Charles Holmes.[21]

The outer compound accommodated a range of buildings essential to the camp's operation—an administrative office, a guardhouse, a garage, the POW galley, a water tower, a pump house, a bathhouse, shops, and warehouses, plus a separate hospital, kitchen, and officers' mess for the Japanese. Four well-positioned guard towers and barracks for the soldiers who manned them stood just beyond the brick wall. Inside the POWs' area, the Japanese thoughtfully converted a large building in the northwest corner into a combined library and recreation hall. As noted earlier, the Red Cross and its supporters augmented the library's holdings over the next two and a half years from more than three thousand volumes to somewhere near six thousand. "One of the redeeming features of this concentration camp is the library," reflected Purser Kantzer. An official from the War Prisoners Department in Tokyo who inspected Kiangwan on March 22, 1944, echoed Kantzer's opinion. The amazed Japanese declared that nothing like the camp library existed in any of his country's other POW facilities.[22]

Kiangwan's attractiveness, however, stemmed mainly from its proximity to Shanghai. "This new site is much more convenient for us as it can be reached from town by motorcar in about half an hour," enthused Edouard Egle, "and this fact greatly facilitates the delivery of relief goods to the camp." Kiangwan sat only five miles north of the International Settlement on the modern Tazang Motor Road. The POWs could easily see the Shanghai skyline whenever they stepped outside the main gate, and this left them feeling less forlorn and forgotten.[23]

Though not immediately apparent, the move to Kiangwan increased the possibility of the Wake Islanders and their comrades becoming victims of friendly fire. The new camp lay between two enemy airfields—one 2 miles to the north, and another 4 miles to the south. A Japanese army training camp stood right next door to Kiangwan, and the troops rotating through there occupied the same type of barracks as the POWs. The presence of such installations turned the entire area into a prime target for air raids. Since the Japanese refrained from marking their prison camps, Kiangwan looked exactly like any other enemy base from the air, which could make it a magnet for Allied bombs or strafing. The Japanese seemed to deliberately invite attack by emplacing antiaircraft machine guns immediately outside the camp's brick wall. Fortunately for the inmates' peace of mind, the USAAF did not start demonstrating the camp's perilous situation until the summer of 1944. The threat seemed so remote before then that the POWs took no alarm when the Japanese imposed blackout precautions on December 17, 1942. Thereafter, camp authorities required that blankets be hung over all barracks windows from dark until lights-out. The Japanese also placed boxes of sand around camp for extinguishing fires caused by bombs.[24]

As soon as each newly arrived POW contingent learned its barracks assignments, the men went to work making Kiangwan more habitable. They began by cleaning and repairing their quarters. The winter cold spurred them to replace broken or missing window panes as quickly as possible, and the Japanese contributed unexpectedly to everyone's comfort by installing small potbellied stoves in every section by December 18, 1942. The expense of coal compelled Colonel Otera to limit stove use to the periods of 7:15 to 9:00 AM and 4:30 to 7:00 PM each day. Sections that exceeded the commandant's restrictions or tried to raise heat levels by burning loose boards pried off their barracks or other buildings risked the loss of their stoves and other penalties.[25]

Even before the POWs finished putting the barracks and hospital in order, work details ventured outdoors for other tasks. They dug drainage ditches or laid out brick walkways to keep inmates out of the mud during rainfalls. Other prisoners equipped the benjos with proper flooring. As the weather warmed, many in the camp's population became landscapers and gardeners. By May 16, 1943, Purser Kantzer was singing a different tune about Kiangwan's appearance. "It has a cultivated look now," he wrote, "with strips of vegetable and flower gardens on the sides of the barracks, . . . and the front of the barracks set out in formal arrangement of circles, ovals, and squares. Between these designs have been dug water pits for fire fighting, and plenty of frogs now inhabit them." American POWs also cleared and leveled sufficient ground for baseball diamonds. The combined effects of Japanese benevolence, Red Cross charity, and POW industry led the official from Tokyo's War Prisoners Department to confide something remarkable to camp librarian Howard Cook. As William Kantzer heard the story, "He said what Col. Odera and Ishihari have been saying for a long time: that this camp is the best one that the japs have."[26]

One feature that did not enhance Kiangwan's showcase image was the cemetery that the Japanese allowed the POWs to establish in May 1943. By that time two Americans had already died at the new camp. Pneumonia killed Pfc. Robert I. Wiskochil, a Wake Marine, on December 16. Joseph Williams, a Contractor from California, succumbed on March 9 to a ruptured spleen induced by malaria. The Japanese conveyed both corpses to Shanghai for cremation as usual. With the next POW death, however, camp authorities adopted a new policy. After Contractor Leo Pat Driscoll expired from stomach ulcers on May 20, Colonel Otera decided to inter deceased prisoners at Kiangwan. CPNAB carpenters took on the task of making concrete crosses reinforced by bamboo to mark each grave. They also constructed wooden boxes to hold the latest dead man's bones or ashes.[27]

Those losses were more than offset by the arrival of two new batches of prisoners within less than three weeks of Kiangwan's activation. On December 7, 1942, four USAAF airmen—the survivors from a B-25 bomber shot down near Canton several weeks earlier—entered camp. The Japanese released them into the general population the following day. Second Lt. Murray Lewis, the B-25's navigator, and Sgt. Paul Webb and Sgt. James Young arrived in reasonably good shape, but a bullet had mangled the left foot of their pilot, 1st Lt. Howard Allers. The enemy had denied Allers all but the most perfunctory treatment. That changed once the lieutenant fell into the hands of Kiangwan's talented U.S. Navy doctors. While Allers convalesced, the Wake Islanders and the other POWs besieged him and his crewmates for uncensored information about home and the fighting fronts. "The piolets shot down over Canton passed out a little good news on how the war was progressing," Private First Class Pearsall scrawled happily in his diary on the first anniversary of the Pearl Harbor attack.[28]

The thirty-four British and Canadian prisoners who joined the Kiangwan community on December 19 had a much more harrowing story to tell. The men belonged to the Hong Kong garrison and had been in enemy custody almost as long as the Wake Islanders. On September 25, 1942, a small freighter named the *Lisbon Maru* embarked 1,865 Hong Kong defenders chosen for slave labor in Japan. The enemy crammed them into three holds, where they suffered torments similar to the Wake Islanders' ordeal on the *Nitta Maru*. The *Lisbon Maru* put out to sea two days later with nearly eight hundred homeward-bound Japanese soldiers also on board, but no markings indicated the presence of POWs. Around 4:00 AM, October 1, the ship crossed the path of the American submarine USS *Grouper*, whose captain mistook it for just another enemy troop transport. The *Grouper* attacked three hours later at a point east of Shanghai, not far from the Zhoushan Archipelago. The submarine fired six torpedoes at its prey. Three torpedoes missed the *Lisbon Maru*, one clanged into its hull without detonating, and a sharp-eyed Japanese gunner disabled another, but the ship was already past saving. The fourth torpedo fired by the *Grouper* had blasted a big enough hole in the transport's stern to cause the *Lisbon Maru* to sink slowly.

A Japanese destroyer, five gunboats, and three other vessels hastened to the stricken transport's aid. The Japanese easily evacuated their own soldiers and the *Lisbon Maru*'s crew, but they had no intention of saving the POWs. Enemy sailors callously locked the hatches on the prisoners' holds, and six suicide guards remained on board to shoot any Britons or Canadians who got loose. Desperate to avoid drowning, the POWs burst free on the morning of October 2. They overran and killed the six guards and then jumped into the sea, hoping to reach the Japanese vessels still hovering in the vicinity. Enemy sailors responded by firing machine guns at the men struggling in the water, and the rescued Japanese soldiers followed suit with their rifles. The skippers of the ships deliberately plowed through groups of swimmers. Unwilling to sit and watch such savagery, valiant Chinese fishermen steered their boats into the chaos and carnage and began pulling survivors out of the water. This courageous compassion seemed to shame the Japanese, and they turned from being murderers into rescuers.

Of the 1,865 POWs who left Hong Kong on the *Lisbon Maru*, 828 went down with the ship, fell victim to hostile fire, or drifted away and were never seen again. The Japanese assembled the survivors they recovered at Shanghai, herding most of them onto the *Shinshei Maru* to resume their voyage north on October 7. Fifty *Lisbon Maru* survivors, the majority of them too sick to travel, remained at Shanghai. Fifteen perished over the next two and a half months, and the Japanese ultimately confined the remainder at Kiangwan. This group recorded its sixteenth death on December 26, one week after entering Japan's model camp. All sixteen deceased prisoners were consigned to a mass grave in the camp cemetery the following day.[29]

The newcomers represented some of the British army's most legendary units—the Royal Scots, Middlesex Regiment, Royal Artillery, Corps of Royal Engineers, and Royal Corps of Signals—not to mention two Royal Navy ratings and one Royal Marine. Without a doubt, however, Kiangwan's original occupants reserved their heartiest welcome for the one officer and four men belonging to the Royal Army Medical Corps. Captain Maurice G. Lynch hailed from Canada. His fellow prisoners called him "Benny Lynch" after the champion flyweight boxer from Scotland. Dr. G. Mason Kahn, who was notoriously hard to please in all matters medical, lauded his Canadian colleague as "the most brilliant doctor I think I ever met." As for the four British medical corpsmen accompanying Lynch, Kahn said, "They were the best men I ever worked with."[30]

Kiangwan took in one more ravaged castoff on March 26, 1943. Vice Squadron Leader Lewis S. Bishop, formerly an ensign in the U.S. Navy, had gone on extended leave before Pearl Harbor to battle the Japanese in China as a fighter pilot with the American Volunteer Group (AVG)—a unit better known to the world as the Flying Tigers. Bishop attained ace status with 5.2 victories before he led a flight of four other P-40s over French Indochina on May 17, 1942. A faulty bomb exploded right after he released it, crippling his plane. Bishop succeeded in bailing out, but troops loyal to Vichy France took him prisoner and turned him over to the Japanese. The Japanese hated the AVG for its aerial prowess, and they despised its members as mercenaries. Consequently, Bishop's treatment ranged from cruel to indifferent.

Following initial detention at Hanoi, the Japanese sent Bishop to Shanghai, where they flung him into the notorious Bridgehouse Jail, the local headquarters of the Kempeitai. During Bishop's first nine months as a prisoner, he got to bathe only twice, and his rations were always meager and sometimes inedible. Ten days after Bishop arrived at the Bridgehouse, the Japanese clapped him into solitary for sixty-nine days. The sequestered American soon grew seriously ill. Beriberi made his body swell from head to toe and hindered his breathing. A Japanese nurse saved him by administering injections of vitamin B1 and glucose, but diarrhea caused weight loss at an alarming rate. Bishop grew so weak that he would faint every time he tried to cross his cell to use the bucket serving as his benjo.

The man the Japanese hauled into Kiangwan on March 26 had dwindled to eighty pounds and hovered on the verge of death. Cpl. Thomas Johnson saw Bishop shortly after the flier's arrival. "He was sitting there on this chair," Johnson related, "and he still had his original tunics. It was all bloody—dried blood. And he was just a walking mass of lice. His hair hadn't been cut at all and his whiskers hadn't been cut or anything." The Wake Marine called Bishop "probably the most pitiful sight that I seen of somebody that was actually alive."[31]

Dr. Kahn decided that only blood transfusions could save Bishop's life, but the procedure carried risks. In those days, doctors had only a rough crossmatch for blood types—A, B, O, and AB. Bishop received as many as five transfusions, the blood drawn from the different nationalities among the confined. To Kahn's relief, Bishop exhibited no adverse reactions. The other prisoners contributed to this curative campaign by giving up enough rice to feed Bishop double portions. In three months the grounded Flying Tiger was as healthy as any other man in camp. A grateful Kahn ascribed the happy turnaround to a higher power: "God is with you many times."[32]

"WE ARE EATING LIKE KINGS"

First Lieutenant Allers and his crewmates, the *Lisbon Maru* survivors, and Lewis Bishop could not have chosen a more propitious time to find refuge at Kiangwan. Right after the Shanghai War Prisoners Camp changed location, the repatriation ship *Conte Verde* docked at Woosung village with a large shipment of Red Cross relief supplies from the United States it had picked up at Lourenço Marques the previous July. On December 7, 1942, Colonel Otera dispatched one hundred

POWs to unload that cargo. They returned to camp that evening with stirring news. "They say there is enough comfort kits for everyone here and enough food packages to go around twice," Purser Kantzer gushed to his diary. "The food packages sound pretty good. The packing list for them . . . said they had canned meat, sweet chocolate, coffee, cocoa, pipe tobacco, cigarettes, powdered orange concentrate and margarine." The prisoners' eyes bulged as the Japanese hauled this bounty into camp and locked it away in a warehouse. Kantzer and the others soon realized that the shipment was much larger than first reported. Lieutenant Polkinghorn later learned that the camp received at least 5,264 American Red Cross food boxes and another 5,621 from Canada. "The red cross boxes keep piling up," an elated Kantzer wrote. "Truck after truck of boxes come in consisting of food, medicines, comfort kits and tobacco galore. We will certainly be well off if we get it." The sudden eruption of Allied munificence left Ishihara incredulous. "I don't understand you Americans," he spluttered. "Your countrymen send all these good things to you prisoners who surrendered. You didn't die for your country."[33]

Camp authorities granted the POWs their first taste of the Red Cross windfall on December 9, but it was a small one. Each section received seven to eight Canadian food boxes, which broke down roughly to one box for every five to six men. Japanese stinginess could not curb the resulting joy as each group of prisoners tore open its eleven-pound container of manna from heaven. "Everyone so happy some men actually cried," Contractor Herb Papock reported. "Sure had a picnic," agreed Emmett Newell. According to William Kantzer, the typical Canadian box contained "15 items of canned goods, condiments and the like plus a bar of soap." A box's edible contents included a pound of butter; a pound of powdered milk; one can each of sardines; salmon, corned beef, and lunch meat; a box of hardtack crackers; a quarter pound of tea; a bar of concentrated chocolate; and assorted quantities of salt, sugar, prunes, and raisins. The lunch meat was new to the Wake Islanders. "We hadn't heard of Spam until then," quipped Sgt. Donald Malleck. "It was an immediate & large success."[34]

The women who packed both the Canadian and American food boxes crammed packs of American cigarettes in the spaces between the food containers. The number of cigarettes found in a particular box depended on the skill of whoever filled it. The relief shipment also brought the POWs a large additional quantity of cigarettes and pipe tobacco to supplement the smokes stuffed in the food boxes. More conducive to the prisoners' health were the one hundred newly arrived cases of American medications, including quinine and all-purpose sulfa drugs.[35]

The Japanese treated the POWs to feasting on a grander scale on December 12 by issuing each man his own food box. Private First Class Pearsall closed his diary entry that evening with words he never thought he would write while in Japanese custody: "Went to bed feeling content." William Kantzer felt good enough to crow the next day, "We got a full Canadian Red Cross food package apiece yesterday evening.... We are eating like kings." Contractor Herb Papock felt equally satisfied after camp authorities issued everyone a second Canadian food box five days later. He noted the occasion by scratching one word in his diary: "HEAVEN."[36]

The prisoners' spirits soared again, appropriately enough, when the Japanese distributed the camp's first batch of American food boxes on Christmas Eve. Aside from substituting instant coffee for tea and including such extras as instant cocoa and orange concentrate, American boxes held pretty much the same things as the Canadian variety. The guards compounded the thrill produced by all that tasty nutrition by presenting every inmate with a second Christmas present from the United States—a comfort kit. Originally designed for participants in the Civilian Conservation Corps, the New Deal's most popular work relief program, a comfort kit contained a safety razor with five blades, a shaving brush, shaving cream, a toothbrush, toothpaste, some soap, a soap container, a comb, and a small sewing kit consisting of needles, thread, and a thimble. To the prisoners' amazement, they also received one pound of candy apiece, plus a plug of American chewing tobacco, some loose smoking tobacco, and an extra pack of Lucky Strike cigarettes. FN1C William Plate could not remember a happier holiday. "We were just having a wonderful time," he recalled, "fixing ourselves hot chocolate, eating out of Red Cross boxes, and smoking cigarettes and just celebrating as only an American celebrates Christmas."[37]

Camp authorities released a second American food box on New Year's Eve, which set off another festive night in the barracks. The POWs had to wait a full month for their next installment. The Japanese withheld it to signalize the first anniversary of the camp's opening, which they arbitrarily designated as February 1. The prisoners received a full issue of Canadian boxes late on February 10, 1943, in observance of the 2,603rd anniversary of the founding of the Japanese Empire, which fell on the following day. March 9 heralded the end of fat times at Kiangwan. The Japanese ostensibly distributed the last of the food boxes, and there were only enough on hand for a partial issue. In Barracks O, each officer took possession of three-quarters of a box. In the rest of the camp, however, one box had to be split by three or four men. As compensation, every inmate received fifty American cigarettes and one can of loose tobacco.[38]

The prisoners greeted the final dispersal of Red Cross food boxes with sadness and suppressed anger. They knew they had not received everything to which they were entitled. Telltale signs of Japanese thievery began cropping up with the arrival of the relief shipment in December 1942. "Empty cans—not ours, and American cigarettes being smoked by the Japanese were evidence of pilfering," recalled Sergeant Malleck. Observant inmates spotted food boxes in the quarters of enemy officers. Members of a detail sent to perform yard work and other chores around Colonel Otera's house in Shanghai reported that the commandant dined regularly on American food. Captain Endo turned out to be even more rapacious than his commanding officer. Colonel Ashurst estimated that one-third of the food boxes in the first relief shipment from America never reached the prisoners. That accounts for why Lieutenant Polkinghorn's totals failed to jibe with Red Cross manifests.[39]

An exact count of food box losses surfaced later thanks to the diligence of PlSgt. Jack R. Bishop, a North China Marine. Bishop worked as an assistant to a senior enemy NCO named Goto who oversaw the warehouse containing the Red Cross supplies. Keeping tabs with a ledger, Bishop immediately noticed "discrepancies between the supplies we were supposed to have and the actual amount on hand." He watched as Captain Endo personally removed 1,056 food boxes from the warehouse over the course of two months. Endo also broke into several medical cases to filch sulfa drugs and other medications. When Endo transferred to a prison camp in Manchuria in early 1944, he left Kiangwan with two 3-ton tucks piled with American and Canadian relief stores. Second Lt. Richard Huizenga figured that the camp's former executive officer got away with enough loot to earn a fortune on the black market. Goto not only gave Endo the run of his warehouse, but he also followed his superior's crooked example. He often opened food and medical boxes, helping himself to whatever he wanted. He once had Bishop and ten other POWs carry 452 Canadian food boxes to his room.[40]

Colonel Ashurst protested the thefts, requesting that he and his officers be given custodianship over all Red Cross supplies that came into camp. Colonel Otera rejected this proposal on the grounds that his guards had as much right to savor Western delicacies as did POWs—if not more. Things might have been worse had Ashurst not adamantly refused to sign vouchers for any food boxes or other items unless the enemy actually turned them over to the inmates. This imposed a ceiling on pilfering, as the receipts were supposed to be referred to Shanghai's Red Cross delegate. Camp authorities did not want Edouard Egle and the Swiss consul general asking any awkward questions. In fact, that possibility worried Otera so much that he returned 150 food boxes on August 30, 1943. That unexpected attack of conscience resulted in the POWs enjoying slightly richer stews for several days thereafter. The commandant also removed four Taiwanese guards from camp on October 15, 1944, after they were caught swiping some of the prisoners' medical stores.[41]

"LOTS OF DEALING GOING ON"

Knowing that the Japanese were taking their cut did not detract from the psychological benefits of the *Conte Verde*'s relief cargo. "It was tremendously uplifting to have this tangible evidence that we had not been forgotten" testified 2nd Lt. John Kinney, "that people in America cared about us and were doing what they could to ease our difficult situation." Second Lt. Robert Hanna deemed the food boxes "a big morale booster." Cpl. Bernard Richardson recalled his feelings as he opened his first box: "God, the highlight of the year. . . . Powdered milk, . . . candy bars, four packs of cigarettes, little goodies, just a touch of home." Pfc. Mackie Wheeler discerned a residual effect in the new hopefulness that swept the camp. "And I imagine," he opined, "that's [what] brought some of us through."[42]

How quickly a POW consumed his food box spoke volumes about his degree of self-restraint and other aspects of his character. Some inmates could not withstand the temptation to gorge and stuffed themselves with as much Western food as their stomachs could hold. "I was hungry," confessed Pvt. Ewing LaPorte. "I ate it." The sudden ingestion of too much rich food could sicken a malnourished man. Several prisoners remembered their reaction to wolfing down a single bar of concentrated chocolate. "I ate one of them whole things one night," admitted Pfc. Calvin L. Permenter from North China, "and I lay awake all night long burning up with energy—12,000 calories at one time. I couldn't close an eye all night." Pfc. Willie Benton, another North China Marine, found his chocolate highs more comforting than disturbing. "Man, you could just sit there in them cold barracks and eat them chocolate bars, and you could just feel the heat," Benton exclaimed. "Actually, it would make you feel warm—that energy coming into your blood."[43]

Most POWs consumed the contents of their food boxes in smaller increments to prolong their solace and pleasure. An individual prisoner might derive a week's use out of a small tin of butter by taking just a dab to flavor his daily rice ration. Conservation could also take a communal approach. Four or five inmates might split one can of meat per day. The more ingenious prisoners would cut up a can's worth of Spam, combine it with rice and bread issued by the Japanese, and turn these ingredients into a passable meatloaf. Even the most disciplined POWs felt too famished to make a food box last much more than a week, but each day it did was special. A frugal prisoner had a reason to get out of bed because he knew a treat awaited him. Such simple joys made it easier to put up with the frustrations of life behind barbed wire.[44]

In addition to morale surges, each newly released batch of Red Cross food boxes unleashed a round of intensified economic activity inside camp. "Issued another box," Private First Class Pearsall noted on New Year's Eve, 1942. "Lots of dealing going on." Contractor Alec Pay offered this more explicit description of the market bazaar the POWs staged one day later: "Food box issued to all men yesterday evening. Today spent by most of us in bartering & swapping various food items & tobaccos."[45]

This barracks commerce originated innocently enough. A POW who did not smoke or drink coffee would trade his cigarettes or a can of Nescafé for more food. Some preferring canned meat to fruit jam would strike a deal with a buddy possessing opposite tastes.

In a short time, however, trading assumed a ruthless character that disturbed Colonel Ashurst and his officers. Some aspiring capitalists employed slick talk or other ploys to do more than just break even. Other inmates, spoiled by the sensation of a full stomach for the first time in a year, began pledging the contents of food boxes they expected to receive in return for eating a comrade's Japanese-issued stew, rice, or bread today. At least one con man sold the same items from a single box to several different prisoners, cheating the majority of his creditors of their payoff. Greed or boredom induced many POWs to gamble with Red Cross food, to the glee of camp cardsharps, who left their victims with little beside a few minutes of suspense and excitement.

It did not take the Marine officers long to realize they had to save their subordinates from themselves. They forbade gambling with Red Cross food and exchanging such items for cigarettes or cash. They also prevailed on Colonel Otera to endorse the gambling ban. Colonel Ashurst and Major Brown threatened offenders with the loss of future food boxes. The Marine brass demonstrated their earnestness by administering a public paddling to the double-dealing inmate who had fooled several comrades into thinking they had purchased his food box. When these measures failed to stamp out underground gaming and trading, Ashurst announced two standing orders on December 24, 1943: "All gambling debts are repudiated. Payment of all honorable debts is postponed until after the war."[46]

The wheeling and dealing precipitated by the food boxes did not worry most prisoners half as much as the spread of thievery. Until December 1942 few prisoners aside from the North China Marines owned much worth stealing. "Now when we got the Red Cross food packages, why, you know, guys watched everyone like a hawk," admitted Pfc. James Venable. Inmates returning from work details began detecting that items had been taken from their boxes. The POWs prevented theft from getting out of hand by posting trusted comrades as barracks guards whenever the rest went out to work.[47]

The Red Cross food boxes stimulated an additional form of illicit activity most Wake Islanders and their comrades preferred to gloss over in postwar interviews and memoirs—namely sex. With few exceptions, men would insist that malnutrition deprived them of their sex drive throughout their long imprisonment. "You'd go months and months and not think about sex," asserted Private First Class Benton. "It never entered your mind. You'd walk up to a group of men, and they were talking about food." SSgt. Clifford Hotchkiss insisted, "I never had a desire for a woman . . . from the day I entered prison camp till the day I left." Contractor Charles R. Milliken, a section leader, used to joke that if a POW got home and found a beautiful naked blonde in his bed and two pork chops on the table, he would pounce on the pork chops.[48]

While much truth dwells in these statements, an inmate's yearnings changed abruptly once he filled his belly with a can of Spam or corned beef. As Capt. John White of the North China Marines explained, "In Kiangwan, with rice 'skoshi' or scarce, the talk turned to chow. When food became 'toksan' or plenty, . . . chatter invariably changed to the subject to sex." Cpl. Bernard Richardson, one of Devereux's Marines, addressed this topic in frank terms: "Those of my former colleagues who say 'starvation robbed them of the sex urge' are, I believe, flat-ass lying. . . . You must remember that [we] were almost all of an age Kinsey reported to be the peak of a man's sexuality. . . . Recalling endless conversations with friends while we were POWs makes me certain that neither I nor they were that different from the total population."[49] Private First Class Pearsall felt these stirrings keenly enough to compose a love poem that began

>Come kiss me, Love?
>No, you never would
>We were not meant for kissing[50]

Many prisoners sought more satisfying outlets for reawakened sexual urges than mere words. Corporal Richardson had been a professional actor in civilian life, and he exuded a worldlier air than most Marines his age. A lot of younger Leathernecks regarded him as a father figure and came to him with their problems. "In matters of sexual need," Richardson related, "I advised masturbation as often as necessary to relieve tensions."[51]

Physical release without intimacy did not alleviate every POW's frustrations. Following the lead of the Guamanians that Pan Am had abandoned on Wake, some civilian prisoners organized stag dances, where men danced with men. "There is a minor rage around camp—dancing," Purser Kantzer declared on April 17, 1944. The day before, he attended "a full fledged square dance" in the recreation hall. "They had a pretty good string orchestra assisted by a bass drum," he commented. "You brought your own partner."[52]

An uncertain number of inmates went further and tried to fill the emotional void by experimenting with homosexuality. Such liaisons among men who had spent almost a year together in close confinement—sharing their fears, hardships, blankets, and body heat—should come as no surprise. "Our mode of living was comparable to a four year mass marriage," Bernard Richardson remarked shortly after the war. Many years later, he wrote an unpublished novel titled "Serenade to the Tree Toad" in which he depicted homosexual couplings as fairly common in the Shanghai War Prisoners Camp. "In today's gay world," he elaborated, "they would be called marriages. Some of them lasted for years in POW camps. Those men are fathers and grandfathers today."[53]

According to the testimony of other equally candid Wake Islanders, however, Richardson's recollections may verge on exaggeration. Pfc. Henry Chapman insisted that the Wake Island Detachment, 1st Defense Battalion, contained only two confirmed homosexuals. "There were a certain two that I know were homosexuals," agreed Private LaPorte. "I know for a fact they were. And I know people who fooled with them." One Contractor's diary reveals that he traded cigarettes for "womens undies" that somehow got into camp. Purser Kantzer reported that "some of the boys did a little female impersonating, to add spice and variety to the promenading" when the POWs took their accustomed constitutional around the compound on Easter Sunday, April 1, 1945. A persistent camp rumor held that either Major Devereux or Major Brown caught a pair of Marines committing sodomy in the benjo and punched them both in the face. A more disturbing story alleged that some Marines, attracted by the girlish looks and manner of the Guamanians, subjected them to gang rape. If any consensual or forced gay relations actually occurred at Kiangwan, the weight of evidence indicates that relatively few inmates took part. Furthermore, the frequency of such interactions dwindled whenever food grew scarce again.[54]

"THE BEST CHRISTMAS DINNER I EVER HAD"

The cornucopia of aid unloaded by the *Conte Verde* did not lull the local Red Cross chapter into scaling back in its efforts to support the Shanghai War Prisoners Camp. Edouard Egle persisted in sending biweekly deliveries of food, clothing, care packages, and other comforts to Kiangwan. "Red cross truck arrived on Th[ursday] with cracked wheat[,] oranges etc.," Private First Class Pearsall scribbled in his diary in early 1943. Half a year later Sgt. Jack Cook reassured his loved ones, "WE RECEIVE A LOT OF GOODS FROM THE RED CROSS EVERY TWO WEEKS." The POWs took a close interest in the size and composition of every shipment and relished speculating about what their cooks would do with it. "Red Cross came across with an excellent shipment yesterday," Purser Kantzer recorded on September 11. "We shall eat fine for the next two weeks, for we got approximately 2000 lbs of lima beans, 750 pounds of ham, 25 sacks of cracked wheat, some noodles, fat and tomato sauce for flavoring. I hear that the galley is going to make doughnuts once again now that they have some fat."[55]

The most spectacular manifestation of local charity transformed Kiangwan into a truly happy place on Christmas Day, 1942. "A very merry Xmas from what we had last year," proclaimed Private First Class Pearsall. "Prisoners enjoyed a very plentiful Christmas," chimed in Cpl. John Johnson. "A festive spirit prevailed during the entire day and evening," confirmed Alec Pay.[56]

The distribution of American food boxes on Christmas Eve sent the POWs to bed in a celebratory mood, and more delights awaited them after they awoke to carolers early the following day. For starters, each inmate received a personally addressed Christmas card from an American woman or girl residing in Shanghai. "Mine came from someone . . . named Anne Carr," reveled Purser Kantzer, "and in my imagination I see her as pretty as her name and the sentiment she expressed."[57]

The high point of that day—and for some Wake Islanders, the high point of their entire captivity—came in the form of a sumptuous Christmas dinner. "You can judge all Christmas dinners from that one," reflected Pfc. George Hubley. "Any Christmas dinner we've ever had before or since then, compared with that one, they just don't have a showing." The mess details for the day served one roast turkey with all the trimmings to every five to seven inmates. William Kantzer and four shipmates from the *President Harrison* dined on "a full-grown, golden-brown, crisp-skinned, stuffed turkey, with giblet gravy, cranberry sauce and sweet potatoes to accompany it." The jubilant Americans and Britons downed this rich repast with cups of hot coffee and then enjoyed slices of mince pie for dessert. "It was just like a family dinner," Kantzer marveled, "with turkey sitting there on the table like an advertisement in a magazine. . . . I figure they must have had every Allied household in Shanghai busy stuffing these birds for us and roasting them."[58]

The founder of this magnificent feast was not Edouard Egle, but Jimmy James, an American expatriate and one of Shanghai's most colorful characters. A Minnesota native and U.S. Army veteran who went on to dabble in several business ventures, James struck gold by reinventing himself as a rollicking restaurateur called "Shanghai Jimmy." By the time his native land entered World War II, he owned four American-style restaurants in Shanghai, plus the Mandarin Club, one of the exotic city's fanciest nightspots. With the opening of the Shanghai War Prisoners Camp, James turned into a one-man Red Cross. He gladly donated substantial sums of money to purchase extra food for ailing prisoners. As the camp's first Christmas rolled around, James obtained permission from the Japanese to provide more than 1,400 inmates with a hot turkey dinner. He also shipped the POWs candy, nuts, powdered milk, coffee, cigars, cigarettes, and a Christmas tree with decorations. "It was the best Christmas dinner I have ever had, before or since," rhapsodized Sergeant Holmes, "and the most appreciated one. After that, every man in the Shanghai War Prisoners Camp worshiped Shanghai Jimmy and we don't understand to this day how he talked the Japanese military into letting him send the dinner in to us. It was a miracle as far as we were concerned."[59]

As Holmes and his comrades would learn all too soon, however, their season of miracles was destined to be short-lived, and their little slice of heaven would deteriorate into another Japanese-run hell on earth.

CHAPTER THIRTEEN

"a hellacious damn deal till we finished"
pushed to the edge on mount fuji

"LAYED AROUND . . . AND WATCHED THE OFFICERS WORK"

When Colonel Otera warned his charges "you must work hard and diligently," he meant it. The Japanese began sending POWs on work details outside Kiangwan within days of the camp's opening. Road repair efforts resumed as early as December 10, 1942. Other prisoners commuted by train to Woosung village to dig a canal. A sudden cold snap turned that task into a stinging ordeal. After returning to camp on January 11, 1943, Contractor Alec Pay griped to his diary, "Worked on Canal Job at Woosung. Weather most severe since internment. A cold, hard, north wind." Two days later, camp authorities issued Japanese army overcoats to inmates assigned to the canal job, making the POWs' workdays more bearable.[1]

The Wake Islanders also returned to a familiar chore after Colonel Otera set up facilities for polishing expended artillery shell casings at Kiangwan. On days the commandant deemed too rainy or muddy to march the prisoners to a distant work site, varying numbers of POWs reported to the shell-polishing shed. Anywhere from a full barracks to half the camp might be found there at the same time. This detail continued off and on until the Japanese finally ended it on May 2, 1944.[2]

During the nine months that the Wake Islanders and their comrades lived at Woosung, the only American and British officers who took part in daily work details were the few who occasionally went out as nominal supervisors. This situation did not escape Colonel Otera's notice, and he reacted on December 7, 1942, the day after the POWs finished moving into Kiangwan. Captain Endo, the camp's executive officer, announced that Allied officers would henceforth perform manual labor alongside their inferiors in rank. Colonel Ashurst responded to this attempt to expand the POW workforce just as he had when Colonel Yuse broached the subject at Woosung. He reminded Endo that the Geneva Convention exempted captured officers from having to work for their keepers. Endo snapped back that the Japanese considered commissioned inmates "only as Prisoners of War and not as officers." The captain threatened POW officers with being "stood at attention in front of the guard house if they did not volunteer to work."[3]

Ashurst was smart enough to know when he faced immovable opposition, but he sought to mollify the enemy without forfeiting his officers' status and dignity. Camp authorities intended to reestablish the garden that had supplemented the prisoners' diet at Woosung, and that gave Ashurst a bargaining chip. He offered to have the POW brass assume full responsibility for that operation. Such work was less exhausting than digging ditches and less demeaning than filling potholes. Ashurst sold the idea to his commissioned subordinates by depicting such toil as health-building exercise.

Camp authorities wasted no time transforming Ashurst and his officers into gentlemen farmers. Armed with spades and three-pronged hoes, the camp's newest laborers braved frigid temperatures and assembled on a six-acre plot just beyond the outer compound. It took the officers four months to turn over the soil in that area and dig the requisite drainage ditches. Some enlisted personnel enjoyed seeing their superiors getting their hands dirty. Pfc. John Pearsall missed a day on the canal detail in mid-December 1942 to have his blood type tested. "Layed around the barracks in the afternoon and watched the officers work," he purred contentedly to his diary. In the opinion of many other POWs, however, gardening represented light duty, and the officers enjoyed a lucky break by landing that assignment. Purser William Kantzer of the *President Harrison* carped that Ashurst and his fellow farmers spent their days at Kiangwan "not doing anything much except loafing."[4]

Although the officers were mostly city boys, their agricultural pursuits paid off for the common good. The local Red Cross kept sending seeds to the POWs and also equipped them by March 27, 1943, with a crude plow and a horse, a mule, and two water buffalo to pull it. MSgt. Reuben E. "Pop" Wiserman, a U.S. Army radar technician captured on the *Malama*, built his own forge and fabricated an improved plow for the officers. The brass entrusted that instrument and the water buffalo to three senior Marine NCOs burly enough to plow straight furrows. The officers augmented the natural fertility of the soil with applications of animal manure, and they reaped a rich harvest. "Chow is a little better," Contractor Emmett Newell commented on August 1, 1943. "They have weighed 3 tons

[of] vegetables out of our garden." Later that month, Sgt. Jack Cook informed his family, "ARE EATING FROM OUR OWN GARDENS LOTS OF TOMATOES AND PUMPKIN."[5]

Among the other vegetables the officers grew were different types of beans, including string, pole, lima, and soy; potatoes; sweet potatoes; cabbage; spinach; beets; onions; garlic; turnips; rutabaga; okra; eggplant; and the ubiquitous daikon. The officers took particular pride in bumper crops of big beefsteak tomatoes. They increased their yield by placing five additional acres under cultivation. The Red Cross gave the Kiangwan gardening operation the appearance of a real farm by shipping in edible livestock—chickens, hogs, goats, and rabbits. These additions permitted Major Devereux to renew his longtime interest in animal husbandry. "I now supervise the raising of pigs," he wrote his son on April 14, 1944. "So far we have butchered about six hogs and should have more in the fall."[6]

Colonel Otera and Captain Endo encouraged gardening and raising livestock for expediency's sake. Permitting the POWs to raise their own food reduced the cost of feeding them. The Japanese also helped themselves to the prisoners' harvests. Colonel Ashurst later asserted that the enemy ate nearly two-thirds of the hogs the Red Cross delivered to Kiangwan. When vegetables were in season, the POWs noticed more of them in their stew, but the difference always seemed slim. According to one report, "They drew only enough tomatoes to flavor the soup." Yet even a slight improvement mattered a lot to undernourished men, as Purser Kantzer bore witness on May 5, 1944: "At the moment, . . . celery takes a bow as a new and refreshing flavor from our farm. It's the first time in almost 3 years that anyone here has met up with this good old relish, and it deserves the fine reception it's getting."[7]

"EIGHTEEN MONTHS OF DAILY, BACK BREAKING MANUAL LABOR"

On January 17, 1943, Isamu Ishihara opened the darkest chapter in Kiangwan's history with a seemingly innocuous announcement. Adopting an eerily pleasant tone, the chief interpreter informed section leaders from the different barracks that the POWs were about to embark on a major new work project. Ishihara said they would "dig a lake and build a mountain" for a playground where children "would run and play and enjoy themselves." He characterized that mountain as a memorial to Japan's war dead, "a miniature of Mount Fujiyama, our beautiful, glorious and sacred mountain in Japan." Once the other inmates got wind of the interpreter's spiel, someone dubbed the detail the "Mount Fuji Project." That moniker promptly became universal usage.[8]

While the Mount Fuji Project lasted, the Wake Islanders learned that building a mountain was essentially the same thing as moving one. "God, it was hard work," exclaimed Pvt. Ewing LaPorte. "It was a hellacious damn deal till we finished." Cpl. Robert F. Haidinger would always remember the "day by day drudgery" of "that damned Mount Fuji." Cpl. Bernard Richardson aptly referred to the detail as "eighteen months of daily, back breaking manual labor."[9]

The Japanese set aside forty acres of flat ground nearly two miles from Kiangwan for the Mount Fuji Project. Enemy surveyors marked off an area around seven hundred feet long and two hundred feet wide. The POWs received instructions to fill that spot with a packed, earthen mound sixty-five feet to eighty feet high, with the sides sloping at sharp 45-degree angles. As the work proceeded, the Japanese decided to restrict Mount Fuji's height to forty feet. Corporal Richardson ascribed that change to fear that the mound would crumble if it got much taller.

Even with a height reduction, Mount Fuji remained a formidable job. Richardson figured that it required 7,246,746 cubic feet of black delta soil to erect the massive eminence. The prisoners had to move at least 200 percent more dirt after their keepers directed them to build a dozen additional mounds. These "12 small Fujis," as Contractor Herb Papock called them, were each supposed to reach a height of twenty-five feet. The project's planners arrayed the smaller mounds in three separate rows set at right angles to the main dirt pile. Containing four mounds apiece, the earthen rows stretched more than 1,300 feet to 1,600 feet in length.[10]

As the second phase of the Mount Fuji Project got under way, the Wake Island and North China Marines discerned that they were not creating a playground. "It was then that we realized the project was a rifle range," TSgt. Charles Holmes wrote after the war. The big mound turned out to be the butt, or backstop, against which targets would stand. The small mounds divided the range into two lanes, which the POWs marked with firing lines that ran parallel to the butt at different ranges. As the project entered its final phase, the Japanese brought in brick masons to construct square barriers along the base of the main mound to shield personnel handling the range's target frames.[11]

It nettled the prisoners—the Marines especially—to discover that Ishihara's talk about "sacred Mount Fujiyama" and frolicking children had been a ruse to trick them into building a training facility for enemy recruits. "The Japanese have lied again," fumed Cpl. John Johnson. The true nature of the Mount Fuji Project also raised a legal complication. Article 31 of the Geneva Convention prohibited the use of POW labor for any task directly related to "war operations." Colonel

Ashurst and Major Brown duly protested this latest violation of international law but received no redress.[12]

As much as the prisoners despised Mount Fuji's purpose, nothing could exceed their loathing for the construction process. It became, as Purser Kantzer phrased it in late July 1943, "an everpresent hell." Except for the officer gardeners, the seriously ill, and a few men excused for cooking, hospital duty, and essential camp maintenance, the Japanese wanted every inmate working on the rifle range. The guards normally marched their charges to Mount Fuji six days a week, giving them only Sundays off. Colonel Otera knew better than to send inmates to the work site when heavy rains turned it into a sea of mud, but he did not spare them when the temperature plunged and snow fell. Not counting the trek to Fuji and back, the standard workday lasted eight hours to ten hours. It could stretch even longer if the prisoners lagged in meeting the quotas their taskmasters set for them. These longer-than-usual days added an extra layer to the POWs' misery. They ate breakfast in camp before heading to Fuji, and they carried their lunch ration with them, but they got no dinner until they returned from work at night.[13]

Compared with other work details, the time the POWs devoted to the Mount Fuji Project passed with excruciating slowness. Every aspect of the job demanded brute physical strength, and the work grew more arduous as it progressed. "Each day seemed interminable," asserted Corporal Richardson. The Japanese directed the prisoners to dig up tons of dirt and transport it to dump sites at the base of the future Mount Fuji and its subsidiary mounds. That sounded simple enough, but the work entailed unexpected complications. The soil surrounding the rifle range defied easy excavation. "That dirt was just cohesive clay," Richardson recalled. "In order to get a shovel full you have to cut it loose on all sides and then pry it up." Due to Japanese stinginess, the POWs battled this stubborn substance with too few tools. The guards issued one short-handled shovel or a Chinese forked hoe to every third man. The other prisoners had to use their bare hands to scoop out dirt and pat it down on the mounds.[14]

The POWs commenced the soil displacement phase of the Mount Fuji Project by digging long ditches. The area's high water table quickly caused the ditches to flood at a depth of five or six feet, however, turning them into useless canals. The prisoners started on the lake that the enemy desired in May 1943 by excavating an area roughly six hundred feet in diameter and six feet down.

The POWs initially hauled dirt to the dump sites in baskets suspended from yo-ho poles, but the Japanese soon introduced a slightly more modern form of transport. Chinese laborers from Shanghai laid movable, narrow-gauge railroad tracks from the excavation areas to the mounds. Ultimately, ten to twelve tracks led to the main mound alone. The Chinese also delivered four-wheeled mining handcars to run on the tracks. These conveyances were miniature flatcars mounted with wooden boxes with removable sides. The boxes measured four feet long, two feet wide, and eighteen inches high. The Japanese assigned six POWs to each car, with orders to fill it, push it to the end of the tracks, pull out the sides, dump the dirt, and then bring back the empty car for another load.[15]

When the mining cars first arrived, the Japanese required only fourteen loads a day from each crew. The work was monotonous, but not too grueling. The Japanese even permitted their charges to rest fifteen minutes every hour. Things changed for the worse, however, as Mount Fuji grew. The Japanese placed tracks up the sides of the rising mound, forcing the POWs to push handcars up an increasingly steep grade before dumping their contents at the top. With each passing day, the hill climbed higher, and reaching the summit required more energy and suffering, which sank the prisoners deeper into perpetual fatigue. "Work became harder and harder as the height of the mountain increased," related Sergeant Holmes. "If you can imagine pushing a car load of coal up a 45 degree incline to a height of 45 feet you can visualize the difficulty of the job. Long ramps had to be buil[t] with pick and shovel to get the cars up to the top of the mountain by the time it was finished." For Pfc. George Hubley, the Mount Fuji Project settled into a nightmarish routine that would haunt him for decades. "It was load 'em and push 'em," Hubley recounted. "Load 'em again and push 'em up the hill and dump 'em."[16]

Each trip up Mount Fuji turned into an onerous test of strength and will. Cpl. Guy Kelnhofer likened the detail to "Hollywood's version of enslavement in Ancient Egypt or someplace like that, with the long lines of slaves . . . carrying big loads up and down." POWs developed agonizing leg cramps as they rolled cars up the slope. An afflicted man did not dare to stop pushing, though, lest a car break loose and roll over him or other members of his crew. "So you just hung on," remembered Pfc. Artie Stocks, "and hollered." Sometimes shouting was not enough. A POW or two would falter, a car would careen down the hill, and men got hurt. Some suffered lacerated fingers, and others sustained painful hand, arm, or leg fractures. No one was killed outright by a runaway car, but the prisoners took little consolation from that. The cruelest truth about Mount Fuji was that it murdered its victims slowly.[17]

What really turned the Mount Fuji Project into a modern Calvary was the enemy's insistence that the prisoners quicken their tempo as the work grew more difficult. Colonel Otera and his staff gave maximum priority to the rapid completion of the rifle range. They tried motivating an unwilling workforce with carrot-and-stick tactics. POWs laboring on Mount Fuji received a double portion of rice for lunch. Those who remained sick in camp were supposed to have their rations cut by 20–50 percent.[18]

To ensure that the prisoners never slackened their pace, Colonel Otera put Ishihara in charge of Mount Fuji. The commandant could not have selected a more diligent slave driver. The chief interpreter gloried in his new assignment and the power it brought him. At Mount Fuji, he reigned as master. Nothing could shield the POWs from his spiteful whims. "He would get out there on the mountain, and he would scream and holler and rave," grumbled Pfc. Willie Benton from North China.

Ishihara demanded that the POWs fill their handcars to overflowing before they started the next uphill push. From his customary perch atop a Chinese burial mound, the Beast of the East watched his charges like a hawk, often dismounting to move stealthily among them as they toiled. Ishihara expanded his supervisory capabilities by designating a pair of zealous Japanese NCOs as special assistants. The POWs called those two tormentors the "gestapoes," distinguishing one from the other as "G-1" and "G-2." In addition, Ishihara hired some Chinese men to verify that no car crews cheated on their daily quotas.[19]

The Beast of the East pounced fiercely on POWs who tried to get away with light loads, denouncing them as dishonorable. "Full dirt," he screeched at them. "No excuses." He usually forced the men he caught to stand at attention while he lashed them with his riding crop. Ishihara once administered that chastisement to a group of fifty prisoners, giving each a stripe or two. He also struck POWs with bamboo poles or his fists for not working fast enough.[20]

Ishihara's responsibilities encompassed more than maintaining POW output at respectable levels. "I gradually increased the work load as the men became used to the work," he admitted after the war. He neglected to mention, however, the various ploys he devised to trick prisoners into boosting their productivity. He approached his job as if it were a game, manipulating his Allied underlings with the cunning of a malicious cat toying with a cornered mouse.[21]

Ishihara instinctively grasped the value of playing his charges off against one another. He launched a seduction campaign aimed at co-opting POW foremen into giving their first loyalty to his agenda instead of their men's welfare. He pretended to honor these honchos by handing them extra cigarettes or inviting them into the shack housing his field office for tea and snacks. Ishihara won over some Wake Marine NCOs so completely that they threatened to report shirkers to Major Devereux. When Cpl. Jesse D. "Pappy" Sorrel collapsed in front of an oncoming handcar one day, a staff sergeant rasped this callous command: "Roll him off the track and keep the carts moving!!"[22]

Ishihara next aimed his charm offensive at the entire Mount Fuji workforce. He frequently promised additional food and other rewards for turning out a few more loads on a specific day. On January 26, 1944, Purser Kantzer heard Ishihara tantalize the prisoners with a guarded prediction: "He stated that perhaps there would be a raise in pay, an increase in breakfast rice twice a week, and mail distribution soon." The interpreter also assured "diligent" workers that they would receive five letters apiece, but that did not fool Kantzer. "Well," he snorted, "I wouldn't hold my breath waiting for any of the aforementioned events."

Pfc. Erwin D. Pistole and his buddies also greeted Ishihara's blandishments with skepticism, but for a different reason. "We were smart enough to know," Pistole bragged, "that if you produced more you was going to go the next day for nothing." Surprisingly, many POWs trusted in Ishihara's honeyed words and insincere smile. FN2C Dare Kibble tried setting them straight. "I always believed we should accomplish as little as possible for the 'Great East Asia Co-Prosperity Sphere,'" he explained. But not everyone agreed. "Some prisoners and 'honchos' worked like hell for them," Kibble griped. "The hotshots were always mad at our team for holding up the production." And that was not the worst result of Ishihara's machinations. Just as Pistole feared, the POWs would return to work the day after moving a record number of loads to find their quota adjusted to that higher amount and their rations down to normal levels.[23]

As temperatures warmed through the spring of 1943, Ishihara cooked up a new ruse to deceive the prisoners. He informed American personnel that he would permit those meeting their quota early to return to camp and play baseball. Experience should have told the POWs that the Beast of the East was much less interested in rewarding nimble workers than ascertaining how much dirt they could move if they gave the job everything they had. When Major Brown heard of Ishihara's proposition, he urged Kiangwan's Marines, "Don't work a damn bit faster than you have to." Gullibility still existed among the lower ranks, however, and the lure of America's favorite pastime trumped too many men's common sense. Some crews went out and finished three hours ahead of schedule. Watching other prisoners racing to win an early release stimulated the competitive urges of their comrades, and even doubters ended up doing exactly what Ishihara wanted.[24]

The POWs got to play some extra ball games, but they paid dearly for the privilege. Ishihara simply used his dupes' enhanced performance to steadily hike their workload. By April 26, 1943, each car crew was expected to make twenty-seven trips per day to the top of Mount Fuji or a smaller mound. It became increasingly common for the POWs to put in overtime at the rifle range to complete their quotas. "Didn't get in from Fuji till 7:00 PM yesterday," Emmett Newell lamented on November 3. Ultimately, Ishihara raised each crew's quota to forty-two carloads, which left the POWs with little time or energy for baseball, especially on workdays. "Our athletic program continued," observed Captain Godbold, "but not at the same pace because we really didn't have the stamina."[25]

As the prisoners' plight worsened, their antipathy for Ishihara reached new heights. "We . . . are working for a 'beast,'" Corporal Johnson exploded to his diary. The POWs also blamed each other for playing into Ishihara's hands. Corporal Richardson paid grudging tribute to the interpreter's divide-and-conquer strategy. "Cleverly, insidiously, he created rivalries that developed into hatreds among the prisoners," Richardson reflected. "Instead of exerting every effort toward outwitting and aggravating the Japs, we fought among ourselves."[26]

Like Satan presiding over Hell, Ishihara exhibited an inexhaustible genius for augmenting his victims' agony. From time to time, Corporal Richardson recounted, the interpreter would decree "a special Front Day in memory of our sons and brothers and relatives who were dying all over the world while we . . . led a good, safe life courtesy of kindly Japan." Ishihara later corroborated Richardson's recollection. "About twice a month," he confessed, "I increased the work considerably (for that day only) because I considered that these men were safe away from the front lines, and in exchange for that safety they should do hard work." On these Front Days Ishihara obliged every handcar crew to move five additional loads as "a memorial to our dead comrades." Prisoners failing to meet the day's altered standard before the normal quitting time had to keep working until they did. With Ishihara gradually raising the men's standard quota, Front Days grew particularly arduous. "On front day we worked extra hard," noted Contractor Warren G. Anderson, "and until after dark so we would not be able to clean up after a day's work."[27]

According to POW testimony, Front Days occurred more frequently than the rate indicated by Ishihara. Front Days soon became a weekly event at Mount Fuji. Ishihara also scheduled additional Front Days to mark special events. He proclaimed a Super Front Day on December 8, 1943, the second anniversary of the Pacific War. He did the same whenever Japanese and American forces clashed in the world's largest ocean. Ishihara always claimed those battles as Japanese victories, but the POWs noticed that each alleged American defeat occurred closer to Japan than the last, which indicated the enemy was giving ground. These deductions pumped up POW morale, but only momentarily. The extra work ahead stifled the men's joy just as surely as it drained them of strength and hope. Pfc. Carl Stegmaier could barely stand to think about each successive Front Day. "Gee," he despaired, "at this rate I ain't going to last."²⁸

"IN '43 WE LIKE TO STARVE TO DEATH"

In addition to ignoring the Geneva Convention's injunction against using POW labor on enemy military installations, the Mount Fuji Project flouted Article 32, which began, "It is forbidden to use prisoners of war at unhealthful or dangerous work." A second cup of rice for lunch did not compensate the POWs for all the work Ishihara squeezed out of them. Straining every muscle and nerve six days a week to keep up with the interpreter's merciless regimen, the prisoners burned many more calories than they consumed. PlSgt. Bernard Ketner, Ishihara's old adversary, summed up things in a single sentence: "The men were forced to work to a point almost beyond endurance at the Fujiyama project." Corporal Kelnhofer spoke more graphically about the toll Mount Fuji exacted from its builders. "We were working like fools out there," he blurted. "It was just terrible. We became automatons. Didn't know what was going on or what day it was or anything else anymore."²⁹

As Kiangwan's arch villain, Ishihara made a natural scapegoat for all the evils associated with the Mount Fuji Project, but much of the prisoners' suffering emanated from forces beyond his control. Exploitative Japanese economic policies, energy reductions, and a booming black market that siphoned off agricultural commodities plagued Shanghai with severe food shortages from 1942 to 1944. The occupants of the Shanghai War Prisoners Camp lived in relative insulation from the city's food crisis for more than a year thanks to the Red Cross and their own industry. On November 13, 1944, Purser Kantzer explained the degree to which those two factors held down Japan's expenses for feeding Kiangwan's inmates: "For better than a year now, the jap contribution to our diet has been a quantity of . . . very inferior bread and two tin cups lightly packed with cooked rice per man per day, plus a cross between a radish and a turnip together with a slimy green onion . . . for vegetables. Everything else that we eat is given by the Red Cross or furnished out of our garden."³⁰

The starvation that had been dogging Shanghai's poorest residents finally penetrated the Kiangwan compound in June 1943. "Chow very short," Emmett Newell confided to his diary on the thirteenth. "Chow is really short," he added sixteen days later. On July 6, another Contractor, Herb Papock, jotted "50% cut in food rations." Twenty-four hours later William Kantzer remarked, "The food has been cut again. We get only gruel for breakfast instead of rice and slum [stew].

We get only 3/4 of a loaf of bread per man every two days instead of a loaf a day that we got a year ago. There are no more seconds of rice." That same day, Emmett Newell protested, "Its slow starvation."[31]

The rations ladled into the inmates' mess bowls declined in quality, too. On July 4, 1943, Kantzer damned "the tough bamboo shoots, the hard tasteless lotus bulbs, the eternal, worm-eaten turnips and the stunted carrots plus the cabbage stalks that are all we ever see in the slum." POW cooks tried thickening this unappetizing mixture by adding flour, but that only produced what Kantzer called "a murderous, disgusting paste that I prefer not to eat, even though hungry."[32]

Scarcity, runaway inflation, and the Japanese internment of Shanghai's British and American nationals hampered Edouard Egle's campaign to send Kiangwan twice-monthly shipments of foodstuffs and other relief supplies. During a camp visit on June 19, 1943, Egle briefed Colonel Ashurst and the latter's officers on meat supplies in Shanghai: "Bacon was available, ham was hard to get, and sausage was unobtainable." Two weeks later, William Kantzer reported more bad news: "The red cross goods have dropped way down. We got no beans for the last month."[33]

Undaunted by escalating difficulties, Egle kept striving to supplement the Kiangwan diet. The Red Cross man called on all his finely honed talents as a scrounger, and he sometimes surpassed what he had accomplished when pickings were easier. "Best R.C. day we've had," Emmett Newell exulted on December 10, 1943, "1 ton beans, 25 sacks corn meal, 25 sacks cracked wheat, 50 boxes of noodles, 100 gallons of lard, 100 lbs. of tongue, 4 cases tomato puree & some winter cloth[e]s." On other occasions, however, Egle fell short. Newell branded October 25 as a "Poor R.C. day—no beans." On November 10, the Contractor registered his disappointment yet again, writing, "Very poor R.C. day. 1000 lb. balony; 100 sweet spuds; 400 lbs. greese; some winter clothing." The POWs' year ended on a dismal note after Egle failed to send Kiangwan a food delivery in the second half of December.[34]

When Sergeant Cook addressed a letter to his parents and siblings on August 24, 1943, he put up a brave front to allay their fears for his welfare: "WE RECEIVE A LOT OF GOODS FROM THE RED CROSS EVERY TWO WEEKS." Cpl. Charles Camp, another Wake Marine, would speak nearly four decades later with greater candor about life at Kiangwan. "In '43 we like to starve to death," Camp attested. "I remember people eating snakes and snails or anything."[35]

Isamu Ishihara cannot be blamed for Kiangwan's starving time, but it gave him no pause in piling more burdens on his prisoners. The interpreter's fanaticism combined with famine to forge an unholy alliance. The Wake Islanders had

Employees of Contractors Pacific Naval Air Bases clutch their few meager belongings in homemade bundles as they leave Wake Island's Camp 2 to board the *Nitta Maru* on January 12, 1942, for a hellish voyage to Japan and China. *National Archives and Records Administration*

A prewar photograph of the *Nitta Maru*, the Japanese luxury liner converted into a troop transport that carried most of the Americans captured on Wake Island to Yokohama, Japan, and Shanghai, China, in January 1942. *Author's collection*

Wearing dress blues, Cdr. Winfield Scott Cunningham leads a group of Wake Islanders past Japanese press photographers and newsreel cameras after the *Nitta Maru*'s arrival at Yokohama on January 17, 1942. Nathan D. "Dan" Teters is visible just over Cunningham's right shoulder. The smiling prisoner in the sun helmet and civilian sports jacket is Lt. (j.g.) G. Mason Kahn, the Wake Island Detachment's Navy surgeon. *Courtesy of Gregory R. Cunningham*

Maj. James P. S. Devereux, the commander of the Wake Island Detachment, 1st Defense Battalion, photographed at the Woosung site of the Shanghai War Prisoners Camp in late February 1942. *Author's collection*

Col. William W. Ashurst commanded the North China Marines and served as the senior Allied prisoner at the Shanghai War Prisoners Camp from his arrival on February 1, 1942, to that installation's dissolution on May 9, 1945. *Author's collection*

Maj. Luther A. Brown, the executive officer of the North China Marines and the man who enforced discipline among the Allied personnel at the Shanghai War Prisoners Camp, had his photograph taken by the Japanese at Woosung in late February 1942. *Author's collection*

Second Lieutenant M. Matsuda informs scruffy Wake Island POWs of recent Allied defeats during a Japanese general's inspection visit to Woosung on February 26, 1942. Matsuda also told the prisoners that the Japanese intended to turn Woosung into a model camp. *Author's collection*

Wake Island Marines wait in line at Woosung on February 26, 1942, to record radio messages notifying their loved ones that they are alive and well. These Leathernecks wear wool Japanese army uniforms, which the enemy issued to provide better protection from the winter cold. *Author's collection*

Colonel Goichi Yuse, Woosung's commandant, presents Col. William W. Ashurst and the shorter Maj. James P. S. Devereux with compact shortwave radios designed to pick up only stations in Japanese-run Shanghai in mid-March 1942. *Author's collection*

This Japanese propaganda photograph shows the POW mess crew preparing a meal at Woosung. The Marine in the wool uniform, scarf, and fur cap belongs to the North China Marines. POW cooks often received fewer vegetables per meal when cameras were not present. *Author's collection*

Colonel Satoshi Otera, instantly recognizable from his luxuriant handlebar moustache, served as the second commandant of the Shanghai War Prisoners Camp from October 20, 1942, to May 9, 1945. He stands here with two of his officers and two Allied civilians from an internment camp he also ran.
Author's collection

Capt. Herbert C. Freuler of Marine Fighting Squadron (VMF) 211 received this card for Christmas 1942 from an American socialite living in Shanghai's International Settlement while he was at Kiangwan.
Courtesy of Anne Freuler Loring

Two friendly Japanese medical corpsmen pose with Marine volunteers in front of the POW hospital at Kiangwan. Pfc. Carl E. Stegmaier Jr., a Wake Island Marine, stands second from left. *Author's collection*

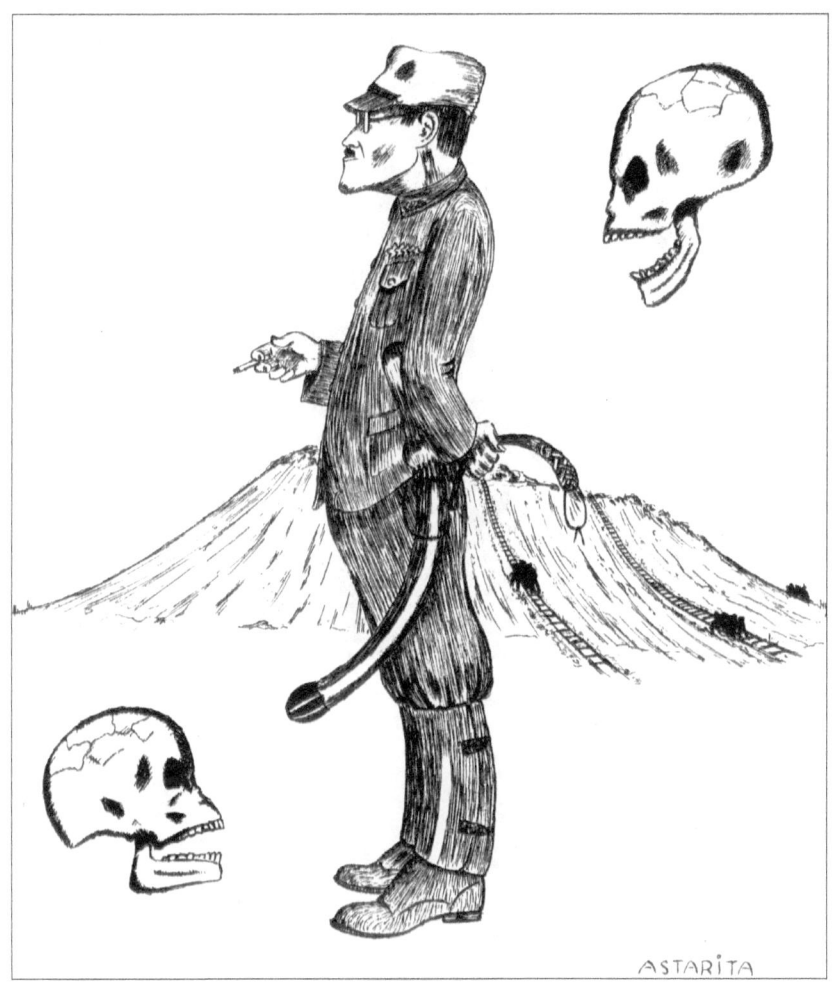

Contractor Joseph J. Astarita sketched this portrait of the interpreter Isamu Ishihara, the hated "Beast of the East," with the rifle range dubbed Mount Fuji rising in the background. *Author's collection*

The ingenious Capt. Herbert C. Freuler of VMF-211 won warm praise from both his fellow prisoners and Japanese prison camp authorities for his efficient and scrupulously fair performance as mess officer at Kiangwan. *Courtesy of Anne Freuler Loring*

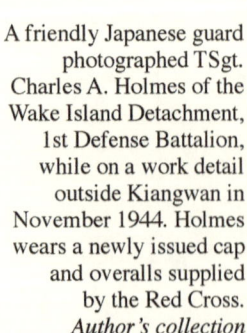

A friendly Japanese guard photographed TSgt. Charles A. Holmes of the Wake Island Detachment, 1st Defense Battalion, while on a work detail outside Kiangwan in November 1944. Holmes wears a newly issued cap and overalls supplied by the Red Cross. *Author's collection*

Five American officers who escaped from the train carrying the former occupants of the Shanghai War Prisoners Camp the night of May 10–11, 1945, pose for a photograph with their Chinese protectors from the Communist New Fourth Army. Seated from left to right are 2nd Lt. John F. Kinney, 2nd Lt. James D. McBrayer, 2nd Lt. Richard M. Huizenga, a senior Communist official, Vice Squadron Leader Lewis S. Bishop, and 2nd Lt. John A. McAlister. The Americans all wear blue uniforms furnished by their hosts. *Author's collection*

The "Diddled Dozen" consisted of twelve pilots from the U.S. Army Air Forces imprisoned at Kiangwan and Fengtai after being shot down at various locations in China. They were separated from the Wake Islanders and North China Marines on Hokkaido in July 1945 and spent the rest of the war at Sapporo. *Author's collection*

American and Australian officers gathered at Nishiashibetsu on September 2, 1945. Capt. Herbert C. Freuler of VMF-211 stands third from left, and his squadron mate, Capt. Frank C. Tharin, stands second from right in a sailor's cap. Another Wake Marine officer, 1st Lt. William W. Lewis of the 1st Defense Battalion, kneels at the far right. *Courtesy of Anne Freuler Loring*

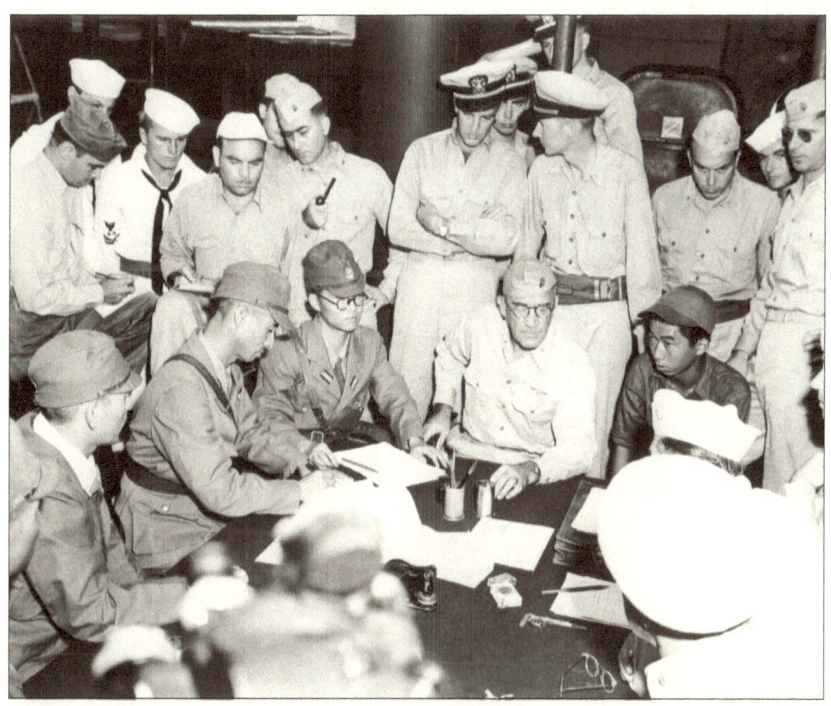

Rear Admiral Shigematsu Sakaibara signs the document surrendering Wake Island to the American military aboard the destroyer USS *Levy* on September 4, 1945. Sakaibara's complicity in the execution of ninety-eight American civilians on Wake would soon be exposed, and the Americans hanged him on Guam on June 19, 1947. *National Archives and Records Administration*

Pfc. Wiley W. Sloman of the Wake Island Detachment, 1st Defense Battalion, at Zentsuji in October 1942. He weighed only 112 pounds when he posed for this photograph. *Author's collection*

Pfc. Jack R. Skaggs shown with his identity number at Osaka Camp 13-B, better known as Tsumori, in February 1944. The twenty-one-year-old Wake Marine weighed only 105 pounds at the time. *Courtesy of Jack R. Skaggs*

Pfc. Fenton R. Quinn (far left) and Pfc. Joseph E. Borne (far right) pose with a Japanese family they befriended after news of the war's end reached their camp at Naoetsu in August 1945. The two Marines wear airdropped uniforms. *Author's collection*

Pfc. Wiley W. Sloman of the Wake Island Detachment, 1st Defense Battalion (seated second from right) celebrates his liberation with two fellow Marines at a West Coast bar in October 1945. *Author's collection*

This postwar publicity photograph shows Wake Marines MGySgt. Bernard O. Ketner and Capt. John A. Hamas. Ketner suffered grievous injuries at the hands of the sadistic Isamu Isihara, the chief interpreter at the Shanghai War Prisoners Camp. Hamas oversaw POW gardening efforts at Woosung.
U.S. Marine Corps

known many rough stretches during their imprisonment, but their previous trials were relatively short-lived. The ration fluctuations of 1943–1944 and the ever crueler grind of Mount Fuji subjected the POWs to almost indescribable physical misery. As early as April 26, 1943, Herb Papock wrote, "Men are thin and underfed. Work now very hard." On June 2 Papock further noted that the laborers from Mount Fuji "look thin and worn out." Just one month later, Purser Kantzer raged after another day on short rations, "This isn't enough to eat, and the work during the summer constitutes an atrocity." Private First Class Stegmaier became certain his body was feeding off its own tissue and bone marrow. Contractor Edward Cook estimated that each man assigned to the Mount Fuji detail dropped an average of forty pounds, weight these already emaciated wretches could ill afford to lose.[36]

Corporal Johnson spoke for hundreds of Kiangwan residents when he characterized the Mount Fuji Project as "probably the very worst time we saw in prison camp." Johnson blamed the rifle range for "our complete deterioration due to the extreme hard work and lack of sufficient food." Famished prisoners began fainting at the work site in the late spring of 1943, and it soon became something of an epidemic. "One or more pass out every day now," Emmett Newell related on July 17. "The men are 'passing out' at work due to lack of nourishment," Corporal Johnson told his diary half a year later. "It was so bad that many people collapsed," confirmed Corporal Kelnhofer. "They were just pushed aside so they would not interfere with the rhythm of work."[37]

Johnson, Newell, Kelnhofer, and Kiangwan's other living skeletons found the mere act of walking home after work a challenge. "Every day," recounted Corporal Richardson, "I would tell myself I would surely fall by the wayside. Each step became an agony of weariness." Defying the guards' best efforts to maintain a tight formation, the plodding column stretched to almost a mile in length. After the POWs finally staggered into their barracks, most were too numb to do much more than eat dinner, talk a little, and fall asleep.[38]

For prisoners who could muster the energy, commuting to and from Mount Fuji furnished opportunities for foraging. The route to the rifle range passed through cultivated areas and a small rural village. In the summertime the POWs plucked the heads off rice and wheat stalks, stuffing their pockets with grain to boil into something edible back at their barracks. When autumn rolled around they pulled the pods off bean plants growing beside the road. The aforementioned village had a chicken house, and a few brazen prisoners snatched some of the birds without being spotted. An experienced chicken thief knew how to grasp his prey tight by the throat to keep it from squawking. Pvt. Joe Reeves may have set the camp record by successfully smuggling a total of four chickens into Kiangwan. One morning the outward-bound column flushed a pheasant from the roadside. A quick-acting Wake Marine killed it with a stone before it had barely cleared the ground. A Japanese soldier appropriated the bird, but Ishihara, impressed by the American's aim, returned it to him as a point of honor.[39]

The POWs' need for nourishment grew so acute that they devoured any animal they could catch, including sparrows, cats, and dogs. Some men went fishing for eels and minnows in the canals they had dug at Mount Fuji. Others gathered the small wild onions growing in fields around the work site. Pfc. Henry Chapman belonged to a group of Leathernecks so desperate that the men tried eating grass. "If cows eat grass," those Americans reasoned, "why the hell can't we?" The grass went right through their digestive systems without any noticeable benefits, which wrote a quick finish to the pathetic experiment. Corporal Richardson saw other comrades gobbling livestock feed stolen from the officers' farm.[40]

The camp canteen offered the prisoners a more dignified form of relief, but its inventory proved beyond the easy reach of most. That institution's prices reflected Shanghai's soaring inflation. A pound of peanut butter cost CRB$25 as of May 3, 1943, CRB$39 in early October, and CRB$41 by November 20 of that year. The price jumped to CRB$52 on March 5, 1944, then to CRB$62 eight days later, and finally leveled off at CRB$64 per pound on March 16. By the latter date, a small bottle of pepper sold for CRB$52, and lard retailed at CRB$92 a pound. With the majority of POWs each earning only CRB$25 to CRB$30 a month, they either had to accumulate this pittance for several paydays or pool their resources to fund even minor purchases at the canteen.[41]

Several nervy prisoners circumvented steep canteen prices by establishing an illicit trade with the Chinese load checkers Ishihara had installed at Mount Fuji. The Japanese issued dire warnings against black market dealing, but the practice promised irresistible savings. Smuggled peanut butter went for less than half of what it cost in the canteen. Leading participants in this underground commerce included those POWs receiving care packages from friends in Shanghai and the North China Marines, who enjoyed the luxury of cash reserves and spare clothing. "Dealing has been hot and heavy at Fuji," Purser Kantzer observed on June 30, 1943. "Everything from neckties and socks to soap trades for eggs and cigarettes. I sent down two bars of Lever Bros. Chinese brand imitation Lifebuoy soap and got five eggs in return."[42]

Among the few inmates able to shop in the canteen whenever they liked were the North China Marine officers, who entered the Shanghai War Prisoners Camp with plenty of money and other valuables. The Japanese had disallowed canteen purchases with American dollars at Woosung in late June 1942, but the exchange rate in occupation script was unattractive. Consequently, the Marine brass from North China hoarded much of their currency until they heard about the black market at Mount Fuji. They then promptly deputized trusted NCOs to act as their middlemen in bartering American dollars, rings, and other jewelry for CRB notes. The consequent surge in canteen sales attracted the attention of camp authorities, who soon realized that the store was taking in more money than entered Kiangwan through approved channels.[43]

"WE HAD A CHICKEN SHIT BUNCH OF OFFICERS"

Rampant debilitation left the greater number of POWs susceptible to various maladies. These included such deficiency diseases as beriberi and pellagra. Tuberculosis also swept the civilian and enlisted men's barracks. "The men became so run down that they had no resistance to the disease," stated Second Lieutenant Huizenga, "and the weather was perfect for the development of tuberculosis." Five inmates died of tuberculosis at Kiangwan. Three were Wake Marines—Pfc. Ralph E. Phipps, Cpl. Frank A. Guthrie, and Sgt. Alton J. Bertels. A fourth tuberculosis victim was Contractor Abner Smith. On January 17, 1945, Cpl. Clyde E. Roark became the sole tuberculosis death suffered by the North China Marines. Prisoners exhibiting no tuberculosis symptoms during confinement returned home lifelong carriers.[44]

The POWs interred other comrades in the Kiangwan cemetery, but not all those deaths could be attributed to Mount Fuji. Contractor John R. Garrison succumbed to stomach cancer on September 2, 1943. Heart trouble and hardened arteries killed Chief Engineer R. W. Hansen from the Norwegian merchant ship *Dukat* on March 17, 1944. Jerry Tijeron, a Pan American employee from Guam, died of cancer on September 19. PlSgt. Holland Cash of the North China Marines expired suddenly from a ruptured appendix on November 18. First Sgt. Paul R. Agar, the most trusted NCO on Major Devereux's staff, endured excruciating pain from beriberi swelling before his demise on November 19. To everyone's surprise, POW doctors identified Agar's primary cause of death as cirrhosis of the liver. John H. Eliassen, a CPNAB canteen clerk, lost his battle with dropsy nine days before Christmas 1944.[45]

These six men might all have died had they never seen Mount Fuji, but Kiangwan's Allied doctors rightly regarded that odious detail as the chief threat to the camp's health. After Navy medical officer Cdr. Leo Thyson visited the rifle range, he beat a path straight to Colonel Ashurst's door. "That work is the hardest manual labor I have *ever* seen any men do," Thyson informed his commanding officer. "Will you please protest to Colonel Otera?" The commandant referred Ashurst to his executive officer, Captain Endo, and the two officers met on July 10, 1943. The American colonel argued that long hours, too little food, and heavy work quotas were undermining his men's health. Endo listened politely, but his reply was inscrutable. He suggested appeals to the Japanese high command in China, which controlled the camp's food supply, and to Colonel Otera, who set the POWs' workload. Then, pretending as if no problem existed, Endo told Ashurst that inmates "will get their three bowls of rice per day . . . and ounce of vegetables that regulations call for, and work for ten hours a day."[46]

To save lives, Dr. Thyson and his medical colleagues issued rest chits to ailing men to excuse them from work or restrict them to light duty. This brought those affected only a temporary respite, if that. Ishihara presumed to be the final judge of who was fit to work, and he tolerated no substantial cuts in the size of the Mount Fuji Project workforce. Ishihara and the guards swept through the barracks every morning on the lookout for prisoners who felt too weak to get out of bed. "Anyone not at death's door felt the whip unmercifully," related Corporal Richardson. "This behavior earned him a new title, Wave of Destruction." If a prisoner produced a rest chit, the interpreter often tore it up and sent him to Mount Fuji anyway. Ishihara once dragged several men with severe diarrhea out of the hospital and forced them to march to the rifle range. Ignoring repeated pleas and protests, the Beast of the East kept Corporal Guthrie pushing dirt up the mountain until the tubercular Wake Marine could no longer stand unassisted. Only then did Ishihara permit the dying man to spend his remaining days in the hospital.[47]

Alerted by Dr. Shindo, camp authorities tempered Ishihara's heartlessness by authorizing the POW doctors to hand out a maximum of twenty-five rest passes as of November 30, 1943. The Japanese thought that a gracious concession, but demand for those passes far exceeded the supply. Dr. Thyson and his colleagues had to adopt a harsh triage policy. If a prisoner reported for sick call without evincing the symptoms of a serious illness, the doctors treated him as a malingerer. Dr. Kahn, the Wake Island Detachment's surgeon, alienated many would-be patients with his hard-nosed attitude. A few mistaken diagnoses further tarnished Kahn's reputation. In one case, he rescinded a rest pass issued to a *President Harrison* crewman who complained of a cardiac condition only to have that poor soul suffer two heart attacks between July and December 1943. Many civilian inmates concluded that the doctors favored military personnel over the rest of Kiangwan's residents. Purser Kantzer complained bitterly about "camp medical treatment and politics." Another civilian muttered ominously, "Some of the worst crimes committed in this place haven't been done by the japs."[48]

Dissatisfaction over medical care helped stoke growing resentment for the POW brass in general, and that feeling blazed more furiously among lower-ranking inmates the longer the Mount Fuji Project lasted. "The officers did not share the hardships the enlisted rank[s] had to endure," grumbled Pfc. Jesse Nowlin. As far as Corporal Richardson was concerned, "The officers never did a single day's work. They puttered around in their barracks and a few each day puttered around in the garden." A third Wake Marine, Private Reeves, leveled a harsher accusation: "I think we had a chicken shit bunch of officers that lived for themselves, that . . . had the choice of food from our galleys, . . . and had to exercise in order to keep from getting fat while we were starving." No one thought less of the POWs' commissioned leaders than Purser Kantzer, who painted them in these venomous colors on July 13, 1943: "They are universally held in deep contempt for their actions here in camp, and they make a tra[v]esty of the high aims that we are supposed to stand for as a people." This bitterness manifested itself in the nicknames the common prisoners tagged on their superiors. They called them "demigods," "belly robbers," and the "pompous buffoons in zero barracks."[49]

Officer prisoners who left accounts of their experiences at Kiangwan conveyed the impression that they shared the same basic rations and privations as their men, but this egalitarian posturing does not withstand close scrutiny. Second Lt. Robert Hanna, who had received his commission after serving as an enlisted man, conceded that there were "some differences in the treatment of the officers and the enlisted. . . . And I'd be the first to admit it." The Marine officers from Wake and North China had come up through the Old Corps of the 1920s and 1930s, whose leadership embraced an aristocratic outlook that would recede during the branch's rapid expansion between 1941 and 1945. Insulated from that massive cultural shift, officers confined at Kiangwan clung tenaciously to the privileges of rank as their right under both military tradition and the Geneva Convention. Colonel Ashurst, Major Brown, and Major Devereux regarded the maintenance of those perquisites as a moral victory, and they set the lead for their commissioned subordinates. POW officers occupied roomier and better-furnished quarters. They drew pay on the same scale as Japanese army officers, according to rank. They had their food cooked separately, which ensured greater quality control in its preparation. They enjoyed the services of enlisted orderlies known variously as "dog robbers," "strikers," and "stooges," who cleaned their rooms, made their beds, brought them boiled drinking water, served their meals, emptied their toilet buckets, and washed their laundry. Instead of standing nightly fire watches in their own barracks, the officers relegated this duty to enlisted servicemen who had been slaving all day on Mount Fuji.[50]

Incredible as it many sound, quite a few of the rank and file accepted this situation as part of the military caste system. "That's the way an officer's supposed to be," remarked Cpl. Frank Gross, a career Marine. Gross dismissed the officers' critics with this indignant challenge: "Did they expect them officers to come down on our level, to live with us as enlisted men?"[51]

Yet scores of Leathernecks who entered confinement thinking like Gross became disillusioned by seeing certain officers take unfair advantage of their status. Aside from workload inequities, no other issue touched a rawer nerve in officer–enlisted relations than differences in food rations. Numerous prisoners swore that the officers received bigger portions at mealtime than their men did. First Lieutenant Kessler countered that accusation with a refrain repeated by the rest of the brass: "Officers received the same rations as the enlisted." Second Lieutenant Hanna made the officers sound less privileged by noting they went without the second cup of rice supposedly reserved for Mount Fuji workers. Both responses were disingenuous. The residents of Zero Barracks arranged for the equal distribution of all food cooked in the camp galley with no consideration for workload. This ploy benefited both the officers and POW hospital patients.[52]

Commissioned inmates also devised ways to ensure they ate considerably more than men who worked much harder. The stew that the galley sent to Zero Barracks contained a greater share of vegetables than the weak broth usually ladled out to ordinary prisoners. The officers' comparative affluence allowed them to purchase many more items from the canteen, and none of those goodies went into the common pot. Although the officers forbade trading or gambling with the contents of Red Cross food boxes, they did not hesitate to buy Western food from anyone willing to sell. Major Brown once had some dried beef and beans from one of Egle's relief shipments hauled to his room for the officers' exclusive consumption. Another time, one American merchant sailor spotted Dr. Thyson smuggling twenty donuts intended for the sick from the hospital. According to Purser Kantzer, such abuses of authority were systemic rather than isolated aberrations. "Some of the officers would get a whole red cross ham at a time when the camp got a couple of slices," he wrote. "They had red cross cereals every morning when we only got it occasionally. . . . The same thing goes on with jap issued bread." No wonder the officers lost weight less quickly than everyone else.[53]

The American brass stooped to a scandalous low in arrogant self-indulgence when Colonel Otera infringed on one of their most cherished perks. A decree from the commandant's office obligated orderlies to labor at Mount Fuji. That threatened Marine officers with losing their servants' ministrations except on Sundays and workday evenings. Shortly thereafter, the POW doctors took to issuing several rest passes to the officers' orderlies despite the fact that they were no worse off than those prisoners sent to the rifle range. The doctors granted two-week exemptions to just enough dog robbers to attend to the officers' daytime needs. At the expiration of that time, the medical staff pronounced those men fit to return to Mount Fuji, and a different set of orderlies would rotate onto the sick list for the next fortnight. The officers could have made orderlies out of enlisted personnel ground down by the rigors of Mount Fuji, but the commissioned gentry preferred to retain experienced help. "This prevented sick men entitled to a rest from obtaining a rest slip," spluttered Corporal Richardson, "an orderly was already using the rest slip he might have had."[54]

Cpl. Carroll E. Trego of VMF-211 grew so disgusted that he stopped saluting his officers, and that insubordinate stand earned him a prominent place on Major Devereux's court-martial list. "I got fifty citations . . . in his little book for not saluting," Trego spat. Contractor Pat N. Herndon's assault on his section leader in early July 1943 so shocked the American officers that they turned him over to the Japanese. Prizing order as essential to the swift completion of the Mount Fuji Project, camp authorities sentenced Herndon to close confinement for two years in Shanghai. Angered by another incident in which Major Brown had the enemy discipline eight other prisoners, Purser Kantzer scoffed, "Well you know the battle cry of the marine officers: 'I'll turn you in to the japs!'"[55]

Most of the Allied servicemen were too disciplined, and most civilian prisoners were too smart, to flirt openly with mutiny. Still, those unable to stomach their disapproval of POW command personnel lashed out covertly. Marines avoided saluting unpopular officers by pretending not to see them or shunning their company. More than once, quick-fingered inmates misappropriated buckets of vegetable stew meant for Zero Barracks, which roused vocal consternation among officers forced to dine on enlisted fare. Other daredevils raided the officers' garden through the spring and summer of 1943 to grab a few more mouthfuls to supplement their substandard diet.[56]

"COOPERATE ENOUGH TO STAY ALIVE SO THAT YOU CAN SEE THIS WAR TO THE END"

The majority of prisoners were either too sensible or lethargic to pull rebellious pranks. They took each day as it came, praying for the abatement of their suffering. After several months of Mount Fuji, however, some POWs yearned so ardently for a change of scene that they began exaggerating their technical attainments on the endless stream of background questionnaires the Japanese had them answer. Camp authorities rewarded this dissembling on August 20, 1943, by removing 520 inmates from Kiangwan for shipment to Japan. This draft was three times as large as the two transferred from Woosung the previous autumn, and it contained a higher proportion of enlisted servicemen, including 110 from Wake Island. Major Devereux handed each of the latter the customary identity slip to remind them of their unit affiliations. Colonel Ashurst waited until the eve of the group's departure to give its members this parting advice: "Don't do too much for the war effort of the Japanese. . . . Cooperate enough to stay alive so that you can see this war to the end."[57]

Colonel Otera's staff sent an even more closely screened contingent to Japan on November 20, 1943. Contractors Jack D. Taylor, Stephen H. Shattles, Mark E. Streeter, and Larry E. Quille, along with Cpl. Albert P. "Bud" Rickert of the Wake Marines, foolishly revealed that they possessed journalistic experience. They joined a select group of fifty-three Allied POWs assembled at the Surnagi Technical Research Center near Tokyo between December 1943 and February 1944 to work for the Japanese Broadcasting Corporation, which is known in Japanese as Nippon Hoso Kyokai, or NHK. This move reunited the five with another Wake Islander, Ens. George H. Henshaw, who had been taken off the *Nitta Maru* at Yokohama in January 1942. Threatened with death if they did not cooperate, the POWs generated radio programming meant to demoralize Allied servicemen combating Japanese forces. One of these men collaborated willingly with the Japanese. Before Mark Streeter left Kiangwan, he denounced the United States and offered his allegiance to the enemy. His fellow prisoners damned him as a "white rat" after he wrote a poem mocking President Roosevelt, which the *Nippon Times* published in June 1943. Streeter and his coerced companions worked side by side with Iva Toguri, a Japanese American woman stranded in Japan by the outbreak of war. She would become infamous as "Tokyo Rose."[58]

The transfer of more than one-third of Kiangwan's occupants impacted those left behind in various ways. The Japanese rearranged quartering assignments, abandoning thirty-six-man sections for groups of twenty-eight. The reconsolidation freed so much space in Barracks 5 that the inmates later converted the building into a four hundred-seat theater for choir concerts and talent shows.

Uncharacteristically, the Japanese did not seize on Kiangwan's population drop as an excuse for slashing the ration budget. "Since the 520 left camp, . . . we have been eating too well," Purser Kantzer crowed on Wednesday, August 25, 1943, "and now, to top it off, a super-super red cross shipment from the local branch arrived. Since Friday [August 20], we have gotten bread a couple of times a day on two occasions, had so much corn one meal that we couldn't eat it all, and had more rice than we could for a couple of days." Kantzer and his comrades ate relatively well for the next month and beyond.[59]

Perversely, Ishihara and his superiors expected 900 POWs to move as much dirt at the Mount Fuji Project as 1,400. The Beast of the East raised quotas while cutting the number of men assigned to each mining car from six to four, then to three, and ultimately to two for the smaller mounds. On the big mountain, Ishihara stationed squads of three to four prisoners partway up the slope. These men met the oncoming cars and helped push them to the top. "It was a tough pace," recalled Corporal Richardson. "When you happened to be one of a cart crew you cursed the pushers for not pushing as hard as they could. When you were a pusher you cursed the cart crews for expecting you to do all the work."[60]

To save time and conserve strength, POWs rode empty cars down the mounds. One man would try to control the car's speed with a two-by-four thrust through a hole in the floor beside a rear wheel, but a little piece of wood made a ludicrously feeble brake. "That thing [the car] would come down and they would all scream and the guys down below would take off," recounted SSgt. Clifford Hotchkiss. For a few thrilling seconds the POWs forgot their aches and worries and enjoyed the ride. "It was like a roller coaster ride coming down," Hotchkiss added. If a hurtling car took a turn too quickly, it would jump the track, flip over, and launch its occupants into brief flights that ended in bone-jarring landings. Miraculously, only a few prisoners suffered fractures or other serious injuries in handcart derailments, and they would repeat this reckless, self-destructive stunt many times a day. It was as if those wasted, overworked men wanted to finish what Mount Fuji was achieving by painful degrees.[61]

A major defection from the Axis coalition enabled the Mount Fuji workforce to briefly recoup some of its lost numbers. Two weeks following the Allied invasion of Sicily on July 10, 1943, Italy's King Victor Emanuel III demanded Benito Mussolini's resignation as head of state. A new Italian government placed Mussolini under house arrest and conducted secret negotiations with the Allies for a separate peace. News of the Italian armistice broke on September 8. That morning in Shanghai, where it was the ninth, the officers of the *Conte Verde* complied with orders radioed from Rome to scuttle their ship. The crews of two Italian warships moored nearby—the gunboats *Lepanto* and *Carlotto*—followed suit. The Japanese took those Italian sailors into custody, along with the crew of the gunboat *Tambien*, which they seized intact. Over the next three days, Japanese army units subdued and captured small garrisons from the Carlotto Battalion of the San Marco Regiment of Italian marines at Tientsin, Shanghai, Peking, and Shan-Hai-Kwan.

On October 10, five Imperial Japanese Navy trucks carrying 201 Italians rolled into Kiangwan. The strangers belonged to two ships—12 officers and 185 crewmen from the *Conte Verde* and one officer and three sailors from the *Tambien*. Camp authorities lodged the Italians by themselves in Barracks 5. Because Italy had yet to conclude a formal peace with the Allies, Colonel Ashurst classified the newcomers as enemies. He asked the camp's previous occupants to refrain from fraternizing with them, but many American civilians thought the colonel's stance too punctilious. Contractor Herb Papock joined other Yanks in making the Italians feel welcome. "Nice fellows," he noted. "Odd having axis prisoners in with Allied prisoners." To the Japanese, however, foreigners were foreigners, and prisoners were cheap labor. Colonel Otera put the Italians to work on Mount Fuji within four days of their arrival.[62]

A bold airborne raid by German commandos liberated Mussolini on November 12, and Adolf Hitler placed him atop a puppet regime that sanctioned Nazi control of Italy. Two months later the Japanese offered freedom to their Italian internees if they swore an oath of loyalty to Mussolini's Fascist republic. The Italian seamen at Kiangwan, many of them along in years, had gotten their fill of building Mount Fuji, and all 201 leaped at this chance to obtain release. The Japanese removed the born-again Fascists from camp on December 12. Stung by the Italians' about face, the Allied POWs bid them good riddance. "Everyone glad," observed Herb Papock. "Means more food as rations were not increased when they arrived."[63]

By this juncture the Shanghai War Prisoners Camp housed a different breed of Italian who got along better with Americans and Britons. On November 30, 1943, the Japanese moved twenty-nine San Marco Marines who refused to renounce their loyalty to Victor Emmanuel from Shanghai to Kiangwan. The enemy also transferred eleven additional Italians from a Shanghai prison and turned them over to Colonel Otera on April 7, 1944. Those men were all officers, including the captain of the *Conte Verde* and the commander of the Carlotto Battalion. Thirty-four more Italian marines, four of them officers, arrived from Tientsin less than half a year later. With many Italian Americans on hand, Kiangwan's residents easily assimilated the new additions. The Italians took as well to confinement as the circumstances allowed, making their presence felt in the camp's a cappella choir and by dominating POW volleyball matches.[64]

Aside from the Italians, Kiangwan's population was periodically bolstered by Allied airmen who had been shot down while conducting operations over

China. Between October 30, 1943, and April 15, 1945, the Japanese caged twenty-one more American fliers and one Chinese pilot there. All but seven of those flyboys were officers, which provided the camp with more potential gardeners but hardly mitigated the rank and file's burdens. Six Norwegian and seven British merchant marine officers originally held in Shanghai made things a little more crowded when they moved into Zero Barracks on June 12, 1943. Finally, Dan Teters, Wake's head Contractor, completed his sentence at the Ward Road Jail for his escape attempt two years earlier and rejoined his comrades at Kiangwan on June 2, 1944. "D. Teters arrived in camp O.K.," rejoiced Alec Pay. "Big morale booster for most Wake Is. civilians." The Wake Islanders would have fresh reasons to celebrate as their long, dreary war inched into its final year.[65]

CHAPTER FOURTEEN

"optimism . . . is running high"
hope revives at kiangwan

"YOU MUST TALK OR I WILL KILL YOU"
The privileges of rank undoubtedly buffered Kiangwan's Allied officers from much adversity during their captivity. With Ishihara on the prowl, however, the POW brass could not count on blanket immunity from the indignities the camp's chief interpreter heaped on the lower ranks six days a week at Mount Fuji. Ishihara despised officers in general, including his own. He nursed a particular animus for the North China Marine officers, viewing them as arrogant and pampered. Ishihara vented his hostility in a speech at Mount Fuji on July 12, 1943, denouncing all the Marine officers for taking more than their share of food and Red Cross supplies.[1]

Colonel Ashurst and Major Brown dismissed those charges as a facile stratagem meant to divide the POWs, but Ishihara's superiors knew he had a point. Later that year the Japanese replaced Ashurst's choice as camp mess officer with a Wake Islander, Capt. Herbert Freuler of VMF-211. Freuler believed that an officer's first duty was to care for his men. He won the trust of the civilian prisoners by naming Edward S. Clancy, the Contractors' leader in Dan Teters' absence, as his second in command and filled other positions on the galley staff with men of unimpeachable probity. Freuler's team improved food preparation for all hands and ended uneven distribution. The captain acted with the support of Major Devereux, who disapproved of officers receiving extra nourishment. Devereux had previously refrained from clashing with Ashurst over this issue, but Freuler's appointment created an opportunity for reform. At Christmastime 1943, Freuler received the written thanks of the enlisted Wake and North China Marines, as well as several groups of civilians.[2] Forty-four Contractors in Barracks 3 signed a homemade Christmas card for the mild-mannered mess officer that read in part:

> The food you've served us is well prepared
> And we know darn well it's fairly shared.
> Now all of us, we like fair play—
> We're back of you in every way.[3]

Edouard Egle sweetened the camp's disposition by providing the ingredients for a bountiful Christmas dinner featuring split pea soup, sweet potatoes, beef pot roast with gravy, a loaf of bread per man, and apple pie. Ration cuts kicked in immediately afterward, but at least the rank and file knew that the officers were no longer receiving more rice or thicker stews. Colonel Otera recognized Freuler's contributions to camp harmony with a certificate of merit written in both Japanese and English.[4]

Ishihara desired changes less benign than galley reform. He wanted to strip the American officers of their haughtiness and grind them into the dust. Ever since Colonel Yuse had disciplined Ishihara for the attempted murder of Sir Mark Young at Woosung, the interpreter had been biding his time, looking for an opening to reclaim his lost power. That finally happened in early January 1944.

As noted earlier, a surprisingly heavy volume of canteen sales at Kiangwan tipped off enemy authorities to the possible existence of black marketeering at Mount Fuji. They placed Ishihara's Chinese load checkers under surveillance and concentrated on one whose behavior appeared especially suspicious. A search of the man's rooms in Shanghai uncovered a record of his transactions, including the names of his imprisoned clients. The Japanese tortured confessions out of the other checkers and then executed them all. Colonel Otera did not contemplate such a fate for the POWs involved in this affair, but he wanted them identified and punished. The commandant deputized a newly arrived lieutenant named Miasaki to conduct a full investigation with Ishihara's assistance. Miasaki's childlike face caused the POWs to call him "Tiny Tim," but his strict adherence to Bushido earned him a reputation as a tireless upholder of the pettiest regulations. Because of Ishihara's language skills, however, he took the lead in questioning POW suspects, which he did with ruthless zeal. The interpreter's victims and their friends would henceforth refer to this period as Ishihara's "inquisition" or "purge."[5]

Ishihara launched his probe on January 8, 1944. Over the next five days, he relied on the assistance of his Mount Fuji henchmen G-1 and G-2, Corporal

Tushihiko Yazawa, a civilian aide named Fukutome, fellow interpreter Kazunori Morisako, and Lieutenant Miasaki. Ishihara initially targeted three American NCOs—SSgt. John C. Minnick, a U.S. Army radar technician taken with the SS *Malama*, and two Marines, SupSgt. Michael J. Schick from North China and PlSgt. Joe M. Stowe from Wake. The interpreter interrogated these men on three successive days. He opened each session with feigned cordiality, posing questions to which he already knew the answers. When a suspect lied, which invariably happened, Ishihara whipped him with a riding crop before resorting to more extreme tortures.[6]

The Beast of the East turned to a barbaric procedure called the "water cure"—known today as waterboarding—to extract information. He began by tying an American to a table, bench, or ladder. Then, while one assistant pinched the helpless man's nose closed and another forced his mouth open, Ishihara would take a teapot and start filling him with water. The interpreter kept pouring, pausing intermittently to ask a question or two, until his victim choked, gagged, and then either vomited or fainted. During Sergeant Stowe's interrogation, Ishihara introduced a variation to the water cure by slapping a wet towel across the Marine's mouth and dousing it with water. In either form, the exercise simulated drowning, which exacerbated the pinioned man's agony with surges of panic. After the prisoner revived, he received more of the water cure until he divulged everything he knew about the black market. Whenever the interpreter upended the teapot, he would coo, "If there is anything you want to say, shake your head." The longer the sergeants held out, the more incensed Ishihara grew. "God damn it," he shouted, "I'll make you talk." Ishihara would continue this for up to three and a half hours before releasing a prisoner from his bonds.[7]

Once it became clear that Ishihara already possessed a detailed knowledge of the three sergeants' complicity, they admitted to trading a few items for their own benefit. But guarded disclosures failed to satisfy the Beast of the East. He wanted these culprits to implicate the North China Marine officers on whose behalf they exchanged currency at Mount Fuji. The interpreter yearned most of all to incriminate Lt (j.g.) William Foley, one of the Navy surgeons who issued rest slips that excused many POWs from working on the rifle range. "You must talk or I will kill you," Ishihara hissed in Sergeant Stowe's ear. "You must tell me about the money you received for Dr. FOLEY."[8]

After Ishihara finished savaging Minnick, Schick, and Stowe, Colonel Otera sentenced them to ten to twenty days in the guardhouse on short rations. Though battered and bloodied, the American NCOs bravely risked further punishment by whispering warnings to the comrades who brought them their meals. Capt. John

White from North China remembered one of those messages: "Ishihara knows the whole story. Don't lie or try to conceal anything or he will torture you."[9]

In the meantime, Ishihara widened his dragnet and hauled in more Yanks for questioning. He tortured three Contractors, one of whom was Ambrose C. Lum, a Chinese American from Hawaii who had attached himself to Major Devereux's CP on Wake. The interpreter also grilled two American officers—Ens. J. J. Davis, and his chief prey, Dr. Foley. Foley fared worse than Ishihara's other victims. The doctor's interrogation began at 10:00 PM, January 12, and lasted until 9:00 the next morning, when the Japanese had some Navy medics carry Foley's unconscious form from the camp office.[10]

The ferocity of Ishihara's inquisition unnerved those North China Marine officers with something to hide. Foley's mauling also showed that the interpreter enjoyed carte blanche to ferret out the truth. It was just a matter of time before someone cracked and the trail of evidence led to them. On the evening of January 13, five of these officers cheated Ishihara of the pleasure of torturing them by confessing to conspiracy to violate Japanese currency regulations. That capitulation soothed Colonel Otera's injured sense of honor, and he ended Ishihara's reign of terror. The following day the Japanese commandant sentenced the guilty American officers to five to thirty days of house arrest. These were much softer penalties than those imposed on the officers' lower-ranking confederates, who served their time in cramped, unheated cells. Purser William Kantzer voiced mock sympathy for the officers' treatment: "What a horrible fate!! They can't leave their rooms to talk to anyone. . . . But they may pull thru alright, in as much as they can't have any loss of chow, or of blankets, or their mattresses, like the others."[11]

Despite the inequities Colonel Otera had written a strangely civil finale to Ishihara's most infamous rampage. The interpreter's victims were less forgiving, but their revenge would have to wait.

"IT'S WONDERFUL TO HAVE AMERICAN FOOD AGAIN"

For the majority of Kiangwan's residents, Ishihara's inquisition provided a brief diversion from their standard regimen of too much work and too little food. Shortages still hobbled Edouard Egle's relief work, but a thin ray of hope staved off total despair between August 1943 and March 1944. Cpl. John Johnson greeted the new year with this thought that kept him and his comrades from giving up during hard times: "We anxiously await Red Cross Supply ship [from] America."[12]

On September 4, 1943, the POWs heard that the *Gripsholm* had left Jersey City a day earlier with more than 1,330 Japanese nationals and a huge consignment of mail, food, and other humanitarian aid for American service personnel and civilians confined throughout East Asia. The Japanese repatriation ship *Teia Maru* steamed westward later that month with 1,500 American, Canadian, and Latin American internees. The two ships rendezvoused at Goa, a Portuguese colony on India's west coast, where they exchanged their passengers and the contents of their holds.

The *Teia Maru* took an inordinate amount of time to wend its way back to the Shanghai area. Kiangwan did not open its gates to the freighter's long-awaited cargo until March 16, 1944. Word flashed through every barracks that the camp held 6,012 Red Cross food boxes, 117 cases of medical supplies, 1,022 pairs of heavy GI shoes, 300 pairs of dress shoes, 6 cases containing shoe repair kits, 1,200 overcoats, 143 cases of adult male clothing, 50 cases of thick wool blankets, 1,000 new American books, 9 cases of toiletries, and 8 cases full of such sundries as sewing kits.[13]

The POW medical officers assumed control of the food boxes and calculated they had a sufficient supply to provide six for each inmate. They gave all hands a tremendous shot in the arm by releasing the first issue on St. Patrick's Day. "Everyone very excited," Contractor Herb Papock scribbled in his diary. "Biggest day in camp. People eating all night. It's wonderful to have American food again."[14] Those boxes contained more items, and the quality was finer, than the ones the POWs had received more than a year earlier. That discovery dissipated Purser Kantzer's usual cynicism, and he rhapsodized

> This time, the boxes are real boxes: 2 quarter pound bars of emergency ration army issue chocolate, doped up with vitamin B1; 4 quarter pound tins of butter that doesn't need refrigeration, 5 12 oz cans of corned willy [corned beef] or spiced ham; 2 cans of powdered coffee; 1 pound of raisins or prunes, 1/2 pound of sugar cubes, 1/4 pound of liver paste, 1/4 pound of jam; 1 pound of powdered milk, 1/2 pound of processed american cheese, 1/2 pound of salmon, and from 6 to 8 packs of American cigarettes.[15]

Once again, the Japanese appropriated numerous boxes, leaving their prisoners just enough to have four more apiece. Not knowing when the next civilian exchange would bring the camp any more food boxes, the POW doctors decided to make those on hand stretch for nine months. They issued the second batch on April 3. When the time came for the third issue at the end of April, Colonel Otera tried to cover up the pilferage by demanding that Colonel Ashurst sign a receipt acknowledging that the prisoners had received the entire shipment.

Ashurst refused, and Otera retaliated by withholding all boxes from the prisoners. The standoff ended after a few days, with the Japanese returning the stolen food but delaying the next issue until May 30 just to save face. Each POW received his fourth box on July 4, his fifth on September 2, and his sixth on November 29.[16]

The Japanese decision to postpone issuing the third box temporarily damaged POW morale, but Ashurst's successful stand against Japanese pilfering redeemed his credibility in the eyes of many subordinates. The prisoners also got a hearty laugh at the enemy's expense from the Old Gold cigarettes stuffed in their boxes. Reflecting the boisterous patriotism that permeated the American home front, each pack had the following message printed on its wrapper: "Our heritage has always been freedom. We can not afford to relinquish it. Our armed forces will safeguard the heritage if we, too, do our share to preserve it."[17]

These sentiments escaped the notice of Ishihara and other Japanese personnel until after the distribution of the first two boxes. Old Gold's appeal to American pride upset them, and they felt mortified that it had reached the prisoners. Determined to squelch the spread of enemy propaganda, camp authorities required the POWs to open their boxes on each subsequent issue and produce all Old Gold packs so the offending passage could be clipped off. The prisoners thought it silly to go to such lengths to destroy words they had already read, but the Japanese obsession with saving face fueled the senseless censorship.[18]

Chuckles over the enemy's petty sensibilities did little to ease the strain of waiting a month or two for the next Red Cross food box. Some men found it more than they could stand and stole American food from their comrades. The most egregious offender was a young sailor from Wake who had become a habitual thief in prison camp. While his section mates slumbered one night, he stealthily removed a freshly issued box from the shelf over another man's sleeping space. The sailor was caught sometime after that lifting a can of corned beef and rice that a medical corpsman had left to heat in a hospital sterilizer.

Colonel Ashurst and his officers decided to quash Kiangwan's latest crime wave by making an example of the repeat offender. They turned the sailor over to two of the toughest Marine gunners in the Corps—William Lee from North China and Clarence McKinstry from Wake—with orders to have him paddled from one end of camp to the other. Stripped down to a pair of light khaki summer shorts, the thief received a portion of his penalty in every barracks but the officers' after evening inspection on April 24. The punishment detail bent the sailor over a chair, strapped him in place with belts, and whacked him across the buttocks with a pair of three-foot pine paddles. Purser Kantzer watched the man receive thirty-four savage strokes, while Lee or McKinstry instructed the paddlers to drag out his suffering by taking "a slight pause between stripes to let the sting go." Before the punishment party headed toward its next stop, someone pulled down the sailor's shorts to display his buttocks. "It was an awful sight," Kantzer testified. "His rump had been literally beaten flat into a mass of red and blue and green and yellow tortured flesh that looked like nothing human." As a crowning touch, the sailor had each buttock marked with a large *T* in silver nitrate—a badge of shame that took six weeks to fade. Pvt. Ewing LaPorte never forgot that humiliating public spectacle, and he affirmed it had a "damned good effect" on him and his campmates. They had learned a valuable lesson the Marine Corps way: "And that's what you get for stealing."[19]

Two other Wake servicemen had gotten their fill of slavery at Kiangwan, but they sought a more honorable release from their troubles. Sgt. Raymond L. Coulson had commanded the four .50-caliber machine guns that did such fearful damage to the Japanese invaders on Wilkes Island on December 23, 1941, and PhM2C Artis T. Brewer was one of Dr. Kahn's trustiest medical corpsmen. The pair decided to bust out of camp, and they put together escape kits by saving canned goods from the Red Cross food boxes issued on April 8, 1944. Brewer also pocketed some medical supplies that might be useful after he and Coulson got loose. On the evening of April 16 the two Wake Islanders secreted themselves in the back of the hospital to await darkness before making their move. Their carefully laid plans fizzled, however, when the Japanese held evening inspection forty-five minutes earlier than usual. The officer of the day raised a shrill alarm as soon as he discovered the two Americans missing from their section. Swarming guards caught Coulson and Brewer red-handed with their escape kits. Colonel Otera ordered the pair spirited to Shanghai for confinement with Commander Cunningham and other would-be escape artists at the Ward Road Jail.

Coulson and Brewer's aborted breakout reverberated unpleasantly among the POWs left at Kiangwan. Convinced that the men who lived in the would-be escapees' section had advance knowledge of the plot, Otera punished them for one week with a 20 percent ration cut. The incident also took the entire camp's morale down a peg. Not only did the fate of Coulson and Brewer reinforce the supposed impossibility of escape, but their misfortune broadened the gulf between POW officers and their inferiors. The Japanese tended to be creatures of habit. Their pulling an early inspection on the same night as an attempted escape inclined many civilian prisoners to conclude that the enemy had been tipped off by American Marine officers. The different versions of this rumor cited no plausible motive for such treachery, but Purser Kantzer claimed that camp authorities rewarded two barracks adjutants with a carton of cigarettes apiece for squealing.

Some American servicemen also believed that Coulson and Brewer had been betrayed by their officers, but most preferred to think the collaborator responsible was a Contractor. Accordingly, those POWs serious about escape concealed their plans from all except their closest friends or a few other comrades who commanded their absolute trust.[20]

Two months later camp authorities freed a specially qualified Contractor from Kiangwan for a softer life in Japan. Colonel Otera and his staff somehow learned that Darwin H. Dodds, a twenty-five-year-old timekeeper from Boise, had worked before the war as a radio announcer. The guards peremptorily pulled him out of Barracks 3 right after morning inspection on June 21. "Dar Dodds leaves camp presumably for Japan & Radio broadcasting," Alec Pay noted later in the day. As assumed, Dodds ended up joining Tokyo Rose and the POW production team broadcasting propaganda aimed at Allied servicemen.[21]

"AT LAST OUR DRUD[G]ERY IS FINISHED"

Ironically, Sergeant Coulson and Pharmacist's Mate Brewer jumped from the frying pan into the fire just as the Mount Fuji Project began winding down. The POWs dumped their last carloads of dirt on the rifle range's sole unfinished mound between April 14 and 19, 1944. "Only mopping up operations left," commented Herb Papock, as he and his comrades took up less-demanding activities. The prisoners pulled up the miles of track intersecting the work site, smoothed firing lines, set range markers, and installed target frames. These tasks did not require a large workforce, and the Japanese gradually diverted more and more men to new assignments. By June 21, the number of POWs trudging to the rifle range had shrunk to 115. That skeleton crew assisted with the brickwork around the target areas and put down sod on the mounds and surrounding spaces. Cpl. John Johnson celebrated his release from Mount Fuji by taking his diary from its hiding place and penciling, "At last our drud[g]ery is finished temporarily."[22]

Johnson's forebodings about the return of drudgery proved unfounded for the remainder of the POWs' stay at Kiangwan. None of the new work details duplicated the Mount Fuji Project's oppressive character. The worst that can be said of them is that some forced the Wake Islanders and their friends to render direct aid to the Japanese military. In fact, the cagey Ishihara began soliciting recruits during the worst of Mount Fuji for a shamelessly blatant violation of the Geneva Convention.[23]

Early in 1944 Ishihara asked for volunteers to work in a Japanese army garage near Shanghai where trucks and automobiles were repaired and refitted for use at the front. Despite the lure of getting away from Mount Fuji, most prisoners balked at servicing vehicles destined to carry enemy troops and supplies in combat zones. By March 1 only fifty men had volunteered for the detail, but Ishihara wanted 150. He switched abruptly to coercion to fill that complement. Colonel Ashurst tendered another protest, but Colonel Otera threatened punishment for any prisoners trying to weasel out of the garage detail. A North China Marine told Major Brown he would rather be shot than cooperate with the Japanese in that way. The major's face creased into a wry smile, and he advised the man to perform repairs "so as to hinder rather than help their war effort."[24]

The POWs staffing the motor pool took Brown's words to heart. They practiced subtle sabotage, doing things that would cause enemy vehicles to break down after they left the garage. Some captive mechanics put sand inside engines as they reassembled them. Others inserted connecting rods that did not fit properly, which caused an engine's pistons to blow off their heads. The most common ploy simply resembled negligence—leaving a part loose or forgetting to tighten a bolt or connect a hose securely.[25]

Many other new work details drew on the pick-and-shovel skills the POWs had perfected at Mount Fuji. They dug several reservoirs near Kiangwan to provide water for Japanese fire trucks. Beginning on May 1 twenty men reported each workday to a Japanese army radio station, which they proceeded to encircle with an earthen wall ten feet tall and a ditch ten feet deep and twenty feet wide. Seventy-five Wake Marines headed by QmSgt. Vincent Kleponis and TSgt. Charles Holmes made up a "Godown Detail" organized in September 1944. Camp authorities trucked them to a sprawling godown, or warehouse, complex, housing supplies for the Japanese Thirteenth Army, which garrisoned Shanghai and the surrounding area. The enemy set Kleponis, Holmes, and their men to digging a ditch eight feet deep with sloping 45-degree sides along the fence that enclosed the supply depot. The Godown Detail temporarily ceased ditchdigging in January 1945 to throw up earthen revetments around the warehouses. The barriers were meant to check the spread of fire in case the buildings took hits from Allied bombs. Other contingents of Kiangwan inmates wove cut grass into rope or resumed such familiar chores as road repair and polishing artillery shell casings.[26]

One of the most distinctive work details that replaced Mount Fuji brought numerous POWs to the storied Kiangwan race course. Built by the British to entertain the International Settlement's horsey crowd, the spacious and opulent facility incorporated a golf course in its design. The race course sat adjacent to the fashionable village of Kiangwan and near the estate where Madame Chiang Kai-shek, the former Soong May-ling, spent her childhood. The track was valued at US$1 million before it became a battlefield for Japanese and Chinese forces in 1932, and it remained an impressive sight when the Wake Islanders and their comrades worked there twelve years later. "The grounds are very beautiful," Cpl. John Johnson confided to his diary.[27]

In the spring of 1944 Shanghai's occupiers decided to convert the Kiangwan race course into a primitive underground fuel dump. By that point in the war, excessive demand and the U.S. Navy's ever-tightening submarine and aerial blockade afflicted the Japanese Empire with a worsening oil crisis. Japanese army units stationed in the Shanghai area resorted to powering their vehicles with grain and sugar alcohol. The POWs drafted into the race course detail dug up the grounds with holes deep enough to hold fifty-five–gallon drums full of alcohol. Then they split bamboo poles and wove the pieces into big mats that they placed over the drums and covered with sod. This simple arrangement concealed the fuel drums from Allied observation planes while allowing the Japanese to retrieve them easily any time they wanted.

Whenever something distracted the guards, bolder POWs dabbled in covert resistance. They would loosen the bunghole on a fuel drum and place the drum in the ground headfirst, which would cause the alcohol to ooze out. Pfc. Leonard Mettscher reckoned that the prisoners performed that prank at least three hundred times, but his estimate may be too conservative.[28]

Much of the alcohol that the POWs denied the Japanese army passed through their kidneys and bladders before it touched Chinese soil. No sooner did the prisoners get a whiff of what their keepers were using for gasoline than some dared to swallow it. "A small sip of the liquor tasted good and was very smooth," recalled Contractor Theodore Abraham, "but when it reached the pit of your stomach, it felt like someone had fueled a furnace inside you." The POWs not only sneaked drinks at the race course, but also at the motor pool, where they drained alcohol from crankcases, fuel tanks, and other sources. They especially liked the sugar-based alcohol, which tasted like fermented pineapple juice. "That was quite an experience, pineapple alcohol," recalled Cpl. Thomas Johnson. "It was good. . . . Of course, I think anything would have tasted good." Private First Class Mettscher felt just as partial to alcohol derived from rice. "It was not too bad drinking that grain alcohol," he confessed.[29]

It only took a few sips of 190-proof spirits to intoxicate malnourished men. Realizing it was safer to drink in the barracks than on the job, alcohol thieves started smuggling the stuff into camp in small glass or rubber bottles. A few prisoners, bolder than the rest, carried a five-gallon can through the gates on a daily basis, which the unsuspecting guards neglected to search for months. The

POWs employed at the motor pool fabricated the cleverest smuggling device. They would cut a segment from a stolen rubber inner tube, vulcanize one end shut, fill the tube with alcohol, and plug a stopper in the other end. A bootlegger could hide the tube under his shirt by wrapping it around his waist or let it dangle inside a trouser leg.

Bootlegging led to several nights of riotous drunkenness in the barracks, which occasionally ended in nasty brawls. Many more inmates ended up with equally fierce hangovers and bellyaches. The camp medical department put out health advisories labeling the fuel alcohol as tainted and unfit for human consumption. Dr. Kahn warned that blindness could result from drinking the stuff. When the rank and file ignored this advice, the POW doctors announced on December 14, 1944, that they would no longer treat hangovers. Colonel Ashurst and his officers threatened to let the enemy punish anyone found drunk. Major Brown had the Japanese clap a Marine relapsing into alcoholism in solitary confinement until he dried out.

The guards at Kiangwan eventually caught several alcohol smugglers by periodically searching returning work parties. Colonel Otera, an alcoholic himself, seemed to sympathize with this class of wrongdoer. Nonetheless, he made a show of chastising bootleggers with stints of fourteen to twenty days in the guardhouse. The commandant asked one offender, a Wake Marine, why he stole alcohol. The quick-thinking rascal answered that he had rheumatism or arthritis and needed something to rub on his sore joints. Otera threw the Leatherneck in the guardhouse, but he sent him a pint of alcohol every day, which made for the merriest spell that anybody at Kiangwan ever spent in solitary.[30]

Ordinarily, the prisoners' high jinks with contraband alcohol were just the sort of thing to provoke one more of Ishihara's inquisitions. In the months following the Mount Fuji Project, however, the Beast of the East lapsed into a state of odd quiescence. He ceased accompanying work details outside camp and acted as if he had lost his relish for persecuting Caucasians. By late 1944 the reason for Ishihara's subdued behavior became clear. He had lost faith in Japan's ability to win the war. The same man who boasted he would celebrate his country's victory by soiling the American flag abruptly changed his tune. "He now says," Purser Kantzer recorded on December 27, "that Japan can quit without losing face, because she has fought two major powers for 3 years. He also says that Japan will fight for 2 years more, but that he, himself, is willing to step back into civilian clothes at any time." Ishihara resigned his post a little more than a month later and quietly left Kiangwan on February 4, 1945. Kantzer penned this epilogue to the Ishihara years that captured the fondest wish of every man the interpreter ever abused: "Thus passeth one fanatic who, I certainly hope, will not be able to slip off to anonymity when this is over."[31]

With the war's end, the men Ishihara had tormented promptly reported him to Allied authorities and swore out affidavits documenting his crimes. On March 7, 1946, an American military commission sitting at Shanghai condemned the erstwhile interpreter to life at hard labor for "cruel, inhuman and brutal atrocities against certain American prisoners of war." Ishihara died of liver cancer on October 23, 1956, a decade into his imprisonment.[32]

"I WONDER WHERE THE ALLIES IS?"

With Ishihara's malignant influence on the wane, the Japanese soldiers who oversaw Kiangwan and the work details that succeeded Mount Fuji behaved with remarkable equanimity. Colonel Otera acquiesced in the hospitalization of sixty ailing inmates and permitted one hundred more to remain in camp for treatment. The commandant also reduced the prisoners' working hours until most were toiling a mere five hours a day by February 10, 1945, less than a week after Ishihara's departure.[33]

The guards assigned to the Godown Detail transcended polite forbearance and assumed the role of hospitable friends. They took their lead from Sergeant Major Tomokethi Takahashi. "He treated us like human beings," testified Sergeant Holmes. "He didn't harrass the sentries . . . he had over us. He let them be friendly also." Takahashi dipped into Japanese stores to supplement the POWs' lunch ration, giving them tasty vegetables not normally available in Kiangwan, sugar, a better grade of tea, and soy sauce to flavor their rice. One of Takahashi's privates regularly broke into the godowns to bring the prisoners additional rice, vegetables, and cigarettes. Takahashi regarded Sergeant Holmes as a peer, and the two of them had many chats about their homes, families, and other concerns. Delighted to learn that Holmes hailed from Texas, the sergeant major pumped him for tales about cowboys and farming. Another guard at the supply depot snapped Holmes' photograph and later surprised the Marine by handing him a print as a keepsake. Takahashi also presented a photograph of himself to his Texan friend. All the Americans with Holmes would have nodded in vigorous assent when he called the Godown Detail the "most humane part of my 44 months as a POW."[34]

Another happy event that coincided roughly with Ishihara's departure was the arrival of a third batch of Red Cross relief supplies from the United States. "*THE SHIP'S IN*!!" Purser Kantzer cheered on January 11, 1945. "Officially, truly and no fooling, the relief ship arrived yesterday, culminating a month of scuttlebutt and rumor that we had learned never to quite believe until we can see and feel it." The POWs received substantial quantities of warm clothing, medical supplies, and cigarettes, but a third fewer food boxes than they had months earlier. A work detail deposited 3,800 American and 300 British food boxes in a camp warehouse—enough to issue four to each of Kiangwan's 1,041 inmates and still leave an emergency reserve of nineteen boxes. The American boxes did not contain as much coffee or canned meat as those of the previous year, but they easily outclassed the British boxes, which were only half as large. Packed in June 1942, the British boxes had taken quite a beating in the interim, and the Yanks in camp sneered at their contents. An appalled William Kantzer captured the general reaction: "Imagine presenting a war prisoner in the far east with a can of creamed rice!, when he has only been eating the damned stuff twice a day for 3 years. And the rest of the stuff was just about as ridiculous: turkey and tongue paste, carrot dumplings or curried mutton."[35]

The POWs received their first issue of boxes—all of them American—on January 15 or 16, 1945. Colonel Ashurst released the next issue on February 1, including all the substandard British boxes. "Unfortunate was the poor person that had to take one," shuddered Kantzer. Ashurst intended to distribute the remaining boxes over two 1-month intervals, but the Japanese scrapped that schedule. Camp authorities delayed the third issue until March 31, the day before Easter, and insisted on saving the fourth until August. Despite those frustrations and disappointments, the renewed availability of food from home imparted both a physical and mental lift to Kiangwan's inmates.[36]

As far as ordinary rations went, inflation and shortages continued to hobble Japanese logistics, but camp authorities and the local Red Cross succeeded every so often in giving the prisoners' diet an upward bump. Faced with astronomical bread prices on the Shanghai market, Colonel Otera had his charges build a bakery with a coal-fired oven. The prisoners began baking their own bread with Red Cross flour on March 2, 1944. By the year's end Edouard Egle could no longer send Kiangwan wheat flour, and the POWs had to chew on black bread. The dark brown loaves were tasty enough, but they were also heavy and soggy, and the inmates did not like them as much as white bread. Egle never stopped trying, however, and he enabled the camp's cooks and bakers to pull off a few culinary miracles. On February 11, 1945, for instance, the bakery astounded its clientele by producing mounds of chocolate covered cream puffs. As William Kantzer marveled, "And imagine the size of them: each one was over a foot long, and every person in camp got half of one. Where they got the frosting and the filling, I don't know."[37]

Egle also sent Kiangwan the fixings for a pleasant dinner of roast beef, vegetables, and pie to celebrate Christmas 1944. Additional gifts of candy and Chinese cigarettes, along with swigs of stolen alcohol, added to the merriment. So did a lavish minstrel show staged in the Barracks 5 theater on Christmas Eve.[38] With the horrors of Mount Fuji consigned to the past, the POWs could poke fun at their ordeal. One of the evening's hit numbers was a song titled "Fujiyama" with lyrics set to the tune of "There's a Gold Mine in the Sky," an old Gene Autry standard:

> There's a mountain in the sky far away
> Where we pushed up forty loads every day
> With a front day every one day out of nine
> While the flag's down, run a short load while there's time
>
> (Chorus)
> *Yasume . . . . . . Yasume. . . .*
> To our children we will sit down and we'll say
> That we sat there and watched the cars roll by
> As we built Mt. Fujiyama to the sky.[39]

"Yasume" means "rest" in Japanese, which partially explains why the POWs related to the lyric so strongly.

It took more than a single holiday and a decent meal to stoke such lightheartedness. By that point in the Wake Islanders' captivity, they and their comrades could sense the war was in its final phase. The Allies stood poised to roll over the Third Reich from both the east and the west. At the same time, American task forces had knifed through Japan's lines of island outposts and were closing in on the enemy's homeland. "Optimism as to the end of the war is running high," Purser Kantzer noted on July 26, 1944. "A few days ago, I was collecting opinions as to the duration, and reports ran from 3 months to a year. Now practically everyone feels we will be home for Xmas, and the end of the war is quite probable within six weeks." The fact that the Japanese were fortifying Shanghai's approaches and burying their fuel supply pointed to an imminent Allied invasion and swift liberation for the POWs.[40]

To be sure, rumors that the Allies would soon crush the Axis had been swirling around the Shanghai War Prisoners Camp since it opened in February 1942. In late March 1943 Pfc. John Pearsall predicted, "The War will be over by Nov." Colonel Ashurst and Major Brown proclaimed on September 2 that the POWs would all be free in Shanghai awaiting a boat home by Christmas 1943. During a visit to Kiangwan that December 3, Edouard Egle assured inmates that they could expect release by Christmas 1944. Contractor Herb Papock heard on June 30, 1944, that the U.S. Navy had placed a "ring of steel around Japan," with thirty aircraft carriers and one hundred troop transports hovering just 250 miles off enemy shores. One month later, an unnamed Marine officer warned a different civilian prisoner, "Everything points to September."[41]

The repeated failure of these prophecies infused numerous POWs with varying degrees of wariness. In the spring of 1943, one Wake Islander teased the camp's Pollyannas with this bit of doggerel: "Spring is sprung. The grass is riz. I wonder where the Allies is?" Cynical prisoners resurrected that irreverent verse to greet the next two springs they spent behind barbed wire. Purser Kantzer whistled a similar tune on February 8, 1945: "We have Berlin fallen now, and the war over again, for the nth time."[42]

Yet, when Kantzer committed those jaded words to paper, he and the men around him understood that such hopes now rested on a more solid footing than desperation and fancy. In spite of Japanese efforts to censor war news, the POWs were amazingly well informed. They knew the outcomes of the Solomon Islands and New Guinea campaigns, the American amphibious assaults on the Gilbert and Mariana islands, and the crushing defeat of Japan's Combined Fleet at Leyte Gulf. In the spring of 1945 the prisoners heard that U.S. Marines had stormed ashore at Iwo Jima, followed by a combined Army–Marine Corps landing on Okinawa. They also followed Allied advances in the European theater from North Africa to Italy, and from the Normandy invasion to the Battle of the Bulge.[43]

As in any other effective intelligence operation, the POWs gathered information from different sources. One of the most useful came courtesy of the enemy. The three shortwave radios presented to the prisoners at Woosung in March 1942 were supposed to receive only stations in Japanese-controlled Shanghai. The city's White Russian station, however, regularly ran reports of Red Army victories over Hitler's Wehrmacht in its English news broadcasts. In addition, a little discreet fiddling with those radios rewarded the Wake Islanders and their campmates with Allied news programming from Chunking, Calcutta, and somewhere in Australia. When the Japanese got wind of this, Colonel Otera had the three shortwave sets confiscated on February 4, 1943.[44]

That action fell short of its intended purpose. Rather than isolate the entire camp from forbidden information, Otera had merely restricted access to a handful of daring and ingenious prisoners. The North China Marines reassembled the shortwave radio they had smuggled into Woosung on their arrival in February 1942. They monitored the news from the BBC in New Delhi and KGEI outside San Francisco until an irreplaceable tube burned out in the summer of 1943. Deeming a knowledge of Japanese and friendly troop positions essential to escape planning, 2nd Lt. John Kinney of VMF-211 began building his own crystal set after the Japanese repossessed their three radios. For seven months, he scrounged and experimented until his homemade earphones picked up an announcement of Italy's surrender. First Lt. Woodrow Kessler and 2nd Lt. John McAlister of Devereux's Wake Island Detachment constructed another crystal set, but its limited range yielded only enemy propaganda. By investing eight months of steady, surreptitious work, the two officers put together a shortwave set that caught the signal from a San Francisco station on New Year's Eve, 1944. Sgt. Frederick B. Mohr, a radio technician with the North China Marines, stole enough parts from the Shanghai motor pool to make either a crystal or shortwave set capable of receiving KGEI. At least one Wake Contractor, a foreman named Don Ludington, made yet another crystal set to correct distortions from enemy news sources.

All these prisoners realized the wisdom of concealing their radios from the enemy and all but a few discreet friends. The last thing they wanted was for some gabby POW to let slip that the camp was getting war news from the Allies. They operated their sets in secluded spots, often after lights-out or with sentinels posted. They also devised alternate hiding places, moving their radios around as an extra precaution against detection. When they obtained news worth sharing with the general population, they spread it in the form of rumors. Over time, however, the Japanese came to suspect the presence of secret radios. Too many inmates knew too much about the actual state of things at the front. Camp authorities sprang many surprise shakedowns in hopes of finding this pernicious contraband, but they succeeded only in uncovering Kessler and McAlister's discarded crystal set. Otera let off the two Wake Marines with a light punishment, and they soon resumed listening to their shortwave.[45]

The POWs gleaned additional information from the English-language newspapers *Shanghai Times* and *Nippon Times*, which the Japanese allowed to circulate in camp. Both publications initially reported only Axis victories, but the prisoners learned to read between the lines. From the names of successive battles, they could tell that the U.S. Navy was driving ever westward into the heart of the Japanese Empire. By the summer of 1943, however, enemy editors began giving their readers glimpses of the truth. They admitted that the Allies had taken the Solomons, New Guinea, and "other places." Subsequent references to more "temporary reverses," culminating in an article listing heavy ship and aircraft losses from an American raid on Truk, elicited this conclusion from Purser Kantzer on March 6, 1944: "They know that they cannot keep up their lies about their losses and claim victory on the one hand while losing base after base in the Pacific on the other, and try to make the public, whom they play for awful suckers, swallow all their bull."[46]

The Wake Islanders' grip on the big picture received occasional jolts of clarity from what is known today as human intelligence. The Allied personnel who entered camp between late 1942 and early 1945—mainly shot-down airmen and the Italians—confirmed what the larger group had already learned through other means. In an ironic twist the POWs received some of their freshest news from their keepers. Ishihara revealed the Marine landings at Tarawa while proclaiming another Front Day at Mount Fuji in late 1943. On April 13, 1945, Colonel Otera's office informed the camp of President Roosevelt's death. Kiangwan's occupants sometimes learned more from the enemy's behavior than their words. Nothing better indicated Japan's sinking military fortunes than the comparatively relaxed atmosphere that prevailed in camp through the latter half of 1944 and into the new year. "It goes to show how our little friends have changed toward us in 3 years," Kantzer commented on January 25, 1945. "No more slave labor now, no more work conscription and purges, a holiday or two a week per man, besides Sundays with no kicks from the japs . . . all show the trend of things. They know what's happening as well as we do."[47]

"WE WAITED OVER 3 YRS. FOR THIS"

Even if the Japanese had clamped an airtight news blackout on Kiangwan, its occupants would have divined sooner or later that their day of delivery was nigh. From Chinese bases hundreds of miles to the west, the U.S. Fourteenth Air Force began testing Shanghai's air defenses in the second half of 1944. Camp authorities sensed what was coming, and they betrayed their dread shortly before the blow fell. For ten days in late March and early April of that year, they kept half the Mount Fuji workforce in camp to erect air raid shelters for the guards—but none for the prisoners. By June 17 Colonel Otera had abandoned his Shanghai residence to stay overnight at Kiangwan. The commandant directed CPNAB carpenters a few weeks later to convert a big concrete water pipe into a bomb shelter for him and his officers. Visibly nervous guards and recently captured American airmen talked about the USAAF's new strategic bomber—the Boeing B-29 Superfortress—but the Wake Islanders and other POWs taken early in the war found it hard to believe any aircraft that massive could get off the ground.[48]

That skepticism persisted until the night of July 5, 1944. A little past 11:00 PM, Kiangwan's inmates awoke to the deep drone of mighty Wright Cyclone air-cooled radial engines belonging to one or two B-29s. The POWs heard five explosions roughly ten miles away, and then the engines receded into the distance. That incident kicked off a series of sporadic nighttime raids conducted by one, two, or three bombers at a time. A few minutes after midnight on August 27, six bombs fell too close to camp for comfort. "We heard no planes either before or after," recounted Purser Kantzer, "but we could hear and see and feel the explosion—the lightening like flash followed not over a second later by the thunder like crack; the shaking of the building and of the sleeping platforms we lay on."[49]

This taste of a terror already known to millions around the globe sent Colonel Ashurst scurrying over to the commandant's office to demand air raid shelters for the prisoners. Downed American fliers had revealed that the Fourteenth Air Force did not know Kiangwan's purpose and assumed the unmarked POW camp was part of the adjacent enemy training complex. It later came out that USAAF intelligence officers had marked Kiangwan as a supply depot on their maps and reconnaissance photographs, and they intended to bomb it after flattening targets of greater strategic value. To Ashurst's consternation, the American aerial campaign against Shanghai had robbed Colonel Otera of his customary affability. The Marine colonel emerged from their meeting to report the commandant had snapped angrily "that if we were injured by our own bombers, it was their fault, not his."[50]

Otera brooded over the matter for several nights until his alcoholic brain struck on a way to teach Ashurst a lesson. At 10:30 PM, October 4—just thirty minutes after lights-out—shouting guards in helmets and full field kit burst into the prisoners' barracks. The Japanese herded the POWs outside, had them count off, and then double-timed them to the baseball diamond in the outer compound, where Handlebar Hank and his officers were waiting. The commandant ordered the mystified prisoners to lie face down on the cold, wet ground while he unleashed a tirade. "A hundred bombers are coming," he stormed. "They are expected in 2 hours. Until then you must stay here quiet, face to the ground. Col. Ashurst requested that you be removed from the barracks during air raids, so we acceded to his suggestion. If you stay in the barracks it will be your blame if you get bombed. But you can have your choice." With that, Otera dissolved into drunken laughter. He kept the prisoners exposed to the night air for fifteen minutes before permitting them to return to their quarters, stand inspection, and climb back into bed.[51]

Twenty days later the Fourteenth Air Force started subjecting the Shanghai area to daylight raids that the POWs could hear but not see. This shift in tactics reached a crescendo on Armistice Day, November 11, in an almost leisurely show of force that made a mockery of Japanese power in full view of Kiangwan's inmates. The raid lasted from 8:30 AM to 1:30 PM, with a flight of three B-29s passing over camp every hour en route to bomb along the Whangpoo River. The Superfortresses cruised at an altitude of approximately 20,000 feet, which put them beyond the range of Japanese antiaircraft fire. A lone enemy fighter rose from a nearby airfield to challenge one flight, but a burst or two from a pair of turret guns caused the would-be interceptor to hurry home trailing smoke.

The demonstration of apparent American invincibility sent shivers of pride and joy through the watching POWs. "To see our own planes coming over made people begin to feel that the war was really getting to the Japanese," recalled Captain Godbold. S2C Cassius Smith thought the B-29s looked "like battleships up there in the sky. I'd never seen anything so huge." To Cpl. Thomas Johnson, the silvery bombers resembled "white angels," and he gasped when they dropped their payloads. "It looked like a ladder reaching from the earth all the way up to those aircrafts," he attested.[52]

Four hours into the Armistice Day raid the guards finally snapped out of their shock and brusquely shooed the POWs into the barracks. This became the standard Japanese response to air strikes. Camp authorities instructed the prisoners to head for their quarters as soon as the air raid sirens sounded or risk being shot. Instead of letting the inmates seek safety through dispersion, this policy massed them into a convenient target that could be annihilated by a few well-placed bombs.[53]

The B-29s abruptly ceased menacing Shanghai in early January 1945. The winged titans withdrew from China to India for transfer to safer, easier-to-supply bases in the Marianas, which had been chosen as the new staging ground for the strategic bombardment of Japan. Shanghai escaped high-altitude bombing for the next two months until the USAAF began sending B-24 and B-25 bombers to disturb the city's peace with a string of raids. In the meantime, American airmen had another nasty surprise up their sleeves for Shanghai's occupiers.[54]

The P-51 Mustang, the USAAF's best long-range fighter escort, made a spectacular debut over Kiangwan on the afternoon of January 17, 1945. Twenty sleek, swift P-51s swooped down on the Japanese airfields near camp, surprising a flight of enemy trainers in the air. The American pilots showed those unarmed two-man crates no mercy. With the POWs as a rapt and appreciative audience, the nimble fighters flamed two clumsy trainers and forced the rest to execute hasty emergency landings. The P-51s also shot down an unlucky transport plane and then emptied their .50-caliber machine guns by strafing the airfields. The Mustang pilots reminded S2C Julian Sandvold of "wild cowboys in the sky. They flew like they didn't have a care in the world." The aerial acrobatics also thrilled Purser Kantzer. "They zoomed down so low that at times they disappeared below the west wall of our compound," he wrote, "and a second later they would flash up again into the sky, going like bats out of hell." Those flyboys were straight shooters, too. The two squadrons that executed that raid claimed a total of sixty-five enemy aircraft destroyed, most on the ground.[55]

That explosive show set off a wild celebration inside Kiangwan. "We almost lost our reason," remembered Cpl. Bernard Richardson. "We screamed our lungs out, waved and shouted to the pilots. We cheered when smoke and destruction followed their wake." Seven words in Cpl. John Johnson's diary preserved his feelings that day: "We waited over 3 yrs. for this." Fifty-five years after the fact, Contractor Bill Charters described the emotional charge from his first sight of a P-51 this way: "God, that was the most beautiful thing I ever saw. It made me think Uncle Sam wasn't too far away." A fourth Wake Islander, Sgt. Jack Cook, emphasized Charters' last point by saying, "It's very exciting to see your own fighter planes come into an area." It meant a lot to those caged men to know that Allied forces stood within fighter range of their prison.[56]

Intent on denuding Shanghai of its fighter screen, the hard-hitting Mustangs returned often to Kiangwan. They struck again at the airfields straddling the camp on January 20. The P-51s zoomed into view that afternoon a minute or two after a twin-engine Japanese bomber took off, and they overtook it at four hundred feet right over camp. Three fighters latched onto the bomber's tail, and Cpl. Guy Kelnhofer's eyes widened as "this P-51 came up behind him, and . . . the little red dots coming out—machine guns. And see the [bomber's crew] in the bubbles running around and trying . . . to get out of there, trying . . . to escape." But there was no escape for those frantic Japanese airmen. The bomber burst into flames within seconds, nosed downward, and exploded either slightly above or on impact with the ground.[57]

The guards chased the POWs indoors at the raid's outset, but many of the latter watched the fireworks from their barracks windows. The Mustangs pounded their targets for a full twenty-five minutes, pulling out of their strafing runs over Kiangwan and circling back for more. All the while the elated Americans and Britons leaned from their windows, screaming encouragement to their champions. The roar of low-flying Merlin engines, the chatter of American machine guns, the cheers from the prisoners, and the humiliation of watching the annihilation of Japanese airpower became too much for some guards to bear. They fired their rifles at the Mustangs, heedless that such futile gestures might provoke retaliation against the camp. More than one leveled his weapons at the POWs and discharged a few wild shots to silence the cheering and drive them from the windows.

In the midst of the clamorous excitement, a guard nicknamed "Sugar" rushed into the barracks housing the Wake Marines and demanded to know who had been cheering. When nobody answered, the berserk Japanese lunged at Pfc. Carl Stegmaier, sinking his bayonet into the surprised Leatherneck's left hip. Sugar turned next on Pfc. Robert L. Frey and beat him unconscious with his rifle butt. Then he stabbed Pfc. Marshall Fields in the upper thigh just below his crotch. Sugar's fury propelled him through three more barracks. Along the way, he bayoneted Pfc. Leonard B. Harbison from North China and two Wake Contractors. The wounds Sugar inflicted were superficial, and all his victims recovered. Colonel Ashurst protested this outrage, but the guard got off with only a transfer. An unapologetic Colonel Otera simply issued a set of regulations forbidding POWs to peer out barracks windows during air raids.[58]

Although the Wake Islanders and their comrades learned to contain their glee, their spirits soared each time the P-51s paid Kiangwan a visit. One memorable raid on Easter Sunday, April 1, caught the POWs and their keepers outdoors around 3:00 PM watching a softball game. The inmates retreated to their barracks as ordered, but they defied the enemy by stealing glances at the action from their windows. The guards scampered about the compound, pointing their rifles at rule breakers, and one angry Japanese corporal punched Contractor Theodore Abraham in the face for daring to look outside.[59]

As the spring of 1945 tightened its gentle grip on eastern China, the Wake Islanders and their comrades faced the future confidently, certain that their lives were about to undergo a drastic change. They expected to hear the guns of an American fleet off Shanghai and see friendly paratroopers raining from the sky. Some POWs urged the guards they liked to save themselves by surrendering to the inevitable invaders. Change did come, but it took a different form than the prisoners expected.[60]

Sustained American aerial activity caused the Japanese high command to reclassify Shanghai as a war zone, which made it an unsuitable locality for lodging POWs. Kiangwan's occupants sensed something was brewing when the enemy closed the training center next door. On April 7 Colonel Ashurst broke the news that the Japanese planned to move the camp in ten to fifteen days to a place they refused to name for the time being. Rumors had already circulated that the prisoners were headed to Mukden in Manchuria or to Soviet Vladivostok for repatriation. Purser Kantzer feared his keepers would take the prisoners to a secure area further inland and hold them as hostages to extract favorable peace terms from the Allies. That same thought may have induced Ashurst to request that the twenty-five sickest POWs in the camp hospital be spared the stress of a long journey. He proposed that those men, including some mental cases and incurable tuberculosis sufferers, be placed in a Shanghai hospital under the protection of the Swiss consul general. Colonel Otera reverted to his agreeable old self, and he arranged things as Ashurst desired.[61]

By April 15 the Japanese had organized one hundred POWs into an advance party. That group consisted of civilian carpenters, electricians, and other specialists, plus a good number of stronger Marines for heavy labor. They were to precede the remainder of their comrades to Camp Hata, which sat a few miles outside Peking, and prepare it for habitation. Within two or three days, however, the prisoners heard that their departure had been canceled, and life at Kiangwan slid back into something resembling routine. Rumors that the move had been reauthorized surfaced on April 30. The POWs resumed their preparations for evacuation, and nothing arose to derail them.[62]

In the Japanese army vacating a facility meant stripping it of anything usable, and that became the order of the day at Kiangwan. The POWs removed the wires from telephone poles, glass panes from windows, and doors and other fixtures from all camp buildings. Contractor carpenters yanked boards off the barracks for lumber to build boxes and packing crates for shipping furniture, tools, brooms, buckets, mops, and the contents of the library and recreation hall. Capt. Frank A. Tharin of VMF-211, who had followed Captain Freuler as camp mess officer, received orders to bake large quantities of hardtack to sustain his comrades on the trip. Each prisoner was also issued his last Red Cross food box for the same purpose. As a farewell gift, Edouard Egle brought the POWs three months' worth of bulk foodstuffs.[63]

On May 4 the one hundred prisoners composing the advance party boarded a train bound for Peking. Before they left Colonel Otera exhorted them, "You must be loyal.... You must take care of your health. You must obey the regulations." One buddy of the departing Marines got hold of a bugle and taunted them by sounding "Taps." He paid for the joke by getting thrown into a fire pond.[64]

By May 8 the Wake Islanders and their campmates were ready to go. "This camp," Purser Kantzer joked, "looks like a field of packing cases in front of the barracks, behind the barracks, and just about everywhere." Thirteen Japanese trucks hauled the POWs' heavy baggage to a nearby railroad station, where a long train of boxcars waited to carry them north, and a somber mood fell over Kiangwan. "We move out early tomorrow morning," Alec Pay scribbled in his diary. "We expect an uninterrupted but uncomfortable trip." Kantzer forced his mind to focus on a more comforting thought: "I don't think this war has very long to run, so it doesn't matter very much whether we get better or worse conditions out of it."[65]

CHAPTER FIFTEEN

"the pleasure of raising our flag over the enemy's homeland"
to japan and liberation

"WEDGED IN LIKE EMPTY BEER BOTTLES IN A BEER CASE"
Reveille sounded for the last time at the Shanghai War Prisoners Camp around 3:30 AM, May 9, 1945. More than 950 inmates rose from their bunks and consumed a simple breakfast of tea and leftover donuts—a parting treat from the camp bakery. At 5:00 AM, the POWs assembled on Kiangwan's baseball diamond to watch the first glimmerings of dawn while drowsy guards conducted a final nose count. The Wake Islanders and their comrades presented a heterogeneous appearance. They wore surviving bits of Allied or Japanese uniforms supplemented by Red Cross clothing, and they carried their personal effects in blanket rolls, homemade knapsacks or cardboard suitcases, and bags of varying sizes.

Following a quick baggage check, the POWs marched five abreast to a railroad station one and a half miles away. The guards had them line up before the twenty-odd boxcars prepared for their use. Built with thin metal sides and wooden floors, the cars were similar in design to those seen in the United States in the 1930s and 1940s, only smaller. The Japanese had divided every car into three compartments by stretching two latticework barbed wire barricades from the floor to the ceiling. Five guards occupied the center section, which was flanked by the car's two steel sliding doors. The Japanese crammed twenty-five Allied enlisted men or civilians, along with their hand luggage, into each end section— making for a total of fifty POWs per car. This arrangement left the majority of prisoners with hardly enough space for everyone to sit at once, let alone lie down and sleep. The two boxcars set aside for the Allied officers were less crowded; they held thirty-three to forty prisoners apiece.

The Japanese covered the boxcar floors with their charges' sleeping mats. They also placed a large can of drinking water, a mailbag and a packing case filled with hardtack, a tray loaded with soft bread, and a five-gallon benjo can in each POW section. Every boxcar had four small windows, two at each end. The windows came equipped with sliding metal doors, and the Japanese propped those open to provide fresh air for the men inside. Since thick steel bars blocked almost every window in the prisoners' cars, this humane gesture did not seem to pose a security risk. Several boxcars offered an additional source of ventilation that made their occupants shudder. Rows of jagged holes half an inch in diameter through their sides and roofs revealed that the railcars had been strafed by American P-51s on previous trips. The Wake Islanders and the other prisoners could not help wondering if they would finish their train ride safely or perish from friendly fire.

Japanese authorities added a coach car to the prison train for Colonel Otera and his officers. Ten more freight cars transported the camp's heavy baggage. One day into the trip, the enemy hitched an additional car containing more soldiers and some dogs to the rear of the train.[1]

By 10:20 AM, prisoners, guards, and impedimenta were all on board, and the train chugged out of the station. It crawled along at speeds rarely as high as ten miles per hour, giving the POWs a good look at the fertile, heavily cultivated region north of Shanghai. Rations for the first day consisted of three small loaves of bread and one bowl of beans per man, augmented by whatever a prisoner chose from his Red Cross food box. For the rest of the trip, the Japanese issued everyone just a single piece of hardtack for breakfast, lunch, and dinner. Crowding in the POW sections made all hands miserable. Few got much sleep that first night on the rails, and tempers frayed. "We are a pretty sad looking lot of boys this morning after 22 hours of being locked up in this miserable boxcar," Purser William Kantzer wrote on May 10. "We are sweaty and hot, stink in competition with the Johnny in the corner, have no more drinking water, much less water for washing either ourselves or our dishes." By the second night, fortunately, the prisoners figured out they could sleep better if they did it in two or more shifts. "We slept wedged in like empty bottles in a beer case," Kantzer quipped. "But having somebody's feet in my face on both sides didn't detract from the relaxation we got by being able to stretch out."[2]

The POWs pulled into Nanking, roughly one hundred miles from Shanghai, at 10:00 AM on May 10. There, they detrained and marched half a mile to a fenced-in field. Over the next three hours the prisoners ate lunch and refilled their water bottles with unboiled water, which their medical corpsmen treated with iodine. While the Wake Islanders and their friends enjoyed a modest picnic, their keepers ferried the prison train's locomotive and cars across the Yangtze

River—a laborious and time-consuming procedure necessitated by the absence of a railroad bridge. The guards started the POWs toward the river at 1:00 PM, shipping them to the north bank in two contingents on a tender that took twenty minutes to negotiate a crossing.

After the train trip resumed, the POWs noted changes in the countryside. "The crops thinned," scribbled Contractor Alec Pay, "the clay soil was drier & low mountains and hills in the distance combined with dry river beds indicated a country more arid & less fertile than the Yangtse valley." A rush of suppressed excitement gripped some prisoners, but that emanated from their knowledge of the military situation rather than the landscape. American fliers incarcerated at Kiangwan before its close had revealed that the enemy's hold over the region north of Nanking was tenuous at best. The Japanese army patrolled a narrow corridor along the railroad, but its control was far from total even there. Chinese guerrillas operated on both sides of the tracks, crossing them with impunity. The irregulars grew so bold that they occasionally attacked passing trains. If a POW could get free of the prison train on this leg of the route, the men surmised, he stood a good chance of finding protection and assistance in reaching Allied forces.[3]

Four daring young Marine second lieutenants put this theory to the test on the night of May 10–11. John Kinney of VMF-211 and John McAlister of the 1st Defense Battalion ranked among the leading heroes of Wake Island's defense, while Richard Huizenga and James McBrayer belonged to the North China Marines. Kinney became obsessed with escape planning within days of his capture in December 1941. While confined at Shanghai, he identified McAlister, Huizenga, and McBrayer as kindred souls, and the four cast their lots together.

On the day the main group of POWs left Shanghai, Kinney and his friends made sure they ended up in the same boxcar section. They immediately spied that the windows on their end lacked the customary two steel bars and were barricaded solely by a few flimsy strands of barbed wire. Figuring out which window would face west once the train got under way, the four plotters rearranged their surroundings to facilitate escape. Feigning consideration for their keepers, the officers suggested moving their benjo can from next to the guards' enclosure to the far corner, right under the Americans' intended exit. "You don't want the smell of POW crap in your face," they told the gullible soldiers. Fortune smiled on the conspirators a second time when the Japanese stowed some doors from the Kiangwan barracks in their car. The fast-thinking Yanks offered to spare their guards the sight of prisoners relieving themselves by enclosing the benjo with a stall. They explained they could fix one door in an upright position as a wall and use a blanket to rig a door. The appreciative Japanese assented once again, unaware they had just given their charges the gift of a concealed escape hatch.[4]

Kinney, McAlister, McBrayer, and Huizenga enjoyed a final stroke of luck on the night of May 10, when the train entered a stretch of hilly territory. Each upward grade slowed the speed of the underpowered locomotive, which reduced the risk of injury from leaping from a moving boxcar. The four lieutenants waited until nearly midnight, when almost everyone in their car had dozed off. Huizenga entered the stall first, cleared the barbed wire from the window with a pair of pliers, and then went out the window. McAlister, Kinney, and McBrayer followed him at varying intervals and jumped clear of the train without mishap. The guards had grown so complacent that they failed to notice when four prisoners went into the benjo without coming out. One person in that boxcar fully aware of the escape was Vice Squadron Leader Lewis S. Bishop, the downed Flying Tiger who had entered Kiangwan in March 1943. No sooner did the four Marines depart than Bishop copied their example.

The five fugitives would go through a succession of harrowing adventures before they reunited and found refuge with the Communist New Fourth Army. Next came a trek of close to one thousand miles—much of it behind enemy lines and punctuated by a tense turnover to the Chinese Nationalists. Finally on June 23, 1945, the five jubilant Americans boarded a C-47 transport plane at a U.S. Army weather station, and Second Lieutenant Kinney and Second Lieutenant McAlister became the first Wake Islanders to successfully escape from the enemy.[5]

The Japanese did not discover the escapees' absence until the morning of May 11, when they stopped the train to let the prisoners stretch their legs and conducted a routine head count. Colonel Otera and his subordinates raised a commotion and uttered some threats, but they did not retaliate directly against the remaining POWs. The colonel simply ordered the doors on the car windows closed two-thirds of the way and chided his guards to exercise greater vigilance. Those precautions intimidated Pfc. Jesse Nowlin and two Marine buddies into aborting their own escape plans.[6]

The train was not rendered as secure as Otera desired, however. That very night, Contractors William L. Taylor and Jack Hernandez crawled out a boxcar window right under their keepers' noses. Unlike most of the other windows in the prisoners' cars, the one in Taylor and Hernandez's section had one bar instead of two. The two Contractors waited for the rhythm of the rails to lull the one guard still awake in their car into a semihypnotic trance. With a stolen pair of pliers, they wrenched away the barbed wire stretched across the window and pushed down its door. That gave them just enough room to squeeze through. Hernandez broke his leg when he hit the ground and urged Taylor to leave him behind. The Japanese recaptured Hernandez and tortured him so badly that he went temporarily insane. Taylor had wrenched his left ankle in his own jump, but he gamely struck out on his own. A devout Mormon and self-described survivor, he eventually linked up with the Chinese Communists, who escorted him to freedom. Prior to leaving China, Taylor met Mao Tse-tung and Chu Teh, Mao's senior military commander.[7]

This second escape stung Colonel Otera more deeply than the first, and he took strict steps to ensure there would never be a third one. From 7:00 PM to 6:00 AM each remaining day of the trip, the Japanese placed the train under maximum lockdown. "They closed all the windows and nailed and blocked them from the outside so that they couldn't be opened," complained Purser Kantzer. "And they kept both doors closed to boot." Along with the overcrowding, heat, humidity, and stench from the benjos, the measures turned the boxcars into nauseating sweatboxes for both their Allied and Japanese occupants, but no more prisoners got away.[8]

"THE MOST PRIMITIVE CAMP WE HAVE HAD TO ENDURE"

Having traveled nine hundred miles in five days, the Shanghai POWs reached their destination, Fengtai, China, around 7:00 AM, May 14. Situated eight miles southwest of Peking, Fengtai was an important railway junction and the site of a huge Japanese army supply depot. Its proximity to the Gobi Desert placed it astride ancient trade routes, which Mongol merchants continued to ply with trains composed of shaggy camels. The prisoners gratefully emerged from their fetid conveyances and marched half a mile to join the one hundred-man advance party at what turned out to be a poor excuse for a camp. The place was nothing more than a cavernous warehouse with a slate roof and red-brick walls fifty feet tall.

As Purser Kanzter stepped through the two sliding doors that flanked the building's only entrance, he could see that the advance party had been issued no materials to create a decent billet. "By far the most primitive camp we have had to endure," he fumed, "it is unfit for human habitation even by oriental standards." One thousand POWs occupied a dimly lit area that afforded each man a sleeping space of six feet by two feet. Denied any furnishings, the Wake Islanders and their comrades had only thin mats to cushion their bony bodies when they sprawled on the concrete brick floor to rest. A single spigot served as the sole water source for the prisoners and their one hundred-odd guards. The benjo consisted of an open trench barely thirty yards from the warehouse door. The enemy's disregard for basic hygiene appalled Major Devereux. "My God, conditions like this are frightful," he exclaimed to Colonel Ashurst. "The flies are all over the place, and . . . you have to have cover on a slit trench like that . . . to keep the flies from breeding. People are going to get sick." Devereux was right. Scores of men came down with dysentery, diarrhea, and other complaints.[9]

Ashurst prepared a detailed proposal for improved facilities, but the Japanese dragged their feet in allocating the necessary resources. "We are very disappointed with the new camp," commented a glum Alec Pay, "& see no prospects of any improvement for a long time if at all." By May 20 the Japanese had begun work on a galley, guardhouse, and latrine for themselves, as well as an electric fence to encircle the warehouse, which made little difference to the prisoners' situation. Work on the fence ceased by June 1, but the unavailability of a transformer forced Colonel Otera to order the erection of an inner barbed wire fence as added insurance against escape.[10]

The POWs' residence at Fengtai coincided with the onset of summer weather. Rising temperatures and cramped accommodations fostered a stifling atmosphere within the prisoners' quarters. "It was hot as the devil," remembered Pfc. Henry Chapman. The warehouse windows sat forty-five feet off the floor, which meant the only place a man could catch a cool breeze while inside was near the doorway. Colonel Ashurst and his officers immediately appropriated this prime area as their billet. The colonel directed that the camp hospital be established next to officers' country. He had the fit enlisted men and civilians occupy floor space further away from the door. He organized those prisoners into three segregated groups, and their distance from the warehouse entrance signified their position in the camp pecking order. The Wake and North China Marines composed the first group; the white Contractors the second; and all U.S. Navy and U.S. Army personnel, American merchant sailors, Britons, Norwegians, Italians, and Contractors of Chinese descent were lumped together in the third. These housing arrangements drew protests from the POW medical staff, who argued that sick prisoners had the greatest need of fresh air. Ashurst turned a deaf ear to this appeal, and put the privileges of rank ahead of the needs of his neediest men.[11]

As long as Fengtai remained unfenced, however, this haughty arrogance benefited the POW brass only during the daytime. At night, the guards shut the warehouse doors, and any prisoners who needed to urinate or defecate before dawn had to make use of one of the five-gallon benjo cans scattered through their quarters. Things eased up a little with the completion of the second fence on June 10. The Japanese left the sliding doors partway open at night and permitted prisoners to visit the latrine outside at any time.

Sometime after the tenth, the officers paid a fitting penalty for their self-indulgence. One night around midnight, the slumbering prisoners awoke to a shrill cry of pain: "Oy, yoi, yoi, yoi, yoi, yoi!" The howls came from a hospitalized Norwegian sailor beset by a dysentery attack. Racked with pain and unable to control his bowels, the Norwegian bolted toward the benjo, trampling the recumbent officers. "He was loose as a damn goose," chuckled Private First Class Chapman. Each time the sailor's feet slapped the concrete floor, his rectum sprayed the officers with watery feces. The next day Colonel Ashurst told his officers to surrender their places beside the door to the camp's sick. The colonel never referred to this incident when he reported on his captivity, but he made a point of complaining that the Japanese insisted POW officers share "the same space with the hospital."[12]

Along with substandard housing, the prisoners' chief gripe at Fengtai concerned rations, which were skimpy at best. The diet consisted mainly of noodles, weak soup, and almost unnoticeable fragments of beef or camel meat, plus whatever individuals had saved from their Red Cross food boxes. The Japanese supplied their charges with flour instead of rice, which seemed a cruel joke since the camp had no bakery. POW cooks used the flour to thicken the soup and experimented with making steamed bread or dumplings, but the latter had a sour taste that repulsed even hungry men. First Lieutenant Kessler saw some inmates seek additional nourishment from "worms, slugs, snakes or anything that moved." Captain Tharin, still the camp mess officer, lobbied his keepers incessantly for an oven. The Japanese found one by May 24 and installed it in another warehouse, allowing the prisoners to dine thereafter on baked rolls and hardtack. Edouard Egle also got word to the POWs on June 13 that delivery of their accustomed bulk food shipments from the Red Cross would resume on the twenty-fifth. "So we ought to start to eat better real soon now," wrote an upbeat Purser Kantzer.[13]

Even before the food situation showed signs of improvement, camp authorities required Fengtai's imprisoned residents to earn their sustenance. The Japanese employed the POWs as stevedores among the godowns in the adjoining supply depot, moving supplies and equipment to a railroad dock for shipment elsewhere. The prisoners also stacked wood in a lumberyard and dug defensive ditches and foxholes around the depot. Some Americans obtained permission to take dirt they removed from a trench and use it to lay out a baseball diamond. Other POWs began fashioning furniture from packing cases, spare bricks, and locally procured mats. Contractor carpenters hammered together a wash rack, and they received enough lumber to start constructing a decent enclosed latrine by June 10.[14]

Despite these belated improvements, a rising number of prisoners became impatient to get free of the Japanese. They fantasized about reaching a camel train and being smuggled across the Gobi Desert. After nearly three weeks at Fengtai, one Contractor tried turning that dream into reality. Raymond "Cap" Rutledge was a CPNAB office clerk and World War I veteran who had flung hand grenades into an enemy landing craft during the final fighting at Wake. On June 3, 1945, he hid under a pile of straw matting outside the POW quarters and waited for darkness. The plan fell apart when Rutledge emerged from the mats and bumped into a guard. The Japanese shackled Rutledge's wrists and took him to Peking, where he spent the remainder of the war in solitary confinement.[15]

Fengtai experienced a slight population boom with the introduction of three more USAAF fighter pilots whose condition registered the fierce hatred the Japanese harbored toward the men who brought them terror and death from the sky. Second Lt. Sam E. Chambliss entered camp on May 20. He had bailed out of his flaming P-51 after it connected with antiaircraft fire over Hankow—now Wuhan—on April 14. "Legs badly burned," noted Alec Pay, "& his emaciated gaunt appearance indicates starvation & bad treatment." First Lt. Harry J. Klota and 1st Lt. James E. Wall arrived on June 10. Klota had taken a bullet through the right ankle when the enemy shot down his Mustang on April 2. He damaged the wounded limb more severely by taking to his parachute at a low altitude. The Japanese who captured him amputated the leg below the right knee. Purser Kantzer tersely described the two pilots' appearance after the enemy released them into the general population on June 12: "Both were terribly emaciated, lousy and dirty."[16]

"WE ARE ANXIOUS TO . . . GET OUT OF THIS PIG STY"

The Shanghai POWs thought they would see the war through to its end at Fengtai, but the Japanese had other plans. Fengtai was merely a transit camp. The prisoners rose at 4:00 AM, June 19, 1945, downed a breakfast of bread and beans, and then boarded another freight train for the next phase of their travels. Once again, fifty prisoners and five guards shared a boxcar. Colonel Otera and his officers did not accompany their longtime charges but stayed behind to facilitate the transfer of civilian internees from Shanghai to Fengtai. Before Otera bade farewell to the POWs, he confiscated Colonel Ashurst's records for the past three years. With Japan's defeat in sight, Handlebar Hank did not want such incriminating evidence reaching the Allies.[17]

At 7:30 AM, the prison train pulled out of Fengtai and headed east across the flat, rolling expanses of North China and Manchuria. The weather turned mild after the first day, which lessened the POWs' misery. They enjoyed an added treat by getting to eat the same travel rations issued to Japanese troops. "At various stops, three times a day," penned Purser Kantzer, "two wooden food boxes were delivered to each of us; rice was in one and various cold vegetables, pickles, seaweed, fish, beans, or the like were in the other. We even got hot tea." By Kantzer's count, the train passed 233 different stations while covering more than one thousand miles in four days. On the last day of the trip the train crossed the Yalu River and plunged southeast into the lush and mountainous Korean Peninsula. According to Contractor Al O'Guinn, the POWs went through eighty-three tunnels as they proceeded toward Korea's tip.[18]

Amid clouds of hissing steam from an overworked locomotive, the train jolted to a halt at the port city of Fusan—known today as Pusan or Busan—at 5:00 AM, June 23. The stiff, sore, and travel-weary POWs hopped from the boxcars into a driving rain and a wind so stiff it threatened to sweep men off their feet. Clutching their hand luggage, the prisoners tramped nearly a mile to a large wooden shed. A plank fence enclosed this ramshackle building and a sea of mud that answered for a parade ground. For the second time since leaving Kiangwan, the Wake Islanders and their comrades had to squeeze into cramped quarters, sleeping on a dirt floor strewn with straw. "It looks like we have hit a new low," grumbled Purser Kantzer, "for there isn't even sleeping space for all the men in this one wooden barracks." The new camp was filthy and abounded with flies. With only three water spigots available, most POWs had to endure long waits to fill the cloth-covered bottles they used as canteens. Four days of this sufficed to set Alec Pay wailing, "We are anxious to move on & get out of this pig sty."[19]

The enemy intended to grant Pay's wish as soon as shipping became available to convey the POWs to Japan. Pay and his campmates got a good indication of what their captors had in store for them a day after detraining at Fusan. The Japanese herded them for three miles along the waterfront to a delousing station, where they had to strip and hand over their clothing and shoes to be steamed clean. While the naked men waited to redress, an enemy medical corpsman took a stool specimen from each one by poking a slender glass rod with a cupped end up his anus. "How comforting to know," growled Captain White from North China, "that the Japanese wanted [us] to enter their country free of any germs."[20]

Camp authorities also put the Shanghai POWs to work. Beginning on June 27 the Japanese sent five hundred enlisted men and civilians to a dock to load a broken-down freighter with bulk salt. The prisoners toted hefty loads with yoke-like yo-ho poles or in bags fitted onto forked stick carriers. Private First Class Nowlin found the task uncomfortably reminiscent of the Mount Fuji Project.

As he related, "When we started walking up this huge, heavy [gang]plank—one going up, one coming down . . ., we were walking up at about a 45° angle. . . . They had to have cleats on there . . . so your feet would catch and you wouldn't slip down the board." The POWs repaid themselves for these exertions by stealing salt by the handful.[21]

Late on the afternoon of June 27, an enemy interpreter alerted the denizens of the Fusan camp to be prepared to depart that night. Without explaining why, the Japanese divided the Shanghai POWs into three contingents designated A, B, and C. Roughly five hundred strong, A Group contained most of the Wake and North China Marines, their comrades from the U.S. Navy, other Allied military personnel, and the merchant marine officers. Seventy-two Italian servicemen, 5 Norwegians, and 228 Contractors and American merchant sailors constituted B Group. C Group encompassed 186 Contractors, 7 U.S. Marines and sailors, and 4 U.S. Army personnel commanded, improbably enough, by Navy surgeon Lt. (j.g.) William Foley.[22]

Beginning at 10:00 PM the Japanese shepherded the three groups to the docks, where a pair of gray, four hundred-foot passenger ferries stood by to embark them and their baggage. One steamer took on A Group, while B Group and C Group boarded the other. The enemy also meant to cross one thousand of their own troops on the first ship and a comparable number of Japanese and Korean civilians on the second. These passengers received accommodations on the main and second decks, while the POWs were packed into the poorly ventilated confines of the third. "There wasn't even room for all to sit," complained Purser Kantzer of C Group. "We had to station some men in the hallway leading to the toilet. Others had to stand. Of course, the place was stifling hot." On the other ship with A Group, RM3C John B. L. Anderson testified, "We were jammed in so solidly that it was necessary for us all to stand." Some of Anderson's comrades got stuck beneath a leaky toilet on the second deck that dripped urine on them. The plight of A Group worsened when the third-deck benjo overflowed early in the trip. "So gradually," noted Cpl. Guy Kelnhofer, "we're standing in deeper and deeper levels of shit." The vessel carrying B Group and C Group developed similar toilet problems. "God," thought Contractor Al O'Guinn, "this must be what hell is really like."[23]

The two ferries got under way at 6:00 AM, June 28, and picked up a destroyer for an escort on exiting Fusan's harbor. Normally, the little convoy could have crossed the Tsushima Strait in eight hours, but that was before nine American submarines had sunk twenty-eight ships in the Sea of Japan earlier that month. The ferry captains wisely steered a zigzag course, elongating the trip by two hours. They also opted to avoid running a possible American submarine or aerial gauntlet at the mouth of Shimonoseki's harbor and detoured northward to Susa, a small resort and fishing village. The ferries dropped anchor in a cove at 4:00 PM and debarked the upper-deck passengers before dark. The POWs had to wait until the following day for the Japanese to move them ashore using lighters. The Wake Islanders and other Shanghai POWs were on Honshu, Japan's main island, but they were too tired, hungry, and sick to evince much excitement.[24]

"I NEVER SAW SUCH DESTRUCTION IN ALL MY LIFE"

On the night of June 29–30, the Japanese lodged the POWs in a school auditorium, the only facility in Susa big enough to contain them all. As the prisoners settled in, word spread that their keepers intended to divide and scatter them across Honshu. Purser Kantzer and one hundred men from B Group were destined for Omori No. 1, a camp on a manmade island in Tokyo Bay midway between Yokohama and the Japanese capital. The Italian marines would end up at Kawasaki No. 2 in a Tokyo suburb south of Omori. The remainder of B Group went to Niigata Camp 5-B, approximately 160 miles northwest of Tokyo. As for the members of A Group and C Group, none of them knew that night where they were bound or how they would be split.[25]

The guards rousted A Group and C Group hours before dawn on the thirtieth to commence the next phase of their journey. A one-mile hike brought the groggy column to a train station, where the POWs entered third-class passenger coaches. This was the first rolling stock with actual seats the Wake Islanders had occupied, but the Japanese forced 140 persons to ride in cars designed for 80. "Men were sitting in the aisles," remembered Private First Class Chapman. "Men were sitting in each other's laps." A relatively brief trip delivered the seven hundred prisoners to Shimonoseki, where they detrained for a layover that consumed almost the entire rest of the day. They finally left at 9:30 PM, enduring the same crowded conditions in which they arrived.[26]

The train carrying A Group and C Group followed a route that led east along Honshu's southern coast and then swung northeast to pass through many of Japan's principal cities. Although the Japanese provided their charges with scant elbow room, they fed them well. The POWs received tasty Japanese army box lunches three times a day for the length of the train trip.[27]

The ride across Honshu treated these prisoners to something even more satisfying than ample rations—copious evidence of the devastation that American B-29s were inflicting on Japan. As the train rolled out of Shimonoseki, enemy soldiers closed the blinds on all windows and commanded their charges to keep

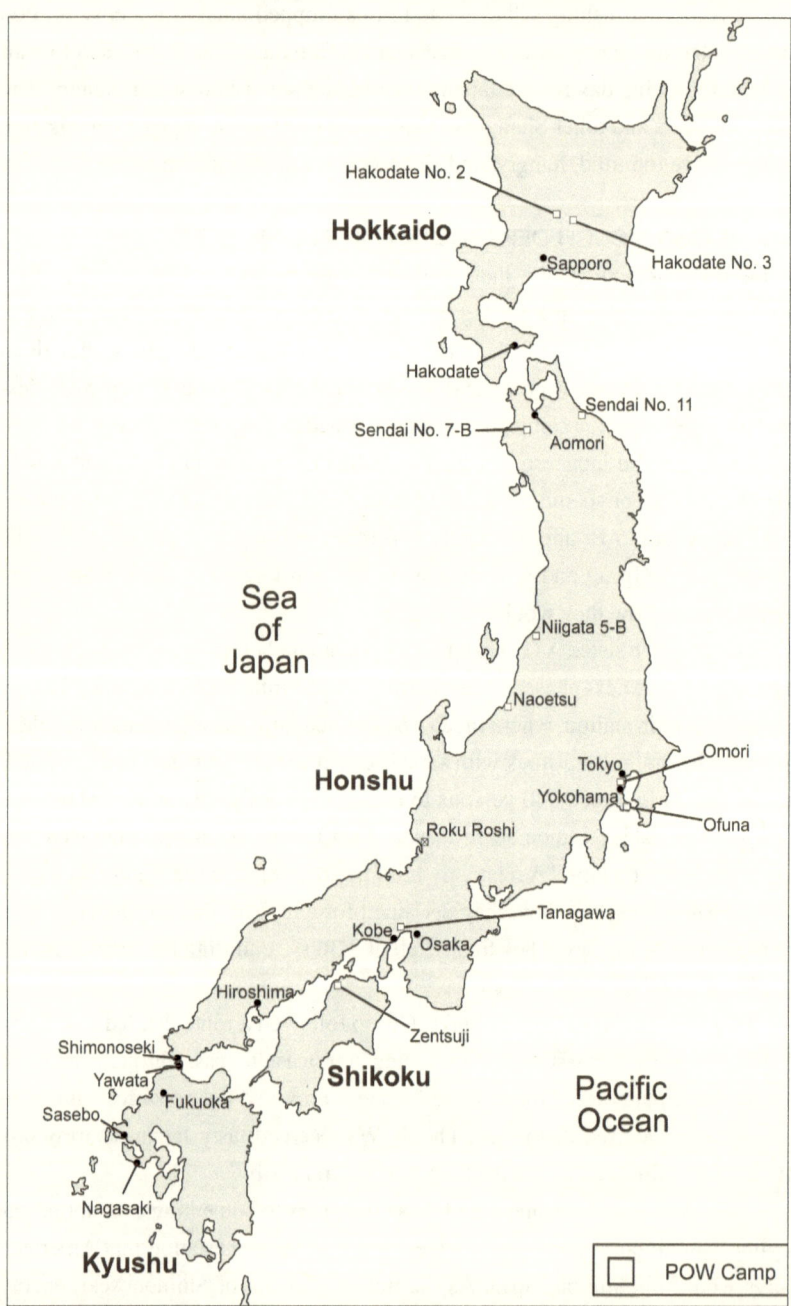

them shut. The Japanese explained this measure was for the POWs' own protection, and they threatened to shoot any man caught peering out. The guards could not watch everyone at once, however, and the Wake Islanders and their friends constantly sneaked peeks from the nearest windows. The terrible sights that greeted the prisoners' eyes stunned them and set their pulses racing. "I never saw such destruction in all my life," swore Private First Class Nowlin. Between Shimonoseki and Tokyo, Cpl. John Dale surveyed stretches of "burned earth" for miles at a time. The smell of razed buildings and cooked human flesh let the POWs know they were approaching a town. "All you'd see was burnt areas," recalled Cpl. Thomas Johnson, "or a [factory] smokestack standing, large smokestacks and just rubble—block after block of rubble, of bricks and bent beams." "It was just . . . unimaginable that everything had been burned out, destroyed," Corporal Kelnhofer confirmed. "I don't know what cities they were, but they were gone." At night, the prisoners felt like their way was being lit by the red glow of flame-wrapped homes and industrial plants. Cpl. John Johnson slipped the folded pages of his diary out of his shoe on the trip's third day and jotted these hasty notes: "Continued to peep under blinds. Such devastation unimaginable. Railroad engines and cars distorted like broken toys."[28]

After stomaching three years of deprivation, degradation, and slave labor, many Wake Islanders relished seeing their captors in such desperate straits. "This made us very happy," confessed Cpl. Bernard Richardson, "and it was difficult to restrain our happiness." Few, however, could remain completely untouched by the tragic spectacle of Japan's obliteration by incendiary bombs and the widespread suffering that entailed. During one brief stopover, Private First Class Chapman beheld a Japanese woman cradling a dead baby in her arms. "Everything else," he added, alluding to the disconsolate mother's surroundings, "was disruption— still burning." Much of the hate Chapman harbored against the Japanese people oozed out of him at that moment. The enemy now had a new face—a woman's face, a child's face—chiseled in the universal language of grief and pain. Men like Chapman still nursed grudges against certain guards and interpreters, but they had learned to distinguish between individuals and nations.[29]

That newborn sensitivity coexisted with the prisoners' rising awareness that they were also possible targets for American bombs. The train reached Osaka at 8:45 PM, July 1, at the height of an air raid. Guards hustled the POWs out of their cars, and they spent an uneasy six hours huddling under a concrete railroad overpass. B-29s passed above them in a steady stream to drop incendiaries somewhere in the distance. Experiences like these left Pvt. Ewing LaPorte wondering if he and his comrades had been transported to the enemy's homeland to act as human shields.[30]

After A Group and C Group arrived at Tokyo on the evening of July 2, the Japanese had them vacate their cars and move to a different station to catch another train for the next part of their trip. During the transfer the Wake Marines and their fellow servicemen developed an instant appreciation for the guards' solicitude in concealing their presence on the train from Shimonoseki. A teenage Japanese girl spotted the prisoners en route to the second station. Screaming hysterically, she began hurling rocks at the Americans and Britons. The commotion attracted the attention of passersby and the girl's neighbors, who reacted to the POWs as she did. Maddened by months of bombing and the deaths of hundreds of thousands of their own countrymen, Japanese civilians of all ages and both sexes snatched umbrellas, sticks, bricks, chunks of concrete, and other debris and flung themselves on the hated white men. As Private First Class Nowlin, one of the crowd's intended victims, realized, "Mob action is instantaneous and . . . absolutely terrifying."

Aided by the guards, the prisoners fought their way through a sea of snarling faces and climbed the platform beside their new train. The mob followed in the POWs' wake, showering them with stones and other missiles. Y3C Robert C. Mayhew from Wake, reported the effects of this barrage: "This added to our casualty list; a broken arm here, a bad scalp wound here, a torn ear there and a good many bruises." The raging civilians also shattered quite a few windows on the waiting passenger cars.[31]

Seven or eight POWs collapsed unconscious when rocks thrown by howling civilians hit them in the head. Nearby Marines or other comrades automatically grabbed their fallen comrades and carried them toward the train. One of those good Samaritans was Carl H. "Dutch" Schulze, a tough sergeant with the 1st Defense Battalion. As Schulze heaved an injured buddy into a passenger car, an old Japanese man whacked the sergeant on the head with an umbrella. Schulze retaliated with a single punch to the face that propelled his tormentor back into the crowd. The car doors closed a second or two later, saving the feisty Leatherneck from additional abuse. Before the train cleared the station, however, a woman ran up to a broken window and shrieked in perfect English at a seated Pfc. James Venable, "You damn Yankee!"[32]

Grateful to see the last of Tokyo, the members of A Group and C Group continued north to Yamagata, where they finally parted company on the afternoon of July 3. The Japanese diverted C Group to Sendai No. 11, a mining camp a dozen miles from the seaport of Aomori on Honshu's northern end. Yeoman Mayhew took a last look at Dr. Foley and his civilians as A Group's train left Yamagata. "They looked a sorry outfit, tired, dirty, and hungry," Mayhew told his journal. "But they were Americans all, and we were sorry to lose them."[33]

The enemy kept A Group riding northward the rest of July 3 and well into the fourth. The military prisoners' transit through Honshu ended at Aomori at 6:30 AM. The Japanese fed them a breakfast that featured a novel entrée—fried grasshoppers. The Marines who dared to taste that local delicacy liked it. The insects reminded Corporal Richardson of potato chips—crisp, greasy, and salty.

Later that morning A Group boarded a steam ferry for an eight-hour voyage across the Tsugaru Strait to Hakodate, the gateway port to Hokkaido, Japan's second largest island. A sixteen-hour ride on one more overcrowded train deposited these POWs at a small mining village near the island's mountainous center. There, A Group sustained its first split. The Japanese called out at least a dozen USAAF pilots and sent them south for confinement in Sapporo, Hokkaido's capital city. The Wake Marines, North China Marines, and remaining Allied military and merchant marine personnel trudged a short distance into the hills to Hakodate Branch Camp No. 2, which lay one hundred miles on a straight line northeast of Hakodate.[34]

Hakodate No. 2 was not much for looks. It sat perched on the edge of a cliff so steep that the Japanese bothered to enclose it only on the other three sides with a board fence eleven feet high. That barrier created a compound measuring 180 feet by 120 feet, into which the enemy squeezed three wooden barracks. Each of those sixty-by-forty-feet structures had sleeping platforms built into the side walls with an even wider platform set between them. This configuration permitted the POWs to sleep side by side in four ranks. Every barracks had its own latrine, which was attached to the back end with only a sliding door and a wash rack separating it from the men's quarters. Consequently, all three of these buildings teemed with flies, fleas, lice, and rats.[35]

Following two uncomfortable, chilly nights huddling in what Cpl. John Johnson characterized as "vermin infested billets [once] used by Korean forced labor," A Group underwent two final divisions on July 7. Sometime that morning the Japanese singled out Colonel Ashurst, Major Brown, Major Devereux, and thirty other military officers and dispatched them with three American pharmacist's mates to a camp twenty miles away at Nishiashibetsu. Those new arrivals from Shanghai joined forty-five Australian officers in a single low barracks intended for sixty men. Around noon that same day, the Japanese selected 310 more members of Hakodate No. 2's population for a ten-mile trek to another branch camp, Hakodate No. 3. Headed by American medical officers Lt. (s.g.)

Eric Pollard and Lt. (j.g.) G. Mason Kahn, this party included 145 enlisted Wake Marines, some 60 North China Marines, 12 to 18 U.S. Navy Bluejackets, 53 merchant marine officers, and 4 to 6 rankers from the U.S. Army. The enlisted British sailors and soldiers from Kiangwan made up the rest of the party. This separation left 130 Shanghai prisoners at Hakodate No. 2 under Captain Maurice "Benny" Lynch, the Canadian surgeon from Hong Kong who had been at Kiangwan since before Christmas 1942. Lynch's short-lived command consisted of sixty-one Wake Marines, a similar number of North China Marines, five American sailors from Wake, and a few American soldiers. Hakodate No. 2's population more than doubled between July 9 and July 12, when it opened its gates to 150 British, Australian, and American soldiers taken at Hong Kong, Singapore, Bataan, and Corregidor. A British army doctor named Murray with the rank of major then superseded Lynch as the camp's senior Allied officer.[36]

"MOST HORRIBLE CAMP I HAVE HAD THE MISFORTUNE TO ENCOUNTER"

Walking briskly, the Pollard–Kahn party made it to Hakodate No. 3 by 5:30 PM on July 7. The POWs entered an installation nestled at the bottom of a narrow valley no more than two hundred yards wide, with hills and snowcapped mountains looming up on either side. The setting may have been scenic, but Hakodate No. 3 was not. As Cpl. John Johnson vented to his diary, "Most horrible camp I have had the misfortune to encounter." Hakodate No. 3 occupied the same total area as its sister camp, but its location atop a leveled-off slag heap dictated a different layout. A wooden palisade fence enclosed a compound nearly 90 feet wide and 240 feet long. A single barracks stood inside the fence. This shoddily built, two-story edifice contained eight sleeping sections. One section measured fifty feet by twenty-three feet on the ground floor and had two lofts, or galleries, with ladders providing easy access for prisoners. Although built with a capacity for 160 men, the barracks had to accommodate nearly twice that many inmates. Camp authorities resolved that difficulty by assigning forty POWs to each section, with twenty in the two galleries and the same number on the lower level. The Japanese neglected to issue their charges furniture or sleeping mats, forcing them to snooze on hardwood floors.[37]

The POWs found their benjo installed in the center of the barracks, dividing the building into two dilapidated wings. "Two open urinal troughs and ten Japanese-style latrines were available," reported Cpl. Robert Brown. "They were indoors, immediately adjacent to [our] sleeping quarters, and due to complete lack of disinfectants or deodorants, the men suffered from the continual stench." The Americans and Britons also suffered from the six-legged pests that bred in the benjo. Sgt. Jack Cook thought captivity had accustomed him to vermin, but the insects were so thick at Hakodate No. 3 that he got little rest. "Fleas and bedbugs interrupts our sleep," reads an entry in Cpl. John Johnson's diary. Many of the unwelcome companions were gifts from the camp's previous inhabitants, slave laborers imported from Korea to work central Hokkaido's coal mines. A thousand of those oppressed and exploited people dwelled in a cluster of hovels to the west and southwest of the camp.[38]

One month after the POWs set foot in Hakodate No. 3, they also became coal miners. The Sorachi Mining Company, a subsidiary of the Hokkaido Mining Company, controlled all industrial, communications, and transportation facilities in the vicinity. The Japanese army leased the Wake Marines and their comrades to the company to operate a mine near Hakodate No. 3. Camp authorities organized the prisoners into a day shift and a night shift. One worked while the other rested, with the day shift putting in twelve hours a day, and the night shift eight and a half. The administrators of Hakodate No. 3 acknowledged no such thing as weekends. They intended the POWs to toil nine days straight, with the tenth day off to bathe and do laundry. On the day following their break, the prisoners would switch shifts and return to work.[39]

Nothing about coal mining appealed to the Wake Marines and their campmates. The mine seemed to plunge forever into the earth. The main shaft inclined at a 45-degree angle for six hundred yards, which made for a long, trying climb, especially at the end of a shift. The prisoners used small air-powered jackhammers to remove raw coal from the shaft facings. After eight or ten hours of chipping rock and coal, Private First Class Nowlin felt like his jackhammer weighed four hundred pounds.

Mining exposed these POWs to the most hazardous working conditions of their captivity. The mine at Hakodate No. 3 was reputedly one of the oldest in Japan. Many of its supporting timbers had cracked or rotted. Somebody always seemed to be getting struck in the head or face by falling rock. The Japanese handed the POWs cloth caps with battery-operated headlamps attached, but no hard hats or other protective gear. The prisoners faced an additional danger from a long copper wire that ran along the ceiling for about half the length of the main shaft. That wire supplied electrical power to a "mechanical donkey"—a train of small cars that conveyed mined coal to the surface. The wire carried a heavy current, but the mine company had failed to either insulate or screen it. That omission posed little threat to the shorter Japanese and Koreans, but the wire hung head high for most of the Americans. With the shaft floor always awash with a thin stream of water, the Asian workers wore rubber-soled shoes as an additional safeguard against electric shock. The POWs received no such footgear, and they had to constantly remember to work stooped over when near the wire if they did not want to risk instant death.[40]

Rations at Hakodate No. 3 fit two negative extremes—wretched and scarce. "The food of this camp was atrocious," stated Cpl. Carroll Trego of VMF-211. "It was by far the worst feeding camp of all that I was in." Each man received one small teacup of unripe rice and a cup of vegetable stew thrice daily. The stew was made from a local weed-like stalk called *fuki*, which possessed a high cellulose content but negligible nutritional value. The only regular supplement to this pathetic fare consisted of small amounts of dried fish in varying forms of decomposition. The Japanese occasionally created a minor sensation by dragging a horse carcass into camp. The meat invariably went to the guards and enemy mine workers, while the POWs got the bones to flavor their fuki stew. The only beverage available was boiled water, but even that never came in plentiful quantities. According to Dr. Kahn, this diet was "wholly lacking in vital food elements, there being no protein or fat, and was about 2,000 calories per day deficient for minimum maintenance of health for the type of work done." The POWs felt the effects of the niggardly regimen right away. As Cpl. John Johnson recorded soon after his arrival, "We are losing weight rapidly. . . . Silver cigarette cases are sold for a rice ball."[41]

Things would have gone far worse had camp authorities not waited a month before turning over the POWs to the coal mine. In Dr. Pollard's opinion, only that grace period saved them from dying before the war's end. Until the enemy started sending the prisoners underground, they laid out a garden and dug so-called "vegetable cellars" on the side of an adjoining hill. Those excavations were really air raid shelters for the Japanese and probing shafts for possible new coal mines. Once mining operations began in earnest on August 9, older POWs and those partially disabled by sickness tended the garden or ventured into the countryside to harvest wild fuki.[42]

The Japanese personnel staffing Hakodate No. 3 behaved like they had learned their trade from the detested Isamu Ishihara. Captain Kinsaburo Niizuma, the camp commandant, was inoffensive enough, but he was too weak or uncaring to restrain his underlings, who seized on any excuse to terrorize the prisoners. Any inmate who neglected to salute a guard within a range of fifty feet could expect to be pounded into the ground by rifle butts, clubs, or fists. Had those Japanese not fled their posts after their country's surrender, "there would have been some killings going on," as Private First Class Nowlin put it. The Wake Islanders would later single out two of these malefactors for prosecution as war criminals—Corporal Unesaku Nakao and civilian Kenichi Kikuchi.[43]

Though only a medical corpsman, Corporal Nakao functioned as Hakodate No. 3's medical officer. A self-important bully, he seemed to do everything in his power to undermine the POWs' health. He confiscated the Red Cross medical supplies the Americans and Britons had lugged along from Shanghai, locking those precious substances in a storeroom. Nakao frequently rejected Dr. Kahn's requests for drugs and vitamins to treat ailing prisoners, but he readily shared those items with his Japanese friends. Nakao also made a habit of looking over Kahn's shoulder, overruling so many of his diagnoses that the latter chafed at the corpsman's "utter disregard of my status as a doctor most of the time." Unmoved by Kahn's protests, Nakao ordered many sick men to keep working as miners. He even refused to let Kahn treat dysentery victims unless they were running fevers. Nakao continued to pester the POWs at night, ranging through the barracks to wake exhausted men and slap those who complained.[44]

Kikuchi, a former Japanese army sergeant, served as the camp mess officer. He was a sadistic loudmouth with an undisguised hatred for Caucasians. Marine Gunner John Hamas, one of the two warrant officers who assisted Dr. Pollard and Dr. Kahn with the interior management of Hakodate No. 3, labeled Kikuchi as "the greatest single source of beatings and unwarranted physical violence in this camp." The mess officer abused his position by shorting the POWs' rice ration and appropriating the surplus for his own purposes. A few days after the Wake Islanders and their comrades arrived at Hakodate No. 3, some Red Cross food that had followed them from Fengtai reached camp. Instead of issuing this godsend to the famished inmates, Kikuchi shut it in a storeroom. POW cooks often saw Kikuchi enter the storeroom to help himself to the beans, sugar, and hardtack meant for his charges.[45]

Life at Hakodate No. 3, with its starvation rations, gratuitous cruelty, and return to long hours of unremitting toil, struck the POWs as a repeat of the Mount Fuji Project. By the summer of 1945, however, these men no longer possessed the stamina or will to stand another such ordeal. Some Marines began to talk about staging a mass escape while they still had the strength to attempt it. They figured the ideal moment for an uprising would come at sunset, when the Japanese changed shifts in the mine—the only time all the prisoners would be together. It was a far-fetched scheme that betrayed its fomenters' desperation. Even if the prisoners overpowered their guards, they would still have to contend with the entire Hokkaido garrison. Yet, each passing day seemed to leave the Americans and Britons with no other choice. In the barracks and mine shafts, men muttered ominously, "We would rather be shot than starve."[46]

Before the conspirators could get properly organized, four Wake Islanders stole their thunder. On the night of August 12 Pfc. John P. Moore and Pfc. Delmar Cooley from the 1st Defense Battalion and two sailors—BM2C Kirby Ludwick Jr. and S1C Clarence E. Wolfe—slipped over the stockade. Moore and Cooley hoped to reach the Sea of Japan thirty-five miles to the west, steal a fishing boat, and pilot it to Vladivostok. The Japanese caught the two Marines in less than twelve hours and returned them to camp, where they were denied food and subjected to other casual tortures. The enemy apprehended Ludwick and Wolfe, too, but took those Bluejackets to Sapporo for close confinement.[47]

On top of everything else, the POWs worried about weathering a Hokkaido winter. Some Japanese told Pfc. Carl Stegmaier to expect temperatures to plunge to 30° below zero Fahrenheit and for snow levels of twelve to sixteen feet. Sergeant Cook noted that the locals stored sleds on the roofs of their homes to keep them from being buried in a sudden blizzard. The prisoners did not own enough warm clothing to suit the climate, and their resistance to cold temperatures was low. Stegmaier and Cook both feared that few of Hakodate No. 3's current residents would live to see the spring of 1946, and numerous campmates felt likewise.[48]

Conditions at Hakodate No. 2 mirrored those at Hakodate No. 3 and were even more dismal in some ways. An old, played-out coal mine too expensive to operate in peacetime lay a mile from camp, and the Japanese let only a week elapse before they began tapping cheap POW labor to reactivate it. By July 13 the occupants of Hakodate No. 2 were at work in that facility, the men alternating between day and night shifts on a nine-days-on, one-day-off schedule. The Japanese had the POWs drill holes in the tunnel walls and ignite light dynamite charges. That kind of mining raised choking clouds of coal dust that encrusted the prisoners' bodies, filled their mouths and nostrils, stung their eyes, and blackened their lungs. "You'd go in there," remarked Pfc. Luther Williams, "and stay twelve hours and the only thing white would be your teeth and your eyeballs."[49]

The residents of Hakodate No. 2 actually received less food after they shouldered the burdens of mine work than before their keepers had put them to work. On July 13 Yeoman Mayhew spelled out the daily menu: "We get a small ration of rice and thin green soup for breakfast, a small bowl of rice to take to work, and, for supper, another small ration of rice with perhaps a soup that is a bit thicker than what we have for breakfast." The galley usually brewed the soup from fuki, but the Japanese sometimes substituted seaweed. Private LaPorte fancied that the latter concoction tasted like something fished from a sewer. Cpl. Floyd H. Davis characterized the quality of the entire diet as "poor—almost too poor[,] but when one is starved a man eats anything." Yet even those inmates who shared Davis' pragmatism could not ingest enough nourishment to keep going for long. In a case later cited as typical by the American Prisoner of War Information Bureau, one Yank dropped from 154 pounds to 139 pounds during his first month in camp.[50]

Hakodate No. 2's medical officer, another overbearing Japanese corporal, acted much like Unesaku Nakao did at Hakodate No. 3. He also kept the POWs' Red Cross medications under lock and key. Whenever Dr. Lynch requested access to those supplies, the corporal would bark, "You are not in China now. You from this date on will have to change your ways." Dr. Murray and Dr. Lynch had to break into the storeroom containing the medical stores and steal what they needed for their patients. Both doctors avoided taking too much lest they arouse the suspicions of their nemesis. In addition to impounding the Allied doctors' pills and drugs, the corporal refused to let them treat anybody before he reviewed their diagnoses. He also insisted that a prisoner had to have a fever to be classified as ill. Camp authorities exhibited the same callousness by decreeing that no more than fifteen sick men could be released from work on any one day. That heartless posture compelled Cpl. Robert Page of VMF-211 to dig coal for weeks while shivering with malarial fever. Men too weak for mining but strong enough to stay on their feet had to dig ditches and air raid shelters.[51]

Many Japanese civilian supervisors in the coal mine exceeded the cruelty of Hakodate No. 2's military guards. Those honchos routinely beat prisoners to accelerate productivity, and sometimes just for the fun of it. They played with the POWs' lives by sending them to retrieve unexploded dynamite sticks from blast sites. A foreman that the Wake Marines nicknamed "Pasty Face" once clobbered Private First Class Williams on the head with a geologist's hammer for a minor rule infraction. That blow left a dent in the lanky Louisianan's skull that remained visible until his death from cancer in July 1982. During one particularly ugly incident, three Japanese beat Sgt. Bernard H. Manning so badly it looked like he might die before they finished. Pfc. Norman N. Kaz, a friend of Manning's from Wake, forgot about his own safety and shouted at the Japanese to stop. This so angered Manning's assailants that they turned on Kaz and beat him senseless. When the gutsy little Jewish Marine finally emerged from the mine, he sported a pair of black eyes, a broken nose, and several broken or missing teeth. Private LaPorte captured the prisoners' feelings for their civilian overseers when he assured American war crimes investigators, "If you need me to find them I could show you the place free of charge. I will gladly pay for the ammo. to shoot them with. Just get me these Gentlemen."[52]

Twenty miles away at Nishiashibetsu, Colonel Ashurst's officers experienced a rude awakening by finally getting a full taste of what prison life was like for the lowly enlisted man. The officer prisoners from Shanghai no longer had orderlies to fetch and carry for them; their new camp also lacked a garden to supplement the scanty rations their captors spared them. Moreover, camp authorities demanded that they work like enlisted men. Officers young and strong enough to bear the strain unloaded massive wooden beams from boxcars at a railroad siding. They also shoveled gravel from freight cars, piling it beside the tracks for transportation to the mines. On some days the Japanese set those commissioned slaves to clearing land for a garden or combing the woods to pick fuki. In common with the inmates of Hakodate No. 2 and Hakodate No. 3, the residents of Nishiashibetsu labored nine days straight and had every tenth day off.

Low rations and excessive toil made the officers increasingly touchy about the subject of food. Stripped of their cherished privileges, they grew as suspicious and quarrelsome as their men. Arguments over the distribution of the rice ration became regular occurrences. Workers felt they should eat more than older and infirm officers who stayed in camp. One junior officer dared to express this opinion to Colonel Ashurst, only to earn a tongue-lashing for his temerity. Ashurst's rebuke temporarily stilled the malcontents, but there was no telling when those grievances might surface again.[53]

"SOON YOU GO HOME"

Regardless of rank or location, every Wake Island defender languishing on Hokkaido prayed for one thing—a speedy end to the war. They all lived to see that day, and it came much more quickly than they or their captors believed possible. Ironically, the Wake Islanders and their comrades became some of the last people in Japan to learn about the war's end. Having played the haughty master race for so many years, the Japanese running the Hokkaido camps had a hard time admitting their country's defeat to beings they despised as much as POWs. Nevertheless, camp administrators could not keep such momentous news secret for long. The Wake Islanders would deduce what had happened well before their captors announced Japan's surrender.

The first tangible signs of the war's close cropped up on August 15, 1945. Early that afternoon, an official from the Sorachi Mining Company visited the coal mine near Hakodate No. 3. He came across Pfc. Leonard Mettscher in a new tunnel that had yet to be braced by overhead beams. The official told Mettscher to leave that part of the mine, adding that the Marine would be better off if he worked where supports had been installed. This unexpected solicitude for POW safety left Mettscher and his buddies gaping at each other in amazement. What could it mean?[54]

The Japanese shattered precedent a second time that day. A little while after Mettscher's encounter with the concerned executive, Japanese foremen bade the day shift to cease working and return to camp. This was the first time inmates from Hakodate No. 3 had ever exited the mine ahead of quitting time. As Private First Class Nowlin plodded up the main shaft, he noticed a coat belonging to a civilian honcho hanging from a nail on a support beam. Eight or ten pieces of newspaper cut into six-inch squares for toilet paper protruded from one pocket. With toilet paper virtually an unknown commodity back in camp, Nowlin stole the strips for himself. Before he put them to use, however, he showed them to Pfc. Charles C. Hill, a Wake Marine who read Japanese. Hill's face lit with a smile, and he informed Nowlin that the Soviet Union had entered the war and was bombing Japanese positions in Manchuria.

When the hour arrived for the night shift to enter the mine, the Japanese kept the POWs in camp. They stated that the machinery had broken down and it would have to be repaired before work resumed. Every prisoner saw through that lie. The day shift had just been in the mine, and its members testified that the mechanical donkey and other apparatuses were functioning as well as ever. What could account for the enemy's increasingly bizarre behavior?[55]

Hakodate No. 2 experienced a similarly abrupt work stoppage on August 15, and camp authorities blamed it on a nonexistent typhus epidemic. That night, the inmates at both Hakodate No. 2 and Hakodate No. 3 noticed that nearby Japanese villages were no longer observing blackout precautions. The following day, the POWs began receiving oversized rations, with servings three times greater than before. The Japanese also ceased denying sick men appropriate medical care. Camp authorities offered no explanation for their sudden and uncharacteristic outpouring of generosity. In conversations with the prisoners, however, certain guards and other Japanese personnel dropped some illuminating hints. At Hakodate No. 3 an interpreter entered a corner of the barracks Dr. Kahn had marked off as a sick bay and told its occupants, "Soon you go home." At Hakodate No. 2 an agitated guard blurted in broken English to Private First Class Williams, "One bomb—kill everybody!" Williams, of course, knew nothing about the Manhattan Project or the use of atomic bombs on Hiroshima or Nagasaki earlier that month. He thought the guard was exaggerating the effects of a large conventional bomb.[56]

Unable to stand the suspense any longer, a British POW at Hakodate No. 2 reassembled the parts of a small smuggled radio and coaxed it back to life on the evening of August 18. Sometime before midnight he tuned in a news broadcast from San Francisco that stated Gen. Douglas MacArthur, the newly appointed supreme commander for the Allied Powers in Japan, would soon arrive in Tokyo to arrange for the enemy's surrender. "This indeed is a red-letter day," Yeoman Mayhew gushed to his diary on the nineteenth, but he appended an urgent caveat from Major Murray: "Our orders are that we say nothing to the japs or do nothing to let them know we have this information." From the moment the Wake Islanders realized the war had turned against Japan, they feared their captors might slaughter prisoners of war rather than see them liberated. Revealing they had cracked the enemy's secret could trigger a massacre.[57]

Less than a week later, however, four inmates at Hakodate No. 3 got fed up with this charade and boldly tested the peace rumors and Japanese intentions. On August 23 Cpl. Winford McAnally and three other Marines went over the fence in broad daylight and headed for the outlying hills. Several distraught guards ran after the escapees, imploring them to come back. The Japanese fired a few shots at the four Leathernecks but aimed well over their heads. McAnally and his accomplices remained at large for two hours. When they strolled back into camp, the enemy refrained from punishing them, which reassured the other inmates about their situation.[58]

Within the next twenty-four hours the enemy finally dropped all pretenses to secrecy. A Japanese army colonel drove into Hakodate No. 3 on August 24 and had a table placed in the compound. After the prisoners assembled, the colonel mounted the table and announced that the war was over. Rather than admit to military defeat, the colonel insisted that "America had dropped a cruel and inhuman atom bomb and had threatened to annihilate the Japanese race if they did not surrender." Tokyo had decided to submit, but only out of an altruistic desire to save mankind and civilization and keep the world from getting blown out of its orbit. The colonel ended his speech by bidding the guards to pour each POW a small cup of sake or Japanese wine. Then an interpreter informed the bemused crowd, "The colonel wants all of us to drink a toast to peace between our nations."

Hakodate No. 2 witnessed an identical version of this ceremony that same day. In addition Lieutenant Jiro Tendo, the camp commandant, distributed a printed statement containing this clumsily worded appeal: "As the War came to an end, so let it be with Enmity, if any of you happens to hold a grudge against any particular man of the Staff or Sentries, let us shake hands and forget the dark hours for the sake of peace and love." Fearing POW retaliation, the guards slipped away from Hakodate No. 2 and Hakodate No. 3 that night. The Japanese replaced them with detachments of schoolboys in baggy uniforms who were hardly as tall as the rifles they carried.[59]

Once the Japanese promulgated their capitulation, they underwent a striking transformation. From imperious conquerors and snarling slave drivers, they morphed into humble and obsequious servants. Some Marines at Hakodate No. 2 tried to heal their psychic wounds by kicking the boy guards or knocking them down. The scrawny young Japanese simply got back up and bowed to their assailants, which filled those POWs with shame. Most prisoners could no longer actively hate people who fawned over them and stood ready to attend to their every material need. The Japanese also relayed messages to the POWs from Allied occupation authorities or provided radios so inmates could receive that information firsthand.[60]

General MacArthur's headquarters instructed all POWs in Japan to stay put and let Allied recovery teams come to them. Prisoners would be easier to find in their camps and safer from possible retribution by the Japanese populace. MacArthur wanted liberation to proceed on an orderly, camp-by-camp basis. It would not do to have bands of prisoners roaming the countryside, terrorizing the inhabitants or provoking attacks from last-ditch fanatics. MacArthur's staff directed Japanese military and civil officials to shield prison camps and their occupants. Those officials also received a warning that they would be held to strict account for the life and health of every prisoner in their care.[61]

It took the Allies about a month to retrieve their POWs from Manchuria, Korea, China, Formosa, and the outlying districts of Japan such as Hokkaido. In the meantime the USAAF and U.S. Navy airlifted supplies to the waiting prisoners. An armistice agreement bound the Japanese to provide MacArthur's staff with the names, locations, and populations of all prison camps under their control. The Japanese were also told to mark those camps conspicuously enough to be easily spotted from the air. The mayor of Utashinai brought the inmates at Hakodate No. 3 a huge pile of white bedsheets. The Americans and Britons took this fabric and laid out a *P* twenty feet to thirty feet long on a nearby hill. The officer prisoners painted *PW* in six-foot yellow letters on the barracks roof at Nishiashibetsu, and the enlisted men at Hakodate No. 2 fabricated what Yeoman Mayhew called "three large P.O.W. signs."[62]

When three B-29 bombers from the U.S. Twentieth Air Force rumbled over Hakodate No. 2 for the first time on August 25, Mayhew gazed transfixed at "those big, beautiful planes." The B-29s returned to that camp on the twenty-eighth, and small flights of Superfortresses located Hakodate No. 3 on that second date and again forty-eight hours later. On each of those visits, the mammoth silver birds opened their bomb bay doors as they swept over the camps, and out fell odd-looking objects trailing colorful parachutes. Down they dropped into the fields and rice paddies beyond—fifty-five–gallon drums welded together in pairs and lashed to wooden pallets. American airmen had stuffed many of those steel containers with all sorts of food, including canned beef, ham, corned beef, Spam, beef stew, soup, vegetables, fruit, bars of concentrated Hershey's chocolate, cocoa, sugar, powdered milk, cheese, dried fruit, and K rations. Other drums held shoes, socks, underwear, hats, handkerchiefs, and khaki uniform shirts, slacks, and caps. Some drums offered the POWs fresh medical supplies. "And they didn't forget cigarettes and plenty of candy and gum," noted a delighted Yeoman Mayhew. Cpl. Robert Brown claimed the B-29s dropped enough provisions at Hakodate No. 3 "to keep a regiment supplied for twenty years." Sgt. Jack Cook, a campmate of Brown's, said something similar but in more conservative terms: "We didn't want for too much—except to get on the way out." The five naval aircraft from the USS *Hancock* that buzzed Nishiashibetsu on August 26 delivered the same sort of items, but their payloads were much smaller. For the moment at least, rank had lost its privileges.[63]

Regardless of size, the airdrops did wonders for the POWs' health and morale. Most felt reborn once they got some American food in their bellies and new clothes on their backs. In some ways, however, the drops represented a mixed blessing. The prisoners were not used to rich food, and more than a few got violently sick from even small portions. The concentrated chocolate bars, in particular, touched off an epidemic of nausea and diarrhea. Private First Class Nowlin compared his reaction to the candy as "kinda like being on a drunk. Lay there and just quiver and shake and bounce." Dr. Kahn ordered the POWs at Hakodate No. 3 to bring him all the American food they found. "Be careful," he warned his subordinates. "Your stomachs are not up to anything." Kahn had camp cooks mix a little bit of canned meat or vegetables with everybody's rice. He steadily upped the servings of American food with each successive meal until the prisoners' systems could tolerate it.[64]

The POWs had something more serious to worry them than digestive problems. Every time American planes flew over these camps, they inadvertently endangered the men they came to aid. The B-29 crews had trained to drop bombs, not relief supplies. For all their good intentions, the flyboys' performance left much to be desired. Sometimes the pilots released their loads at such low altitudes the cargo chutes had no time to open. In addition, the fifty-five–gallon drums proved too heavy and unwieldy for this kind of work. The majority tore loose from their parachutes, plummeting like unarmed bombs to bounce across the landscape for hundreds of feet. Often, the B-29s missed the narrow drop zones. On August 28 several drums crashed through the quarters of Korean slave laborers and the mine office at Hakodate No. 3. Eleven Korean and Japanese civilians—seven men, three women, and one child—suffered gruesome deaths. One drum bearing five hundred pairs of shoes landed on a cow. "They practically made hamburger of her," gasped Pfc. James Venable. More civilians died this way at Nishiashibetsu and Hakodate No. 2.[65]

Although the cargo chutes usually failed to serve their intended purpose, the inmates at Hakodate No. 3 put them to good use. Those POWs learned from radio reports that the Japanese were going to surrender formally to General MacArthur aboard the battleship USS *Missouri* in Tokyo Bay on September 2. The Marine prisoners decided the camp should observe the occasion with a military assembly and a flag raising. The only trouble was that they had no flag. It just so happened, however, that the B-29s' cargo chutes were made of red, white, and blue silk. On September 1, fifteen Leathernecks gathered this material and set to work. They cut out stripes, stars, and a blue field, and sewed through the night. By morning, the POWs possessed their own American flag. All they needed was a flagpole. A detail went out before breakfast, felled a tall tree, cut away its limbs, dragged it into camp, and erected it in the compound. Then some inventive soul rigged a halyard for the new flagpole.

When all was ready, the POWs fell into formation. They came to attention, and a small color party marched in hushed cadence to the flagpole. The three senior enlisted men in the camp—a Marine, a sailor, and an Army airman—attached the flag to the halyard, and one of them gave a brisk tug on the line. As that patch of red, white, and blue flew from its handlers' grasp, a Marine field musician stepped forward with a confiscated Japanese bugle, raised the instrument to his lips, and sounded "To the Colors." At the first note, every American's right hand snapped to his forehead in salute. Men who had denied themselves the luxury of tears for most of the past three and half years wondered why their vision was blurring, and then they felt the hot drops rolling down their cheeks. They could cry now. They had done it. They had come through hell and lived to tell about it. America was five thousand miles away, but the Stars and Stripes waved overhead, and that made the foreign soil on which they stood feel like home.[66]

After the formation dismissed, the ever conscientious Cpl. John Johnson wiped his eyes, opened his diary, and scratched these words: "3 years 9 months and 21 days ago our flag was lowered by the enemy on Wake Is. [T]o-day we have the pleasure of raising our flag over the enemy's homeland."[67]

CHAPTER SIXTEEN

"98 US PW, 5-10-43"
the wake island diaspora, 1942–1945

"YOU'RE A MARINE, AND DON'T FORGET IT"
Revitalized by airdropped American food, the inmates at the three Hokkaido camps grew restless sitting around their barracks day after day. The enlisted personnel at Hakodate No. 2 and Hakodate No. 3 began venturing beyond the palisades to tour nearby Japanese villages and Korean workers' settlements. Some felt strong enough to brave a longer jaunt to visit friends in the other camp. At first, those POWs took the precaution of carrying clubs or requisitioning Japanese policemen or firefighters as escorts. The prisoners soon realized, however, that they had nothing to fear from the locals, who greeted them with cringing docility or professions of friendship.

With food no longer a concern, many POWs rediscovered an interest in sex. The Korean conscript laborers had suffered even more atrociously than Allied personnel, and no one was flying relief supplies to those oppressed Asians. A few cans of food could easily purchase the services of a starving Korean woman. Lust blinded the POWs to the fact that they were exploiting fellow victims of Japanese inhumanity.[1]

Following Japan's capitulation on the *Missouri*, Colonel Ashurst bade two of his officers to leave Nishiashibetsu and assume command of the enlisted men's camps. Capt. John White took charge at Hakodate No. 2 on September 4, 1945, and Major Devereux arrived at Hakodate No. 3 the next day. Ever the martinet, Devereux heralded his resumption of command by putting all the Leathernecks in camp through close order drill bright and early on September 6. "You've been away from it too long," he chided his subordinates, "but you're a Marine, and don't forget it." The men complied with Devereux's orders, but they grumbled about having to play soldier again. "Our moral[e] seems to be going down," Cpl.

John Johnson observed after the drill session. "Our Major has returned to camp but the men are disappointed and seem to be disliking him."[2]

Both Devereux and White disarmed the Japanese guards at their respective camps in staged surrender ceremonies. Devereux would cherish the receipts for the six swords, nineteen rifles, and twenty-four bayonets that Hakodate No. 3's former commandant yielded on September 14. Well before those formalities played out, however, Devereux and White took over the complete administration of their camps. POWs could now depart the premises only in authorized liberty parties, but leave was freely granted.[3]

The two enlisted men's camps received their final airdrops within a week of the Devereux and White takeovers. This time, the mercy runs came courtesy of the U.S. Navy. More than a dozen Grumman TBF Avenger torpedo bombers visited Hakodate No. 3 on September 11, and a comparable number did the honors at Hakodate No. 2 on the twelfth. On both occasions the Avengers released auxiliary fuel tanks stuffed with food from their wings and similarly packed fifty-five–gallon drums from their bomb bays. Dropped without parachutes, the containers struck the ground at such velocity that they either went bouncing for a hundred yards or burst open, shooting their contents in all directions like shrapnel. As the Avengers swooped over Hakodate No. 2, some twenty famished Koreans dashed onto the drop zone to steal American food and cigarettes. The sight of those scavengers infuriated Pfc. Darrell L. Beaver, a Wake Marine, and two American soldiers captured on Corregidor. Forgetting the danger, the three Yanks rushed into the field to chase away the Koreans. Seconds later, the last Avenger to execute its pass cleared the POW barracks and dropped its payload. A drum landed near Beaver and his companions, barraging them with canned goods. Blows to the head immediately killed Beaver and an Army sergeant. A can struck the second soldier in the stomach, prostrating him with several internal injuries. After three and a half years of captivity—and with home just weeks away—Darrell Beaver became the last Wake Islander to die in prison camp.[4]

Rescue teams from the U.S. Army's 1st Cavalry Division finally reached Hokkaido in the second week of September, and they evacuated the occupants of Nishiashibetsu and the enlisted men's camps between the thirteenth and fifteenth. The Wake Islanders and their friends traveled by train to the Chitose Air Base near Sapporo. They climbed aboard C-47 transport planes and flew in groups of forty to Tokyo. There, having come so far together, the POW officers parted company with their men. Colonel Ashurst, Major Brown, Major Devereux, and the lesser brass flew back to the United States ahead of the rank and file. The enlisted Americans proceeded to Yokohama, where they bid adieu to their British and Australian comrades. The Yanks boarded the USS *Hyde*, a combination troop transport and hospital ship bound for San Francisco. The *Hyde*'s passengers faced a long and languorous ocean voyage, punctuated by a stopover of four or five days at Guam, but none of that fazed the Wake Island Marines. They had transcended the consequences of defeat and clinched the sweetest victory of all. They were headed home.[5]

"WE PLAYED SANTA CLAUS ON THE ROAD TO THE STATION TO ALL THE KIDS WE SAW"

Half of the inmates from the Shanghai War Prisoners Camp who landed at Susa on June 29, 1945, spent the remainder of their war on Honshu. Like their military brethren on Hokkaido, these men occupied camps that lacked most of the amenities available at Woosung and Kiangwan. They faced harsher guards, ate less food, suffered from diminished medical care, and frequently endured working conditions that matched the agonies of the Mount Fuji Project. Fortunately for the Wake Contractors and the other prisoners accompanying them, their ordeal lasted only a month and a half and they all came through it alive.[6]

The one hundred Contractors and merchant sailors from B Group sent to Omori No. 1, the island camp in Tokyo Bay, encountered a frosty welcome from the American, British, and Dutch prisoners who had arrived there before them. Relegated to a bowl of tasteless noodles for breakfast, a small loaf of moldy bread for lunch, and noodles again for dinner, the newcomers fished heavy logs out of the bay or worked in local industries. Purser William Kantzer of the *President Harrison* deduced that living between Tokyo and Yokohama placed him on a bull's-eye for American bombs. "It's as if the japs are deliberately trying to get us knocked off," he fussed. Camp authorities compounded Kantzer's fears on August 13 by announcing the existence of a new American weapon, which they called "an acid bomb." The Japanese responded to the threat with these standing orders: "In the future, all war prisoners must take a blanket to cover all exposed surfaces of the body to the dugouts with them during air raids, and . . . must not wait for orders to take to the shelters upon hearing planes of the enemy, especially if it is a single plane in the air."[7]

Two days later the enemy transferred the Shanghai POWs to a clean, freshly built camp at Warabi, northeast of Tokyo. Kantzer and his comrades made the move on the same day that Emperor Hirohito ordered his people to embrace defeat. Although camp authorities concealed the surrender until August 23, they tipped their hand by increasing rations and assigning their charges no work. Airdrops conducted by the U.S. Navy and the USAAF on August 28, 29, and 31 brought the POWs so much food that they wished the planes would stop coming. Full stomachs fostered magnanimity, which these men exhibited as they exited Warabi on the thirty-first to catch a train back to Omori for evacuation by sea. "We played Santa Claus on the road to the station to all the kids we saw, passing out gum and candy by the handful," Kantzer related.[8]

Split in early July from the one hundred Shanghai POWs with Kantzer and the Italian marines sent to Kawasaki No. 2, the other one hundred or so members of B Group went to Niigata Camp 5-B. The installation took its name from a nearby seaport in northwest Honshu that had thus far escaped the attention of American B-29s. Unbeknownst to the POWs, that made Niigata one of the four leading candidates for the atomic bomb. The camp had been open for nearly two years and had acquired a run-down appearance. The POWs toiled from 7:30 AM to 5:00 PM at the Rinko coal yard or Marutsu dockyard with only two days off each month. First Lieutenant Tetsutaro Karo, the camp commandant, disclosed Japan's surrender on August 16, the day after the emperor announced that decision in a radio broadcast to the nation. Relief drops by B-29s began soon thereafter at Niigata 5-B. The prisoners vacated the camp in two contingents on September 4 and 5, respectively, and took a train to Tokyo for repatriation.[9]

The 197 Americans composing C Group ended up at Sendai No. 11 in the mountains of northern Honshu near Aomori. A few weeks after the 186 Contractors and 11 servicemen settled into their two-story frame barracks, the guards stripped them of everything but the clothes on their backs. The Japanese also hassled their charges for the most trivial reasons, driving Alec Pay to write on July 23, 1945, "Conditions are getting worse. These people are not only very strict, they are making it a point to find fault with our every action. The mental strain is as difficult to bear as the physical."[10]

Sendai No. 11 sat in mining country. Starting on July 10 the POWs had to walk four miles up and down mountainsides to an open-pit iron mine, where the already weary men would dig iron ore. After the first day on the job, Pay told his diary, "Tonite we are dead tired." The Japanese ceased mine work on July 29, but they set the prisoners to cutting and gathering firewood while granting them only two days off a month. A ration of rice, soybeans, and fuki soup afforded each man two thousand calories per day, but Dr. Foley figured that the workload easily burned four thousand. Inmates lost weight at an average of three pounds a week. They began collapsing while merely standing inspection and a growing number swelled with beriberi. Two Contractors—Robert P. "Cowboy" Head and "Shorty"

Martin—rebelled against a slow death by starvation, and they went over the fence on August 12. Fortunately, they stayed at large until the sixteenth, which meant the suddenly tame Japanese returned them to camp without the usual abuse.

Sendai No. 11 had already welcomed a friendly new camp director a day earlier. He immediately placed his guards on a tight leash and promised the prisoners more food. Supply drops by the USS *Bennington*'s air group on August 26 and 27 and by B-29s on September 2 and 4 enabled the POWs to gorge on American chow. On the latter date the camp's original commandant committed hari-kari to escape prosecution for war crimes. The men of C Group finally left camp around 5:00 PM, September 12, and enjoyed an overnight train ride to the port of Sendai. There, the Americans boarded a hospital ship appropriately christened the USS *Rescue* for the first leg in their voyage home.[11]

"A WARNING TO SOME WHO STILL FEEL THEY HAVE SOME RIGHTS HERE"

Up to now, this book has focused on the main group of Wake Islanders, which endured most of its captivity at the Shanghai War Prisoners Camp. Yet close to four hundred Americans taken at Wake never set foot in China. Those men either stayed on the atoll or sailed, sooner or later, straight to Japan. Hundreds more were removed from Woosung or Kiangwan and sent to the enemy's homeland well ahead of the main group. Before evaluating the Wake Islanders' POW survival success, it is necessary to briefly chronicle that diaspora and make an overall count of those who lived and those who died.

The Wake Islanders' first major separation occurred less than three weeks into their captivity. When the *Nitta Maru* pulled away from the atoll on January 12, 1942, with 1,235 POWs bound for Yokohama and Shanghai, it left behind 387 Americans. Twenty of them were servicemen judged too ill or badly wounded to stand a sea voyage. The Japanese sequestered those invalids in a separate hospital compound overseen by Dr. Lawton Shank, the Contractors' devoted surgeon. Shank's most serious military cases included Cpl. Ralph Holewinski, whose legs had been mangled by a strafing dive-bomber the day Wake fell, and Pfc. Wiley Sloman, who had been shot in the head and left for dead on Wilkes Island. The Japanese also retained 367 Contractors on the atoll. They chose those men for their skill at operating heavy machinery and other trades required to convert Wake into an advanced outpost for Japan's newly enlarged empire. Leal Henderson Russell, a forty-two-year-old CPNAB buildings superintendent, shouldered the unwelcome responsibility of motivating this unwilling work force to serve its new masters. The Japanese issued him a blue armband to signify his status.

The Japanese put Russell and his subordinates to work almost immediately. The Contractors repaired existing buildings, filled bomb craters in roads and on the airfield, and unloaded cargo from calling ships. For the most part, however, the civilians applied their talents to preparing Wake to withstand anticipated American attacks. They dug tank traps, slit trenches, and rifle pits; set up barbed wire entanglements; and mined probable landing beaches. The Contractors linked these defenses to a network of two hundred coral and concrete pillboxes, two concrete fire control centers, twenty-five bombproof shelters, fifteen CPs, and a new concrete magazine in addition to the seven built under American auspices. The Japanese also gave the prisoners permission to construct a large bomb shelter for their own use.[12]

The Japanese army and navy contributed increments that raised their garrison on Wake to a peak strength of 4,100 men by 1943. Those sailors and soldiers armed the atoll with four 8-inch and four 6-inch coastal guns, a wide assortment of antiaircraft weaponry, thirty-six field pieces, and two dozen light tanks. They also returned to operable condition half of the artillery from Major Devereux's 1st Defense Battalion. In addition, the Japanese stationed four motor torpedo boats and a large complement of land-based aircraft on the atoll.[13]

As long as the Contractors did their work and observed regulations, their captors ruled them with a comparatively light hand. Prisoners caught shirking could expect to stand at attention for prolonged periods or spend a couple of days in close confinement. "The treatment we receive is fair," Russell decided, "and, I think, quite reasonable." The Japanese also refrained from punishing three Contractors who hid in the brush in hopes of evading capture until the U.S. Navy liberated the atoll. Lloyd S. McKeehan, a structural steel worker from San Francisco, turned himself in on January 20, 1942. Fred J. Stevens, a sheet metal worker, and Logan Kay, a carpenter, remained at large for more than another month, foraging and constantly changing their hiding places. Worn down by the stress and privations of a fugitive's life, they finally surrendered on March 10.[14]

All during this time the Japanese continued to feed their known prisoners pretty well, drawing on the caches of American canned goods scattered across the atoll. On May 13 Leal Russell rejoiced over a "very good meal of baked ham, fruit sauce and spinach at noon, also corn bread." Thanks in part to this nutritious diet, the hospitalized American servicemen recuperated quickly. By mid-February all of Dr. Shank's military patients except Corporal Holewinski could get out of bed and move about on their own. Holewinski grew well enough to travel in three months. On May 11 the Japanese embarked him and his nineteen formerly hospitalized comrades on the *Asama Maru*, another luxury liner pressed into naval service, and shipped them to Japan.[15]

Before the last members of Wake's American garrison quitted their old post, they saw their country strike back at Japan. The U.S. Navy never attempted to retake the atoll, but it did not forget the enemy stronghold perched one thousand miles from Midway. On February 24, 1942, Task Force 16—the carrier USS *Enterprise*, two heavy cruisers, and seven destroyers under Vice Adm. William F. "Bull" Halsey Jr.—raided Wake. The cruisers USS *Northampton* and USS *Salt Lake City*, accompanied by two destroyers, started bombarding Peale Island at 7:42 AM. Eight minutes later, the *Enterprise* air group weighed in with thirty-five SBD Dauntless dive-bombers, nine TBD Devastator torpedo bombers, and six Grumman F4F-3 Wildcat fighters. "At last something," scribbled Leal Russell. "We were bombed, shelled, and machine gunned starting somewhere around 7:00 AM." The Contractors and convalescing servicemen safely weathered an hour of such pounding in their respective bomb shelters, but the Japanese lost three Mavis flying boats, a captured CPNAB dredge, a motor torpedo boat, and a barge.[16]

The POWs prayed that this thunderous onslaught betokened an imminent invasion, but the only Yanks to come ashore were Ens. Percy W. Forman and AMM2C John E. Winchester, whose SBD had its fuel line cut by antiaircraft fire. The two *Enterprise* fliers ditched their spluttering plane, inflated a rubber life raft, and paddled to Wilkes Island, where they made landfall around 2:00 AM on February 25. The Japanese took Forman and Winchester into custody and sent them away a few days later on a merchant ship. Tragically for Wake Island's two newest prisoners, both died when an American submarine sank their ship in Japan's Inland Sea on March 13.[17]

Back on the atoll 387 other Americans realized their deliverance had been postponed to a later date. "It is my firm belief that the U.S. forces will not come here unless they need the island," wrote Leal Russell, "and from all appearances, they do not." A pair of Russell's subordinates soon tired of waiting for their navy to free them. Burned-out dredge crewmen Elmer E. Mackie and Donald Sullivan decided to steal a motorized sailboat that CPNAB had brought to the atoll. For two weeks, the conspiring duo accumulated diesel fuel and provisions. Mackie and Sullivan put their plan in motion on the night of April 25, 1942. The Japanese did not notice their absence until roll call the following morning. Nine days later an enemy interpreter read a proclamation to the assembled POWs in Camp 2. He announced that the escapees' boat had run out of fuel and drifted south to the Marshall Islands, where they were recaptured and executed. Some Contractors scoffed at this tale, but others believed it. Wherever the truth actually lay, Mackie and Sullivan were never heard from again.[18]

Two weeks after the Mackie–Sullivan escape, Captain Susumu Kawasaki, the atoll's Japanese commander, subjected the POWs to a stomach-churning demonstration of the limits of their captors' patience. Sometime on the night of May 7–8 enemy guards caught Julius M. Hofmeister, a thirty-two-year-old roofer from San Francisco, drunk and singing at the top of his lungs inside a Japanese canteen, where he had forced entry to slake his thirst for liquid depressants. Hofmeister was a burly man who stood six feet six, which caused his buddies to tag him with the ludicrous nickname "Babe." A jovial giant afflicted with alcoholism, Hofmeister took a job on Wake to dry out, but the cure did not stick. After the atoll changed owners, Babe habitually slipped out of the prisoners' compound after sundown to steal food, liquor, and other things from the Japanese. Too big and heavy to sneak around unnoticed, he received repeated warnings to mend his ways, but he would only laugh in his keepers' faces. Exasperated by the recent escape and Hofmeister's recalcitrance, Captain Kawasaki hauled him before a Japanese court-martial on May 9. The court found Hofmeister guilty and sentenced him to death. The Japanese forced Leal Russell and twenty CPNAB supervisors to watch as they beheaded Babe the morning of the tenth. Russell correctly gauged the impact of this harsh measure by telling his diary, "Possibly it will serve as a warning to some who still feel they have some rights here."[19]

Death did not revisit Russell's flock until the night of July 15, 1942, when William Miles, a San Francisco carpenter in his mid-fifties, succumbed to cardiac arrest. Miles' comrades mourned his passing, but they were also worried about their own health. The atoll's stocks of canned food and American cigarettes had grown short. In addition the absence of fresh vegetables in the Contractors' diet deprived them of vitamin K and caused a jaundice epidemic that persisted until mid-September.[20]

Most of those men blessed their lucky stars when they learned a few days later that the Japanese had decided to evict them from Wake Island. On September 30, 1942, Russell and 264 of his subordinates boarded the *Tachibana Maru*, a combination freighter and tanker, and steamed away toward Japan. The Japanese kept ninety-eight Americans on the atoll for additional base construction and maintenance. Murray Kidd, a common laborer from Boise, called the men he left behind a "skeleton crew"—dragline operators, electricians, concrete specialists, and a couple of cooks. Dr. Shank remained on Wake to keep the other ninety-seven Americans healthy. Shank would lose no patients to natural causes, but he and his companions had little more than a year to live.[21]

There is little to tell of the final months of those ninety-eight doomed Yanks. They left just one cryptic record, and it survived only because it was carved in stone. While tending to some job on Wilkes Island in the spring of 1943, one or more Contractors etched this message on a coral boulder: "98 US PW, 5-10-43." Captain Kawasaki no longer commanded the Japanese garrison by that time. He had been relieved on December 13, 1942, by Captain Shigematsu Sakaibara, a stocky, broad-shouldered officer around fifty years of age. A champion swordsman, Sakaibara cracked down on rule breakers with less hesitation than his predecessor. In July 1943 he had an ensign behead a Contractor caught stealing food from a Japanese warehouse.[22]

The ninety-seven remaining Americans evidently took care to avoid angering Sakaibara, but their mere presence soon became an itch that the atoll's commander longed to scratch. The captain's testiness mounted with the pressure that the Contractors' countrymen placed on his exposed domain. On July 8, 1943, eight Consolidated B-24 Liberator bombers based on Midway delivered the first in a series of intermittent strikes on Wake. American submarines also prowled the waters around the atoll that summer, waiting to ambush enemy supply ships. One of them put two torpedoes through the guts of the *Suwa Maru*, a 10,000-ton merchantman whose captain ran the dying ship onto a reef to save at least some of its cargo. On October 5, 1943, all hell seemed to break loose as an American task force built around the carrier USS *Yorktown* unleashed its firepower on Sakaibara's garrison. Grumman F6F-3 Hellcat fighters announced the task force's arrival at dawn, roaring over the airfield to disable the atoll's air force. The Americans destroyed thirty-one planes on the ground. The *Yorktown* air group logged a total of 510 murderous sorties, scorching Wake with 340 tons of bombs. At the same time American cruisers and destroyers rocked that cramped coral strip with 3,198 shells from their 5-inch and 8-inch guns. Holed up in a dugout, Petty Officer Hisao Tsuji, one of the atoll's shaken defenders, would later testify that the explosions and terror went on without a break for two days.[23]

The intensity of the bombardment, the heaviest that Wake had sustained thus far, convinced Captain Sakaibara that American troops were about to storm ashore. The last thing he needed was to keep one eye open for an amphibious assault and the other on nearly one hundred POWs. As American fire subsided on the raid's second and final day, Sakaibara issued orders to execute the prisoners. Seamen belonging to the garrison's headquarters company herded the Contractors to a beach on the northwestern tip of the main islet within sight of Sakaibara's CP. As a late afternoon sun bore witness, the Japanese directed the Americans to sit in a line along an antitank ditch facing out to sea. They blindfolded the perplexed civilians and bound them hand and foot. Then three platoons positioned behind the prisoners opened fire with rifles and machine guns. After the shooting stopped, the Japanese rolled the murdered men into the ditch and covered them with white coral sand. Sakaibara justified his crime with this disingenuous radio dispatch to his superiors: "Riotous conduct among prisoners. Have executed them." Petty Officer Tsuji knew the truth, however, and he felt his commander had gone too far.

The day after the execution a Japanese enlisted man reported that one American had somehow escaped the slaughter. A frantic Sakaibara ordered the POWs exhumed and confirmed that one was still alive and on the loose. The Japanese caught the lone fugitive a week later and brought him to Sakaibara. The captain seized on the situation to show off his dexterity at kendo, his favorite sport. He unsheathed his sword and personally decapitated the last American prisoner on Wake Island.[24]

The invasion dreaded by Sakaibara never materialized, but what actually happened was arguably worse. The American military subjected Wake's defenders to a slow death. The *Yorktown* and its consorts had destroyed two years' worth of Japanese food stores on October 6, which imposed drastic ration cuts on the atoll's garrison. Mounting aerial harassment by land-based bombers and PBYs from Midway sapped the Imperial Japanese Navy's willingness to risk surface vessels to resupply Wake. Five Japanese submarines visited the atoll between December 1943 and August 1945, but they delivered minuscule relief. By April 1944 aircraft based on America's new conquests in the Marshall Islands were flying missions against Wake, and bombings became an almost daily occurrence.[25]

Sakaibara's sailors and soldiers burrowed as deep as they could beneath Wake's gritty coral surface, emerging between air raids to hunt for food. "It was like being in hell every day," remembered Petty Officer Tsuji. On July 20, 1944, Lance-Corporal Misumasa Watanabe, an antitank gunner stationed on Wake by the Japanese army, vented to his diary, "Our food is terrible: three small crackers and a few beans. We are getting accustomed to tree leaves." Starving men wiped out the atoll's rat population, along with its flightless rails. They also devoured all the seabirds they could catch and scoured the brush for the creatures' eggs. Some Japanese planted gardens, using their own feces to fertilize closely watched plots that yielded puny tomatoes, melons, and squash. The stronger fellows went fishing from reefs or small boats, often throwing dynamite into the ocean to kill anything swimming in the vicinity. When those efforts failed to save all from hunger, several desperate enlisted men started stealing from the few warehouses holding any food. The officers condemned those they caught to death by starvation. Food thieves took to carrying their rifles on their nocturnal forays so they could shoot themselves if a superior spotted them, thus avoiding a far worse fate.[26]

Virtually abandoned by Japan, an estimated 1,288 members of Sakaibara's wilting command died of malnutrition or disease. That was more than twice the number of Japanese who perished on Wake from American raids. By the time the destroyer USS *Levy* appeared offshore to accept Sakaibara's surrender on September 4, 1945, most of his subordinates were too weak, sick, and demoralized to feel anything but relief.[27]

Sakaibara, who had been promoted to rear admiral before the war's end, tried to conceal his complicity in the murder of the ninety-eight Americans entrusted to his care. His officers claimed that half of the POWs had died during the *Yorktown* raid of October 5–6, 1943, after a bomb scored a direct hit on one of their bomb shelters. The other Contractors in a second dugout allegedly killed their guard, stole two rifles, and fought to the death when the Japanese tried to recapture them. The obviously rehearsed nature of the story aroused American suspicions, and a full-fledged investigation ensued. One of Sakaibara's officers, a key player in the massacre, eventually committed suicide, but not before leaving a written confession. An American military commission convened on Kwajalein on December 21, 1945, tried Sakaibara and found him guilty. The Americans hanged him along with five other Japanese war criminals on Guam on June 19, 1947. Before the rear admiral ascended the gallows, he uttered this final stoic statement: "I think my trial was entirely unfair . . . , and the sentence too harsh, but I obey with pleasure."[28]

"THE FOOD CONTINUES GOOD (FOR JAPANESE PRISON FOOD)"

The twenty American servicemen who departed Wake Island on May 11, 1942, experienced a pleasant passage to Japan. They traveled on the former luxury liner *Asama Maru*, and the ship's captain permitted them access to some of its amenities. He quartered the prisoners in the swimming pool area, where they could enjoy fresh air and sunshine. A steward who liked Americans attended to their needs, which was a far cry from the vengeance-crazed guards who had savaged their charges on the *Nitta Maru*.[29]

The *Asama Maru* delivered the twenty fortunate Yanks to Yokohama in less than a week, and they boarded a train to continue their journey. The train stopped briefly a few miles outside town while the Japanese removed six prisoners for transfer to the Ofuna Naval Interrogation Center. Two of the Wake Islanders diverted to Ofuna were officers—Capt. Henry S. Wilson, the commander of the atoll's tiny Army radio detail, and 2nd Lt. Henry G. Webb, a baby-faced pilot from VMF-211. Four enlisted Marines from the 1st Defense Battalion—Cpl. Ralph Holewinski, Pfc. Wiley Sloman, Pfc. Charles E. Tramposh, and Pvt. Berdyne Boyd—accompanied them.

Inmates at Ofuna faced a bleak and isolated existence. The Japanese lodged them in two-man cells, and guards chosen for their height enforced a strict no-talking rule. Intelligence officers in civilian suits employed sophisticated techniques while interrogating the prisoners individually. They habitually timed these sessions to interrupt meal times, banking on hunger to make their victims more malleable.[30]

After two and a half months the Imperial Japanese Navy decided that these Americans had divulged all the worthwhile information in their possession. It turned them over to the Imperial Japanese Army, which deposited them in the Zentsuji POW camp on the island of Shikoku. When Captain Wilson and his five Marine companions entered their new camp on August 3, they rejoined the fourteen friends with whom they had spent their first five months in captivity. They also received a hearty welcome from the twenty Wake Islanders taken from the *Nitta Maru* during that hellship's three-day layover at Yokohama in January 1942. The earlier arrivals included Maj. George Potter, Major Devereux's affable executive officer; Maj. Paul Putnam, VMF-211's intrepid commanding officer; and Cdr. Campbell Keene, Commander Cunningham's second in charge on Wake.

In addition to this unexpected reunion, Wilson, Webb, Holewinski, Sloman, Tramposh, and Boyd rejoiced in their changed surroundings. First established during the Russo–Japanese War, Zentsuji was the oldest POW camp in Japan. It also rivaled the Shanghai War Prisoners Camp in the humane treatment of inmates. Located in the midst of a large Japanese army training center, Zentsuji reopened its doors as a prison on January 15, 1942, taking in 268 British and Dutch subjects captured in the Gilbert Islands and 450 Americans seized on Guam. Nearly 145 of the latter were U.S. Marines, which provided a ready-made support network for many of the Wake Islanders.[31]

The Japanese troops who ran Zentsuji were reservists, and they exhibited less ferocity than the guards most Allied POWs encountered elsewhere. On occasion those older enemy soldiers felt mellow enough to share their leftover food with sick prisoners. Zentsuji's commandant set a benign example by respecting some of the rights guaranteed by the Geneva Convention, and he tried to provide his charges with the same food and accommodations authorized for the emperor's soldiers. Prisoners could borrow books and magazines from a fine library built around the print materials removed from the U.S. Embassy in Tokyo. The camp boasted a post exchange that even sold limited quantities of soda pop. The Japanese also allowed inmates to form a choral group dubbed the Bathhouse Gang that buoyed morale with regular concerts called "sing-songs."[32]

Compared with those at other camps, POW rations at Zentsuji could actually qualify as ample, tasty, and nutritious. Inmates even got accustomed to eating fresh donuts on Sundays. Camp authorities wisely allowed prisoners to supplement their diet in assorted ways. Gardening details composed of both officers and enlisted men cultivated Irish potatoes and other crops that made a notable difference in their caloric intake. "The food continues good (for Japanese prison food)," Major Putnam jotted on May 8, 1943, "and the work continues about the farm." Three months later, he celebrated, "For dinner tonight, we had the usual rice and beans and in place of soup there was a big dish of potato salad!!" On August 23 Putnam recorded a complaint that would have flabbergasted Allied POWs confined almost anywhere else in the Japanese Empire: "Food continues plentiful and is good except that many are beginning to gag whenever they see an egg-plant." A month earlier, the Japanese had presented Putnam and his comrades with eight hundred baby chicks to raise for eggs and meat. The POWs also tended a large herd of rabbits, whose quick reproductive capacity provided the camp with a sustained source of meat, gravy, and fur for winter caps.[33]

Zentsuji's occupants benefited from greater amounts of outside aid than was the norm at most other POW camps. Despite the usual enemy pilfering, each prisoner received the equivalent of twenty-one Red Cross food boxes between December 24, 1942, and May 28, 1945. During the same period, mail delivery averaged seventy to eighty letters per man, with many receiving personal packages from home.[34]

Yet as the war progressed, feasting alternated with famine. American advances across the South Pacific and Central Pacific played havoc with Japanese logistics, and Zentsuji's inmates felt the pinch in the form of periodic ration cuts. Conditions deteriorated to an alarming extent during the first half of 1944, which exposed the POWs to prolonged malnutrition. "Our food is getting worse and worse," Major Putnam noted on July 2. "The ration of rice and beans is quite noticeably cut, and vegetables are scarce indeed. Since the first of the year and particularly since March, losses of weight among the officer prisoners of as much as 40 or more pounds was not uncommon." A feed shortage killed off the rabbits. Scurvy and beriberi broke out among the camp's human populace. Men lost the strength to work, with increasing numbers suffering dizziness and blackouts. Capt. H. J. Van Peenen, a U.S. Navy doctor from Guam, managed to keep beriberi in check with vitamins from the post exchange and Red Cross. Thanks to his ministrations and the camp administration's efforts to bring in more food, only ten POWs died at Zentsuji. None of the deceased were Wake Islanders, and three might have survived had they clung to life a little tighter.[35]

Major Putnam and Major Potter belonged to that class of officer who believed that the men should come first. Both regularly visited the rank and file to check on their welfare and lift their spirits. Potter also made sure that no POW officers exploited the enlisted Wake Islanders. Private First Class Sloman did Potter's laundry for nearly three years at Zentsuji, but he volunteered for the job because the major paid well. Like Putnam and Potter, all other U.S. Marine and Navy officers in camp maintained an open-door policy, encouraging the lower ranks to drop by any time to discuss their problems. The Leathernecks at Zentsuji appreciated this paternal command style, and they responded with filial devotion. On November 10, 1943, for instance, the NCOs threw a party to mark the 168th birthday of the Marine Corps. They treated their superiors to coffee sweetened with saccharine and gave them American cigarettes—both rare and treasured commodities among the prisoners. A touched Major putnam expressed the officers' feelings: "It made us feel quite small that they had been able to beat us to the draw on the party. We shall certainly have to make their Christmas a good one." True to his word, Putnam hoarded a few cans of meat from two Red Cross food boxes and some candy from his wife as Christmas presents for his men.[36]

Enlightened Japanese administration, superior American leadership, and POW camaraderie, industry, and discipline turned Zentsuji into a true island of mutual support. The camp had a capacity for fewer than eight hundred inmates, however, and the enemy repeatedly filled it with more men than it could hold. Sixty-five Australians taken at Rabaul on New Britain Island in Papua New Guinea gave Zentsuji's population an upward bump on June 15, 1942. One hundred and eighty more POWs shuffled into camp on January 16, 1943, all but thirty of them half-starved Americans from the Philippines. Major Putnam recorded the arrival of 180 new officer prisoners on August 1—84 Americans, 80 Dutchmen, 11 Australians, and 5 Britons. Yet another 122 POWs followed that group by August 9.[37]

With the entry of each additional cohort, camp authorities transferred out a corresponding number of prisoners, primarily enlisted men. That led to an eventual scattering of the lower-ranking Wake Islanders. S1C James Darden exited Zentsuji on July 1, 1942, with 150 other prisoners. Darden ended up at the Osaka Main POW Camp—a facility also known as Osaka No. 1-B—on Honshu, along with Sgt. Edwin M. Ackley of VMF-211, Aerog1C Walter J. Cook, and PhM2C

Lawrence M. Atwood. Corporal Holewinski and eleven more Wake Islanders transferred from Zentsuji to Tanagawa, another camp in the Osaka area, in mid-January 1943. After four months or so, the Japanese relocated Holewinski to a nearby facility called Umeda Bunsho. The Japanese moved the tall Marine to Osaka No. 1-B in late May 1945, reuniting him with Seaman First Class Darden. Shortly after Holewinski's arrival, incendiary bombs dropped by B-29s on June 1 razed the camp and the surrounding area. The Japanese sent Holewinski, Darden, and about half of the camp's six hundred dehoused occupants to Fushiki, a small installation on Honshu's north coast that overlooked the Sea of Japan. There they ended the war.[38]

The escalating American air raids also impelled the Japanese to evacuate Zentsuji's higher-ranking prisoners. Major Putnam, 332 other American officers, and 2 civilians marched out of camp on June 23, 1945. The Japanese intended to send this contingent to Hiroshima, but they abruptly changed their minds and transported the 335 Yanks to Roku Roshi on Honshu. Putnam experienced dramatic revelations during his two days in transit. "The trip was miserable and tiring in the extreme," he scribbled, "but I didn't feel so bad about it after the things we saw on the way. Okayama was packed ... with refugees who were in [a] much worse plight than we were, and Osaka and Kobe were nothing more than piles of rubbish. Apparently our raids have been doing things in a big way." Heartened by the certainty of the enemy's imminent defeat, Putnam weathered the next few months until Roku Roshi's commandant announced Japan's surrender on August 22. That news had already reached Private First Class Sloman and the 108 POWs left at Zentsuji a good four days earlier.[39]

Wherever the Wake Islanders torn from Zentsuji's protective embrace happened to land, they had to adjust to inferior accommodations, scantier rations, and harsher working conditions. Seaman Darden lost one hundred pounds in three years at Osaka No. 1-B, and Pharmacist's Mate Second Class Atwood picked up a case of tuberculosis that killed him shortly after the war. Those men and their comrades survived as long as they did by stealing food from the enemy and black market trading with corruptible Japanese. They also displayed a noble spirit that reflected well on their training and discipline. AMM1C James P. Hesson, who had helped keep VMF-211 flying over Wake Island as a volunteer mechanic, headed the fifty Zentsuji inmates bundled off to Tanagawa in January 1943. Hesson found himself thrust into a veritable hell on earth populated by more than five hundred ailing and dispirited U.S. Army officers from the Philippines. With five to six prisoners expiring per day, it seemed just a matter of time before the whole camp ended up in a cemetery. "It was just filthy dirty," recalled an appalled Corporal Holewinski. "Nobody was taking care of anybody." Each of Hesson's men had left Zentsuji with half a Red Cross food box. He persuaded them to donate their cheese and powdered milk to nourish POWs lying sick in the hospital and their canned corn to cook a hearty stew for all hands. Hesson's party also cleaned up the hospital and exhorted Tanagawa's original inmates to take better care of themselves and each other. Thanks to these and other sensible measures, the camp's death rate declined within a week to one man a day.[40]

"I ATE GARBAGE WHILE AT CAMP 18"

Leal Henderson Russell and the 264 other Contractors who bid farewell to Wake Island from the *Tachibana Maru* on September 30, 1942, hoped they were headed for pleasanter surroundings, but they only exchanged a monotonous and sometimes dangerous life for a slow boat to perdition. The Japanese clapped the Americans below decks with little food or water. Temperatures soared as the ship steamed west, turning the prisoners' crowded compartments into pressure cookers. Charles L. Myers soon felt like he was lying in a pool of sweat. The luckier men around him fainted, which made their eleven days at sea seem shorter.[41]

The *Tachibana Maru* disgorged its dazed passengers at Yokohama at noon on October 11. All the POWs boarded the same train, but they did not remain together for long. Less than thirty minutes into the trip, the train stopped to hand over Leal Russell and four subordinates for questioning at the Ofuna Naval Interrogation Center. That was the last contact Russell had with most of the men he led through their first ten months of captivity. The enemy detained Russell at Ofuna until December 3, when they sent him to a waterfront camp that supplied slave labor to a Yokohama shipyard. Twelve underfed and exhausted POWs died in the month following Russell's arrival, and he suffered a near-fatal physical collapse on January 12, 1943. Inexplicably, the Japanese provided the stricken man with decent hospital care, and he regained his strength and a great deal of the weight he had lost. Russell finally returned to the waterfront camp in November 1944, but the Tokyo area's vulnerability to B-29 attack caused the Japanese to send him with a one hundred-man draft to Kamaishi to help operate a steel mill. The U.S. Navy shelled Kamaishi on July 14 and August 9, 1945, killing thirty-two prisoners. Russell survived to be transferred to the POW camp at Ohashi, and an American liberation team found him there on September 15.[42]

Far too many Contractors who parted company with Russell outside Ofuna never saw home again. The Japanese transported those 260 Yanks to Fukuoka

No. 18-B, a mountain camp overlooking the major Japanese naval base at Sasebo on Kyushu. Aside from the view, nothing about the place appealed to the POWs. The Wake Islanders set up housekeeping in an old cement warehouse that lacked heat and had a leaky roof. They bedded down on thin mats and huddled under cotton blankets swarming with fleas and lice. An inmate's daily ration amounted to three small bowls of rice, accompanied by a watery slop masquerading as soup. Every three or four days, the prisoners would discover a small piece of fish in their meager repast.

Sasebo Naval District Headquarters opened Fukuoka No. 18-B and initially supplied its guard detachment. Haseo Igawa, the camp's first commandant, was a warrant officer devoid of compassion for POWs. His motto was "One man bad, all men bad," and he routinely ordered collective punishment for individual transgressions. The Japanese army assumed control of the camp a year into its existence, and the inmates prayed their new keepers would exhibit some glimmerings of humanity. To the POWs' dismay, Lieutenant Uichi Ikegama, Fukuoka No. 18-B's second commandant, was as heartless as his predecessor. Under both regimes, the guards freely beat their charges with clubs and baseball bats for even minor infractions. "You had to let them knock you down a few times and stay down in order to make them quit," recalled electrician Robert Maple.[43]

The enemy established Fukuoka No. 18-B to house forced labor for the construction of Soto Dam. They organized the POWs into twenty-man gangs, each tended by a civilian honcho armed with a sledgehammer handle. Work often involved toting one hundred-pound bags of cement for hundreds of yards while making repeated trips up and down a steep trail—an operation hard on the Contractors' backs, legs, lungs, and hearts. The Japanese insisted that the prisoners toil through all types of weather without regard for their health. On February 8, 1943, Franklin B. Miller Jr., an asphalt technician from California, wrote in his diary, "Snowy and cold and muddy across the canyon today, yet this morning I saw two of our men being half dragged out to work—the Nips thought they weren't sick enough to stay in our nice warm barn." Some honchos matched the military guards in viciousness. A supervisor nicknamed "Grandma" habitually picked on George O. Dillon, a driller from Metalline Falls, Washington. Grandma pushed Dillon too far one day, and the latter whacked his tormentor with a shovel. Camp authorities condemned Dillon after a swift trial and removed him to an undisclosed location. His fellow POWs never heard from him again, and assumed that the Japanese killed him.[44]

Assisted by malnutrition, overwork, and exposure, death began stalking Fukuoka No. 18-B's other occupants. In the frantic scramble to see another miserable tomorrow, numerous Contractors jettisoned their dignity. "*I hate to admit it*," confessed Claude Davis Howes, "*but I ate garbage while at Camp 18. A man will do anything for food if he is really hungry.*" Such pathetic means saved some, but they could not stop the grim reaper from fastening his bony fingers on others. More than forty Contractors perished at Fukuoka No. 18-B by July 18, 1943. Among the doomed was diarist Frank Miller, who first felt death's chilly breath in the latter half of February. "I'm so darned weak these days that I teeter back and forth when I stand up," Miller wrote on the nineteenth, adding, "hope I don't get any weaker." Two days later, Miller scratched, "I'm still afflicted with diarrhea, consequently feeling weak all the time. Hope I and my bowels return to normal soon." Hope and little else kept Miller going until April 27. Before the Japanese finally closed that joyless camp, the Contractors interred Miller and fifty-two more of their number in cedar boxes on a hill near the dam for which they died.[45]

None of Fukuoka No 18-B's inmates felt a twinge of regret when their keepers directed them to vacate the premises in April 1944. The famished Contractors moved into Fukuoka No. 1, a camp situated between the city of Fukuoka and the northern suburb of Kashii, on the twenty-fifth of that month. They found the place occupied by several hundred British, Australian, Dutch, and American POWs. Housing consisted of bark-and-grass huts better suited for the tropics than Kyushu winters. The flimsy, unheated structures had leaky straw roofs that harbored numerous rats. The guards could be as nasty as those at the Wake Islanders' previous camp, but most Japanese at Fukuoka No. 1 preferred slapping errant prisoners to beating them.

Food at the new camp remained meager. The Japanese allotted each prisoner 1,500 calories a day, dished up in three small bowlfuls of a boiled mess composed of rice, kafir corn, rolled barley, greens, and a sprinkling of fish slivers. The occupants of Fukuoka No. 1 also received a slight taste of the Red Cross aid that entered Japan. Camp authorities permitted only two issues of the lifesaving food boxes, but three men had to split the contents of one parcel. This compared favorably, however, with what occurred at Fukuoka No. 18-B. The administrators of that camp had also released two batches of food boxes, but they had forced twenty POWs to share one parcel on the first occasion and gave one box to every ten men on the second. The administration of Fukuoka No. 1 handed out only a minuscule amount of the Red Cross medical supplies at its disposal. Such stinginess led prisoners to treat their maladies with bizarre home remedies. "Many men would urinate on the scurvy sores to try to heal them," reported Warren O. Rogge, a carpenter from Watsonville, California.[46]

Incredibly, only seven Wake Islanders died at Fukuoka No. 1. The majority probably owed their salvation to a less strenuous workload. During their confinement at this camp, the Japanese had them lay out an airfield.[47]

In January 1945 the Japanese transplanted the camp to a grove of pine trees on the northern outskirts of Fukuoka city. Before the month closed, another 193 half-dead Yanks from the Philippines came shuffling into the compound. The new installation offered the POWs real barracks, but its proximity to the city and some military bases put the prisoners in jeopardy. During several American air raids on the area, fragments from bombs aimed at the aforementioned targets ripped through the tar paper roofs on the prisoners' quarters. On one especially traumatic day, a naval mine dropped into the compound without detonating.[48]

In December 1944 the Japanese moved approximately two hundred prisoners from Fukuoka No. 1 to a branch camp called Fukuoka No. 23. Fifteen Wake Contractors accompanied that draft, including Claude Howes, who gave thanks on beholding his latest accommodations. "Camp No. 23 was paradise in comparison with the others," Howes wrote. "We had good quarters, a pad to sleep on, five blankets each, and every man had a hot water bottle. We had a very good bathhouse and plenty of hot water." The Japanese let the POWs bathe every day and wash their clothes regularly, which kept down vermin. During the war's remaining eight months, each inmate received three Red Cross food parcels. The Japanese commandant increased rations in honor of Christmas and treated his charges to a brief concert and a drink of sake. This same officer also exempted the fifty-four-year-old Howes and other older prisoners from working in a coal mine half a mile away, which ensured those men would live to see peace.[49]

Two months prior to Japan's surrender, the enemy moved fourteen disabled Contractors from Fukuoka No. 1 to Fukuoka No. 9, a coal mining camp two miles south of Miyata. British and Dutch servicemen constituted the bulk of the inmates, and Korean guards beat them every day for sport. Conditions in the mine were so abysmal that many prisoners deliberately broke their arms or legs to gain an extended rest from the oppressive place. Camp authorities judged the Wake Islanders unfit for mining but kept them busy for the rest of the war as carpenters, cooks, tailors, and cobblers.[50]

"THEY CAN'T WORK US ANY HARDER OR FEED US ANY LESS"

Three times before the Shanghai War Prisoners Camp closed in May 1945, it sent contingents totaling 660 men to bolster the workforce manning Japan's war industries. The first group of sixty-nine Wake Contractors and one North China

Marine left Woosung on September 18, 1942. The Japanese removed seventy more POWs from Woosung on November 3. That draft possessed a more military character, as its numbers included twenty-four Marines, four sailors, and one soldier from the Wake Island garrison, four crewmen from the American gunboat *Wake*, and sixteen North China Marines. The enemy took their biggest bite out of the Shanghai camp's population at the height of the Mount Fuji Project on August 30, 1943, when they pulled 520 prisoners out of Kiangwan.[51]

Many Allied personnel selected for transfer sailed from Shanghai with high hopes for a better life. Colonel Otera assured the members of the third draft that they would receive improved treatment and more food in Japan. Cpl. Frank Gross knew better than to believe everything Otera said, and he cracked to another Leatherneck, "Well, one thing for sure. They can't work us any harder or feed us any less." Contractor John Burton, who belonged to the first draft from Woosung, learned otherwise a year earlier than Gross. "Every time we thought things couldn't get any worse," Burton remembered, "we were shown how wrong we were."[52]

The 140 POWs drawn from Woosung in the fall of 1942 went to Yawata, an important steel city on Kyushu. The Japanese billeted them at Fukuoka No. 3, a large three-story concrete building that sat atop a towering hill. Inmates variously christened the place the "Castle," "Citadel," and "White House," with the latter tag being inspired by the edifice's whitewashed exterior. The enemy ultimately confined 1,200 prisoners at Fukuoka No. 3, including crewmen from the captured submarine USS *Grenadier*, American soldiers from the Philippines, European and Javanese troops from the Dutch East Indies, and merchant sailors from several Allied countries and colonies.

The Citadel, with steam heat and glass covering its barred windows, offered a snug refuge from cold winter nights, but other comforts were scarce and grew scarcer as time passed. The prisoners slaved nine to ten hours a day at a steel plant some two miles from camp. Sometimes they acted as stevedores at nearby docks, unloading coal, coke, jagged iron ore, and other raw materials, which they placed on flatcars for transport to the mill. POW laborers unloaded those cars, too, and also staffed various shops and departments around the plants as needed. "Skinned my hands all up," Pfc. John Himelrick griped on December 4, 1942. "Work rain or shine. . . . Loaded some rock today that was just unloaded yesterday."[53]

A man required ample rations to withstand such a regimen, but Major Yaichi Rikitake, the camp commandant, started shorting his charges to sell food on the black market. Eventually, a U.S. Navy doctor informed Pfc. Dennis Conner that the POWs were living on a pitiful eight hundred calories a day. Fukuoka No.

3 received a large shipment of Red Cross food boxes less than a week before Christmas 1942, but it did not do the camp much good. Each POW received half a box, and the remaining stock mysteriously disappeared. The Japanese inexplicably issued their charges another half a box on June 6, 1944, and a quarter of a box on New Year's Day, 1945, but such stinginess brought the POWs scant relief. On July 22, 1945, S1C Norris H. Troney, a young sailor taken on Wake, scribbled this lament: "Chow is low and going lower all the time. If this doesn't end soon these Sons of Bitches will starve us to death."[54]

It is surprising that death did not gather a richer harvest from Fukuoka No. 3. Private First Class Himelrick, the sole Wake Marine to perish in that camp, succumbed to pneumonia. The same disease killed two North China Marines and at least four of the ten Contractors who died there. Other groups in the camp, particularly the Dutch and Javanese, arrived in much worse shape than the Shanghai POWs, and they consequently suffered many more fatalities. The mortality rate for the winter of 1943–1944 ranged from one to five men a day. The guards, most of them veterans sidelined by combat injuries, would visit the hospital to mock dying prisoners.[55]

In the scramble to survive, inmates traded whatever they had for food, dealing most frequently with the Japanese and Korean civilians with whom they worked. Cpl. Terence S. Kirk, a North China Marine, sold a green woolen uniform blouse for five pounds of beans. Some POWs turned on their own kind and stole their food. The Wake Contractors cleansed their sections of that incipient crime wave by forming a "goon squad" to physically chastise malefactors.

Amid the misery and squalor, certain Shanghai POWs performed noble acts that shone like inspiring beacons. Corporal Kirk, a section leader, stubbornly disregarded an enemy order to place men too ill for work on half rations, and his section mates went along without serious protest. Sometime in December 1944 the Japanese caught a young POW trying to smuggle a bag of beans into camp. Pfc. Max H. Neuse, another North China Marine, saved his comrade from a beating by claiming the beans were his. The Japanese not only thrashed Neuse, but they forced him to stand for three hours in a cistern of ice-cold water. The valiant Leatherneck came down with pneumonia and died in a matter of days. Contractor John Burton, a practicing Mormon, observed "fast day" by giving one breakfast meal each month to a sick buddy.[56]

On December 15, 1943, the Japanese moved the occupants of Fukuoka No. 3 to a freshly built camp in the suburbs of Tobata, just west of Yawata, on land overlooking Moji Bay and the Sea of Japan. The POWs called their new home

Tobata and also Kokura after a nearby arsenal. Tobata featured a much more traditional layout than the Citadel, with tall outer walls, guard towers, and ten 2-story wooden barracks. Aside from the different location, unheated quarters, and another ration cut, little changed in the prisoners' grim lives. They continued to die by inches in the Yawata steel mills, which they now reached via a thirty-minute commute by rail.[57]

In the spring of 1944, however, the POWs noticed something that gave them new hope. Their Japanese and Korean co-workers took to gathering in small knots to speak in hushed tones about some horror called a *B-ni-ju-kyu*, which was the Japanese transliteration of B-29. The Yawata steel mills experienced their first B-29 raid around midday on June 15. By some lucky stroke, none of the eight hundred to nine hundred POWs at work that day were killed or maimed. Although streams of Superfortresses passed repeatedly over Yawata for more than a year, the city escaped a second daylight raid until August 8, 1945. On that day American incendiaries devastated the steel production facilities, killing one prisoner and wounding several others.

The POWs never returned to their mill jobs. Fukuoka No. 3's commandant informed his charges of the war's end promptly on August 15, and the guards deserted their posts that night. The thirty-seven surviving Wake and North China Marines took over security duties while the camp awaited airdrops and a liberation team.[58]

"GETTING WEAKER EVERY DAY"

The 520 POWs expelled from Kiangwan on August 20, 1943, set foot on Honshu scarcely four days later. They came ashore at Osaka, Japan's second largest city, which sat in the heart of the country's industrial belt. Most of these white coolies went to Tsumori, which was known officially as Osaka Camp 13-B, but the Japanese detached 120 prisoners to Dispatch Camp 5-D in the Tokyo Area Command. The Wake Islanders and the other Kiangwan exiles shortened the latter's unwieldy name to Kawasaki.[59]

Kawasaki was smaller and less pleasant than Kiangwan. The Shanghai prisoners found the premises already inhabited by a slightly higher number of U.S. Army personnel from the Philippines. One look at those men filled FN2C Dare Kibble with foreboding. "They were in such bad shape," he stated, "they looked like ghouls returning from the dead." Kawasaki's inmates subsisted mainly on musty barley and kafir corn. The unappetizing fare factored in recurring bouts of dysentery that drained the POWs of their vigor and morale. Kibble testified that one friend had to bring along some comrades whenever he visited the benjo "to push his guts back into his rectum." Squatting over a slit trench to defecate so exhausted numerous men that they had to call for help to stand up again.[60]

Camp authorities tried varying this diet with infusions of beans, rice, potatoes, fish, noodles, bread, sweet potatoes, and even the occasional donut, tangerine, pear, or cookie. These efforts faltered, however, in the face of nationwide food shortages that hit with increasing frequency. "Food our big trouble here, is the same as always; not enough," Cpl. Henry Durrwachter complained on April 3, 1944. "The last few meals we have had greens in our soup but they have been just enough to flavor and not satisfy." Whatever nourishment the prisoners ingested was often shared with parasites. "We had worms so badly," explained Fireman Second Class Kibble, "you could feel them in your throat and actually reach down with your fingers and pull them out of your mouth." Malnutrition led to beriberi and other deficiency diseases, and it also left the POWs woozy and unable to concentrate. "Getting weaker every day," Contractor Conrad Johnson wrote on March 30, 1944. "Can't keep this up much longer on the chow we are getting."[61]

The Americans received little sympathy from their keepers. The Japanese expected all but the sickest inmates to slave eight hours at a stretch on alternating day and night shifts in a nearby steel mill. The prisoners had to put in nine days or nights before they got one off. "It seems," Conrad Johnson joked, "they don't know the difference between Sunday or Monday in Japan." Aside from iodine, camp authorities released few medical supplies to the POWs. The Japanese exhibited the same miserly attitude with respect to Red Cross food boxes. Corporal Durrwachter recorded that each prisoner received two-thirds of a box for Christmas 1943, a whole box a little later, and a third issue amounting to two boxes for every five men in early May 1944. A large shipment of additional boxes entered Kawasaki between November 20 and 23, 1944, but it appears the POWs received only one box apiece for Christmas and one-third of a box per man on May 14, 1945.[62]

Hunger turned the POWs into inveterate food thieves. They stole anything edible from the enemy wherever they found it—in camp, at work, and throughout the area surrounding camp. One Wake Marine regularly broke out of Kawasaki at night to go foraging. The guards caught him a minimum of twenty times and beat him unmercifully, but he persisted with his nocturnal excursions. By the last spring of the war, however, the Japanese seemed to cease caring if their ravenous charges temporarily left camp to swipe produce from local gardens. "Practically half the camp could be found in some poor Jap['Js potatoe field," Corporal Durrwachter observed on April 20, 1945. "The funny part is that no one ever came in with less than 50 lbs. of spuds. One night 3 fellows actually butchered a goat and brought it in."⁶³

The spotty records that still exist indicate that those forays may have staved off death for all but a couple of Shanghai men, but they afforded the POWs no protection from the B-29 raids that gutted the industrial corridor between Kawasaki and Tokyo in the spring of 1945. Night after night the Wake Islanders and their comrades looked in the direction of the enemy capital and drank in the spectacle of Japan's aerial annihilation. "We could lay . . . in our bunk and look out and see Tokyo burning," claimed Pfc. George Hubley. "You could see the whole skyline over there, it was burning." A nighttime strike on the Kawasaki area in mid-April caused so much damage that the steel mill employing the POWs had to shut down. "The area around us looks like a city dump," observed Corporal Durrwachter, "and several of the fellows who have made the trip from here to Tokyo and Yokohama say it looks that way for 15 miles." Kawasaki's inmates spent nearly a month clearing bomb wreckage from the city that gave its name to their camp. Ultimately, the Japanese transferred these prisoners to locales where they could be of greater use to the war effort.⁶⁴

When Kawasaki closed on May 13, 1945, the enemy split up its occupants and dumped them in three different camps. FN2C Dare Kibble and FN1C James Cox joined a few other campmates for a long train ride that ended at Niigata 5-B on the northwest coast of Honshu. Contractor Joe Goicoechea and another small party traveled a shorter distance to Omori No. 1, the headquarters camp on a man-made island in Tokyo Bay. Those men would reunite by early July with many old friends from China. That fortuitous circumstance occurred with the arrival of elements of B Group, part of the main body of Wake Islanders that had dwelled at Kiangwan until its closure on May 10. The story of those prisoners' final days of captivity at Niigata and Omori has already been told earlier in this chapter.⁶⁵

The greater portion of Kawasaki's residents—two hundred Yanks in all—watched the war wind down from Sendai No. 7-B, a copper mining camp in the mountains of northern Honshu. There, they assimilated into an international community composed of Australians, Dutchmen, and Americans from the Philippines. The prisoners' living conditions gave new meaning to the word primitive. "Of course this place is way behind the times," grumbled Corporal Durrwachter. "The camp isn't even completed yet and as a result everything is scarce, especially food." Private First Class Hubley wrote off copper mining as "miserable"—largely because it reminded him of the Mount Fuji Project. "I don't like a thing about mines either," confessed Durrwachter. Nevertheless, the certainty that hostilities would cease well before Christmas kept Durrwachter and most of his comrades from losing hope. No Wake Islanders or any other Shanghai men expired at Sendai No. 7-B before camp authorities admitted their country's defeat on August 20, 1945.[66]

The four hundred Kiangwan prisoners assigned to Tsumori in August 1943 entered a camp designed to confine one thousand souls. The compound accommodated five wooden barracks capacious enough to shelter two hundred men apiece. The Shanghai POWs shared the structures with European and native troops from the Dutch East Indies. Smaller contingents of Americans from the Philippines and of British Commonwealth personnel boosted Tsumori's population to the 1,100 range, but the camp's worrisome death rate alleviated overcrowding.

Lieutenant Habe Toshitaro, Tsumori's commandant, despised POWs and felt they should not lead a restful existence. He regularly awoke his charges for roll call in the middle of the night, and he disturbed their waking hours with frequent inspections and drill sessions. Close order drill was still second nature to the Wake and North China Marines, but the Contractors often confused the commands barked at them by Japanese NCOs. The civilians paid for every mistake with a beating. Ordinarily, the Leathernecks would have gotten a laugh out of this, but they realized that Toshitaro's harassment policy deprived all inmates of precious energy needed for a more important purpose. Tsumori supplied Allied laborers for several shipyards in Osaka, and the Shanghai men discovered that the demands placed on them in those facilities exceeded even the rigors of Mount Fuji.

Cpl. Frank Gross summed up a year and a half of shipbuilding at Osaka in six words: "It was nothing other than slavery." The Japanese consistently pushed their charges beyond all reasonable limits of endurance, driving Gross to splutter, "They thought cuz we was Americans we was superman." The POWs filled various jobs in the shipyards. Some ran heavy lathes or drills, preparing large steel parts for installation on vessels under construction. Others worked as riveters or as machinists, regrinding nuts and bolts in the machine shop. For the most part, however, the prisoners strained at tasks requiring brute strength. The enemy organized them into six-man crews equipped with poles to move heavy steel plates to different work stations in the yards. A single day of such exertion left a POW ready for little else by quitting time besides food and sleep.[67]

The scanty rice-and-soup ration at Tsumori replenished a mere fraction of the calories that inmates expended in the shipyards. Having to work ten days before getting one off afforded them hardly any respite. The POWs received only one day off some months, and Lieutenant Toshitaro's maniacal drill festivals dissipated the benefits of every holiday. It comes as no surprise that thirty-four Americans perished at Tsumori. Thirty-one of them were Wake Islanders—five Marines from the 1st Defense Battalion or VMF-211, three sailors, and twenty-three Contractors.[68]

Some of the men who died might have fared better had not the Kiangwan contingent gotten off to a bad start at Tsumori. A dysentery epidemic broke out shortly after the group's arrival, and that impaired everyone's ability to face the trials ahead. BM1C James E. Barnes, a stout, muscular sailor, had bravely hurled hand grenades into enemy landing craft during the final fighting for Wake. Tsumori's administrators named this tough natural leader the senior prisoner in Barracks 3, but Barnes never rebounded from his first bout with dysentery in Japan. He remained flat on his back in the makeshift sick bay that the enemy set aside for ailing prisoners. Like others unfit for work, Barnes received half rations, but he had lost his taste for Japanese food. "See if you can get me some eggs," he begged his friend, Army radioman SSgt. Clifford Hotchkiss. "I know they'll fix me up." Unable to gratify that request, Hotchkiss watched helplessly as the depressed hero dwindled away. Barnes drew his last breath on March 2, 1944. "I've never seen a man die so horribly in my life," Hotchkiss grieved.[69]

For a few Wake Islanders, death came with merciful swiftness. Charles B. Robertson, a Contractor and beriberi sufferer, keeled over from a heart attack after just a couple of weeks at Tsumori. Pfc. Lloyd G. Lane of the 1st Defense Battalion died immediately when a toppling generator crushed him at his workstation on January 11, 1944. Most doomed inmates, however, expired slowly like James Barnes. Two Wake survivors—Contractor George E. Keyser and RM3C Edwin A. Bird—starved themselves to death by trading their rations for cigarettes. Bereft of hope, they chose to exchange their lives for the fleeting comfort of additional nicotine.[70]

Numerous POWs at Tsumori attempted to evade death by turning into black marketers. Army Sergeant Hotchkiss developed into one of the camp's leading businessmen, earning the sobriquet "Jungle Bum." Hotchkiss first dealt in condiments—salt, pepper, red pepper, and mustard—which he purchased from Japanese workers in the shipyards. He eventually branched out into yeast tablets, vitamins, and bowls of rice. As Hotchkiss grew prosperous, he acquired a snazzy wardrobe at the expense of a North China Marine in his barracks section. The shrewd soldier justified his profits in terms of economic necessity. "If you give it away, you put yourself out of business," he rationalized. "Because the Japanese wouldn't buy anything for you if you didn't have any money." Hotchkiss also insisted that the risks he took justified certain rewards.[71]

The American firebombing campaign that rendered Kawasaki untenable did the same to Tsumori. One or more of the 274 B-29s that the Twentieth Air Force directed to Osaka on the night of March 13–14, 1945, unknowingly released their payloads over the camp. Bomblets filled with napalm set three barracks ablaze, forcing the POWs to form bucket brigades to save their homes. One bomb casing crushed the chest of Cpl. Richard Rider, a North China Marine, before he could roll off his bunk and seek shelter. Two Wake Islanders—Pfc. Joseph C. Culp of the 1st Defense Battalion and Contractor Donald H. Rienks—sustained injuries that eventually killed them. In addition to these three fatalities, several inmates suffered burns.[72]

With Osaka's industrial center reduced to ashes, it no longer served Japan's economic interests to keep prisoners at Tsumori. Officials bedeviled by American air strikes needed two months to arrange the necessary transport. On May 15 Tsumori's occupants boarded a train that hauled them up much of Honshu's length to Naoetsu, a camp on the island's northwest coast that stood near unbombed steel mills and a carbide factory. The prisoners from Tsumori prayed for a softer life at Naoetsu, but that wish evaporated as they entered their verminous barracks and met the remnants of the Australian and British drafts that had preceded them there. "Food was as bad if not worse than any other camp," remarked Contractor John Young. "The treatment was about the same except it was a little more harsh." The POWs lost track of all the blows they absorbed, but they coined unforgettable nicknames for the guards and interpreters who introduced them to new standards of cruelty. They called the worst of the lot the "Bull," "Casey at the Bat," the "Bird," "Little Caesar," and the "Healer."[73]

Prisoners intent on surviving at the Naoetsu camp kept an eye open for anything edible they could steal from their keepers. Pvt. Earl Broyles of the 1st Defense Battalion had been the champion thief at Tsumori, where guards expressed grudging admiration for his incorrigible cheek by giving him the nickname "Zoomy." While working the night shift in a Naoetsu steel mill, Broyles figured out how to sneak into an untended mess hall for Korean conscript workers. Zoomy and his friend, Sergeant Hotchkiss, absconded with large quantities of the Koreans' rice, smuggling some into camp and stashing the rest in tin cans hidden on girders running under the mill roof. Hotchkiss lived down much of his sordid reputation as a profiteer by sharing extra food with his buddies. Other Wake Islanders exhibited identical deviousness and resolve, which kept them alive until August 15, when guards informed the night shift that it did not have to go to work. The POWs realized that Japan had lost the war after most enemy personnel fled before morning and the remainder then announced no work for the day shift.[74]

One and a half months before that fortuitous turn of events, fifteen lucky POWs received an unexpected reprieve from the grinding existence at Naoetsu. The transfer of 333 officer prisoners and two Allied civilians from Zentsuji to Roku Roshi in late June 1945 caused the Japanese to round up a few captive carpenters to put some finishing touches on the latter camp. Accordingly, Corporal Gross and fourteen other inmates with the requisite skills left Naoetsu. Having spent nearly two years separated from his officers, Gross lived out his final weeks in confinement under the gaze of Major Potter and Major Putnam.[75]

"AS FAR AS SPIV CUNNINGHAM WAS CONCERNED, THE WAR WAS OVER"

Cdr. Winfield Scott Cunningham, foremost among the daring handful to break out of the Shanghai War Prisoners Camp, regained his freedom ahead of most of the men he had led on Wake Island. Though a fitting happenstance, that jubilant day did not come soon enough to suit the dauntless naval officer.

As related in chapters 11 and 14, Cunningham and the ten other POWs who tried escaping from Woosung and Kiangwan were court-martialed for desertion from the Japanese army and locked up in Shanghai's Ward Road Jail. Retaliatory treatment failed to shatter Cunningham's defiant spirit, and life in maximum security further whetted his desire to give his captors the slip. In the fall of 1944 he and seven comrades engineered a new escape attempt. The eight conspirators made their move on the night of October 6, 1944. Armed with hacksaw blades smuggled to them by a Danish contact on the outside, they sawed their way out of their cells and climbed over the jail wall in two groups. Lt. Cdr. C. D. Smith of the gunboat *Wake*, Commander John Woolley of the Royal Navy, and Cpl. Jerold Story of the North China Marines went first. Cunningham followed a little later with Sgt. Raymond Coulson and PhM2C Artis Brewer from Wake, plus Cpl. Charles Brimmer and Pfc. Charles Stewart from North China. Incredibly, the first group avoided detection and passed safely through Shanghai. Assisted by friendly Chinese, the lucky trio made its way to friendly forces by November 3. Unfortunately for Cunningham and his party, they attracted the notice of enemy police a mile away from the Ward Road Jail. The Japanese gave chase, cornered the fugitives in a cul-de-sac, and took them back into custody.

Dragged before another court-martial, Cunningham received a sentence of "unlimited confinement"—meaning life. The Japanese first held this confirmed hard case in a military prison in Shanghai and then moved him to Nanking on January 19, 1945. Cunningham transferred to Peking and a third military prison on August 1, unaware that hostilities had only two more weeks to run. On the eighteenth the commander's jailers informed him that peace reigned once more in East Asia and the Pacific. They took him at once to a civilian internment camp at Fengtai. Cunningham flew out of Peking on a B-24 Liberator six days later— the first in a series of hops that carried him over China, India, Africa, and the Atlantic Ocean to New York, where he touched down on September 7. Less than two hours later, he fell into his wife's arms at an airport outside Washington, D.C., and she drove him to their home in Annapolis. Cunningham never forgot how sweet his long-deferred homecoming tasted. "I was still suffering from beri-beri," he subsequently told readers of his memoirs, "and was gaunt and haggard, but I felt wonderful. As far as Spiv Cunningham was concerned, the war was over."[76]

CHAPTER SEVENTEEN

"we had a bond there that's still going"
why so many came home

"I THINK WE GOT PREFERRED TREATMENT, ACTUALLY"

Determining the exact number of Wake Islanders to die in Japanese custody entails multiple challenges. Although the American military accounted for servicemen lost from the atoll's garrison, it worried less about verifying the fate of their civilian comrades. This carelessness extended to the war's early days and the exaggerated Contractor casualty statistics that the Navy Department accepted for the fighting on Wake. Col. William Ashurst maintained trustworthy records on both military and civilian deaths at Woosung and Kiangwan, but 367 Contractors never saw China during the conflict. Hundreds of additional Wake civilians left the Shanghai War Prisoners Camp in 1942 and 1943 to toil in Japan. When Kiangwan finally closed in May 1945, Ashurst and almost all the American servicemen still there went to prison camps on Hokkaido, while the remaining Contractors ended up at several different installations on Honshu. The repeated scattering the Wake Islanders experienced over three and a half years impeded an accurate count of their living and dead at the war's end.[1]

The available sources yield the names of 243 Americans and Guamanians captured on Wake who perished before Allied liberation teams reached them. Twenty-six of those unfortunates belonged to the American military—seventeen from the U.S. Marine Corps and nine from the U.S. Navy. Two Guamanians employed by Pan American Airways also expired in Japanese hands, as did 215 Americans who signed with CPNAB to earn big money on Wake.

The Imperial Japanese Navy rounded up 1,621 prisoners after it took possession of Wake Island on December 23, 1941. The loss of 243 men from this quantity means that the Wake Islanders emerged from captivity with an overall death rate of 14.9 percent. The atoll's diverse population did not share evenly in these fatalities. The 1,109 Contractors who survived the siege constituted the largest of these subgroups. They also suffered more deaths than the others. The Contractors' 215 POW fatalities broke down to a death rate of 21.9 percent. The thirty-five Guamanians buried only two men while in enemy custody, or 5.7 percent of their number. The 476 American servicemen captured on Wake saw their ranks thinned by 5.4 percent over the next forty-four months by the deaths of twenty-six enlisted men. The 403 Wake Marines to escape death in battle composed the bulk of the atoll's military POWs, and just 17, or 4.2 percent, never saw home again. Nine out of sixty-six captured naval personnel expired behind barbed wire, which fixed the POW death rate for that part of the American garrison at 13.6 percent.[2]

The Contractors' poorer survival rate resulted from several factors, most of which lay beyond their control. They indisputably absorbed severer applications of Japanese inhumanity than their comrades in uniform. For instance, the enemy executed 101 Contractors—ninety-nine on Wake and two in the Marshall Islands. The Japanese also apparently punished a Contractor at Fukuoka No. 18-B by taking the man's life. In contrast, they executed just five Wake sailors and Marines. Without those murders the Contractors would have suffered only 113 deaths, or 10.2 percent, of their number. Contractors were the only Wake Islanders the Japanese sent to Fukuoka No. 18-B, a virtual death camp, and that doomed more of them to foreign graves. In addition, age contributed to the Contractors' higher mortality. Most servicemen who defended Wake were in their late teens or twenties. Pfc. Eschol Davis observed that "not too many old guys" belonged to the Wake Island Detachment, 1st Defense Battalion. The CPNAB organization, in contrast, assigned numerous older men to the atoll's prewar work force. Those experienced hands were tough enough to withstand heavy labor if they enjoyed plenty of food and decent quarters. Slaving under the deprived circumstances to which the Japanese sentenced them, however, caused many older men to break.[3]

Oscar Claude Lent, a CPNAB deckhand from Portland, Oregon, kept a diary during his eighteen months at Fukuoka No. 18-B. He listed fifty-one Contractor deaths at that camp. In forty-six cases, Lent noted the date of death and age of each fatality. Seven of those men died in their twenties. The rest were older— fourteen in their thirties, twelve in their forties, six in their fifties, six in their sixties, and one in his seventies.[4]

The full significance of these statistics can be seen by placing them in a broader context. The 1,621 Wake POWs represented just a small sample of the Allied personnel taken by Emperor Hirohito's forces. The Japanese army and navy snared some 95,000 American, British, Canadian, Australian, and New Zealander servicemen. More than 28 percent of those prisoners died in captivity, a revelation that casts the Wake Islanders' lower POW casualty figures in a decidedly favorable light. The Wake POWs look even more impressive stacked up solely against their fellow countrymen. Thirty-three thousand, five hundred and eighty-seven American soldiers, airmen, sailors, and Marines fell into Japanese hands. By the time peace returned to the Pacific, 12,909 of those Yanks had died. That amounted to a death rate of 38.4 percent for all American POWs captured in the Pacific, or more than twice that for the Wake Islanders. The 25,580 American servicemen who surrendered in the Philippines made up the largest chunk of U.S. military personnel to enter Japanese custody. Capitulation became a death sentence for an estimated 10,650, or 41.6 percent, of them. Once S2C Julian Sandvold, a Wake sailor who spent most of his war outside Shanghai, got home and met other prisoners held in East Asia, he concluded, "I think we got preferred treatment, actually."[5]

"I THINK THAT WE WERE VERY LUCKY"

On Pfc. Henry Chapman's return to the United States, he convalesced briefly at California's Long Beach Naval Hospital. Granted a ninety-day furlough, the Wake Marine spent that time with his older sister Bee, who lived nearby. Another sister named Dotty, Bee's twin, dropped over one day to ask Chapman's help with a delicate matter.

"Well little brother," Dotty began, "my neighbor has heard about you, and she has a brother who will not leave the kitchen. He was from the Bataan Death March, and all he does is sit there and have her husband buy him whiskey. She wanted to know if you would go over and talk to him."

"Sure," Chapman replied without thinking twice, "I'll see what I can do for him."

Having cruised through hell on the *Nitta Maru* and survived stays at Woosung, Kiangwan, Fengtai, Fusan, and Hakodate No. 3, Chapman thought he had endured the worst the Japanese could do to a man. He expected he could draw on his personal experiences to solve any former prisoner's problems.

Buoyed by self-confidence, Chapman paid a call on the Bataan survivor, a soldier recently discharged from the Van Nuys Army Hospital. The man's condition matched Dotty's description to a T. He spent his days with a bottle in his hands, staring at a blank wall between drinks.

Chapman wasted no time on ceremony. He introduced himself, sat down, poured himself a drink, and started talking. The soldier recognized Chapman as a kindred soul, and the two veterans were soon swapping stories about their

POW days. Chapman entered the conversation certain he had seen it all, but what he heard from the Bataan defender shook his composure. "I realized that I had a picnic compared to him," he admitted later. "All in all, I think that we [Wake Islanders] were very lucky."[6]

Chapman was not the only Wake defender to have his eyes opened on that score. In 1966 James Devereux, by then a retired brigadier general and former Republican U.S. congressman from Maryland, reviewed a draft on POW life intended for the official history of Marine Corps operations during World War II. Devereux not only digested the material bearing on his own experiences, but also those of Leathernecks captured on Guam and Corregidor. His comments to the authors of that manuscript closed with this admission: "I would like to add that . . . I cannot but conclude that we [Wake Islanders] were probably the best-treated of all the POWs in the hands of the Japanese." Other Wake Marines readily echoed their chief's judgment. "I think we got better treatment than the average Japanese prisoner of war," volunteered Pfc. Luther Williams. Asked to explain the Wake Islanders' 85.1 percent survival rate, Private First Class Chapman gave a modest shrug and replied, "There was a lot of luck involved."[7]

Luck is indispensable to success and survival in war. The Wake Islanders knew that better than anyone. During much of their imprisonment, they benefited from advantages denied to most other Allied POWs in the Pacific theater. Toiling to convert a coral strip into a fortified base left both the atoll's military and civilian occupants in prime physical shape when hostilities commenced in December 1941. The Navy Department's ban on women, hard liquor, and narcotics from Wake removed the usual vices that might have undermined this bodybuilding regimen. Cpl. Bernard Richardson aptly characterized his prewar life as "lots of hard physical labor, no drinking, [and] no whoring allowed of any kind."[8]

From the defenders' perspective, the Wake Island campaign ended with merciful swiftness and light losses. Sixteen days of Japanese pounding killed no more than eighty-six Americans and ten Guamanians. Fewer than two dozen Yanks suffered wounds serious enough to require extended hospitalization. Thanks to the Contractors' volunteer catering service, the Marines and their auxiliaries usually received two hot meals a day throughout the siege. Adequate nourishment, a brief period of fighting, and lulls permitting attention to sanitary needs kept the Wake garrison largely disease free.[9]

The Wake Island experience contrasted starkly with the struggle for the Philippines. American media portrayed both campaigns as heroic last stands, but each assumed a distinctive character that impacted on the survivors' future as POWs.

When Gen. Douglas MacArthur's American and Filipino troops dug in for their three-month defense of the Bataan Peninsula in January 1942, he halved each man's rations from four thousand to two thousand calories a day. The approved daily intake dwindled to 1,500 calories by February, and it dropped to 1,000 the following month. Men with a normal weight of 175 to 200 pounds wasted away to 135 or 145. Malaria, dysentery, and other diseases preyed on those walking skeletons. In some outfits, the number of personnel fit to carry a rifle shrank by 50 to 70 percent.

Bataan's Fil-American defenders held out until April 9, 1942, but surrender shoved them only deeper into the bowels of hell. Depending on the enfeebled prisoners' point of capture, the Japanese made them walk 70 to 140 miles to a railroad station 20 miles northeast of the peninsula. This trek became the infamous Bataan Death March. Denied medical care, shelter, and sufficient rest, the Americans and Filipinos tramped for days under a tropical sun with little or nothing to eat or drink. An estimated 10,650 POWs never reached the trains waiting to transport them to Camp O'Donnell, their first prison camp. Many who died received the coup de grâce from Japanese bayonets, bullets, or rifle butts after illness, exhaustion, hunger, dehydration, or sunstroke caused them to faint or refuse to take another step.

The Death March kept killing men long after it ended. A minimum of 17,600 Bataan survivors arrived at Camp O'Donnell so depleted that they died over the next seven weeks. The ultimate toll of the Bataan Death March may have topped 32,250 dead. Between April 26 and June 3, 1942, Lt. John E. Olson, Camp O'Donnell's assistant adjutant, reported 1,103 American deaths, an average of thirty a day. A much larger number of Filipino soldiers expired during the same period.[10]

The Japanese staged other deadly forced marches during the war. They also built more camps like O'Donnell—virtual charnel houses surrounded by barbed wire. In the typical Japanese-run camp, callousness and cruelty combined with overcrowding and the denial of sufficient food, potable water, medical care, and sanitary facilities to shorten the lives of thousands of Allied personnel.[11]

Fortunately for the Wake Islanders, their atoll was too small for a death march. As soon as the SNLF men who took Wake finished securing their objective and their combat frenzy waned, they treated their prisoners decently. The POWs moved into American-built barracks, enjoyed the use of flush toilets and salt-water showers, and ate two hot meals a day cooked by Contractor chefs. The Japanese refrained from overworking their charges for those first weeks and rarely beat them. Yanks needing medical attention received it as a matter of course.

This idyllic introduction to POW life ended abruptly for the 1,235 Wake Islanders who boarded the *Nitta Maru* on January 12, 1942. That trip revealed the Japanese at their worst, but the voyage lasted less than two weeks, and the only prisoners to die were the five selected for execution. The *Nitta Maru*'s passengers recovered from their sufferings in facilities that were the closest the Japanese army ever came to running model prison camps. Twenty American officers and enlisted men removed for interrogation at Yokohama ended up at Zentsuji, the most admirably managed POW installation in Japan proper. Their 1,200-odd shipmates proceeded to China for internment in the Shanghai War Prisoners Camp, which turned out to be as good a place as Zentsuji to be a prisoner.[12]

The Japanese did the Wake Islanders a tremendous favor by concentrating the majority of them just outside Shanghai. This applied preeminently to the Wake Marines and their fellow servicemen, but also—to a slightly lesser degree—their civilian comrades. Unlike many other captured Allied commands, Wake's defenders entered confinement in cohesive units. Those men had worked side by side for months—if not years—as the United States drifted toward war. Combat strengthened preexisting bonds and forged new ones between men who had been strangers before Japan struck. Hence, the Wake Islanders passed through captivity surrounded by friends—men who cared about them and would not desert or betray them under any circumstances. Studies of unit cohesion during World War II revealed that a soldier remained on his best behavior if he was part of a primary group of men he knew, liked, and trusted. Men cast among strangers tended to think only of themselves, especially when the going got rough.[13]

Residence at the Shanghai War Prisoners Camp made a positive difference to the main group of Wake Islanders in countless additional ways. Even at the malaria-ridden Woosung site, the installation boasted a healthier climate than the jungle settings where the enemy confined so many other prisoners. Proximity to a commercial metropolis filled with affluent Allied and neutral civilians eager to assist POWs improved the Wake Islanders' chances of returning home alive. Those men also owed a debt to Edouard Egle of the Red Cross for coordinating relief efforts on their behalf. Egle and Shanghai's Swiss consulate general additionally exercised firm but tactful diplomacy to ensure most of the aid reached its intended recipients. That humanitarian alliance enriched the POWs' diet and also provided them with recreational supplies, new and hand-me-down clothing, and possibly the best-equipped health care facility in a Japanese prison camp. Moreover, Shanghai's location in a fertile rice-producing area facilitated the POWs receiving enough food to stay alive. That situation also shortened the duration of the recurring food shortages that plagued the prisoners as Japan's fortunes declined.[14]

Statistics mesh with anecdotal evidence in substantiating Shanghai's reputation as a model camp. Only twenty-three inmates died in that facility in the three years it existed. That many Americans—and more—frequently perished in a single day at Camp O'Donnell. Although Dr. G. Mason Kahn, the Wake Islanders' Navy surgeon, got his numbers slightly wrong in a 1979 interview, his main point is incontestable: "I think the total [dead] was twenty-one in four years, and that ain't bad." Capt. Bryghte Godbold offered a similar perspective on the benefits of imprisonment at Shanghai: "The mortality rate among this group . . . was probably less than it would have been in a civilian situation."[15]

None of the outside aid trucked to the Shanghai War Prisoners Camp would have done the inmates any good had not their keepers allowed them to have it. The personnel the Japanese army assigned to Woosung and Kiangwan generally behaved with a rough restraint that puts the lie to any idea that the Japanese acted solely according to a fiercely militant national creed. Despite the bastardization of Bushido in the 1930s, individual Japanese chose to act chivalrously either in deference to conscience or dictates from above. Colonel Goichi Yuse and Colonel Satoshi Otera, the two commandants who oversaw the Shanghai camps, complied with their superiors' desire to maintain them as showplaces. Yuse and Otera cooperated with the Red Cross to obtain extra resources to enhance Japan's image by keeping his POWs healthy. Both commandants could exhibit a harsh side, but that usually occurred when the prisoners misbehaved. Colonel Yuse did a better job of curbing sadistic subordinates. Though Colonel Otera appeared much more affable, his lifestyle as an absentee commandant made him a less-reliable protector. He granted Isamu Ishihara, the sadistic interpreter, too much freedom in managing Kiangwan. Otera also permitted the Mount Fuji Project to burgeon into an ongoing threat to the prisoners' welfare. Nonetheless, Otera would step in before his charges reached the limits of their endurance, sanctioning ration hikes or other measures to alleviate their suffering. The Wake Islanders appreciated those gestures, but they frequently credited shows of Japanese humanity to the influence of Dr. Yoshiro Shindo. Many came to revere the enemy medical officer as their guardian angel.[16]

By all accounts the Japanese administered Zentsuji according to the same enlightened standard. Maj. Paul A. Putnam, VMF-211's commander, spent all but a few months of his confinement at that camp, and he developed a healthy respect for his guards. "I was surprised at how good we were treated," the major declared. "There were two nasty little bastards there, and whenever they could manage not to get caught by their boss, they could make life miserable for us. But I was really surprised by the decency they did give us."[17]

Sheer luck spared the Wake Islanders from death by friendly fire—a fate that claimed a tragically high number of prisoners. When the Japanese moved their charges by water, they crammed them onto unmarked ships and neglected to notify Allied authorities who was on board. The enemy also transported POWs on vessels carrying their own troops and war materials, almost as if daring the U.S. Navy to sink them. Thus, when American submarines and aircraft sighted those vessels, they assumed they were fair game and attacked. In such incidents, the POWs found themselves caught between two fires. Not only did the Japanese make no provisions for rescuing prisoners from stricken ships, but they often shot at those who tried swimming to safety. Historian Gregory F. Michno determined that 21,039 Allied personnel perished on those hellships, making ocean travel the most dangerous aspect of being a prisoner of the Japanese. Yet, aside from the five men murdered on the *Nitta Maru*, no Wake Islanders were lost at sea while in enemy custody.[18]

"NO . . . MILITARY ORGANIZATION CAN BE SUCCESSFUL WITHOUT DISCIPLINE"

Fortune may have smiled on the Wake Islanders, but that was not all that kept most of them alive. The group contained many sons of the Great Depression— men who had felt the bite of hard times—but prison life under the Japanese took them to a lower living standard than they had ever known. The POWs quartered at Woosung and Kiangwan never dreamed they inhabited model camps until the enemy sent them elsewhere. Until then, the Wake Islanders regarded the Shanghai camps as hellholes. After all, inmates died in both places from disease, overwork, or Japanese carelessness, and they all watched their bodies deteriorate from malnutrition. The Wake Islanders grasped early on that survival required struggle, and that this involved both self-help and mutual assistance. It was not enough to be lucky; they had to make their own luck, too.[19]

The presence of the North China Marines and their brothers from Wake embedded a large and powerful cadre within the Shanghai War Prisoners Camp whose discipline and cohesion set the tone for all the other inmates. In prison pens across East Asia, Leathernecks withstood confinement more successfully than other American servicemen. Even in the Philippines, Marines stuck together and achieved a survival rate of 68.2 percent—10 percent higher than their Army comrades. The Wake and North China Marines outdid that feat with their combined survival rate of nearly 96 percent. That fell just 1 percent below the survival rate of American troops taken in North Africa and Europe, where Hitler's Wehrmacht endeavored to treat Yanks and Britons according to the Geneva Convention.[20]

The main advantage the Shanghai POWs derived from a sizable Marine contingent was strong leadership. Wherever the Japanese permitted Marine officers freedom of action, the latter assumed control of their camps' interior management, reestablishing order and directing their subordinates to work for the common good. Colonel Ashurst, Maj. Luther A. Brown, and Major Devereux instituted such a regime at Woosung and Kiangwan. By insisting that their men act in a military fashion, those officers provided a comforting sense of normality and pride that helped the former rise above the humiliations and hardships of imprisonment. Discipline also furnished the structure that converted the Marines and other servicemen into a community dedicated to bringing out every member with his life and dignity. "No . . . military organization can be successful without discipline," acknowledged Cpl. Frank Gross from Wake. Although Ashurst and Brown ran things after the North China Marines arrived at Woosung, Devereux exerted a pervasive influence over his Wake Island Detachment. The little major's ability to keep his people in line impressed the most respected Marine in camp, Gunner William Lee from North China. "I personally believe," Lee confided to a journalist, "that . . . Major James P. S. Devereux was one of the greatest leaders of the war."[21]

Colonel Ashurst and his command team actively intervened to prevent the prisoners from harming themselves or each other. Those officers cracked down hard on theft and tried to stop weak-willed inmates from gambling or trading away their food. The brass may have gone too far in discouraging escape, but that policy rested on a realistic appraisal of the improbability of success, not to mention a desire to shield the innocent from Japanese retaliation. Marine leadership at Woosung and Kiangwan also helped stabilize the prisoners' relations with their keepers. Dealing with a largely orderly inmate population reduced the enemy's resort to punitive controls and enabled the POWs to obtain more concessions.[22]

Junior Marine officers in the Shanghai camps ordinarily kept a low profile, leaving disciplinary decisions and negotiations with camp authorities to their seniors. Some, however, went out of their way to comfort the lower ranks. A few officers gave their men bits of extra food acquired through legal purchase or shadier means. Some taught night school classes to help enlisted men pass their time more fruitfully. Capt. Wesley Platt persisted with the heroic behavior that made him the idol of the Wake Island Detachment when he wiped out the Japanese beachhead on Wilkes Island on December 23, 1941. Platt put his life on the line in prison camp by stopping an enraged guard from beating a fellow

POW. On another occasion, the captain removed his own shoes and gave them to a destitute enlisted man whose feet were bleeding. Such selfless actions prompted 1st Lt. Woodrow Kessler to say of his friend, "Platt's sense of concern for his men frequently led him to disregard his own welfare in many situations." At Zentsuji, Maj. George Potter and Major Putnam matched Platt with exhibitions of concern for their men's health and morale.[23]

The dearth of such leadership in numerous Japanese-operated prison camps spelled disaster for thousands of Allied POWs. First Lt. Jack Hawkins of the 4th Marines, the only Leatherneck regiment with MacArthur in the Philippines, recounted what could happen to prisoners whose officers shirked their duty: "There were many indeed who became so demoralized that they abandoned every tenet of personal integrity, honor, loyalty and the accepted standards of human behavior. These sank to the level of animals or worse. There was a selfish dog-eat-dog, every man for himself attitude among the prisoners and little group spirit. . . . Many of the men would no longer obey the orders of officers. Many of the officers, on the other hand, abandoned all responsibility to take care of the men."[24]

The protracted fight for Bataan and the subsequent Death March morally shattered the American troops who reached Camp O'Donnell. As Lieutenant Hawkins testified, something similar befell the garrison of Corregidor, the island fortress controlling access to Manila Bay that fell on May 6, 1942. For months afterward, U.S. Army officers taken at Bataan and Corregidor wallowed in self-pity. They balked at reasserting their authority and restoring order. "There was a lot of breakdown in discipline and cussing by enlisted men to officers and blaming them for the predicament we were in," admitted Capt. Harcourt G. Bull, a Citadel graduate captured on Corregidor. Bull tried to exculpate himself and his brother officers for passively accepting this unseemly anarchy. "Our hands were tied," he protested, "and there was no effective way to punish men, so it was an impossible situation."[25]

Denied direction and inspiration, many Army survivors from Bataan and Corregidor turned on each other. The strong preyed on the weak, stealing rations from anyone unable to stop them. Second Lt. Charles W. Burris, a USAAF fighter pilot, witnessed this sort of degradation at Cabanatuan, a large POW complex in the Philippines: "That was . . . where I learned that a human being is a marauder. I believe he would steal from his own mother if he was starving hard enough. You couldn't keep food around because they'd steal it. . . . They didn't mind seeing a guy die. They just wanted his food. Everybody was concerned about themselves."[26]

Col. J. V. Collier, a senior staff officer at Camp O'Donnell, detailed the consequences of that leadership vacuum. "Food and water details were not supervised," he related. "Thirst crazed men were drinking the stream water. Food was not equally distributed to messes, and it looked as tho the main officer's mess was never the loser. Care of the sick was haphazard if at all. Men were found dead who had apparently died alone and unnoticed until the odor called attention to the decaying body." Maj. Alva R. Fitch, an Army artilleryman, also depicted O'Donnell as devoid of discipline and decency: "I have seen men try to go from barracks to the latrine who were too weak to walk and would fall in the mud and rain, unable to rise—their friends, officers, or enlisted men would sit in the barracks sheltered from the rain and look at them without moving to help them. I have seen men, not one but 50 or more at a time, lying in their own feces too weak to move and no one to move them."[27]

The same story could be told of innumerable Japanese-run POW camps. Things rarely improved until the weak died off and the strong realized that they stood a better chance of living if they helped each other. That turnaround occurred sooner at Cabanatuan No. 1, one of the worst POW facilities in the Philippines, thanks to Marine leadership. When Lt. Col. Curtis T. Beecher of the 4th Marines assumed command of that camp in late October 1942, more than two thousand of its inmates had died since the previous June. Beecher conducted a quick inspection, taking note of overflowing latrines and the mud-choked paths hampering movement between barracks. He immediately formed clean-up, maintenance, and sanitary squads to install dry walkways, dig deeper drainage ditches, and provide more latrines. Beecher's reforms paid off dramatically. On January 18, 1943, Cabanatuan No. 1 passed its first day without a single POW death. By February of that year the camp's death rate had shrunk to ten men a month. On June 21 Capt. William H. Owen Jr. of the U.S. Army Coast Artillery lauded Beecher and his Marine staff for their "high sense of duty and long hours of work."[28]

Although Colonel Ashurst, Major Brown, and Major Devereux warrant kudos for not letting their men degenerate into an ungovernable mob, the challenges facing them paled beside those that overwhelmed their equivalents elsewhere. Conditions at the Shanghai camps rarely approached the deprivation and dehumanization common in the Philippines. Ashurst, Brown, and Devereux also headed a much more tractable POW population. Officers can lead only as far as their men will follow. Ashurst's command team could have accomplished little without the cooperation of their enlisted men, the British and Italian servicemen, the crews from captured Allied merchant ships, and the Wake Contractors.

Those disparate clusters maintained remarkable self-discipline, and they usually responded well to orders from above.[29]

To be sure, however, Woosung and Kiangwan never became saintly sanctuaries. Brown and Devereux had to punish subordinates who stopped toeing the mark or threaten them with court-martial. The Contractors sometimes rebelled against what they considered petty regulations, prompting Major Brown to resort to strong-arm tactics to compel compliance. Despite that friction—an inevitable consequence of keeping so many men caged together for so long—the Marine hierarchy at the Shanghai camps never encountered an organized mutiny. Most POWs confined there recognized that the existing system offered them their best possible path to survival.[30]

Still, even the best-behaved Wake Islanders and other Shanghai prisoners grumbled about the Marine officers' insistence on the privileges of rank. The enlisted men and Contractors resented the brass for evading hard labor, having access to more food and other creature comforts, and retaining enlisted orderlies. Those perquisites clashed with the officers' endless talk about shared sacrifice. The inability of Ashurst and his commissioned subordinates to jettison a prewar caste system tarnishes their reputation, but it does not negate the fact that they basically did what POW officers were supposed to do. No one at Woosung and Kiangwan expressed greater scorn for the officers' self-indulgence than Purser William Kantzer of the *President Harrison*. At the war's end Kantzer resided at Warabi, where a committee of captive civilians regulated POW life. A brief taste of that management style had the purser singing a different tune. "We used to talk about how nice it would be to get away from the American officers in Shanghai," Kantzer mused, "but no sooner did we do it that we got civilian substitutes that left us just as bad off as before. We actually need one leader and only one."[31]

As irksome as the Ashurst regime felt at times, it conditioned the Wake Islanders and their fellow POWs to handle the harsher conditions they eventually confronted in Japan. Camp authorities began transferring drafts to the home islands as early as the fall of 1942, and ultimately all but twenty-five seriously ill inmates shipped out for the enemy homeland. Many of those transferees found billets in camps without the American officers they had known in China, but most showed they had internalized the principles practiced at Woosung and Kiangwan. Marine NCOs or their Navy counterparts seized the reins of leadership, reinforcing their men's sense of unit identity and prodding them to stand by each other. When the war ended at Fukuoka No. 3, Lt. Col. William Dorris, a U.S. Army officer from the Philippines, feared that local Japanese might seek revenge for their country's defeat by harming POWs. He also worried about his men leaving camp and causing trouble in nearby towns. To Dorris' relief, the three dozen North China and Wake Marines under his command took it upon themselves to maintain security. The Marine NCOs automatically mustered their men and scheduled rotating guard details to patrol the camp's perimeter. Dorris validated that show of initiative by designating the Leathernecks as his military police. Reflecting on why Dorris did not order American soldiers to share that duty, Pfc. James King declared, "We were more cohesive. We stayed together as a group and recognized our senior NCOs as in charge."[32]

The 265 Contractors who went straight from Wake to Japan in September 1942 demonstrated similar group solidarity. During their bleakest days at Fukuoka No. 18-B, those Americans called on their ebbing reserves of strength to give their many dead decent burials. They would build a cedar box filled with straw in which they placed each man's remains for interment. Oreal Johnson of Boise assumed the role of chaplain and conducted funeral services over the deceased. The Freemasons and World War I veterans in camp made sure their departed comrades received the appropriate final honors. Leo W. Wilcox's diary describes the rites performed for George E. Bailey on February 6, 1943: "I put on my VFW emblem, last night. . . . I called all veterans together and read the burial ritual out of the VFW Ritual. Oral Johnson gave a short service and a solo 'I Need Thee Every Hour' was sung."[33]

"DESTINY FORGED INEXTRICABLE BONDS OF FRIENDSHIP"

Superior leadership was vital, but that was not the only weapon the Wake Islanders and their fellow inmates brought to the struggle for survival. The communal bonds that steeled those men against years of privation, uncertainty, and monotony drew on more than formal military strictures or company affiliations. Acting on their own, the POWs instituted a network of intimate alliances that constituted a mutual aid system more effective than anything decreed by Ashurst and his officers. "As a whole," insisted Cpl. Bernard Richardson, "we didn't care for the thousand, or twelve hundred, or three hundred men who were in any particular prison we were in. But there were cadres of caring people, your close friends." Most Wake Islanders used a commonplace name for Richardson's "caring cadres." They called the resilient cliques that pulled them through the worst days of their lives the "buddy system."[34]

Buddy systems sprang into existence early in the Wake Islanders' confinement, with some originating at the moment of capture and others emerging later as compatible POWs grew better acquainted. "I would say," ventured Pfc. Leonard Mettscher, "that the reason there wasn't more prisoners that died . . . was the fact we looked out for each other." Private First Class Chapman agreed, saying, "A lot of us were helped by buddies or friends." Pfc. Joseph Borne, another Leatherneck captured on Wake, grasped this essential lesson: "In order to survive, you couldn't be an island." Cpl. Robert Brown put it more emphatically: "In our group there were no individuals. We were all buddies."[35]

A buddy system could consist of an entire barracks section of up to thirty-six men. Sometimes everyone in camp might work together at critical junctures. More often than not, however, such alliances encompassed a small circle of friends or just one man and his bunkie. Corporal Richardson identified eight other Marines as his caring cadre. Pfc. Robert Shores stuck by three men from his battery in the 1st Defense Battalion. Pvt. Ewing LaPorte gave his primary loyalty to a few fellow machine gunners. "We had a bond there," he boasted in 1998, "that's still going."[36]

For the Wake Marines, the buddy system emanated from the peculiar recent history of their branch of the armed services. During the first four decades of the twentieth century Leathernecks regularly acted as America's imperial light infantry—the first to fight in distant trouble spots around the globe. Battling insurgents and bandits in Nicaragua, Haiti, and China exposed the Marine Corps to foes who did not usually take prisoners, and that bush war experience fostered a distinctive institutional culture. The Marines posted on Wake Island had been indoctrinated in three inviolable maxims since basic training:

Marines don't surrender.
Marines bring out their wounded.
Marines don't desert their buddies.

That code also regulated those men's conduct after they became prisoners of war. Cpl. Robert Brown described how the formula applied to POW life: "When your buddy's down you picked him up—when you were down he picked you up. It happened all the time." The North China Marines believed in the same creed, and they embraced the buddy system as firmly as their Wake comrades. "During our imprisonment, almost everyone teamed up with someone else," explained Pfc. Chester Biggs, who had served in Peking before the war. "They shared what they had and looked after one another."[37]

Buddy systems also proliferated among the Contractors. John Burton, a plumber from Salt Lake City, Utah, named the members of the "tribe" that assured his salvation. "Walter Gable slept on the one side of me, Reed [Catmull] on the other," Burton wrote in his memoirs. "Emmett Newell, and his brother

Glenn, slept next to Reed. I don't suppose a person could ask for dearer friends than these." As that passage indicates, some Contractors could count on family members—fathers, sons, brothers, uncles, nephews, and cousins—to sustain them. Herb Jaffe and Tex Aiken, two ruthless POW entrepreneurs, formed a partnership cemented by shared greed and the enmity of men they fleeced or bullied. "We stuck together," Jaffe reminisced, "we stayed together . . . as close as we could to protect each other."[38]

A buddy system's primary attraction lay in its obvious tangible advantages. If a POW fell ill, sustained a serious injury, or pulled a stint in solitary confinement with little or no food, his buddies frequently pooled small amounts of their own rations to sneak him additional nourishment. Those voluntary assessments went on until the man in trouble could stand on his own feet again. On June 15, 1942, Colonel Yuse seized on an infraction at Woosung to deny dinner to Barracks 7. The merchant sailors from another barracks saved enough soup from their evening meal to give half a ladle to each seaman in Barracks 7. John Burton's friends Emmett and Glenn Newell donated some cash they earned through trading to purchase additional food for Contractors with tuberculosis. As Emmett Newell informed his diary on December 22, 1943, "Eddie Cook is a T.B. [tuberculosis] suspect. We're taking up a collection to get him food. Got him 2 lbs. of peanut butter." SSgt. Bernard Ketner proudly reported on what the POWs decided to do with a relief shipment from Shanghai that reached Fengtai in the spring of 1945: "They thought what little food which came in from the Red Cross wasn't going to do them much good and they voted to give it to the men in the hospital."[39]

Often, the most valuable assistance a POW extracted from his buddy system was psychological. This entry from Cpl. Henry Durrwachter's diary illustrates the power of the slightest supportive gesture to raise a man's spirits: "Yesterday was my birthday and believe it or not I had a party. There wasn't much to it as we only had bread and sugar to eat for cake. I thought it was swell for the fellows to remember. They gave me a couple of packs of cigarettes and a ring made out of a quarter. It made me feel fine to think I had friends like that." When Contractor James Allen turned twenty-six, a buddy in the Kiangwan carpentry shop scrounged a special meal consisting of lima bean soup, salad, buttered toast, corn, fried potatoes, fried Spam, steamed rice, and pumpkin pie that he and Allen ate together. Such displays of camaraderie underlined a hopeful message, which Cpl. James Brown captured in six words: "You're not deserted by your buddies."[40]

Pfc. Jesse Nowlin joined other Wake Islanders in paying tribute to the buddy system, but he inserted a frank caveat. "We looked out . . . for each other," Nowlin stated, "in spite of the fact . . . the first order of business was to look out for yourself. I know that we collectively at times helped people with our food who were in serious trouble. . . . There was a lot who were saved by our collective . . . physical as well as moral support." Nowlin rightly emphasized the need for individual effort. "It was just as simple as that," he argued. "You took care of yourself or you died, and that was about the size of it." Yet even this hard-boiled Texan had to concede, "Had we not hung together we would have certainly fallen apart. That was one of our strengths." The buddy system became the glue that held the Wake Islanders and their fellow prisoners in a lifesaving community.[41]

More than one POW found the moral courage to face each day's trials in the knowledge that they were surrounded by friends who cared if they lived or died. In numerous cases mentally resolute prisoners devoted their spare time to rallying comrades they saw slipping into despair. A man felt obligated to stay alive to justify the sacrifices buddies made on his account. The buddy system also imbued its beneficiaries with a desire to help others. "It was the kind of morale," remarked Cpl. James Brown, "that brought most of them back with their morals." Group aid could not save everyone—even at Woosung and Kiangwan—but more Wake Islanders would have perished without it.[42]

Cpl. Robert Brown enlisted in the Marines in 1939 to dodge a paternity suit. Despite getting captured on Wake, he stayed in the Corps for thirty years, retiring as a major. Brown served with many different outfits, but none meant more to him than the Wake Island Detachment, 1st Defense Battalion. Those feelings gushed out shortly after he joined his old comrades at a reunion in June 1980. "I don't know any other unit cohesion . . . that works quite as well as this did," Brown said at that time. "In the very bitterest days we had . . . by and large, this group got through what they went through, with the number of casualties en route by . . . one of the greatest cases of friendship the world has ever known."[43]

❖ ❖ ❖

History remembers Wake Island primarily for the valiant stand an outnumbered American garrison made there in December 1941. Those U.S. Marines, sailors, soldiers, and their civilian auxiliaries handed Japan its first tactical defeat of the Pacific War, stirring a nation staggered by the devastation at Pearl Harbor. Heavy newspaper coverage, reinforced by radio broadcasts, magazine articles, and a 1942 feature film, fixed Wake Island in the American people's psyche as a symbol of heroism and defiance. The memory of that fight remains surprisingly fresh more than sixty years since the end of World War II. Major academic and commercial publishers have released five books on the Wake Island campaign since 1995. It has also been the subject of two nationally broadcast documentaries produced since 2003.

The Americans captured on Wake Island found that confluence of history and memory highly ironic. Their sixteen days in combat constituted a minute portion of their World War II experience, and as celebrated as it was, their defensive effort ended in defeat. For the next three and a half years, the Wake Islanders waged an equally intensive struggle as POWs. Unarmed and at their enemy's mercy, they achieved victory in defeat by emerging with one of the highest survival rates of any group of Caucasian POWs held by the Japanese.

The Wake Islanders have always been quick to claim credit for their own salvation, and their largely honorable conduct certainly warrants commendation. At the same time they enjoyed greater amounts of luck than most other groups of Allied POWs devoured by the Japanese juggernaut. The Wake Islanders' survival owed much to an international effort coordinated by the Red Cross, the Swiss government, and the American and British nationals of Shanghai.

In the final analysis, the Wake Islanders' survival also reflected well on portions of the Japanese military. The decision to turn the Shanghai War Prisoners Camp into a showplace spared the Americans confined there from much of the barbarism inflicted on their counterparts elsewhere in East Asia. Many Wake Islanders also benefited from encountering a disproportionately high number of individual Japanese officers and enlisted men who either treated POWs kindly or did not go out of their way to persecute them.

At the same time the comparatively gentle handling the Wake Islanders received constitutes an indictment. What happened at Camp 2 on Wake, Woosung and Kiangwan in China, and Zentsuji on Shikoku showed that Japanese soldiers and sailors knew how to behave humanely. The atrocities that occurred at so many other camps were not inevitable. They did not stem solely from an ancient culture unable to adapt to modern standards. They represented deliberate choices informed by current considerations. The Japanese military opted to commit war crimes in certain locales and to perform acts of mercy in others. The Wake Island defenders and their companions just happened to be in the right place at the right time more often than not. That good fortune, combined with the Wake Islanders' talent for capitalizing on any advantage by living the golden rule, kept their POW losses much lower than the norm.

The Defenders of Wake Island, the veterans' organization formed by the atoll's military survivors, chose this fitting motto: "Destiny Forged Inextricable Bonds of Friendship." With most of these men resting now in American cemeteries, those words serve as an appropriate eulogy.[44]

notes

CHAPTER 1

1. For a broad historical overview of the fight for Wake Island, see Gregory J. W. Urwin, *Facing Fearful Odds: The Siege of Wake Island* (Lincoln: University of Nebraska Press, 1997), particularly at 7–9, 14–17, 19, 21–35, 37, 39, 42, 44–46, 48–50, 51–53, 55–59, 62, 64–66, 73–89, 82, 84, 91–94, 96–97, 105, 107–116, 114–120, 126–132, 133–134, 137–141, 155–160, 162–164, 167–168, 170–178, 180, 183, 185–200, 201–202, 206, 209, 212, 225–226, 231–237, 241–242, 264–273, 274–279, 282–284, 286–287, 288–292, 299–305, 306, 309–314, 316–334, 341, 342, 350, 358, 385–395, 396–400, 406–420, 426–430, 431–440, 445–448, 451–454, 455–458, 495–506, 532; Lt. Col. Arthur A. Poindexter, USMC, "Informal Report on the Operations of the .30 Caliber MG Battery and the Mobile Reserve During the Defense of Wake Island," April 4, 1947, 3–7, Papers Relating to the Defense of Wake Island, Box 12, File 1m-2a, 1st DefBn—Reports of Individuals (1947), Marine Corps Historical Archives, Marine Corps Historical Center, Washington, DC (hereinafter MCHA); Arthur A. Poindexter, "Our Last Hurrah on Wake," *American History Illustrated*, February 1992, 66–67, 74; Arthur A. Poindexter to author, 18 November 1992; Arthur A. Poindexter, telephone interviews with author, May 17, 1986, and March 26, 1993; William F. Kauffman, ed., "Interview With Arthur A. Poindexter," December 8, 1999, 28, 30–32, Aviator Pictures, Santa Monica, CA (hereinafter Aviator Pictures); John M. Valov to Lt. Col. James P. S. Devereux, USMC, 18 April 1946, B.1, F.4, James P. S. Devereux Collection, Howard Gotlieb Archival Research Center, Boston University, Boston, MA (hereinafter Devereux Collection); John Toland, *But Not in Shame: The Six Months After Pearl Harbor* (New York: Random House, 1961), 115–116; Gregory R. Cunningham, "The Life of Rear Admiral Winfield Scott Cunningham" (unpublished monograph in the author's possession, ca. 2005), 1–20;

Winfield Scott Cunningham, interview by author, March 30, 1985; Donald R. Malleck to author, April 1980; Wiley W. Sloman, interview by author, September 12, 1986; *St. Louis Post-Dispatch*, October 29, 1945; *Cleveland News*, November 9, 1945; Jack R. Skaggs, taped reply to author's questionnaire, December 28, 1981; James O. King, interview by author, October 17, 1998.

2. Ewing E. LaPorte, interview by author, October 16, 1998; Earl R. Row, interview by author, June 19, 1981; Mackie L. Wheeler, interview by author, October 8, 1994.

3. Robert Shores, interview by author, September 11, 1986; Bernard E. Richardson, taped reply to author's questionnaire, October 31, 1986; Robert McCulloch Brown, interview by author, June 21–22, 1980; James R. Brown, interview by author, June 20, 1981; Henry H. W. Chapman, interview by author, February 20, 1982; Charles A. Holmes to author, 23 June 1978. See also Dennis E. Showalter, "Evolution of the U.S. Marine Corps as a Military Elite," *Marine Corps Gazette*, November 1979, 44–58.

4. Ronald E. Marcello, ed., "Interview With Bryghte D. Godbold, April 7, 1972," 5, University of North Texas Oral History Collection, University of North Texas, Denton, TX (hereinafter UNT Oral History Collection); John F. Dolezal to Col. James P. S. Devereux, USMC, 29 March 1946, B.1, F.4, Devereux Collection; Cora E. Bronner to Col. James P. S. Devereux, USMC, 4 September 1947, Personal Correspondence, B.40 B, Devereux Collection; Valov to Devereux, 18 April 1946; William F. Kauffman, ed., "Interview With Don Ludington," March 2000, 4, Aviator Pictures: 11; William F. Kauffman, ed., "Interview With Charles Loveland," March 2000, 9, Aviator Pictures; William F. Kauffman, ed., "Interview With Joe Goiceochia," March 2000, 5, Aviator Pictures; L. A. Magnino, *Jim's Journey: A Wake Island Civilian POW's Story* (Central Point, OR: Hellgate Press, 2001), 40–42. See also Gregory J. W. Urwin, "The Wake Island Militia," *Naval History* 11, no. 5 (1997): 39–42; Robert J. Cressman, *"A Magnificent Fight": The Battle for Wake Island* (Annapolis: Naval Institute Press, 1995), 86–87; Wheeler, interview; LaPorte, interview; Magnino, *Jim's Journey*, 50–51, 316; William F. Kauffman, ed., "Interview With Leo Nonn," August 2000, 13–18, 21, Aviator Pictures; Kauffman, "Goiceochia Interview," 7; Kauffman, "Loveland Interview," 11–12; Marcello, "Godbold Interview," 18; John R. Hoskins, "Memoir" (unpublished manuscript in the author's possession, ca. 2002), 4–5, 20; Maj. Walter L. J. Bayler, USMC, to Commander-in-Chief, U.S. Pacific Fleet, "Wake Island, Report on. Period of the 7th to 20th December, 1941," 7 January 1942, 3, Papers Relating to the Defense of Wake Island, Box 12, File 1M-1, Reports of Individuals, VMF-211, MCHA; R. D. Heinl Jr., *The Defense of Wake* (Washington, DC: Historical Section, Division of Public Information, Headquarters, U.S. Marine Corps, 1947), 17–18; Robert

M. Hanna, interview by author, September 10,1986; H. O'Guinn, "V.O.C.," (unpublished manuscript, n.d.), 22–23, Allan O'Guinn Papers, Hoover Institution Archives, Stanford University, Stanford, CA; Glenn E. Tripp to author, 14 November 1979; Otis T. Jones to Winfield Scott Cunningham, 16 December 1967, B.2, F.1, Winfield Scott Cunningham Collection, Howard Gotlieb Archival Research Center, Boston University, Boston, MA (hereinafter Cunningham Collection); Shores, interview; Kauffman, "Goiceochea Interview," 13; Kauffman, "Loveland Interview," 22, 26.

5. Urwin, *Facing Fearful Odds*, 477–492; Shigeyoshi Ozeki, "Wake Island in Sight," trans. and ed. Daniel King, Gregory J. W. Urwin, Department of History, Temple University, http://astro.temple.edu/~gurwin/ffoozeki.htm (accessed July 21, 2006).
6. Urwin, *Facing Fearful Odds*, 495–506.
7. Ibid., 455–473.
8. Ibid., 482–483, 492–495, 500–501, 507–508, 510–523.
9. Urwin, *Facing Fearful Odds*, 515, 524; Frank B. Miller Jr., Diary, 23 December 1941 (unpublished transcript in the author's possession, 2006).

CHAPTER 2

1. *Honolulu Sunday Star Bulletin & Advertiser*, September 23, 1962; W. Scott Cunningham and Lydel Sims, *Wake Island Command* (1961; paperback ed., New York: Popular Library, 1962), 106; Cunningham, interview; *Washington Post*, October 14, 1945; R. Brown, interview; Chet Cunningham, *Hell Wouldn't Stop: An Oral History of the Battle of Wake Island* (New York: Carroll & Graf Publishers, 2002), 111.
2. James P. S. Devereux, *The Story of Wake Island* (Philadelphia: J. B. Lippincott, 1947), 173–176, 178, 197–198; R. Brown, interview; Second Lt. John Hamas, USMC, "Report on What Happened and What Each Officer Did on Wake Island During Period 7 December to 24 December, 1941," 12 October 1945, 8, Papers Relating to the Defense of Wake Island, Box 12, File 1m-2b, 1st DefBn, Informal Reports of Individuals (1945), MCHA.
3. Devereux, *Story of Wake*, 176, 178–179; Woodrow M. Kessler, *To Wake Island and Beyond: Reminiscences* (Washington, DC: History and Museums Division, Headquarters, U.S. Marine Corps, 1988), 69–70; Charles A. Holmes to author, 19 November 1978; Maj. C. A. Barninger Jr., USMC, "Memorandum to Lt. Col. James P. S. Devereux," 8 October 1945, 8, Papers Relating to the Defense of Wake Island, Box 12, File 1m-2b, 1st DefBn, Informal Reports of Individuals (1945), MCHA; G. Mason Kahn, interview by author, June 15, 1979; Franklin D. Gross, interview by author, October 13, 1984.
4. Joseph E. Borne, interview by author, October 17, 1998; Holmes to author, 19 November 1978; Carl E. Stegmaier Jr., interview by author, June 16,

1979; Joe M. Reeves, interview by author, September 13, 1986; Hanna, interview; Franklin A. Gross, interview by author, October 22, 1983; Thomas H. Miller, ed., "An Interview With Thomas W. Johnson at His Home in Saint Joseph, Missouri, 29 May 2001," 9, Oral History Program, Collection No. 3975, Missouri Ex-POWs, State Historical Society of Missouri, Columbia, MO (hereinafter Missouri Oral History); J. Brown, interview; Eschol E. Davis, interview by author, October 8, 1994; Guy J. Kelnhofer Jr., interview by author, September 13, 1986; Cunningham, *Hell Wouldn't Stop*, 117; John R. Himelrick, Diary, 23 December 1941, Personal Papers, MCHA; Holmes to author, 19 November 1978.

5. Guy J. Kelnhofer Jr., *Understanding the Former Prisoner of War: Life After Liberation* (St. Paul, MN: Banfil Street Press, 1992), 3; Winston S. Churchill, *London to Ladysmith via Pretoria* (London: Longmans, Green, 1900), 96; Ozeki, "Wake Island in Sight."

6. Urwin, *Facing Fearful Odds*, 526, 540; Devereux, *Story of Wake*, 199; Ralph J. Holewinski, interview by author, June 20, 1980; Woodrow M. Kessler to author, 18 November 1992; Kessler, *To Wake Island and Beyond*, 77; Gross, interview, October 13, 1984; Bonnie Gilbert, "Wake Deaths CPNAB," (electronic copy in author's possession, May 12, 2009); "Extracts From Letter From CPNAB to Mr. Ferris," 17 May 1952, B.F, F.4, Cunningham Collection.

7. John F. Kinney and James M. McCaffrey, *Wake Island Pilot: A World War II Memoir* (Washington, DC: Brassey's, 1995), 81; Gross, interview, October 13, 1984; Chapman, interview; LaPorte, interview; William F. Kauffman, ed., "Interview With Bill Charters," March 2000, 4: 20, Aviator Pictures; Kelnhofer, interview; Borne, interview; Julian K. Sandvold, interview by author, June 20, 1980; Bernard E. Richardson, "Initiation" (unpublished manuscript in the author's possession, n.d.), 21; Edward V. Sturgeon, interview by author, October 13, 1984. See also Iris Chang, *The Rape of Nanking: The Forgotten Holocaust of World War II* (New York: Basic Books, 1997), and John W. Dower, *War Without Mercy: Race and Power in the Pacific War* (New York: Pantheon Books, 1986).

8. Sylvester Gregouire to author, March 1979; Hanna, interview; Sturgeon, interview, October 13, 1984; Gross, interview, October 22, 1983; Ronald E. Marcello, ed., "Interview With Mr. James C. Venable, April 13, 1971," 29, UNT Oral History Collection.

9. Chapman, interview; LaPorte, interview; Kelnhofer, interview; Victor V. Skaggs to Winfield Scott Cunningham, 4 September 1946, B.1, F.1, Cunningham Collection; Davis, interview; Thomas H. Miller, ed., "An Interview With Thomas W. Johnson at His Home in St. Joseph, Missouri, 16 July 2001," 35, Missouri Oral History.

10. Walter A. Bowsher, interview by author, June 18, 1981; Shores, interview; William F. Kauffman, ed., "Interview With John Rogge," March 2000, 17,

Aviator Pictures; Edwin Darby Nye, interview by author, February 13, 1982. See also Bernard C. Nalty, *Strength for the Fight: A History of Black Americans in the Military* (New York: Free Press, 1986).

11. Ronald E. Marcello, ed., "Interview With Marshall E. Fields, February 13, 1972," 17, UNT Oral History Collection; E. Davis, interview; Henry L. Durrwachter, Diary, 26 February 1942, Henry L. Durrwachter Papers, Eugene C. Barker Texas History Center, General Libraries, University of Texas at Austin, Austin, TX; Dare Kibble, "My War" (unpublished manuscript in the author's possession, 2002), 59; Cunningham, *Hell Wouldn't Stop*, 117; Holmes to author, 19 November 1978.

12. Devereux, *Story of Wake*, 179; George H. Potter Jr. to author, 28 October 1982; Donald R. Malleck to author, October 1980.

13. Devereux, *Story of Wake*, 179–180; John S. Johnson, taped reply to author's questionnaire, April 25, 1981; T. Miller, "T. Johnson Interview, 29 May 2001," 20; Leonard G. Mettscher, taped reply to author's questionnaire, February 1980; Malleck to author, October 1980; Grover E. Thaire to author, September 1981. See also Gary Nila and Robert A. Rolfe, *Japanese Special Naval Landing Forces: Uniforms and Equipment 1932–45* (Botley, Oxford: Osprey Publishing, 2006).

14. Kinney and McCaffrey, *Wake Island Pilot*, 79; Kahn, interview; Herbert C. Freuler, interview by author, June 16, 1979; William F. Kauffman, ed., "Interview With Bill Gooding," March 2000, 12, Aviator Pictures.

15. Devereux, *Story of Wake*, 180–181; Malleck to author, October 1980; Cunningham and Sims, *Wake Island Command*, 107.

16. Devereux, *Story of Wake*, 181–196; Ralph J. Holewinski, interview by author, June 20, 1980; Kauffman, "Poindexter Interview," 31–32; Marcello, "Godbold Interview," 29–30; Cassius E. Smith, interview by author, June 20, 1981; Chapman, interview; Arthur A. Poindexter to author, 16 September 1981.

17. Himelrick, Diary, 23 December 1941; John S. Johnson, taped reply to author's questionnaire, May 9, 1981; Smith, interview; Marcello, "Fields Interview," 8.

18. Devereux, *Story of Wake*, 183–184; Malleck to author, October 1980; Holewinski, interview, June 20, 1980; Hanna, interview; James H. Cox, interview by author, June 20, 1980; Kelnhofer, interview.

19. Devereux, *Story of Wake*, 185; Kauffman, "Poindexter Interview," 32; Gavan Daws, ed., "Transcript of Interview With Herb Jaffe," n.d., 8, Gavan Daws Papers, U.S. Army Military History Institute, Carlisle Barracks, PA (hereinafter USAMHI); Kelnhofer, interview.

20. George G. Hubley, interview by author, October 15, 1998; Smith, interview; Devereux, *Story of Wake*, 185.

21. Bernard E. Richardson, "Wake Island: End of Combat," 17–18 (unpublished manuscript in the author's possession, ca. 1945); Devereux, *Story of*

Wake, 186, 194; Chapman, interview; J. Johnson, reply, April 25, 1981; Artie Stocks, interview by author, June 14, 1979; Richardson "Initiation," 20; Edwin F. Hassig, interview by author, June 21, 1980; Stegmaier, interview.
22. *Washington Times-Herald*, July 21, 1945.
23. Mettscher, reply; J. Brown, interview; Row, interview; Bowsher, interview; Kessler, *To Wake Island and Beyond*, 70–71; Sturgeon, interview, October 13, 1984; Wheeler, interview; Luther Williams, interview by author, June 21, 1980; Gregouire to author, March 1979; Jack B. Cook, interview by author, June 19, 1981; Cunningham, *Hell Wouldn't Stop*, 129; R. Brown, interview.
24. Holmes to author, 19 November 1978; Terrence T. McAmis, interview by author, June 16, 1979; Kelnhofer, interview; Marcello, "Venable Interview," 28; Robert F. Haidinger, interview by author, June 15, 1979.
25. Holmes to author, 19 November 1978; McAmis, interview; Kelnhofer, interview.
26. *Washington Post*, October 14, 1945; Barninger, "Memorandum," 8; Kessler, *To Wake Island and Beyond*, 71–72; J. Cook, interview; Ernest G. Rogers, interview by author, June 21, 1980.
27. Marcello, "Godbold Interview," 30–31; Holmes to author, 19 November 1978; Magnino, *Jim's Journey*, 65.
28. Marcello, "Godbold Interview," 31; R. Brown, interview; LaPorte, interview; Magnino, *Jim's Journey*, 71; Nye, interview; Charles H. Camp, interview by author, June 21, 1980; Row, interview; Ozeki, "Wake Island in Sight."
29. Kinney and McCaffrey, *Wake Island Pilot*, 80; McAmis, interview; J. Johnson, reply, April 25, 1981; Shores, interview; Stegmaier, interview; Kauffman, "Nonn Interview," 26; Cunningham, *Hell Wouldn't Stop*, 112, 120; Williams, interview; Earl M. Broyles, taped reply to author's questionnaire, March 28, 1986.
30. Kahn, interview; Freuler, interview; Kinney and McCaffrey, *Wake Island Pilot*, 80; Theodore A. Abraham Jr., *"Do You Understand, Huh?" A POW's Lament, 1941–1945* (Manhattan, KS: Sunflower University Press, 1992), 18; T. Miller, "T. Johnson Interview, 29 May 2001," 20–21; Hamas, "Report," 8; Row, interview; Durrwachter, Diary, 26 February 1942; Mettscher, reply; Kelnhofer, interview; Haidinger, interview; Holmes to author, 19 November 1978; Magnino, *Jim's Journey*, 65, 67; Marcello, "Venable Interview," 30–32; Kauffman, "Ludington Interview," 5: 2.
31. Kinney and McCaffrey, *Wake Island Pilot*, 80; T. Miller, "T. Johnson Interview, 29 May 2001," 20–21; Marcello, "Venable Interview," 31; LaPorte, interview; Holmes to author, 19 November 1978; Camp, interview; Hamas, "Report," 8.
32. R. Brown, interview; Magnino, *Jim's Journey*, 65; Kauffman, "Ludington Interview," 5: 2; Kelnhofer, interview.

33. Durrwachter, Diary, 26 February 1942; Bowsher, interview; J. Brown, interview; Magnino, *Jim's Journey*, 66; Marcello, "Venable Interview," 32.
34. Ronald E. Marcello, ed., "Interview With George W. McDaniel, October 23, 1973," 37, UNT Oral History Collection; Marcello, "Fields Interview," 7–8; Magnino, *Jim's Journey*, 65–67; Haidinger, interview; LaPorte, interview; John F. Kinney, "P.O.W. Survival and Escape," 23 (unpublished manuscript in the author's possession, ca. 1972); Holmes to author, 19 November 1978.
35. For a description of the same passivity many European Jews exhibited during the Holocaust, see Raul Hilberg, *The Destruction of the European Jews*, 3 vols. (New York: Holmes & Meier, 1985). Kelnhofer, interview; Durrwachter, Diary, 26 February 1942; Haidinger, interview; McAmis, interview; Marcello, "Venable Interview," 32.
36. Holmes to author, 19 November 1978; R. Brown, interview; Kelnhofer, interview; Kauffman, "Ludington Interview," 5: 2; Devereux, *Story of Wake*, 201.
37. J. Brown, interview; Kauffman, "Ludington Interview," 5: 2; Hamas, "Report," 8; Charles A. Holmes to author, 19 November 1978; Haidinger, interview; Magnino, *Jim's Journey*, 67; Kelnhofer, interview.
38. Holmes to author, 19 November 1978, and 27 December 1978; Abraham, *Do You Understand*, 19; Haidinger, interview; T. Miller, "T. Johnson Interview, 29 May 2001," 21; Kelnhofer, interview; Mettscher, reply; Camp, interview.
39. Cunningham and Sims, *Wake Island Command*, 109; Capt. W. S. Cunningham, USN, "Narrative of Cruise in Japanese Prison Ship *NITTA MARU*, 12–24 January 1942," October 31, 1946, 5, B.3, F.6, Cunningham Collection; Sturgeon, interview, October 13, 1984; Kauffman, "Goiceochea Interview," 13; William F. Kauffman, ed., "Interview With Swede Hokanson," June 2000, 12, Aviator Pictures; Wheeler, interview; J. Cook, interview; Cox, interview; Skaggs, reply; J. Johnson, reply, April 25, 1981; "Perpetuation of Testimony of Chew Bock Teung Civilian Employee," n.d., 1, File 67-75, Bk. 1 (1–2), POWs on the *Nitta Maru*, Records of the Office of the Judge Advocate General, Record Group 153, National Archives, Washington, DC (hereinafter RG 153); Rogers, interview; Claude Davis Howes, "Testimony of Claude Davis Howes," 6 (unpublished manuscript in the author's possession, n.d.).
40. Smith, interview; Cox, interview; Hubley, interview; J. Johnson, reply, April 25, 1981; Hassig, interview; Stegmaier, interview; Chapman, interview; Shores, interview; Bernard E. Richardson, "Initiation," 21 (unpublished manuscript in the author's possession, n.d.); Stocks, interview; Skaggs, reply; Erwin D. Pistole, interview by author, June 21, 1980; Williams, interview; Wheeler, interview; Sturgeon, interview, October 13, 1984.
41. Barninger, "Memorandum," 8; Gregouire to author, March 1979; J. Cook, interview.

42. *Washington Post*, October 14, 1945.
43. F. Miller, Diary, 23 December 1941; William F. Kauffman, ed., "Interview With Murray Kidd," March 2000, 20, Aviator Pictures; William F. Kauffman, ed., "Interview With Charles Leroy Myers," March 2000, 20, 24, 35–36, Aviator Pictures; Nye, interview; Kauffman, "Loveland Interview," 17–18; Kauffman, "Goiceochea Interview," 11; John H. Burton, *Traveling Life's Twisting Trails* (New York: Vantage Press, 1992), 66–68; Howes, "Testimony," 7–8; Arthur V. Caps to Winfield Scott Cunningham, n.d., B.1, F.2, Cunningham Collection; Alexander E. Pay, Diary, 23 December 1941 (unpublished transcript in the author's possession, n.d.); Leal Henderson Russell, "War Diary of Leal Henderson Russell, 1940–1945," 10 March 1942 (unpublished transcript in the author's possession, 1987).
44. Richardson, "Initiation," 24; J. Johnson, reply, April 25, 1981; John O. Young, "John O. ("J.O.") Young: WWII Japanese POW," 5 (unpublished manuscript in the author's possession, n.d.) (hereinfter Young, "WWII POW").
45. Hassig, interview; Richardson, "Initiation," 24–25; Stegmaier, interview; Chapman, interview; Nye, interview; T. Miller, "T. Johnson Interview, 29 May 2001," 22; J. Johnson, reply, April 25, 1981; Devereux, *Story of Wake*, 198.
46. Bowsher, interview.
47. Stocks, interview; John R. Dale, interview by author, June 14, 1979; Donald R. Malleck to author, October 1980; J. Johnson, reply, April 25, 1981.
48. Mettscher, reply; Richardson, "Initiation," 26; J. Johnson, reply, April 25, 1981; Chapman, interview; William O. Plate, taped reply to author's questionnaire, February 2, 1982; Row, interview; R. Brown, interview; Hubley, interview; Kauffman, "Myers Interview," 21.
49. J. Cook, interview; Clifford E. Hotchkiss, interview by author, October 22, 1982; Rogers, interview; Plate, reply.
50. Chapman, interview; Williams, interview.
51. Shores, interview; R. Brown, interview; Marcello, "Venable Interview," 35–36; Reeves, interview.
52. R. Brown, interview; Marcello, "Venable Interview," 36; Kinney and McCaffrey, *Wake Island Pilot*, 81.
53. Kinney and McCaffrey, *Wake Island Pilot*, 81; Devereux, *Story of Wake*, 210; Howes, "Testimony," 7.
54. Kinney, "P.O.W. Survival," 24. See also Devereux, *Story of Wake*, 202.
55. Chapman, interview; J. Brown, interview; Mettscher, reply.
56. Kinney and McCaffrey, *Wake Island Pilot*, 82.

CHAPTER 3

1. Bruce Lamberto, ed., "Interview With Dr. Shigeyoshi Ozeki in New Orleans, La. on May 31, 1998 as told to Bruce Lamberto," 1 (transcript in the author's possession, 1998); Ozeki, "Wake Island in Sight"; Shigeyoshi Ozeki, "Dr.

Shigeyoshi Ozeki's Second Account of the Fall of Wake Island," trans. and ed. Daniel King, Gregory J. W. Urwin, Department of History, Temple University, http://astro.temple.edu/~gurwin/ffoozeki.htm (accessed July 21, 2006).
2. Ozeki, "Dr. Shigeyoshi Ozeki's Second Account."
3. Allied Translator and Interpreter Section (ATIS), South West Pacific Area (SWPA), "Research Report No. 76 (Part II): The Emperor Cult as a Present Factor in Japanese Military Psychology, 21 June 1944," 1–28, Records of the Adjutant General's Office, Record Group 94, National Archives, Washington, DC (hereinafter RG 94); ATIS, SWPA, "Research Report, No. 76 (Part IV): Prominent Factors in Japanese Military Psychology, 7 February 1945," 7, RG 94; Saburo Ienaga, *The Pacific War: World War II and the Japanese*, trans. Frank Baldwin (New York: Pantheon Books, 1978), 13–53, 97–128, 153–202; David Bergamini, *Japan's Imperial Conspiracy*, vol. 1 (New York: William Morrow, 1971), 243–485; Ichiro Kawasaki, *Japan Unmasked* (Rutland, VT: C. R. Tuttle, 1969), 151–152; Robert C. Christopher, *The Japanese Mind* (New York: Simon & Schuster, 1983), 44–45; Takie Sugiyama Lebra, *Japanese Patterns of Behavior* (Honolulu: University of Hawaii Press, 1976), 24; Ozkei, "Wake Island in Sight," 6.
4. Conrad Totman, *Japan Before Perry: A Short History* (Berkeley: University of California Press, 1981), 4–5, 15, 58–59, 127–128; ATIS, SWPA, "Research Report, No. 76 (Part VI): Defects Arising From the Doctrine of 'Spiritual Superiority' as Factors in Japanese Military Psychology, 10 October 1945," 18, RG 94; Stanley L. Falk, *Bataan: The March of Death* (New York: W. W. Norton, 1962), 226–227; Christopher, *Japanese Mind*, 268; Kawasaki, *Japan Unmasked*, 97–98, 114; Edwin T. Layton, *"And I Was There": Pearl Harbor and Midway—Breaking the Secrets* (New York: William Morrow, 1985), 40. See also Emiko Tierney-Ohuki, *Illness and Culture in Contemporary Japan* (New York: Cambridge University Press, 1984).
5. ATIS, SWPA, "Research Report, No. 76 (Part III): The Warrior Tradition as a Present Factor in Japanese Military Psychology, 30 October 1944," 4, RG 94; Lebra, *Japanese Patterns*, 25–26, 28–29, 34, 67–68, 82–83; Christopher, *Japanese Mind*, 51, 55, 268–269.
6. ATIS, SWPA, "Warrior Tradition," 3–4; Yuki Tanaka, *Hidden Horrors: Japanese War Crimes in World War II* (Boulder, CO: Westview Press, 1996), 207; Meirion Harries and Susie Harries, *Soldiers of the Rising Sun: The Rise and Fall of the Imperial Japanese Army* (New York: Random House, 1991), 3–4, 5, 7.
7. ATIS, SWPA, "Research Report, No. 76 (Part I): Self-Immolation as a Factor in Japanese Military Psychology, 4 April 1944," 16, RG 94; Tanaka, *Hidden Horrors*, 206–209; Harries and Harries, *Soldiers*, 24–25, 40–41, 101–102; Lebra, *Japanese Patterns*, 190–191.

8. ATIS, SWPA, "Warrior Tradition," 5, 9; ATIS, SWPA, "Self-Immolation," 12–13, 16, 34; Tanaka, *Hidden Horrors*, 195, 198; Harries and Harries, *Soldiers*, 24–25; Kiyoshi Ibushi, "A Detailed Report on the Capture of Wake Island," in ATIS, SWPA, "Enemy Publications No. 6: Hawaii–Malaya Naval Operations, 27 March 1943," 28, Records of the Adjutant General's Office, 1917–, Record Group 407, National Archives, Washington, DC.
9. Rogers Interview; ATIS, SWPA, "Prominent Factors," 9–10; ATIS, SWPA, "Defects of 'Spiritual Superiority,'" 20; Ienaga, *Pacific War*, 51–54; Clifford E. Hotchkiss, interview by author, October 21, 1983; Rogers, interview; John A. White, *The United States Marines in North China* (Millbrae, CA: privately printed, 1974), 38; Richardson, reply; Benis M. Frank, ed., "Brigadier General James P. S. Devereux, U.S. Marine Corps (Retired): Oral History Transcript," 1973, 125, Marine Corps Oral History Collection, Historical Division, Headquarters, U.S. Marine Corps, Washington, DC; Tanaka, *Hidden Horrors*, 40, 202–203.
10. Kahn, interview; ATIS, SWPA, "Defects of 'Spiritual Superiority,'" 18–20; Tanaka, *Hidden Horrors*, 160–161; Harry L. McDonald, Affidavit, December 17, 1947, 2–3, File 67-75, Bk. 2 (1–5), POWs on the *Nitta Maru*, RG 153.
11. ATIS, SWPA, "Prominent Factors," 7; Rogers, interview; Ozeki, "Dr. Shigeyoshi Ozeki's Second Account," 16; Allison B. Gillmore, *You Can't Fight Tanks With Bayonets: Psychological Warfare Against the Japanese Army in the Southwest Pacific* (Lincoln: University of Nebraska Press, 1998), 94–98.
12. International Committee of the Red Cross. *Report of the International Committee of the Red Cross on Its Activities during the Second World War (September 1, 1939–June 30, 1947)*, vol. 1 (Geneva: ICRC, 1948), 438–39; ATIS, SWPA, "Japanese Military Psychology," 7; J. Johnson, reply, April 25, 1981.
13. Richardson, "Initiation," 24–25; Ozeki, "Dr. Shigeyoshi Ozeki's Second Account"; Ozeki, "Wake Island in Sight."
14. "Convention of July 27, 1929, Relative to the Treatment of Prisoners of War," 1932, in U.S. Congress, Senate, *Treaties, Conventions, International Acts, Protocols and Agreements Between the United States of America and Other Powers*, vol. 4, *1923–1937*, ed. Edward J. Trenwith (Washington, DC: U.S. Government Printing Office, 1938), 5224–5236 (hereinafter Geneva Convention).
15. Benis M. Frank and Henry I. Shaw Jr., *History of U.S. Marine Corps Operations in World War Two*, vol. 5, *Victory and Occupation* (Washington, DC: Historical Branch, G-3 Division, Headquarters, U.S. Marine Corps, 1968), 739; Tanaka, *Hidden Horrors*, 73; *Red Cross Activities*, vol. 1, 437–438; Ronald H. Bailey, *Prisoners of War*, World War II (Alexandria, VA: Time-Life Books, 1981), 9–12; Col. William W. Ashurst, USMC, "Record of In-

ternment, 10 September 1945," 2, Fengtai, China, Records of the Provost Marshal General, Record Group 389, National Archives, Washington, DC (hereinafter RG 389); Cunningham and Sims, *Wake Island Command*, 129.
16. Devereux, *Story of Wake*, 220; Charles A. Stenger, *American Prisoners of War in WWI, WWII, Korea and Vietnam: Statistical Data Concerning Numbers Captured, Repatriated, and Still Alive* (Washington, DC: Veterans Affairs Advisory Committee on Former Prisoners of War, 1981), 3–4; Bailey, *Prisoners of War*, 13; Gavan Daws, *Prisoners of the Japanese: POWs of World War II in the Pacific* (New York: William Morrow, 1994), 360–361; Dower, *War Without Mercy*, 48; Van Waterford, *Prisoners of the Japanese in World War II: Statistical History, Personal Narratives and Memorials Concerning POWs in Camps and on Hellships, Civilian Internees, Asian Slave Laborers and Others Captured in the Pacific Theater* (Jefferson, NC: McFarland, 1994), 141–146.
17. For an early indictment of Japanese conduct, see Lord Edward Russell, *The Knights of Bushido: A Short History of Japanese War Crimes* (London: Cassell, 1958). A recent variation on Russell's approach is Linda Goetz Holmes' *Unjust Enrichments: How Japan's Companies Built Postwar Fortunes Using American POWs* (Mechanicsburg, PA: Stackpole Books, 2001). See also Charles W. Sanders Jr., *While in the Hands of the Enemy: Military Prisoners in the Civil War* (Baton Rouge: Louisiana State University Press, 2005).
18. Tanaka, *Hidden Horrors*, 72–73, 208; Harries and Harries, *Soldiers*, 60, 70, 96, 110–111; Philip A. Towle, "Japanese Treatment of Prisoners in 1904–1905—Foreign Officers Reports," *Military Affairs* 39, no. 3 (1975): 115–117; Kawasaki, *Japan Unmasked*, 202–203; Christopher, *Japanese Mind*, 315; Dower, *War Without Mercy*, 48–52; John S. Johnson Jr., Diary, 6 March 1942 (transcript in the author's possession, 1979); Donald R. Malleck to author, 29 August 1981; Devereux, *Story of Wake*, 224; Ashurst, "Record," 7.
19. A. B. Henningsen, "Report of Shanghai War Prisoners," n.d., 9, Conditions at Kiangwan (Folder I), RG 389; Kinney, "P.O.W. Survival," 55; Harries and Harries, *Soldiers*, 111.
20. Emile Fontanel, "Report on Visit to Camp of Prisoners of War at Kiangwan on November 26th, 1944," n.d., 2, Kiangwan Prisoner of War Camp, Shanghai, RG 389; Holmes to author, December 27, 1978; Row, interview; H. Jay Tice, interview by author, June 14, 1979; Ashurst, "Record," 5.
21. Chapman, interview; Rogers, interview; J. Brown, interview; Cunningham and Sims, *Wake Island Command*, 118; White, *United States Marines*, 36; J. Johnson, reply, April 25, 1981; Hoskins, "Memoir," 22; Shores, interview.
22. Devereux, *Story of Wake*, 220, 222; Kinney, "P.O.W. Survival," 67, 79; Chapman, interview; Nye, interview; Kibble, "My War," 152; Floyd Herman Comfort, "In the Matter of the Cruel Beating of American Prisoner of

362   *notes to pages 49–52*

War Marine B. O. Ketner, at Woo Sung . . . About August 1942," December 14, 1945, Prosecution Exhibit No. 15, "*United States of America vs. Isamu Ishihara*: Public Trial before the Military Commission Convened by the Commanding General, United States Army Forces, China Theater," April 5, 1946, 59, RG 153; Capt. Richard M. Huizenga, USMC, 1st Lt. John F. Kinney, USMC, Capt. James D. McBrayer Jr., USMC, and 1st Lt. John A. McAlister, USMC, "Escape Report No. 665: Kiangwan—Shanghai, 12 July 1945," 4, Conditions at Kiangwan, China (Folder No. I), RG 389.

23. Brig. Gen. Paul A. Putnam, USMC (Ret.). to Col. F. C. Caldwell, USMC, 8 October 1966, Wake Island and North China Marine POW Comments (Letters), Correspondence Relating to the Marine Corps Official History of World War II and the Captivity of the Wake Island Marines, the North China Marines, the Guam Marines, and the 4th Marines (hereinafter Correspondence), MCHA.

24. Holewinski, interview, June 20, 1980; Ralph J. Holewinski, interview by author, September 11, 1986.

25. Ozeki, "Dr. Shigeyoshi Ozeki's Second Account"; Joseph E. Borne, "My Memories: Early Days in the USMC" (unpublished manuscript in the author's possession, February 22, 2001), 16–21.

26. Richardson, "Initiation," 23–24.

27. Rogers, interview; R. Brown, interview; T. Miller, "T. Johnson Interview, 29 May 2001," 21; *Washington Post*, October 14, 1945; Kibble, "My War," 95; Magnino, *Jim's Journey*, 70; Kelnhofer, interview.

28. Nye, interview; Row, interview; Young, "WWII POW," 5; Kauffman, "Nonn Interview," 27; Hubley, interview; Burton, *Life's Twisting Trails*, 68; Shores, interview; J. Johnson, reply, 25 April 1981; Kauffman, "Ludington Interview," 5: 3.

29. J. Cook, interview; Young, "WWII POW," 5; Stegmaier, interview; Kibble, "My War," 97; Rogers, interview; J. Johnson, reply, 25 April 1981.

30. Holewinski, interview, June 20, 1980; Smith, interview; Kibble, "My War," 63: Pistole, interview; Burton, *Life's Twisting Trails*, 68; Rogers, interview.

31. Durrwachter, Diary, 26 February 1942; J. Johnson, reply, April 25, 1981; Smith, interview; Row, interview; Pay, Diary, 24 December 1941; Russell, Diary, 23 December 1941; Kauffman, "Loveland Interview," 19; Shores, interview; Pistole, interview; Kauffman, "Goicecochea Interview," 12; Rogers, interview.

32. Hotchkiss, interview, October 22, 1982; Mettscher, reply; Marcello, "Venable Interview," 33–34; Kauffman, "Loveland Interview," 19; Kelnhofer, interview; Charles A. Holmes to author, 3 December 1978; Kibble, "My War," 95; T. Miller, "T. Johnson Interview, 29 May 2001," 21.

33. Magnino, *Jim's Journey*, 70–71; Rogers, interview; Sturgeon, interview, October 13, 1984; Wheeler, interview; Fred R. Rumpel, "My Experience" (unpublished manuscript in the author's possession, n.d.), 3; Kinney and McCaffrey, *Wake Island Pilot*, 82–83; Young, "WWII POW," 5; F. Miller, Diary, 23 December 1941.
34. Cunningham and Sims, *Wake Island Command*, 109–110; Devereux, *Story of Wake*, 201–203; Cunningham, "Narrative of Cruise," 2; Kessler, *To Wake Island and Beyond*, 76; Donald R. Malleck to author, 16 April 1981; Kauffman, "Poindexter Interview," 28.
35. Malleck to author, 16 April 1981.
36. Russell, Diary, 24 December 1941; Barninger, "Memorandum," 9.
37. Holmes to author, 27 December 1978; Barninger, "Memorandum," 9; Cunningham, *Hell Wouldn't Stop*, 124; Reeves, interview; Hanna, interview.
38. Kinney, "P.O.W. Survival," 26; Kinney and McCaffrey, *Wake Island Pilot*, 83; O'Guinn, "V.O.C.," 20; Russell, Diary, 24 December 1941.
39. Stegmaier, interview; Barninger, "Memorandum," 9; Kibble, "My War," 95; Shores, interview; Rogers, interview; Gregouire to author, March 1979; Plate, reply; Broyles, reply; Cox, interview; Nye, interview; Row, interview; Doris Miller, *Doc Miller: Wake Survivor* (n.p.: privately printed, n.d.), 7; Holmes to author, 3 December 1978.
40. Kinney, "P.O.W. Survival," 26; Kinney and McCaffrey, *Wake Island Pilot*, 83.
41. Kinney, "P.O.W. Survival," 26–27; Kinney and McCaffrey, *Wake Island Pilot*, 83; Barninger, "Memorandum," 9; Bowsher, interview; Raymond R. Rutledge, "Mistreatment of American Prisoners of War," September 13, 1945, 2, File 67-75, Bk. 1 (1–2), POWs on the *Nitta Maru*, RG 153.
42. Kinney, "P.O.W. Survival," 27; Durrwachter, Diary, 26 February 1942; Pay, Diary, 24 December 1941; Nye, interview; Row, interview; Kauffman, "Nonn Interview," 28.
43. Himelrick, Diary, 24 December 1941; O'Guinn, "V.O.C.," 20; Hotchkiss, interview, October 22, 1982; Pistole, interview; Mettscher, reply; Stocks, interview; Camp, interview; Rogers, interview; Kinney and McCaffrey, *Wake Island Pilot*, 82–83; Kinney, "P.O.W. Survival," 25, 40; Marcello, "Venable Interview," 34.
44. Russell, Diary, 24 December 1941; Chapman, interview; Holewinski, interview, September 11, 1986; Eric Niderost, "Wake Island Survivor," *WWII History*, January 2006, 82.
45. Hamas, "Report," 8–9; R. Brown, interview; Camp, interview; Cunningham, *Hell Wouldn't Stop*, 124; J. Johnson, Diary, 24 December 1941.
46. Kinney and McCaffrey, *Wake Island Pilot*, 84.
47. Chapman, interview; Rumpel, "My Experience," 3.

CHAPTER 4

1. Russell, Diary, 25 December 1941; F. Miller, Diary, 25 December 1941.
2. J. Johnson, Diary, 25 December 1941; Durrwachter, Diary, 26 February 1942; Herbert Papock, Diary, 25 December 1941 (transcript in the author's possession, n.d.); Nye Interview; Russell, Diary, 25 December 1941; F. Miller, Diary, 25 December 1941; Wheeler, interview; McAmis, interview; Magnino, *Jim's Journey*, 72; O'Guinn, "V.O.C.," 20; Pay, Diary, 25 December 1941; Himelrick, Diary, 25 December 1941; T. Miller, "T. Johnson Interview, 29 May 1941," 21–22; Borne, interview; Herbert C. Freuler, Diary (photostat copy in the author's possession); Ralph J. Holewinski, "The Works of Dr. Shank on Wake Island During December 1941 thru May 1942," n.d., 1–2, B.5, F.4, Cunningham Collection; Huizenga, Kinney, McBrayer, and McAlister, "Escape Report No. 665: Kiangwan–Shanghai, 12 July 1945," 1; Smith, interview.
3. Abraham, *Do You Understand*, 19; Young, "WWII POW," 5.
4. Kibble, "My War," 97; Kelnhofer, interview; Kauffman, "Nonn Interview," 28; Chapman, interview; Abraham, *Do You Understand*, 20; Marcello, "Venable Interview," 37–38; Freuler, Diary, 25 December 1941; Kahn, interview; Holewinski, interview, June 20, 1980; Holewinski, "Dr. Shank," 2.
5. Russell, Diary, 25 December 1941; Kauffman, "Kidd Interview," 6; Kauffman, "Nonn Interview," 8; Nye, interview; Ozeki, "Wake Island in Sight"; Ozeki, "Dr. Shigeyoshi Ozeki's Second Account."
6. Himelrick, Diary, 25 December 1941; F. Miller, Diary, 25 December 1941; O'Guinn, "V.O.C.," 20–21; Kelnhofer, interview; Rogers, interview; Row, interview; Ozeki, "Wake Island in Sight"; Ozeki, "Dr. Shigeyoshi Ozeki's Second Account."
7. Russell, Diary, 25 December 1941; Reeves, interview; Nye, interview; Kauffman, "Goiceochea Interview," 13; Cox, interview; T. Miller, "T. Johnson Interview, 29 May 2001," 22; J. Johnson, reply, April 25, 1981.
8. Durrwachter, Diary, 26 February 1942; Himelrick, Diary, 26 December 1941–12 January 1942; Nye, interview; O'Guinn, "V.O.C.," 21; J. Johnson, replies, April 25, 1981, and May 9, 1981; *Washington Post*, October 14, 1945; Freuler, Diary, 25 December 1941; Skaggs, reply; William F. Kauffman, ed., "Interview With Ralph Pete Ingram," March 2000, 13–14, Aviator Pictures; F. Miller, Diary, 27–31 December 1941, and 1 and 3–10 January 1942; Russell, Diary, 26 and 29 December 1941.
9. Russell, Diary, 5, January 8, 1942; LaPorte, interview; Abraham, *Do You Understand*, 20.
10. Durrwachter, Diary, 26 February 1942; J. Johnson Reply, 25 April 1981; Rogers, interview; Stegmaier, interview; George G. Hubley, Affidavit, November 18, 1947, 2, File 67-75, Bk. (1–5), POWs on the *Nitta Maru*, RG 153.

11. Wiley W. Sloman, taped reply to author's questionnaire, June 24, 1986; Bill Sloan, *Given Up for Dead: America's Heroic Stand at Wake Island* (New York: Bantam Books, 2003), 1–4, 269–270, 273–274, 291–292, 321–325; Holewinski, interviews, June 20, 1980, and September 11, 1986; Holewinski, "Dr. Shank," 2–3.
12. Sturgeon, interview, October 13, 1984; Russell, Diary, 27 December 1941, and 8 January 1942; Kelnhofer, interview; Marcello, "Godbold Interview," 33; Marcello, "McDaniel Interview," 38; Wheeler, interview; R. Brown, interview; Kauffman, "Loveland Interview," 23; Papock, Diary, 26 December 1941; Himelrick, Diary, 26 December 1941–12 January 1942.
13. Ozeki, "Wake Island in Sight"; Ozeki, "Dr. Shigeyoshi Ozeki's Second Account."
14. Kauffman, "Myers Interview," 22.
15. Papock, Diary, 26 December 1941; Kelnhofer, interview; Russell, Diary, 29 December 1941; J. Johnson, reply, 25 April 1981; Howes, "Testimony," 7; Abraham, *Do You Understand*, 20; O'Guinn, "V.O.C.," 21, 23–24; Plate, reply; T. Miller, "T. Johnson Interview, 29 May 2001," 22; Magnino, *Jim's Journey*, 75.
16. Cunningham and Sims, *Wake Island Command*, 110; Kauffman, "Rogge Interview," 6–7, 15.
17. Russell, Diary, 28 and 30 December 1941, and 3 January 1942; Kauffman, "Myers Interview," 21; Kauffman, "Ludington Interview," 5: 6; Burton, *Life's Trails*, 70; Gross, interview, October 13, 1984.
18. O'Guinn, "V.O.C.," 21–23; Row, interview; Kauffman, "Nonn Interview," 28–29; Nye, interview; Howes, "Testimony," 7; Magnino, *Jim's Journey*, 74.
19. Marcello, "McDaniel Interview," 36; Rogers, interview; LaPorte, interview; Hubley, interview; Gregouire to author, March 1979; Hassig, interview; Otis T. Jones to Winfield Scott Cunningham, 9 August 1969, pts. 1–3, B.2, F.1, Cunningham Collection; Otis T. Jones to author, 15 September 1981.
20. McAmis, interview; Haidinger, interview; Cox, interview; J. Johnson, reply, May 9, 1981.
21. Russell, Diary, 5 January 1942; J. Johnson, reply, May 9, 1981; Rogers, interview; Himelrick, Diary, 26 December 1941–12 January 1942; O'Guinn, "V.O.C.," 21; Kelnhofer, interview; Abraham, *Do You Understand*, 20; Wheeler, interview; Howes, "Testimony," 7.
22. Durrwachter, Diary, 26 February 1942; Himelrick, Diary, 26 December 1941–12 January 1942.
23. Rogers, interview; Reeves, interview; Kelnhofer, interview; LaPorte, interview; Sturgeon, interview, October 13, 1984.
24. Himelrick, Diary, 26 December 1941–12 January 1942; Kauffman, "Ludington Interview," 5: 6; Kauffman, "Goicecochea Interview," 14; Kauffman, "Charters Interview," 5: 5.

25. Holmes to author, 3 and 27 December 1978; Skaggs, reply; Mettscher, reply; Hassig, interview; Russell, Diary, 26 December 1941.
26. Robert C. Maple, taped reply to author's questionnaire, April 24, 1984; Mettscher, reply; J. Johnson, replies, April 25 and May 9, 1981; LaPorte, interview; Camp, interview; Marcello, "Venable Interview," 38; Kibble, "My War,"99; Russell, Diary, 3 January 1942.
27. Nye, interview; Chapman, interview; O'Guinn, "V.O.C.," 25, 42; Jack Snipes, "Los Adventureros," 11 (unpublished manuscript in the author's possession, 1989); Daws, "Jaffe Interview," 11.
28. Russell, Diary, 31 December 1941, and 1 and 5 January 1942.
29. E. Davis, interview; Hotchkiss, interview, October 22, 1982; Kinney and McCaffrey, *Wake Island Pilot*, 85; Kinney, "P.O.W. Survival," 31–33.
30. Russell, Diary, 27 December 1941; Freuler, interview; Frank, "Devereux Transcript," 124; Cunningham, interview; Hanna, interview.
31. Cunningham and Sims, *Wake Island Command*, 111–112; Cunningham, "Narrative of Cruise," 4.
32. Devereux, *Story of Wake*, 207–208; Frank, "Devereux Transcript," 124; Kessler, *To Wake Island and Beyond*, 79–81.
33. Shores, interview; Hanna, interview; O'Guinn, "V.O.C.," 22–23; Tripp to author, 14 November 1979; Kauffman, "Goiceochia Interview," 13; Jones to Cunningham, 16 December 1967; Jones to Cunningham, 9 August 1969, pt. 4; Kauffman, "Loveland Interview," 22, 26.
34. Kauffman, "Nonn Interview," 29; Magnino, *Jim's Journey*, 75; Kauffman, "Goiceochia Interview," 13–14; Russell, Diary, 7 January 1942.
35. Holmes to author, 3 December 1978; CW04 Charles A. Holmes to Winfield Scott Cunningham, 12 October 1962, B.2, F.1, Cunningham Collection; Kelnhofer, interview; Russell, Diary, 5 January 1942; Marcello, "Venable Interview," 38; Stegmaier, interview.
36. Kinney, "P.O.W. Survival," 33–38; Kinney and McCaffrey, *Wake Island Pilot*, 85–88.
37. Russell, Diary, 9 January 1942.
38. J. Johnson Reply, 9 May 1981.
39. Commander of the Prisoner Escort, Navy of the Great Japanese Empire, "Regulations for Prisoners," January 11, 1942, File 67-75, Bk. 1 (1–2), POWs on the *Nitta Maru*, RG 153.
40. J. Johnson Reply, 9 May 1981.

CHAPTER 5

1. Kinney, "P.O.W. Survival," 38; Holmes to author, 3 December 1978; O'Guinn, "V.O.C.," 25; Snipes, "Adventureros," 11; Kauffman, "Nonn Interview," 34.

2. O'Guinn, "V.O.C.," 25; Kauffman, "Ludington Interview," 5: 8–9; *Washington Times-Herald*, July 21, 1945.
3. Stegmaier, interview; Wheeler, interview; R. Brown, interview.
4. Russell, Diary, 11 January 1942; Hubley, interview; Kelnhofer, interview; Holmes to author, 3 December 1978; Kauffman, "Ludington Interview," 5: 7–8; Abraham, *Do You Understand*, 20; O'Guinn, "V.O.C.," 24–25; Kauffman, "Kidd Interview," 21.
5. Russell, Diary, 12 January 1942; F. Miller, Diary, 12 January 1942; O'Guinn, "V.O.C.," 25; Kauffman, "Ingram Interview," 14; Pay, Diary, 12 January 1942; Camp, interview.
6. Holewinski, interviews, June 20, 1980, and September 11, 1986; Holewinski, "Dr. Shank," 3; Fukashi Sakurai, Testimony, January 6, 1948, "Record of Trial of Usaji Hida et 4 by Military Commission Appointed by the Commanding General, Headquarters Eighth Army, Tried at Yokohama, Japan, 19 December 1947–2 February 1948," RG 153 (hereinafter "Hida et 4"); Tsumori Misaka, Reinterrogation, September 8, 1947, Prosecution Exhibit No. 1, "Hida et 4"; Russell, Diary, 12 January 1942.
7. Kinney and McCaffrey, *Wake Island Pilot*, 89; Bernard E. Richardson, "The Voice of the Cornet," 8–9 (unpublished manuscript in the author's possession, n.d.); Kauffman, "Ingram Interview," 14; Kauffman, "Goiceochea Interview," 14–15; Clifford E. Hotchkiss, interview by author, October 13, 1984; "Wake Island Personnel, 12 September 1945," 6, 10, 11, 13, Papers Relating to the Defense of Wake Island, Box 12, File 1L—Wake Island Personnel, MCHA; Freuler, Diary, 25 January 1942; James B. Darden III, *Guests of the Emperor: The Story of Dick Darden* (Clinton, NC: Greenhouse Press, 1990), 172, 177.
8. First Lieutenant Henry T. Omachi, AUS, "Additional Information Pertaining to Name-List of POWs Captured on Wake Island and Transferred to Shanghai POW Camp," November 24, 1947, Prosecution Exhibit No. 20; Nishiki Juta, Testimony, December 29 1947, "Hida et 4"; Tamotsu Takezoe, Confession, December 11, 1946, Prosecution Exhibit No. 32, "Hida et 4"; Sakurai, Testimony, "Hida et 4"; Toshio Jinno, Testimony, January 7, 1948, "Hida et 4"; Hansgeorg Jentschura, Dieter Jung, and Peter Mickel, *Warships of the Imperial Japanese Navy, 1869–1945* (Annapolis: Naval Institute Press, 1982), 58–59; Kinney and McCaffrey, *Wake Island Pilot*, 93; Legal Section Informational Summary No. 168, General Headquarters, Supreme Commander for the Allied Powers, Legal Section, December 22, 1947, B.3, F.6, Cunningham Collection.
9. Narakazu Yonetani, Testimony, January 12, 1948; Prosecution Opening Statement, January 23, 1947; Jinno, Testimony, January 7, 1948; Misaka, Reinterrogation; Yoshiharu Takahasi, Testimony, January 5, 1948; Mori Mitsuzo,

Testimony, December 30, 1947; Tokuichi Takamura, Confession, June 30, 1947, Prosecution Exhibit, No. 24; Tamotsu Takezoe, Confession, December 11, 1946, Prosecution Exhibit, No. 32; Asaichi Yoshimura, Confession, December 2, 1947, Prosecution Exhibit No. 34, all in "Hida et 4"; Legal Section Informational Summary No. 168; Cunningham, "Narrative of Cruise," 1; Abraham, *Do You Understand*, 42; Kauffman, "Nonn Interview," 36.

10. Misaka, Reinterrogation, "Hida et 4"; Toshio Jinno, Testimony, January 8, 1948, "Hida et 4"; Nishiki Juta, Testimony, December 30, 1947, "Hida et 4"; Ritaro Koga Interrogation, October 29, 1946, Prosecution Exhibit No. 4, "Hida et 4"; Statement of Usaji Hida, n.d., Defense Exhibit B, "Hida et 4"; Statement of Asaichi Yoshimura, n.d., Defense Exhibit C, "Hida et 4."

11. O'Guinn, "V.O.C.," 25; Kinney and McCaffrey, *Wake Island Pilot*, 90; Plate, reply; LaPorte, interview; Pay, Diary, 12 January 1942; Papock, Diary, 12 January 1942; Holmes to author, 3 December 1978; Takamura, Confession, June 30, 1947, "Hida et 4."

12. Sturgeon, interview, October 13, 1984; Edward V. Sturgeon, interview by author, October 13–14, 1984; Stegmaier, interview; Richardson, "Voice," 2; Burton, *Life's Trails*, 70; Marcello, "Venable Interview," 39–40; Kauffman, "Charters Interview," 5: 8.

13. Takezoe, Confession, "Hida et 4"; Plate, reply; Nye, interview; Magnino, *Jim's Journey*, 83; Mettscher, reply; Chapman, interview; Cox, interview; Wheeler, interview; Camp, interview; Gross, interview, October 13, 1984; Rogers, interview; Borne, interview; Kauffman, "Nonn Interview," 35; Burton, *Life's Trails*, 70.

14. Nye, interview; Stegmaier, interview.

15. J. Johnson, reply, May 9, 1981; Borne, interview.

16. Sturgeon, interview, October 13, 1984; Kelnhofer, interview; Hassig, interview; E. Davis, interview; Reeves, interview; Papock, Diary, 12 January 1942; Bernard O. Ketner, "In the Matter of the . . . Mistreatment of Prisoners of War Aboard the POW Ship *Nitta Maru* by Captain Saito, His Cohorts, and Other Unidentified Japanese Guards . . . Between 12 January and 24 January 1942," January 29, 1947, 3, File 67-75, Bk. 1 (1–2), POWs on the *Nitta Maru*, RG 153; Chapman, interview; O'Guinn, "V.O.C.," 27; Magnino, *Jim's Journey*, 83; Holmes to author, 3 December 1978.

17. Marcello, "McDaniel Interview," 39; LaPorte, interview; Borne, interview; Hubley, interview; J. Johnson, reply, May 9, 1981; Conner, interview; Rogers, interview; Nye, interview; Robert McCulloch Brown, "In the Matter of the Mistreatment of American Prisoners of War Aboard the TSS *Nitta Maru* . . . 12 January 1942 to 24 January 1942," March 18, 1947, 2, File 67-75, Bk. 1 (1–2), POWs on the *Nitta Maru*, RG 153; Eugene Weslie Shugart, "In the Matter of the Mistreatment of Allied Prisoners of War Aboard the S.S.

NITTA MARU ... ," July 9, 1947, 1–2, File 67-75, Bk. 1 (1–2), POWs on the *Nitta Maru*, RG 153.

18. Sturgeon, interview, October 13, 1984; Misaka, Reinterrogation, "Hida et 4"; Mettscher, reply; Thaire to author, September 1981; Kelnhofer, interview; Wheeler, interview; Bowsher, interview; Holmes to author, 3 December 1978.

19. Cunningham, "Narrative of Cruise," 2; Kauffman, "Rogge Interview," 15; Malleck to author, 16 April 1981; Kinney and McCaffrey, *Wake Island Pilot*, 90; Devereux, *Story of Wake*, 212–214; Wesley M. Platt, "In the Matter of Atrocities ... Committed Aboard the POW Ship *Nitta Maru*," February 13, 1947, 2, File 67-75, Bk. 1 (1–2), POWs on the *Nitta Maru*, RG 153; MIS-X Section, CPM Branch, "Ex Reports 665–668 (CHINA)," Appendix E, July 12, 1945, 1, Escape Reports, 654–671, RG 389; Malleck to author, 16 April 1981; Woodrow M. Kessler to author, 4 November 1989; Kessler, *To Wake Island and Beyond*, 83.

20. Cunningham, "Narrative of Cruise," 3; Kauffman, "Rogge Interview," 15; Marcello, "Godbold Interview," 34; Platt, "Atrocities Aboard *Nitta Maru*," 2; Devereux, *Story of Wake*, 213–214; MIS-X Section, CPM Branch, "Ex Reports 665–668 (CHINA)," Appendix E, 1; Freuler, Diary, 12 January 1942; Malleck to author, 16 April 1981; Kauffman, "Rogge Interview," 15–16.

21. Misaka, Reinterrogation, "Hida et 4"; Takezoe, Confession, "Hida et 4"; Nishiki Juta, Testimony, December 29, 1947, "Hida et 4"; Pay, Diary, 12 January 1942; Kauffman, "Nonn Interview," 25; O'Guinn, "V.O.C.," 28; Magnino, *Jim's Journey*, 84; Kauffman, "Loveland Interview," 26; S. L. Baker, "In the Matter of the Transportation Under Improper Conditions ... From Wake Island to Woosung, China, in January 1942," December 29, 1945, 2, File 67-75, Bk. 1 (1–2), POWs on the *Nitta Maru*, RG 153.

22. Hubley, interview; Pistole, interview; Plate, reply; Nye, interview; Conner, interview; Marcello, "Venable Interview," 41; William J. Hamilton, "In the Matter of the Improper Transfer of Prisoners of War ... on the Japanese Ship *Nitta Maru*, ... 12 to 17 January 1942," October 31, 1945, 2; R. Brown, "Mistreatment Aboard *Nitta Maru*," 2; Benjamin F. Comstock Jr., "In the Matter of the Improper Transportation of ... Prisoners of War Aboard the *Nitta Maru* ... From 12 January 1942 to 24 January 1942," December 26, 1945, 2; Baker, "Transportation Under Improper Conditions," 2; Raymond R. Rutledge, "In the Matter of the Mistreatment of American Prisoners of War ... at Wake Island and During Transfer by Steamer From Wake Island to Woo Sung, China Between 27 December 1941 and 24 January 1942 ... ," September 13, 1945, 2–3, all in File 67-75, Bk. 1 (1–2), POWs on the *Nitta Maru*, RG 153; Rumpel, "My Experience," 3; Kauffman, "Ludington Interview," 5:10.

23. Durrwachter, Diary, 27 February 1942; Pay, Diary, 12 January 1942; Malleck to author, 16 April 1981; Richardson, "Voice," 6; Rogers, interview; Kauffman, "Nonn Interview," 35; Skaggs, reply; Charles A. Holmes to author, 19 August 1983; R. Brown, "Mistreatment Aboard *Nitta Maru*," 2; O'Guinn, "V.O.C.," 32.
24. Camp, interview; R. Brown, "Mistreatment Aboard *Nitta Maru*," 2–3; Stegmaier, interview; Mettscher, reply; O'Guinn, "V.O.C., 31; Abraham, *Do You Understand*, 24; Magnino, *Jim's Journey*, 84, 87.
25. Reynold Carr, "Tales of Woe," n.d., B.5, F.2, Cunningham Collection; Rumpel, "My Experience," 4; Holmes to author, 3 December 1978; Himelrick, Diary, 12 January 1942; Ketner, "Mistreatment Aboard *Nitta Maru*," 2; Shugart, "Mistreatment Aboard *Nitta Maru*," 1–2; Borne, interview; Rutledge, "Mistreatment of Prisoners," 3; Young "WWII POW," 6; Wheeler, interview; Hamilton, "Improper Transfer on *Nitta Maru*," 2; Skaggs, reply; Reeves, interview; LaPorte, interview; R. Brown, "Mistreatment Aboard *Nitta Maru*," 2; Richardson, "Voice," 7; Baker, "Transportation Under Improper Conditions," 3.
26. Misaka, Reinterrogation, "Hida et 4"; Durrwachter, Diary, 27 February 1942; Rumpel, "My Experience," 4; Papock, Diary, 17 January 1942; Baker, "Transportation Under Improper Conditions," 3.
27. Malleck to author, 16 April 1981; McAmis, interview; Young, "WWII POW," 6; Stegmaier, interview; Gross, interview, October 13, 1984; Nye, interview; Magnino, *Jim's Journey*, 88; Kinney, "P.O.W. Survival," 43.
28. "Regulations for Prisoners"; Marcello, "McDaniel Interview," 40; Kauffman, "Goiceochea Interview," 15; Magnino, *Jim's Journey*, 87; R. Brown, "Mistreatment Aboard *Nitta Maru*," 2; Baker, "Transportation Under Improper Conditions," 2–3; Rutledge, "Mistreatment of Prisoners," 1; Nye, interview; Holmes to author, 3 December 1978; Chapman, interview; Rogers, interview; LaPorte, interview; Abraham, *Do You Understand*, 27, 28; Kauffman, "Loveland Interview," 26; Gregouire to author, March 1979; Kibble, "My War," 105–106.
29. Cox, interview; Kauffman, "Ludington Interview," 5: 10; Rogers, interview; McAmis, interview; Hubley, interview; Borne, interview; Magnino, *Jim's Journey*, 87; Kauffman, "Goiceochea Interview," 15; Hubley, Affidavit, 3, File 67-75, Bk. 2 (1–5), POWs on the *Nitta Maru*, RG 153; Vincent H. Verga, Affidavit, March 5, 1948, 1–2, File 67-75, Bk. 2 (1–5), POWs on the *Nitta Maru*, RG 153; Plate Reply; Thomas H. Miller, ed., "An Interview With Thomas W. Johnson at His Home in Saint Joseph, Missouri, 1 June 2001," 1, Missouri Oral History Program; Gross, interview, 13 October 1984.
30. Rogers, interview; Broyles, reply; Young, "WWII POW," 6; Kibble, "My War," 112; Mettscher, reply; R. Brown, "Mistreatment Aboard *Nitta Maru*,"

2–3; Thaire to author, September 1981; Stegmaier, interview; Shores, interview; R. Brown, interview; Hubley, interview; Nye, interview; Williams, interview.
31. Rogers, interview; Baker, "Transportation Under Improper Conditions," 3; Richardson, "Voice," 7.
32. Cunningham and Sims, *Wake Island Command*, 114; Cunningham, "Narrative of Cruise," 3, 6; Platt, "Atrocities Aboard *Nitta Maru*," 2; Kinney and McCaffrey, *Wake Island Pilot*, 92.
33. Cunningham, "Narrative of Cruise," 5; Kessler, *To Wake Island and Beyond*, 84; Kinney and McCaffrey, *Wake Island Pilot*, 92.
34. William D. Beck, "In the Matter of the Mistreatment of American Prisoners of War Aboard the *Nitta Maru* . . . From 12 January 1942 to 24 January 1942," May 13, 1946, 2, File 67-75, Bk. 1 (1–2), POWS on the *Nitta Maru*, RG 153; O'Guinn, "V.O.C.," 28–30; Chapman, interview; Kibble, "My War," 105; Thaire to author, September 1981; R. Brown, "Mistreatment Aboard *Nitta Maru*," 2; E. Davis, interview; J. Cook, interview; Smith, interview; Marcello, "Field Interview," 12; Richardson, "Voice," 7.
35. Chapman, interview; Holmes to author, 27 December 1978; Nye, interview; Magnino, *Jim's Journey*, 85–86; Ketner, "Mistreatment Aboard *Nitta Maru*," 2; J. Johnson, reply, May 9, 1981; Frank H. Houseschildt, "In the Matter of Atrocities Committed Aboard the POW Ship *NITTA MARU* and at Hakodate POW Camp No. 2, Akariba, Japan," January 9, 1948, 2, File 67-75, Bk. 2 (1–5), POWs on the *Nitta Maru*, RG 153; Herman A. Todd, Affidavit, October 8, 1945, File 67-75, Bk. 1 (1–2), POWs on the *Nitta Maru*, RG 153; Cassius E. Smith, Affidavit, October 8, 1945, 1, File 67-75, Bk. 1 (1–2), POWs on the *Nitta Maru*, RG 153.
36. Thomas J. Andrews, "In the Matter of Atrocities Committed Aboard the Japanese Ship *NITTA MARU*, Between 23 December 1941 and 24 January 1942," April 27, 1946, 1, File 67-75, Bk. 1 (1–2), POWs on the *Nitta Maru*, RG 153; Beck, "Mistreatment Aboard *Nitta Maru*," 1; J. Johnson, reply, May 9, 1981; Richardson, "Voice," 8–9.
37. Richardson, "Voice," 8; Shores, interview; John F. Blandy, Affidavit, September 23, 1947, 1, File 67-75, Bk. 1 (1–2), POWs on the *Nitta Maru*, RG 153.
38. Shores, interview; Richardson, "Voice," 8; Rutledge, "Mistreatment of Prisoners," 3; Smith, interview; Dave Rush, "In the Matter of Atrocities Committed at Prisoner of War Camp Hakodate No. 2, Akariba Japan and Aboard Prisoner of War Ship *NITTA MARU*," March 13, 1947, 1–2, POWs on the *Nitta Maru*, RG 153; Platt, "Atrocities Aboard *Nitta Maru*," 2.
39. Platt, "Atrocities Aboard *Nitta Maru*," 1–2; Clarence B. McKinstry, Affidavit, n.d., 1, File 67-75, Bk. 1 (1–2), POWs on the *Nitta Maru*, RG 153; Kahn, interview.

40. Kauffman, "Loveland Interview," 26; Richardson, "Voice," 9; Borne, interview; Earl M. Broyles, "In the Matter of Mistreatment of American Prisoners Aboard the Japanese Vessel '*NITTA MARU*' Enroute From Wake Island to Shanghai," October 10, 1947, 2, File 67-75, Bk. 2 (1–5), POWs on the *Nitta Maru*, RG 153; McDonald, Affidavit, 2–3; Houseschildt, "Atrocities Aboard *Nitta Maru*," 1, 3; Rogers, interview; LaPorte, interview; Himelrick, Diary, 12 January 1942; R. Brown, "Mistreatment Aboard *Nitta Maru*," 2–3; Nye, interview; Ketner, "Mistreatment Aboard *Nitta Maru*," 2–3; Blandy, Affidavit, 1; Papock, Diary, 12 January 1942; Marcello, "Venable Interview," 41.
41. Takamura, Confession, 2, "Hida et 4"; Asaichi Yoshimura, Confession, December 2, 1947, Prosecution Exhibit No. 34, "Hida et 4"; Yasuo Kohara, Confession, November 19, 1946, Prosecution Exhibit No. 27, "Hida et 4"; Cunningham, "Narrative of Cruise," 5; Cunningham and Sims, *Wake Island Command*, 116; *Washington Daily News*, November 15, 1945; Kinney and McCaffrey, *Wake Island Pilot*, 91; McDonald, Affidavit, 2; Winford J. McAnally, "In the Matter of Mistreatment of Joseph TERFANSKY, Private First Class, and Evan RICHTER, Private First Class, . . . Aboard . . . *NITTA MARU* During January 1942, and Other Incidents . . . ," January 8, 1948, 4, File 67-75, Bk. 2 (1–5), POWs on the *Nitta Maru*, RG 153; Statement of Toshio Saito, October 4, 1946, File 67-75, Bk. 2 (1–5), POWs on the *Nitta Maru*, RG 153.
42. Hubley, Affidavit, 3; Misaka, Reinterrogation, 3, "Hida et 4."
43. Carr, "Tales of Woe"; Chapman, interview; J. Johnson, reply, May 9, 1981.
44. Statement of Glenn E. Tripp, October 31, 1947, 1, Prosecution Exhibit No. 6, "Hida et 4"; Misaka, Reinterrogation, 2, 3, "Hida et 4"; Kauffman, "Rogge Interview," 16.
45. Freuler, Diary, 17 January 1942; Papock, Diary, 17 January 1942; Himelrick, Diary, 12 January 1942; Cunningham and Sims, *Wake Island Command*, 188; Mettscher, reply; Gregouire to author, March 1979.
46. Cunningham, "Narrative of Cruise," 6; Cunningham and Sims, *Wake Island Command*, 118; Hanna, interview; Marcello, "Godbold Interview," 37; Kahn, interview; King, interview; Broyles, reply; Winfield S. Cunningham, Affidavit, November 10, 1947, 6, B.3, F.6, Cunningham Collection; "War-Weary American Prisoners Find Peace Once Again on the Shores of Dai Nippon," *Freedom*, Third Impress, 1942, 37.
47. Broyles, reply; King, interview; Malleck to author, 16 April 1981.
48. "Prisoners Find Peace," 37; Kibble, "My War," 106; Rumpel, "My Experience," 4; Borne, interview; E. Davis, interview; Magnino, *Jim's Journey*, 88; Plate, reply; Malleck to author, 16 April 1981; Kessler, *To Wake Island and Beyond*, 84–85.

49. Cunningham and Sims, *Wake Island Command*, 119; Devereux, *Story of Wake*, 215; Freuler, Diary, 17 January 1942; "Wake Personnel," September 12, 1945, 6, 10, 12, 13; Rogers, interview; Hubley, interview; Freuler, interview.
50. J. Johnson, Diary, 20–24 January 1942; Pay, Diary, 12 January 1942.

CHAPTER 6

1. Jinno, Testimony, January 7, 1948, "Hida et 4"; Takahashi, Testimony, "Hida et 4."
2. Jinno, Testimony, January 7, 1948, "Hida et 4"; Prosecution Opening Statement, December 23, 1947, "Hida et 4"; "Wake Personnel, 12 September 1945," 10, 12.
3. Yoshimura, Confession, "Hida et 4"; Yoshimura, Statement, "Hida et 4"; Misaka, Reinterrogation, "Hida et 4"; Shoze Imamura, Testimony, December 29, 1947, "Hida et 4."
4. Yoshimura, Confession, "Hida et 4"; Jinno, Testimony, January 7, 1948, "Hida et 4"; Tripp, Statement, "Hida et 4"; E. Davis, interview; Kauffman, "Nonn Interview," 36.
5. Yonetani, Testimony, "Hida et 4"; Takahashi, Testimony, "Hida et 4"; Juta, Testimony, "Hida et 4"; Sakurai, Testimony; Takezoe, Confession, "Hida et 4"; Misaka, Reinterrogation, "Hida et 4"; Jinno, Testimony, January 7–8, 1948, "Hida et 4."
6. Takahashi, Testimony, "Hida et 4"; Jinno, Testimony, January 7–8, 1948, "Hida et 4"; Inamori, Testimony, "Hida et 4"; Misaka, Reinterrogation, "Hida et 4."
7. Yoshimura, Confession, "Hida et 4"; Takezoe, Confession, "Hida et 4"; Takahashi, Testimony, "Hida et 4"; Inamori, Testimony, "Hida et 4"; Koga, Interrogation, "Hida et 4"; Imamura, Testimony, "Hida et 4."
8. Jinno, Testimony, January 8, 1948, "Hida et 4"; Takezoe, Confession, "Hida et 4"; Sakurai, Testimony, "Hida et 4"; Inamori, Testimony, "Hida et 4"; Tokuichi Takamura, Confession, July 3, 1947, Prosecution Exhibit No. 25, "Hida et 4."
9. Kohara, Confession, "Hida et 4"; Inamori, Testimony, "Hida et 4"; Jinno, Testimony, January 8, 1948, "Hida et 4"; Takezoe, Confession, "Hida et 4"; Sakurai, Testimony, "Hida et 4"; Yonetani, Testimony, "Hida et 4"; Misaka, Reinterrogation, "Hida et 4"; Takahashi, Testimony, "Hida et 4"; Usaji Hida, Confession, July 9, 1947, Prosecution Exhibit No. 36, "Hida et 4."
10. Yonetani, Testimony, "Hida et 4"; Jinno, Testimony, January 8, 1948, "Hida et 4"; Takezoe, Confession, "Hida et 4."
11. Toshio Jinno, Testimony, January 9, 1948, "Hida et 4"; Yonetani, Testimony, "Hida et 4"; Takezoe, Confession, "Hida et 4"; Tamotsu Takezoe, Testimony, January 16, 1948, "Hida et 4"; Misaka, Reinterrogation, "Hida et 4."

12. Freuler, Diary, 17 January 1942; Kinney and McCaffrey, *Wake Island Pilot*, 99; Cunningham and Sims, *Wake Island Command*, 121; Tripp, Statement, "Hida et 4"; Jinno, Testimony, January 8, 1948, "Hida et 4."
13. Lt. Col. Richard E. Rudesill, USA, Testimony, December 23, 1947, "Hida et 4"; Alva C. Carpenter to Capt. John Hamas, USMC (Ret.), 3 February 1948, B.3, F.6, Cunningham Collection; Capt. Winfred Hearn, USN, to Rear Adm. W. S. Cunningham, USN (Ret.), 9 July 1958, B.3, F.6, Cunningham Collection; *Washington Daily News*, November 15, 1945.
14. Cunningham, "Narrative of Cruise," 1; Himelrick, Diary, 12 January 1942; "Shanghai," *Fortune*, January 1935, 30–40; Ernest G. Heppner, *Shanghai Refuge: A Memoir of the World War II Jewish Ghetto* (Lincoln: University of Nebraska Press, 1995), 37–39; Beatrice G. Coyle to Col. John P. Welsh, USA (ret.), 6 December 1943, B.1, F.1, Devereux Collection; *Washington Post*, October 14, 1945; Kinney and McCaffrey, *Wake Island Pilot*, 95.
15. Peter Oldham, *Lieutenant Stephen Polkinghorn, D.S.C., R.N.R.* (Auckland: New Zealand Military Historical Society Inc., 1984), 4, 12; David H. Grover, "Naval Battle off Shanghai," *Pacific War*, November/December 2004, 19; "Wake Personnel, 12 September 1945," 14. See also Gregory Haines, *Gunboats on the Great River: A History of the Royal Navy on the Yangtse* (London: MacDonald and Jane's, 1976).
16. Grover, "Naval Battle," 19–20; Layton, *And I Was There*, 360; Quentin Reynolds, *Officially Dead: The Story of Commander C. D. Smith* (New York: Random House, 1945), 3–7, 27; Devereux, *Story of Wake*, 216.
17. Oldham, *Lieutenant Stephen Polkinghorn*, 4–7; Grover, "Naval Battle," 19–21; Reynolds, *Officially Dead*, 8–9.
18. Oldham, *Lieutenant Stephen Polkinghorn*, 6, 8–9; Grover, "Naval Battle," 21; Reynolds, *Officially Dead*, 34; J. Johnson, Diary, 24 January 1941.
19. White, *United States Marines*, 29; Magnino, *Jim's Journey*, 90–91; Oldham, *Lieutenant Stephen Polkinghorn*, 12; Pay, Diary, 12 [sic] January 1942; Kelnhofer, interview; Papock, Diary, 24 January 1942; Cunningham, "Narrative of Cruise," 4; O'Guinn, "V.O.C.," 36; Kessler, *To Wake Island and Beyond*, 86–87; Kibble, "My War," 114; Tripp, Statement, "Hida et 4."
20. Richardson, "Voice," 9–10; J. Johnson, reply, May 9, 1981; Papock, Diary, 24 January 1942; Nye, interview; T. Miller, "T. Johnson Interview, 29 May 2001," 24; Hassig, interview; Mettscher, reply; Plate, reply; Wheeler, interview; Williams, interview; Burton, *Life's Trails*, 73; O'Guinn, "V.O.C.," 36; Holmes to author, 3 December 1978; Stocks, interview; Thaire to author, September 1981.
21. Holmes to author, 3 December 1978; Kelnhofer, interview; Richardson, "Voice," 9–10; Skaggs, reply.

22. Richardson, "Voice," 9; J. Johnson, reply, May 9, 1981; Oldham, *Lieutenant Stephen Polkinghorn*, 12; Burton, *Life's Trails*, 73; Papock, Diary, 24 January 1942.
23. Richardson, "Voice," 10.
24. Papock, Diary, 24 January 1942; Skaggs, reply; Durrwachter, Diary, 27 February 1942; Snipes, "Adventureros," 11; Williams, interview; Nye, interview; King, interview; Marcello, "Fields Interview," 14; Bernard E. Richardson, "Front Man on a Yaho Pole," 1 (unpublished manuscript in the author's possession, January 21, 1947).
25. Magnino, *Jim's Journey*, 92; Kauffman, "Ludington Interview," 5: 10; Kauffman, "Loveland Interview," 26; Rumpel, "My Experience," 4; Kauffman, "Charters Interview," 5: 10–11; Papock, Diary, 24 January 1942; Williams, interview; Hubley, interview; Holmes to author, 3 December 1978; Abraham, *Do You Understand*, 31.
26. Abraham, *Do You Understand*, 31; Kauffman, "Charters Interview," 5: 10–11; Magnino, *Jim's Journey*, 90; Baker, "Transportation Under Improper Conditions," 3; Kauffman, "Goiceochea Interview," 17; Kauffman, "Gooding Interview," 15; Ramon Menique, Affidavit, 20 February 1947, 2, File 67-75, Bk. 1 (1–2), POWs on the *Nitta Maru*, RG 153.
27. Marcello, "McDaniel Interview," 41–42; Borne, interview; Sturgeon, interview, October 13–14, 1984; Richardson, "Voice," 10; Kelnhofer, interview; Richardson, reply.
28. Marcello, "Venable Interview," 45; Mettscher, reply; Richardson, "Voice," 11; Himelrick, "Diary." 12 [*sic*] January 1942; Bernard E. Richardson, "The Bread of Idleness," 2 (unpublished manuscript in the author's possession, March 10, 1947); Kibble, "My War," 116; John F. Kinney, Affidavit, August 2, 1945, 2, File 101-59, Box 1584, Japanese War Crimes at Woosung, RG 153; Abraham, *Do You Understand*, 31; Kessler, *To Wake Island and Beyond*, 87; Marcello, "Godbold Interview," 39; Kelnhofer, interview.
29. "SHANGHAI WAR-PRISONERS CAMP: Directions for the Daily Life of the War-Prisoners," 1–4 (photostat copy in the author's possession, ca. 24 January 1942); Kinney, Affidavit, 2; Menique, Affidavit, 2; J. Johnson, reply, May 9, 1981; Cox, interview; Magnino, *Jim's Journey*, 95; Durrwachter, Diary, 27 February 1942; Skaggs, reply; Rumpel, "My Experience," 4; Nye, interview.
30. Oldham, *Lieutenant Stephen Polkinghorn*, 12; Marcello, "Venable Interview," 45, 59; Richardson, reply; Richardson, "Voice," 12; O'Guinn, "V.O.C.," 37, 50; Kelnhofer, interview; Nye, interview; Tice, interview; Skaggs, reply; J. Johnson, reply, May 9, 1981; Menique, Affidavit, 2.
31. LaPorte, interview; O'Guinn, "V.O.C.," 43; King, interview; Richardson, reply; Smith, interview.

32. Mettscher, reply; Nye, interview; Magnino, *Jim's Journey*, 95; Kinney, "P.O.W. Survival," 51; Cunningham and Sims, *Wake Island Command*, 128; Holmes to author, 3 December 1978; Stocks, interview; Hotchkiss, interview, October 22, 1982; Kibble, "My War," 117; Burton, *Life's Trails*, 75; Young, "WWII POW," 6.
33. Mettscher, reply; Holmes to author, 3 December 1978.
34. Capt. James L. Norwood, USA, and Capt. Emily L. Shek, USA, "Prisoner of War Camps in Areas Other Than the Four Principal Islands of Japan," July 31, 1946, 27, RG 389; Roy M. Stanley, *Prelude to Pearl Harbor: War in China, 1937–41; Japan's Rehearsal for World War II* (New York: Charles Scribner's Sons, 1982), 102; Kinney, "P.O.W. Survival," 52; Plate, reply; Hotchkiss, interview, October 22, 1982; Magnino, *Jim's Journey*, 93–94; O'Guinn, "V.O.C.," 37; Snipes, "Adventureros," 11; Kauffman, "Goiceochea Interview," 17; Marcello, "Fields Interview," 13; White, *United States Marines*, 34–36; Kinney, Affidavit, 2; Hubley, interview.
35. Norwood and Shek, "POW Camps," 28; Floyd H. Comfort, "In the Matter of Improper . . . Care . . . of American Prisoners of War at Woo Sung and Kang Won . . . 1942 to 1945," December 14, 1945, 2, File 101-150, Box 1584, Japanese War Crimes at Woosung, RG 153; Herman Davis, "In the Matter of the Imprisonment Under Improper Conditions . . . at Shanghai War Prisoners Camp, Woosung, China, From on or About 3 February 1942 to 4 December 1942," June 11, 1946, 2, File 101-150, Box 1584, Japanese War Crimes at Woosung, RG 153; Richard M. Huizenga, Affidavit, August 14, 1945, File 101-150, Box 1584, Japanese War Crimes at Woosung, RG 153; Kelnhofer, interview; Mettscher, reply; Kibble, "My War," 118; Hubley, interview; Papock, Diary, 24 January 1942; Marcello, "Godbold Interview," 39; Magnino, *Jim's Journey*, 95; O'Guinn, "V.O.C.," 38; Stocks, interview; Pay, Diary, 13 February 1942.
36. Norwood and Shek, "POW Camps," 28; H. Davis, "Improper Conditions at Woosung," 2; Mettscher, reply; Marcello, "Fields Interview," 13; Abraham, *Do You Understand*, 32–33; Kessler, *To Wake Island and Beyond*, 87–88; Henningsen, "Shanghai Prisoners," 1, 2; Hotchkiss, interviews, October 22, 1982, and October 21, 1983; Shores, interview; Kibble, "My War," 118; Stocks, interview; Plate, reply; Ashurst, "Record," 5; White, *United States Marines*, 31; Kinney, Affidavit, 3; Marcello, "Godbold Interview," 39; Oldham, *Lieutenant Stephen Polkinghorn*, 12.
37. O'Guinn, "V.O.C.," 36, 41; Abraham, *Do You Understand*, 41; Holmes to author, 3 December 1978; Burton, *Life's Trails*, 72; James D. McBrayer Jr., Affidavit, September 18, 1945, 2, File 101-156, Box 1584, Miscellaneous Reports on Atrocities in the Shanghai Camps, RG 153; Roger Dick Bamford, "In the Matter of the Failure of the Japanese to Furnish Proper . . . Care

to American Prisoners of War at Woosung, China, Between 1 February 1942 and March 1943," February 15, 1946, 2, File 101-150, Box 1584, Japanese War Crimes at Woosung, RG 153.
38. White, *United States Marines*, 34; Holmes to author, 21 January 1979; O'Guinn, "V.O.C.," 42; Richardson, reply; Kessler, *To Wake Island and Beyond*, 109; Richardson, "Voice," 17; Abraham, *Do You Understand*, 54.
39. McBrayer, Affidavit, 2; Kessler, *To Wake Island and Beyond*, 109; Kinney and McCaffrey, *Wake Island Pilot*, 104; Kibble, "My War," 118.
40. White, *United States Marines*, 34; Richardson, "Voice," 17; Abraham, *Do You Understand*, 54; Young, "WWII Japanese POW," 9; Gross, interview, October 13, 1984; Holmes to author, 21 January 1979; Hoskins, "Memoir," 21; John E. Pearsall, "Diary of My Last Year 1942–43 A United States Marine," 10 November 1942, John E. Pearsall, WWII, POW Diary & Notes, Personal Papers, MCHA; Kibble, "My War," 134; Tice, interview.
41. Holmes to author, 3 December 1978; Sturgeon, interview, October 13, 1984; Huizenga, Affidavit, 5; White, *United States Marines*, 34; Haidinger, interview.
42. Holmes to author, 3 December 1978; Magnino, *Jim's Journey*, 94–95; White, *United States Marines*, 52; Kinney, "POW Survival," 51; O'Guinn, "V.O.C.," 41–42.
43. Stegmaier, interview; Pay, Diary, 12 [sic] January 1942; Papock, Diary, 24 January 1942; Menique, Affidavit, 2; Richardson, "Voice," 12; Plate, reply; Durrwachter, Diary, 27 February 1942; Reeves, interview; Kelnhofer, interview; Rumpel, "My Experience," 4; Holmes to author, 3 December 1978; Hubley, interview; T. Miller, "T. Johnson Interview, 1 June 2001," 5; Kauffman, "Ludington Interview," 5: 11.
44. Marcello, "Fields Interview," 13; Huizenga, Affidavit, 2; Kinney and McCaffrey, *Wake Island Pilot*, 96; Magnino, *Jim's Journey*, 96.
45. Papock, Diary, 24 January 1942; Pay, Diary, 12 [sic] January 1942; Menique, Affidavit, 2; Richardson, "Voice," 14; Cox, interview; T. Miller, "T. Johnson Interview, 1 June 2001," 5; Magnino, *Jim's Journey*, 95; Kauffman, "Charters Interview," 5: 11; Kauffman, "Ludington Interview," 5: 11; Stegmaier, interview; Kibble, "My War," 128.
46. Young, "WWII POW," 6; Chapman, interview; Richardson, reply; Kauffman, "Goiceochea, interview," 17; Mettscher, reply; Shores, interview; Stegmaier, interview; Reeves, interview; Hassig, interview; T. Miller, "T. Johnson Interview, 1 June 2001," 5; Kibble, "My War," 128.
47. Young, "WWII POW," 6; Cox, interview; Broyles, reply; Kelnhofer, interview; Kauffman, "Loveland Interview," 27; Smith, interview; Richardson, reply; Richardson, "Voice," 14; Tice, interview; Mettscher, reply.
48. Carr, "Tales of Woe"; Oldham, *Lieutenant Stephen Polkinghorn*, 12; Kelnhofer, interview.

CHAPTER 7

1. Richardson, "Voice," 15; Pay, Diary, 12 January 1942; Abraham, *Do You Understand*, 43–54; Chapman, interview; Kinney, "P.O.W. Survival," 57.
2. Bamford, "Failure of Japanese at Woosung," 2; Shores, interview; Abraham, *Do You Understand*, 43; Mettscher, reply; Charles A. Holmes to author, 25 March 1979; Durrwachter, Diary, 1, 6, and 22 March and 18 and 22 April 1942; Pay, Diary, 22, 24, and 28 March and 15 April 1942; Papock, Diary, 30 March 1942; Kibble, "My War," 139; Kessler, *To Wake Island and Beyond*, 88.
3. Reeves, interview; Plate, reply; Hotchkiss, interview, October 21, 1983; Kelnhofer, interview; Malleck to author, 16 April 1981; Wheeler, interview; O'Guinn, "V.O.C," 50; LaPorte, interview; Kauffman, "Goiceochea Interview," 17; Kauffman, "Rogge Interview," 16; Stocks, interview; Kinney and McCaffrey, *Wake Island Pilot*, 96–97; Kessler, *To Wake Island and Beyond*, 88–89; Hanna, interview; Kibble, "My War," 128.
4. Abraham, *Do You Understand*, 34, 57–58; Plate, reply; Jesse E. Nowlin to author, 24 November 1979; Holmes to author, 3 December 1978, and 25 March 1979; Hotchkiss, interview, October 21, 1983; O'Guinn, "V.O.C.," 36; Burton, *Life's Trails*, 72; Richardson, "Voice," 16.
5. Abraham, *Do You Understand*, 57; Kessler, *To Wake Island and Beyond*, 88; Stegmaier, interview; E. Davis, interview; Richardson, "Voice," 15–16; T. Miller, "T. Johnson Interview, June 1, 2001," 6; Kauffman, "Charters Interview," 5: 10; Daws, "Jaffe Interview," 13; Richardson, reply; Kelnhofer, interview; Magnino, *Jim's Journey*, 105–106.
6. Richardson, "Voice," 15–16; T. Miller, "T. Johnson Interview, June 1, 2001," 5–6; Stegmaier, interview; Gross, interview, October 13, 1984; Daws, "Jaffe Interview," 18.
7. Richardson, "Voice," 15; Nye, interview; Kauffman, "Gooding Interview," 15; White, *United States Marines*, 63; Newell, Diary, 10 October 1942; Gross, interview, October 22, 1983; Marcello, "McDaniel Interview," 68.
8. "Directions for War-Prisoners," 2; Kinney, "P.O.W. Survival," 48; Kinney and McCaffrey, *Wake Island Pilot*, 98; White, *United States Marines*, 36; Magnino, *Jim's Journey*, 99.
9. White, *United States Marines*, 36; Kinney and McCaffrey, *Wake Island Pilot*, 98; Nye, interview; Durrwachter, Diary, 27 February 1942; Cox, interview; Young, "WWII POW," 6; Wheeler, interview; Magnino, *Jim's Journey*, 99; Carr, "Tales of Woe"; Richardson, "Voice," 25.
10. Richardson, "Voice," 13–14; Chapman, interview.
11. Richardson, "Voice," 115; Richard M. Huizenga, Affidavit, August 14, 1945, 2, File 101-150, Box 1584, Japanese War Crimes at Woosung, RG 153; Har-

ries and Harries, *Soldiers*, 478; Isamu Ishihara, Testimony, March 6, 1946, "*USA vs. Ishihara*," 114.

12. MIS-X Section, CPM Branch, "Ex Reports 665–668 (CHINA)," Appendix C, July 12, 1945, 2, Escape Reports Nos. 654–671, RG 389; James D. McBrayer Jr., Affidavit, September 18, 1945, Prosecution Exhibit No. 31, "*USA vs. Ishihara*," 86; Huizenga, Affidavit, 2; J. Johnson, Diary, 25 January 1942.
13. J. Cook, interview; Richardson, "Bread," 1; Sturgeon, interview, October 13, 1984; J. Johnson, reply, May 9, 1981.
14. Holmes to author, 3 December 1978, and 25 March 1979; Kinney and McCaffrey, *Wake Island Pilot*, 100; Shores, interview; Chapman, interview; J. Johnson, reply, May 9, 1981; Snipes, "Adventureros," 11; Rumpel, "My Experience," 4; Kibble, "My War," 127; Borne, interview; Nowlin to author, 24 November 1979.
15. E. Davis, interview; Hotchkiss, interview, October 21, 1983; Nowlin to author, 24 November 1979; Chapman, interview; Gross, interview, October 22, 1983; Kauffman, "Goiceochea Interview," 17; Plate, reply; Mettscher, reply.
16. Richardson, "Voice," 16; Durrwachter, Diary, 27 February 1942; Kinney and McCaffrey, *Wake Island Pilot*, 104; Kibble, "My War," 118.
17. Durrwachter, Diary, 27 February 1942; Pay, Diary, 1 February 1942; J. Johnson, Diary, 25 January 1942; William K. Kantzer, "Imperial Guest," 72–73 (unpublished manuscript in the author's possession, n.d.); Abraham, *Do You Understand*, 58.
18. Burton, *Life's Trails*, 76; Abraham, *Do You Understand*, 58; Bamford, "Failure of Japanese at Woosung," 2.
19. MIS-X Section, CPM Branch, "Ex Reports 665–668 (CHINA)," Appendix C, 2; Oldham, *Lieutenant Stephen Polkinghorn*, 12; White, *United States Marines*, 31, 44; Carr, "Tales of Woe"; O'Guinn, "V.O.C.," 38; Kantzer, "Imperial Guest," 71; Gross, interview, October 22, 1983; Holmes to author, 3 December 1978, and 21 January 1979; Magnino, *Jim's Journey*, 133; Hotchkiss, interview, October 21, 1983.
20. J. Johnson, Diary, 25–26 January 1942.
21. Richardson, "Voice," 18; MIS-X Section, CPM Branch, "Ex Reports 665–668 (CHINA)," Appendix C, 5; J. Johnson, reply, May 9, 1981; Papock, Diary, 18 February 1942; Durrwachter, Diary, 27–28 February 1942; Pay, Diary, 11 February 1942; Cox, interview; H. Davis, "Improper Conditions at Woosung," 11; White, *United States Marines*, 44; Carr, "Tales of Woe."
22. Huizenga, Affidavit, 3; Skaggs, reply; Kinney and McCaffrey, *Wake Island Pilot*, 121; Nye, interview; Row, interview; Sturgeon, interview, October 13, 1984; Freuler, interview; White, *United States Marines*, 31; Gregouire to

author, March 1979; Tice, interview; Comfort, "Improper Care at Woo Sung and Kang Wan," 2; Kessler, *To Wake Island and Beyond*, 112; Magnino, *Jim's Journey*, 102–103; Stocks, interview.

23. Huizenga, Affidavit, 3; Holmes to author, 3 December 1978; Marcello, "Godbold Interview," 51; Mettscher, reply; White, *United States Marines*, 31; Hubley, interview; T. Miller, "T. Johnson Interview, 1 June 2001," 6; Row, interview; Richardson, "Voice," 18, 20; Marcello, "McDaniel Interview," 68; Freuler, interview; Charles W. Brimmer, "Prisoner of War Report," September 21, 1945, 1, Woosung, Shanghai, China, RG 389.

24. White, *United States Marines*, 34; Nye, interview; John Brown Leslie Anderson, Affidavit, January 23, 1946, 1, File 67-75, Bk. 1 (1–2), POWs on the *Nitta Maru*, RG 153; T. Miller, "T. Johnson Interview, 1 June 2001," 9.

25. Pay, Diary, 11 February 1942; Daws, "Jaffe Interview," 91–92; Skaggs, reply; Kessler, *To Wake Island and Beyond*, 113.

26. Shores, interview; Magnino, *Jim's Journey*, 98, 101; Hubley, interview; Carr, "Tales of Woe"; Holmes to author, 3 December 1978, and 25 March 1979; Hotchkiss, interview, October 21, 1983; Young, "WWII POW," 6; Nye, interview; Gavan Daws, ed., "Transcript of Interview With Shirley 'Tex' Akin," n.d., 28, Daws Papers; T. Miller, "T. Johnson Interview, 1 June 2001," 7; Skaggs, reply; Sturgeon, interview, October 13, 1984.

27. Richardson, "Voice," 18; Hubley, interview; Daws, "Akin Interview," 14, 18; Kinney and McCaffrey, *Wake Island Pilot*, 103; Magnino, *Jim's Journey*, 103–104; Nye, interview; Hotchkiss, interview, October 21, 1983; LaPorte, interview; Snipes, "Adventureros," 11–12; Young, "WWII POW," 6.

28. Hotchkiss, interview, October 21, 1983; White, *United States Marines*, 31; O'Guinn, "V.O.C.," 40; Nye, interview.

29. Burton, *Life's Trails*, 75; Row, interview; MIS-X Section, CPM Branch, "Ex-Reports 665–668 (CHINA)," Appendix C, 5; Norwood and Shek, "POW Camps," 29; Kibble, "My War," 129; Ashurst, "Record," 5; O'Guinn, "V.O.C.," 40; Kinney, "P.O.W. Survival," 50; Marcello, "Fields Interview," 35; Falk, *Bataan*, 36; Shirley Akin, Affidavit, December 19, 1945, Prosecution Exhibit No. 29, "*USA vs. Ishihara*," 83.

30. Donald R. Malleck to author, 10 October 1981; Stocks, interview; Smith, interview; Chapman, interview; J. Johnson, reply, May 9, 1981; Kinney, "P.O.W. Survival," 113; Hoskins, "Memoir," 22; Mettscher, reply; Shores, interview; Kibble, "My War," 129.

31. Newell, Diary, 16 February 1942; Ashurst, "Record," 9; Oldham, *Lieutenant Stephen Polkinghorn*, 13; Pay, Diary, 18 February 1942; Papock, Diary, 18 February 1942; Pay, Diary, 19 February 1942; Menique, Affidavit, 2; Magnino, *Jim's Journey*, 97–98.

32. J. Johnson, reply, May 9, 1981; Abraham, *Do You Understand*, 59; Chapman, interview; Holmes to author, 3 December 1978; Kinney, "P.O.W. Survival," 55; Richardson, "Voice," 25; Camp, interview.
33. Kinney, "P.O.W. Survival," 55; Plate, reply; Chapman, interview; Holmes to author, 3 December 1978; Shores, interview; Kibble, "My War," 127; Urwin, *Facing Fearful Odds*, 103, 142–143.
34. Jesse E. Nowlin to author, 21 July 1979; Sloman, interview; Chapman, interview; Holewinski, interview, September 11, 1986; Frank, "Devereux Transcript," 135a, 165–166.
35. Holmes to author, 3, 27 December 1978; King, interview; Cox, interview; Chapman, interview; LaPorte, interview; Hanna, interview; Hassig, interview; Sloman, reply; Frank, "Devereux Transcript," 168; Kauffman, "Poindexter Interview," 6.
36. Devereux, *Story of Wake*, 222.
37. Devereux, *Story of Wake*, 225–226; R. Brown, interview.
38. Holmes to author, 27 December 1978, and 19 August 1983; Camp, interview; Hassig, interview; LaPorte, interview; Marcello, "Venable Interview," 55; Marcello, "Godbold Interview," 60–61; Gross, interview, October 22, 1983.
39. Hotchkiss, interview, October 21, 1983; Hanna, interview; Bowsher, interview; Nye, interview.
40. Gross, interview, October 22, 1983; Hotchkiss, interview, October 13, 1984; Sloman, reply; Sandvold, interview; Wheeler, interview; R. Brown, interview; King, interview; Marcello, "McDaniel Interview," 56; E. Davis, interview; Jesse E. Nowlin, taped reply to author's questionnaire, March 18, 1980.
41. Shores, interview; Borne, interview; Sturgeon, interview, October 13, 1984; Gross, interview, October 22, 1982; Thaire to author, September 1981; Donald R. Malleck to author, 27 July 1981; Plate, reply.
42. Woodrow M. Kessler to Gavan Daws, 15 April 1987, Daws Papers; Cox, interview; J. Cook, interview; Camp, interview; Frank, "Devereux Transcript," 133, 166–167; Chapman, interview; Conner, interview.
43. Holmes to author, 27 December 1978; Malleck to author, 27 July 1981; Devereux, *Story of Wake*, 225.
44. Frank, "Devereux Transcript," 166; LaPorte, interview; Borne, interview.
45. R. Brown, interview; Malleck to author, 27 July 1981; Hotchkiss, interview, October 21, 1983.
46. Frank, "Devereux Transcript," 166; O'Guinn, "V.O.C.," 60; Abraham, *Do You Understand*, 93–94.
47. Marcello, "Godbold Interview," 42; Newell, Diary, 2 May 1942; Kauffman, "Goiceochea Interview," 19; Daws, "Akin Interview," 27; Row, interview; Nye, interview; Daws, "Akin Interview," 13, 14, 27, 28; Lloyd O. Nelson to

Gavan Daws, n.d., Daws Papers; Sandvold, interview; Sturgeon, interview, October 13, 1984.

48. Charles A. Holmes to author, 1 October 1982.

49. Papock, Diary, 1 February 1942; Pay, Diary, 1 February 1942; J. Johnson, Diary, 1 February 1942; White, *United States Marines*, 25, 27–29, 136; Marcello, "Venable Interview," 47; Chapman, interview; Sturgeon, interview, October 13, 1984; Marcello, "McDaniel Interview," 45; Hubley, interview; Daws, "Jaffe Interview," 15; Harold E. Lochridge to Col. James P. S. Devereux, USMC, 8 May 1946, B.1, F.4, Devereux Collection; Charles W. Brimmer, Affidavit, September 21, 1945, 2, File 101-150, Box 1854, Japanese War Crimes at Woosung, RG 153; Malleck to author, 27 July 1981.

50. Norwood and Shek, "POW Camps," 26; Huizenga et al., "Escape Report No. 665," 3; White, *United States Marines*, 2–10; James D. McBrayer Jr., *Escape! Memoir of a World War II Marine Who Broke Out of a Japanese POW Camp and Linked Up With Chinese Communist Guerrillas* (Jefferson, NC: McFarland, 1995), 74, 85–91; Terrence S. Kirk, *The Secret Camera* (Redwood Valley, CA: Owl Wise Publishing, 1982), 16–18, 30–31; William Howard Chittenden, *From China Marine to Jap POW: My 1,364 Day Journey Through Hell* (Paducah, KY: Turner Publishing, 1995), 48–111; Chapman, interview.

51. Huizenga, Kinney, McBrayer, and McAlister, "Escape Report No. 665," 3–4; Chester M. Biggs Jr., *Behind the Barbed Wire: Memoir of a World War II U.S. Marine* (Jefferson, NC: McFarland, 1995), 10–11; White, *United States Marines*, 11–18; Chittenden, *From China Marine*, 112–113, 117–118; Kirk, *Secret Camera*, 9–27; McBrayer, *Escape*, 74–76; Chapman, interview.

52. White, *United States Marines*, 13–14, 22, 60–61; Ashurst, "Record," 3; J. Johnson, reply, May 9, 1981; Kessler, *To Wake Island and Beyond*, 115; Huizenga, Kinney, McBrayer, and McAlister, "Escape Report No. 665," 3–4.

53. Brimmer, Affidavit, 2–3; Huizinga et al., "Escape Report No. 665," 3–4; White, *United States Marines*, 24–28, 37–40.

54. Richardson, reply; Reeves, interview; Tice, interview; Hotchkiss, interview, October 21, 1983; Hubley, interview; John White to Charles A. Holmes, 13 February 1981 (photostat copy in the author's possession); Marcello, "Godbold Interview," 41; Kahn, interview.

55. Henry I. Shaw Jr., *Opening Moves: Marines Gear Up for War*. Marines in World War II Commemorative Series (Washington, DC: History and Museums Division, Headquarters, U.S. Marine Corps, 1991), 1, 19; Sturgeon, interview, October 13, 1984; Kinney and McCaffrey, *Wake Island Pilot*, 100; Richardson, reply; Borne, interview.

56. Papock, Diary, 1 February 1942; E. Davis, interview; T. Miller, "T. Johnson Interview, 1 June 2001," 9–10; Kelnhofer, interview; Reeves, interview; Mar-

cello, "Venable Interview," 47; Richardson, reply; Kauffman, "Goiceochea Interview," 18; Sturgeon, interview, October 13, 1984; Shores, interview.
57. Jack R. Williamson to Gavan Daws, 4 November 1991, Daws Papers; Kauffman "Goiceochea Interview," 18; T. Miller, "T. Johnson Interview, 1 June 2001," 10; Richardson, reply; Kelnhofer, interview; Chapman, interview; Reeves, interview; Gross, interview, October 22, 1983; Charles A. Holmes to author, 20 February 1981; Marcello, "Godbold Interview," 41; Nye, interview; Daws, "Akin Interview," 13; Daws, "Jaffe Interview," 15; O'Guinn, "V.O.C.," 44; Burton, *Life's Trails*, 76–77; Marcello, "Venable Interview," 48; LaPorte, interview; Hubley, interview; White, *United States Marines*, 59.
58. Marcello, "Venable Interview," 48, 68; Sturgeon, interview, October 13, 1984; T. Miller, "T. Johnson Interview, 1 June 2001," 9; Wheeler, interview; Skaggs, reply; Reeves, interview.
59. Hubley, interview; Reeves, interview; Victor V. Skaggs to Winfield Scott Cunningham, 7 November 1946, B.1, F.1, Cunningham Collection.

CHAPTER 8

1. Hotchkiss, interviews, October 22, 1982, and October 21, 1983; Jack R. Williamson to author, 7 February 1981; Brimmer, Affidavit, 3.
2. White, *United States Marines*, 30, 37; Kinney, "P.O.W. Survival," 49; Kinney and McCaffrey, *Wake Island Pilot*, 100; Freuler, interview; Sturgeon, interview, October 13, 1984; Richardson, reply; Marcello, "McDaniel Interview," 45–46; Marcello, "Venable Transcript," 47; Charles A. Holmes to author, 7 February 1981; Hubley, interview; V. Skaggs to Cunningham, 7 November 1946; Biggs, *Behind the Barbed Wire*, 82, 91, 209; Kirk, *Secret Camera*, 51–52.
3. Frank, "Devereux Transcript," 130–131; T. Miller, "T. Johnson Interview, 1 June 2001," 9; Hubley, interview.
4. Hotchkiss, interviews, October 22, 1982, and October 21, 1983; T. Miller, "T. Johnson Interview, 1 June 2001," 10; Reeves, interview; Marcello, "Venable Interview," 48–49; Kelnhofer, interview; Kantzer, "Imperial Guest," 70.
5. Ronald E. Marcello, ed., "Interview With Henry B. Stowers, May 25, 1973," 48–49, UNT Oral History Collection; Biggs, *Behind the Barbed Wire*, 73, 91, 114–115; McBrayer, *Escape*, 122; Jon T. Hoffman, *Chesty: The Story of Lieutenant General Lewis B. Puller, USMC* (New York: Random House, 2001), 71–73, 77–78, 80–83, 90–96, 98, 102, 103, 135.
6. Cunningham, interview; Biographical Files, Reference Section, MCHC; White, *United States Marines*, 77–78.
7. *Washington Post*, October 14, 1945; White, *United States Marines*, 9; Williamson to author, 7 February 1981; Kirk, *Secret Camera*, 10, 32, 62–64; Biggs, *Behind the Barbed Wire*, 91, 203; Borne, interview; Nowlin, reply,

March 18, 1980; Marcello, "Venable Interview," 63; McBrayer, *Escape*, 122–123. See also L. A. Brown, *The Marine's Handbook* (Annapolis: United States Naval Institute, 1940).
8. Daws, "Akin Interview," 13; Kantzer, "Imperial Guest," 157; Henningsen, "Shanghai Prisoners," 1.
9. Kantzer, "Imperial Guest," 157; Daws, "Akin Interview," 13; Rumpel, "My Experiences," 6.
10. Chapman, interview; White, *United States Marines*, 37–38; Hassig, interview; Kirk, *Secret Camera*, 39–40; Biggs, *Behind the Barbed Wire*, 91, 205; Chittenden, *From China Marine*, 133.
11. Lt. Glenn E. Tripp, USN, to Winfield Scott Cunningham, 5 July 1961, B.1, F.2, Cunningham Collection; Holmes to author, 7 February 1981; LaPorte, interview; Nowlin, reply, March 18, 1980; Conner, interview; Borne, interview.
12. Biggs, *Behind the Barbed Wire*, 205; Conner, interview.
13. White, *United States Marines*, 125; Gavan Daws, ed., "Interview With Dr. William T. Foley," 3 October 1984, 2, Daws Papers; Kantzer, "Imperial Guest," 130; Clyde F. Lawrence to Winfield Scott Cunningham, 25 April 1960, B.1, F.2, Cunningham Collection; Hanna, interview; Kahn, interview.
14. Kahn, interview; Kinney, "P.O.W. Survival," 70; Davis, "Improper Conditions at Woosung," 3.
15. Kahn, interview; Biggs, *Behind the Barbed Wire*, 90; DMI/3751/50/GSI(e), General Headquarters, India, General Staff Branch, November 28, 1942, 2, 3, Conditions at Kiangwan (Folder No. I), RG 389; Kessler, *To Wake Island and Beyond*, 108; White, *United States Marines*, 30; Pay, Diary, 28 February 1942.
16. Kahn, interview; Daws, "Foley Interview," 1; Pay, Diary, 28 February 1942; Cox, interview; Gregouire to author, March 1979; *Kalamazoo Gazette*, December 2, 1991; Sturgeon, interview, October 13, 1984; *East Hampton Star*, October 11, 1945; Young, "WWII POW," 7–8.
17. Kahn, interview; Cox, interview; Gregouire to author, March 1979; Daws, "Foley Interview," 1.
18. Daws, "Akin Interview," 11; Daws, "Jaffe Interview," 48; Kantzer, "Imperial Guest," 105, 108, 125, 132, 136; Pearsall, Diary, 9 and 11 November 1942; Hanna, interview; Reeves, interview; T. Miller, "T. Johnson Interview, 1 June 2001," 21; Nye, interview; White, *United States Marines*, 125; Richardson, reply.
19. Oldham, *Lieutenant Stephen Polkinghorn*, 12; Magnino, *Jim's Journey*, 107; White, *United States Marines*, 38; Norwood and Shek, "POW Camps," 27; Kinney, Affidavit, 3; Chapman, interview; Hotchkiss, interview, October 21, 1983; Nowlin to author, 24 November 1979; Tanaka, *Hidden Horrors*, 37–38.

20. White, *United States Marines*, 37; Abraham, *Do You Understand*, 30; Kinney and McCaffrey, *Wake Island Pilot*, 96, 117; Kantzer, "Imperial Guest," 86; Pay, Diary, 3 October 1942; Richardson, "Voice," 29; Hubley, interview.
21. Richardson, "Voice," 29; Hanna, interview; White, *United States Marines*, 68, 79; Kinney and McCaffrey, *Wake Island Pilot*, 117; Sturgeon, interview, October 13, 1984.
22. Kinney, "P.O.W. Survival," 76.
23. J. Johnson, Diary, 6 March 1942; Cunningham and Sims, *Wake Island Command*, 129; Ashurst, "Record," 6; White, *United States Marines*, 46, 56–57, 78; Kirk, *Secret Camera*, 59–60; Richardson, "Voice," 30.
24. MIS-X Section, CPM Branch, "Ex-Reports 665–668 (CHINA)," Appendix C, 10; Kinney and McCaffrey, *Wake Island Pilot*, 103; Chapman, interview; Nye, interview; Conner, interview; White, *United States Marines*, 31, 44–45; Row, interview; Magnino, *Jim's Journey*, 158–159; Kinney, "P.O.W. Survival," 116–117.
25. Pay, Diary, 9 February 1942; Papock, Diary, 9 February 1942; Holmes to author, 3, 27 December 1978; Kantzer, "Imperial Guest," 72; O'Guinn, "V.O.C.," 51; Nowlin to author, 24 November 1979; Richardson, reply; Hubley, interview; Marcello, "Fields Interview," 36–37; Magnino, *Jim's Journey*, 112; Plate, reply; Kinney and McCaffrey, *Wake Island Pilot*, 100.
26. Magnino, *Jim's Journey*, 99.
27. Marcello, "Fields Interview," 20–21; William L. Taylor, interview by author, August 28, 2002; Richardson, "Voice," 30; Hanna, interview; Sturgeon, interview, October 13, 1984; Warren G. Anderson, Affidavit, September 5, 1946, 1, File 101-150, Box 1584, Japanese War Crimes at Woosung, RG 153.
28. McAnally, "Mistreatment Aboard *NITTA MARU*," 6; Kahn, interview; Young, "WWII POW," 7; Burton, *Life's Trails*, 77–78.
29. Richardson, reply; Kahn, interview; White, *United States Marines*, 124, 126; Abraham, *Do You Understand*, 98; Stegmaier, interview; Daws, "Jaffe Interview," 37; Daws, "Foley Interview," 1; LaPorte, interview; Reeves, interview; Hanna, interview; Stegmaier, interview; Kessler, *To Wake Island and Beyond*, 92; Kahn, interview; Menique, Affidavit, 2; Marcello, "Venable Interview," 60–61; Sturgeon, interview, October 13, 1984; 124; O'Guinn, "V.O.C.," 51.
30. Pay, Diary, 29 March, 5 and 30 April, 17 May, and 19 August 1942; Newell, Diary, 29 March, 5 and 30 April, 17 May, and 19 August 1942; Papock, Diary, 29 March and 26 April 1942; Kantzer, "Imperial Guest," 77; Kessler, *To Wake Island and Beyond*, 111; Hanna, interview.
31. Pay, Diary, 21 April, 29 May, 30 July, and 11 September 1942; Newell, Diary, 20 April, 29 July, 11 September, and 25 November 1942; Papock, Diary, 29 July 1942; Chapman, interview; Kantzer, "Imperial Guest," 80, 84; Durrwachter, Diary, 18 April 1942; White, *United States Marines*, 126.

32. Huizenga, Affidavit, 5.
33. Ronald E. Marcello, ed., "Interview With T. G. Crews, January 22, 1972," 20–21, UNT Oral History Collection; Biggs, *Behind the Barbed Wire*, 79; Chittenden, *From China Marine*, 122.
34. Allan R. Millett, *Semper Fidelis: The History of the United States Marine Corps*, rev. ed. (New York: Free Press, 1991), 220–235; J. Michael Miller, *From Shanghai to Corregidor: Marines in the Defense of the Philippines*. Marines in World War II Commemorative Series (Washington, DC: History and Museums Division, Headquarters, U.S. Marines Corps, 1997), 1–2; White, *United States Marines*, 59–60.
35. Oldham, *Lieutenant Stephen Polkinghorn*, 12–13; Pay, Diary, 17 February 1942; O'Guinn, "V.O.C.," 44; White, *United States Marines*, 108, 138–139, 142; Oscar G. Jacobson, Affidavit, October 12, 1945, Prosecution Exhibit No. 39, "*USA vs. Ishihara*," 97–98.
36. Papock, Diary, 21 February 1942; Pay, Diary, 21 February 1942; Bernard E. Richardson, "Outpost of Empire" (unpublished manuscript in the author's possession, n.d.), 1–2; Keith Hindell, "Conquest of Hong Kong," *History of the Second World War*, October 4, 1973, 724–728.
37. White, *United States Marines*, 49, 52; Abraham, *Do You Understand*, 61; Kauffman, "Goiceochea Interview," 18; Holmes to author, 25 March 1979.
38. Richardson, "Outpost of Empire," 2, 3; Holmes to author, 25 March 1979; Oldham, *Lieutenant Stephen Polkinghorn*, 13; White, *United States Marines*, 51–52; MIS-X Section, CPM Branch, "Ex-Reports 665–668 (CHINA)," Appendix C, 9.
39. Papock, Diary, 21 February 1942; Burton, *Life's Trails*, 78; Durrwachter, Diary, 1 March 1942.
40. Holmes to author, 25 March 1979; Kauffman, "Goiceochea Interview," 18; White, *United States Marines*, 78; Magnino, *Jim's Journey*, 108; Hotchkiss, interview, October 21, 1983.
41. Durrwatcher, Diary, 26–27 February 1942; Richard Fuller, *Shōkan: Hirohito's Samurai; Leaders of the Japanese Armed Forces* (London: Arms & Armour Press, 1992), 96–97; Holmes to author, 21 January 1979; White, *United States Marines*, 42.
42. "War Prisoners Are Given Bad News regarding Allied Calamities . . . but the Blow Is Softened by Unexpected Japanese Kindness," *Freedom*, Third Impress, 1942, 46–47; Holmes to author, 21 January 1979; White, *United States Marines*, 42.
43. "Tell the Public We Are Receiving Good Treatment," *Freedom*, Third Impress, 1942, 44–45.
44. "War Prisoners Given Bad News," 47; "Captured Commanders Put Views on Record," *Freedom*, Third Impress, 1942, 48; White, *United States*

Marines, 43; Kessler, *To Wake Island and Beyond*, 95–96; Stegmaier, interview; Hassig, interview; Plate, reply; Hotchkiss, interview, October 13, 1984.
45. Janet Morison to Louise Cunningham, 3 April 1942, B.2, F.4, Cunningham Collection.
46. Pay, Diary, 18 March 1942; "Music and Merriment Reigns in Shanghai Concentration Camps Through Radios Presented by the Japanese Army Authorities," *Freedom*, Third Impress, 1942, 42–43; Kinney and McCaffrey, *Wake Island Pilot*, 112; White, *United States Marines*, 44; J. Cook, interview; Williams, interview; Durrwachter, Diary, 22 March 1942.
47. MIS-X Section, CPM Branch, "Ex-Reports 665–668 (CHINA)," Appendix C, 9; Marcello, "Godbold Interview," 62; Kessler, *To Wake Island and Beyond*, 97, 99; Holmes to author, 27 December 1978, and 21 January 1979; Kinney and McCaffrey, *Wake Island Pilot*, 112–113; Snipes, "Adventureros," 12; Nowlin to author, 24 November 1979; Kantzer, "Imperial Guest," 75; White, *United States Marines*, 65; Gavan Daws, ed., "Interview With Victor F. Ciarrachi," December 1986–January 1987, 2, Daws Papers.
48. White, *United States Marines*, 114; Holmes to author, 21 January and 25 March 1979; *St. Louis Star Times*, October 29, 1945; Magnino, *Jim's Journey*, 114; Chapman, interview; Kinney and McCaffrey, *Wake Island Pilot*, 112; Nye, interview.
49. White, *United States Marines*, 42–43; Pay, Diary, 25 March 1942; Durrwachter, Diary, 30 March and 27 May 1942; Newell, Diary, 12 June 1942.
50. Pay, Diary, 5, 15, and 29 April 1942; Papock Diary, 5 and 29 April 1942; Newell, Diary, 5, 14, 29, and 30 April 1942; Durrwachter, Diary, 29 April 1942; Camp, interview.
51. Holmes to author, 25 March 1979; E. Davis, interview; Pay, Diary, 18 March 1942; White, *United States Marines*, 55; Newell, Diary, 25 March 1942; Richardson, "Bread," 1.
52. Richardson, "Bread," 1–3; Chapman, interview; Pay, Diary, 21 and 30 March 1942; Abraham, *Do You Understand*, 48; Norwood and Shek, "POW Camps," 30; White, *United States Marines*, 56; Rumpel, "My Experience," 4; MIS-X Section, CPM Branch, "Ex-Reports 665–668 (CHINA)," Appendix C, 12; King, interview; Kantzer, "Imperial Guest," 71, 74; Durrwachter, Diary, 12 April 1942.
53. Pay, Diary, 17 and 20 March and 3 June 1942; O'Guinn, "V.O.C.," 47; Oldham, *Lieutenant Stephen Polkinghorn*, 13–14, 38; Papock, Diary, 17 March 1942; Newell, Diary, 3 June 1942; Kantzer, "Imperial Guest," 70.
54. Pay, Diary, 10 May 1942; see also, Papock, Diary, n.d., and Oldham, *Lieutenant Stephen Polkinghorn*, 14.
55. J. M. Miller, *From Shanghai to Corregidor*, 1–3; W. Pat Hitchcock, *Forty*

Months in Hell (Jackson, TN: Page Publishing, 1996), 14–15; Kantzer, "Imperial Guest," 15–16.
56. Kantzer, "Imperial Guest," 17–20, 24, 38, 64, 70.
57. Ibid., 71.

CHAPTER 9
1. Edna Lee Booker and John S. Potter, *Flight From China* (New York: Macmillan, 1946), 11–12, 138–140.
2. E. Bartlett Kerr, *Surrender & Survival: The Experience of American POWs in the Pacific 1941–1945* (New York: William Morrow, 1985), 38–39, 43–44; "Geneva Convention," 5244–5245; Special Division, Department of State, to War Department (hereinafter Special Div., State Dept., to War Dept.), "American Interests—China: Report No. 1 on Kiangwan Camp: Visit Made November 4, 1943, by Mr. Fontanel," 13 January 1944, 1, Conditions at Kiangwan (Folder No. I), RG 389; Fontanel, "Report on Visit to Kiangwan, November 26th, 1944," 1–4; Ashurst, "Record," 8; MIS-X, CPM Branch, "Ex-Reports 665–668 (CHINA)," Appendix C, 4–5; Minister C. Gorgé, Swiss Legation to Japan, to Foreign Minister Tani Masayuki, 23 December 1942, Diplomatic Record Office of the Ministry of Foreign Affairs, Documents Relating to Greater East Asia War, Treatment of Nationals of Enemy Countries and Prisoners of War Between Belligerent Countries, General and Specific Problems, Protests against Japan, Vol. 4, Japan Center for Asian Historical Records, National Archives of Japan, Tokyo, Japan.
3. Ashurst, "Record," 7–8; J. Johnson, reply, May 9, 1981; MIS-X, CPM Branch, "Ex-Reports 665–668 (CHINA)," Appendix C, 4–5; Warren G. Anderson, Affidavit, September 5, 1946, 2, File 101-150, Box 1584, Japanese War Crimes at Woosung, RG 153.
4. Henningsen, "Shanghai Prisoners," 3; Kantzer, "Imperial Guest," 78.
5. Durrwachter, Diary, 3 October 1942; Huizenga, Affidavit, 5.
6. *Red Cross Activities*, vol. 1, 441–463, 500–503; Bailey, *Prisoners of War*, 21–22.
7. *Red Cross Activities*, vol. 1, 447–448, 473; J. Johnson, Diary, 6 March 1942; White, *United States Marines*, 66–67; Daws, "Foley Interview," 1; MIS-X Section, CPM Branch, "Ex-Reports 665–668 (CHINA), Appendix C, 4; Special Div., Department of State, to War Dept. Information Bureau, 15 September 1942, 2–3, Woosung, Shanghai, China, RG 389.
8. Huizenga, Affidavit, 5; *Red Cross Activities*, vol. 1, 470–472; Pay, Diary, 18 August 1942; Papock, Diary, 18 August 1942; Kantzer, "Imperial Guest," 88–89.
9. Special Div., State Dept., to War Dept., Information Bureau, 15 September 1942, 2–3; Kinney, "P.O.W. Survival," 88–89; White, *United States Marines*,

66; Kinney and McCaffrey, *Wake Island Pilot*, 121; *Red Cross Activities*, vol. 1, 471. See also Christian Henriot and Wen-Hsin Yeh, eds., *In the Shadow of the Rising Sun: Shanghai Under Japanese Occupation* (Cambridge: Cambridge University Press, 2004).
10. Special Div., State Dept., to War Dept. Information Bureau, 15 September 1942, 2; Booker and Potter, *Flight From China*, 128–129; Henningsen, "Shanghai War Prisoners," 5–6; Oldham, *Lieutenant Stephen Polkinghorn*, 15; *East Hampton Star*, October 11, 1945; Coyle to Welsh, 6 December 1943; MIS-X Section, CPM Branch, "Ex-Reports 665–668 (CHINA)," Appendix C, 4.
11. Announcement from *Shanghai Evening Post & Mercury*, April 4, 1942, quoted in Pay, Diary, n.d.
12. Coyle to Welsh, 6 December 1943; Col. James P. S. Devereux, USMC, to P. D. Brown, 14 March 1946, B.3, F.1, Devereux Collection; Henningsen, "Shanghai Prisoners," 5; Hotchkiss, interview, October 22, 1982, and October 21, 1983; J. Johnson, Diary, 28 August 1942; Kantzer, "Imperial Guest," 78, 84; King, interview.
13. Special Div., State Dept., to War Dept. Information Bureau, 15 September 1942, 2; Henningsen, "Shanghai Prisoners," 5; White, *United States Marines*, 66; MIS-X Section, CPM Branch, "Ex-Reports 665–668 (CHINA)," Appendix C, 6; Kantzer, "Imperial Guest," 83; E. Egle, "Notes Regarding Visit to Camp of Prisoners of War at Shanghai, on 10th November 1942," n.d., 3, Conditions at Kiangwan, China (Folder No. I), RG 389.
14. Devereux to Brown, 14 March 1946; Richardson, "Voice," 20; Comfort, "Improper Care at Woo Sung and Kang Won," 2; Marcello, "Fields Interview," 17–18.
15. Kelnhofer, interview; Kinney and McCaffrey, *Wake Island Pilot*, 188; Hotchkiss, interview, October 21, 1983; John F. Kinney, Affidavit, August 2, 1945, 4, File 101-59, Box 1584, Japanese War Crimes at Kiangwan, RG 153; Huizinga, Affidavit, 3; Ashurst, "Record," 7.
16. Egle, "Vist to Camp, 10th November 1942," 4; Kinney and McCaffrey, *Wake Island Pilot*, 118; Kelnhofer, interview.
17. Huizenga, Affidavit, 3; Ashurst, "Record," 7.
18. MIS-X Section, CPM Branch, "Ex-Reports 665–668 (CHINA), 6; Newell, Diary, 11–12 November 1942; White, *United States Marines*, 66.
19. Ashurst, "Record," 5; Kantzer, "Imperial Guest," 80–81; Kinney and McCaffrey, *Wake Island Pilot*, 122; Oldham, *Lieutenant Stephen Polkinghorn*, 45; Newell, Diary, 25 November 1942; Pearsall, Diary, 30 November 1942; Egle, "Visit to Camp, 10th November 1942," 3.
20. Kantzer, "Imperial Guest," 79; Newell, Diary, 10 July 1942.
21. White, *United States Marines*, 66; Newell, Diary, 26 September and 1

November 1942; Kantzer, "Imperial Guest," 85; Kinney and McCaffrey, *Wake Island Pilot*, 121; LaPorte, interview; Hanna, interview; Wheeler, interview; Richardson, reply; Young, "WWII POW," 6.

22. Hanna, interview; Richardson, reply; Young, "WWII POW," 6; Kinney and McCaffrey, *Wake Island Pilot*, 121–122; Gross, Interview, October 22, 1983; Kessler, *To Wake Island and Beyond*, 112–113.
23. Richardson, reply.
24. Ibid.
25. Richardson, reply; Pay, Diary, 21 August 1942; Newell, Diary, 20 August 1942; H. Davis, "Improper Conditions at Woosung," 2.
26. Kibble, "My War," 142–144; J. Johnson, Diary, 6 March 1942; King, interview; Kantzer, "Imperial Guest," 71, 74; Sturgeon, interview, October 13, 1984; Pay, Diary, 21 March 1942; Hotchkiss, interview, October 22, 1982; Cox, interview; Chapman, interview; Burton, *Life's Trails*, 79–80; Broyles, reply; Newell, Diary, 1, 7, and 17 May, 28 June, 3 and 11 July, and 6 October 1942; *East Hampton Star*, October 11, 1945; Special Div., State Dept., to War Dept. Information Bureau, 15 September 1942, 2–3; Richardson, reply; Mettscher, reply.
27. Sturgeon, interview, October 13, 1984; Magnino, *Jim's Journey*, 103; Mettscher, reply; Pearsall, Diary, 7 November 1942.
28. Special Div., State Dept., to War Dept. Information Bureau, 15 September 1942, 2–3; Kantzer, "Imperial Guest," 71; *East Hampton Star*, October 11, 1945; Kibble, "My War," 144–145; Hotchkiss, interview, October 21, 1983.
29. Pay, Diary, 21 March 1942; Kelnhofer, interview; Tice, interview; Ashurst, "Record," 7; Sturgeon, interview, October 13, 1984; Kibble, "My War," 144.
30. Deut. 8: 2–3; Matt. 4: 4; Luke 4: 4 (New American Bible).
31. Kantzer, "Imperial Guest," 85, 87; Newell, Diary, 11, 13, and 29 July, 1, 4, 13, and 29 August, 13 September, and 27 and 28 November 1942; Special Div., State Dept., to War Dept. Information Bureau, 15 September 1942, 2–3; MIS-X Section, CPM Branch, "Ex-Reports, 665–668 (CHINA)," Appendix C, 6; Pearsall, Diary, 29 November 1942; Egle, "Visit to Camp 10th November 1942," 2; Wheeler, interview; Oldham, *Lieutenant Stephen Polkinghorn*, 45.
32. Newell, Diary, 11, 13, and 29 July, 1, 4, 13, and 29 August, 13 September, 20 and 28 October, and 27 and 28 November 1942; Kantzer, "Imperial Guest," 87.
33. Newell, Diary, 4 and 21 April, 16 May, 5, 13, 15, and 21 July, 29 August, 13 September, and 13 November 1942; Smith, interview; Kinney and McCaffrey, *Wake Island Pilot*, 128; Oldham, *Lieutenant Stephen Polkinghorn*, 43, 45; Durrwachter, Diary, 1 March 1942.
34. MIS-X Section, CPM Branch, "Ex-Reports 665–668 (China)," Appendix C, 10; Kantzer "Imperial Guest," 85; Egle, "Visit to Camp, 10th Novem-

ber 1942," 1; Kahn, interview; Young, "WWII POW," 7–8; Magnino, *Jim's Journey*, 190–191; Hotchkiss, interview, October 21, 1983; Rumpel, "My Experience," 6; Newell, Diary, 12 June 1942; T. Miller, "T. Johnson, Interview, 1 June 2001," 19–21; D. Miller, *Doc Miller*, 15.

35. Newell, Diary, 17 June, 4 and 13 July, 1 August, and 9 October 1943.
36. Kelnhofer, interview; Hotchkiss interviews, October 22, 1982, and October 21, 1983; MIS-X Section, CPM Branch, "Ex-Reports 665–668 (CHINA)," Appendix C, 4; Henningsen, "Shanghai Prisoners," 5; Oldham, *Lieutenant Stephen Polkinghorn*, 15.
37. Kantzer, "Imperial Guest," 78, 82, 84, 85, 89.
38. Coyle to Welsh, 6 December 1943; *East Hampton Star*, October 11, 1945; Marcello, "Godbold Transcript," 58; Huizinga, Affidavit, 3; Shores, interview.
39. Capt. James L. Norwood, USA, "Colonel Devereux: Notes Taken by Capt. Norwood," n.d., 3, Conditions at Hakodate Branch Camp No. 3, RG 389; Marcello, "Godbold Interview," 47; White, *United States Marines*, 124; Burton, *Life's Trails*, 77; Hanna, interview; MIS-X Section, CPM Branch, "Ex-Reports 665–668 (CHINA)," Appendix C, 8; Pay, Diary, 20 March and 16 May 1942; Newell, Diary, 29 April 1942.
40. Magnino, *Jim's Journey*, 195; Oldham, *Lieutenant Stephen Polkinghorn*, 46, 49; Kantzer, "Imperial Guest," 81; Special Div, State Dept., to War Dept. Information Bureau, 15 September 1942, 2–3.
41. MIS-X, Section, CPM Branch, "Ex-Reports 665–668 (CHINA)," Appendix C, 8; Norwood, "Devereux Notes," 3; Marcello, "Godbold Interview," 47, 56; D. Miller, *Doc Miller*, 15; White, *United States Marines*, 124; Snipes, "Adventureros," 12; Daws, "Akin Interview," 28a; O'Guinn, "V.O.C.," 59; Richardson, reply; Nye, interview.
42. Daws, "Akin Interview," 28a; D. Miller, *Doc Miller*, 15; Kinney and McCaffrey, *Wake Island Pilot*, 128; Marcello, "Godbold Interview," 56.
43. White, *United States Marines*, 124; MIS-X Section, CPM Branch, "Ex-Reports 665–668 (CHINA)," Appendix C, 8; Newell, Diary, 29 April, 10 and 15–16 August, and 10 and 15 October 1942; Snipes, "Adventureros," 12; Durrwachter, Diary, 3 October 1942; Oldham, *Lieutenant Stephen Polkinghorn*, 49; Marcello, "Godbold Interview," 47; Pearsall, Diary, 15 and 22 November 1942.
44. O'Guinn, "V.O.C.," 59; Kantzer, "Imperial Guest," 80, 81, 84; White, *United States Marines*, 67–68; Reeves, interview; Nye, interview; Hotchkiss, interview, October 22, 1982; Richardson, reply; Oldham, *Lieutenant Stephen Polkinghorn*, 53; Kauffman, "Rogge Interview," 2; Kinney and McCaffrey, *Wake Island Pilot*, 127; Young, "WWII POW," 7; T. Miller, "T. Johnson Interview, 1 June 2001," 19; Newell, Diary, 24 January, 1, 11, 14, 21, and 28 February, 14 March, 18, 23, and 30 April, 14 and 25 May, 5 and 29 June, 6

and 25 July, 8, 16, 21, and 30 August, 11, 19, and 24 September, 2 October 1943, and 17 April 1944; O'Guinn, "V.O.C.," 59.
45. O'Guinn, "V.O.C.," 59; Ishihara, Testimony, "*USA vs. Ishihara*," 115; Kantzer, "Imperial Guest," 84; Newell, Diary, 5 June 1943, and 23 April 1944.
46. Chapman, interview; White, *United States Marines*, 67; Sandvold, interview; Richardson, reply; Kinney and McCaffrey, *Wake Island Pilot*, 127.
47. Gross, interview, October 22, 1983; Sturgeon, interview, October 13, 1984; Kessler, *To Wake Island and Beyond*, 115–116; Holmes to author, 3 December 1978; Richardson, reply; Durrwachter, Diary, 27 May 1942; Freuler, interview; Nye, interview; E. Davis, interview; Stegmaier, interview; Tice, interview; Kinney and McCaffrey, *Wake Island Pilot*, 127; Pearsall, Diary, 9, 11, 13, 17, and 19 November 1942.
48. Durrwachter, Diary, 27 May 1942; Richardson, reply; Pearsall, Diary, 17, 19, and 21 November 1942.
49. Holmes to author, 21 January 1979; Young, "WWII POW," 7; Freuler, interview; Magnino, *Jim's Journey*, 110; Marcello, "Godbold Interview," 57; Stegmaier, interview; Gross, interview, October 13, 1984; Kinney and McCaffrey, *Wake Island Pilot*, 107.
50. White, *United States Marines*, 43; O'Guinn, "V.O.C.," 45; Pay, Diary, 21 February and 21 April 1942.
51. Snipes, "Adventureros," 12; Kantzer, "Imperial Guest," 75, 78; Nowlin, reply, March 18, 1980; J. Johnson, reply, May 9, 1981; Pay, Diary, 29 April 1942; Newell, Diary, 7 May, 5 and 12 July, 10 August, and 15 November 1942; Hassig, interview; Special Div., State Dept, to War Dept. Information Bureau, 15 September 1942, 2–3.
52. White, *United States Marines*, 127–128.
53. Himelrick, Diary, n.d.
54. *Washington Post*, October 14, 1945; Reeves, interview; Snipes, "Adventureros," 12; Nowlin, reply, March 18, 1980; Marcello, "Godbold Interview," 58; Oldham, *Lieutenant Stephen Polkinghorn*, 15; Kauffman, "Ludington Interview," 5: 26.
55. Hotchkiss, interview, October 21, 1983; Pearsall, Diary, 6, 13, and 19 November 1942; Hoskins, "Memoir," 8; Shores, interview; Tex Akin to Gavan Daws, 21 March 1985, Daws Papers; Reeves, interview; Kauffman, "Ludington Interview," 5: 26.
56. Carr, "Tales of Woe"; Shores, interview; Tex Akin to Gavan Daws, March 21, 1985; Pearsall, Diary, 11 November 1942; Frank, "Devereux Transcript," 131–132.
57. Richardson, "Front Man," 1, 5; Kinney and McCaffrey, *Wake Island Pilot*, 117; Young, "WWII POW," 9.
58. Stocks, interview; LaPorte, interview; Kibble, "My War," 140; J. Johnson, reply, May 9, 1981; Young, "WWII POW," 7; Burton, *Life's Trails*, 81.

59. Gregouire to author, March 1979; MIS-X Section, CPM Branch, "Ex-Reports 665–668 (CHINA)," Appendix C, 12; Newell, Diary, 10 and 31 May 1942; J. Johnson, reply, May 9, 1981; Joe Goicoechea to Gavan Daws, 12 February 1992, Daws Papers; *Cleveland Catholic Universe Bulletin*, November 9 and 16, 1945; *St. Louis Post-Dispatch*, October 28, 1945; *Queen's Work*, December 1945, n.p., clippng in B.2, F.2, Devereux Collection.
60. Newell, Diary, 12 July and 10 August 1942; Kantzer, "Imperial Guest," 79–80; Ashurst, "Record," 6; Pearsall, Diary, 16 November 1942.
61. King, interview; Kelnhofer, interview; Marcello, "Venable Interview," 66–67; Durrwachter, Diary, 26 February and 30 March 1942; Daws, "Jaffe Interview," 40; Kantzer, "Imperial Guest," 80–81; Richardson, reply; Stegmaier, interview; Shores, interview; Marcello, "Fields Interview," 33–34; D. Miller, *Doc Miller*, 19; Rumpel, "My Experience," 13.
62. Chapman, interview; Marcello, "Venable Interview," 66–67; Magnino, *Jim's Journey*, 113–114; Hotchkiss, interview, October 21, 1983; Marcello, "McDaniel Interview," 56–57; Snipes, "Adventureros," 13; Hoskins, "Memoir," 12; Durrwachter, Diary, 27 May 1942, and n.d.
63. Pearsall, Diary, 16 and 18 November 1942; Durrwachter, Diary, 6 and 30 March and 10 May 1942; Skaggs, reply; Shores, interview; Marcello, "Fields Interview," 14; White, *United States Marines*, 64; Freuler, interview; LaPorte, interview.

CHAPTER 10

1. Chapman, interview; Hotchkiss, interview, October 21, 1983; Jesse E. Nowlin to author, 24 November 1979; Kessler, *To Wake Island and Beyond*, 126; Marcello, "Venable Interview," 60; Nye, interview; LaPorte, interview; John Brown L. Anderson, Affidavit, 23 January 1946, 1, File 67-75, Bk. 1 (1–2), POWs on the *Nitta Maru*, RG 153; Williams, interview.
2. Kelnhofer, interview; Kessler, *To Wake Island and Beyond*, 199; White, *United States Marines*, 36; Ashurst, "Record," 2; LaPorte, interview; Broyles, reply; Floyd H. Hilberg, Affidavit, December 14, 1945, Prosecution Exhibit No. 15, "*USA vs. Ishihara*," 59; Chapman, interview; D. Miller, *Doc Miller*, 13; Hotchkiss, interview, October 21, 1983.
3. Smith, interview; Camp, interview; Richardson, "Voice," 13; Young, "WWII POW," 9; J. Cook, interview; Wheeler, interview.
4. *Washington Post*, October 14, 1945; Hoskins, "Memoir," 22; Conner, interview; Chapman, interview; Kauffman, "Gooding Interview," 11; Richardson, reply.
5. Richardson, reply; Reeves, interview; Marcello, "Venable Interview," 59; Marcello, "Godbold Interview," 42–43.

6. Mettscher, reply; Magnino, *Jim's Journey*, 108, 241; Hassig, interview; Skaggs, reply; Sandvold, interview; Nye, interview; Broyles, reply; Hoskins, "Memoir," 23.
7. Gross, interview, October 22, 1983; Hanna, interview; Stegmaier, interview; Nye, interview; J. Cook, interview; Row, interview; Pistole, interview; Robert J. Hardy to Lt. Col. James P. S. Devereux, USMC, 1 May 1946, B.1, F.4, Devereux Collection; Tushihiko Yazawa, Testimony, March 4, 1946, "*USA vs. Ishihara*," 49.
8. Row, interview; Sturgeon, interview, October 13–14, 1984; Gross, interview, October 13, 1984; Nye, interview; Marcello, "Fields Interview," 38.
9. Kazunori Morisako, Testimony, March 4, 1946, "*USA vs. Ishihara*," 54; Abraham, *Do You Understand*, 63; Richardson, reply; Sturgeon, interview, October 13, 1984; Nye, interview; J. Johnson, reply, May 9, 1981; White, *United States Marines*, 57; Marcello, "Fields Interview," 38; Bowsher, interview; Rumpel, "My Experience," 6–7.
10. White, *United States Marines*, 57; Sturgeon, interview, October 13, 1984; Hotchkiss, interview, October 21, 1983; Chapman, interview; Nye, interview; Smith, interview; Sandvold, interview.
11. Stegmaier, interview.
12. Chapman, interview; Magnino, *Jim's Journey*, 183.
13. Newell, Diary, 18–19 June 1942; J. Johnson, Diary, 18 June 1942; Papock, Diary, 19 June 1942; Pay, Diary, 19 June 1942; Kantzer, "Imperial Guest," 76; Durrwachter, Diary, 27 June 1942; Tice, interview; Nye, interview; Ashurst, "Record," 3, 9.
14. Ashurst, "Record," 6; "Geneva Convention," 5232; Chapman, interview; Marcello, "Godbold Interview," 59–60.
15. Richard P. Adams, "In the Matter of the Mistreatment of an American . . . at Whu Sung (phonetic) Prison Camp in Approximately October 1942," January 30, 1946, 2–3, File 101-150, Box 1584, Japanese War Crimes at Woosung, RG 153.
16. O'Guinn, "V.O.C.," 75; Kinney and McCaffrey, *Wake Island Pilot*, 114; Reeves, interview; T. Miller, "T. Johnson Interview, 1 June 2001," 6; Malleck to author, 27 July 1981; Bowsher, interview; Jones to author, 15 September 1981.
17. Kelnhofer, interview; Kessler, *To Wake Island and Beyond*, 199; Kauffman, "Gooding Interview," 11; Magnino, *Jim's Journey*, 108; Reeves, interview; Nye, interview; Sturgeon, interview, October 13, 1984; Stocks, interview; Kibble, "My War," 152; Broyles, reply.
18. White, *United States Marines*, 56–57; Kinney and McCaffrey, *Wake Island Pilot*, 107–108; "Geneva Convention," 5234; Freuler, interview; Shores, interview.

19. "Geneva Convention," 5234; Ashurst, "Record," 6.
20. Richardson, "Bread," 2–3; Chapman, interview; Norwood and Shek, "POW Camps," 30; Edward L. Cook, Affidavit, October 26, 1945, Prosecution Exhibit No. 36, "*USA vs. Ishihara*," 94; Pay, Diary, 30 March 1942; Kantzer, "Imperial Guest," 72; Durrwachter, Diary, 28 April 1942.
21. Kinney, "P.O.W. Survival," 79; MIS-X Section, CPM Branch, "Ex-Report No. 670 (CHINA)," August 20, 1945, 1, Escape Reports, Nos. 654–671 (G-2), RG 389; Kantzer, "Imperial Guest," 72, 85; Mettscher, reply; Carr, "Tales of Woe"; Gross, interview, October 22, 1983; Marcello, "McDaniel Interview," 54; Abraham, *Do You Understand*, 65; Durrwachter, Diary, 10 May 1942.
22. Lester LeRoy Barger, "In the Matter of the Use of American Prisoners of War in Polishing Artillery Shells at Shanghai, China," March 28, 1946, 1–2, File 101-59, Japanese War Crimes at Kiangwan, RG 153; Kibble, "My War," 153; Holmes to author, 21 January 1979; Kantzer, "Imperial Guest," 73; Wheeler, interview; Magnino, *Jim's Journey*, 111–112; T. Miller, "T. Johnson Interview, 1 June 2001," 11–12; William Krenistki, "Improper Imprisonment and Lack of Food," September 29, 1945, 2, File 101-150, Box 1584, Japanese War Crimes at Woosung, RG 153; "Geneva Convention," 5234.
23. Kinney and McCaffrey, *Wake Island Pilot*, 113; La Porte, interview; MIS-X, Section CPM Branch, "Ex-Reports 665–668 (CHINA)," Appendix C, 7; Barger, "Polishing Artillery Shells," 1–2; Norwood and Shek, "POW Camps," 30; Pay, Diary, 24 March 1941; Krenistki, "Improper Imprisonment," 6; Kauffman, "Ludington Interview," 5: 20.
24. Kantzer, "Imperial Guest," 73, 74; T. Miller, "T. Johnson Interview, 1 June 2001," 11–12; Marcello, "Venable Interview," 65–66; Kauffman, "Ludington Interview," 5: 19; Hubley, interview; Kauffman, "Goiceochea Interview," 18; Wheeler, interview; Richardson, reply; Barger, "Polishing Artillery Shells," 1–2; Newell, Diary, 10 May 1942; Magnino, *Jim's Journey*, 111–112; Pay, Diary, 24 and 26 March 1942.
25. Reeves, interview; Chapman, interview; Smith, interview; Kauffman, "Ludington Interview," 5: 19–20; Kantzer, "Imperial Guest," 74; Barger, "Polishing Artillery Shells," 1–2.
26. J. Johnson, reply, May 9, 1981; Chapman, interview; Pearsall, Diary, 12 November 1942.
27. Kelnhofer, interview; Nowlin, reply, March 18, 1980; Pearsall, Diary, 20 and 27 November 1942; Abraham, *Do You Understand*, 56; Chapman, interview.
28. Plate, reply; Kibble, "My War," 141; Marcello, "McDaniel Interview," 53; Mettscher, reply; Reeves, interview; Holmes to author, 3 December 1978; Bowsher, interview; LaPorte, interview.

29. Plate, reply; Mettscher, reply; Holmes to author, 3 December 1978; Bowsher, interview; Richardson "Bread," 3; LaPorte, interview.
30. Pearsall, Diary, 10, 18, 20, and 23 November 1942; Kibble, "My War," 141.
31. Kantzer, "Imperial Guest," 87, 88; J. Johnson, reply, May 9, 1981; Newell, Diary, 19, 20, and 22 October 1942; Marcello, "McDaniel Interview," 52; Richardson, "Bread," 4.
32. MIS-X Section, CPM Branch, "Ex-Reports 665–668 (CHINA)," Appendix C, 5; Daws, "Foley Interview," 1; Henningsen, "Shanghai Prisoners," 6–7.
33. Kantzer, "Imperial Guest," 74; Magnino, *Jim's Journey*, 112, 136–137; Young, "WWII POW," 6; Valov to Devereux, 18 April 1946; Nye, interview.
34. White, *United States Marines*, 70–73; Richardson, "Bread," 3.
35. "Geneva Convention," 5233, 5235; Pay, Diary, 18 September 1942; Durrwachter, Diary, 3 October 1942; Newell, Diary, 28 November 1942.
36. White, *United States Marines*, 97; Norwood and Shek, "POW Camps," 31; Gross, interview, October 22, 1983; Magnino, *Jim's Journey*, 138; John Ahlers, "Shanghai at the War's End," *Far Eastern Survey*, 14 (1945), 332–333; Kelnhofer, interview; MIS-X Section, CPM Branch, "Ex-Reports 665–668 (CHINA)," Appendix C, 8; Marcello, "Fields Interview," 32; Ashurst, "Record," 6; Bruce Elleman, *Japanese–American Civilian Prisoner Exchanges and Detention Camps, 1941–45*, Routledge Studies in the Modern History of Asia (London: Routledge, 2006), 51; Greg Leck, *Captives of Empire: The Japanese Internment of Allied Civilians in China, 1941–1945* (Bangor, PA: Sandy Press, 2006), 300.
37. Chapman, interview; Kessler, *To Wake Island and Beyond*, 136; White, *United States Marines*, 97; Norwood and Shek, "POW Camps," 30.
38. "Geneva Convention," 5233, 5235; Durrwachter, Diary, 28 February 1942; Pay, Diary, 5, 23, 25, and 26 March and 26 April 1942; Kantzer, "Imperial Guest," 72, 78; MIS-X Section, CPM Branch, "Ex-Reports 665–668 (CHINA)," Appendix C, 8; Newell, Diary, March, 27 April, 2 and 3 June, 6 and 15 July, and 14 and 17 September 1942; Papock, Diary, 25 March 1942; Special Div., State Dept., to War Dept. Information Bureau, 15 September 1942, 1–2; Ashurst, "Record," 5.
39. Kantzer, "Imperial Guest," 72, 78, 86; Newell, Diary, March, 27 April, 3 June, and 15 July 1942; Kauffman, "Loveland Interview," 28.
40. Pay, Diary, 5 and 26 March and 26 April 1942; Newell, Diary, March and 6 and 15 July 1942; Durrwachter, Diary, 28 April 1942; Kantzer, "Imperial Guest," 77.
41. Ashurst, "Record," 5; Chapman, interview.
42. Nye, interview; Marcello, "Fields Interview," 29–30; Kinney and McCaffrey, *Wake Island Pilot*, 115; Abraham, *Do You Understand*, 77; Kantzer, "Imperial Guest," 77; Holmes to author, 27 December 1978.

43. Kinney and McCaffrey, *Wake Island Pilot*, 115; White, *United States Marines*, 61, 63; Abraham, *Do You Understand*, 77; Chapman, interview; Kessler, *To Wake Island and Beyond*, 109–111; Daws, "Foley Interview," 1; Burton, *Life's Trails*, 80; Hassig, interview; H. Davis, "Improper Conditions at Woosung," 2–3; Newell, Diary, 3 April 1942; Richardson, "Voice," 28.
44. Kessler, *To Wake Island and Beyond*, 109–110; Richardson, "Voice," 28; Newell, Diary, 6 and 12 May 1942; Papock, Diary, 7 May 1942; Abraham, *Do You Understand*, 77; Chapman, interview; Kessler, *To Wake Island and Beyond*, 109–110; Richardson, "Voice," 28; Kinney and McCaffrey, *Wake Island Pilot*, 115; O'Guinn, "V.O.C.," 53; White, *United States Marines*, 62.
45. H. Davis, "Improper Conditions at Woosung," 2–3; Marcello, "Fields Interview," 29; Marcello, "Venable Interview," 57; Newell, Diary, 24 June 1942; Kantzer, "Imperial Guest," 76; Durrwachter, Diary, 27 June 1942.
46. T. Miller, "T. Johnson Interview, 1 June 2001," 21.
47. Kantzer, "Imperial Guest," 81; Newell, Diary, 7 August 1942; O'Guinn, "V.O.C.," 53.
48. Kantzer, "Imperial Guest," 81.
49. Kantzer, "Imperial Guest," 81, 88; White, *United States Marines*, 63.
50. Newell, Diary, 2 August 1942; Richardson, reply; Rumpel, "My Experience," 5, 7; J. Cook, interview; Daws, "Foley Interview," 1.
51. For surveys of conditions in different Japanese POW camps, see Norwood and Shek, "POW Camps," 1–81, and John M. Gibbs, "Prisoner of War Camps in Japan and Japanese Controlled Areas as Taken From Reports of Interned American Prisoners," July 31, 1946, 1–200, RG 389.

CHAPTER 11

1. Freuler, Diary, 8–13 February 1942; Kinney and McCaffrey, *Wake Island Pilot*, 104–106; Cunningham and Sims, *Wake Island Command*, 131–132; Kinney, "P.O.W. Survival," 58–60; Cunningham, interview.
2. Kessler, *To Wake Island and Beyond*, 94–95.
3. Kantzer, "Imperial Guest," 71, 74, 81; Richardson, "Voice," 26–27; King, interview; E. Davis, interview; J. Johnson, reply, May 9, 1981; Conner, interview.
4. J. Johnson, reply, May 9, 1981; Shores, interview; Marcello, "McDaniel Interview," 70; Richardson, "Voice," 27.
5. Richardson, "Voice," 26–27; Kantzer, "Imperial Guest," 74; J. Johnson, reply, May 9, 1981; Shores, interview.
6. Hassig, interview; King, interview; J. Johnson, reply, May 9, 1981.
7. Kinney, "P.O.W. Survival," 34, 61–62; Kinney and McCaffrey, *Wake Island Pilot*, 116; White, *United States Marines*, 157; Nowlin, reply, March 18, 1980.

8. Hotchkiss, interviews, October 22, 1982, and October 21, 1983; Kelnhofer, interview; *Washington Post*, October 14, 1945; Smith, interview.
9. R. Brown, interview; Hotchkiss, interview, October 22, 1982; Marcello, "Godbold Interview," 67; Mettscher, reply; Reeves, interview; *Washington Post*, October 14, 1945; Pistole, interview; Richardson, reply; Marcello, "McDaniel Interview," 91; Marcello, "Fields Interview," 22; Chapman, interview; Reynolds, *Officially Dead*, 49; Burton, *Life's Trails*, 81.
10. R. Brown, interview; Gregouire to author, March 1979.
11. Pay, Diary, 27 February 1942; Durrwachter, Diary, 28 February and 1 March 1942; White, *United States Marines*, 46, 50; Reynolds, *Officially Dead*, 41–43.
12. Cunningham, interview; Cunningham and Sims, *Wake Island Command*, 132–143; Reynolds, *Officially Dead*, 4, 44; Richardson, reply; Kinney and McCaffrey, *Wake Island Pilot*, 108; White, *United States Marines*, 46–47.
13. Cunningham and Sims, *Wake Island Command*, 135–138, 141–142; Reynolds, *Officially Dead*, 45–48, 53–54; Pay, Diary, 12 and 14 March 1942; Papock, Diary, 12 March 1942; Durrwachter, Diary, 12 March 1942; *Oakland Post Enquirer*, September 8, 1945; Kinney and McCaffrey, *Wake Island Pilot*, 108; Holmes to author, 21 January 1979; Abraham, *Do You Understand*, 59–60; Ashurst, "Record," 2; Oldham, *Lieutenant Stephen Polkinghorn*, 13–14; O'Guinn, "V.O.C.," 46; Kessler, *To Wake Island and Beyond*, 90–91.
14. Cunningham and Sims, *Wake Island Command*, 137–141, 143–144; Reynolds, *Officially Dead*, 49–50, 53–54; Papock, Diary, 13 March 1942; Pay, Diary, 13–14 March 1942; White, *United States Marines*, 47; Kessler, *To Wake Island and Beyond*, 90; Winfield Scott Cunningham to Col. James D. McBrayer, USMC, 17 April 1962, B.1, F.3, Cunningham Collection.
15. Cunningham and Sims, *Wake Island Command*, 145–151; Reynolds, *Officially Dead*, 54–122; Kay Nogami, "Memoirs," 1963, 1–8, B.2, F.1, Cunningham Collection; John Bumgarner, *Parade of the Dead: A U.S. Army Physician's Memoir of Imprisonment by the Japanese, 1942–1945* (Jefferson, NC: McFarland, 1995), 102–103; Samuel C. Grashio and Bernard Norling, *Return to Freedom* (Tulsa, OK: MCN Press, 1982), 65–66; Lester I. Tenney, *My Hitch in Hell: The Bataan Death March* (Washington, DC: Brassey's, 1995), 111–113; Donald Knox, *Death March: The Survivors of Bataan* (New York: Harcourt Brace Jovanovich, Publishers, 1981), 179–184; Robert S. LaForte, Ronald E. Marcello, and Richard L. Himmel, eds., *With Only the Will to Live: Accounts of Americans in Japanese Prison Camps, 1941–1945* (Wilmington, DE: SR Books, 1994), 29–32.
16. Pistole, interview; Pay, Diary, 14, 17, 25, and 26 March 1942; Marcello, "McDaniel Interview," 64.

17. Pay, Diary, 17 March 1942; O'Guinn, "V.O.C.," 47; White, *United States Marines*, 48–51; Kinney and McCaffrey, *Wake Island Pilot*, 111; "Geneva Convention," 5237–5238; Ashurst, "Record," 4; Richardson, "Outpost of Empire," 4.
18. Richardson, "Outpost of Empire," 4; Durrwachter, Diary, 22 March 1942; Hanna, interview; LaPorte, interview; Kinney and McCaffrey, *Wake Island Pilot*, 111.
19. White, *United States Marines*, 49; Holmes to author, 25 March 1979; Kauffman, "Ludington Interview," 5: 19; Richardson, "Outpost of Empire," 5.
20. Woodrow M. Kessler to Gavan Daws, 25 April 1987, Daws Papers; White, *United States Marines*, 50–52; LaPorte, interview.
21. Papock, Diary, 30 March 1942; Pay, Diary, 30 March 1942; Durrwachter, Diary, 30 March 1942; Newell, Diary, 30 March 1942; Brimmer, Affidavit, 3–6; White, *United States Marines*, 53–54.
22. Richardson, "Voice," 30; Pay, Diary, 31 March and 2 April 1942; Papock, Diary, 31 March 1942; Sturgeon, interview, October 13, 1984; Ashurst, "Record," 7; John Francis Ryan, "In the Matter of the Mass Punishment of American Prisoners . . . at Woosung, . . . September 1942," February 12, 1946, 1–2, File 101-150, Box 1584, Japanese War Crimes at Woosung, RG 153.
23. Papock, Diary, 31 March 1942; Pay, Diary, 2 April 1942; Durrwachter, Diary, 12 April 1942; Kinney and McCaffrey, *Wake Island Pilot*, 109; Kessler, *To Wake Island and Beyond*, 91; Richardson, reply; White, *United States Marines*, 34.
24. Ashurst, "Record," 4; Pay, Diary, 15 August 1942; Papock, Diary, 15 August 1942; J. Johnson, Diary, 15 August 1942; Kantzer, "Imperial Guest," 81; Durrwachter, Diary, 17 August 1942; Newell, Diary, 15 and 16 August 1942; Nye, interview.
25. Kantzer, "Imperial Guest," 76, 81; Newell, Diary, 24 August 1942; White, *United States Marines*, 136; Herman Raspe to Col. James P. S. Devereux, USMC, 30 June 1946, B.1, F.4, Devereux Collection; Young, "WWII POW," 7.
26. Newell, Diary, 28 August 1942; J. Johnson, Diary, 28 August 1942; Pay, Diary, 28–29 August 1942; White, *United States Marines*, 65–66; Hubley, interview.
27. White, *United States Marines*, 65–66; Kantzer, "Imperial Guest," 84; Ashurst, "Record," 4.
28. Pay, Diary, 21 August, 5 and 31 October, and 13–14 November 1942; Newell, Diary, 20 August, 5–6 October, and 1 and 13 November 1942; Oldham, *Lieutenant Stephen Polkinghorn*, 15; Papock, Diary, 5 October 1942; H. Davis, "Improper Conditions at Woosung," 2; Daws, "Akin Interview," 36.
29. Elleman, *Japanese–American Exchanges*, 2–4, 9, 11, 18, 29–30, 33, 36, 41; Leck, *Captives*, 283–285; Papock, Diary, 29 June 1942; Pay, Diary, 29 June

1942. For more on this subject, see P. Scott Corbett, *Quiet Passages: The Exchange of Civilians Between the United States and Japan During the Second World War* (Kent, OH: Kent State University Press, 1987).
30. Pay, Diary, 14 and 30 April and 9 and 29 June 1942; Ronald E. Marcello, "Interview With Willie L. Benton, March 10, 1975," 99, UNT Oral History Collection; Kantzer, "Imperial Guest," 73; J. Johnson, Diary, 9 June 1942; Oldham, *Lieutenant Stephen Polkinghorn*, 14; Holmes to author, 25 March 1979; O'Guinn, "V.O.C.," 58; Newell, Diary, 14 April and 9 May 1942; Kinney and McCaffrey, *Wake Island Pilot*, 116; Hanna, interview.
31. Elleman, *Japanese-American Exchanges*, 33, 34, 43, 53; Leck, *Captives*, 288; Hanna, interview.
32. Pay, Diary, 29 May and 7 August 1942; Oldham, *Lieutenant Stephen Polkinghorn*, 14, 15; Leck, *Captives*, 290–294; Newell, Diary, 7 August 1942; Papock, Diary, 7 and 16 August 1942.
33. Magnino, *Jim's Journey*, 120; Kantzer, "Imperial Guest," 71, 84; Devereux, *Story of Wake*, 224; Holmes to author, 21 January 1979; Herbert C. Freuler to Lucille M. Freuler, 30 May 1942 (photostat copy in the author's possession).
34. Nye, interview; Stegmaier, interview; Kinney, "P.O.W. Survival," 85; Hotchkiss, interview, October 22, 1982; Plate, reply; Kantzer, "Imperial Guest," 85; J. Cook, interview.
35. H. Freuler to L. Freuler, 30 May 1942; Jack B. Cook to Mrs. John B. Cook, ca. late May–early June 1942 (author's transcription of original in Cook's possession).
36. *Washington News*, July 23, 1942; Special Div., State Dept., to War Dept. Information Bureau, 15 September 1942, 1–3; Henningsen, "Shanghai Prisoners," 4–5; White, *United States Marines*, 80; Nye, interview; Jack B. Cook to Mr. and Mrs. John B. Cook, 29 April 1943 (author's transcription of original in Cook's possession).
37. *Red Cross Activities*, vol. 1, 452–461; Henningsen, "Shanghai Prisoners," 4; White, *United States Marines*, 79.
38. "Form 1698," n.d. (author's transcription of Japanese document in Jack B. Cook's possession); Oldham, *Lieutenant Stephen Polkinghorn*, 57; Holmes to author, 27 December 1978, and 21 January 1979; J. Cook, interview; Marcello, "Venable Interview," 68; T. Miller, "T. Johnson Interview, 1 June 2001," 22; O'Guinn, "V.O.C.," 67.
39. John Cotton, "How the Japanese Treat Prisoners," *Marine Corps Gazette*, March 1945, 30; "Form 1698"; White, *United States Marines*, 80; Nye, interview; Magnino, *Jim's Journey*, 120; Kantzer, "Imperial Guest," 180; Papock, Diary, 23 June 1944; Holmes to author, 21 January 1979.
40. Louise Hotchkiss to Clifford E. Hotchkiss, 15 October 1943 (photostat copy in author's possession); Holmes to author, 21 January 1979; Hotchkiss, interview, October 22, 1982; Nye, interview.

41. Ashurst, "Record," 7; MIS-X Section, CPM Branch, "Ex-Report No. 670 (CHINA), Appendix C, July 24, 1945, 5, Escape Reports, Nos. 654–671 (G-2), RG 389; MIS-X Section, CPM Branch, "Ex-Report, No. 669 (CHINA), Appendix C, July 12, 1945, 8–9, Escape Reports, Nos. 654–671 (G-2), RG 389; Newell, Diary, 14 August, 22, 26, 27, and 28 September, 15 October, and 17 November 1942; Magnino, *Jim's Journey*, 125; Kantzer, "Imperial Guest," 85; J. Johnson, Diary, 30 September 1942; White, *United States Marines*, 79; Durrwachter, Diary, 3 October 1942; Pay, Diary, 29 October 1942; Devereux, *Story of Wake*, 224; Malleck to author, 29 August 1981; Special Division, Department of State, to War Department (PMG), "International Red Cross Committee Memorandum of the Visit by Mr. Egle to the Prisoners of War Camp at Shanghai, on January 9, 1943," 23 September 1943, 1–2, Conditions at Kiangwan, China (Folder No. II), RG 389.
42. Kinney, "P.O.W. Survival," 14, 195; Jesse E. Nowlin to author, 5 February 1980; MIS-X Section, CPM Branch, "Ex-Report No. 670 (CHINA)," Appendix C, 5; White, *United States Marines*, 80; Hassig, interview; Marcello, "Venable Interview," 67; Marcello, "McDaniel Interview," 56; D. Miller, *Doc Miller*, 15; Chapman, interview; Wheeler, interview; Smith, interview; Jack B. Cook to Mrs. John B. Cook, 12 April 1944 (author's transcription of original in Cook's possession); Nye, interview; *San Francisco Chronicle*, February 11, 1945; Alvin H. Blahuta, Affidavit, November 2, 1945, 1, File 101-59, Box 1584, Japanese War Crimes at Woosung, RG 153.
43. American Legation, Bern, to Special War Problems Division, Department of State, "Despatch No. 11768: American Interests—Shanghai Intercross Report regarding Visit to Haiphong Road Civilian Internment Camp and Kiangwan Prisoner of War Camp," 23 May 1945, 5, Kiangwan Prisoner of War Camp, Shanghai, RG 389; Office of Censorship, "Record No., NY PW 14617: American Prisoners of War and Civilian Internees in Shanghai War Prisoners' Camp," ca. September 1943, 1–2, Conditions at Kiangwan, China (Folder No. II), RG 389; Nowlin to author, 5 February 1980; Kinney, "P.O.W. Survival," 195; Jack B. Cook to Mr. and Mrs. John B. Cook, 29 April and 24 August 1943; Jack B. Cook to Mrs. John B. Cook, ca. late May–early June 1942, 1 January, 29 April, 23 June, and 24 August 1943, ca. December 1943, 6 February, 12 April 1944, and 16 July 1945 (all author's transcriptions from originals in Cook's possession).
44. Huizenga, Affidavit, 7; Kantzer, "Imperial Guest," 85; Pay, Diary, 18 September 1942; Papock, Diary, 18 September 1942; Newell, Diary, 18 September 1942; Oldham, *Lieutenant Stephen Polkinghorn*, 15; Magnino, *Jim's Journey*, 124; Norwood and Shek, "POW Camps," 31.
45. Newell, Diary, 23, 25, and 27 October and 3 November 1942; Kantzer, "Imperial Guest," 88; King, interview; Kirk, *Secret Camera*, 70; Conner, interview.

46. Devereux, *Story of Wake*, 225–226; R. Brown, interview; Phillip W. Johnson to Lt. Col. James P. S. Devereux, USMC, ca. June 1946, B.1, F.3, Devereux Collection.
47. Richardson, "Voice," 30; J. Cook, interview; Camp, interview; Young, "WWII POW," 9; Cox, interview.
48. White, *United States Marines*, 46, 69–70, 76; Sturgeon, interview, October 13, 1984; R. Brown, interview; J. Cook, interview; J. Johnson, reply, May 9, 1981; Clarence E. Wolfe, Affidavit, October 4, 1945, Prosecution Exhibit No. 12, "*USA vs. Ishihara*," 41; Isamu Ishihara, Affidavit, January 3, 1946, Prosecution Exhibit No. 40, "*USA vs. Ishihara*," 108; E. Cook, Affidavit, "*USA vs. Ishihara*," 94; Huizenga, Affidavit, "*USA vs. Ishihara*," 2; Marcello, "Fields Interview," 20; Chapman, interview; Marcello, "McDaniel Interview," 51; Conner, interview; Camp, interview; Holmes to author, 25 March 1979.
49. Bernard E. Richardson, "Fanatic With Cropped Hair" (unpublished manuscript in the author's possession, November 17, 1954), 5; White, *United States Marines*, 69–70; Abraham, *Do You Understand*, 47–48, 55; O'Guinn, "V.O.C.," 56–57; Richard O. Bone, Affidavit, January 2, 1946, Prosecution Exhibit No. 28, "*USA vs. Ishihara*," 81; Holmes to author, 25 March 1979.
50. R. Brown, interview; Huizenga, Affidavit, 2; Holmes to author, 25 March 1979; Camp, interview; Williams, interview; Nowlin, reply, March 18, 1980; White, *United States Marines*, 69; T. Miller, "T. Johnson Interview, 1 June 2001," 12; James N. Young, Affidavit, September 29, 1945, Prosecution Exhibit No. 9, "*USA vs. Ishihara*," 36; S. L. Baker, Affidavit, December 29, 1945, Prosecution Exhibit No. 22, "*USA vs. Ishihara*," 73; Oscar G. Jacobson, Affidavit, October 12, 1945, Prosecution Exhibit No. 39, "*USA vs. Ishihara*," 99; Akin, Affidavit, "*USA vs. Ishihara*," 84; E. Cook, Affidavit, "*USA vs. Ishihara*," 69–70; Comfort, Affidavit, "*USA vs. Ishihara*," 59; Yazawa, Testimony, "*USA vs. Ishihara*," 47; Ishihara, Testimony, "*USA vs. Ishihara*," 110–111, 114, 116–117; James S. Browning, "In the Matter of the Torture of Approximately 50 American Prisoners . . . by . . . Ishihari," December 29, 1945, 1, File 101-150, Box 1584, Japanese War Crimes at Woosung, RG 153.
51. Hubley, interview; Williams, interview; Holmes to author, 25 March 1979; Sturgeon, interview, October 13, 1984; Marcello, "McDaniel Interview," 50–51; Abraham, *Do You Understand*, 106–107; T. Miller, "T. Johnson Interview, June 1, 2001," 13; Richardson, "Fanatic," 3.
52. Shores, interview; Holmes to author, 25 March 1979; Plate Reply; Nowlin, reply, March 18, 1980; R. Brown, interview; Richardson, reply; J. Cook, interview; Pistole, interview; Stocks, interview; Hanna, interview; Abraham, *Do You Understand*, 62; Williams, interview; Joseph T. Chudzik, Affi-

davit, October 6, 1945, Prosecution Exhibit No. 21, "*USA vs. Ishihara,*" 71; Alvin H. Blahuta, Affidavit, October 6, 1945, Prosecution Exhibit No. 37, "*USA vs. Ishihara,*" 95; McBrayer, Affidavit, "*USA vs. Ishihara,*" 86; Baker, Affidavit, "*USA vs. Ishihara,*" 73; Ishihara, Testimony, "*USA vs. Ishihara,*" 113, 118; Camp, interview; Freuler, interview; Hassig, interview; Hubley, interview; Haidinger, interview; Wheeler, interview; Reeves, interview; Tice, interview.

53. Marcello, "Venable Interview," 61–62; Richardson, "Fanatic," 5; Hanna, interview; Marcello, "Godbold Interview," 44–45; White, *United States Marines*, 69, 80; Abraham, *Do You Understand*, 106–107; LaPorte, interview; Isamu Ishihara, Affidavit, January 6, 1946, Prosecution Exhibit No. 40, "*USA vs. Ishihara,*" 108, 110; Ishihara, Testimony, "*USA vs. Ishihara,*" 114; Blahuta, Affidavit, "*USA vs. Ishihara,*" 96; American Legation, Bern, to Special War Problems Div., State Dept., "Despatch No. 11768," 4–5; Kinney and McCaffrey, *Wake Island Pilot*, 126; Bowsher, interview.

54. Williams Interview; Shores Interview; Abraham, *Do You Understand*, 135–136; R. Brown, interview; Freuler, interview; Marcello, "Fields Interview," 20; Defense Closing Arguments, March 6, 1946, "*USA vs. Ishihara,*" 120; Huizenga, Affidavit, 2; Hassig, interview.

55. Row, interview; Dower, *War Without Mercy*, 237–249; Richardson, "Fanatic," 9; Williams, interview; Charles R. Milliken, Affidavit, August 1946, 3, File 101-56, Box 1584, Miscellaneous Reports on Atrocities in the Shanghai Camps, RG 153; D. Miller, *Doc Miller*, 13; White, *United States Marines*, 70; Shores, interview; Holmes to author, 25 March 1979.

56. Ishihara, Affidavit, "*USA vs. Ishihara,*" 109–110; Yazawa, Testimony, "*USA vs. Ishihara,*" 51; Daws, "Jaffe Interview," 91; Kessler, *To Wake Island and Beyond*, 92–93; White, *United States Marines*, 69; Richardson, "Fanatic," 3–4, 6; Plate, reply; Richardson, reply.

57. Richard M. Huizenga, Affidavit, August 14, 1945, Prosecution Exhibit No. 18, "*USA vs. Ishihara,*" 65; McBrayer, *Escape*, 118–121.

58. Victor F. Ciarrachi, Affidavit, October 6, 1945, Prosecution Exhibit No. 16, "*USA vs. Ishihara,*" 61; Bernard O. Ketner, Affidavit, October 12, 1945, Prosecution Exhibit No. 17, "*USA vs. Ishihara,*" 62–63; Ralph Y. Williams, Affidavit, n.d., Prosecution Exhibit No. 35, "*USA vs. Ishihara,*" 92; Comfort, Affidavit, "*USA vs. Ishihara,*" 59; Ishihara, Affidavit, "*USA vs. Ishihara,*" 109; Ishihara, Testimony, "*USA vs. Ishihara,*" 112; White, *United States Marines*, 75; Haidinger, interview.

59. Ciarrachi, Affidavit, "*USA vs. Ishihara,*" 61; Ketner, Affidavit, "*USA vs. Ishihara,*" 63; Comfort, Affidavit, "*USA vs. Ishihara,*" 59; Ashurst, "Record," 3; White, *United States Marines*, 75.

60. Raymon Gragg, Affidavit, October 6, 1945, Prosecution Exhibit No. 19, "*USA vs. Ishihara,*" 68; Edward Clancy, Affidavit, September 9, 1945, Pros-

ecution Exhibit No. 23, "*USA vs. Ishihara*," 75; Don Walmer, Affidavit, October 12, 1945, Prosecution Exhibit No. 24, "*USA vs. Ishihara*," 76; Charles H. Darr, Affidavit, October 12, 1945, Prosecution Exhibit No. 27, "*USA vs. Ishihara*," 80; Huizenga, Affidavit, "*USA vs. Ishihara*," 65; E. Cook, Affidavit, "*USA vs. Ishihara*," 69; Bone, Affidavit, "*USA vs. Ishihara*," 81; Blahuta, Affidavit, "*USA vs. Ishihara*," 96; Ishihara, Affidavit, "*USA vs. Ishihara*," 109; Ishihara, Testimony, "*USA vs. Ishihara*," 113; MIS-X Section, CPM Branch, "Ex-Reports 665–668 (CHINA)," Appendix C, 2–4; Ashurst, "Record," 3; Menique, Affidavit, 2; Conner, interview; Shores, interview.
61. Huizenga, Affidavit, "*USA vs. Ishihara*," 65; Clancy, Affidavit, "*USA vs. Ishihara*," 75; White, *United States Marines*, 76–79; Daws, "Foley Interview," 1.
62. White, *United States Marines*, 76–78; *Washington Post*, October 14, 1945; Ashurst, "Record," 3; Richardson, "Fanatic," 4; Hotchkiss, interview, October 21, 1983.
63. White, *United States Marines*, 78–79; Oldham, *Lieutenant Stephen Polkinghorn*, 15; J. Johnson, Diary, 13 September 1942; Papock, Diary, 14 September 1942.
64. Kantzer, "Imperial Guest," 86; Papock, Diary, 3 October 1942; Oldham, *Lieutenant Stephen Polkinghorn*, 15; Newell, Diary, 3–4 October 1942; Pay, Diary, 3–4 October 1942; White, *United States Marines*, 78–79; Magnino, *Jim's Journey*, 124–125; Durrwachter, Diary, 3 October 1942; Mettscher, reply.

CHAPTER 12

1. White, *United States Marines*, 38; Abraham, *Do You Understand*, 79–80; James D. McBrayer Jr., Affidavit, 18 September 1945, Prosecution Exhibit No. 31, "*USA vs. Ishihara*," 86; Clancy, Affidavit, "*USA vs. Ishihara*," 75; Milliken, Affidavit, 1; Huizinga, Affidavit, 3; Ashurst, "Record," 7.
2. Satoshi Otera, Testimony, March 5, 1946, "*USA vs. Ishihara*," 100, 107; Newell, Diary, 20 October 1942; Pay, Diary, October 1942; White, *United States Marines*, 79, 111; Leck, *Captives*, 449; Young, Affidavit, "*USA vs. Ishihara*," 36; Kantzer, "Imperial Guest," 151–152; James S. Browning, "In the Matter of the Use of United States Prisoners of War on Enemy Military Works . . . ," December 29, 1945, 2, File 101-59, Box 1584, Japanese War Crimes at Kiangwan, RG 153; Camp, interview; Kessler, *To Wake Island and Beyond*, 92.
3. Kantzer, "Imperial Guest," 87; Richardson, "Bread," 4.
4. Frank, "Devereux Transcript," 134; Philip Speck Chambers, "In the Matter of the Use of Corporal Philip Speck Chambers . . . on Military Works . . . ," February 12, 1946, 2, File 101-59, Box 1584, Japanese War Crimes at Kiang-

wan, RG 153; Henningsen, "Shanghai Prisoners," 3–4; Kantzer, "Imperial Guest," 87, 133, 177; Pay, Diary, 4 February 1945; Milliken, Affidavit, 1; Magnino, *Jim's Journey*, 183–184; Marcello, "Godbold Interview," 46–47; Sturgeon, interview, October 13, 1984.

5. Frank, "Devereux Transcript," 134; Hotchkiss, interview, October 21, 1983; Camp, interview; Hubley, interview; T. Miller, "T. Johnson Interview, June 1, 2001," 16–17.

6. Marcello, "Godbold Interview," 46; Milliken, Affidavit, 1; LaPorte, interview; Shores, interview; Frank, "Devereux Transcript," 134; Leck, *Captives*, 207.

7. White, *United States Marines*, 79; Marcello, "Benton Interview," 83; LaPorte, interview; Sturgeon, interview, October 13, 1984; Chambers, Affidavit, 2; Richardson, "Bread," 18; Marcello, "Godbold Interview," 46–47.

8. Otera, Testimony, "*USA vs. Ishihara*," 100; Marcello, "Benton Interview," 77, 83; Ronald E. Marcello, ed., "Interview With C. L. Permenter, October 25, 1972," 94, UNT Oral History Collection; Marcello, "McDaniel Interview," 50; Kantzer, "Imperial Guest," 97, 111, 139, 186; Charles A. Holmes to author, 17 July 1979; Ashurst, "Record," 3; Newell, Diary, 16 February, 25 May 1943; Huizenga, Affidavit, 7; Shores, interview; Richardson, "Fanatic," 5; Menique, Affidavit, 2–3; Mettscher, reply; Pearsall, Diary, 8 January 1943.

9. Huizenga, Affidavit, 7; Milliken, Affidavit, 1; Otis T. Jones to author, August 1981; Papock, Diary, 26 March 1943; Pay, Diary, 23–24 April 1943; J. Johnson, Diary, 24 April 1943; Kantzer, "Imperial Guest," 106, 143; William F. Clubb, "In the Matter of the Collective Punishment of the Group for the Offense of Others," January 9, 1946, 2, File 101-150, Box 1584, Japanese War Crimes at Woosung, RG 153; Newell, Diary, 20 May 1943.

10. *Red Cross Activities*, 1: 471–472; Marcello, "Permenter Interview," 51; International Red Cross, Shanghai, "Prisoner of War Camp at Shanghai Visited by Mr. Egle on March 24, 1943," November 3, 1943, 1–2, Conditions at Kiangwan, China (Folder II), RG 389; Edouard Egle, "POW Camp at Shanghai Visited by Mr. E. Egle on the 24th March 1943," n.d., 9, Conditions at Kiangwan, China (Folder II), RG 389; Egle, "Visit to Camp, 10th November 1942," 1, 5; Special Div., State Dept., to War Dept., PMG, "Egle Visit, January 9, 1943," 23 September 1943, 1–2; Special Div., State Dept., to War Dept., "Fontanel Visit, November 4, 1943," 13 January 1944; Newell, Diary, 19 June and 3 December 1943; Pay, Diary, 15 September 1944; Kantzer, "Imperial Guest," 97, 105, 121, 123, 124, 164, 180.

11. Kantzer, "Imperial Guest," 121, 164; Pay, Diary, 27 November 1944.

12. Marcello, "Permenter Interview," 51; Egle, "Camp Visit, 24th March 1943," 1, 2; Special Div., State Dept., to War Dept., "Fontanel Visit, November 4, 1943," 13 January 1944; Kantzer, "Imperial Guest," 97, 121, 164–165,

179–180; Newell, Diary, 4 November 1943; Pay, Diary, 15 September 1944; Oldham, *Lieutenant Stephen Polkinghorn*, 26; American Legation, Bern, to Special War Problems Div., State Dept., "Enclosure No. 1 to Despatch No. 11046," 2 March 1945, 2, Conditions at Kiangwan, China (Folder No. I), RG 389.
13. Kantzer, "Imperial Guest," 89; Huizenga, Affidavit, 5; LaPorte, interview; Oldham, *Lieutenant Stephen Polkinghorn*, 16; Chapman, interview; Norwood and Shek, "POW Camps," 16, 27.
14. Kantzer, "Imperial Guest," 90; Pay, Diary, 3 December 1942; Papock, Diary, 3 December 1942; Newell, Diary, 3 and 5 December 1942; Pearsall, Diary, 5 December 1942; J. Johnson, Diary, 5 December 1942.
15. White, *United States Marines*, 82; Kantzer, "Imperial Guest," 90; Pay, Diary, 3 December 1942; Pearsall, Diary, 3 and 5 December 1942.
16. Master Gunnery Sgt. Edwin F. Hassig, USMC, to Capt. Willard A. Smith, USA, 25 March 1946, 6, RG 389; Newell, Diary, 3 December 1942.
17. Kantzer, "Imperial Guest," 90; J. Johnson, reply, May 9, 1981; Pearsall, Diary, 5 December 1942.
18. Richardson, reply; Nye, interview; Marcello, "Godbold Interview," 63; Holmes to author, 25 March 1979; Marcello, "Benton Interview," 100; Magnino, *Jim's Journey*, 130; Kessler, *To Wake Island and Beyond*, 101; Kinney and McCaffrey, *Wake Island Pilot*, 119; White, *United States Marines*, 82; Joseph J. Astarita, *Sketches of P.O.W. Life* (Brooklyn, NY: Rollo Press, 1947), 34; Kinney, "P.O.W. Survival," 81; Norwood and Shek, "POW Camps," 17; Pearsall, Diary, 29 March–1 April 1943; Kantzer, "Imperial Guest," 133; James P. S. Devereux to Annie S. Devereux, 3 January 1943, B.1., F.1, Devereux Collection.
19. Kantzer, "Imperial Guest," 101, 141, 185; Norwood and Shek, "POW Camps," 18; American Legation, Bern, to Special War Problems Div., State Dept., "Enclosure No. 1 to Despatch No. 11046," 2 March 1945, 1; Egle, "Camp Visit, 24th March 1943," 3; Special Div., State Dept., to War Dept., (PMG), "Egle Visit, 9 January 1943," 1; International Committee of the Red Cross to American Red Cross National Headquarters, "Relief for Prisoners of War SHANGHAI," 31 May 1944, 3–4, Conditions at Kiangwan, China (Folder No. II), RG 389; Fontanel, "Report on Visit to Kiangwan, November 26th, 1944," 2.
20. Ashurst, "Record," 5; Marcello, "Venable Interview," 52.
21. Mettscher, reply: Nye, interview; Otera, Testimony, "*USA vs. Ishihara*," 103; White, *United States Marines*, 82; Huizenga, Affidavit, 5; Kinney, "P.O.W. Survival," 80; Chapman, interview; Kauffman, "Rogge Interview," 17; Marcello, "Godbold Interview," 68; Kelnhoffer, interview; Holmes to author, 25 March 1979.

22. Astarita, *Sketches*, 34; Kinney, "P.O.W. Survival," 81; Row, interview; Chapman, interview; Norwood and Shek, "POW Camps," 2, 7; Fontanel, "Report on Visit to Kiangwan, November 26th, 1944," 4; Kantzer, "Imperial Guest," 99, 115, 141, 176.
23. Edward [Edouard] Egle, "Memorandum of the Visit Made by Mr. Egli, Delegate of the IRCC [*sic*], to the Camp of Prisoners of War at Shanghai, on the 9th January 1943," n.d., 1, Conditions at Kiangwan, China (Folder No. I), RG 389; Lt. Col. John A. White, USMC, "Kiangwan," n.d., 1, Conditions at Kiangwan, China (Folder No. II), RG 389; Marcello, "Godbold Interview," 63; Norwood and Shek, "POW Camps," 16; Kantzer, "Imperial Guest," 90; Hoskins, "Memoir," 7; Astarita, *Sketches*, 34.
24. Norwood and Shek, "POW Camps," 16; Chapman, interview; Marcello, "Permenter Interview," 52; Huizenga, Affidavit, 6; Pfc. William Krenistki, USMC, "In the Matter of the Exposure of American Prisoners of War to Bombing . . . ," September 29, 1945, 1, File 101-59, Box 1584, Japanese War Crimes at Kiangwan, RG 153; SSgt. Steven Penka, USAAF, "In the Matter of Exposure of American Prisoners of War to Bombing . . . ," October 26, 1945, 2, File 101-59, Box 1584, Japanese War Crimes at Kiangwan, RG 153; Newell, Diary, 17 December 1942; Kantzer, "Imperial Guest," 93; Pay, Diary, 17 December 1942.
25. Pearsall, Diary, 5–7, 9, 19, 22, and 27 December 1942; Kantzer, "Imperial Guest," 91, 93, 97–98; Row, interview; Kinney and McCaffrey, *Wake Island Pilot*, 122; Pearsall, Diary, 10 January 1943; MIS-X Section, CPM Branch, "Ex-Reports 665–668 (CHINA)," Appendix C, July 12, 1945, 6; Newell, Diary, 10 January 1943; Pay, Diary, 25 January, 8 February, and 3 March 1943.
26. Kantzer, "Imperial Guest," 91, 101; Marcello, "Permenter Interview," 65–66; Newell, Diary, 10 March 1943; Marcello, "Benton Interview," 100.
27. Abraham, *Do You Understand*, 143; Pay, Diary, 16–17 December 1942, and 9 and 11 March 1943; Papock, Diary, 16 December 1942, and 14 March 1943; Russell de Ritis to author, 25 June 2008; Newell, Diary, 15 December 1942, and 20 May 1943; Elezak, Diary, 20 May 1943; Oldham, *Lieutenant Stephen Polkinghorn*, 16; Magnino, *Jim's Journey*, 155–156.
28. Egle, "Camp Visit, 24th March 1943," 1; Pay, Diary, 7 December 1942; Newell, Diary, 7–8 December 1942; Kantzer, "Imperial Guest," 91; Kinney and McCaffrey, *Wake Island Pilot*, 133; Oldham, *Lieutenant Stephen Polkinghorn*, 16; Nye, interview; Pearsall, Diary, 8 December 1942; Prisoners of War Information Bureau, "List of Prisoners of War," October 19, 1943, Diplomatic Record Office of the Ministry of Foreign Affairs, Documents Relating to Greater East Asia War, Treatment of Nationals of Enemy

Countries and Prisoners of War Between Belligerent Countries, Nationals of Enemy Countries Within Empire, Vol. 5, Japan Center for Asian Historical Records.

29. Pay, Diary, 19 and 27 December 1942; Kantzer, "Imperial Guest," 93; Newell, Diary, 19 and 27 December 1942; Oldham, *Lieutenant Stephen Polkinghorn*, 16, 40; Tony Banham, *The Sinking of the* Lisbon Maru*: Britain's Forgotten Wartime Tragedy* (Hong Kong: Hong Kong University Press, 2006), 1, 15–16, 38, 40–42, 44, 60–61, 64–69, 71–73, 78, 80, 82–83, 89, 91, 93–96, 102, 115, 118–120, 127, 253; Papock, Diary, 27 December 1942.

30. Kahn, interview.

31. Papock, Diary, 26 March 1943; Newell, Diary, 27 March 1943; MIS-X Section, CPM Branch, "Ex-Report No. 669 (CHINA), Appendix C," July 12, 1945, 1–6, Escape Reports, Nos. 654–71 (G-2), RG 389; MIS-X Section, CPM Branch, "Ex-Report No. 669 (CHINA), Appendix E," July 12, 1945, 1–2, Escape Reports, Nos. 654–71 (G-2), RG 389; Lewis Sherman Bishop and Shiela Bishop Irwin, *Escape From Hell: An AVG Flying Tiger's Journey* (Bloomington, IL: Tiger Eye Press, 2004), 1–35, 73–144; Kinney and McCaffrey, *Wake Island Pilot*, 132; Kahn, interview; Sturgeon, interview, October 13, 1984; T. Miller, "T. Johnson Interview, 16 July 2001," 3–4. See also Wanda Cornelius and Thayne Short, *Ding Hao: America's Air War in China, 1937–1945* (Gretna, LA: Pelican Publishing Company, 1980).

32. Kahn, interview; Kinney and McCaffrey, *Wake Island Pilot*, 132–133.

33. Leck, *Captives*, 288–89; Pay, Diary, 7 December 1942; Newell, Diary, 7 December 1942; Kantzer, "Imperial Guest," 91; Oldham, *Lieutenant Stephen Polkinghorn*, 50; White, *United States Marines*, 83–84.

34. J. Johnson, Diary, 9 December 1942; Newell, Diary, 9 and 12 December 1942; Papock, Diary, 7 December 1942; Kantzer, "Imperial Guest," 91; Marcello, "Permenter Interview," 73; Malleck to author, 29 August 1981.

35. White, *United States Marines*, 83–84; White, "Kiangwan," 2; Young, "WWII POW," 8; Archie Satterfield, ed., *The Home Front: An Oral History of the War Years in America* (New York: Playboy Press, 1981), 101; Stegmaier, interview; Kahn, interview; Special Div., State Dept., to War Dept., (PMG), "Egle Visit, January 9, 1943," 1.

36. Newell, Diary, 12 December 1942; Pearsall, Diary, 12–13 December 1942; Kantzer, "Imperial Guest," 92.

37. Kantzer, "Imperial Guest," 95; Newell, Diary, 24 December 1942; Papock, Diary, 24 December 1942; Pay, Diary, 24 December 1942; Pearsall, Diary, 24 December 1942; Plate, reply.

38. Papock, Diary, 31 December 1942, 11 February, and 9 March, 1943; Newell, Diary, 31 December 1942, 31 January, 10 February, and 9 March 1943; Kantzer, "Imperial Guest," 97, 98–99; Pearsall, Diary, 31 December 1942;

Pay, Diary, 1 February and 9 March 1943; Oldham, *Lieutenant Stephen Polkinghorn*, 16.
39. *Kalamazoo Gazette*, December 2, 1991; Malleck to author, 29 August 1981; Ashurst, "Record," 7; Milliken, Affidavit, 1; McBrayer, Affidavit, 3; Huizenga, Affidavit, 3; Kinney, Affidavit, 4; Kinney and McCaffrey, *Wake Island Pilot*, 120.
40. Jack Roland Bishop, "In the Matter of the Theft of American and Canadian Red Cross Relief Supplies by Capt. Endo and Sgt. Major Goto . . . ," April 5, 1946, 1–2, File, 101-150, Box 1584, Japanese War Crimes at Woosung, RG 153; Huizenga, Affidavit, 3.
41. Ashurst, "Record," 7; Maj. Gen. Frank C. Tharin, USMC, to Col. F. C. Caldwell, USMC, 19 October 1966, Correspondence, MCHA; First Lt. John A. McAlister, USMC, "In the Matter of the Mistreatment of American Prisoners . . . From January 1942 to May 1945," September 11, 1945, 2, File 101-59, Box 1584, Japanese War Crimes at Kiangwan, RG 153; McBrayer, *Escape*, 115–16; Bishop, "Theft of Supplies," 2; Capt. James L. Norwood, USA, "Colonel Devereux: Notes Taken by Capt. Norwood," n.d., 3–4, Conditions at Hakodate Branch Camp No. 3, RG 389; John Brown L. Anderson, Affidavit, January 23, 1946, 2, File 67-75, Bk. 1 (1–2), POWs on the *Nitta Maru*, RG 153.
42. Kinney and McCaffrey, *Wake Island Pilot*, 119–20; Hanna, interview; Chapman, interview; Nye, interview; Richardson, reply; Wheeler, interview.
43. Marcello, "McDaniel Interview," 48; Hotchkiss, interview, November 21, 1983; Marcello, "Stowers Interview," 34; LaPorte, interview; Kinney and McCaffrey, *Wake Island Pilot*, 120; Kelnhofer, interview; Marcello, "Permenter Interview," 73; Abraham, *Do You Understand*, 124; Marcello, "Benton Interview," 67–68.
44. Wheeler, interview; Kantzer, "Imperial Guest," 91; Pearsall, Diary, 14 December 1942; Newell, Diary, 26 March 1944; Marcello, "Benton Interview," 67; Marcello, "McDaniel Interview," 48; Hotchkiss, interview, October 21, 1983; Kelnhofer, interview; Kinney, "P.O.W. Survival," 80; Nye, interview; Marcello, "Stowers Interview," 34.
45. Nye, interview; Kantzer, "Imperial Guest," 92; Pearsall, Diary, 31 December 1942, and 31 January 1943; Pay, Diary, 1 February 1942.
46. Hotchkiss, interview, October 21, 1983; Nye, interview; Marcello, "McDaniel Interview," 49; Newell, Diary, 7 and 15 November 1943; Kelnhofer, interview; Snipes, "Adventureros," 12; Kantzer, "Imperial Guest," 92, 95, 105, 126, 144, 157.
47. Nye, interview; Kibble, "My War," 137; Marcello, "Venable Interview," 68; J. Cook, interview; Kantzer, "Imperial Guest," 143.
48. Hubley, interview; Marcello, "Stowers Interview," 64; Hoskins, "Memoir,"

12–13; Chapman, interview; Marcello, "Benton Interview," 63; Hotchkiss, interview, October 21, 1983; Nye, interview.
49. LaPorte, interview; Nye, interview; Magnino, *Jim's Journey*, 133; White, *United States Marines*, 198; Bernard E. Richardson to author, 17 November 1986.
50. John E. Pearsall, "This Love We Hold," in "John Edward Pearsall, Virginia, Minnesota, Section 5, Barracks 2, U.S.M.C.," (Notebook), ca. 1942–1945, Personal Papers, MCHC.
51. Richardson to author, 17 November 1986.
52. Newell, Diary, 9 April 1944; Kantzer, "Imperial Guest," 143.
53. Richardson permitted the author to read "Serenade to the Tree Toad" on the condition that he took no notes from it. Richardson, "Voice," 22; Bernard E. Richardson to author, 31 October, 17 November 1986. For more on homosexual culture during this period, see George Chauncey, *Gay New York: Gender, Urban Culture, and the Making of the Gay Male World, 1890–1940* (New York: Basic Books, 1994) and Allan Berube, *Coming Out Under Fire: The History of Gay Men and Women in World War Two* (New York: Free Press, 1990). Glimpses of homosexual relations in the Marine Corps during World War II appear in William Manchester's *Goodbye Darkness: A Memoir of the Pacific War* (Boston: Little, Brown, 1979).
54. Kelnhofer, interview; Chapman, interview; LaPorte, interview; Newell, Diary, 9 April 1944; Nye, interview.
55. Newell, Diary, 18 December 1942, 14, 15, 18, and 23 January, 25 and 26 February, 13 March, 25 May, 21 August, 10, and 26 September 1943; Kantzer, "Imperial Guest," 100, 101, 106, 117, 119, 120; Pearsall, Diary, undated entry between 3 February and 29 March–3 April 1943; Jack B. Cook to "Dearest Family," 24 August 1943.
56. Pearsall, Diary, 25 December 1942; J. Johnson, Diary, 25 December 1942; Pay, Diary, 25 December 1942.
57. Pearsall, Diary, 25 December 1942; Kantzer, "Imperial Guest," 95, 96; Newell, Diary, 25 December 1942; Magnino, *Jim's Journey*, 132.
58. Hubley, interview; Pay, Diary, 25 December 1942; Papock, Diary, 25 December 1942; Durrwachter, Diary, 14 March 1943; Kantzer, "Imperial Guest," 96.
59. *Dallas Times Herald*, November 2, 1980; White, *United States Marines*, 123; J. Johnson, Diary, 28 August and 5 December 1942; *Dallas Times Herald*, undated clipping attached to Charles A. Holmes to author, 16 November 1980.

CHAPTER 13

1. Kantzer, "Imperial Guest," 78; Richardson, "Bread," 4; Pearsall, Diary, 10, 15, 18, 24, and 28 December 1942, and 3–6 January 1943; Newell, Diary,

14 and 15 December 1942; Pay, Diary, 22 December 1942, and 11 and 13 January 1943.
2. Marcello, "Venable Interview," 65; Newell, Diary, 29 March, 7 April, and 20 October 1943, and 4 January 1944; Pay, Diary, 23 April 1943, and 2 May 1944; Kantzer, "Imperial Guest," 131; Elezak, Diary, 2 May 1944.
3. White, *United States Marines*, 83; Marcello, "Godbold Interview," 48; Ashurst, "Record," 4, 6.
4. White, *United States Marines*, 83, 89; Marcello, "Godbold Interview," 48, 63–64; Freuler, interview; MIS-X Section, CPM Branch, "Ex-Reports 665–668 (CHINA)," Appendix C, 7; Pearsall, Diary, 11 December 1942; Williams, interview; Nye, interview; Kantzer, "Imperial Guest," 136.
5. White, *United States Marines*, 89–90; Newell, Diary, 27 March and 1 August 1943; Hanna, interview; LaPorte, interview; J. Cook to "Dearest Family," 24 August 1943.
6. White, *United States Marines*, 89, 91, 92; MIS-X Section, CPM Branch, "Ex-Reports 665–668 (CHINA)," Appendix C, 7; *Burlingame (CA) Advance*, December 16, 1943; Norwood and Shek, "POW Camps," 20; Kantzer, "Imperial Guest," 101; *San Francisco Chronicle*, February 11, 1945.
7. Magnino, *Jim's Journey*, 149; LaPorte, interview; Marcello, "Benton Interview," 68; Kinney, Affidavit, 4; Ashurst, "Record," 7; Richardson, reply; MIS-X Section, CPM Branch, "Ex-Reports 665–668 (CHINA)," Appendix C, 7; Kantzer, "Imperial Guest," 146.
8. Newell, Diary, 17 January and 16 February 1943; Durrwachter, Diary, 14 March 1943; Holmes to author, 25 March 1979; Marcello, "McDaniel Interview," 60; Haidinger, interview; Kessler, *To Wake Island and Beyond*, 106; White, *United States Marines*, 83.
9. LaPorte, interview; Haidinger, interview; Richardson, "Bread," 4.
10. Richardson, "Bread," 4–5; Rumpel, "My Experience," 5–6; James N. Young, Affidavit, "*USA vs. Ishihara*," 36; E. Cook, Affidavit, "*USA vs. Ishihara*," 94; Durrwachter, Diary, 28 May 1943; Mettscher, reply; Stegmaier, interview; Papock, Diary, 13 July 1943; Stocks, interview; Holmes to author, 25 March 1979; Richardson, reply; Papock, Diary, 13 July 1943; MIS-X Section, CPM Branch, "Ex-Reports 665–668 (CHINA)," Appendix C, 7; White, *United States Marines*, 88; Raymond Osborne Bennett, "In the Matter of the Use of Prisoners of War on Enemy Military Works or Operations," May 25, 1946, File 101-59, Box 1584, Japanese War Crimes at Kiangwan, RG 153.
11. Pearsall, Diary, undated entry between those for 3 February and 29 March–2 April 1943; Pistole, interview; Holmes to author, 25 March 1979; White, *United States Marines*, 88; Marcello, "McDaniel Interview," 60; Mettscher, reply; Pay, Diary, 21 June 1944.

12. J. Johnson, Diary, August 1944; Holmes to author, 25 March 1979; "Geneva Convention," 5234; Kinney and McCaffrey, *Wake Island Pilot*, 131.
13. Kantzer, "Imperial Guest," 106, 111; Newell, Diary, 29 June and 1 December 1943, and 10 March 1944; Haidinger, interview; Shores, interview; Marcello, "Venable Interview," 52–53; *Washington Post*, October 14, 1945; Yazawa, Testimony, "*USA vs. Ishihara*," 53; E. Cook, Affidavit, "*USA vs. Ishihara*," 94.
14. Richardson, "Bread," 5, 6; Richardson, reply; Marcello, "McDaniel Interview," 61; Holmes to author, 25 March 1979; White, *United States Marines*, 85.
15. Durrwachter, Diary, 28 May 1943; Mettscher, reply; Chapman, interview; Richardson, reply; White, *United States Marines*, 85–86; Richardson, "Bread," 5–6; R. Brown, interview; Nye, interview; Marcello, "Stowers Interview," 51; Hotchkiss, interview, October 21, 1983; Marcello, "McDaniel Interview," 61; Abraham, *Do You Understand*, 89; Hubley, interview.
16. Richardson, "Bread," 6; Holmes to author, 25 March 1979; Hubley, interview.
17. Kelnhofer, interview; Stocks, interview; Bernard O. Ketner, Affidavit, October 12, 1945, 1, File 101-150, Box 1584, Japanese War Crimes at Woosung, RG 153; Browning, "Use of Prisoners," 2; Stegmaier, interview; Sandvold, interview.
18. Sturgeon, interview, October 13, 1984; Browning, "Use of Prisoners," 2; Richardson, "Bread," 6, 19; R. Brown, interview; Marcello, "Venable Interview," 52; Marcello, "McDaniel Interview," 47; Chapman, interview; White, *United States Marines*, 86; LaPorte, interview; Magnino, *Jim's Journey*, 149; Kessler, *To Wake Island and Beyond*, 107; Norwood and Shek, "POW Camps," 18.
19. Richardson, "Bread," 11–12; Richardson, "Fanatic," 8; Marcello, "Benton Interview," 103; Ketner, Affidavit "*USA vs. Ishihara*," 63; Irving B. Silverlieb, Affidavit, October 12, 1945, Prosecution Exhibit No. 34, "*USA vs. Ishihara*," 91; Abraham, *Do You Understand*, 76; Sturgeon, interview, October 13, 1984; Nowlin to author, 24 November 1979.
20. Warren G. Anderson, Affidavit, September 5, 1946, 2, File 101-150, Box 1584, Japanese War Crimes at Woosung, RG 153; Ketner, Affidavit, "*USA vs. Ishihara*," 63; Clyde W. Hannah, Affidavit, October 12, 1945, Prosecution Exhibit No. 30, "*USA vs. Ishihara*," 85; Lorel J. Bragg, Affidavit, December 17, 1945, Prosecution Exhibit No. 32, "*USA vs. Ishihara*," 88–89; Silverlieb, Affidavit, "*USA vs. Ishihara*," 91; Ralph Y. Williams, Ernest I. Reece, Claude N. Conaway, and Alfred J. V. Herbert, Affidavit, n.d., Prosecution Exhibit No. 35, "*USA vs. Ishihara*," 92; E. Cook, Affidavit, "*USA vs. Ishihara*," 94; Blahuta, Affidavit, "*USA vs. Ishihara*," 95; Chapman, interview.
21. Richardson, "Bread," 6; Ishihara, Affidavit, "*USA vs. Ishihara*," 110; Hassig, interview; Nye, interview.

22. Richardson, "Bread," 12, 13, 21–22.
23. J. Johnson, reply, May 9, 1981; Kantzer, "Imperial Guest," 133; Pistole, interview; Haidinger, interview; Nye, interview; Dale, interview; Stocks, interview; Chapman, interview; Kibble, "My War," 150.
24. Hassig, interview; Nye, interview; Stocks, interview; Dale, interview; J. Johnson, reply, May 9, 1981; Kelnhofer, interview.
25. Williams, interview; Marcello, "Venable Interview," 50; Papock, Diary, 26 April 1943; Newell, Diary, 13 July, 2 August, and 3 November 1943; White, *United States Marines*, 88; Stocks, interview; Nye, interview.
26. J. Johnson, Diary, January 1944; Richardson, "Bread," 12.
27. Richardson, reply; Ishihara, Affidavit, "*USA vs. Ishihara*," 110; Newell, Diary, 22 May and 8 December 1943; Chapman, interview; White, *United States Marines*, 86; Richardson, "Fanatic," 8; Abraham, *Do You Understand*, 75; Kantzer, "Imperial Guest," 125; Marcello, "Venable Interview," 50–51; Haidinger, interview; Nye, interview; Anderson, Affidavit, 2.
28. Richardson, "Fanatic," 8; Newell, Diary, 8 December 1943; Kantzer, "Imperial Guest," 117, 125, 138, 153–154; Anderson, Affidavit, 2; Marcello, "Venable Interview," 51; Hanna, interview; White, *United States Marines*, 115–116; Stegmaier, interview.
29. "Geneva Convention," 5234; Stegmaier, interview; Ketner, Affidavit, "*USA vs. Ishihara*," 63; Kelnhofer, interview.
30. Christian Henriot and Wen-hsin Yeh, "Introduction," in Henriot and Yeh, *Shadow of the Rising Sun*, 4–5, 11; Christian Henriot, "Shanghai Industries Under Japanese Occupation: Bombs, Boom, and Bust (1937–1945)," in Henriot and Yeh, *Shadow of the Rising Sun*, 37; Frederic Wakeman Jr., "Shanghai Smuggling," in Henriot and Yeh, *Shadow of the Rising Sun*, 123, 125–26; Kantzer, "Imperial Guest," 163.
31. Newell, Diary, 13 and 29 June and 7 July 1943; Papock, Diary, 6 July 1943; Kantzer, "Imperial Guest," 106–107.
32. Kantzer, "Imperial Guest," 106.
33. Newell, Diary, 6 March 1943; Kantzer, "Imperial Guest," 99, 105, 107, 108, 123, 124, 174, 180; Oldham, *Lieutenant Stephen Polkinghorn*, 15.
34. Richardson, "Bread," 19–20; Newell, Diary, 11, 27, and 28 July, 21 August, 10, 26 September, 12, 25, and 26 October, 10 and 25 November, and 10 and 26 December 1943, 24 January, 9 and 25 February, 10 and 25 March, and 8 and 25 April 1944; Kantzer, "Imperial Guest," 106, 117, 119, 120, 122, 125, 157.
35. J. Cook to "Dearest Family," 24 August 1943; Camp, interview.
36. Papock, Diary, 26 April and 2 June 1943; Kantzer, "Imperial Guest," 108; J. Johnson, Diary, September 1943; Stegmaier, interview; E. Cook, Affidavit, "*USA vs. Ishihara*," 94.
37. J. Johnson, reply, May 9, 1981; Newell, Diary, 27 June and 17 July 1943; J. Johnson, Diary, January 1944; Kelnhofer, interview.

38. Richardson, "Bread," 7, 13; Marcello, "Venable Interview," 52–53.
39. Chapman, interview; Marcello, "Venable Interview," 65; Shores, interview; Kelnhofer, interview; Newell, Diary, 2, 7, and 17 October 1943; Reeves, interview; Richardson, "Bread," 14–19.
40. Richardson, "Bread," 18–20; Newell, Diary, 10 January 1943.
41. American Legation, Bern, to Special War Problems Div., State Dept., "Despatch No. 11768," 5–6; White, *United States Marines*, 98; MIS-X Section, CPM Branch, "Ex-Report No. 669 (China), Appendix 'C,'" 7–8; Newell, Diary, 17 April, 28 July, 7, 11, 14, 16, 20, and 26 October, 20 November, 22, 25, and 31 December 1943, and 15 February and 5 and 13 March 1944; J. Johnson, Diary, April 1943; Kantzer, "Imperial Guest," 100, 114, 117, 139.
42. Marcello, "McDaniel Interview," 57; Marcello, "Godbold Interview," 65; Chester M. Biggs Jr., Affidavit, January 3, 1946, Prosecution Exhibit No. 7, "*USA vs. Ishihara*," 31–32; Clarence E. Wolfe, Affidavit, October 4, 1945, Prosecution Exhibit No. 12, "*USA vs. Ishihara*," 41; Kantzer, "Imperial Guest," 105.
43. White, *United States Marines*, 98–99, 104–105, 130–131; Hotchkiss, interview, October 21, 1983; Nye, interview; T. Miller, "T. Johnson Interview, June 1, 2001," 16; Papock, Diary, 2 June 1943; Kantzer, "Imperial Guest," 77; Biggs, Affidavit, "*USA vs. Ishihara*," 31; Robert M. Brown, Affidavit, October 8, 1945, Prosecution Exhibit No. 11, "*USA vs. Ishihara*," 38–39.
44. Kessler, *To Wake Island and Beyond*, 106–107; J. Johnson, reply, May 9, 1981; Marcello, "McDaniel Interview," 64; Abraham, *Do You Understand*, 80; Huizenga, Affidavit, 5; Devereux, *Story of Wake*, 231; Pay, Diary, 1–2 June, 10–11 August, and 15–16 September 1944, and 29–30 January and 23 and 26 March 1945; Elezak, Diary, 1 June, 10 August, and 15 September 1944, and 22 January and 23 March 1945; Papock, Diary, 11 August and 15 September 1944; Kantzer, "Imperial Guest," 158, 177, 186; Oldham, *Lieutenant Stephen Polkinghorn*, 24, 27, 28; Stocks, interview.
45. Elezak, Diary, 2 September 1943, 17 March, 19 September, 18, 20, and 29 November, and 16 December 1944; Pay, Diary, 2 September 1943, and 17 March, 19–20 September, 18 and 29 November, and 16 and 20 December 1944; Kantzer, "Imperial Guest," 140, 159, 166, 167; Oldham, *Lieutenant Stephen Polkinghorn*, 24, 27; R. Brown, interview; Hotchkiss, interview, October 22, 1982.
46. White, *United States Marines*, 88; Ashurst, "Record," 6; Kantzer, "Imperial Guest," 107–108.
47. Ketner, Affidavit, "*USA vs. Ishihara*," 63; E. Cook, Affidavit, "*USA vs. Ishihara*," 94; Blahuta, Affidavit, "*USA vs. Ishihara*," 96; Williams, Reece, Conaway, and Herbert, Affidavit, "*USA vs. Ishihara*," 93; Richardson, "Fanatic," 4; Richardson, "Bread," 23.

48. *Memphis Press-Scimitar*, October 30, 1961; White, *United States Marines*, 127; Kahn, interview; Richardson, reply; Hoskins, "Memoir," 7; Newell, Diary, 1 December 1943; Richardson, "Bread," 23–25; Kelnhofer, interview; Kantzer, "Imperial Guest," 104, 105, 108, 125, 132, 136.
49. Nye, interview; Kelnhofer, interview; Borne, interview; Nowlin to author, 24 November 1979; Richardson, "Bread," 25; Reeves, interview; Kantzer, "Imperial Guest," 109, 116, 130, 143.
50. Devereux, *Story of Wake*, 218; White, *United States Marines*, 31–34; Kinney and McCaffrey, *Wake Island Pilot*, 103; Kessler to Daws, 15 April 1987; Marcello, "Godbold Interview," 49; Freuler, interview; Hanna, interview; Hoffman, *Chesty*, 145–146; Richardson, reply; Richardson, "Bread," 25; Ashurst, "Record," 6; Chapman, interview; LaPorte, interview; Sturgeon, interview, October 13, 1984; Hubley, interview; Nowlin, reply, March 18, 1980; Kantzer, "Imperial Guest," 94, 188; Lt. Col. James D. McBrayer, USMC, to Col. James P. S. Devereux, USMC, February 24, 1946, B.1, F.3, Devereux Collection; Kelnhofer, interview.
51. Hubley, interview; Chapman, interview; Williams, interview; Shores, interview; Nowlin, reply, March 18, 1980; Gross, interview, October 22, 1983.
52. Nowlin, reply, March 18, 1980; LaPorte, interview; Pay, Diary, 11 April 1943; Kibble, "My War," 151–152; Kessler to Daws, 25 April 1987; Hanna, interview; Borne, interview.
53. Chapman, interview; Borne, interview; Magnino, *Jim's Journey*, 211–12; Frank, "Devereux Transcript," 130; Marcello, "Godbold Interview," 49; Kantzer, "Imperial Guest," 109, 129–130.
54. Ashurst, "Record," 6; Kantzer, "Imperial Guest," 109; Richardson, "Bread," 24.
55. Cunningham, *Hell Wouldn't Stop*, 219; Richardson, "Bread," 22; Elezak, Diary, 5 July 1943; Newell, Diary, 15 July 1943; Kantzer, "Imperial Guest," 104.
56. Chapman, interview; Newell, Diary, 23–24 April and 13 August 1943; Wheeler, interview.
57. Hotchkiss, interviews, October 22, 1982, and October 21 1983; Snipes, "Adventureros," 13; J. Johnson, reply, May 9, 1981; Hubley, interview; Abraham, *Do You Understand*, 83; Kantzer, "Imperial Guest," 112–114; Pay, Diary, 12, 15, and 20 August 1943; Papock, Diary, 13–14, 16, and 20 August 1943; Elezak, Diary, 20 August 1943; "Wake Personnel," September 12, 1945, 1; Oldham, *Lieutenant Stephen Polkinghorn*, 18; White, *United States Marines*, 95–96.
58. Papock, Diary, 21 November 1943; Elezak, Diary, 20 November 1943; Pay, Diary, 20 November 1943; Newell, Diary, 18 June and 20 November 1943; James Wood, *History of International Broadcasting* (London: P. Peregrinus Ltd., 1992), 84–95; Frank Fujita, *Foo: A Japanese–American Prisoner of the Rising Sun: The Secret Prison Diary of Frank "Foo" Fujita*, ed. Stanley L.

Falk (Denton, TX: University of North Texas Press, 1993), 195–225; Gavan Daws, "Recorded Notes on Fujita Diary," August 16, 1984, Daws Papers; White, *United States Marines*, 64, 141; Col. Luther A. Brown, USMC, to Stanley T. Blaszek, 7 March 1950, Box 5, File No. 205, Luther A. Brown Collection, Personal Papers, MCHA; Jesse E. Nowlin, taped reply to author's questionnaire, n.d.

59. Papock, Diary, 1 September 1943; Newell, Diary, 20–21 August and 24 September 1943; Kantzer, "Imperial Guest," 114–115, 168.
60. Abraham, *Do You Understand*, 89; Richardson, "Bread," 6, 11, 13.
61. Richardson, reply; Kauffman, "Goicoechea Interview," 20; Stegmaier, interview; Hotchkiss, interviews, October, 22, 1982, and October 21, 1983; Marcello, "McDaniel Interview," 62; Sandvold, interview; Newell, Diary, 17 July 1943; Stocks, interview.
62. Enrico Cernushi and Vincent P. O'Hara, "Italy and the Pacific War," *World War II Quarterly* 3, no. 1 (2006): 14–18; Nowlin, reply, March 18, 1980; Kantzer, "Imperial Guest," 119; Pay, Diary, 10 October 1943; Newell, Diary, 10 and 14 October 1943; Elezak, Diary, 10 October 1943; Papock, Diary, 10 October 1943; J. Johnson, Diary, 10 October 1943; Abraham, *Do You Understand*, 101; J. Cook, interview; Magnino, *Jim's Journey*, 130.
63. Cernushi and O'Hara, "Italy and the Pacific War," 18; Kantzer, "Imperial Guest," 123; Oldham, *Lieutenant Stephen Polkinghorn*, 19; Nowlin, reply, March 18, 1980; Elezak, Diary, 12 December 1943; Pay, Diary, 12 December 1943; Newell, Diary, 12 December 1943; Papock, Diary, 13 December 1943; Abraham, *Do You Understand*, 101–102.
64. Elezak, Diary, 20 November 1943, and 7 April and 19 September 1944; Pay, Diary, 30 November 1943, and 7 April and 19 September 1944; Kantzer, "Imperial Guest," 122–23, 143, 158–59; Chapman, interview; Papock, Diary, 7 April and 20 September 1944; Oldham, *Lieutenant Stephen Polkinghorn*, 19, 24, 26; Nowlin, reply, March 18, 1980; White, *United States Marines*, 124–125.
65. Elezak, Diary, 12 June, 30 October, and 31 December 1943, and 1 June and 30–31 December 1944; Kantzer, "Imperial Guest," 103–4, 120, 129, 149, 171, 179, 181, 191; Oldham, *Lieutenant Stephen Polkinghorn*, 18, 24, 37; Newell, Diary, 30 October 1943, and 1 and 4 January 1944; James M. Taylor to Charles A. Holmes, ca. January 1980 (photostat copy in author's possession); Charles A. Holmes to author, 21 January 1980; *Nashville Tennessean*, January 14, 1946; Papock, Diary, 2 June 1944; Pay, Diary, 12 June and 31 December 1943, 22 May, 2 June, and 30–31 December 1944, and 18 February 1945; Prisoners of War Information Bureau, "List of Prisoners of War," March 25, 1944, Diplomatic Record Office of the Ministry of Foreign Affairs, Documents Relating to Greater East Asia War, Treatment of Nationals

of Enemy Countries and Prisoners of War Between Belligerent Countries, Nationals of Enemy Countries Within Empire, Vol. 5, Japan Center for Asian Historical Records.

CHAPTER 14

1. Pearsall, Diary, 8 December 1942; Kantzer, "Imperial Guest," 109.
2. Kantzer, "Imperial Guest," 109; Freuler, interview; Frank, "Devereux Transcript," 132; R. E. Forsythe to "Captain Herbert C. Freuler, et al.," 24 December 1943 (photostat copy in the author's possession); Sgt. Maj. C. M. Dietz, USMC, to "Mess Officer and Members of the Galley Force," 25 December 1943 (photostat copy in the author's possession); First Sgt. Paul R. Agar, USMC, M. Gunnery Sgt. John W. Krawie, USMC, and QM Sgt. Vincent Kleponis, USMC, to "Mess Officer and the Galley Force," 25 December 1943 (photostat copy in the author's possession); Section 7, Barracks 4, to "Captain Freuler, Staff & Employees," 30 December 1943 (photostat copy in the author's possession).
3. Sections 5 and 6, Barracks No. 3, to Capt. Herbert C. Freuler, USMC, Edward S. Clancy, Supply Sgt. James A. Callis, USMC, Lloyd Gordon, "and Crew," Christmas Card, n.d. (photostat copy in the author's possession).
4. Papock, Diary, 25 and 31 December 1943; Newell, Diary, 25 December, 1943, and 7 January 1944; Kantzer, "Imperial Guest," 126–128, 130; S. Otera to "Captain H.C. Freuler," Certificate of Merit, n.d. (photostat copy in the author's possession).
5. Kantzer, "Imperial Guest," 130–131; Ashurst, "Record of Internment," 3; White, *United States Marines*, 64, 99; Joseph M. Stowe, Affidavit, October 8, 1945, Prosecution Exhibit No. 3, "*USA vs. Ishihara*," 24–25; W. T. Foley, Affidavit, September 15, 1945, Prosecution Exhibit No. 4, "*USA vs. Ishihara*," 27; Clancy, Affidavit, "*USA vs. Ishihara,* 37"; R. Brown, Affidavit, "*USA vs. Ishihara*," 38–39; T. Miller, "T. Johnson interview, 16 July 2001," 8; Abraham, *Do You Understand*, 77; Robert M. Brown, "In the Matter of the Mistreatment of American Prisoners . . . at the Shanghai War Prisoners Camp in January 1944," February 7, 1946, 2, File 101-150, Box 1584, Japanese War Crimes at Woosung, RG 153; Papock, Diary, 5 January 1944.
6. John C. Minnick, Affidavit, December 13, 1945, Prosecution Exhibit, No. 1, "*USA vs. Ishihara*," 19–20; Michael J. Schick, Affidavit, October 12, 1945, Prosecution Exhibit No. 2, "*USA vs. Ishihara*," 22; Stowe, Affidavit, "*USA vs. Ishihara*," 24–25; Foley, Affidavit, "*USA vs. Ishihara*," 27.
7. Minnick, Affidavit, "*USA vs. Ishihara*," 20; Schick, Affidavit, "*USA vs. Ishihara*," 22; Stowe, Affidavit, "*USA vs. Ishihara*," 24–25; Bernie Bergman, Affidavit, September 15, 1945, Prosecution Exhibit No. 5, "*USA vs. Ishihara*," 28.

8. Schick, Affidavit, "*USA vs. Ishihara*," 22; Stowe, Affidavit, "*USA vs. Ishihara*," 24–25.
9. Minnick, Affidavit, "*USA vs. Ishihara*," 20; Schick, Affidavit, "*USA vs. Ishihara*," 22; Stowe, Affidavit, "*USA vs. Ishihara*," 25; Biggs, Affidavit, "*USA vs. Ishihara*," 31–32; White, *United States Marines*, 100.
10. Stowe, Affidavit, "*USA vs. Ishihara*," 26; Foley, Affidavit, "*USA vs. Ishihara*," 27; Bergman, Affidavit, "*USA vs. Ishihara*," 28–29; Wesley W. Carter, Affidavit, Prosecution Exhibit No. 6, "*USA vs. Ishihara*," 30; Clancy, Affidavit, "*USA vs. Ishihara*," 37; R. Brown, Affidavit, "*USA vs. Ishihara*," 39; Ashurst, "Record, 3; Kantzer, "Imperial Guest," 131.
11. White, *United States Marines*, 101, 104–105; Bergman, Affidavit, "*USA vs. Ishihara*," 29; Elezak, Diary, 14 January 1944; Pay, Diary, 14 January 1944; Newell, Diary, 13 January 1944; Kantzer, "Imperial Guest," 131.
12. James P. S. Devereux to Annie S. Devereux, August 25, 1943; Newell, Diary, 3 December 1943; Kantzer, "Imperial Guest," 123; J. Johnson, Diary, January 1944.
13. Papock, Diary, 4 September 1943, and 17 March 1944; Leck, *Captives*, 296–299, 302–303; Elleman, *Japanese–American Exchanges*, 55, 79–80, 91–92; Magnino, *Jim's Journey*, 146–147; Newell, Diary, 13–15 March 1944; Kantzer, "Imperial Guest," 140–141; J. Johnson, Diary, 17 March 1944; White, *United States Marines*, 122.
14. J. Johnson, Diary, 18 March 1944; Kantzer, "Imperial Guest," 140; *San Francisco Examiner*, February 11, 1945; Papock, Diary, 17 March 1944.
15. Kantzer, "Imperial Guest," 140–141.
16. Camp, interview; Kantzer, "Imperial Guest," 143, 145, 147, 148, 156, 166; Pay, Diary, 8 April, 6 and 30–31 May, 4 July, 3 September, and 29 November 1944; Newell, Diary, 8 April 1944; Elezak, Diary, 8 April, 6 and 30 May, 4 July, and 30 November 1944; Papock, Diary, 30 May and 4 July 1944; J. Johnson, Diary, 18 March 1944.
17. Magnino, *Jim's Journey*, 147–148; White, *United States Marines*, 122; Abraham, *Do You Understand*, 134.
18. Kantzer, "Imperial Guest," 148; Pay, Diary, 4 July 1944; Papock, Diary, 4 July 1944.
19. Marcello, "Fields Interview," 25; Richardson, "Bread," 20; Kantzer, "Imperial Guest," 143–145; Biggs, *Behind the Barbed Wire*, 91; Borne, interview; LaPorte, interview. For starvation's effect on human morals, see Ancel Keys and others, *The Biology of Human Starvation*, vol. 2 (Minneapolis: University of Minnesota Press, 1950), 784–785, 789, 822–823, 828.
20. Urwin, *Facing Fearful Odds*, 455–457, 459–463; Pay, Diary, 16 April and 2 May 1944; Elezak, Diary, 16 April and 2 May 1944; Newell, Diary, 16 April 1944; Papock, Diary, 17 April 1944; Kantzer, "Imperial Guest," 143;

Oldham, *Lieutenant Stephen Polkinghorn*, 24; Cunningham and Sims, *Wake Island Command*, 160; Chapman, interview.
21. Pay, Diary, 21 June 1944; Elezak, Diary, 21 June 1944; Kantzer, "Imperial Guest," 150; Oldham, *Lieutenant Stephen Polkinghorn*, 25.
22. Newell, Diary, 14 April 1944; Papock, Diary, 19 April 1944; Richardson, "Bread," 27; Pay, Diary, 21 June 1944; Elezak, Diary, 21 June 1944; J. Johnson, Diary, June 1944.
23. Reeves, interview; Richardson, "Bread," 26, 30.
24. J. Johnson, Diary, January 1944; Newell, Diary, 1 March 1944; Kelnhofer, interview; Richardson, "Bread," 26; T. Miller, "T. Johnson Interview, 1 June 2001," 17; Ashurst, "Record," 7; Browning, "Use of Prisoners," 2; White, *United States Marines*, 94–95.
25. Richardson, "Bread," 26–27; Stocks, interview; Mettscher, reply.
26. Papock, Diary, 1 May 1944; J. Johnson, Diary, September 1944; Holmes to author, 17 July 1979; Richardson, "Bread," 27–30; Mettscher, reply; J. Johnson, reply, May 9, 1981; Chapman, interview; Bowsher, interview; Ishihara, Affidavit, "*USA vs. Ishihara*," 110; Newell, Diary, 2 February 1944.
27. J. Johnson, Diary, 10 June 1944; Nye, interview; "Japan Shanghaied," *Time*, February 29, 1932, 21–22.
28. Nye, interview; Smith, interview; Bowsher, interview; Mettscher, reply; Nowlin, reply, March 18, 1980; Magnino, *Jim's Journey*, 138; T. Miller, "T. Johnson Interview, 16 July 2001," 5.
29. J. Johnson, Diary, September 1944; Magnino, *Jim's Journey*, 137; Abraham, *Do You Understand*, 72; T. Miller, "T. Johnson Interview, July 16, 2001," 5–6; Mettscher, reply.
30. Kantzer, "Imperial Guest," 162–163, 167, 170–171, 192; Abraham, *Do You Understand*, 71–72; Nye, interview; White, *United States Marines*, 95; Camp, interview; Nowlin, reply, March 18, 1980; Hubley, interview; T. Miller, "T. Johnson Interview, 16 July 2001," 5; Nye, interview; Oldham, *Lieutenant Stephen Polkinghorn*, 27; Pay, Diary, 29 and 31 December 1944; Kessler, *To Wake Island and Beyond*, 104–105.
31. Kantzer, "Imperial Guest," 170, 176, 178; Richardson, "Fanatic," 10; Ishihara, Affidavit, "*USA vs. Ishihara*," 108.
32. Col. Edward H. Young, JAGD, Maj. Paul J. Driscoll, JAGD, and First Lt. Jacob I. Isaacs, USA, "Review of the Record of Trial by a Military Commission of Ishihara, Isamu, Civilian Interpreter, Armed Forces of Japan," April 30, 1946, "*USA vs. Ishihara*," 1–7; Afternoon Session, March 7, 1946, "*USA vs. Ishihara*," 123; White, *United States Marines*, 112–113.
33. Kantzer, "Imperial Guest," 176; American Legation, Bern, to Special War Problems Div., State Dept., "Enclosure No. 1 to Despatch No. 11046," 2 March 1945, 1.

34. Charles A. Holmes to author, 17 July and 11 August 1979; Richardson, "Bread," 29; Mettscher, reply.
35. Kantzer, "Imperial Guest," 173–175, 177; White, *United States Marines*, 122–123; American Legation, Bern, to Special War Problems Div., State Dept., "Enclosure No. 1 to Despatch No. 11046," 1.
36. Kantzer, "Imperial Guest," 175, 177, 182, 186; Pay, Diary, 16 January, 1 February, and 31 March 1945; Elezak, Diary, 16 and 31 January and 31 March 1945; White, *United States Marines*, 123.
37. Kantzer, "Imperial Guest," 103, 137, 161, 163–164, 179; Magnino, *Jim's Journey*, 156–157; Kinney and McCaffrey, *Wake Island Pilot*, 122; Newell, Diary, 8 January, 12 and 14 February, and 2 March 1944.
38. Pay, Diary, 25 December 1944; Elezak, Diary, 25 December 1944; Oldham, *Lieutenant Stephen Polkinghorn*, 26; Kantzer, "Imperial Guest," 168–169.
39. Kantzer, "Imperial Guest," 168a.
40. Hanna, interview; Kantzer, "Imperial Guest," 152–153; Kinney, "P.O.W. Survival," 123.
41. Durrwachter, Diary, 6 June 1943; Pearsall, Diary, 29 March–1 April 1943; Papock, Diary, 28 September 1943, and 30 June 1944; Kantzer, "Imperial Guest," 116, 125, 140, 141, 153, 154, 156.
42. Magnino, *Jim's Journey*, 139; Kantzer, "Imperial Guest," 153, 178.
43. White, *United States Marines*, 115, 116; Kinney and McCaffrey, *Wake Island Pilot*, 130–131; LaPorte, interview; Mettscher, reply; Kantzer, "Imperial Guest," 101, 112, 116–117, 138, 149, 152, 170–171; Magnino, *Jim's Journey*, 167–170; Papock, Diary, 6 June 1944; Pay, Diary, 8 and 10 June 1944.
44. Pay, Diary, 13 January 1943; White, *United States Marines*, 115; Papock, Diary, 4 February 1943; Newell, Diary, 21 February 1943; Kantzer, "Imperial Guest," 99; Durrwachter, Diary, 14 March 1943.
45. White, *United States Marines*, 117–121, 154; Kinney and McCaffrey, *Wake Island Pilot*, 129–131; John F. Kinney, "POW Radio," *Combat Illustrated*, Winter 1979, 67–71; John F. Kinney, "Building a Radio in a Japanese POW Camp," *Foundation*, Spring 1985, 20–26, 75; Kessler, *To Wake Island and Beyond*, 119–120; Chittenden, *From China Marine*, 135–137; Kauffman, "Ludington Interview," 5: 13–15; Hanna, interview; Kauffman, "Ludington Interview," 5: 13–16; Marcello, "Godbold Interview," 61–62; Magnino, *Jim's Journey*, 124, 169; Smith, interview; R. Brown, interview; Sandvold, interview; LaPorte, interview; Kessler, *To Wake Island and Beyond*, 120–123, 126.
46. Magnino, *Jim's Journey*, 169–170, 193–194; White, *United States Marines*, 115–116; Kantzer, "Imperial Guest," 111, 112, 117, 137, 138.
47. Marcello, "Venable Interview," 63; Newell, Diary, 30 October 1943, and 4 January 1944; White, *United States Marines*, 115; Pay, Diary, 13 April 1945;

O'Guinn, "V.O.C.," 75–76; Magnino, *Jim's Journey*, 198–199; Kantzer, "Imperial Guest," 171–172, 176, 181, 183.

48. Kantzer, "Imperial Guest," 142, 149–150; Newell, Diary, 2 April 1944; Magnino, *Jim's Journey*, 194; Nye, interview; Nowlin to author, 5 February 1980.

49. Elezak, Diary, 5 July and 8 August 1944; Pay, Diary, 5 and 9 July and 8 August 1944; Papock, Diary, 6 and 7 July and 27 August 1944; Oldham, *Lieutenant Stephen Polkinghorn*, 26; Kinney and McCaffrey, *Wake Island Pilot*, 134; Kantzer, "Imperial Guest," 151, 154, 156.

50. Huizenga, Affidavit, 7; John F. Kinney, Affidavit, August 2, 1945, 4, File 101-59, Box 1584, Japanese War Crimes at Woosung, RG 153; T. Miller, "T. Johnson Interview, 16 July 2001," 4; Marcello, "Godbold Interview," 69–70; Ashurst, "Record," 8.

51. Pay, Diary, 5 October 1944; Elezak, Diary, 5 October 1944; Oldham, *Lieutenant Stephen Polkinghorn*, 26; Huizenga, Affidavit, 7; Kantzer, "Imperial Guest," 159.

52. Elezak, Diary, 24 October and 11 November 1944; Pay, Diary, 25 October and 11 November 1944; Kinney, "P.O.W. Survival," 110–111; Kantzer, "Imperial Guest," 161–162; J. Cook, interview; J. Johnson, Diary, 11 November 1944; White, *United States Marines*, 131; Marcello, "Venable Interview," 64; Oldham, *Lieutenant Stephen Polkinghorn*, 26; Holmes to author, 17 July 1979; Marcello, "Godbold Interview," 69; Smith, interview; T. Miller, "T. Johnson Interview, 16 July 2001," 3.

53. Kantzer, "Imperial Guest," 162; Huizenga, Affidavit, 7; Chapman, interview; Marcello, "Fields Interview," 46; Kessler, *To Wake Island and Beyond*, 125; Ashurst, "Record," 8.

54. Daniel L. Haulman, *Hitting Home: The Air Offensive Against Japan*, The U.S. Army Air Forces in World War II (Washington, DC: Air Force History and Museums Program, 1999), 7–14; Trevor Dupuy, "The U.S. at War in China," *History of the Second World War*, July 18, 1974, 1853; Ronald H. Spector, *Eagle Against the Sun: The American War With Japan* (New York: Free Press, 1985), 489–492; Pay, Diary, 23 March and 14, 15, and 29 April 1945; Kantzer, "Imperial Guest," 186, 187; Elezak, Diary, 24 and 31 March, 13, 14, 20–21 and 23–29 April, and 1 May 1945; J. Johnson, Diary, 2 April 1945.

55. Elezak, Diary, 17 January 1945; Pay, Diary, 17 January 1945; Oldham, *Lieutenant Stephen Polkinghorn*, 27; J. Johnson, Diary, 17 January 1945; Marcello, "Venable Interview," 64; Holmes to author, 17 July 1979; J. Cook, interview; Kantzer, "Imperial Guest," 174–175; Sandvold, interview; Cornelius and Short, *Ding Hao*, 461.

56. Richardson, "Bread," 31; J. Johnson, Diary, 17 January 1945; Kauffman, "Charters Interview," 5: 12; J. Cook, interview; Chapman, interview.

57. William Hess, *P-51: Bomber Escort* (New York: Ballantine Books, 1971), 135; Kantzer, "Imperial Guest," 175; J. Johnson, Diary, 20 January 1945; MIS-X Section, CPM Branch, "Ex-Reports 665–668 (CHINA)," Appendix C, 5; Elezak, Diary, 20 January 1945; Kelnhofer, interview; Huizenga, Affidavit, 7–8; Pay, Diary, 20 January 1945.
58. Kantzer, "Imperial Guest," 175–176; Ashurst, "Record," 3, 8; Marcello, "McDaniel Interview," 66; Pay, Diary, 20 January 1945; Carl E. Stegmaier Jr., Affidavit, November 29, 1945, 1–2, File 101-59, Box 1584, Japanese War Crimes at Kiangwan, RG 153; J. Johnson, Diary, 20 January 1945; Holmes to author, 17 July 1979; Oldham, *Lieutenant Stephen Polkinghorn*, 27; Marcello, "Fields Interview," 23–24; MIS-X Section, CPM Branch, "Ex-Reports 665–668 (CHINA)," Appendix C, 5.
59. Pay, Diary, 1 April 1945; Elezak, Diary, 1 April 1945; Kantzer, "Imperial Guest," 187; Magnino, *Jim's Journey*, 195–196; LaPorte, interview; White, *United States Marines*, 131–132; Abraham, *Do You Understand*, 154–156; J. Johnson, Diary, 1 April 1945.
60. T. Miller, "T. Johnson Interview, 1 June 2001," 45; T. Miller, "T. Johnson Interview, 16 July 2001," 2; Marcello, "McDaniel Interview," 66.
61. White, *United States Marines*, 154; Kinney, "P.O.W. Survival," 124; Kantzer, "Imperial Guest," 184, 189–190, 193, 194; Pay, Diary, 23 March 1945; Kinney and McCaffrey, *Wake Island Pilot*, 135, 137; Oldham, *Lieutenant Stephen Polkinghorn*, 29; Pay, Diary, 8 May 1945.
62. Kantzer, "Imperial Guest," 192–193; Pay, Diary, 4 May 1945; Huizenga, Kinney, McBrayer, and McAlister, "Escape Report No. 665," 5; J. Johnson, Diary, 4 May 1945; Chapman, interview; Bowsher, interview.
63. Magnino, *Jim's Journey*, 199–202; Kantzer, "Imperial Guest," 193–194; Kinney and McCaffrey, *Wake Island Pilot*, 137; LaPorte, interview; MIS-X Section, CPM Branch, "Ex-Reports 665–668 (CHINA)," Appendix C, 13; O'Guinn, "V.O.C.," 79; Mettscher, reply.
64. Kantzer, "Imperial Guest," 192–193; Pay, Diary, 4 May 1945; J. Johnson, Diary, 4 May 1945; Chapman, interview; Bowsher, interview.
65. Kantzer, "Imperial Guest," 194; Pay, Diary, 8 May 1945.

CHAPTER 15

1. Kantzer, "Imperial Guest," 195; Ashurst, "Record," 1; American Legation, Bern, to Special War Problems Div., State Dept., "Enclosure No. 1 to Despatch No. 11046," 2 March 1945, 1; Abraham, *Do You Understand*, 160–163; White, *United States Marines*, 154–155; Kinney and McCaffrey, *Wake Island Pilot*, 138–140, 142; Kessler, *To Wake Island and Beyond*, 127–128; Marcello, "Venable Interview," 69; Magnino, *Jim's Journey*, 204–205;

Huizenga, Kinney, McBrayer, and McAlister, "Escape Report No. 665," 5; O'Guinn, "V.O.C.," 78, 82; Pay, Diary, 9 May 1945; Kinney, "P.O.W. Survival," 128–129, 132.
2. Kantzer, "Imperial Guest," 196–197; Pay, Diary, 15 May 1945; O'Guinn, "V.O.C." 79–81; Abraham, *Do You Understand*, 163.
3. Kantzer, "Imperial Guest," 196–197; Kinney and McCaffrey, *Wake Island Pilot*, 140; O'Guinn, "V.O.C.," 80; Pay, Diary, 10 and 14 May 1945; Frank and Shaw, *History of U.S. Marine Corps Operations*, vol. 5, 758–759; Marcello, "Godbold Interview," 70.
4. Kinney and McCaffrey, *Wake Island Pilot*, 85–88, 100, 107, 112–113, 116, 127–131, 133–134, 136, 138–141; McBrayer, *Escape*, 6–8, 10–11; Bishop and Irwin, *Escape From Hell*, 48–50; Marcello, "Godbold Interview," 71; Kessler, *To Wake Island and Beyond*, 128.
5. Kessler, *To Wake Island and Beyond*, 129; Kinney, "P.O.W. Survival," 131–183; Kinney and McCaffrey, *Wake Island Pilot*, 140–160; McBrayer, *Escape*, 18–78, 103, 117, 132–146, 157–207; Bishop and Irwin, *Escape From Hell*, 50–69. See also Gregory Urwin, "The Road Back From Wake Island, Part II," *American History Illustrated*, January 1981, 43–49.
6. Kantzer, "Imperial Guest," 197; O'Guinn, "V.O.C.," 82–83; White, *United States Marines*, 156; Williams, interview; Abraham, *Do You Understand*, 163; Smith, interview; Sandvold, interview; Nowlin to author, 5 February 1980; Hanna, interview.
7. Taylor, interview, August 28, 2002; William L. Taylor, interview by author, August 29, 2002; William Taylor, *Rescued by Mao: World War II, Wake Island, and My Remarkable Escape to Freedom Across Mainland China* (Sandy, UT: Silverleaf Press, 2007), 219–297; Raymond R. Rutledge, "In the Matter of the Mistreatment of American Prisoners of War at Feng Tai . . . between 8 May 1945 and August 1945 . . . ," September 13, 1945, 2, File 101-165, Box 1585, War Crimes at Fengtai, RG 153.
8. Kantzer, "Imperial Guest," 197; Abraham, *Do You Understand*, 163; Marcello, "Venable Interview," 70–71; Freuler, interview; Oldham, *Lieutenant Stephen Polkinghorn*, 29; Magnino, *Jim's Journey*, 208.
9. Pay, Diary, 14 May 1945; Norwood and Shek, "POW Camps," 1–2, 12; Director, Far East Division, International Committee of the Red Cross, to George Tait, 7 August 1945, Fengtai, China, RG 389; Richardson, reply; LaPorte, interview; Abraham, *Do You Understand*, 164; Marcello, "Godbold Interview," 73; Kantzer, "Imperial Guest," 198; Ashurst, "Record," 5; J. Johnson, reply, May 9, 1981; Chapman, interview; Sandvold, interview; Nowlin, reply, March 18, 1980; Frank, "Devereux Transcript," 144; Carroll E. Trego to Capt. Willard A. Smith, CMP, 25 March 1946, Fengtai, China, RG 389.

10. Pay, Diary, 14 and 20 May and 10 June 1945; J. Johnson, Diary, 14 May 1945; Kauffman, "Ludington Interview," 5: 17; Kantzer, "Imperial Guest," 200–202.
11. Chapman, interview; Magnino, *Jim's Journey*, 209–211; Kantzer, "Imperial Guest," 201; Kauffman, "Ludington Interview," 5: 127–128.
12. Kantzer, "Imperial Guest," 198, 200–202; Chapman, interview; Magnino, *Jim's Journey*, 211; Marcello, "Benton Interview," 119; Ashurst, "Record," 5.
13. Magnino, *Jim's Journey*, 213, 215; Abraham, *Do You Understand*, 167; Trego to Smith, 25 March 1946; Kantzer, "Imperial Guest," 198–199, 203; Nowlin, reply, March 18, 1980; Kessler, *To Wake Island and Beyond*, 130; Richardson, reply; Kahn, interview; Maj. Gen. Frank C. Tharin, USMC, to Col. F. C. Caldwell, USMC, 19 October 1966, Correspondence, MCHA.
14. Kantzer, "Imperial Guest," 199; White, *United States Marines*, 158–159; Pay, Diary, 20 May 1945; Nowlin, reply, March 18, 1980; Chapman, interview; LaPorte, interview; Trego to Smith, 25 March 1946.
15. Kelnhofer, interview; Elezak, Diary, 3 June 1945; Rutledge, "Mistreatment of American Prisoners," 2–3; Ashurst, "Record," 2.
16. Elezak, Diary, 20 May and 12 June 1945; Pay, Diary, 20 May and 10 June 1945; Taylor to Holmes, ca. January 1980; Kantzer, "Imperial Guest," 199, 203.
17. Pay, Diary, 19 June 1945; Kantzer, "Imperial Guest," 204; J. Johnson, Diary, 19 June 1945; Director, Far East Division, ICRC, to George Tait, 7 August 1945; Leck, *Captives*, 890; Ashurst, "Record," 1.
18. Kantzer, "Imperial Guest," 204–205; Pay, Diary, 20 and 27 June 1945; Mettscher, reply; Nowlin, reply, March 18, 1980; Magnino, *Jim's Journey*, 219–220; Kessler, *To Wake Island and Beyond*, 131; Abraham, *Do You Understand*, 172; Chapman, interview.
19. Kantzer, "Imperial Guest," 205–207; Pay, Diary, 27 June 1945; Mettscher, reply; Nowlin, reply, March 18, 1980; Magnino, *Jim's Journey*, 219–220; Kessler, *To Wake Island and Beyond*, 131; Abraham, *Do You Understand*, 172; Chapman, interview.
20. Kantzer, "Imperial Guest," 206; Richardson, reply; Abraham, *Do You Understand*, 171; Kessler, *To Wake Island and Beyond*, 132; White, *United States Marines*, 160.
21. Kantzer, "Imperial Guest," 207; Marcello, "McDaniel Interview," 75; Smith, interview; Marcello, "Venable Interview," 71; J. Johnson, reply, May 9, 1981; Magnino, *Jim's Journey*, 220–221; Nowlin, reply, March 18, 1980.
22. White, *United States Marines*, 162; Magnino, *Jim's Journey*, 216, 224; Abraham, *Do You Understand*, 168; Ashurst, "Record," 1; Richard C. Mayhew, "Northern Exposure," 241 (photostat copy in author's possession); Pay, Diary, 27 June 1945; John M. Gibbs, "Prisoner of War Camps in Japan and Japanese Controlled Areas as Taken From Reports of Interned Ameri-

can Prisoners," July 31, 1946, 1, RG 389; Davis, "Improper Conditions at Woosung," 2; Ryan, "Mass Punishment of American Prisoners," 1.
23. White, *United States Marines*, 161–166; Kantzer, "Imperial Guest," 207–208; Pay, Diary, 27 June 1945; J. Johnson, Diary, 28 June 1945; Hanna, interview; Nowlin, reply, March 18, 1980; Kelnhofer, interview; O'Guinn, "V.O.C.," 88.
24. Pay, Diary, 27 and 29 June 1945; Kantzer, "Imperial Guest," 208–209; Clay Blair Jr., *Silent Victory: The U.S. Submarine War Against Japan* (Philadelphia: J. B. Lippincott, 1975), 859–865; Camp, interview; Mettscher, reply; White, *United States Marines*, 163, 167; J. Johnson, reply, May 9, 1981; J. Cook, interview; Magnino, *Jim's Journey*, 226–227; Nowlin, reply, March 18, 1980; Kelnhofer, interview; Oldham, *Lieutenant Stephen Polkinghorn*, 29; J. Johnson, Diary, 29 June 1945.
25. Kantzer, "Imperial Guest," 208, 212, 222; Ashurst, "Record," 1; Richardson, reply; Magnino, *Jim's Journey*, 1; Knox, *Death March*, 402; Gibb, "POW Camps in Japan," 66–173; Norwood and Shek, "POW Camps," 15.
26. Kantzer, "Imperial Guest," 210; J. Johnson, Diary, 30 June 1945; Mayhew, "Northern Exposure," 241; Oldham, *Lieutenant Stephen Polkinghorn*, 30; Pay, Diary, 30 June 1945; Ashurst, "Record," 4; J. Cook, interview; Ketner, "Mistreatment Aboard *Nitta Maru*," 1.
27. Ketner, "Mistreatment Aboard *Nitta Maru*," 1; Marcello, "Fields Interview," 40; Kahn, interview; White, *United States Marines*, 168–170; J. Johnson, Diary, 30 June–2 July 1945; Oldham, *Lieutenant Stephen Polkinghorn*, 30; Camp, interview; Richardson, reply.
28. J. Johnson, Diary, 30 June and 2 July 1945; Sandvold, interview; Camp, interview; Mettscher, reply; Nowlin, reply, March 18, 1980; J. Cook, interview; Dale, interview; LaPorte, interview; Williams, interview; T. Miller, "T. Johnson Interview, 16 July 2001," 13; Kelnhofer, interview; J. Johnson, reply, May 9, 1981.
29. Richardson, reply; LaPorte, interview; Chapman, interview.
30. J. Johnson, Diary, 1–2 July 1945; Reeves, interview; Kessler, *To Wake Island and Beyond*, 134; Mettscher, reply; J. Cook, interview; LaPorte, interview.
31. J. Johnson, Diary, 2 July 1945; Oldham, *Lieutenant Stephen Polkinghorn*, 30; Nowlin, reply, March 18, 1980; Kessler, *To Wake Island and Beyond*, 134; LaPorte, interview; Stocks, interview; Chapman, interview; Kauffman, "Poindexter Interview," 42; Williams, interview; Marcello, "Venable Interview," 73; Mayhew, "Northern Exposure," 241. Authoritative treatments of the American air offensive against Japan include Wesley Frank Craven and James Lea Cate, eds., *The Army Air Forces in World War II*, vol. 5, *The Pacific: Matterhorn to Nagasaki, June 1944 to August 1945* (1953; repr., Washington, DC: Office of Air Force History, 1983) and Kenneth P. Werrell,

Blankets of Fire: U.S. Bombers Over Japan During World War II (Washington, DC: Smithsonian Institution Press, 1996).

32. Marcello, "Venable Interview," 73–74; Marcello, "Fields Interview," 51–52; LaPorte, interview; Mettscher, reply; Williams, interview; J. Johnson, reply, May 9, 1981; Richardson, reply; Nowlin, reply, March 18, 1980; Chapman, interview.

33. White, *United States Marines*, 171; O'Guinn, "V.O.C.," 88; Pay, Diary, 4 and 10 July 1945; Abraham, *Do You Understand*, 175–176; Gibbs, "POW Camps in Japan," 73; Mayhew, "Northern Exposure," 241.

34. J. Johnson, reply, May 9, 1981; J. Johnson, Diary, 3–5 July 1945; Oldham, *Lieutenant Stephen Polkinghorn*, 30; Mayhew, "Northern Exposure," 241–242; Marcello, "Fields Interview," 40; Richardson, reply; Mettscher, reply; Taylor to Holmes, ca. January 1980; Kessler, *To Wake Island and Beyond*, 135; Gibbs, "POW Camps in Japan," 174; White, *United States Marines*, 172.

35. Gibbs, "POW Camps in Japan," 174–176; Marcello, "Fields Interview," 58; M. W. Shellhorn, "Check List, Hakodate No. 2," n.d., 1–2, Conditions at Hakodate Branch Camp 2, RG 389; Robert E. L. Page, "Check List, Hakodate No. 2," n.d., 1–2, 5, Conditions at Hakodate Branch Camp 2, RG 389.

36. J. Johnson, Diary, 6–7 July 1945; Mayhew, "Northern Exposure," 242–244; Oldham, *Lieutenant Stephen Polkinghorn*, 30, 32; "Report of Interview With Comdr. Eric G. F. Pollard, USN, DC," April 22, 1946, 1–2, Conditions at Hakodate Branch Camp No. 3, RG 389; Capt. James L. Norwood, USA, "Colonel Devereux: Notes Taken by Capt. Norwood," n.d., 1, Conditions at Hakodate Branch Camp No. 3, RG 389; Thomas R. Carpenter, "Check List, Hakodate No. 2," n.d., 2, Conditions at Hakodate Branch Camp 2, RG 389; Shellhorn, "Check List, Hakodate No. 2," 2; LaPorte, interview; Devereux, *Story of Wake*, 236–237; White, *United States Marines*, 173; Gibbs, "POW Camps in Japan," 174, 201–202; "Wake Personnel," September 12, 1945, 11, 13–18.

37. Marine Gunner John Hamas, USMC, "Report on Branch Camp No. 3, Hakodate War-Prisoner's Camp, Uteshinal, Hokkaido, Japan," September 14, 1945, 1, Conditions at Hakodate Branch Camp No. 3, RG 389; Chester M. Biggs Jr., "Check List, Hakodate No. 3," n.d., 1–2, 4–5, Conditions at Hakodate Branch Camp No. 3, RG 389; Victor V. Skaggs, "Check List, Hakodate No. 3," n.d., 1, 5, Conditions at Hakodate Branch Camp No. 3, RG 389; "Pollard Interview," 1; J. Johnson, Diary, 7–8 July 1945; Richardson, reply; Nowlin, reply, March 18, 1980; R. Brown, interview.

38. Robert M. Brown, "Check List, Hakodate No. 3," n.d., 2, Conditions at Hakodate Branch Camp No. 3, RG 389; Hamas, "Hakodate No. 3," 1; J. Cook, interview; J. Johnson, Diary, 9 August 1945; Kelnhofer, interview; Nowlin, reply, March 18, 1980.

39. J. Johnson, Diary, 9 August 1945; Hamas, "Hakodate No. 3," 2–3; R. Brown, "Hakodate No. 3," 2, 4; Smith, interview; Nowlin, reply, March 18, 1980; Kelnhofer, interview.
40. Hamas, "Hakodate No. 3," 3; "Pollard Interview," 3–4; Stegmaier, interview; Marcello, "McDaniel Interview," 79; Marcello, "Benton Interview," 131; Nowlin, reply, March 18, 1980; Chapman, interview; T. Miller, "T. Johnson Interview, 16 July 2001," 16–17.
41. Trego to Smith, 25 March 1946; G. Mason Kahn, "Check List, Hakodate No. 3," n.d., Conditions at Hakodate Branch Camp No. 3, RG 389; Clarence B. McKinstry, "Check List, Hakodate No. 3," n.d., 2, Conditions at Hakodate Branch Camp No. 3, RG 389; Hamas, "Hakodate No. 3," 3–4; Nowlin, reply, March 18, 1980; Kahn, interview; J. Cook, interview; Stegmaier, interview; J. Johnson, Diary, 8 July 1945.
42. "Pollard Interview," 3; J. Johnson, Diary, 8 July–9 August 1945; Sandvold, interview; Hamas, "Hakodate No. 3," 3; Kahn, "Hakodate No. 3," 3.
43. Gibbs, "POW Camps in Japan," 202, 205; Hamas, "Hakodate No. 3," 3, 7–8; Biggs, "Hakodate No. 3," 3; J. Johnson, Diary, 7 July 1945; Nowlin, reply, March 18, 1980.
44. Hamas, "Hakodate No. 3," 6–7; Kahn, "Hakodate No. 3," 2–3; McAnally, "Mistreatment Aboard *NITTA MARU*," 6; J. Johnson, Diary, 9 August 1945.
45. Hamas, "Hakodate No. 3," 5–6; McKinstry, "Hakodate No. 3," 3; J. Johnson, Diary, 8 July–9 August 1945; Kahn, interview; Nowlin, reply, March 18, 1980.
46. Marcello, "Benton Interview," 131; Ronald E. Marcello, ed., "Interview With Henry B. Stowers, May 25, 1973," 84, UNT Oral History Collection; Kelnhofer, interview; Richardson, reply; J. Johnson, reply, May 9, 1981; J. Johnson, Diary, 11–12 August 1945.
47. Nowlin, reply, March 18, 1980; J. Johnson, Diary, 12 August 1945; "Wake Personnel," 12 September 1945, 11.
48. Marcello, "McDaniel Interview," 82; Marcello, "Benton Interview," 131, 134; J. Johnson, reply, May 9, 1941; R. Brown, interview; Stegmaier, interview; J. Cook, interview.
49. Mayhew, "Northern Exposure," 244; Gibbs, "POW Camps in Japan," 179–180; LaPorte, interview; Marcello, "Fields Interview," 54; Camp, interview; Williams, interview.
50. Mayhew, "Northern Exposure," 244; Gibbs, "POW Camps in Japan," 176–177; Marcello, "Fields Interview," 57; Ewing E. LaPorte, "Check List, Hakodate No. 2," n.d., 2, Conditions at Hakodate Branch Camp 2, RG 389; Floyd H. Davis, "Check List, Hakodate No. 2," n.d., 2, Conditions at Hakodate Branch Camp 2, RG 389; Shellhorn, "Hakodate No. 2," 2; Page, "Hakodate No. 2," 2; Williams, interview; Carpenter, "Hakodate No. 2," 3.

51. David A. Timpany, "Check List, Hakodate No. 2," n.d., 2, Conditions at Hakodate Branch Camp 2, RG 389; Carpenter, "Hakodate No. 2," 2; LaPorte, "Hakodate No. 2," 2; Shellhorn, "Hakodate No. 2," 2; Page, "Hakodate No. 2," 2; Gibbs, "POW Camps in Japan," 180.
52. Williams, interview; Norman Kaz to author, 17 July 1982; Lester C. Owens, Affidavit, April 17, 1981, 1 (photostat copy in author's possession); Timpany, "Hakodate No. 2," 3; Page, "Hakodate No. 2," 3; LaPorte, "Hakodate No. 2," 3, 5.
53. Tharin to Caldwell, 19 October 1966; White, *United States Marines*, 173–178; Devereux, *Story of Wake*, 237; Hanna, interview; Kessler, *To Wake Island and Beyond*, 138–139; Marcello, "Godbold Interview," 79–80; Ashurst, "Record," 6.
54. Mettscher, reply.
55. Nowlin, reply, March 18, 1980; Mettscher, reply, J. Cook, interview; Reeves, interview; Stegmaier, interview; J. Johnson, Diary, 15 August 1945.
56. Mayhew, "Northern Exposure," 244–245; Williams, interview; LaPorte, interview; Camp, interview; Marcello, "McDaniel Interview," 84; J. Johnson, Diary, 16 August 1945; Marcello, "Venable Interview," 77; T. Miller, "T. Johnson Interview, 16 July 2001," 20.
57. Mayhew, "Northern Exposure," 245; LaPorte, interview; Williams, interview; R. Brown, interview; Smith, interview; Sandvold, interview; Kelnhofer, interview.
58. J. Johnson, Diary, 23 August 1945; Nowlin, reply, March 18, 1980; Mettscher, reply.
59. J. Johnson, Diary, 24–25 August 1945; Nowlin, reply, March 18, 1980; Marcello, "Venable Interview," 77–78; T. Miller, "T. Johnson Interview, July 16, 2001," 21–22; Richardson, reply; Mayhew, "Northern Exposure," 245; Marcello, "Fields Interview," 59–60; Lt. Jiro Tendo, IJA, "Announcement," August 24, 1945, 1, B.5, F.5, Cunningham Collection; LaPorte, interview; Sandvold, interview; R. Brown, interview. For more on this national personality change, see John W. Dower, *Embracing Defeat: Japan in the Wake of World War II* (New York: W.W. Norton, 1999).
60. R. Brown, interview; White, *United States Marines*, 189–193; Devereux, *Story of Wake*, 79; J. Johnson, Diary, 24–25 August 1945; Williams, interview; LaPorte, interview; T. Miller, "T. Johnson Interview, July 16, 2001," 20.
61. Bergamini, *Japan's Imperial Conspiracy*, vol. 1, 166–167; Douglas MacArthur, *Reminiscences* (New York: McGraw-Hill Book Company, 1964), 271–272; J. Johnson, reply, May 9, 1981; R. Brown, interview; White, *United States Marines*, 186; Frank and Shaw, *U.S. Marine Corps Operations*, vol. 5, 781–782.
62. Frank and Shaw, *U.S. Marine Corps Operations*, vol. 5, 784; R. Brown,

interview; Williams, interview; White, *United States Marines*, 195; Kessler, *To Wake Island and Beyond*, 142; Mayhew, "Northern Exposure," 245.

63. Mayhew, "Northern Exposure," 245–246; J. Johnson, Diary, 28–30 August 1945; R. Brown, interview; Nowlin, reply, March 18, 1980; Williams, interview; T. Miller, "T. Johnson Interview, July 16, 2001," 24; Sandvold, interview; White, *United States Marines*, 195–196; Kessler, *To Wake Island and Beyond*, 142–143; Oldham, *Lieutenant Stephen Polkinghorn*, 31; J. Cook, interview.

64. Chapman, interview; Nowlin, reply, March 18, 1980; Kahn, interview; R. Brown, interview; Richardson, reply; T. Miller, "T. Johnson Interview, July 16, 2001," 24; Marcello, "McDaniel Interview," 88.

65. Nowlin, reply, March 18, 1980; Chapman, interview; J. Johnson, Diary, 28 August 1945; Camp, interview; J. Johnson, reply, May 9, 1981; Williams, interview; Richardson, reply; Marcello, "Venable Interview," 78; White, *United States Marines*, 196; Frank and Shaw, *U.S. Marine Corps Operations*, vol. 5, 785.

66. J. Johnson, reply, May 9, 1981; Nowlin, reply, March 18, 1980; Marcello, "McDaniel Interview," 85; J. Johnson, Diary, 2 September 1945; "History of Flag Raised Over This Camp on 2nd Sept. 1945," September 14, 1945, B.1, F.2, Devereux Collection.

67. J. Johnson, Diary, 2 September 1945.

CHAPTER 16

1. Hamas, "Hakodate No. 3," 8; Marcello, "Fields Interview," 56; Mayhew, "Northern Exposure," 245–46; Williams, interview; LaPorte, interview; Marcello, "McDaniel Interview," 85–86; J. Johnson, Diary, 4 September 1945; Smith, interview; Camp, interview.

2. White, *United States Marines*, 199–200; Devereux, *Story of Wake*, 239; Marcello, "Venable Interview," 78; Nowlin, reply, March 18, 1980; Richardson, reply; J. Johnson, Diary, 6 September 1945.

3. White, *United States Marines*, 200–212; Devereux, *Story of Wake*, 239–240; Captain Niizuma Kinsaburo, IJA, Receipt for Japanese Army Property, September 14, 1945, B.3, F.2, Devereux Collection; Marine Gunner John Hamas, USMC, Receipt for Japanese Army Property, September 14, 1945, B.3, F.2, Devereux Collection; Reeves, interview; Nowlin, reply, March 18, 1980.

4. J. Johnson, Diary, 11 September 1945; Nowlin, reply, March 18, 1980; T. Miller, "T. Johnson Interview, 16 July 2001," 23; Kelnhofer, interview; Chapman, interview; Mayhew, "Northern Exposure," 246–247; White, *United States Marines*, 208–209; Sandvold, interview; LaPorte, interview; Camp, interview.

5. Devereux, *Story of Wake*, 240; White, *United States Marines*, 212–217; Kahn, "Hakodate No. 3," 3–4; Carpenter, "Hakodate No. 2," 3–4; LaPorte, "Hakodate No. 2," 3–4; Davis, "Hakodate No. 2," 3–4; Nowlin, reply, March 18, 1980; Frank, "Devereux Transcript," 151; J. Johnson, reply, May 9, 1981; Chapman, interview; Haidinger, interview; Kessler, *To Wake Island and Beyond*, 143–144; Williams, interview; Camp, interview; Mayhew, "Northern Exposure," 247.

6. O'Guinn, "V.O.C.," 90; Kantzer, "Imperial Guest," 212, 215; Magnino, *Jim's Journey*, 231, 233–235; Anderson, Affidavit, 2; Pay, Diary, 23 July 1945; Gibbs, "POW Camps in Japan," 74–75; Joseph L. Mendiola, "Check List," n.d., 2–3, Conditions at Fukuoka No. 11, RG 389; Nye, interview.

7. O'Guinn, "V.O.C.," 90–91; Kantzer, "Imperial Guest," 212–214.

8. Kantzer, "Imperial Guest," 224–239; O'Guinn, "V.O.C.," 94–96.

9. Magnino, *Jim's Journey*, 228, 230–271; D. Miller, *Doc Miller*, 15–17; Richard B. Frank, *Downfall: The End of the Imperial Japanese Empire* (New York: Random House, 1999), 149–150.

10. Gibbs, "POW Camps in Japan," 73–75; Pay, Diary, 10, 14, 18, and 23 July 1945; Nye, interview; Mendiola, "Check List," 1–2.

11. Pay, Diary, 10 and 29 July, 1, 12, 16, 21, 26, and 27 August, and 2, 4, and 13 September 1945; Gibbs, "POW Camps in Japan," 73–75; Nye, interview; Kauffman, "Loveland Interview," 31; Kauffman, "Kidd Interview," 30; Kauffman, "Rogge Interview," 24.

12. Leo W. Wilcox, Diary, 12–13 January 1942, POW Conditions on Wake Island, RG 389; Kauffman, "Myers Interview," 23; Kauffman, "Rogge Interview," 20; Maple, reply; Sloman, reply; Russell, Diary, 11–12, 15–17, 19, 21, 24–25, 29, and 31 January, 1 March, and 20 May 1942; E. A. Junghans, "Wake, 1568–1946," n.d., 15, File 1M-5, Wake Island Defenses (Historical Data), Papers Relating to the Defense of Wake Island, MCHA; Kauffman, "Myers Interview," 28; Howes, "Testimony," 19.

13. Junghans, "Wake, 1568–1946," 15; F. Miller, Diary, 20 February 1942.

14. Russell, Diary, 20, 28, and 30–31 January, 10 and 14–15 March, and 5, 13, and 15 April 1942; F. Miller, Diary, 10 March 1942; Sloman, interview; Holewinski, interview, June 20, 1980; Howes, "Testimony," 8; Kauffman, "Myers Interview," 35–36; Kauffman, "Hokanson Interview," 18.

15. Maple, reply; Russell, Diary, 10–11 and 13 May 1942; Holewinski, interviews, September 11, 1986, and June 20, 1980; Holewinski, "Works of Dr. Shank," 3; Darden, *Guests*, 191.

16. John B. Lundstrom, *The First Team: Pacific Naval Air Combat From Pearl Harbor to Midway* (Annapolis: Naval Institute Press, 1984), 137–143; Cressman, *Magnificent Fight*, 253; Junghans, "Wake, 1568–1946," 16; Holewinski, interviews, June 20, 1980, and September 11, 1986; Kauffman, "Myers

Interview," 29–30; Howes, "Testimony," 7; Russell, Diary, 21 and 24–25 February 1942; F. Miller, Diary, 24–25 February 1942.
17. Cressman, *Magnificent Fight*, 254; Holewinski, interview, September 11, 1986; Russell, Diary, 26–27 February and 3 March 1942; F. Miller, Diary, 26–27 February 1942; Howes, "Testimony," 8; Sloman, interview.
18. Kauffman, "Myers Interview," 30–31; Kauffman, "Hokanson Interview," 18–19; Russell, Diary, 26 and 28 April and 5 May 1942; F. Miller, Diary, 26 April and 5 May 1942; Howes, "Testimony," 8; Maple, reply; Sloman, interview.
19. Russell, Diary, 13 and 15 April and 8–10 May 1942; F. Miller, Diary, 8 and 10 May 1942; Wilcox, Diary, 8–9 May 1942; Darden, *Guests*, 173–174, 189; Sloman, interview; Kauffman, "Myers Interview," 29; Howes, "Testimony," 8; Maple, reply.
20. Russell, "War Diary," 16, 24, and 28 July and 20 September 1942; Kauffman, "Myers Interview," 34; Robert C. Maple to Gilbert V. V., 13 December 1952 (audiocassette copy of taped letter in the author's possession); F. Miller, Diary, 9 and 14 April, 16 and 18 July, and 11 September 1942.
21. Russell, Diary, 12 October 1942; F. Miller, Diary, 28–29 September 1942; Kauffman, "Kidd Interview," 25; Maple, reply; Junghans, "Wake, 1568–1946," 46.
22. Mark E. Hubbs, "Massacre on Wake Island," *Naval History* 15, no. 1 (2001): 30, 33; Junghans "Wake, 1568–1946," 49.
23. Junghans, "Wake, 1568–1946," 17, 44, 49; Darden, *Guests*, 204, 236; Hubbs, "Massacre," 33; Tsuji, interview; Jon Guttman, "Carrier Strike on Wake," *World War II*, September 1998, 26–32.
24. Junghans, "Wake, 1568–1946," 50; Earl A. Junghans, "Wake's POWs," *Naval Institute Proceedings* 109, no. 2 (1983): 49–50; Hubbs, "Massacre," 33–34; Tsuji, interview; Darden, *Guests*, 337.
25. Tsuji, interview; E. A. Junghans, ed., "Life on Wake Island—From a Japanese Diary," n.d., 2–13 (photostat copy in the author's possession); Junghans, "Wake's POWs," 44; Junghans, "Wake 1568–1946," 16–17.
26. Junghans, "Life on Wake," 2–4, 6, 8–9, 12; Tsuji, interview; Junghans, "Wake, 1568–1946," 17.
27. Junghans, "Wake, 1568–1946," 17; Ernie Harwell, "The Wake Story," *Leatherneck*, November 1945, 9.
28. Hubbs, "Massacre," 34; Junghans, "Wake's POWs," 46, 49–50; Junghans, "Wake, 1568–1946," 19–20; *Navy News* (Guam, Marianas Islands), June 20, 1947.
29. Sloman, reply; Holewinski, interviews, June 20, 1980, and September 11, 1986.
30. Darden, *Guests*, 195–197; Sloman, reply; Holewinski, interviews, June 20, 1980, and September 11, 1986; Sloman, interview.

31. Gibbs, "POW Camps in Japan," 53–54; Sloman, reply; Sloman, interview; H. J. Van Peenen, "Touchstone From Zentsuji," in *Zentsuji in Kansas: Stories From the POW Reunions*, ed. Joe Brown (Marble Hill, MO: Stewart Publishing & Printing, 1986), 81; Rogers, interview; Donald T. Giles, *Captive of the Rising Sun: The POW Memoirs of Rear Admiral Donald T. Giles* (Annapolis: Naval Institute Press, 1994), 20–59, 78, 102, 189–199; Martin Boyle, *Yanks Don't Cry* (New York: Bernard Geis Associates, 1963), 7; Timothy P. Maga, *Defending Paradise: The United States and Guam, 1898–1950* (New York: Garland, 1988), 179; Frank O. Hough, Verle E. Ludwig, and Henry I. Shaw Jr., *History of U.S. Marine Corps Operations in World War II.*, vol. 1, *Pearl Harbor to Guadalcanal* (Washington, DC: Historical Branch, G-3 Division, Headquarters, U.S. Marine Corps, 1958), 75–78.
32. Giles, *Captive*, 85–86, 98, 130; Frank and Shaw, *U.S. Marine Corps Operations*, vol. 5, 734; Gibbs, "POW Camps in Japan," 63–64; Darden, *Guests*, 197; Sloman, interview; Rogers, interview; "Truman Keck (An Interview)," in Brown, *Zentsuji in Kansas*, 56; "Paul 'Doughbelly' Ritthaler," in Brown, *Zentsuji in Kansas*, 64; "Wiley 'Slick' Sloman," in Brown, *Zentsuji in Kansas*, 73; Paul A. Putnam, "Shorthand Diaries: Book I, February 23, 1943–December 25, 1944," trans. Elizabeth and Rebecca Millard, 13 June, 23 August, and 13 December 1942, Paul A. Putnam Papers (No. 313), Special Collections Department, J. Y. Joyner Library, East Carolina University, Greenville, NC (hereinafter Putnam Papers).
33. Gibbs, "POW Camps in Japan," 58, 62; Rogers, interview; Darden, *Guests*, 198; Putnam, "Shorthand Diary: Book I," 30 March, 18–19 and 29 April, 8 May, 16 June, 14 July, 1, 9, 19, and 23 August, 17 October 1943, and 13 and 20 February 1944; "Paul Albert Putnam Oral History Interview (No. OH0027)," November 13, 1975, 12, Special Collections Department, J. Y. Joyner Library, East Carolina University.
34. Gibbs, "POW Camps in Japan," 58, 60–62; Holewinski, interview, September 11, 1986; Putnam, "Shorthand Diary: Book I," 29 April, 9 August, 15 September, 17 October, 10 and 28 November, and 5, 13, and 19 December 1943, and 24 September, 23 and 30 November, and 23 December 1944; Paul A. Putnam, "Shorthand Diaries: Book II, December 26, 1944–September 20, 1945," trans. Elizabeth and Rebecca Millard, 7, 21 January, 9 March, 24 April, 10 May 1945, Putnam Papers.
35. Gibbs, "POW Camps in Japan," 54, 58–59; Rogers, interview; Giles, *Captive*, 84; Sloman, interview; Putnam, "Shorthand Diary: Book I," 6 April, 30 August, 8 September, and 17 October 1943, 13 and 20 February, 2 July, 19 August, 6 and 28 September, 3 and 29 October, 12, 19, 23, and 30 November, and 10 and 20 December 1944; Putnam, "Shorthand Diary: Book II," 14 February and 16 March 1945.

36. Sloman, interview; Sloman, reply; Holewinski, interview, September 11, 1986; Putnam, "Shorthand Diary: Book I," 10 November and 23 December 1943.
37. Gibbs, "POW Camps in Japan," 54; Sloman, interview; Van Peenen, "Touchstone From Zentsuji," 82; Putnam, "Shorthand Diary: Book I," 31 July, 1 and 9 August, and 19 December 1943, and 28 August and 3 September 1944.
38. Darden, *Guests*, 199, 206, 211, 218, 220, 222–223, 232, 263–266, 268, 272; *Bloomfield (MO) Vindicator*, June 4, 1980; Holewinski, interview, September 11, 1986.
39. Gibbs, "POW Camps in Japan," 54, 64; Sloman, reply; Putnam, "Shorthand Diary: Book II," 23 and 27 June and 22 August 1945; Van Peenen, "Touchstone From Zentsuji," 84; Sloman, interview.
40. Putnam, "Shorthand Diary: Book II," 27 June, 2 and 25 July, and 3–6 August 1945; Darden, *Guests*, 206, 210, 220, 223, 233, 245, 249, 280; Holewinski, interviews, June 20, 1980, and September 11, 1986.
41. Russell, Diary, 12 October 1942; Howes, "Testimony," 8; Kauffman, "Myers Interview," 36; Maple, reply; Kauffman, "Kidd Interview," 27–28.
42. Russell, Diary, 12–13, 16, 20, and 25 October, 12, 14, and 24 November, and 3–4, 8, 11, 14, 25, and 31 December 1943, 8 January, 12 March–13 September, and 30 December 1943, and 24 May 1944; "Prologue," in Russell, Diary, 169–182.
43. Warren O. Rogge to Capt. Willard A. Smith, 22 May 1946, Conditions at Fukuoka No. 9, RG 389; Howes, "Testimony," 8–11, 17, 20–21, 26; F. Miller, Diary, 11, 14, and 20 February 1943; Howes, "Testimony," 9–10, 18; Maple, reply.
44. Howes, "Testimony," 9, 15, 18, 21; Maple, reply; F. Miller, Diary, 8–9 February 1943.
45. Howes, "Testimony," 10–11, 17, 21, 25; Maple, reply; Rogge to Smith, 22 May 1946; F. Miller, Diary, 14, 17, 19, and 21–22 February 1943; Wilcox, Diary, 2 November and 9 December 1942, 11–12 and 26 January, 6–7, 14, 17, 19–20, 22, 25, and 27 February, 1–2, 8–10, 12, 15, 18, 20–23, 25, 27, and 30 March, 3, 8, and 25 April, 1, 4, and 6 May, 4 June, and 4 and 16 July 1943; Center for Research, Allied POWs Under the Japanese, "53 Men Deceased: Fukuoka No. 18 Sasebo," http://www.mansell.com/pow_resources/camplists/fukuoka/fuku_18_sasebo/fuk_18_deceased.html (accessed February 15, 2009).
46. Gibbs, "POW Camps in Japan," 1; Howes, "Testimony," 11, 21; Maple, reply; Rogge to Smith, 22 May 1946.
47. Howes, "Testimony," 11; Rogge to Smith, 22 May 1946.
48. Gibbs, "POW Camps in Japan," 1–2; Maple, reply; Rogge to Smith, 22 May 1946.

49. Howes, "Testimony," 11–13, 22.
50. Rogge to Smith, 22 May 1946; Warren O. Rogge, "Check List, Fukuoka Camp No. 9," n.d., Conditions at Fukuoka No. 9, RG 389.
51. Pay, Diary, 18 September 1942, and 20 August 1943; Papock, Diary, 18 September 1942, and 20 August 1943; Newell, Diary, 18 September and 3 November 1942; Oldham, *Lieutenant Stephen Polkinghorn*, 15, 18; Magnino, *Jim's Journey*, 124; Kantzer, "Imperial Guest," 85, 88, 112–14; Norwood and Shek, "POW Camps," 31; Elezak, Diary, 20 August 1943; "Wake Personnel," 12 September 1945, 1; Kirk, *Secret Camera*, 70; White, *United States Marines*, 95–96.
52. Kirk, *Secret Camera*, 84; Hans Whitney, *Guest of the Fallen Sun* (New York: Exposition Press, 1951), 52; Borne, interview; Hotchkiss, interview, October 21, 1983; Gross, interviews, October 22, 1983, and October 13, 1984; Burton, *Life's Trails*, 85, 90.
53. Gibbs, "POW Camps in Japan," 15–16, 21; Kirk, *Secret Camera*, 74–75, 77–82, 85–88, 94; Conner, interview; Burton, *Life's Trails*, 82–85, 92; King, interview; Himelrick, Diary, 4 and 12, December 1942.
54. Burton, *Life's Trails*, 87–89, 97; King, interview; Conner, interview; Kirk, *Secret Camera*, 91–92, 98, 118–19; Himelrick, Diary, 19 and 23 December 1942; Norris H. Troney, "Norris Troney Diary," 6 June 1944, and 1 January and 22 July 1945, North China Marines, http://www.northchinamarines.com/id73.html (accessed March 20, 2009).
55. Center for Research, Allied POWs Under the Japanese, "Fukuoka No. 3-b: Roster of American POWs & Civilians," http://www.mansell.com/pow_resources/camplists/fukuoka/fusku_3_tobata/fuku_3_yanks.html (accessed November 21, 2008); Conner, interview; White, *United States Marines*, 152; Burton, *Life's Trails*, 84, 90, 99–100; Kirk, *Secret Camera*, 94, 129, 133, 138, 152, 174–175; Gibbs, "POW Camps in Japan," 19, 23; King, interview; Conner, interview.
56. Kirk, *Secret Camera*, 82, 92, 99–100, 103, 174–175; Conner, interview; Burton, *Life's Trails*, 96, 100, 102–103, 108–109.
57. Gibbs, "POW Camps in Japan," 15; Troney, "Diary," 15 and 24 December 1943, and 14 and 22 July 1945; Burton, *Life's Trails*, 91–92; Conner, interview; Kirk, *Secret Camera*, 120, 122, 124–127.
58. Kirk, *Secret Camera*, 157–159, 161, 199–203, 205–207, 209–216; Troney, "Diary," 15 June, 29 July, and 20 August 1944, and 11 February, 1 April, 27 May, 10–11, 18, and 21–22 June, 3 and 10–11 July, and 1 and 7–14 August 1945; Burton, *Life's Trails*, 107–109, 115–117, 119; Conner, interview; King, interview.
59. Young, "WWII POW," 9; John A. Glusman, *Conduct Under Fire: Four American Doctors and Their Fight for Life as Prisoners of the Japanese*

(New York: Viking, 2005), 297–298; Kauffman, "Goicoechea Interview," 21–22; Haidinger, interview; Whitney, *Guest*, 53–54; Gross, interview, October 13, 1984.

60. Durrwachter, Diary, 15 September and 13 October 1943; Joe Goicoechea to Gavan Daws, 10 February 1992, Daws Papers; Hubley, interview; Kauffman; "Goicoechea Interview," 23; Cox, interview; Kibble, "My War," 159, 169.
61. Durrwachter, Diary, 13 and 21 October, 8 November, and 14 December 1943, and 6 January, 19–26 February, 21 March, 3 April, 4 May, 23 and 27 October, and 1 November 1944; Conrad Johnson, "Diary of Conrad Johnson, 1944, Part I," 21–22, 24, 26, and 28 February, 4–5, 7–8, 13, 16, 22–23, and 30 March, and 3–4, 6–11, 13–14, 23, and 25–28 April 1944, Center for Research, Allied POWs Under the Japanese, http://www.mansell.com/pow_resources/camplists/tokyo/kawasaki-5D/conrad%20diary1.html (accessed February 27, 2009); Conrad Johnson, "Diary of Conrad Johnson, 1944, Part II," 1, 4, 6, 9–11, 13, 20, 25, and 27–28 May, 4, 18–20, 22–24, and 29 June, 4, 18, and 28–31 July, 2–4, 7, 20–22, 25, and 31 August, and 1–22 September 1944, Center for Research, Allied POWs Under the Japanese, http://www.mansell.com/pow_resources/camplists/tokyo/kawasaki-5D/conrad%20diary2.html (accessed February 27, 2009); Hubley, interview; Kibble, "My War," 172; Whitney, *Guest*, 59.
62. Durrwachter, Diary, 15 September, 19 November, and 29 December 1943, 15 and 22 January, 4 and 13 May, 20 and 23 November, and 29 December 1944, and 14 May 1945; C. Johnson, "Diary, Pt. I," 26–28 February, 11 March, and 9 and 14 April 1944; C. Johnson, "Diary, Pt. II," 1, 3, 10, and 24 May, 7 June, 4 July, and 17 August 1944; Kauffman, "Goicoechea Interview," 25, 37; Haidinger, interview; Whitney, *Guest*, 54–55; Kibble, "My War," 172.
63. Hubley, interview; Kibble, "My War," 165; C. Johnson, "Diary, Pt. I," 18–20 April 1944; Durrwachter, Diary, 29 December 1943, 25 October and 9 November 1944, and 20 April 1945.
64. Diarists Henry Durrwachter and Conrad Johnson both mourned an unnamed Shanghai POW on March 12, 1944, and Durrwachter also mentioned the loss of Pfc. Ralph H. Goudy of the North China Marines. See Durrwachter, Diary, 12 March, 1 November, and 10 December 1944, 29 April, and 1 and 4 May 1945, as well as C. Johnson, "Diary, Pt. I," 12 March 1944; Cox, interview; Haidinger, interview; Kibble, "My War," 176–179; Hubley, interview.
65. Durrwachter, Diary, 23 April 1945; Cox, interview; Kibble, "My War," 183–190; Kauffman, "Goicoechea Interview," 26; Tice, interview.
66. Hubley, interview; Durrwachter, Diary, 24 June and 20 August 1945; Center for Research, Allied POWs Under the Japanese, "Hanaoka-Sendai No. 7-B,"

http://www.mansell.com/pow_resources/camplists/sendai/sendai_07_hanuoka/hanuoka_7_b.html (accessed January 14, 2009).
67. Glusman, *Conduct*, 296, 299; Gross, interviews, October 22, 1983, and October 13, 1984; Cox, interview; Jack R. Williamson to Gavan Daws, 11 August 1991, Daws Papers; White, *United States Marines*, 150; Wheeler, interview; Borne, interview; Plate, reply; Hotchkiss, interview, October 21, 1983; Broyles, reply; Young, "WWII POW," 9; Sturgeon, interview, October 13, 1984; Frank R. Mace, *The Story of Wake Island: Before, During and After Life as a Prisoner of War of the Japanese* (Spokane, WA: privately printed, n.d.), 48.
68. Borne, interview; Broyles, reply; Snipes, "Adventureros," 13; Wheeler, interview; "Young, "WWII POW," 10; Rumpel, "My Experience," 8–9; Center for Research, Allied POWs Under the Japanese, "Osaka Branch 13—Tsumori: Deceased Americans," http://www.mansell.com/pow_resources/camplists/osaka/tsumori_13B/Tsumori_deceased_yanks.html (accessed January 6, 2009).
69. Hotchkiss, interviews, October 22, 1982, and October 13, 1984; Wheeler, interview; Gross, interview, October 13, 1984; "Osaka Branch 13—Tsumori: Deceased Americans."
70. White, *United States Marines*, 150; Hoskins, "Memoir," 12; Hotchkiss, interview, October 22, 1982; Kauffman, "Ludington Interview," 5: 24–25; Young, "WWII POW," 8; Gross, interview, October 13, 1984; "Osaka Branch 13—Tsumori: Deceased Americans."
71. Hotchkiss, interviews, October 22, 1982, and October 21, 1983; Gross, interview, October 13, 1984; Wheeler, interview.
72. Haulman, *Hitting Home*, 20–25; Sturgeon, interview, October 13, 1984; Broyles, reply; Wheeler, interview; Plate, reply; Borne, interview; Gross, interview, October 22, 1983; White, *United States Marines*, 148; Snipes, "Adventureros," 14; Rumpel, "My Experience," 10; Young, "UWWII POW," 11; "Osaka Branch 13—Tsumori: Deceased Americans."
73. Plate, reply; White, *United States Marines*, 148–152; Richard Williamson to Gavan Daws, 10 February 1992, Daws Papers; Young, "WWII POW," 11–12; Stanley A. Mongrain, Affidavit, June 1, 1946, 1–2, File 101-150, Box 1584, Japanese War Crimes at Woosung, RG 153; Hotchkiss, interview, October 22, 1982; Broyles, reply; Borne, interview; Wheeler, interview; Rumpel, "My Experience," 11; Menique, Affidavit, 3.
74. Broyles, reply; Hotchkiss, interviews, October 22, 1982, and October 21, 1983; Skaggs, reply; Young, "WWII POW," 12–14; Sturgeon, interviews, October 13–14, 1984; Borne, interview; Plate, reply.
75. Gross, interviews, October 22, 1983, and October 13, 1984.

76. Cunningham and Sims, *Wake Island Command*, 149–184; Reynolds, *Officially Dead*, 138–243; Winfield Scott Cunningham, "A Capitulation of the Treatment of Ex-Prisoner-of-War Captain W. S. Cunningham, (56074), U.S. Navy, by the Detaining Power, Japan . . . , 1929," n.d., 7–9, B.3, F.6, Cunningham Collection.

CHAPTER 17

1. Ashurst, "Record," 9; Pacific Island Employees Foundation, *A Report to Returned CPNAB Prisoners of War Heroes and Their Dependents* (Boise, ID: Pacific Island Employees Foundation, 1945), 26–29, 31–49.
2. Survivors of Wake, Guam, and Cavite, "Died in Prison Camps, January 24, 1942–October 1945," n.d., 1–3 (photostat copy in author's possession); Survivors of Wake, Guam, and Cavite, Untitled Roster of Wake Contractors, n.d., 1–45 (photostat copy in author's possession); Roger Mansell, "First Defense Battalion—Wake Island—Surrendered 23 Dec 1941," n.d., 1–16 (copy in author's possession); Roger Mansell, "USMC Air Group 21—VMF-211," n.d., 1–2 (copy in author's possession); Roger Mansell, "Naval Air Station VP-11," n.d., 1–2 (copy in author's possession); Norman Gruenzer, "Marines and Civilians on Wake Island," in *The Japanese Story: History of POWs in Japan and After-Effects*. POW Medsearch Packet 10, ed., Stanley G. Sommers (Marshfield, WI: American Ex-Prisoners of War, 1980), 46; "U.S. Prisoners of War Executed by the Japanese, 7 October 1943," Wake Island Civilian Survivors Association, http:www.wakeisland-csa.com/pdf/98.pdf (accessed May 21, 2009); "Osaka Branch 13—Tsumori: Deceased Americans"; "Fukuoka No. 3-b: Roster"; "53 Men Deceased: Fukuoka No. 18"; Ashurst, "Record," 9; "Wake Personnel," 1–5; Gregory J. W. Urwin, "U.S. Marine Survival Success in Japanese POW Camps," *World War II Quarterly* 4, no. 2 (2007): 5.
3. Richardson, reply; E. Davis, interview; Bowsher, interview; Urwin, *Facing Fearful Odds*, 92–93, 94–95, 194–199, 202.
4. Oscar Claude Lent, Diary, undated entries (photostat copy in author's possession).
5. Stanley G. Sommers, "Introduction to Japanese Story," in Sommers, *Japanese Story*; "World War II, Pacific"; Walter G. Winslow, "Epilogue," in Sommers, *Japanese Story*, D, 46, 80; Knox, *Death March*, xi, 155; Falk, *Bataan*, 194–199; D. Clayton James, ed., *South to Bataan, North to Mukden: The Prison Diary of Brigadier General W. E. Brougher* (Athens: University of Georgia Press, 1971), 41–42; Sandvold, interview.
6. Chapman, interview.
7. James P. S. Devereux to F. C. Caldwell, 5 October 1966, Correspondence, MCHA; Williams, interview; Chapman, interview.

8. Jones to author, 15 September 1981; J. Brown, interview; Benjamin F. Comstock Jr. to author, 19 February 1982; Skaggs, reply; Thaire to author, September 1981; Chapman, interview; Richardson, reply.
9. Williams, interview; Cunningham and Sims, *Wake Island Command*, 55; Nye, interview; Holewinski, interview, June 20, 1980; Richardson, reply.
10. John J. Beck, *MacArthur and Wainwright: Sacrifice of the Philippines* (Albuquerque: University of New Mexico Press, 1974), 64, 71–73, 181, 188, 276; Francis Worthington Lipe, "Food Rations of the Japanese Prisoners of War, W.W. II, During Combat and Captivity," in Sommers, *Japanese Story*, 49–50; Falk, *Bataan*, 17–24, 33, 36–38, 90–199; Jonathan M. Wainwright, *General Wainwright's Story: The Account of Four Years of Humiliating Defeat, Surrender, and Captivity*, ed. Robert Considine (Garden City, NY: Doubleday, 1946), 48, 68; Knox, *Death March*, 53, 56, 65–67, 83–84, 91, 119–169; Sommers, "Introduction," D; William E. Dyess, *The Dyess Story: The Eye-Witness Account of the Death March From Bataan and the Narrative of Experiences in Japanese Prison Camps and of Eventual Escape*, ed. Charles Leavelle (New York: G. P. Putnam's Sons, 1944), 69–95; Melvin H. McCoy and S. M. Mellnik, *Ten Escape From Tojo*, ed. Welburn Kelley (New York: Farrar & Rinehart, 1944), 38–44; John E. Olson, "Daily Journal (April 26, 1942–June 5, 1942)," 28 April–3 June 1942, John E. Olson Papers, USAMHI.
11. Steve Mellnik, *Philippine Diary 1939–1945* (New York: Van Nostrand Reinhold Company, 1969), 167–168; James Bertram, *Beneath the Shadow: A New Zealander in the Far East, 1939–46* (New York: John Day, 1947), 111, 113; Russell, *Knights of Bushido*, 142, 149–185, 191, 203; Dyess, *Dyess Story*, 114–136; McCoy and Mellnik, *Ten Escape From Tojo*, 47–60; Knox, *Death March*, 198–247; Ernest Gordon, *Through the Valley of the Kwai* (New York: Harper & Brothers, 1962), 65–81; Tanaka, *Hidden Horrors*, 45–78.
12. Brian MacArthur, *Surviving the Sword: Prisoners of the Japanese in the Far East, 1942–45* (New York: Random House, 2005), 321–322; White, *United States Marines*, 217.
13. R. Brown, interview; J. Brown, interview; Mettscher, reply; Samuel A. Stouffer and others, *The American Soldier*, Studies in Social Psychology in World War II, 4 vols. (Princeton: Princeton University Press, 1949), 2: 106–130; Edward A. Shils and Morris Janowitz, "Cohesion and Disintegration in the Wehrmacht in World War II," *Public Opinion Quarterly* 12 (1948): 280–315; Robert Sterling Rush, *Hell in Hürtgen Forest: The Ordeal & Triumph of an American Infantry Regiment* (Lawrence: University Press of Kansas, 2001), 8–10. See also Stephen E. Ambrose, *Band of Brothers:*

E Company, 506th Regiment, 101st Airborne From Normandy to Hitler's Eagle's Nest (New York: Simon & Schuster, 1992).
14. Nye, interview; Mettscher, reply.
15. White, *United States Marines*, 217; Kahn, interview; Marcello, "Godbold Interview," 84–85.
16. Chapman, interview; Sandvold, interview; Robert B. Edgerton, *Warriors of the Rising Sun: A History of the Japanese Military* (New York: W. W. Norton, 1997), 305–324; J. Cook, interview; Taylor, interview, August 28, 2002; Kessler, *To Wake Island and Beyond*, 144; R. Brown, interview; Nye, interview; Richardson, reply; Kahn, interview; White, *United States Marines*, 127; *Memphis Press-Scimitar*, October 30, 1961; Marcello, "Venable Interview," 60–61.
17. "Putnam Interview No. 1," November 13, 1975, 11, 17.
18. Gregory F. Michno, *Death on the Hellships: Prisoners at Sea in the Pacific War* (Annapolis: Naval Institute Press, 2001), 3–86, 92–296, 305–317.
19. Kantzer, "Imperial Guest," 152; Plate, reply; Young, "WWII POW," 8; Skaggs, reply; J. Cook, interview; Row, interview; Nowlin, reply, n.d.; Hardy to Devereux, 1 May 1946.
20. Urwin, "U.S. Marine Survival Success," 4–23; Gregory J. W. Urwin, "How Marine POWs Hung Tough," *World War II*, June/July 2008, 32–39; Daws, *Prisoners of the Japanese*, 361.
21. Biggs, *Behind the Barbed Wire*, 19, 90–91; Borne, interview; Kirk, *Secret Camera*, 39–40, 62–64; Chapman, interview; Hassig, interview; Nowlin to author, 24 November 1979; Gross, interview, October 22, 1983; Dolezal to Devereux, 29 March 1946; Eileen Mead, "Pearl Harbor Memories," *Town & Country: The Weekend Magazine of the (Fredericksburg, VA) Free-Lance Star*, December 7, 1991, 15.
22. Devereux, *Story of Wake*, 225.
23. Hassig, interview; Freuler, interview; Kinney and McCaffrey, *Wake Island Pilot*, 106–107; White, *United States Marines*, 165; J. Johnson, reply, April 25, 1981; Borne, interview; Kessler, *To Wake Island and Beyond*, 74.
24. Grashio and Norling, *Return to Freedom*, 56–62, 67–73; Gordon, *Valley of the Kwai*, 90–108, 169–170; Knox, *Death March*, 135–136, 158–159, 166, 207, 251, 265; Jack Hawkins, *Never Say Die* (Philadelphia: Dorrance, 1961), 74–75.
25. Shields Goodman, "A Letter From Bilibid Prison," *Shipmate*, November 1989, 13–14; LaForte, Marcello, and Himmel, *With Only the Will*, 60–64.
26. LaForte, Marcello, and Himmel, *With Only the Will*, 62. See also John M. Wright Jr., *Captured on Corregidor: Diary of an American P.O.W. in World War II* (Jefferson, NC: McFarland, 1988); A. B. Feur, ed., *Bilibid Diary: The Secret Notebooks of Commander Thomas Hayes, POW, the Philippines,*

1942–45 (Hamden, CT: Archon Books, 1987); Bumgarner, *Parade of the Dead*; Robert E. Haney, *Caged Dragons: An American P.O.W. in WWII Japan* (Ann Arbor, MI: Sabre Press, 1991).

27. Collier's account is transcribed in James W. Callahan Jr., "Book No. 6: Boy's Letter," n.d., James W. Callahan Papers in USAMHI and in Alva R. Fitch, "The Siege of Bataan From the Bottom of a Foxhole," April 22, 1943, 31, Alva R. Fitch Papers, USAMHI.
28. Knox, *Death March*, 223–234; Wright, *Captured on Corregidor*, 59; William H. Owen Jr., "Lest We Forget by W. H. Owen Jr., P.O.W., Cabanatuan, Philippine Is.," n.d., 31, William H. Owen Papers, USAMHI.
29. Sloman, reply; Sloman, interview; Reeves, interview; Shores, interview; R. Brown, interview; J. Brown, interview; Chapman, interview; Boshwer, interview; Row, interview; Nowlin, reply, March 18, 1980.
30. Malleck to author, 27 July 1981; Frank, "Devereux Transcript," 166; Nye, interview; Row, interview.
31. Kantzer, "Imperial Guest," 229.
32. Haidinger, interview; Pistole, interview; Skaggs, reply; Plate, reply; Hotchkiss, interview, October 13, 1984; Kirk, *Secret Camera*, 124–126, 210–211; King, interview.
33. Howes, "Testimony," 10–11; Wilcox, Diary, 2 November 1942, and 11 and 26 January, 7, 14, 17, 19–20, 22, and 27 February, 2 March, 8, 23, and 25 April, 6 May, and 16 July 1943.
34. R. Brown, interview; J. Brown, interview; Chapman, interview; J. Johnson, reply, May 8, 1981; Mettscher, reply; Skaggs, reply; Richardson, reply.
35. Daws, *Prisoners of the Japanese*, 135; Smith, interview; Jones to author, August 1981; Skaggs, reply; Mettscher, reply; Chapman, interview; Borne, interview; R. Brown, interview.
36. Kinney, "P.O.W. Survival," 109; Gavan Daws, "Transcript of Interview With Victor F. Ciarrachi," December 1986–January 1987, 7, Daws Papers; Richardson, reply; Shores, interview; LaPorte, interview.
37. Chapman, interview; J. Brown, interview; R. Brown, interview; Marcello, "Permenter Interview," 80–81; Biggs, *Behind the Barbed Wire*, 175–176.
38. Burton, *Life's Trails*, 75–76; Daws, "Jaffe Interview," 11–12.
39. Kinney and McCaffrey, *Wake Island Pilot*, 132–133; Col. Luther A. Brown, USMC (ret.) to Col. F. C. Caldwell, USMC, 5 October 1966, Correspondence, MCHA; Hanna, interview; Daws, "Akin Interview," 15; Borne, interview; R. Brown, interview; Biggs, *Behind the Barbed Wire*, 139; Kantzer, "Imperial Guest," 75; Newell, Diary, 11 May 1942, and 22 December 1943; Ketner, "Mistreatment Aboard *Nitta Maru*," 2.
40. Durrwachter, Diary, 27 June 1942; Magnino, *Jim's Journey*, 176–177; Plate, reply; J. Brown, interview.

41. Nowlin, reply, March 18, 1980; Skaggs, reply; Daws, "Akin Interview," 36; Marcello, "Venable Interview," 81; Hubley, interview; King, interview; Comstock to author, 19 February 1982; Stegmaier, interview; Pistole, interview; Kauffman, "Hokanson Interview," 30.
42. Malleck to author, 10 October 1981; Chapman, interview; J. Johnson, reply, May 8, 1981; Stocks, interview; Bowsher, interview; Smith, interview; J. Brown, interview.
43. R. Brown, interview; Skaggs, interview.
44. That motto appeared atop the front page of the *Wake Island Wig-Wag*, the quarterly newsletter of the Defenders of Wake Island.

bibliography

MANUSCRIPTS IN PUBLIC REPOSITORIES
Eugene C. Barker Texas History Center, General Libraries, University of Texas at Austin, Austin, TX
    Henry L. Durrwachter Papers

Howard Gotlieb Archival Research Center, Boston University, Boston, MA
    Winfield Scott Cunningham Collection
    James P. S. Devereux Collection

Douglas County Museum of History and Natural History, Roseburg, OR
    Curtis T. Beecher, "Experiences in Fighting on Corregidor . . ." Unpublished memoir, n.d.

Hoover Institution Archives, Stanford University, Stanford, CA
    Allan O'Guinn Papers

Japan Center for Asian Historical Records, National Archives of Japan, Tokyo, Japan
    Diplomatic Record Office of the Ministry of Foreign Affairs
        Documents Relating to Greater East Asia War

Marine Corps Historical Center, Washington, DC
    Marine Corps Historical Archives
        Correspondence Relating to the Marine Corps Official History of World War II and the Captivity of the Wake Island Marines, the North China Marines, the Guam Marines, and the 4th Marines

Papers Relating to the Defense of Wake Island
PERSONAL PAPERS
    Gerald L. Beeman Papers
    Walter A. Bowsher Papers
    Luther A. Brown Collection
    James B. Darden Papers
    William A. Diemert Papers
    J. E. DuPont Papers
    John R. Himelrick. "Diary."
    Charles A. Holmes Collection
    Charles R. Jackson. "I Am Alive." Unpublished memoir, n.d.
    Frederick A. Knight. "POW Diaries."
    Ewing E. LaPorte Papers
    Frances M. McKinstry Papers
    Robert B. Murphy. "Scrapbook."
    Thomas C. Nixon Papers
    John E. Pearsall. "POW Diary and Notes."
    Floyd O. Schilling Papers
    Lemuel C. Shepherd Jr., Papers
    James B. Shimel, "Prisoner of War." Unpublished memoir, n.d.
    Carter B. Simpson. "Diary: Bataan/Corregidor, POW Camp." December 8, 1941–October 12, 1944.
    Jack R. Skaggs Papers
    Jerold B. Story Papers
    Joseph L. Walker. "Mad Marine of Mukden." Unpublished memoir, n.d.
    Garden Wendell Papers
    Clifford Wilkening Papers

MARINE CORPS ORAL HISTORY COLLECTION.
    Frank, Benis M., ed. "Brigadier General James P. S. Devereux, U.S. Marine Corps (Retired): Oral History Transcript," 1973.

Marine Corps University Archives, Quantico, VA
Personal Papers
    Elmer E. Long Collection

National Archives, Washington, DC
    Records of the Adjutant General's Office, Record Group 94
    Records of the Office of the Judge Advocate General, Record Group 153
    Records of the Provost Marshal General, Record Group 389
    Records of the Adjutant General's Office, 1917–, Record Group 407

Special Collections Department, J. Y. Joyner Library, East Carolina University, Greenville, NC
Paul Albert Putnam Oral History Interview (No. OH0027). November 13, 1975
Paul A. Putnam Papers (No. 313)

State Historical Society of Missouri, Columbia, MO
Oral History Program, Collection No. 3975, Missouri Ex-POWs
Miller, Thomas H., ed. "An Interview With Thomas W. Johnson at His Home in Saint Joseph, Missouri, 29 May 2001."
———. "An Interview With Thomas W. Johnson at His Home in Saint Joseph, Missouri, 1 June 2001."
———. "An Interview With Thomas W. Johnson at His Home in Saint Joseph, Missouri, 16 July 2001."

U.S. Army Military History Institute, Carlisle Barracks, PA
James W. Callahan Papers
Gavan Daws Papers
Alva R. Fitch Papers
John E. Olson Papers
William H. Owen Papers

University of North Texas Oral History Collection, University of North Texas, Denton, TX
Marcello, Ronald E., ed. "Interview With Billy Allen, March 1, 1976."
———. "Interview With Willie L. Benton, March 10, 1975."
———. "Interview With Boren H. Brantley, November 19, 1971."
———. "Interview With Karl A. Bugbee, December 8, 1971."
———. "Interview With George Burlage, November 18, 1970."
———. "Interview With T. G. Crews, January 22, 1972."
———. "Interview With Marshall E. Fields, February 13, 1972."
———. "Interview With J. B. Garrison, September 18, 1970."
———. "Interview With Bryghte D. Godbold, April 7, 1972."
———. "Interview With Alton C. Halbroch, March 21, 1972, April 18, 1972."
———. "Interview With George W. McDaniel, October 23, 1973."
———. "Interview With C. L. Permenter, October 25, 1972."
———. "Interview With Marvin Robinson, May 25, 1982."
———. "Interview With Rufus Smith, June 13, 1989."
———. "Interview With O. R. Sparkman, May 6, 1971."
———. "Interview With Henry B. Stowers, May 25, 1973."
———. "Interview With Mr. James C. Venable, April 13, 1971."
———. "Interview With John W. Wisecup, July 28, 1987."

TAPED REPLIES TO AUTHOR'S QUESTIONNAIRES

Earl M. Broyles, March 28, 1986.
John S. Johnson, April 25, 1981, and May 9, 1981.
Robert C. Maple, April 24, 1984.
Leonard G. Mettscher, February 1980.
Jesse E. Nowlin, March 18, 1980, November 1982, and n.d.
William O. Plate, February 2, 1982.
Bernard E. Richardson, October 31, 1986.
Jack R. Skaggs, December 28, 1981, and January 24, 1982.
Wiley W. Sloman, June 24, 1986.

INTERVIEWS CONDUCTED BY AUTHOR

Joseph E. Borne, October 4, 1992, January 20, 1993, and October 17, 1998.
Walter A. Bowsher, June 18, 1981.
James R. Brown, June 20, 1981.
Earl M. Broyles, November 23, 1985.
Charles H. Camp, June 21, 1980.
Henry H. W. Chapman, February 20, 1982.
Jack B. Cook, June 19, 1981.
James H. Cox, June 20, 1980.
Winfield Scott Cunningham, March 30, 1985.
John R. Dale, June 14, 1979.
Eschol E. Davis, October 8, 1994.
Jack E. Davis, September 13, 1986.
Herbert C. Freuler, June 16, 1979.
Arnold Green, September 6, 2003.
Franklin A. Gross, October 22, 1983, and October 13, 1984.
Robert F. Haidinger, June 15, 1979.
Robert M. Hanna, September 10, 1986.
Edwin F. Hassig, June 21, 1980.
Ralph J. Holewinski, June 20, 1980, and September 11, 1986.
Clifford E. Hotchkiss, October 22, 1982, October 21, 1983, and October 13, 1984.
George G. Hubley, October 15, 1998.
G. Mason Kahn, June 15, 1979.
Guy J. Kelnhofer Jr., September 13, 1986.
Walter T. Kennedy, September 11, 1986.
James O. King, October 17, 1998.
John F. Kinney, June 16, 1979.
Ewing E. LaPorte, October 16, 1998.
Terrence T. McAmis, June 16, 1979.

Edwin Darby Nye, February 13, 1982.
Shigeyoshi Ozeki, November 1, 1995.
Robert E. L. Page, September 10, 1986.
Erwin D. Pistole, June 21, 1980.
Arthur A. Poindexter, May 17, 1986, November 24, 1992, March 26, 1993, and July 10, 1993.
Joe M. Reeves, September 13, 1986.
Ernest G. Rogers, June 21, 1980.
Earl R. Row, June 19, 1981.
Julian K. Sandvold, June 20, 1980.
Robert Shores, September 11, 1986.
Wiley W. Sloman, September 12, 1986.
Cassius E. Smith, June 20, 1981.
Carl E. Stegmaier Jr., June 16, 1979.
Artie Stocks, June 14, 1979.
Edward V. Sturgeon, October 13, 1984, and October 13–14, 1984.
William L. Taylor, August 28, 2002, and August 29, 2002.
H. Jay Tice, June 14, 1979.
Glenn E. Tripp, September 13, 1986.
Hisao Tsuji, October 31, 1995.
Mackie L. Wheeler, October 8, 1994.
Luther Williams, June 21, 1980.

AVIATOR PICTURES, SANTA MONICA, CA
Interviews Conducted and edited by William A. Kauffman
Bill Charters, March 2000.
Joe Goiceochia, March 2000.
Bill Gooding, March 2000.
Swede Hokanson, June 2000.
Ralph Pete Ingram, March 2000.
Murray Kidd, March 2000.
Charles Loveland, March 2000.
Don Ludington, March 2000.
Charles Leroy Myers, March 2000.
Leo Nonn, August 2000.
Arthur A. Poindexter, December 1999.
John Rogge, March 2000.

NEWSPAPERS AND NEWSLETTERS
Bloomfield (MO) Vindicator, June 4, 1980.
Boston Daily Globe, April 16, 1947.

Burlingame (CA) Advance, December 16, 1943.
Cleveland Catholic Universe Bulletin, November 9 and 16, 1945.
Cleveland News, November 9, 1945.
Dallas Times Herald, November 2, 1980.
East Hampton Star, October 11, 1945.
Honolulu Sunday Star Bulletin & Advertiser, September 23, 1962.
Kalamazoo Gazette, December 2, 1991.
Little Wig-Wag. Survivors of Wake, Guam and Cavite, December 1979–June/July 2001.
Memphis Press-Scimitar, October 30, 1961.
Nashville Tennessean, January 14, 1946.
Navy News (Guam, Marianas Islands), June 20, 1947.
New York Times, December 8, 1941–September 21, 1945.
Oakland Post Enquirer, September 8, 1945.
Prisoners of War Bulletin (Washington, DC), June 1943–June 1945.
St. Louis Post-Dispatch, October 28–29, 1945.
St. Louis Star Times, October 29, 1945.
San Francisco Chronicle, February 11, 1945.
San Francisco Examiner, February 11, 1945.
Wake Island Wig-Wag (Defenders of Wake Island), January 1978–January 2006.
Washington Daily News, November 15, 1945.
Washington News, July 23, 1942.
Washington Post, October 14, 1945.
Washington Times-Herald, July 21, 1945.

INTERNET SOURCES

Center for Research, Allied POWs Under the Japanese. "53 Men Deceased: Fukuoka No. 18 Sasebo." http://www.mansell.com/pow_resources/camplists/fukuoka/fuku_18_sasebo/fuk_18_deceased.html.

———. "Fukuoka No. 3-b: Roster of American POWs & Civilians." http://www.mansell.com/pow_resources/camplists/fukuoka/fuku_3_tobata/fuku_3_yanks.html.

———. "Hanaoka-Sendai No. 7-B." http://www.mansell.com/pow_resources/camplists/sendai/sendai_07_hanuoka/hanaoka_7_b.html.

———. "Osaka Branch 13—Tsumori: Deceased Americans." http://www.mansell.com/pow_resources/camplists/osaka/tsumori_13B/Tsumori_deceased_yanks.html.

Johnson, Conrad. "Diary of Conrad Johnson, 1944, Part I." Center for Research, Allied POWs Under the Japanese. http://www.mansell.com/pow_resources/camplists/tokyo/kawasaki-5D/conrad%20diary1.html.

———. "Diary of Conrad Johnson, 1944, Part II." Center for Research, Allied POWs Under the Japanese. http://www.mansell.com/pow_resources/camplists/tokyo/kawasaki-5D/conrad%20diary2.html.

Ozeki, Shigeyoshi. "Dr. Shigeyoshi Ozeki's Second Account of the Fall of Wake Island." Translated and edited by Daniel King. Gregory J. W. Urwin, Department of History, Temple University. http://astro.temple.edu/~gurwin/ffoozeki.htm.

———. "Wake Island in Sight." Translated and edited by Daniel King. Gregory J. W. Urwin, Department of History, Temple University. http://astro.temple.edu/~gurwin/ffoozeki.htm.

Troney, Norris H. "Norris Troney Diary." North China Marines. http://www.northchinamarines.com/id73.html.

"U.S. Prisoners of War Executed by the Japanese, 7 October 1943." Wake Island Civilian Survivors Association. http://www.wakeislandcsa.com/pdf/98.pdf.

THESES AND DISSERTATIONS

Jones, Waller F. "Japanese Attitudes Toward Prisoners of War: Feudal Resurgence in Kokutai No Hongi." Master's thesis, University of North Texas, 1990.

Urwin, Gregory J. W. "The Defenders of Wake Island: Their Two Wars, 1941–1945." PhD diss., University of Notre Dame, 1983.

OTHER WORKS

Abraham, Theodore A. Jr. *"Do You Understand, Huh?" A POW's Lament, 1941–1945*. Manhattan, KS: Sunflower University Press, 1992.

Ahlers, John. "Shanghai at the War's End." *Far Eastern Survey* 14 (1945), 329–333.

Ambrose, Stephen E. *Band of Brothers: E Company, 506th Regiment, 101st Airborne From Normandy to Hitler's Eagle's Nest*. New York: Simon & Schuster, 1992.

Anselmo, Guy Jr. "Fourth Marines: Bataan & Corregidor." *Leatherneck: Magazine of the Marines*, December 1988, 26–30.

Archer, Bernice. *The Internment of Western Civilians Under the Japanese, 1941–1945: A Patchwork of Internment*. Hong Kong: Hong Kong University Press, 2008.

Ashton, Paul. *Bataan Diary*. Santa Barbara, CA: Paul Ashton, 1984.

Astarita, Joseph J. *Sketches of P.O.W. Life*. Brooklyn, NY: Rollo Press, 1947.

Bailey, Ronald H. *Prisoners of War*. World War II. Alexandria, VA: Time-Life Books, 1981.

Banham, Tony. *The Sinking of the* Lisbon Maru*: Britain's Forgotten Wartime Tragedy*. Hong Kong: Hong Kong University Press, 2006.

Bartlett, Tom. "Reunion of Two Warriors." *Leatherneck: Magazine of the Marines*, January 1983, 34–37.

———. "Wake Island Marine: Still in Love with the Corps." *Leatherneck: Magazine of the Marines*, December 1988, 38–43.

Bayler, Walter L. J. "Wake Surrender." *Marine Corps Gazette*, November 1945, 2–5.

Beck, John J. *MacArthur and Wainwright: Sacrifice of the Philippines*. Albuquerque: University of New Mexico Press, 1974.

Bergamini, David. *Japan's Imperial Conspiracy*. 2 vols. New York: William Morrow, 1971.

Berry, William A. *Prisoner of the Rising Sun*. Norman: University of Oklahoma Press, 1993.

Bertram, James. *Beneath the Shadow: A New Zealander in the Far East, 1939–46*. New York: John Day, 1947.

Berube, Allan. *Coming Out Under Fire: The History of Gay Men and Women in World War Two*. New York: Free Press, 1990.

Biggs, Chester M. Jr. "Surrender at Peiping," *Leatherneck: Magazine of the Marines*, December 1991, 8–11.

———. *Behind the Barbed Wire: Memoir of a World War II U.S. Marine*. Jefferson, NC: McFarland, 1995.

Bischof, Günter, and Robert L. Dupont, eds. *The Pacific War Revisited*. Eisenhower Center Studies on War and Peace. Baton Rouge: Louisiana State University Press, 1997.

Bishop, Lewis Sherman, and Shiela Bishop Irwin. *Escape From Hell: An AVG Flying Tiger's Journey*. Bloomington, IL: Tiger Eye Press, 2004.

Blair, Clay Jr. *Silent Victory: The U.S. Submarine War Against Japan*. Philadelphia: J. B. Lippincott, 1975.

Booker, Edna Lee, and John S. Potter. *Flight From China*. New York: Macmillan, 1946.

Boyle, Martin. *Yanks Don't Cry*. New York: Bernard Geis Associates, 1963.

Boyt, Eugene P., and David L. Burch. *Bataan: A Survivor's Story*. Norman: University of Oklahoma Press, 2004.

Braly, William C. *The Hard Way Home*. Washington, DC: Infantry Journal Press, 1947.

Brill, Norman Q. "Neuropsychiatric Examination of Military Personnel from Japanese Prison Camps." *Bulletin of the U.S. Army Medical Department* 5 (1946): 429–438.

Brown Joe, ed. *Zentsuji in Kansas: Stories From the POW Reunions*. Marble Hill, MO: Stewart Publishing & Printing, 1986.

Brown, L. A. *The Marine's Handbook*. Annapolis: United States Naval Institute, 1940.

Bumgarner, John. *Parade of the Dead: A U.S. Army Physician's Memoir of Imprisonment by the Japanese, 1942–1945*. Jefferson, NC: McFarland, 1995.

Burton, John H. *Traveling Life's Twisting Trails*. New York: Vantage Press, 1992.

"Captured Commanders Put Views on Record." *Freedom*, Third Impress, 1942, 48.

Cernushi, Enrico, and Vincent P. O'Hara. "Italy and the Pacific War." *World War II Quarterly* 3, no. 1 (2006): 14–19.

Chang, Iris. *The Rape of Nanking: The Forgotten Holocaust of World War II*. New York: Basic Books, 1997.

Chauncey, George. *Gay New York: Gender, Urban Culture, and the Making of the Gay Male World, 1890–1940*. New York: Basic Books, 1994.

Chittenden, William Howard. *From China Marine to Jap POW: My 1,364 Day Journey Through Hell*. Paducah, KY: Turner Publishing, 1995.

Christopher, Robert C. *The Japanese Mind*. New York: Simon & Schuster, 1983.

Churchill, Winston S. *London to Ladysmith via Pretoria*. London: Longmans, Green, 1900.

Coleman, John S. *Bataan and Beyond: Memories of an American POW*. College Station: Texas A&M University Press, 1978.

Corbett, P. Scott. *Quiet Passages: The Exchange of Civilians Between the United States and Japan During the Second World War*. Kent, OH: Kent State University Press, 1987.

Cornelius, Wanda, and Thayne Short. *Ding Hao: America's Air War in China, 1937–1945*. Gretna, LA: Pelican Publishing, 1980.

Cotton, John. "How the Japanese Treat Prisoners." *Marine Corps Gazette*, March 1945, 28–30.

Crager, Kelly E. *Hell Under the Rising Sun: Texan POWs and the Building of the Burma–Thailand Death Railway*. College Station: Texas A&M University Press, 2008.

Craven, Wesley Frank, and James Lea Cate. eds. *The Army Air Forces in World War II*. Vol. 5, *The Pacific: Matterhorn to Nagasaki, June 1944 to August 1945*. 1953. Reprint. Washington, DC: Office of Air Force History, 1983.

Cressman, Robert J. *"A Magnificent Fight": The Battle for Wake Island*. Annapolis: Naval Institute Press, 1995.

Cunningham, Chet. *Hell Wouldn't Stop: An Oral History of the Battle of Wake Island*. New York: Carroll & Graf Publishers, 2002.

Cunningham, W. Scott, and Lydel Sims. *Wake Island Command*. 1961. Paperback edition, New York: Popular Library, 1962.

Darden, James B. III. *Guests of the Emperor: The Story of Dick Darden.* Clinton, NC: Greenhouse Press, 1990.

Daws, Gavan. *Prisoners of the Japanese: POWs of World War II in the Pacific.* New York: William Morrow, 1994.

Devereux, James P. S. *The Story of Wake Island.* Philadelphia: J. B. Lippincott, 1947.

Dower, John W. *War Without Mercy: Race and Power in the Pacific War.* New York: Pantheon Books, 1986.

———. *Embracing Defeat: Japan in the Wake of World War II.* New York: W. W. Norton, 1999.

Doyle, Robert C. *Voices From Captivity: Interpreting the American POW Narratives.* Lawrence: University Press of Kansas, 1994.

Drea, Edward J. "In the Army Barracks of Imperial Japan." *Armed Forces and Society* 15 (1989): 329–348.

Dupuy, Trevor. "The U.S. at War in China." *History of the Second World War*, July 18, 1974, 1849–1855.

Dyess, William E. *The Dyess Story: The Eye-Witness Account of the Death March From Bataan and the Narrative of Experiences in Japanese Prison Camps and of Eventual Escape.* Edited by Charles Leavelle. New York: G. P. Putnam's Sons, 1944.

Edgerton, Robert B. *Warriors of the Rising Sun: A History of the Japanese Military.* New York: W. W. Norton, 1997.

Elleman, Bruce, *Japanese–American Civilian Prisoner Exchanges and Detention Camps, 1941–45.* Routledge Studies in the Modern History of Asia. London: Routledge, 2006.

Falk, Stanley L. *Bataan: The March of Death.* New York: W. W. Norton, 1962.

Felton, Mark. *Slaughter at Sea: The Story of Japan's Naval War Crimes.* Annapolis: Naval Institute Press, 2008.

Feur, A. B., ed. *Bilibid Diary: The Secret Notebooks of Commander Thomas Hayes, POW, the Philippines, 1942–45.* Hamden, CT: Archon Books, 1987.

Foley, William T. "A Small Contribution to the Mystery of Peking Man." *Cornell University Medical College Alumni Quarterly*, Winter 1971–1972, 5–12.

Frank, Benis M., and Henry I. Shaw Jr. *History of U.S. Marine Corps Operations in World War Two.* Vol. 5. *Victory and Occupation.* Washington, DC: Historical Branch, G-3 Division, Headquarters, U.S. Marine Corps, 1968.

Frank, Richard B. *Downfall: The End of the Imperial Japanese Empire.* New York: Random House, 1999.

Fujita, Frank. *Foo: A Japanese-American Prisoner of the Rising Sun; The Secret Prison Diary of Frank "Foo" Fujita.* Edited by Stanley L. Falk. Denton, TX: University of North Texas Press, 1993.

Fuller, Richard. *Shōkan: Hirohito's Samurai; Leaders of the Japanese Armed Forces*. London: Arms & Armour Press, 1992.

Giles, Donald T. *Captive of the Rising Sun: The POW Memoirs of Rear Admiral Donald T. Giles*. Annapolis: Naval Institute Press, 1994.

Gillmore, Allison B. *You Can't Fight Tanks With Bayonets: Psychological Warfare Against the Japanese Army in the Southwest Pacific*. Lincoln: University of Nebraska Press, 1998.

Glusman, John A. *Conduct Under Fire: Four American Doctors and Their Fight for Life as Prisoners of the Japanese*. New York: Viking, 2005.

Goodman, Shields. "A Letter From Bilibid Prison." *Shipmate*, November 1989, 13–14.

Gordon, Ernest. *Through the Valley of the Kwai*. New York: Harper & Brothers, 1962.

Grashio, Samuel C., and Bernard Norling. *Return to Freedom*. Tulsa, OK: MCN Press, 1982.

Grover, David H. "Naval Battle off Shanghai." *Pacific War*, November/December 2004, 19–22.

Gruenzer, Norman. "Marines and Civilians on Wake Island." In Sommers, *The Japanese Story*.

Guttman, Jon. "Carrier Strike on Wake." *World War II*, September 1998, 26–32.

Haines, Gregory. *Gunboats on the Great River: A History of the Royal Navy on the Yangtse*. London: MacDonald and Jane's, 1976.

Hales, Edward Everett. "A P.O.W. Remembers Guam: The Paradise, the People, the Pummeling." *Periodical: Journal of America's Military Past* 24, no. 4 (1998): 42–54.

Haney, Robert E. *Caged Dragons: An American P.O.W. in WWII Japan*. Ann Arbor, MI: Sabre Press, 1991.

Harries, Meirion, and Susie Harries. *Soldiers of the Rising Sun: The Rise and Fall of the Imperial Japanese Army*. New York: Random House, 1991.

Harwell, Ernie. "The Wake Story." *Leatherneck*, November 1945, 6–10.

Haulman, Daniel L. *Hitting Home: The Air Offensive Against Japan*. The U.S. Army Air Forces in World War II. Washington, DC: Air Force History and Museums Program, 1999.

Hawkins, Jack. *Never Say Die*. Philadelphia: Dorrance, 1961.

Heilman, Robert. "Lloyd O. Nelson: Wake Island POW." *Table Rock Sentinel*, 11, no. 3/4 (1991): 2–15.

Heinl, R. D. Jr. *The Defense of Wake*. Washington, DC: Historical Section, Division of Public Information, Headquarters, U.S. Marine Corps, 1947.

Henriot, Christian. "Shanghai Industries Under Japanese Occupation: Bombs, Boom, and Bust (1937–1945)." In Henriot and Yeh, *In the Shadow of the Rising Sun*, 17–45.

Henriot, Christian, and Wen-hsin Yeh, eds. *In the Shadow of the Rising Sun: Shanghai Under Japanese Occupation*. Cambridge, UK: Cambridge University Press, 2004.

———. "Introduction." In Henriot and Yeh, *In the Shadow of the Rising Sun*, 1–16.

Heppner, Ernest G. *Shanghai Refuge: A Memoir of the World War II Jewish Ghetto*. Lincoln: University of Nebraska Press, 1995.

Hess, William. *P-51: Bomber Escort*. New York: Ballantine Books, 1971.

Hilberg, Raul. *The Destruction of the European Jews*. 3 vols. New York: Holmes & Meier, 1985.

Hindell, Keith. "Conquest of Hong Kong." *History of the Second World War*, October 4, 1973, 724–728.

Hitchcock, W. Pat. *Forty Months in Hell*. Jackson, TN: Page Publishing, 1996.

Hoffman, Jon T. *Chesty: The Story of Lieutenant General Lewis B. Puller, USMC*. New York: Random House, 2001.

Holmes, Linda Goetz. *Unjust Enrichments: How Japan's Companies Built Postwar Fortunes Using American POWs*. Mechanicsburg, PA: Stackpole Books, 2001.

Hough, Frank O., Verle E. Ludwig, and Henry I. Shaw Jr. *History of U.S. Marine Corps Operations in World War II*. Vol. 1, *Pearl Harbor to Guadalcanal*. Washington, DC: Historical Branch, G-3 Division, Headquarters, U.S. Marine Corps, 1958.

Hubbs, Mark E. "Massacre on Wake Island." *Naval History* 15, no. 1 (2001): 30–35.

Ienaga, Saburo. *The Pacific War: World War II and the Japanese*. Translated by Frank Baldwin. New York: Pantheon Books, 1978.

International Committee of the Red Cross. *Report of the International Committee of the Red Cross on Its Activities During the Second World War (September 1, 1939–June 30, 1947)*. 3 vols. Geneva: ICRC, 1948.

Jacobs, Eugene C. "From Guerrilla to P.O.W. in the Philippines." *Medical Opinion & Review* 5 no. 8 (1969): 99–119.

Jacobsen, Gene S. *We Refused to Die: My Time as a Prisoner of War in Bataan and Japan, 1942–1945*. Salt Lake City: University of Utah Press, 2004.

James, D. Clayton, ed. *South to Bataan, North to Mukden: The Prison Diary of Brigadier General W. E. Brougher*. Athens: University of Georgia Press, 1971.

"Japan Shanghaied." *Time*, February 29, 1932, 21–22.

Jentschura, Hansgeorg, Dieter Jung, and Peter Mickel. *Warships of the Imperial Japanese Navy, 1869–1945*. Annapolis: Naval Institute Press, 1982.

Jones, Wilbur D. Jr. *Gyrene: The World War II United States Marine*. Shippensburg, PA: White Mane Books, 1998.

Junghans, Earl A. "Wake's POWs," *Naval Institute Proceedings* 109, no. 2 (1983): 43–50.

Kawasaki, Ichiro. *Japan Unmasked*. Rutland, VT: C. R. Tuttle, 1969.

Keene, R. R. "Murder on Bataan." *Leatherneck: Magazine of the Marines*, April 1992, 12–17.

———, "The Death March." *Leatherneck: Magazine of the Marines*, April 1992, 17–23.

Kelnhofer, Guy J. Jr. *Understanding the Former Prisoner of War: Life After Liberation*. St. Paul, MN: Banfil Street Press, 1992.

Kerr, E. Bartlett. *Surrender & Survival: The Experience of American POWs in the Pacific 1941–1945*. New York: William Morrow, 1985.

Kessler, Woodrow M. *To Wake Island and Beyond: Reminiscences*. Washington, DC: History and Museums Division, Headquarters, U.S. Marine Corps, 1988.

Keys, Ancel, Josef Brozek, Austin Henschel, Olaf Mickelsen, and Henry Longstreet Taylor. *The Biology of Human Starvation*. 2 vols. With the assistance of Ernst Simonson, Angie Sturgeon Skinner, and Samuel M. Wells. Minneapolis: University of Minnesota Press, 1950.

Kinney, John F. "POW Radio." *Combat Illustrated*, Winter 1979, 67–71.

———, "Building a Radio in a Japanese POW Camp." *Foundation*, Spring 1985, 20–26, 75.

———, and James M. McCaffrey. *Wake Island Pilot: A World War II Memoir*. Washington, DC: Brassey's, 1995.

Kirk, Terrence S. *The Secret Camera*. Redwood Valley, CA: Owl Wise Publishing, 1982.

———, and Carolyn Noonan. "Secret Camera: A Marine's View of Hell," *World War II*, September 2006, 17–18, 20–22.

Knox, Donald. *Death March: The Survivors of Bataan*. New York: Harcourt Brace Jovanovich, Publishers, 1981.

LaForte, Robert S., and Ronald E. Marcello, eds. *Building the Death Railway: The Ordeal of American POWs in Burma, 1942–1945*. Wilmington, DE: SR Books, 1993.

———, Ronald E. Marcello, and Richard L. Himmel, eds. *With Only the Will to Live: Accounts of Americans in Japanese Prison Camps, 1941–1945*. Wilmington, DE: SR Books, 1994.

Lamont-Brown, Raymond. *Kempeitai: Japan's Dreaded Military Police*. Thrupp, Stroud, Gloucestershire, UK: Budding Books, 1998.

Landas, Marc. *The Fallen: A True Story of American POWs and Japanese Wartime Atrocities*. Hoboken, NJ: Wiley, 2004.

Lawton, Manny. *Some Survived*. Chapel Hill, NC: Algonquin Books of Chapel Hill, 1984.

Layton, Edwin T. *"And I Was There": Pearl Harbor and Midway—Breaking the Secrets*. New York: William Morrow, 1985.

Lebra, Takie Sugiyama. *Japanese Patterns of Behavior*. Honolulu: University of Hawaii Press, 1976.

Leck, Greg. *Captives of Empire: The Japanese Internment of Allied Civilians in China, 1941–1945*. Bangor, PA: Sandy Press, 2006.

Lipe, Francis Worthington. "Food Rations of the Japanese Prisoners of War, W.W. II, During Combat and Captivity." In Sommers, *The Japanese Story*.

Lundstrom, John B. *The First Team: Pacific Naval Air Combat From Pearl Harbor to Midway*. Annapolis: Naval Institute Press, 1984.

MacArthur, Brian. *Surviving the Sword: Prisoners of the Japanese in the Far East, 1942–45*. New York: Random House, 2005.

MacArthur, Douglas. *Reminiscences*. New York: McGraw-Hill Book Company, 1964.

Mace, Frank R. *The Story of Wake Island: Before, During and After Life as a Prisoner of War of the Japanese*. Spokane, WA: privately printed, n.d.

Machi, Mario. *The Emperor's Hostages*. New York: Vantage Press, 1982.

Maga, Timothy P. *Defending Paradise: The United States and Guam, 1898–1950*. New York: Garland, 1988.

Magnino, L. A. *Jim's Journey: A Wake Island Civilian POW's Story*. Central Point, OR: Hellgate Press, 2001.

Manchester, William. *Goodbye Darkness: A Memoir of the Pacific War*. Boston: Little, Brown, 1979.

McBrayer, James D. Jr. *Escape! Memoir of a World War II Marine Who Broke Out of a Japanese POW Camp and Linked Up With Chinese Communist Guerrillas*. Jefferson, NC: McFarland, 1995.

McCoy, Melvin H., and S. M. Mellnik. *Ten Escape From Tojo*. Edited by Welburn Kelley. New York: Farrar & Rinehart, 1944.

McDougall, William H. *If I Get Out Alive: World War II Letters & Diaries of William H. McDougall Jr.* Edited by Gary Topping. Salt Lake City: University of Utah Press, 2007.

Mead, Eileen. "Pearl Harbor Memories." *Town & Country: The Weekend Magazine of the (Fredericksburg, VA) Free-Lance Star*, December 7, 1991, 15.

Mellnik, Steve. *Philippine Diary 1939–1945*. New York: Van Nostrand Reinhold, 1969.

Michno, Gregory F. *Death on the Hellships: Prisoners at Sea in the Pacific War*. Annapolis: Naval Institute Press, 2001.

Miller, Doris. *Doc Miller: Wake Survivor*. N.p.: privately printed, n.d.

Miller, J. Michael. *From Shanghai to Corregidor: Marines in the Defense of the Philippines*. Marines in World War II Commemorative Series. Washington, DC: History and Museums Division, Headquarters, U.S. Marine Corps, 1997.

Millett, Allan R. *Semper Fidelis: The History of the United States Marine Corps*. Revised ed., New York: Free Press, 1991.

Moore, Bob, and Kent Fedorowich, eds. *Prisoners of War and Their Captors in World War II*. Oxford: Berg, 1996.

Morgan, Hugh J., Irving S. Wright, and Arie van Ravenswaay, "Health of Repatriated Prisoners of War From the Far East." *Journal of the American Medical Association* 130, no. 15 (1946): 995–999.

"Music and Merriment Reigns in Shanghai Concentration Camps Through Radios Presented by the Japanese Army Authorities." *Freedom*, Third Impress, 1942, 42–43.

Nalty, Bernard C. *Strength for the Fight: A History of Black Americans in the Military*. New York: Free Press, 1986.

Nardini, John E. "Vitamin Deficiency Diseases on Allied Prisoners of the Japanese." *United States Naval Medical Bulletin* 47, no. 2 (1947): 272–278.

———. "Survival Factors in American Prisoners of War of the Japanese." *American Journal of Psychiatry* 109, no. 4 (1952): 241–248.

———. "Psychiatric Concepts of POW Confinement." *Military Medicine* 127 (1962): 299–307.

Niderost, Eric. "Wake Island Survivor." *WWII History*, January 2006, 40–45, 82.

Nila, Gary, and Robert A. Rolfe. *Japanese Special Naval Landing Forces: Uniforms and Equipment 1932–45*. Botley, Oxford: Osprey Publishing, 2006.

Norquist, Ernest O. "Three Years in Paradise: A GI's Prisoner-of-War Diary, 1942–1945." *Wisconsin Magazine of History* 63, no. 2 (1979): 2–35.

Oldham, Peter. *Lieutenant Stephen Polkinghorn, D.S.C., R.N.R.* Auckland: New Zealand Military Historical Society, 1984.

Olson, John E. *O'Donnell: Andersonville of the Pacific*. Lake Quivara, KS: privately printed, 1985.

Pacific Island Employees Foundation. *A Report to Returned CPNAB Prisoner of War Heroes and Their Dependents*. Boise, ID: Pacific Island Employees Foundation, 1945.

Page, William Frank. *The Health of Former Prisoners of War: Results From the Medical Examination Survey of Former POWs of World War II and the Korean Conflict*. Washington, DC: National Academy Press, 1992.

Poindexter, Arthur A. "Wake Island: America's First Victory." *Leatherneck: Magazine of the Marines*, December 1991, 28–35.

———. "Our Last Hurrah on Wake." *American History Illustrated*, February 1992, 64–67, 74.

Reynolds, Quentin. *Officially Dead: The Story of Commander C. D. Smith*. New York: Random House, 1945.

Richardson, Herb. "Jack Hawkins: Escape Artist of the Philippines." *Leatherneck*, June 1982, 24–27.

Roland, Charles G. "Stripping Away the Veneer: P.O.W. Survival in the Far East as an Index of Cultural Atavism." *Journal of Military History* 53, no. 1 (1989): 79–94.

———, and Harry S. Shannon. "Patterns of Disease Among World War II Prisoners of the Japanese: Hunger, Weight Loss, and Deficiency Diseases in Two Camps." *Journal of the History of Medicine and Allied Sciences* 46, no. 1 (1991): 65–85.

Rush, Robert Sterling. *Hell in Hürtgen Forest: The Ordeal & Triumph of an American Infantry Regiment*. Lawrence: University Press of Kansas, 2001.

Russell, Lord Edward. *The Knights of Bushido: A Short History of Japanese War Crimes*. London: Cassell, 1958.

Sanders, Charles W. Jr. *While in the Hands of the Enemy: Military Prisoners in the Civil War*. Baton Rouge: Louisiana State University Press, 2005.

Satterfield, Archie, ed. *The Home Front: An Oral History of the War Years in America*. New York: Playboy Press, 1981.

Saylor, Thomas. *Long Hard Road: American POWs During World War II*. St. Paul: Minnesota Historical Society, 2007.

Schneider, Cece. "Pilgrimage to Wake Island." *Leatherneck: Magazine of the Marines*, January 1992, 36–41.

Schull, William J. *Song Among the Ruins*. Cambridge, MA: Harvard University Press, 1990.

Shaw, Henry I. Jr. *Opening Moves: Marines Gear Up for War*. Marines in World War II Commemorative Series. Washington, DC: History and Museums Division, Headquarters, U.S. Marine Corps, 1991.

Shils, Edward A., and Morris Janowitz. "Cohesion and Disintegration in the Wehrmacht in World War II." *Public Opinion Quarterly* 12 (1948): 280–315.

Showalter, Dennis E. "Evolution of the U.S. Marine Corps as a Military Elite." *Marine Corps Gazette*, November 1979, 44–58.

Sloan, Bill. *Given Up for Dead: America's Heroic Stand at Wake Island*. New York: Bantam Books, 2003.

Smith, Maurice J. "What to Expect if You Are Captured by the Japs!" *Leatherneck*, November 1942, 30–31.

Sommers, Stanley G., ed. *The Japanese Story: History of POWs in Japan and After-Effects*. POW Medsearch Packet 10. Marshfield, WI: American Ex-Prisoners of War, 1980.

———. "Introduction to Japanese Story." In Sommers, *The Japanese Story*.

Spector, Ronald H. *Eagle Against the Sun: The American War With Japan.* New York: Free Press, 1985.

Stanley, Roy M. *Prelude to Pearl Harbor: War in China, 1937–41; Japan's Rehearsal for World War II.* New York: Charles Scribner's Sons, 1982.

Stenger, Charles A. *American Prisoners of War in WWI, WWII, Korea and Vietnam: Statistical Data Concerning Numbers Captured, Repatriated, and Still Alive.* Washington, DC: Veterans Affairs Advisory Committee on Former Prisoners of War, 1981.

Stewart, Sidney. *Give Us This Day.* New York: W. W. Norton, 1956.

Stouffer, Samuel A., and others. *The American Soldier.* Studies in Social Psychology in World War II. 4 vols. Princeton: Princeton University Press, 1949.

Tanaka, Yuki. *Hidden Horrors: Japanese War Crimes in World War II.* Boulder, CO: Westview Press, 1996.

Taylor, Vince. *Cabanatuan—Japanese Death Camp: A Survivor's Story.* Waco, TX: Texian Press, 1985.

Taylor, William. *Rescued by Mao: World War II, Wake Island, and My Remarkable Escape to Freedom Across Mainland China.* Sandy, UT: Silverleaf Press, 2007.

"Tell the Public We Are Receiving Good Treatment." *Freedom*, Third Impress, 1942, 44–45.

Tenney, Lester I. *My Hitch in Hell: The Bataan Death March.* Washington, DC: Brassey's, 1995.

Tierney-Ohuki, Emiko. *Illness and Culture in Contemporary Japan.* New York: Cambridge University Press, 1984.

Timpany, David. "The Life of a POW." *Follow Me*, March/April 2002, 5, 20–21.

Toland, John. *But Not in Shame: The Six Months After Pearl Harbor.* New York: Random House, 1961.

Totman, Conrad. *Japan Before Perry: A Short History.* Berkeley: University of California Press, 1981.

Towle, Philip A. "Japanese Treatment of Prisoners in 1904–1905—Foreign Officers Reports." *Military Affairs* 39, no. 3 (1975): 115–117.

———, Margaret Kosuge, and Yoichi Kibata, eds. *Japanese Prisoners of War.* New York: Hambledon and London, 2000.

U.S. Congress, Senate. *Treaties, Conventions, International Acts, Protocols and Agreements Between the United States of America and Other Powers.* Vol. 4, *1923–1937.* Edited by Edward J. Trenwith. Washington, DC: U.S. Government Printing Office, 1938.

Urwin, Gregory J. W. "The Road Back From Wake Island, Part I," *American History Illustrated*, December 1980, 16–24.

———. "The Road Back From Wake Island, Part II." *American History Illustrated*, January 1981, 43–49.

———. "The Defenders of Wake Island and Their Two Wars, 1941–1945." *Prologue: Quarterly of the National Archives* 23 (1991): 368–381.

———. *Wake Island in World War II: An Annotated Bibliography*. Huntsville, AL: U.S. Army Space and Strategic Defense Command, 1996.

———. *Facing Fearful Odds: The Siege of Wake Island*. Lincoln: University of Nebraska Press, 1997.

———. "The Wake Island Militia," *Naval History* 11, no. 5 (1997): 39–42.

———. "U.S. Marine Survival Success in Japanese POW Camps." *World War II Quarterly* 4, no. 3 (2007): 4–23.

———. "How Marine POWs Hung Tough." *World War II*, June/July 2008, 32–39.

Vance, John R. *Doomed Garrison—The Philippines (A POW Story)*. Ashland, OR: Cascade House, 1974.

Van Peenen, H. J. "Touchstone From Zentsuji." In *Zentsuji in Kansas: Stories From the POW Reunions*, edited by Joe Brown, 81. Marble Hill, MO: Stewart Publishing & Printing, 1986.

Versaw, Donald L. *The Last China Band*. Belmont Shore, CA: Pepper Tree Publications, 1990.

Veterans Affairs, Studies and Analysis Service, Office of Planning and Program Evaluation. *Study of Former Prisoners of War*. Washington, DC: Government Printing Office, 1980.

Wainwright, Jonathan M. *General Wainwright's Story: The Account of Four Years of Humiliating Defeat, Surrender, and Captivity*. Edited by Robert Considine. Garden City, NY: Doubleday, 1946.

Wakeman, Frederic Jr. "Shanghai Smuggling." In Henriot and Yeh, *In the Shadow of the Rising Sun*, 116–155.

"War Prisoners Are Given Bad News regarding Allied Calamities . . . but the Blow Is Softened by Unexpected Japanese Kindness." *Freedom*, Third Impress, 1942, 46–47.

"War-Weary American Prisoners Find Peace Once Again on the Shores of Dai Nippon." *Freedom*, Third Impress, 1942, 37.

Waterford, Van. *Prisoners of the Japanese in World War II: Statistical History, Personal Narratives and Memorials Concerning POWs in Camps and on Hellships, Civilian Internees, Asian Slave Laborers and Others Captured in the Pacific Theater*. Jefferson, NC: McFarland, 1994.

Werrell, Kenneth P. *Blankets of Fire: U.S. Bombers Over Japan During World War II*. Washington, DC: Smithsonian Institution Press, 1996.

White, John A. *The United States Marines in North China*. Millbrae, CA: privately printed, 1974.

Winslow, Walter G. "Epilogue." In Sommers, *The Japanese Story*.
Wodnik, Bob. *Captured Honor: POW Survival in the Philippines and Japan*. Pullman: Washington State University Press, 2003.
"World War II, Pacific." In Sommers, *The Japanese Story*.
Wright, John M. Jr. *Captured on Corregidor: Diary of an American P.O.W. in World War II*. Jefferson, NC: McFarland, 1988.

index

Abraham, Theodore A., Jr., 59, 61, 124, 178–79, 263, 274
Ackley, Edwin M., 316
Adams, Richard P., 174–75
Agar, John R., 112; death, 245
Ahlrich, Wayne H., 192
Akin, Shirley, 118, 119, 162, 166, 198, 347
Akiyama (IJA lieutenant), 136
Allen, James, 64, 104, 142, 347
Allers, Howard, 220, 222
American Prisoner of War Information Bureau, 297
American Volunteer Group (AVG), 221–22
Anderson, John B. L., 286
Anderson, Warren G., 240
Aomori, 290, 291, 307
Araki (IJA sergeant), 175, 203
Arthur, Robert O., 57
Asakawa, Yoshio: and *Nitta Maru* executions, 95
Asama Maru (Japan), 199, 310, 314
Ashurst, William W., 137, 138, 144, 150, 152, 154, 155, 162, 182, 183, 197, 214, 215, 225, 227, 234, 242, 250, 252, 254, 259, 262, 264, 266, 267–68, 274–75, 282, 284, 291, 304, 305, 333, 341, 343, 345; background, 132; discourages escape, 191–92, 341; and no-escape pledge, 191, 194–95; and officers' garden, 232–33; and privileges of rank, 176, 247, 282–83, 298, 344; protests to Japanese, 176, 177, 208, 225, 232–33, 235–36, 245–46, 258–59, 271, 274; senior Allied POW at Woosung, 132
atomic bomb, 299, 300, 306, 307
Atwood, Lawrence M., 318

"Babe Ruth" (IJN guard), 88
Bailey, George E.: death, 345
Bailey, Vincent W.: executed, 92–96
Baker, S. L., 83, 102
Barnes, James E.: death, 329
Barninger, Clarence A., 10, 12, 15, 31, 35, 54
Bataan, 143, 292, 337, 342
Bataan Death March, 335, 337, 342
Battles, Connie G.: escape attempt, 195
Beaver, Darrell L.: killed, 305
Beecher, Curtis T., 343
Beijing. *See* Peking
Ben Nevis, 146
Bennington (CV-20), 308
Bennington (PG-4), 2
Benton, Willie, 226, 228, 238
Bertels, Alton J.: death, 245
Biggs, Chester H., Jr., 133, 346
Bird, Edwin A.: death, 329
"Bird," The (IJA guard), 330
Bishop, Jack R., 225
Bishop, Lewis S., 221–22; abused by Japanese, 222; escape, 280
Blandy, John F., 87
Borne, Joseph E., 80, 94, 123, 124, 128, 346; and Ozeki, xi–xii, 50
Boucher, Carroll W.: electrocuted, 197

Bowsher, Walter A., 12, 37, 205
Boxer Protocol of 1901, 126, 141
Boxer Rebellion, 47
Boyd, Berdyne, 315
Brewer, Artis T.: escape attempts, 260–61, 331
Bridgehouse Jail, 222
Brimmer, Charles W.: escape attempt, 195–96
British army, 142, 147, 220–21
British Broadcasting Corporation (BBC), 144–45, 269
Brown, James R., 347, 348
Brown, Luther A., 135, 137, 138, 146, 154, 208, 214, 239, 247, 248, 254, 262, 267–68, 291, 305; background, 132; friction with Contractors, 132–33; maintains POW discipline, 132–33, 227, 229, 249, 264, 341, 343–44; protests to Japanese, 133–34, 176, 235–36; restrains Ishihara, 208–9
Brown, Robert M., 22, 32, 75, 82, 124, 203, 292–93, 302, 346, 348
Broyles, Earl M., 55, 88, 80, 170, 171, 190, 330
Bull, Harcourt G., 342
"Bull," The (IJA guard), 330
Burris, Charles W., 342
Burton, John H., 51, 119, 139, 167, 191, 323, 324, 346, 347
Bushido, 42–43, 45, 48, 68, 95, 169, 255, 339

Cabanatuan (camp), 342
Cabanatuan No. 1 (camp), 343
Calcutta, 268
Camacho, Jesus: death, 197
Camp, Charles H., 204–5, 242
Camp Hata. *See* Fengtai
Camp O'Donnell, 337, 339, 342–43
Camp 1 (Wake Island), 4, 9, 18, 19; and American surrender, 28–29, 40
Camp 2 (Wake Island), 4, 13, 36, 57, 75; converted into POW camp, 58–59; Contractors depart for Japan, 312, 319; daily routine, 66; escape attempt, 310–11; foraging, 65–66; hygiene, 61; illness and health care, 59, 61–62, 69, 72, 76–77, 308, 336; interrogations, 64, 68; POW accommodations, 59–60, 336; POW background questionnaires, 64, 76; POW deaths and executions, 69, 311, 312–13, 314; rations, 60–62, 309, 311, 336; recovered American military personnel evacuated, 309–10; relations with guards, 62–63, 64, 67–68, 69, 309, 336; rumors, 66–67, 71; secret POW radios, 67–68; work details, 63–65
Canadian army, 142, 220–21
Carlotto (Italy), 251
Carlotto Battalion, San Marco Regiment (Italian marines), 251–52, 287, 307, 343
Carr, Louis: death, 198
Carr, Reynold, 89
"Casey at the Bat" (IJA guard), 330
Cash, Holland, 128; death, 245
Cathay Mansions Hotel, 188–89, 190
Catmull, Reed, 346
Chambliss, Sam E., 284
Chandler, Paul D., 141; repatriated, 198–99
Chapman, Henry H. W., 38, 39, 57, 89, 109, 114, 145, 168, 173, 183, 202, 229, 244, 282, 283, 287, 289, 335–36, 346
Charters, Bill, 111, 273
China, 204; poverty, 100, 102, 178, 191; night soil fertilizer, 107, 117, 183
Chinese Revolution, 141
Chinwangtao, 126, 147
Chitose Air Base, 305
Chunking, 144, 196, 268
Churchill, Winston S.: on becoming a POW, 23–24
Civilian Conservation Corps, 224
Clancy, Edward S., 254
Climie, James F., 137; beaten by Ishihara, 207
collaboration, 249, 250, 260–61
"College, Joe," (IJA interpreter), 103, 112
Collier, J. V., 343
Comfort, Floyd H., 49, 154, 170
Commers, Joseph F.: death, 156
Comstock, Benjamin F., Jr., 82
Conner, Dennis, 170, 323
Conte Verde (Italy): crew imprisoned at Kiangwan, 252; as repatriation ship, 198–99, 222, 229; scuttled, 251
Contractors, 44, 52, 53, 59–60, 66, 88, 105, 137, 144, 146, 162, 164, 180,

181, 190, 213, 220, 254–55, 270, 274, 275, 282, 283, 286, 291, 306, 320–22, 324, 328, 343, 346–47; admire Wake Marines, 124, 128; and American surrender, 29, 35, 36; assist in Wake's defense, 10, 12–13, 18–20, 67, 71, 124–25, 336; classified as POWs, 67; drafts sent to Japan, 202–3, 250–51, 311, 319, 322–23, 345; executions, 311, 312–13, 314, 320, 334; fortify Wake for Japanese, 63–64, 308–9; friction with Luther Brown, 132–33, 344; hopes for repatriation, 66, 67, 75, 198; Japanese retain 367 on Wake, 76, 308; Kiangwan barracks assignments, 216; mock North China Marines, 128; organized on airfield, 55–56; other POW deaths, 119–20, 174, 197–98, 219–20, 245, 311, 321, 322, 324, 329, 330, 333–34; POW leadership, 55–56, 124–25; prewar working conditions, 3–4, 59, 336; train on Marine weapons, 7; Woosung barracks assignments, 104

Contractors Pacific Naval Air Bases (CPNAB). *See* Contractors

Cook, Edward, 243, 347

Cook, Howard, 163, 219

Cook, Jack B., 31, 38, 170, 200, 202, 230, 234, 242, 273, 293, 296, 302

Cook, Walter J., 317

Cooley, Delmar, 296

Corregidor, 141, 143, 292, 305, 342

Coulson, Raymond L.: escape attempts, 260–61, 331

Cox, James H., 55, 327

"Crash Dive" (IJA guard), 171

Culp, Joseph C.: killed, 330

Cunningham, Louise, 144, 332

Cunningham, Winfield S., 85–86, 88, 89–90, 96, 132, 133, 260; aloofness at Woosung, 125; and American surrender, 21–22, 27, 35, 37; background, 5; boards *Nitta Maru*, 81–82; commands Wake, 5, 10–11, 12, 13, 16, 20–21; confined in guest bungalow, 53, 54, 59, 60, 63; escape attempts, 192–94, 331–32; interrogated, 68, 188–89; liberated, 332; records radio messages, 90, 143–44

Dale, John R., 56, 289

Darden, James, 317–18

Davis, Eschol E., 25, 67, 115, 334

Davis, Floyd H., 297

Davis, J. J., 257

Dazang Loyalty Monument, 181

Devereux, James P. S., 7, 44, 85, 131, 144, 146, 153–54, 160–61, 202, 234, 247, 254, 281–82, 291, 336; and American surrender, 2, 22–23, 26–29, 31; background, 5–6; boards *Nitta Maru*, 81–82; commands Wake Island Detachment, 1st Defense Battalion, 5–6, 9; confined in "White House," 53–54, 59, 60; devout Catholic, 5, 6, 167; discourages escape, 191–92, 341; disliked by enlisted men, 6, 305; institutes Woosung POW school, 164–65; interrogated, 68; maintains POW discipline, 120–25, 132, 229, 238, 249, 341, 343–44; maintains unit identity, 121, 164, 191, 203, 250; and no-escape pledge, 195; prepares to get back into war, 124, 191; relations with Otera, 211–12; takes command at Hakodate No. 3, 304–5; and Wake defense, 9–10, 14–15, 17–18, 20–21

Dietz, Cecil M., 128

Dillon, George O.: executed, 320

Dispatch Camp 5-D, Tokyo Area Command. *See* Kawasaki (camp)

Dodds, Darwin H., 261

Dorris, William, 344–45

Driscoll, Leo P., 219–20

Dukat (Norway), 245

Durrwachter, Henry L., 25, 33, 65, 83, 101, 103, 140, 143, 144, 145, 146, 150, 164–65, 168, 176, 181, 183, 185, 195, 209, 326–28, 347

Economou, Michael N., 64–65

Egle, Edouard, 201, 205, 218, 225, 231, 283; background, 151; relations with Japanese officials, 151–52, 154, 182, 213–14; sends POWs relief shipments, 151–66, 168–69, 216, 230, 242, 255, 257, 266–67, 275, 338; sends POWs seed and livestock, 157–58, 233–34; visits

Woosung and Kiangwan, 154, 213–14, 268
Eliassen, John H.: death, 245
Elrod, Henry T., 13, 15, 19
Endo (Yuse and Otera's executive officer), 136, 137, 139, 210, 232–33, 234, 246; steals ICRC supplies, 225
Enterprise: delivers VMF-211 to Wake, 9; raids Wake, 310
Essaff, Thomas G., 197

Fengtai (camp), 275, 295; evacuated, 284; illness and health care, 282, 283; incarceration of American airmen, 284; Japanese security precautions, 282; POW accommodations, 281–82; rations, 283; selfishness of POW officers, 282–83; work details, 283
Fields, Marshall E., 101, 138, 168, 171, 203, 205, 274
First Sino-Japanese War, 47
Fitch, Alva R., 343
Flying Tigers. *See* American Volunteer Group (AVG)
Foley, William T., 134–36, 184, 186, 192, 197, 256–57, 286, 291, 307
Fontanel, Emile: aids POWs at Woosung and Kiangwan, 149–50; camp visits, 149–50, 213–14
Forman, Percy W., 310
Franklin, Theodore: executed, 92–96
Freedom (Japanese magazine), 90, 143
Freuler, Herbert C., 77, 85–86, 130, 199–200, 205; designs rice-cleaner, 137; execution threat, 39; interrogated, 188–89; Kiangwan mess officer, 254–55, 275; and Wake surrender, 27
Frey, Robert L., 274
Fukuoka No. 18-B (camp), 319–21, 334, 345
Fukuoka No. 9 (camp), 322
Fukuoka No. 1 (camp), 321–22
Fukuoka No. 3 (camp), 323–25, 344–45
Fukuoka No. 23 (camp), 322
Fukutome (Ishihara's assistant), 256
Fusan (camp), 285–86; POWs split into three groups, 286
Fusan (city), 285
Fushiki (camp), 318

"G-1" (Ishihara's assistant), 238, 255
"G-2" (Ishihara's assistant), 238, 255
Gable, Walter, 346
Ganci, William B., 160
Garrison, John R.: death, 245
Geneva Convention: and ICRC, 151; Japanese ambivalence, 46, 103; Japanese violations, 137, 142, 174, 176, 177, 194–95, 232–33, 235–36, 241; POW provisions, 45–46, 96, 133, 149, 150, 176, 181–82, 194–95, 235–36, 241, 315
Goa, 258
Godbold, Bryghte D., 7, 102, 122, 162, 170, 174, 191, 206, 211, 212, 240, 272, 339
Goiceochea, Joe, 52, 109, 327
Gonzales, Roy J.: executed, 92–96
Gooding, William, 170
Goto (IJA guard), 225
Gragg, Raymon, 156
"Grandma" (Japanese foreman), 320
Graves, Leon A., 26
Greater East Asia Co-Prosperity Sphere, 46, 100, 103, 176, 182, 189, 206, 239
Greey, Elmer B., 53
Gregouire, Sylvester, 167, 191
Grenadier, 323
Gripsholm (Sweden), 199, 257–58
Gross, Franklin A., 84–85, 113, 122, 165, 248, 323, 328, 331, 341
Grouper: sinks *Lisbon Maru*, 220
Guthrie, Frank A., 246; death, 245

Haidinger, Robert F., 34, 64–65, 207, 235
Haiphong Road Internment Camp, 210, 212
Hakodate (city), 291
Hakodate Branch Camp No. 3: B-29 airdrops, 301–3; coal mining, 293–94; escape attempts, 296, 300; gardening, 294; illness and health care, 295, 299, 302; Japanese security precautions, 292; POW accommodations, 292–93; POW desperation, 294, 295–96; POWs raise American flag, 303; rations, 294, 295; relations with guards, 294–95, 299; revived sexual urges, 304; USN airdrop, 305; and war's end, 298–306

Hakodate Branch Camp No. 2, 292; B-29 airdrops, 301–3; coal mining, 296; illness and health care, 297; Japanese security precautions, 291; POW accommodations, 291; rations, 296–98; relations with guards, 296–98, 299; revived sexual urges, 304; USN airdrop, 305; and war's end, 299–306
Halsey, William F., 310
Hamas, John A., 57, 164, 295; investigates *Nitta Maru* executions, 95; supervises Woosung garden, 157; and Wake surrender, 22–23, 34
Hamilton, William J., 82, 83
Hancock, 302
Hanna, Robert M., 18–19, 25, 49, 54, 68, 134, 139, 140, 155, 195, 226, 247, 248
Hannum, Earl R.: executed, 92–96
Hansen R. W.: death, 245
Harbison, Leonard B., 274
Hardy, Robert J., 171
Hassig, Edwin F., 66, 205, 215; and Wake surrender, 36–37
Hata, Shunroku: inspects Woosung, 143–44
Hawaiian Naval Coastal Frontier, 4
Hawkins, Jack, 342
Hayate (Japan), 15
Head, Robert P., 307–8
"Healer," The (IJA guard), 330
Helander, Charles G.: death, 198
Henningsen, A. B., 132–33
Henshaw, George H., 250
Hepburn, Arthur J., 3
Hepburn Board, 3
Hernandez, Jack: escape attempt, 280–81
Herndon, Pat N., 249
Hesson, James P., 318–19
Hevenor, Herman P., 53, 81–82
Hida, Usaji: and *Nitta Maru* executions, 95, 96
Hill, Charles C., 299
Himelrick, John R., 23, 28, 62, 65, 166, 323; death, 324
Hirohito, Emperor, 39, 86, 145, 206, 306
Hiryu (Japan), 17–18
Hitler, Adolf, 3, 252
Hodgkins, Ray H.: electrocuted, 196–97
Hofmeister, Julius M.: executed, 311
Hokkaido Mining Company, 293

Holewinski, Ralph J., 309–10, 315, 318, 320; barred from *Nitta Maru*, 77, 308; merciful treatment from captors, 49–50, 56–57, 58, 59; wounded, 49–50
Holmes, Charles A., 17, 23, 26, 30, 33, 52, 66, 75, 81, 83, 100, 101, 104, 106, 107, 108, 110, 111, 118, 120, 122, 123, 125, 133, 138, 142, 144, 145, 198, 201, 218, 231, 235, 237, 262, 265
Hong Kong, 142, 151, 220–21, 292
Honolulu, 62, 204
Hoskins, John R., 12, 48, 168, 171
Hotchkiss, Clifford E., 38, 52, 104, 115, 124, 130, 131, 142, 160, 201, 228, 251, 329–30
Hotchkiss, Louise, 201
Howes, Claude Davis, 321, 322
Hubley, George G., 28–29, 51, 80, 82, 89, 101, 118, 129, 136, 230, 237, 327
Huizenga, Richard M., 140, 150, 212–13, 225, 245; beaten by Ishihara, 207–8; escape, 279–80; escape planning, 190
Hyde, 306

Igawa, Haseo, 320
Ikegama, Uichi, 320
Imperial Japanese Army (IJA), 40, 43, 104, 116, 210, 213, 275, 293, 334; assumes control of Wake defenders, 100–101, 315; atrocities in China, 24–25; China Expeditionary Army, 143; garrisons Wake, 309; POW liaison bureau, 152, 218; POW treatment before World War II, 47; POW treatment during World War II, 45, 46, 194, 337, 342–43; preferential treatment for North China Marines, 127, 140–41; Thirteenth Army, 262
Imperial Japanese Navy (IJN), 40, 188, 313, 334; Chitose Air Group, 11, 13–14, 92; Combined Fleet, 268; executes Borneo ICRC delegate, 151; Fourth Fleet, 16; garrisons Wake, 77, 309; humiliated by Wake repulse, 16, 68; intelligence gathering, 68, 189; interrogates Wake defenders, 54, 64, 68, 315; 3rd Replacement Company, 77; turns over Wake defenders to IJA, 100–101, 315; 24th Air Flotilla, 11, 16

International Committee of the Red Cross (ICRC), 48, 150; aids POWs, 151–66, 168–69, 216, 218, 222–27, 229–30, 233–34, 241, 242, 250–51, 255, 257–59, 265–67, 275, 295, 316, 317, 321, 322, 324, 338, 347, 349; hampered by Japanese, 151–52. *See also* Egle, Edouard
Ishihara, Isamu, 211, 212, 213, 219, 223, 234, 244, 254, 259, 261–62, 270, 339; arrives at Woosung, 203; attacks on POWs, 204–5, 206–9, 246, 255; background, 204; conducts "inquisition," 255–57; grows demoralized, 264; hatred for POWs, 203, 204–6, 254, 355; imprisoned for war crimes, 265; leaves Kiangwan, 264–65; oversees Mount Fuji Project, 238–41, 242–43, 246, 251, 254, 270; punished by Yuse, 209, 255

Jaffe, Herbert K., 111–12, 117–18, 125, 206, 347
James, Jimmy, 231
Japan: blockaded by USN, 152, 263, 268; bombed by USAAF, 287–90, 306, 307, 318, 325, 327, 330
Japan Times and Advertiser, 145
Japanese attitudes: toward authority, 42, 137, 174; toward Chinese populace, 157, 178–79; toward corporal punishment, 43–44, 48–49, 175; toward death, 43; toward duty, 42, 44–45, 185; toward the emperor, 41–42, 206; toward family, 44–45; toward Geneva Convention, 46, 48, 103; toward ICRC, 150–52; toward illness and health care, 42, 44, 63, 139, 180, 185, 295, 297; occasional compassion for POWs, 49–50, 56–57, 58, 59, 61–62, 72–74, 137, 138–40, 156, 170, 215, 236, 264, 265, 275, 339–40; toward other foreigners, 42, 47, 150, 161, 211, 213–14, 252; toward POW escapes, 194, 196; toward POWs, 41, 46, 47–49, 154, 158–59, 170, 174–76, 180, 184, 188, 201–2, 204, 211, 213, 220–21, 223, 225, 320; toward surrender, 44. *See also* Bushido
Japanese Broadcasting Corporation. *See* Nippon Hoso Kyokia (NHK)

Jersey City, 199
Jinno, Toshio, 78; and *Nitta Maru* executions, 92, 93, 95
Johnson, Conrad, 326
Johnson, John S., Jr., 28, 37, 51, 60, 71–74, 80, 87, 89, 91, 114, 189–90, 230, 235, 240, 243, 257, 261, 263, 273, 289, 291, 292, 293, 294, 303, 304–5
Johnson, Mick D., 77
Johnson, Oreal, 345
Johnson, Phillip W., 203
Johnson, Thomas W., 25, 52, 84, 99–100, 108, 109, 111–12, 117, 128, 129, 131, 175, 178, 185, 200, 204, 211, 222, 263, 272, 289
Jones, Otis T., 64
Journal of the American Medical Association, 135
Jost, Hans, 151
Juta, Nishiki, 93, 95

Kahn, G. Mason, 67, 86, 111–12, 119, 127, 134, 136, 221, 222, 264, 292, 294, 295, 299, 302, 339; accused of discrimination, 135, 246–47; prison camp surgery, 134–35, 159; relations with Ozeki, 63; relations with Shindo, 138–39; and Wake surrender, 23, 26, 32
Kajioka, Sadamichi, 40, 50; first attempt to capture Wake, 14–16; second attempt to capture Wake, 17–18, 68; prevents executions, 33–34, 38, 92
Kakko Maru (Japan). *See President Harrison*
Kamaishi (camp), 319
Kamakura Maru (Japan), 199
Kantzer, William K., Sr., 148, 153, 155, 158, 160, 162, 164, 165, 167–68, 177, 183–84, 185–86, 197, 199, 209, 213–14, 215, 218, 219, 223, 224, 229, 230, 233, 234, 236, 239, 241–42, 243, 244, 246–47, 248, 249, 250–51, 257, 258, 259–60, 264–66, 267, 268, 270, 271, 273, 275–76, 278, 281, 283, 284, 285, 286, 287, 306–7, 344
Karo, Tetsutaro, 307
Katsumi (IJN interpreter), 39, 50–51, 57, 63–64
Kawasaki (camp), 325–27

Kawasaki No. 2 (camp), 287, 307
Kawasaki, Susumu, 311, 312
Kay, Logan, 309
Kaz, Norman N., 297
Keene, Campbell, 53, 91, 315
Kelnhofer, Guy J., 23, 25, 26, 30–31, 33, 51, 69, 99, 100, 102, 105, 109, 111, 237, 241, 243, 273, 286, 289
Kempeitai, 151, 178–79, 193–94, 222
Kennedy, Walter T.: and Ozeki, xi–xii
Kessler, Woodrow M., 24, 53, 82, 107, 117, 118, 123, 139–40, 143, 155, 156, 164, 189, 193, 248, 283, 342; builds crystal radio, 269; interrogated, 68; and Wake surrender, 31
Ketner, Bernard O., 241, 347; beaten by Ishihara, 206–7
Keyser, George E.: death, 329
KGEI, San Francisco, 67, 269
Kiangwan (camp): alcohol smuggling, 263–64; Allied merchant marine officers incarcerated, 253; American airmen incarcerated, 220, 221–22, 252–53, 270, 279; bakery, 266; Barracks 5 theater, 250 267; biweekly ICRC aid deliveries, 216, 229–30, 242, 250–51, 255, 257, 266–67, 275, 347; canteen, 244–45, 255; cemetery, 219–20, 221, 245; Chinese pilot incarcerated, 253; and Christmas 1942, 230–31; escape attempt, 260–61; evacuated, 274–77; exercise, recreation, and entertainment, 239–40, 267; first shipment of ICRC food boxes, 222–27, 230; food shortages, 241–44, 257, 266; gambling, 227; illness and health care, 216, 217, 219, 220, 222, 223, 245–47, 249, 258, 264, 265, 275; Ishihara's "inquisition," 255–57; Italian merchant sailors released, 252; Italian POWs incarcerated, 252; Japanese censorship, 259; Japanese confiscate radios, 268; Japanese pilfer food boxes, 225–26, 258–59; Japanese pilfer POW produce, 234; Japanese security precautions, 217–19; library, 218; *Lisbon Maru* survivors incarcerated, 220–21, 222; Mount Fuji black market, 244–45, 255–56; POW accommodations, 215–17, 218, 219; POW deaths, 219–20, 221, 245; POW drafts sent to Japan, 250–51, 323; POW foraging, 243–44; POW garden, 233–34; POW sabotage, 262, 263; POW trading, 227; POWs exhausted by Mount Fuji Project, 237, 241, 242–43, 245–46, 251, 339; POWs transfer from Woosung, 214–15; proximity to IJA bases, 218–19; rations, 214, 226, 230, 233–34, 238, 241–43, 246, 247, 248, 250–51, 252, 255, 266, 277; relations with guards, 212–13, 264, 265, 270, 272, 273–74, 339; rest chits controversy, 246–47, 248–49; revived sexual urges, 228–29; rumors, 266, 267–70, 274–75; second ICRC food box shipment, 257–59; and secret POW radios, 268–69; stealing, 227, 259–60; superior location, 214, 218; third ICRC food box shipment, 265–66, 275; work details, 219, 232–41, 245–48, 251, 261–64, 265, 267
Kiangwan (village), 214, 262
Kiangwan race course, 214, 262–63
Kiangwan Road Naval War Prisoners Camp, 99, 188–89
Kibble, Dare, 49, 51, 55, 84, 85, 102, 105, 107, 109, 111, 119, 156, 239, 325–26, 327
Kidd, Murray, 311
Kikuchi, Kenichi, 295
Kimmel, Husband E., 4–5, 7, 9, 16–17, 20
King, James O., 23, 103, 122, 345
Kinney, John F., 48, 55, 56, 110, 115, 120, 130, 144, 164, 202, 226; and American surrender, 33; builds crystal radio, 269; escape, 279–80; escape planning, 69–71, 165, 190, 279; execution threat, 39, 57; interrogated, 57, 188–89; operates secret radio at Camp 2, 67, 69; and Wake defense, 12
Kirk, Terence S., 133, 324
Kisaragi (Japan), 15
Kleponis, Vincent, 262
Kliewer, David D.: execution threat, 39; interrogated, 57
Klota, Harry J., 284

Knox, Frank, 5
Kohara, Yasuo: and *Nitta Maru* executions, 94, 96
Kokura. *See* Fukuoka No. 3 (camp)
Korean conscript laborers, 293, 303, 304, 305
Krawie, John W., 100
Kure Naval Base, 77

Lambert, John W.: executed, 92–96
Lane, Lloyd G.: death, 329
LaPorte, Ewing E., 11–12, 60, 66, 78, 124, 133, 179, 226, 229, 235, 260, 289–90, 296–98, 346
Layton, Edwin T., 42
Lee, William A., 131, 212, 259–60, 341
Lent, Oscar C., 334
Lepanto (Italy), 251
Levin, Maurice, 205
Levy, 314
Lewis, Murray, 220
Lewis, William W., 30
Lexington, 89
Lisbon Maru (Japan): sunk by *Grouper*, 220–21
"Little Caesar" (IJA guard), 330
Liu (Chinese servant), 192–94
Lourenço Marques, 199, 201, 222
Ludington, Don W., 32, 51, 82, 166, 269
Ludwick, Kirby, Jr., 296
Lum, Ambrose C., 257
Lynch, Maurice G., 221, 292, 297

MacArthur, Douglas, 143, 300, 301, 337
Mackie, Elmer E., 310–11
Malama: crew incarcerated at Woosung, 141; scuttled, 141
Malleck, Donald R., 6, 26, 27, 37, 53–54, 81–82, 110, 123, 125–26, 201, 223, 225
Mandarin Club, 231
Manning, Bernard H., 297
Maple, Robert C., 66, 320
Marine's Handbook, The (Luther Brown), 132
Marshall, Donald R., 140–41
Martin, "Shorty," 307–8
Matsuda, M.: visits Woosung, 143, 144, 152
Mayhew, Robert C., 290–91, 296, 300, 302

McAlister, John A., 53, 61, 75; builds crystal radio, 269; escape, 279–80; and Wake defense, 15, 19–20
McAmis, Terence T., 33, 38
McAnally, Winford J., 138; escape attempt, 300
McBrayer, James D., 130, 144, 150; escape, 279–80; escape planning, 165, 190
McDaniel, George W., 113, 122, 180
McKeehan, Lloyd S., 309
McKinstry, Clarence B., 18, 19–20, 61, 259–60
McQuilling, Robert E., 156
Menique, Raymon, 103
Mettscher, Leonard G., 52, 104, 105, 115, 191, 263, 298–99, 345–46
Miasaki (IJA lieutenant), 255–56
Midway Island, 4, 62, 189, 201, 313
Mikani (Japanese interpreter), 203, 208; altercation with Luther Brown, 137
Miles, William M.: death, 311
Miller, Franklin B., Jr., 320; death, 321
Milliken, Charles R., 228
Minnick, John C., 141, 256
Misaka, Tsumori, 78, 81, 89, 93
Missouri, 303, 304
Mohr, Frederick B., 269
Moore, John P., 296
Morisako, Kazunori, 171–72, 184, 208–9, 256; and "Mortimer Snerd" incident, 172–73
Morrison Knudsen Company, 3
Mount Fuji Project. *See* Kiangwan (camp): work details
Murray (British army doctor), 292, 297, 300
Mussolini, Benito, 251, 252
Myers, Charles L., 63, 319

Nakao, Unesaku, 295, 297
Nanking, 181, 278, 332
Naoetsu (camp), 330–31
Nelson, Edward A.: death, 197–98
Neuse, Max H.: death, 324
New Fourth Army (China), 280
Newell, Emmett L., 112–13, 146, 154, 159, 163, 164, 201, 215, 223, 233–34, 240, 241–42, 243, 346–47
Newell, Glenn, 346–47
Niigata Camp 5-B, 287, 307, 327

Niizuma, Kinsaburo, 294
Nippon Hoso Kyokai (NHK), 250
Nippon Times, 269
Nishiashibetsu (camp), 291, 298, 302
Nitta Maru (Japan), 119, 308, 338; arrives at Wake, 76; boarding instructions, 72–75, 84, 86; commandeered by IJN, 77; disembarks POWs at Woosung village, 99–100, 102; embarks guard detail, 77; embarks POWs, 78–82; and executions, 92–96, 338; illness and health care; 83–84, 85–86; POW accommodations, 82–85; rations, 83; Shanghai layover, 96, 99; submarine scares, 90; Yokohama layover, 89–91, 188, 250, 315, 338
Nitta Maru guard detachment, 73, 113–14; animus toward Wake defenders, 78, 90; handpicked men, 77–78; physical abuse of POWs, 80–82, 86–88, 99, 169; psychological abuse, 89; robbery, 86, 88. *See also* Saito, Toshio
Nonn, Leo L., 79
North China Marines, 126, 139, 145, 147, 183, 197, 208, 235, 244–45, 254–55, 282, 291, 292, 325, 328, 330, 340, 345, 346; aid Wake defenders, 130–31; assume POW leadership, 131–34, 137; barracks assignment at Kiangwan, 216; claim diplomatic status, 126–27, 141, 190, 198; concentrated at Tientsin, 127; drafts sent to Japan, 202–3, 322–23; dubbed "Ten-Cent Marines," 128; elite composition, 126; exploited for enemy propaganda, 143–44; incarcerated at Woosung, 125–26, 127; medical officers, 134–36, 159, 184, 186, 197, 216, 245–46, 256; POW deaths, 197, 245, 324, 330; preferential treatment, 126, 127, 140–41; and secret radio, 145, 268–69; shun Wake defenders, 128–29; surrender, 126; trade with Wake defenders, 130, 131; transported to Shanghai, 127
Northampton, 310
Nowlin, Jesse E., 122, 133, 138, 202, 247, 280, 285–86, 289, 290, 293, 294–95, 299, 302, 347–48
Nye, Edwin D., 25, 79–80, 83, 118, 202

Ofuna Naval Interrogation Center, 314–15, 319
Ogawa, Kiyoshi, 77, 93, 95
O'Guinn, Allan A., 59, 82, 111, 124, 285, 286
Ohashi (camp), 319
Olson, James E., 337
Omori No. 1 (camp), 327, 306
"One Round Hogan" (IJA guard), 212
Osaka (city), 318; bombed by USAAF, 289
Osaka (IJA medic), 173
Osaka Camp 13-B. *See* Tsumori (camp)
Osaka Main POW Camp. *See* Osaka No. 1-B (camp)
Osaka No. 1-B (camp), 317–19
Otera, Satoshi, 219, 225–26, 227, 232, 234, 236, 237–38, 246, 248–49, 252, 255, 256, 257, 258–59, 260, 261, 266, 268, 269, 270, 274, 275, 282, 284, 323, 339; affable personality, 211, 212, 264, 275; alcoholism, 212, 264; background, 210–12; confiscates Ashurst's records, 284; cooperates with ICRC, 213–14, 222–23, 339; laid-back management style, 212–13, 339; moves POWs from Woosung to Kiangwan, 214–15; reacts to train escapes, 280, 281; relations with Devereux, 211–12; reliance on collective punishment, 213, 219, 259, 262; succeeds Yuse at Woosung, 210–11; upset by air raids, 270, 271
Owen, William H., Jr., 343
Ozeki, Shigeyoshi, 40, 44, 45, 59–60; relations with POWs, xii, 40–41, 50, 61–63; and Wake's capture, 19, 24, 31–32, 40

Packard, Forrest L., 167
Page, Robert E. L., 297
Pan American Airways (PAA), 12, 70; employee deaths on Wake, 11, 336; establishes Wake airbase, 3; evacuates white employees, 12–13, 53; Guamanian employees as POWs, 147, 165, 229; POW deaths, 197, 245, 333–34
Papock, Herbert, 83, 99, 142, 145, 146–47, 196, 223, 224, 235, 241, 243, 252, 258, 261, 268

"Pasty Face" (Japanese foreman), 297
Patrol Boat 33 (Japan), 17, 19
Patrol Boat 32 (Japan), 17, 19, 37
Pay, Alexander E., 36, 52, 110, 115–16, 135, 139, 146–47, 165, 178, 181, 193, 196, 198, 227, 230, 232, 253, 261, 276, 279, 282, 284, 285, 307
Pearl Harbor, 4, 6, 9–10, 16, 20, 46, 66, 70, 89, 150, 220, 221
Pearsall, John E., 107, 157, 163, 165, 168, 178, 215, 220, 224, 227, 228, 230, 233, 267
Peking (Beijing), 47, 126, 128, 199, 281, 284, 332
Perkins, Frances, 67
Permenter, Calvin L., 226
Peterel (United Kingdom), 96, 147; crew barracks assignment, 104; crew boards *Nitta Maru*, 99; crew marches to Woosung camp, 101; crew receives relief supplies from families, 153, 160; sunk by Japanese, 98–99; surviving crew incarcerated in Shanghai, 99
Philippine Clipper (PAA flying boat), 11, 13, 53
Philippines, 126, 141, 147; POW treatment, 194, 337, 342–43
Phipps, Ralph E.: death, 245
Pierson, Oral A., 147–48
Pistole, Erwin D., 52, 239
Plate, William O., 78, 83, 84, 115, 123, 206, 224
Platt, Wesley M., 53, 81–82, 87; aids enlisted POWs, 341–42; and American surrender, 29; beaten on *Nitta Maru*, 87–88; saves Sloman, 61; and Wake defense, 14, 19–20, 27, 61, 71–72, 341
Poindexter, Arthur A., 5, 53, 121; and American surrender, 2; and Wake defense, 1–2, 12, 18, 19, 28, 56
Polkinghorn, Stephen, 98–99, 192–93, 223, 225
Pollard, Eric G. F., 134–36, 165, 216, 291–92, 294, 295
Potter, George H., Jr., 26, 33, 59, 88, 91, 96, 331; reinstitutes discipline at Wake airfield, 55–56; at Zentsuji, 315, 317, 342
President Harrison, 126, 141, 230; captured by IJN, 147; crew incarcerated in Shanghai, 147–48; crew receives relief supplies from Shanghai friends, 153, 160; senior crew members incarcerated at Woosung, 148
President Madison, 141
prisoner of war camps. *See under individual camp names*
prisoner of war officers, 160–61; accused of collaboration, 249, 260–61; ban food trading, 227, 341; ban gambling, 167, 227, 341; black marketeering, 244–45; and discipline, 54, 55–56, 120–25, 132, 227, 229, 238, 264, 304–5, 341–45; discourage escape, 191–92, 341; friction at Nishiashibetsu, 298; gardening at Kiangwan, 233–34; leadership failures, 120, 248–49, 282, 342–43; leadership successes, 56, 120–24, 164–65, 180, 254–55, 258–59, 317, 341–42, 343–44; placed in separate barracks at Kiangwan, 216; privileges of rank, 142, 155, 161, 176, 224, 247–49, 254, 257, 277, 305, 344; punish stealing, 227, 259–60, 341; quarters at Woosung, 105; selfishness at Fengtai, 282–83
prisoners of war (POWs): Australian, 291, 292, 306, 317, 321, 327, 328, 330, 334; bitterness of captivity, 69, 168, 187; British, 46, 69, 99, 103, 104, 109, 114, 145, 146, 147, 157, 158, 160, 165, 166, 174, 177, 179, 182, 184–85, 195, 215, 216, 220, 221, 230, 232, 252, 253, 282, 290, 292, 296, 300, 301, 306, 315, 317, 321, 322, 328, 334, 343; and buddy system, 58, 102, 290 318–19, 324, 345–48, 349; Canadian, 220–21, 334; Dutch, 306, 315, 317, 321, 322, 324, 327, 328; death rate in U.S. Civil War, 47; European Theater death rates, 46, 340–41; and friendly fire, 340; and Geneva Convention, 45–46, 96, 133, 149, 150, 176, 181–82, 194–95; from Guam, 315, 336; importance of humor, 156, 166, 171–73, 175, 190; Italian, 251–52, 270, 282, 286, 287, 307, 323, 343; and mail, 199; New Zealander, 334–35; Norwegian,

245, 253, 282, 283, 286; obsession with food, 168; Pacific Theater death rates, 46, 334–35, 337, 340; from Philippines, 292, 305, 317, 318, 322, 323, 325, 327, 335–36, 342–43, 344; and sex, 178, 304; vulnerability, 23–24, 49, 171, 187; will to survive, 69, 155–56, 168, 198, 347–48
Puller, Lewis B., 131
Pusan. *See* Fusan (city)
Putnam, Paul A., 49, 53, 91, 331; execution threat, 39, 92; interrogated, 57, 188; leads VMF-211, 9, 10, 12, 15, 19; transferred to Roku Roshi, 318; at Zentsuji, 315, 316, 317, 339–40, 342
Pye, William S., 20

Queen's Work: names Devereux "Catholic of the Month," 167
Quille, Larry E., 250

Raspe, Herman G., 126, 197
Reeves, Joe M., 38, 127, 129, 170, 175, 178, 243–44, 247
Rescue, 308
Richardson, Bernard E., 15, 24–25, 36–37, 43–44, 45, 50, 85, 87, 99, 100, 101, 102, 103, 107, 109, 110, 112, 113–14, 115, 117, 118, 136, 138, 154, 155, 156, 164, 165, 170, 172, 177, 178, 190, 195, 204, 206, 226, 228–29, 235, 236, 240, 243, 244, 246, 247, 249, 251, 273, 289, 291, 336, 345, 346
Rickert, Albert P., 250
Riddle, Lonnie B.: killed, 173–74
Rider, Richard: killed, 320
Riebel, Chester A., 60
Rienks, Donald H.: killed, 330
Rikitake, Yaichi, 323
Roark, Clyde E.: death, 245
Robertson, Charles B.: death, 329
Rogers, Ernest G., 31, 35, 38, 51, 52, 56, 61, 65, 91
Rogge, John D., 63, 81–82, 321
Roku Roshi (camp), 318, 331
Roosevelt, Franklin D., 16, 39, 67, 250, 270
Row, Earl R., 6, 31
Royal Marines (British), 147, 221

Royal Navy (British), 98, 99, 104, 147, 192, 221
Rules for Land Warfare (USA), 133
Rumpel, Fred R., 83, 108, 168, 173
Russell, Leal H., 54–55, 58, 60, 62, 63–64, 66–67, 69, 71, 75–76, 308–9, 310, 311, 319
Russo-Japanese War, 47
"Ruth, Babe" (IJN guard), 88
Rutledge, Raymond R., 144; assists Potter at airfield, 55–56; escape attempt, 284; temporarily heads Contractors, 124–25

Saito, Toshio, 77, 83, 89, 100; animus toward Wake defenders, 78, 86, 88–89, 91; asked to execute Putnam, 92; background, 78; bans sick POWs from ship, 76; collects POW information, 89, 92; covers up executions, 95; evades arrest, 95–96; executes five POWs, 92–95; oversees POW embarkation, 76, 80, 92; robs POWs, 88, 96; taunts POWs, 89
Sakai, Taikashi, 142
Sakaibara, Shigematsu: executed, 314; executes Contractors on Wake, 312–13, 314
Sakurai, Fukashi, 93, 95
Salt Lake City, 310
Sandvold, Julian K., 273, 335
Sapporo, 291, 296, 305
Saratoga, 16, 20
Sasebo Naval District Headquarters, 320
Schick, Michael J., 256
Schulze, Carl H., 290
Second Anglo-Boer War, 23
Second Sino-Japanese War, 24, 104, 126, 181
Sendai No. 11 (camp), 290, 307–8
Sendai No. 7-B (camp), 327–28
Shanghai, 48, 77, 92, 99, 100, 104, 124, 127, 141, 146, 147, 148, 149, 185, 188–89, 194, 198, 199, 212, 216, 218, 219, 220, 222, 230, 253, 260, 262, 274, 275, 331–32, 335; American consulate, 98, 198; British consulate, 98, 147, 192, 199; Bund, 98, 127; food shortages, 145, 152, 182, 241, 338–39; International Settlement, 96, 141, 152, 161, 210,

218; Swiss consulate general, 99, 149–50, 213–14, 338; and USAAF air raids, 218, 270–74
Shanghai American Association, 152–53, 156, 158, 161
Shanghai British Residents Association, 152–53, 156, 158, 160, 161, 163
Shanghai Municipal Jail. *See* Ward Road Jail
Shanghai Times, 145, 181, 269
Shanghai War Prisoners Camp, 212, 229, 338; acquires outstanding library, 163–64, 218; grows dependent on ICRC relief shipments, 152, 213, 241; evacuated, 274–77; IJA intends as model camp, 140, 143, 144, 149, 211, 215, 219, 340, 349; Japanese censorship, 164, 200–201, 205; low death rate, 339; moves to Kiangwan site, 214–15; opens at Woosung site, 102, 104–5; POW exercise, recreation, and entertainment, 122, 146, 160, 161–68, 239–40; and POW mail, 199–202. *See also* Kiangwan (camp); Woosung (camp)
Shan-Hai-Kwan, 252
Shank, Lawton E., 67, 69, 76, 308, 311; executed, 314–15; keeps twenty convalescents off *Nitta Maru*, 76–77; relations with Ozeki, 63
Shattles, Stephen H., 250
Shek, Chiang Kai, 104, 196
Shek, Madame Chiang Kai, 262
Shimonoseki, 287, 289
Shindo, Yoshiro, 184–85, 208; admired by POWs, 138–39, 140; background, 139; compassion, 139–40, 185, 207, 208, 246, 339; monitors POW health, 140; vaccinates POWs, 139–40
Shinshei Maru (Japan), 221
Shores, Robert E., 6, 49, 51, 88, 166, 190, 204, 346
Shugart, Eugene W., 80–81, 83
Silverlieb, Irving R., 135
Singapore, 143, 199, 292
Skaggs, Jack R., 100
Sloman, Wiley W., 315, 317, 318; barred from *Nitta Maru*, 77, 308; left for dead, 61; and Ozeki, xi–xii, 61–62; saved by Platt, 61
Smith, Abner: death, 245

Smith, Cassius E., 29, 58, 103, 202, 272; aborts escape attempt, 190–91
Smith, Columbus D., 98; escape attempts, 192–94, 331
Smith, Raymond E., 137
"Snake," The (IJN guard), 88
Snipes, Jack, 67
Sorachi Mining Company, 293, 298
Sorrel, Jesse D., 238–39
Soryu (Japan), 17–18
Special Naval Landing Force (SNLF): and capture of Wake, 14, 16, 17, 18–21, 23, 24, 27–28, 52–53, 61, 71–72; commits atrocities, 37, 57; concentrates POWs on airfield, 34, 35, 37; kinder treatment for POWs at Camp 2, 62, 63, 69; moves POWs to Camp 2, 58–59; ordered to spare POWs, 33–34, 38–39; 52–53; prepares to execute POWs, 32–33, 37–38; puts POWs to work, 63–65; rounds up POWs, 26–37, 333
Stark, Harold R., 4, 7, 9
Staten, Mark E.: death, 119–20
Stegmaier, Carl E., Jr., 56, 80, 112, 173, 241, 243, 274, 296
Stevens, Fred J., 309
Stewart, Charles A.: escape attempts, 195–96, 331
Stocks, Artie, 237
Stone, George B., 140–41
Story, Jerold B.: escape attempts, 195–96, 331
Stowe, Joe M., 256
Streeter, Mark E., 250
Sturgeon, Edward V., 25, 66, 80, 81, 102, 123, 128, 157, 211
"Sugar" (IJA guard): bayonets POWs during air raid, 274
Sullivan, Donald, 310–11
Surnagi Technical Research Center, 250
Susa, 287, 306
Suwa Maru (Japan), 312
"Sword Waver," The (IJN guard), 88

Tachibana Maru (Japan), 311, 319
Takahashi, Tomokethi, 265
Takamoto (first Woosung commandant), 103, 104, 114, 127; relieved by Yuse, 136
Takamura, Tokuichi, 78, 84; and *Nitta Maru* executions, 94, 96

index 475

Takezoe, Tamotsu, 78; and *Nitta Maru* executions, 95, 96
Tambien (Italy), 251
Tanagawa (camp), 318–19
Tanaka (IJA medic), 173
Task Force 16: raids Wake, 310
Tatsuta (Japan), 17–18
Tatuta Maru (Japan), 199
Taylor, Jack D., 250
Taylor, William L.: escape, 280–81
Tazang Motor Road, 218
Teh, Chu, 281
Teia Maru (Japan), 258
Tendo, Jiro, 300
Tenryu (Japan), 17–18
Terfansky, Joseph E., 77, 87
Teters, Nathan D., 81–82, 89, 124–25, 253, 254; confined in his bungalow, 53, 54; CPNAB general superintendent on Wake, 3–4; escape attempt, 192–94; interrogated, 68; and Wake defense, 12–13
Thaire, Grover E., 81, 85, 100
Tharin, Frank A., 54, 57; escape planning, 70–71; execution threat, 39; interrogated, 57, 188–89; mess officer at Kiangwan and Fengtai, 275, 283
Thyson, Leo C., 134–36, 245–46, 248
Tice, H. Jay, 107
Tientsin, 126, 127, 128, 140
Tijeron, Jerry: death, 245
Tobata. *See* Fukuoka No. 3 (camp)
Todd, Herman A., 86–87
Toguri, Iva, 250, 261
Tokyo, 151, 204, 250, 287, 300, 305, 307, 316; anti–POW riot, 290; bombed by USAAF, 289, 290, 306, 319, 327
"Tokyo Rose." *See* Toguri, Iva
Toshitaro, Habe, 328–29
Tramposh, Charles E., 315
Trego, Carroll E., 249, 294
Tripp, Glenn E., 133
Troney, Norris H., 324
Tse-tung, Mao, 281
Tsugaru Strait, 291
Tsuji, Hisao, 312, 313
Tsumori (camp), 325; black market, 329–30; bombed, 330; evacuated, 330; POW accommodations, 328; POW deaths, 329; rations, 328; work details, 328
Tsushima Strait, 286–87

Umeda Bunsho (camp), 318
U.S. Army (USA), 25, 268, 286, 292; 8th Army, 96; 1st Cavalry Division, 305; POW deaths, 46; POW discipline breakdowns, 342–43; Wake Island radio detachment, 5, 53, 77, 91, 203, 282, 315, 323
U.S. Army Air Forces (USAAF), 220, 301, 307; bombs Japan, 287–90; Fourteenth Air Force, 270–72; raids Shanghai area, 218, 270–74; targets Kiangwan (camp), 271; Twentieth Air Force, 301, 330
U.S. Bureau of the Budget, 53
U.S. Marine Corps (USMC), 4–5, 25, 68, 205, 268, 270, 315, 317; attitudes toward Japanese military, 24–25; discourages surrender, 6–7, 22, 23, 24–25; 1st Marine Division, 145; 4th Defense Battalion, 16; 4th Marines, 141, 147, 198, 336, 342, 343; Marine Air Group 21 (MAG-21), 9; "Old Corps," 122, 126, 131, 247; POW deaths, 69, 92–96, 156, 197, 219, 245, 305, 324, 329, 330, 333, 334; prewar expansion, 7, 128; small wars legacy, 131, 346; superior POW conduct, 36–37, 260, 340–42, 343–45. *See also* North China Marines; VMF-211; Wake Island Detachment, 1st Defense Battalion
U.S. Navy (USN), 25, 68, 152, 198, 263, 268, 282, 286, 292, 307, 340; bombs Wake, 313; Civil Engineers Corps, 53; Pacific Fleet, 4–5, 16, 66–67, 75; Patrol Wing 2, 93; POW deaths, 196–97, 334; Wake Island detachment, 5, 12, 77, 91, 147, 203, 282, 286, 292, 301, 323, 329, 333. *See also* Task Force 16
U.S. State Department, 48, 150
Utashinai, 301

Van Peenen, H. J., 316–17
Venable, Alexander B., Jr.: death, 69
Venable, James C., 25, 33, 38, 79, 128, 170, 200, 205, 227–28, 290, 303

Victor Emanuel III (king), 251, 252
Vincent: crew incarcerated at Woosung, 141; sunk by commerce raider, 141
VMF-211, 9, 53, 54, 57, 128, 147, 340; combat casualties, 11, 13, 19; drafts sent to Japan, 203; leaves seven wounded on Wake, 77; personnel disembark at Yokohama, 91, 188, 314, 315; POW deaths, 92–96, 329, 334; and Wake defense, 10–15, 17, 19, 70

Wake, 96, 98, 147, 192; captured by Japanese, 98; crew boards *Nitta Maru*, 99; crew incarcerated in Shanghai, 99, 147; crew marches to Woosung camp, 101; crew receives relief supplies from families, 153, 160; crewmen sent to Japan, 203, 323; Woosung barracks assignment, 104.
Wake Invasion Force (IJN): captures Wake, 17–21, 34, 40; casualties, 15, 24, 40, 51; first landing attempt, 14–15; reinforced, 16; spares POWs, 33–34, 38–39
Wake Island: as American rallying point, xi, 15–16, 348; and American war plans, 3–5, 7; base development, 3–4; becomes naval air station, 5; bombed by USAAF, 312, 313; bombed by USN, 313; early history, 2–3; first IJN landing attempt, 14–16, 68; fortified by Devereux's Marines, 4, 336; fortified by Japanese, 63–64, 308–9; IJN air raids, 11, 13–14, 16–17; Japanese garrison starves and sickens, 313–14; outbreak of war, 9–11; POW deaths and executions, 69, 311, 312–13, 314; raided by Task Force 16, 310; raided by *Yorktown*, 312, 313, 314; second IJN landing attempt, 1–2, 18–21, 24, 27–28, 71–72, 329, 341; surrenders to Americans, 314; surrenders to Japanese, 21–29
Wake Island (film), xi, 348
Wake Island defenders: airfield rations, 54–55, 58; barracks assignments at Kiangwan, 216; battling cold, 108, 110–11, 115, 138; beaten and abused on *Nitta Maru*, 80–82, 86–88; board *Nitta Maru*, 78–82;

boarding instructions for *Nitta Maru*, 72–75, 84, 86; boarding preparations, 75–77; bury battle dead, 57; Christmas on airfield, 57–58; combat casualties, 11, 13, 24, 37, 57, 336; confined at Camp 2, 58–77; confined on Wake airfield, 34–39, 50–58; constipation epidemic, 83–84, 111–12; cross Tsushima Strait, 286–87; defiant POW attitude, 24, 25, 37, 62, 165, 171–73, 174; disembark at Woosung village, 99–101; drafts sent to Japan, 202–3, 250–51; executed by Japanese, 311, 312–13, 314, 320, 338; exploited for enemy propaganda, 89–90, 143–44; fall into stupor, 84, 85; five executed on *Nitta Maru*, 92–96; foraging on Wake, 65–66; given clothing, 34, 56; good luck as POWs, 69, 335, 336–40, 349; grateful for ICRC relief, 150, 153–54, 226; hatred for Japanese, 165, 289, 294–95, 297–98, 300–301; initial depression, 101, 104, 109, 110, 120; irrepressibility, 41, 45, 62, 175; issued IJA uniforms, 138; liberated, 305–6, 307, 308; maintain discipline as POWs, 120–25, 341–42, 343–44; march to Woosung camp, 101–2; mobbed in Tokyo, 290; move to Kiangwan, 214–15; occasional insubordination, 123, 125, 249, 344; organized on airfield, 55–56; pity Japanese civilians, 289; POW cohesion, 36, 121, 191, 203, 250, 290, 338, 344–45; POW deaths, 69, 92–96, 119–20, 174, 197–98, 219–20, 245, 305, 311, 312–13, 314, 320, 321, 322, 324, 329, 330, 333–34, 338; and POW sabotage, 64–65; POW survival rate, xii, 333–35; put to work, 63–65; recognize Japanese compassion, 49–50, 56–57, 58, 59, 61–62, 72–74, 138–40, 170, 173, 186, 187, 189, 215, 264, 265, 298–99, 339; resent North China Marines, 128; sports rivalries, 162–63; surrender, 22–39; train trip to Fengtai, 278–81; train trip to Fusan, 284–85; train trip across Honshu, 287–91; turned over to IJA, 100–101; twenty leave *Nitta*

Maru, 90–91, 250; unruly behavior, 54–55; Woosung barracks assignments, 103–4
Wake Island Detachment, 1st Defense Battalion, 5, 128, 147, 229, 235, 291, 292, 293, 325, 328, 334, 340, 346, 348; disabled weapons repaired by Japanese, 64–65, 309; drafts sent to Japan, 202–3, 250–51, 323; dubbed "Raggedy-Ass Marines," 128; fortifies Wake, 6; leaves eight wounded on Wake, 77; personnel detained at Ofuna, 314–15; personnel disembark at Yokohama, 91, 314; personnel interrogated, 54, 64, 68; POW deaths, 69, 156, 219, 245, 305, 324, 329, 330, 334; recovers discipline and morale, 120–24, 345; surrenders, 22–39; undermanned, 7; and Wake defense, 9–10, 12–15, 17–20, 49, 68, 260; Woosung barracks assignments; 104
Wall, James E., 284
Waller, J., 142, 147, 209
Warabi (camp), 306–7, 344
Ward Road Jail, 194, 196, 260, 331
Waronker, Alvin C., 9
Watanabe, Misumasa, 313
waterboarding. *See* Ishihara, Isamu: conducts "inquisition"
Webb, Henry G., 315
Webb, Paul, 220
Whangpoo River, 98, 99, 104, 179, 192, 193, 272
Wheeler, Mackie L., 6, 75, 83, 170, 202, 226
White, John A., 130, 164, 185, 186, 228, 256–57, 285, 304, 305
Widdup, Beatrice Coyle: organizes POW officer relief network, 160–61
Wilcox, Leo W., 345
Williams, Joseph: death, 219
Williams, Luther, 38, 296, 297, 299, 336
Williamson, Jack R., 132
Wilson, Henry S., 53, 77, 314–15
Winchester, John E., 310
Wiserman, Reuben E., 233
Wiskochil, Robert I.: death, 219
Wolfe, Clarence E., 203, 296
Woolley, John B., 99; escape attempts, 192–94, 331

Woosung (camp): Allied merchant seamen incarcerated, 141, 146–48; appearance, 102; British consulate personnel incarcerated, 147; camp rumors, 116, 204; canteen, 182–83; carpentry shop, 180, 207–8; Chinese boat boys incarcerated, 147; cobbler's shop, 180; daily schedule, 112–13, 176–77, 179; Devereux reinstitutes discipline, 120–24; escape attempts, 192–94, 195–96; evacuated, 214–15; exercise, recreation, and entertainment, 122, 146, 160, 161–68; fly and mosquito–killing campaign, 184–86; and ICRC aid, 151–66; illness and health care, 111–12, 117, 119, 134–36, 138–40, 156, 173, 183–87, 197–98, 214; impact of ICRC food shipments, 153–56; inspected by Hata, 143–44; Japanese censorship, 164, 200–201, 205; Japanese pilfer ICRC food, 154–55; Japanese pilfer POW produce and livestock, 158; Japanese security precautions, 104–5, 107–8, 190–91, 193, 196–97; library, 163–64; North China Marines arrive, 125–29, 140–41; occasional treats from Japanese, 145–46, 181; POW accommodations, 105–8, 115, 216–17; POW background questionnaires, 189–90, 202, 250; POW barber shop, 159; POW deaths, 119–20, 156, 174, 197–98; POW dental parlor, 159; POW drafts sent to Japan, 198, 202–3, 322–23; POW gambling, 166–67; and POW garden, 156–58; POW hygiene, 111, 115–16, 159; POW interrogations, 188–89; POW mail, 199–202; POW medical staff, 111–12, 134–36, 139, 186, 197; POW pay, 177, 181–83; and POW sabotage, 108, 179, 214; and POW school, 164–65, 341; POW weight loss, 119, 140; POWs issued bedding, 108–9; POWs issued radios, 144–45; POWs receive newspapers, 143, 145; POWs record radio messages, 143–44; POWs' first meal, 109; rat problem, 112–13; rations, 116–19, 137, 145, 152,

155–56, 180; receives permanent guard detachment, 136; recreation hall, 162, 196; relations with guards, 113–14, 131, 133–34, 135, 138, 162, 167, 179–87, 193, 195, 196, 199–202, 203, 339, 347; religious observances, 167–68, 209; Takamura's temporary guard detail, 113–14; work details, 146, 176–81, 184
Woosung (village), 99, 100, 179, 222, 232
World War I, 47, 124, 132, 142, 171, 284, 345
Wright, 5

Yamagata, 290
Yangtze River, 96, 192, 278–79
Yazawa, Tushihiko, 171, 206, 255–56
Yokohama, 89–91, 92, 199, 306, 313, 315, 319, 327
Yorktown, 312, 313, 314
Yoshimura, Asaichi, 78; and *Nitta Maru* executions, 93, 94, 96
Young, James, 220
Young, John O., 59, 118, 135, 139, 142, 170, 330
Young, Sir Mark A., 147; attacked by Ishihara, 208–9, 255; background, 141–42; and no-escape pledge, 191, 195; protests Ishihara's conduct, 208; transferred to Formosa, 209; wins admiration of Woosung POWs, 142, 209
Young, Sir William M., 142
Yubari (Japan), 14–15
Yuse, Goichi, 144, 146, 150, 156, 162, 169, 176, 177, 180–81, 188, 197, 203, 208, 233, 339, 347; background, 136; death, 209; demands excessive military courtesy, 137, 174; earns POWs' grudging respect, 138; micromanager, 136; mocked by POWs, 136–37; nervous temperament, 136–37, 193; and no-escape pledge, 191–92, 194–95; promotes POW health and welfare, 137, 138, 145, 156, 165, 167, 184–87; punishes Ishihara, 209, 255; reacts to escape attempts, 192–96, 203; relations with ICRC, 151–52, 154, 213, 339; relieves Takamoto at Woosung, 136

Zentsuji (camp): evacuated, 318; humane treatment of POWs, 315–16, 338, 339–40; POW deaths, 317; POW transfers, 317–18; rations, 316–17; Red Cross food boxes, 316; work details, 316 *about the author*

GREGORY J. W. URWIN is a professor of history at Temple University in Philadelphia, PA, where he specializes in American and British military affairs. A prize-winning author, he has produced eight other books, including *Facing Fearful Odds: The Siege of Wake Island,* which won the Gen. Wallace M. Greene Jr. Award from the Marine Corps Heritage Foundation. Urwin has also published more than 150 articles and essays and has appeared in numerous historical documentaries.

The Naval Institute Press is the book-publishing arm of the U.S. Naval Institute, a private, nonprofit, membership society for sea service professionals and others who share an interest in naval and maritime affairs. Established in 1873 at the U.S. Naval Academy in Annapolis, Maryland, where its offices remain today, the Naval Institute has members worldwide.

Members of the Naval Institute support the education programs of the society and receive the influential monthly magazine *Proceedings* or the colorful bimonthly magazine *Naval History* and discounts on fine nautical prints and on ship and aircraft photos. They also have access to the transcripts of the Institute's Oral History Program and get discounted admission to any of the Institute-sponsored seminars offered around the country.

The Naval Institute's book-publishing program, begun in 1898 with basic guides to naval practices, has broadened its scope to include books of more general interest. Now the Naval Institute Press publishes about seventy titles each year, ranging from how-to books on boating and navigation to battle histories, biographies, ship and aircraft guides, and novels. Institute members receive significant discounts on the more than eight hundred Press books in print.

Full-time students are eligible for special half-price membership rates. Life memberships are also available.

For a free catalog describing Naval Institute Press books currently available, and for further information about joining the U.S. Naval Institute, please write to:

Member Services
U.S. NAVAL INSTITUTE
291 Wood Road
Annapolis, MD 21402-5034
Telephone: (800) 233-8764
Fax: (410) 571-1703
Web address: www.usni.org

www.ingramcontent.com/pod-product-compliance
Lightning Source LLC
Chambersburg PA
CBHW060347080526
44583CB00012B/211